Cognitive Psychology

Cognitive Psychology

THIRD EDITION

E. Bruce Goldstein
University of Pittsburgh
University of Arizona

Australia • Brazil • Japan • Korea • Mexico • Singapore • Spain • United Kingdom • United States

Cognitive Psychology, Third Edition
E. Bruce Goldstein

Publisher/Executive Editor: Linda Schreiber-Ganster
Acquisitions Editor: Jaime Perkins
Developmental Editor: Kristin Makarewycz
Assistant Editor: Paige Leeds
Editorial Assistant: Philip Hovanessian
Media Editor: Lauren Keyes
Marketing Manager: Elisabeth Rhoden
Marketing Assistant: Anna Andersen
Marketing Communications Manager: Talia Wise
Content Project Manager: Charlene M. Carpentier
Creative Director: Rob Hugel
Art Director: Vernon Boes
Print Buyer: Becky Cross
Rights Acquisitions Account Manager, Text: Roberta Broyer
Rights Acquisitions Account Manager, Image: Robyn Young/Dean Dauphinais
Production Service: Scratchgravel Publishing Services
Text Designer: Liz Harasymczuk
Photo Researcher: Pre-Press PMG
Copy Editor: Margaret C. Tropp/Anne Draus
Illustrator: Precision Graphics
Cover Designer: Denise Davidson
Cover Image: David Wasserman/Brand X; Digital Vision
Compositor: Integra

Library of Congress Control Number: 2010923871

International Student Edition:

ISBN-13: 978-1-111-18588-6
ISBN-10: 1-111-18588-3

Cengage Learning International Offices

Asia
www.cengageasia.com
tel: (65) 6410 1200

Australia/New Zealand
www.cengage.com.au
tel: (61) 3 9685 4111

Brazil
www.cengage.com.br
tel: (55) 11 3665 9900

India
www.cengage.co.in
tel: (91) 11 4364 1111

Latin America
www.cengage.com.mx
tel: (52) 55 1500 6000

UK/Europe/Middle East/Africa
www.cengage.co.uk
tel: (44) 0 1264 332 424

Represented in Canada by Nelson Education, Ltd.
tel: (416) 752 9100 / (800) 668 0671
www.nelson.com

Cengage Learning is a leading provider of customized learning solutions with office locations around the globe, including Singapore, the United Kingdom, Australia, Mexico, Brazil, and Japan. Locate your local office at **www.cengage.com/global.**

For product information: **www.cengage.com/international**
Visit your local office: **www.cengage.com/global**
Visit our corporate website: **www.cengage.com**

AVAILABILITY OF RESOURCES MAY DIFFER BY REGION. Check with your local Cengage Learning representative for details.

Printed in Canada
1 2 3 4 5 6 7 14 13 12 11 10

To Barbara

About the Author

E. BRUCE GOLDSTEIN is Professor Emeritus of Psychology at the University of Pittsburgh and Adjunct Professor of Psychology at the University of Arizona. He has received the Chancellor's Distinguished Teaching Award from the University of Pittsburgh for his classroom teaching and textbook writing. He received his bachelor's degree in chemical engineering from Tufts University and his PhD in experimental psychology from Brown University. He was a post-doctoral fellow in the Biology Department at Harvard University before joining the faculty at the University of Pittsburgh. Bruce has published papers on a wide variety of topics, including retinal and cortical physiology, visual attention, and the perception of pictures. He is the author of *Sensation and Perception*, 8th edition (Wadsworth, 2010) and is the editor of the *Blackwell Handbook of Perception* (Blackwell, 2001) and the two-volume *Sage Encyclopedia of Perception* (Sage, 2010).

Brief Contents

Contents

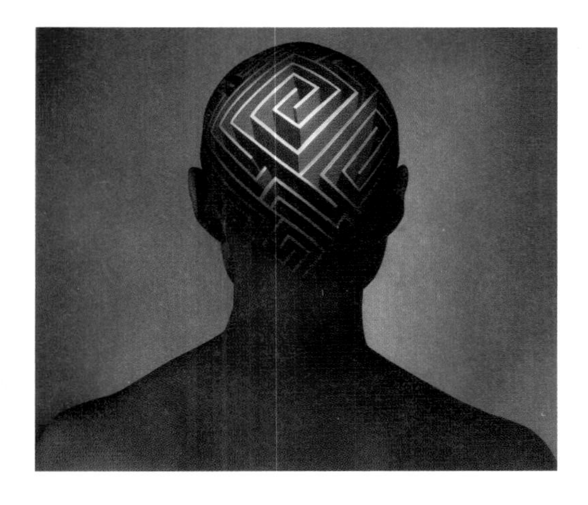

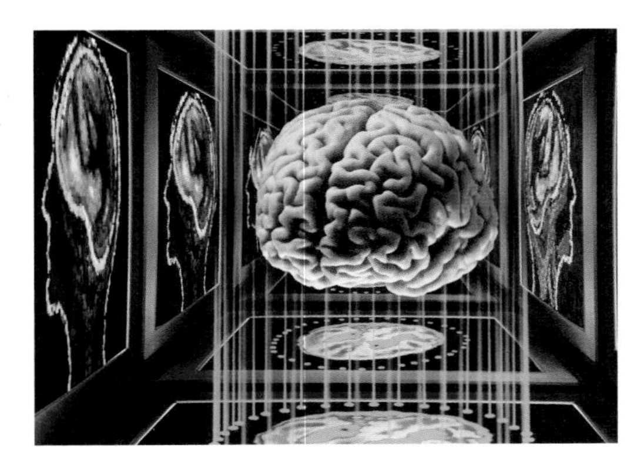

CHAPTER 4

Attention 80

CHAPTER 11

Language 292

CHAPTER 12

Thinking: Problem Solving 324

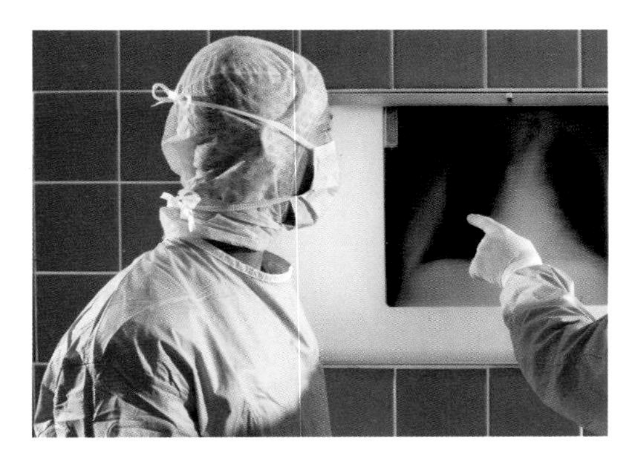

CHAPTER 13

Thinking: Reasoning and Decisions 358

CogLab Experiments

DEMONSTRATIONS

METHODS

Preface to Instructors

The Evolution of a Cognitive Psychology Textbook

This book is the culmination of a process that began in 2002, when I decided to write the first edition of this book. From a survey of more than 500 instructors and my conversations with colleagues, it became apparent that many teachers were looking for a text that not only covers the field of cognitive psychology but is also accessible to students. From my teaching of cognitive psychology, it also became apparent that many students perceive cognitive psychology as being too abstract and theoretical, and not connected to everyday experience. With this information in hand, I set out to write a book that would tell the story of cognitive psychology in a concrete way that would help students appreciate the connections between empirical research, the principles of cognitive psychology, and everyday experience.

I did a number of things to achieve this result. I started by including about a dozen **real-life examples** per chapter, and **neuropsychological case studies** where appropriate. To provide students with firsthand experience with the phenomena of cognitive psychology, I included more than 40 **Demonstrations**—easy-to-do mini-experiments that were contained within the narrative of the text—as well as 20 additional suggestions of things to try, throughout the chapters. The Demonstrations in this edition are listed on page xxii.

Students also received access to more than 45 online **CogLab experiments** that they could run themselves, and then compare their data to the class average and to the results of the original experiments from the literature. In order to ensure that students not only know the results of experiments but also appreciate how these results were obtained, I **described experiments in detail**, so students would understand what the experimenter and participants were doing. In addition, most of these descriptions were supported by illustrations such as pictures of stimuli, diagrams of the experimental design, or graphs of the results.

The first edition (2005) therefore combined many elements designed to achieve the goal of covering the basic principles of cognitive psychology in a way that students would find interesting and easy to understand. My goal was for students to come away feeling excited about the field of cognitive psychology.

The acceptance of the first edition was gratifying, but one thing I've learned from years of teaching and textbook writing is that there are always explanations that can be clarified, new pedagogical techniques to try, and new research and ideas to describe. With this in mind as I began preparing the second edition (2008), I elicited feedback from students in my classes and received more than 1,500 written responses indicating areas in the first edition that could be improved. In addition, I also received feedback from instructors who had used the first edition. This feedback was the starting point for the second edition, so in addition to updating the book, I revised many sections that students and instructors had flagged as needing clarification.

Retained Features

All of the features described above were well received by students and instructors, and so are continued in this new third edition. Additional pedagogical features that have

AVAILABILITY OF RESOURCES MAY DIFFER BY REGION. Check with your local Cengage Learning representative for details.

been retained from previous editions include **Test Yourself** sections, which help students review the material, and **Think About It** questions, which ask students to consider questions that go beyond the material.

Method sections, which were introduced in the second edition, highlight the ingenious methods cognitive psychologists have devised to study the mind. The 27 Method sections, which are integrated into the text, describe methods such as brain imaging, lexical priming, and think-aloud protocols. This not only highlights the importance of the method, but makes it easier to return to its description when it is referred to later in the text. See page xxii for a list of Methods.

The end-of-chapter **Something to Consider** sections describe cutting-edge or controversial research. A few examples of topics covered in this section are "Attention in Social Situations—the Case of Autism," "Are Memories Ever 'Permanent'?" and "Culture, Language, and Cognition." **If You Want to Know More** includes brief descriptions of interesting topics that are related to the chapter but could not be discussed in detail in the text for space reasons. A few references are provided to help students begin exploring this additional material. **Chapter Summaries** provided succinct outlines of the chapters, without serving as a substitute for reading the chapters.

What Is the Same and What Is New in the Third Edition?

An obvious difference between the second edition and this one is that the third edition *looks* different. In response to comments that students didn't like having to refer to the separate "color plates" section when brain scans or other color plates were mentioned, plus my feeling that more color would enhance the book's accessibility and pedagogy, we took the major step of redoing the entire illustration program in full color. The results are obvious, and for me, reinforce the message in the text that cognitive psychology is an exciting and vibrant field.

But this edition is more than a color version of the last one. Material has been extensively updated throughout the text, and in a few cases chapters have been rewritten or reorganized to improve clarity and pedagogy. One significant organizational change was to divide coverage of long-term memory (Chapter 6 of the second edition, Long-Term Memory: Basic Principles) into two chapters of more manageable length (Chapter 6, Structure of Long-Term Memory, and Chapter 7, Encoding and Retrieval). Following is a selective chapter-by-chapter list of a few of the key changes in this edition.

CHAPTER 1 INTRODUCTION TO COGNITIVE PSYCHOLOGY

- Expanded treatment of the nature of the mind to include coverage of different ways of defining "mind."
- Revised section on "Researching the Mind," using research on memory consolidation to illustrate psychophysical and physiological approaches.
- Revised section on "Models of the Mind," using Broadbent's filter model of attention as an example
- New *Something to Consider*: "Learning From This Book," to make students aware that the material is presented as a series of "mini-stories"—description of a phenomenon followed by experimental evidence.

CHAPTER 2 BRAIN AND COGNITION

- Discussion of physiological details that do not appear later in the book has been eliminated.
- Chapter completely rewritten to help students appreciate the relationship between neural representation and cognition.

AVAILABILITY OF RESOURCES MAY DIFFER BY REGION. Check with your local Cengage Learning representative for details.

- Expanded sections on localization of function and the distributed representation in the brain.
- New *Something to Consider*: "'Mind Reading' by Measuring Brain Activity."

CHAPTER 3 PERCEPTION

- Completely rewritten to reflect contemporary research in perception. New topics include the role of context in perception, physical and semantic regularities in the environment, and parallel processing streams.
- Increased focus on top-down versus bottom-up processing.
- New section on the connection between perception and action.
- New *Demonstrations*: "Two Quarters" (size constancy); "Visualizing Scenes and Objects."
- New *Method*: "Brain Ablation."
- New *Something to Consider*: "Mirror Neurons."

CHAPTER 4 ATTENTION

- Material on inattentional blindness and change detection has been moved from the perception chapter to this chapter.
- Section on overt attention (eye movements) rewritten.
- New section on covert attention.
- New *Demonstrations*: "Detecting a Target" (divided attention); "Looking for a Face in the Crowd" (scanning).

CHAPTER 5 INTRODUCTION TO MEMORY

- Rewritten section on how information is coded in STM.
- New *Demonstrations*: "Remembering Letters" (chunking); "Recalling Visual Patterns" (visual coding).
- New *Something to Consider*: "The Advantages of Having a More Efficient Working Memory."
- New *Method*: "Reading Span."

CHAPTER 6 STRUCTURE OF LONG-TERM MEMORY

- This is the first part of the old Chapter 6 in the second edition, which introduces the basic types and dimensions of long-term memory.
- Discussion of conditioning added to section on implicit memory.
- Rewritten section on priming, which distinguishes between repetition priming and conceptual priming.
- Distinction between explicit and implicit memory clarified.
- New *Methods*: "Recognition Memory"; "Avoiding Explicit Remembering in a Priming Experiment."
- New *Demonstration*: "Mirror Drawing."
- New *Something to Consider*: "Memory Loss in the Movies."

CHAPTER 7 ENCODING AND RETRIEVAL

- This is the second part of Chapter 6 from the second edition, which focuses on the interrelationship between encoding and retrieval.

AVAILABILITY OF RESOURCES MAY DIFFER BY REGION. Check with your local Cengage Learning representative for details.

- New explanation of the circularity in the definition of depth of processing, to illustrate why LOP theory became less popular.
- New material on the testing effect in the section "Research Showing That Encoding Influences Retrieval."
- Expanded treatment of how memory principles can be applied to studying.
- "Memory and the Brain" section moved to the end of the chapter to avoid interrupting the narrative describing encoding and retrieval.
- New *Method*: "Cued Recall."

CHAPTER 8 EVERYDAY MEMORY

- Expanded section on the constructive nature of memory.
- Expanded treatment of source monitoring.
- New *Method*: "Testing for Source Monitoring."
- Updated material on memory errors and eyewitness testimony, including a description of the reverse testing effect.

CHAPTER 9 KNOWLEDGE

- Simplified treatment of the connectionist approach to knowledge representation.
- New material on category information in single neurons.
- New material on neuropsychological studies of category-specific knowledge impairment.
- New material discussing how the brain's representation of category knowledge includes activation of areas that respond to properties such as what an object is used for and how it moves.
- New *Demonstration*: "Activation of Property Units in a Connectionist Network."
- New *Something to Consider*: "Categorization in Infants."
- New *Method*: "Familiarization/Novelty Preference Procedure."

CHAPTER 10 IMAGERY

- Minor changes were made in this chapter.
- New *Demonstration*: "Experiencing Imagery."

CHAPTER 11 LANGUAGE

- *Method*: "Word Superiority Effect" moved to this chapter.
- Section on understanding sentences rewritten, focusing on clarifying sections students found difficult. To accomplish this, the section on parsing has been rewritten.
- New *Demonstrations*: "Late Closure"; "Making Up a Story" (inference in story understanding).
- Situation models updated, with new material on mental representations as simulations, and the physiology of simulations.
- *Something to Consider* on the Whorf-Sapir hypothesis has been rewritten to consider research on how Russian names for "blue" affect color categorization and on the relation between brain lateralization and the effect of language on color perception.

AVAILABILITY OF RESOURCES MAY DIFFER BY REGION. Check with your local Cengage Learning representative for details.

CHAPTER 12 THINKING: PROBLEM SOLVING

- Minor changes to this chapter focus on improving pedagogy.
- Newell-Simon approach and analogical problem solving sections rewritten and tables added for increased clarity.
- New *Something to Consider*: "Does Large Working Memory Capacity Result in Better Problem Solving? It Depends" (on the effect of stress on problem solving).

CHAPTER 13 THINKING: REASONING AND DECISIONS

- Section on categorical and conditional syllogisms streamlined in response to feedback that the treatment in the second edition was too detailed.
- Section on decision making updated, with new material on how emotions affect decision making (using, as one example, the *Deal or No Deal* game show).

Ancillaries to Support Your Teaching

COGLAB 2.0 FOR GOLDSTEIN'S *COGNITIVE PSYCHOLOGY*

Free with every new copy of this book, CogLab 2.0 lets your students do more than just think about cognition. CogLab 2.0 uses the power of the web to teach concepts using important classic and current experiments that demonstrate how the mind works. Nothing is more powerful for students than seeing for themselves the effects of these experiments! CogLab 2.0 includes features such as simplified student registration, a global database that combines data from students all around the world, between-subject designs that allow for new kinds of experiments, and a "quick display" of student summaries. Also included are trial-by-trial data, standard deviations, and improved instructions.

BOOK COMPANION WEBSITE (WWW.CENGAGE.COM/INTERNATIONAL)

When you adopt *Cognitive Psychology,* Third Edition, you and your students will have access to a rich array of teaching and learning resources that you won't find anywhere else. This outstanding site features multiple-choice questions, short essay questions, flashcards, crossword puzzles, web links, and a glossary for students to practice, as well as PowerPoints, an Instructor's Manual, and a Test Bank to aid teaching and testing.

AVAILABILITY OF RESOURCES MAY DIFFER BY REGION. Check with your local Cengage Learning representative for details.

Preface to Students

As you begin reading this book, you probably have some ideas about how the mind works from things you have read, from other media, and from your own experiences. In this book, you will learn what we actually do and do not know about the mind, as determined from the results of controlled scientific research. Thus, if you thought that there is a system called "short-term memory" that can hold information for short periods of time, then you are right; when you read the chapters on memory, you will learn more about this system and how it interacts with other parts of your memory system. If you thought that some people can accurately remember things that happened to them as very young infants, you will see that there is a good chance that these reports are inaccurate. In fact, you may be surprised to learn that even more recent memories that seem extremely clear and vivid may not be entirely accurate due to basic characteristics of the way the memory system works.

But what you will learn from this book goes much deeper than simply adding more accurate information to what you already know about the mind. You will learn that there is much more going on in your mind than you are conscious of. You are aware of experiences such as seeing something, remembering a past event, or thinking about how to solve a problem—but behind each of these experiences are a myriad of complex and largely invisible processes. Reading this book will help you appreciate some of the "behind the scenes" activity in your mind that is responsible for everyday experiences such as perceiving, remembering, and thinking.

Another thing you will become aware of as you read this book is that there are many practical connections between the results of cognitive psychology research and everyday life. You will see examples of these connections throughout the book. For now I want to focus on one especially important connection—what research in cognitive psychology can contribute to improving your studying. This discussion appears on pages 187–189 of Chapter 7, but you might want to look at this material now, rather than waiting until later in the course. I invite you to also consider the following two principles, which are designed to help you get more out of this book.

Principle 1: It is important to know what you know.

Professors often hear students lament, "I came to the lecture, read the chapters a number of times, and still didn't do well on the exam." Sometimes this statement is followed by ". . . and when I walked out of the exam, I thought I had done pretty well." If this is something that you have experienced, the problem may be that you didn't have a good awareness of what you knew about the material and what you didn't know. If you think you know the material but actually don't, you might stop studying or might continue studying in an ineffective way, with the net result being a poor understanding of the material and an inability to remember it accurately, come exam time. Thus, it is important to test yourself on the material you have read by writing or saying the answers to the Test Yourself questions in the chapter and also by taking advantage of the sample test questions that are available on the Book Companion Website. To access these questions and other valuable learning aids, go to www.cengage.com/international.

AVAILABILITY OF RESOURCES MAY DIFFER BY REGION. Check with your local Cengage Learning representative for details.

Principle 2: Don't mistake ease and familiarity for knowing.

One of the main reasons that students may think they know the material, even when they don't, is that they mistake familiarity for understanding. Here is how it works: You read the chapter once, perhaps highlighting as you go. Then later, you read the chapter again, perhaps focusing on the highlighted material. As you read it over, the material is familiar because you remember it from before, and this familiarity might lead you to think, "Okay, I know that." The problem is that this feeling of familiarity is not necessarily equivalent to knowing the material and may be of no help when you have to come up with an answer on the exam. In fact, familiarity can often lead to errors on multiple-choice exams because you might pick a choice that looks familiar, only to find out later that although it was something you had read, it wasn't really the best answer to the question.

This brings us back again to the idea of testing yourself. One finding of cognitive psychology research is that the very act of *trying* to answer a question increases the chances that you will be able to answer it when you try again later. Another related finding is that testing yourself on the material is a more effective way of learning it than simply rereading the material. The reason testing yourself works is that *generating* material is a more effective way of getting information into memory than simply *reviewing* it. Thus, you may find it effective to test yourself before rereading the chapter or going over your highlighted text.

Whichever study tactic you find works best for you, keep in mind that an effective strategy is to rest (take a break or study something else) before studying more and then retesting yourself. Research has shown that memory is better when studying is spaced out over time, rather than being done all at once. Repeating this process a number of times—testing yourself, checking back to see whether you were right, waiting, testing yourself again, and so on—is a more effective way of learning the material than simply looking at it and getting that warm, fuzzy feeling of familiarity, which may not translate into actually knowing the material when you are faced with questions about it on the exam.

I hope you will find this book to be clear and interesting and that you will sometimes be fascinated or perhaps even surprised by some of the things you read. I also hope that your introduction to cognitive psychology extends beyond just "learning the material." Cognitive psychology is endlessly interesting because it is about one of the most fascinating of all topics—the human mind. Thus, once your course is over, I hope you will take away an appreciation for what cognitive psychologists have discovered about the mind and what still remains to be learned. I also hope that you will become a more critical consumer of information about the mind that you may encounter on the Internet or in movies, magazines, or other media. Finally, if you have any questions or comments about anything in the book, please feel free to contact me at bruceg@email.arizona.edu.

AVAILABILITY OF RESOURCES MAY DIFFER BY REGION. Check with your local Cengage Learning representative for details.

Acknowledgments

The starting point for a textbook like this one is an author who has an idea for a book, but other people soon become part of the process. Editors first provide guidance regarding the kind of book teachers want and, along with outside reviewers, provide feedback about chapters as they are written. When the manuscript is completed, the production process begins, and a new group of people take over to turn the manuscript into a book. This means that this book has been a group effort and that I had lots of help, both during the process of writing and after submitting the final manuscript. I would therefore like to thank the following people for their extraordinary efforts in support of this book.

- Jaime Perkins, my editor, for his continued support of this book, and particularly for doing what was necessary to make it possible to publish this book in full color.
- Kristin Makarewycz, my developmental editor, who read every word of every chapter and somehow, even after I had "perfected" the writing, found numerous ways to make it better. Also, thank you, Kristin, for the moral support along the way.
- Anne Draus of Scratchgravel Publishing Services, for dealing so expertly with the hundreds of details that have to be dealt with in the process of assembling a book. Thank you, Anne, for making the complex process of assembling all of the various components of this book seem easy, even though I know it wasn't. Also, thanks for your obsession with cats and dogs near the end of the process, which I completely enjoyed (pages 238–239, 263–264). And finally, thanks for the many ways that you supported the book and my efforts.
- Vernon Boes (a.k.a. Pablo), the art director, for directing the team responsible for the look and layout of this book and for being open to suggestions, even from the author!
- Cheryl Carrington, for yet another elegant and beautiful cover.
- Liz Harasymczuk, for the eye-catching and functional interior design.
- Lisa Torri, art editor, for yet again directing the art program for one of my books, this time as director of the illustrators at Precision Graphics, who carried out the daunting task of recreating more than 250 of the illustrations from the second edition in color, plus 80 new ones.
- Charlene Carpentier, content project manager, for making sure everything was done correctly and on time during the production process.
- Philip Hovanessian, editorial assistant extraordinaire, who really meant it when he said, "Let me know if there's anything else I can do for you." Thank you, Philip, for your support.
- Margaret Tropp, for her expert and extremely thorough copy editing that went beyond just "copy editing" to include pointing out places that needed further clarification.
- Martha Hall of Pre-Press PMG, for her photo research, for obtaining permissions, and for patiently waiting for my answers to her questions.
- Martha Ghent, for the essential task of proofreading.
- James Minkin, for creating the index.
- Paige Leeds, assistant editor, for coordinating the supplements for the book.
- Lauren Keyes, media editor, for her work on the media that accompanies the book.
- Carla and Steve Loper and the staff at Sertinos Café in Tucson, for providing the coffee and a writer-friendly environment that were essential for completing this book.

In addition to the help I received from the above people on the editorial and production side, I received a great deal of help from teachers and researchers who gave me feedback on what I wrote and made suggestions regarding new work in the field. I thank the following people for their help:

GENERAL REVIEWERS

Many of these reviewers read multiple chapters. They all provided invaluable input, based both on their expertise in specific areas and on their experience in teaching the course.

Pamela Ansburg
Metropolitan State College of Denver

Teresa A. Hutchens
University of Tennessee–Knoxville

Jerwen Jou
University of Texas–Pan American

Aarre Laakso
University of Michigan, Dearborn

Tracy Lennertz
Florida Atlantic University

Esin Esendal Provitera
Argosy University

Hildur Schilling
Fitchburg State College

Kenith V. Sobel
University of Central Arkansas

Lucy J. Troup
Colorado State University

Jennifer Zapf
University of Wisconsin–Green Bay

SPECIALIST REVIEWERS

A number of experts were commissioned to read one of the chapters from the second edition (indicated in parentheses) and provide suggestions on updating the content for the third edition to include cutting-edge research. What made many of these reviews especially helpful were suggestions that combined the reviewers' expertise with their experience of presenting the material in their classes.

Anne Cleary (Long-Term Memory)
Colorado State University

Nelson Cowan (Working Memory)
University of Missouri

Tim Curran (Long-Term Memory)
University of Colorado

Michael Dodd (Attention)
University of Nebraska

Jason Hicks (Everyday Memory and Memory Errors)
Louisiana State University

Marsha Lovett (Problem Solving)
Carnegie-Mellon University

Richard Marsh (Everyday Memory and Memory Errors)
University of Georgia

Akira Miyake (Working Memory)
University of Colorado

Paul Price (Reasoning and Decision Making)
California State University at Fresno

Michael Tanenhaus (Language)
University of Rochester

Matthew Traxler (Language)
University of California at Davis

In addition, the following reviewers read parts of chapters to check for accuracy in their areas of expertise.

Marlene Behrmann
Carnegie-Mellon University

Sian Beilock
University of Chicago

Alain Brunet
McGill University

Jason C. K. Chan
Iowa State University

Marci DeCaro
Vanderbilt University

David Freedman
University of Chicago

Wayne D. Gray
Rensselaer Polytechnic Institute

Tiago Maia
Columbia University

Jay McClelland
Stanford University

Paul Quinn
University of Delaware

Svetlana Shinkareva
University of South Carolina

I also thank the following people who donated photographs and research records for illustrations that are new to this edition.

Mary Bravo
Rutgers University

Linda Chao
University of California, San Francisco

David Freedman
University of Chicago

Olaf Hauk
Medical Research Council, Cambridge, UK

Mary Hayhoe
University of Texas

Brian Henderson
University of Edinburgh

Andrew Hollingworth
University of Iowa

Brian Levine
University of Toronto

Aude Oliva
Massachusetts Institute of Technology

Friedmann Pulvermuller
Medical Research Council, Cambridge, UK

Svetlana Shinkareva
University of South Carolina

Antonio Torralba
Massachusetts Institute of Technology

Melissa Võ
Harvard University

Jonathan Winawer
Stanford University

Jeffrey Zacks
Washington University

Cognitive Psychology

1 Introduction to Cognitive Psychology

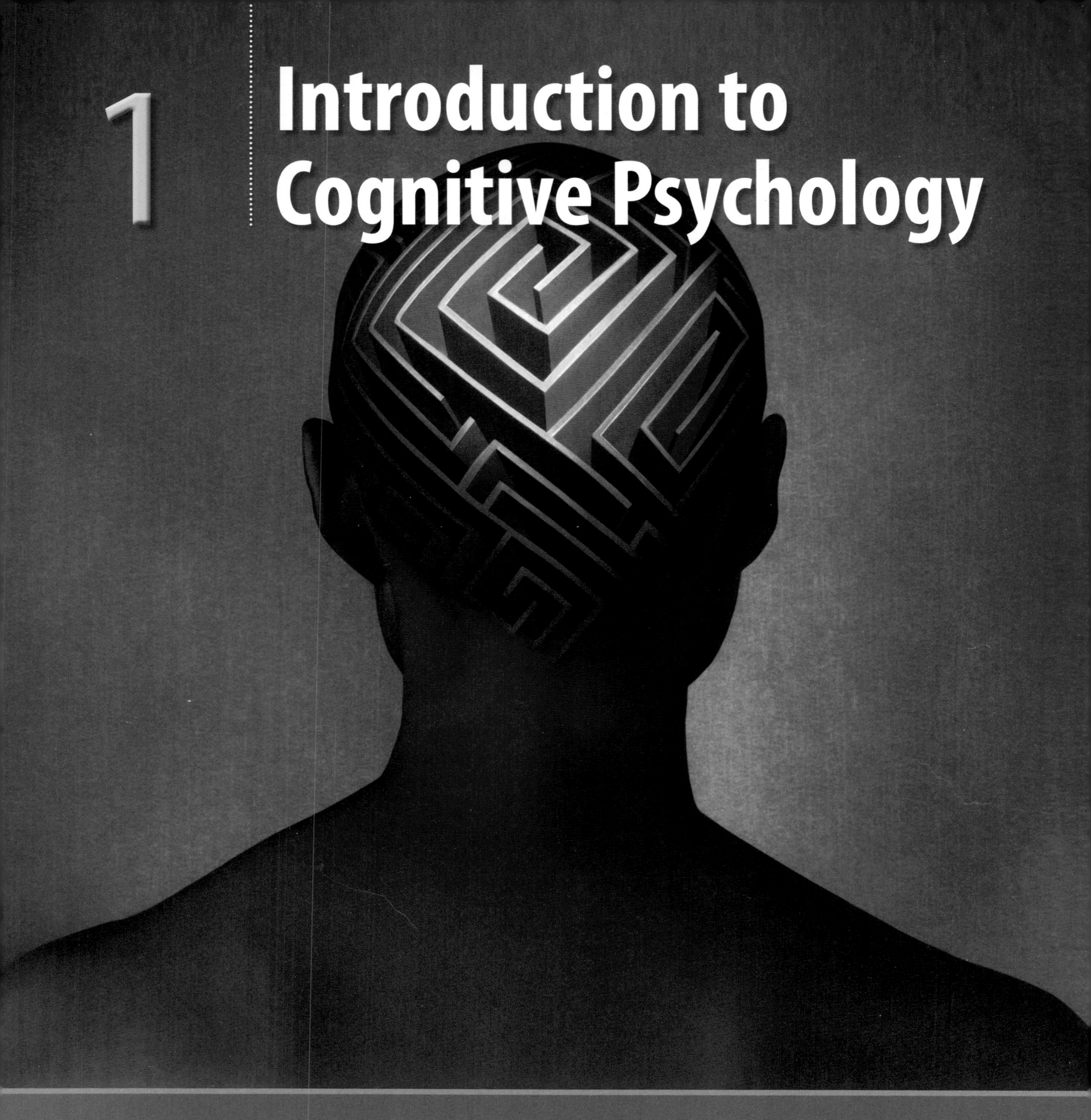

Do we have a maze in our heads? Not really. But this picture represents the idea that the mechanisms responsible for the operation of our minds are complex and a challenge to understand. One of the goals of cognitive psychology is to increase our understanding of how these mechanisms operate and how they affect cognitive processes such as perception, attention, memory, language, and thinking.

Dianna Sarto/CORBIS

Some Questions We Will Consider

- How is cognitive psychology relevant to everyday experience? (4)
- Are there practical applications of cognitive psychology? (4)
- How is it possible to study the inner workings of the mind, when we can't really see the mind directly? (7)
- What is the connection between computers and the study of the mind? (13–14)

As Raphael is walking across campus, talking to Susan on his cell phone about meeting at the student union later this afternoon, he remembers that he left the book she had lent him at home (● Figure 1.1). "I can't believe it," he thinks, "I can see it sitting there on my desk, where I left it. I should have put it in my backpack last night when I was thinking about it."

As he finishes his call with Susan and makes a mental note to be on time for their appointment, his thoughts shift to how he is going to survive after Wednesday when his car is scheduled to go into the shop. Renting a car offers the most mobility, but is expensive. Bumming rides from his roommate is cheap, but limiting. "Perhaps I'll pick up a bus schedule at the student union," he thinks, as he puts his cell phone in his pocket.

Entering his anthropology class, he remembers that an exam is coming up soon. Unfortunately, he still has a lot of reading to do, so he decides that he won't be able to take Susan to the movies tonight, as they had planned, because he needs time to study. As the lecture begins, Raphael is anticipating, with some anxiety, his meeting with Susan.

This brief slice of Raphael's life is noteworthy because it is ordinary, while at the same time so much is happening. Within a short span of time, Raphael does the following things that are related to material covered in chapters in this book:

- *Perceives* his environment—seeing people on campus and hearing Susan talking on the phone (Chapter 3: Perception)
- *Pays attention* to one thing after another—the person approaching on his left, what Susan is saying, how much time he has to get to his class (Chapter 4: Attention)
- *Remembers* something from the past—that he had told Susan he was going to return her book today (Chapters 5–8: Memory)
- *Distinguishes items in a category*, when he thinks about different possible forms of transportation—rental car, roommate's car, bus (Chapter 9: Knowledge)
- *Visualizes* the book on his desk the night before (Chapter 10: Imagery)
- *Understands and produces language* as he talks to Susan (Chapter 11: Language)
- Works to *solve a problem*, as he thinks about how to get places while his car is in the shop (Chapter 12: Problem Solving)
- *Makes a decision*, when he decides to postpone going to the movies with Susan so he can study (Chapter 13: Reasoning and Decisions)

● **FIGURE 1.1** What's happening in Raphael's mind as he walks across campus? Each of the "thought bubbles" corresponds to something in the story in the text.

The things Raphael is doing not only are covered in this book but also have something very important in common: They all involve the mind. **Cognitive psychology** is the branch of psychology concerned with the scientific study of the mind. As you read the story about the quest to understand the mind, you will learn what the mind is, how it has been studied, and what researchers have discovered about how the mind works. In this chapter we will first describe the mind in more detail, then consider some of the history behind the field of cognitive psychology, and finally introduce a few of the ways that modern cognitive psychologists have gone about studying the mind.

Cognitive Psychology: Studying the Mind

You may have noticed that we have been using the term **mind** without precisely defining it. As we will see, mind, like other concepts in psychology, such as intelligence or emotion, can be thought of in a number of different ways.

WHAT IS THE MIND?

One way to approach the question "What is the mind?" is to consider how "mind" is used in everyday conversation. Here are a few examples:

1. "He was able to call to mind what he was doing on the day of the accident." (The mind as involved in memory)
2. "If you put your mind to it, I'm sure you can solve that math problem." (The mind as problem-solver)
3. "I haven't made up my mind yet" or "I'm of two minds about this." (The mind as used to make decisions or consider possibilities)
4. "He is of sound mind and body" or "When he talks about his encounter with aliens, it sounds like he is out of his mind." (A healthy mind being associated with normal functioning, a nonfunctioning mind with abnormal functioning)
5. "A mind is a terrible thing to waste." (The mind as valuable, something that should be used)
6. "He has a beautiful mind." (From Sylvia Nasar's book *A Beautiful Mind*, about Nobel Prize winner John Nash, which was made into an Academy Award–winning movie staring Russell Crowe)

These statements tell us some important things about what the mind is. Statements 1, 2, and 3, which highlight the mind's role in memory, problem solving, and making decisions, are related to the following definition of the mind: *The **mind** creates and controls mental functions such as perception, attention, memory, emotions, language, deciding, thinking, and reasoning.* This definition reflects the mind's central role in determining our various mental abilities, which are reflected in the titles of the chapters in this book.

Statement 4 is related to another definition of the mind: *The mind is a system that creates representations of the world so that we can act within it to achieve our goals.* This definition reflects the mind's importance for functioning and survival, and also provides the beginnings of a description of how the mind achieves these ends. The idea of creating representations is something we will return to throughout this book.

These two definitions of the mind are not incompatible. The first one indicates different types of **cognition**—the mental processes such as perception attention, memory, and so on, that are what the mind does. The second definition indicates something about how the mind operates (it creates representations) and its function (it enables us to act and to achieve goals). It is no coincidence that all of the cognitions in the first definition play important roles in acting to achieve goals.

The final two everyday statements about the mind emphasize the importance and beauty of the mind. The mind is something to be used, and the products of some people's minds are considered extraordinary. But one of the messages of this book is that the "beauty" of the mind is not reserved for "extraordinary" minds, because even the most "routine" things—recognizing a person, having a conversation, or deciding what courses to take next semester—become amazing in themselves when we consider the properties of the mind that enable us to achieve these familiar activities.

What exactly are the properties of the mind? What are its characteristics? How does it operate? Saying that the mind creates cognition and is important for functioning and survival tells us *what the mind does* but not *how it achieves what it does*. Determining the properties and mechanisms of the mind is what cognitive psychology is about. Our goal in the rest of this chapter is to describe how the field of cognitive psychology evolved from its early beginnings to where it is today, and to begin describing how cognitive psychologists approach the scientific study of the mind.

STUDYING THE MIND: EARLY WORK IN COGNITIVE PSYCHOLOGY

The idea that the mind can be studied scientifically is a modern one. In the 1800s, ideas about the mind were dominated by the belief that it is not possible to study the mind. One reason given was that it is not possible for the mind to study itself, but there were other reasons as well, including the idea that the properties of the mind simply cannot be measured. Nonetheless, some researchers defied the common wisdom and decided to study the mind anyway. One of these people was the Dutch physiologist Franciscus Donders, who in 1868, eleven years before the founding of the first laboratory of scientific psychology, did one of the first experiments that today would be called a cognitive psychology experiment. (It is important to note that the term "cognitive psychology" was not coined until 1967, but the early experiments we are going to describe qualify as cognitive psychology experiments.)

Donders' Pioneering Experiment: How Long Does It Take to Make a Decision?

Donders was interested in determining how long it takes for a person to make a decision. He determined this by measuring **reaction time**, how long it takes to respond to presentation of a stimulus. In the first part of his experiment, he asked his participants to press a button upon presentation of a light (● Figure 1.2a). This is called

(a) Press J when light goes on.

(b) Press J for left light, K for right.

● **FIGURE 1.2** A modern version of Donders' (1868) reaction time experiment: (a) the simple reaction time task; and (b) the choice reaction time task. In the simple reaction time task, the participant pushes the J key when the light goes on. In the choice reaction time task, the participant pushes the J key if the left light goes on and the K key if the right light goes on. The purpose of Donders' experiment was to determine the time it took to decide which key to press for the choice reaction time task.

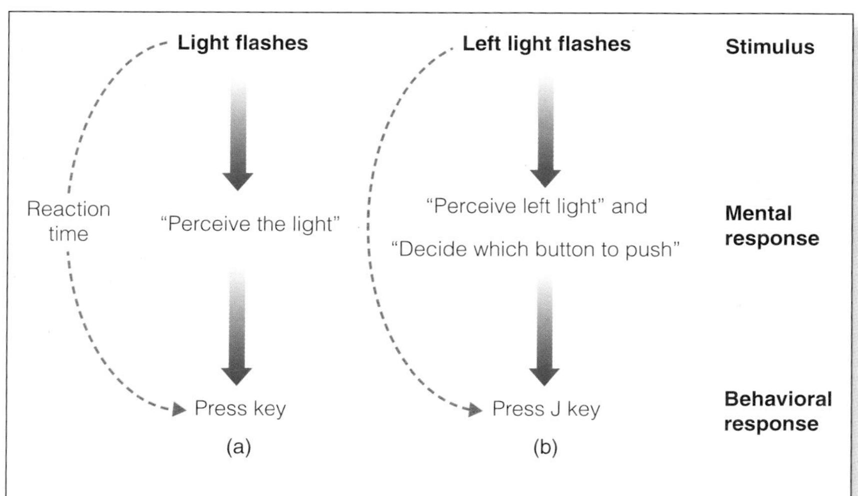

● **FIGURE 1.3** Sequence of events between presentation of the stimulus and the behavioral response in Donders' experiment. The dashed line indicates that Donders measured reaction time, the time between presentation of the light and the participant's response. (a) Simple reaction time task; (b) choice reaction time task.

a **simple reaction time** task. In the second part of the experiment, he made the task more difficult by presenting two lights, one on the left and one on the right. The participants' task in this part of the experiment was to push one button when the light on the left was illuminated and another button when the light on the right was illuminated (Figure 1.2b). This is called a **choice reaction time** task.

The rationale behind the simple reaction time task is shown in ● Figure 1.3a. Presenting the stimulus (the light) causes a mental response (perceiving the light), which leads to a behavioral response (pushing the button). The reaction time (dashed line) is the time between presentation of the stimulus and the behavioral response.

The diagram for the choice reaction time task in Figure 1.3b shows that the mental response includes not only perceiving the light but also deciding which button to push. Donders reasoned that choice reaction time would be longer than simple reaction time because of the additional time it takes to make the decision, and that the difference in reaction time between the simple and choice conditions would indicate how long it took to make the decision. Because the choice reaction time took one-tenth of a second longer than simple reaction time, Donders concluded that it took one-tenth of a second to decide which button to push.

Donders' experiment is important, both because it was one of the first cognitive psychology experiments and because it illustrates something extremely significant about studying the mind: Mental responses (perceiving the light and deciding which button to push, in this example) cannot be measured directly, but must be *inferred* from behavior. We can see why this is so by noting the dashed lines in Figure 1.3. These lines indicate that when Donders measured the reaction time, he was measuring the relationship between the presentation of the stimulus and the participant's response. He did not measure the mental response directly, but *inferred* how long it took from the reaction times. The fact that mental responses can't be measured directly, but must be inferred from observing behavior, is a principle that holds not only for Donders' experiment but for all research in cognitive psychology.

Ebbinghaus's Memory Experiment: What Is the Time-Course of Forgetting? Another pioneering approach to measuring the properties of the mind was devised by Hermann Ebbinghaus (1885/1913). Ebbinghaus was interested in determining the nature of memory and forgetting—specifically, how information that is learned is lost over time. Ebbinghaus determined this by testing himself, using the procedure shown in ● Figure 1.4. He presented nonsense syllables such as DAX, QEH, LUH, and ZIF to himself one at a time, using a device called a memory drum (modern cognitive psychologists would use a computer). He used nonsense syllables so that his memory would not be influenced by the meaning of a particular word.

The first time through the list, he looked at each syllable one at a time and tried to learn them in order (Figure 1.4a). The second time through, his task was to begin by remembering the first syllable on the list, look at it in the memory drum to see if he was correct, then remember the second syllable, check to see if he was correct, and so on (Figure 1.4b). He repeated the procedure, going through the list and trying to remember each syllable in turn, until he was able to go through the list without making any errors. He noted the number of trials it took him to do this.

After learning a list, Ebbinghaus waited, for delays ranging from almost immediately after learning the list to 31 days. He then repeated the above procedure for each

● **FIGURE 1.4** Ebbinghaus's memory drum procedure for measuring memory and forgetting. (a) Initial viewing—going through the list of nonsense syllables for the first time. (b) Learning the list—going through the list a number of times until each syllable can be correctly predicted from the one before. The number of repetitions necessary to learn the list is noted. (c) After a delay, the list is relearned. The number of repetitions needed to relearn the list is noted.

(a) View series of nonsense syllables.

(b) Repeat. Predict what next syllables in list will be, until remember all items correctly.

(c) After delay, repeat step b.

list and noted how many trials it took him to remember all of the syllables without any errors (Figure 1.4c). He used the **savings method** to analyze his results, calculating the savings by subtracting the number of trials needed to learn the list after a delay from the number of trials it took to learn the list the first time. He then calculated a *savings score* for each delay interval, using the following formula:

$$\text{Savings} = [(\text{Initial repetitions}) - (\text{Relearning repetitions})/\text{Initial repetitions}] \times 100$$

Ebbinghaus found that the savings were greater for short intervals than for long. For example, after a short interval it may have taken him 3 trials to relearn the list. If it had taken him 9 trials to learn the list the first time, then the savings score would be 67 percent ($[(9 - 3)/9] \times 100 = 67$ percent). If after a longer interval it took 6 trials to learn the list the second time, his savings score would be 33 percent.

Ebbinghaus's "savings curve" (● Figure 1.5) shows savings as a function of retention interval. The curve indicates that memory drops rapidly for the first 2 days after the initial learning and then levels off. This curve was important because it demonstrated that memory could be quantified and that functions like the forgetting curve could be used to describe a property of the mind—in this case, the ability to retain information. Notice that although Ebbinghaus's savings method was very different from Donders' reaction time method, both measured *behavior* to determine a property of the *mind*.

Wundt's Psychology Laboratory: Structuralism and Analytic Introspection In 1879, Wilhelm Wundt founded the first laboratory of scientific psychology at the University of Leipzig in Germany, with the goal of studying the mind scientifically. Wundt's approach, which dominated psychology in the late 1800s and early 1900s, was called **structuralism**. According to structuralism, our overall experience is determined by combining basic elements of experience the structuralists called *sensations*. Thus, just as chemistry had developed a periodic table of the elements, which organized elements on the basis of their molecular weights and chemical properties, Wundt wanted to create a "periodic table of the mind," which would include all of the basic sensations involved in creating experience. Wundt thought he could achieve this by using **analytic introspection**, a technique in which trained participants described their experiences and

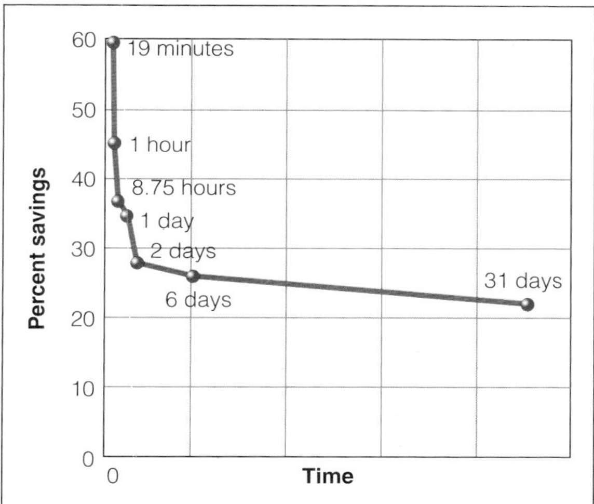

● **FIGURE 1.5** Ebbinghaus's savings (or forgetting) curve. Taking the percent savings as a measure of the amount remembered, Ebbinghaus plotted this against the time interval between initial learning and testing. (Source: Based on data from Ebbinghaus, 1885/1913.)

thought processes in response to stimuli. For example, in one experiment, Wundt asked participants to describe their experience of hearing a five-note chord played on the piano. Wundt was interested in whether they heard the five notes as a single unit or if they were able to hear the individual notes.

Although Wundt never achieved his goal of explaining behavior in terms of sensations, he had a major impact on psychology by establishing the first laboratory of scientific psychology and training PhDs who established psychology departments at other universities, including many in the United States.

William James: *Principles of Psychology* William James, one of the early American psychologists (although not a student of Wundt's), taught Harvard's first psychology course and made significant observations about the mind in his textbook, *Principles of Psychology* (1890). James' observations were based not on the results of experiments, but on introspections about the operation of his own mind. His skill in doing this is reflected in the fact that many of his observations still ring true today, and his book is notable for the breadth of its coverage. In it, James covers a wide range of cognitive topics, including thinking, consciousness, attention, memory, perception, imagination, and reasoning.

The work of Donders, Ebbinghaus, Wundt, James, and others provided what seemed to be a promising start to the study of the mind. However, research on the mind was to soon to be curtailed, largely because of events early in the 20th century that shifted the focus of psychology away from the study of the mind and mental processes. One of the major forces that caused psychology to reject the study of mental processes was a negative reaction to the technique of analytic introspection.

Abandoning the Study of the Mind

Research in many early departments of psychology was conducted in the tradition of Wundt's laboratory, using analytic introspection to reveal hidden mental processes. This emphasis on studying the mind was to change, however, because of the efforts of John Watson, who received his PhD in psychology in 1904 from the University of Chicago.

WATSON FOUNDS BEHAVIORISM

The story of how John Watson founded an approach to psychology called behaviorism is well known to introductory psychology students. We will briefly review it here because of its importance to the history of cognitive psychology.

As a graduate student at the University of Chicago, Watson became dissatisfied with the method of analytic introspection. His problems with this method were (1) it produced extremely variable results from person to person, and (2) these results were difficult to verify because they were interpreted in terms of invisible inner mental processes. In response to what he perceived to be deficiencies in analytic introspection, Watson proposed a new approach called **behaviorism**. One of Watson's papers, "Psychology As the Behaviorist Views It," set forth the goals of this approach to psychology in this famous quote:

> Psychology as the Behaviorist sees it is a purely objective, experimental branch of natural science. Its theoretical goal is the prediction and control of behavior. *Introspection forms no essential part of its methods*, nor is the scientific value of its data dependent upon the readiness with which they lend themselves to interpretation in terms of consciousness. . . . What we need to do is start work upon psychology *making behavior, not consciousness, the objective point of our attack*. (Watson, 1913, pp. 158, 176; emphasis added)

● **FIGURE 1.6** In Pavlov's famous experiment, he paired ringing a bell with presentation of food. Initially, only presentation of the food caused the dog to salivate, but after a number of pairings of bell and food, the bell alone caused salivation. This principle of learning by pairing, which came to be called classical conditioning, was the basis of Watson's "Little Albert" experiment.

This passage makes two key points: (1) Watson rejects introspection as a method, and (2) observable behavior, not consciousness (which would involve unobservable processes such as thinking, emotions, and reasoning), is the main topic of study. In another part of this paper, Watson also proclaims that "psychology . . . need no longer delude itself into thinking that it is making mental states the object of observation" (p. 163). Watson's goal was to eliminate the mind as a topic of study in psychology and replace it with the study of directly observable behavior.

As behaviorism became the dominant force in American psychology, psychologists' attention shifted from asking "What does behavior tell us about the mind?" to "What is the relation between stimuli in the environment and behavior?" Thus, the focus shifted from the mind as the topic of study to behavior (with no reference to the mind) as the topic.

Watson's most famous experiment was the "Little Albert experiment," in which Watson and Rosalie Rayner (1920) subjected Albert, a 9-month-old-boy, to a loud noise every time a rat (which Albert had originally liked) came close to the child. After a few pairings of the noise with the rat, Albert reacted to the rat by crawling away as rapidly as possible.

Watson's ideas are associated with **classical conditioning**—how pairing one stimulus (such as the loud noise presented to Albert) with another, previously neutral stimulus (such as the rat) causes changes in the response to the neutral stimulus. Watson's inspiration for his experiment was Ivan Pavlov's research, begun in the 1890s, that demonstrated classical conditioning in dogs. In these experiments (● Figure 1.6), Pavlov's pairing of food (which made the dog salivate) with a bell (the initially neutral stimulus) caused the dog to salivate to the sound of the bell (Pavlov, 1927).

Watson used classical conditioning to argue that behavior can be analyzed without any reference to the mind. For Watson, what was going on inside Albert's head, either physiologically or mentally, was irrelevant. He only cared about how pairing one stimulus with another affected Albert's behavior.

SKINNER'S OPERANT CONDITIONING

In the midst of behaviorism's dominance of American psychology, B. F. Skinner, a young graduate student at Harvard, provided another tool for behaviorism, which insured this approach would dominate psychology for decades to come. Skinner introduced **operant conditioning**, which focused on how behavior is strengthened by the presentation of positive reinforcers, such as food or social approval (or withdrawal of negative reinforcers, such as a shock or social rejection). For example, Skinner showed that reinforcing a rat with food for pressing a bar maintained or increased the rat's rate of bar pressing. Like Watson, Skinner was not interested in what was happening in the mind, but focused solely on determining the relationship between stimuli and responses (Skinner, 1938).

The idea that behavior can be understood by studying stimulus-response relationships influenced an entire generation of psychologists and dominated psychology in the United States from the 1940s through the 1960s. Psychologists applied the techniques of classical and operant conditioning to things like classroom teaching, treating psychological disorders, and testing the effects of drugs on animals. ● Figure 1.7 is a timeline showing the initial studies of the mind and the rise of behaviorism. We now move beyond this timeline to the 1950s, when changes began to occur in psychology that eventually led to a decline in the influence of behaviorism.

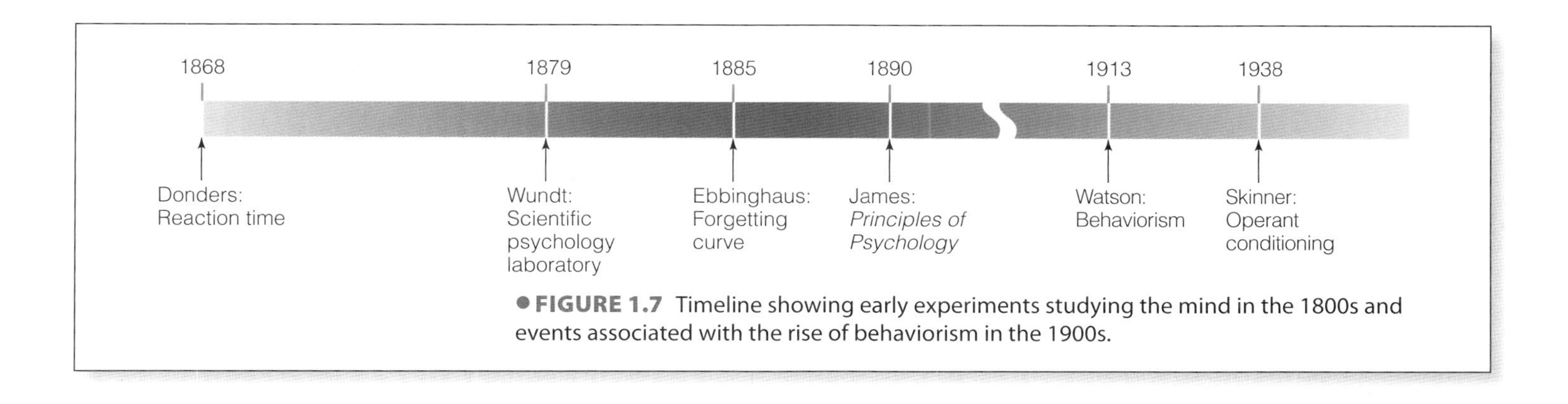

● **FIGURE 1.7** Timeline showing early experiments studying the mind in the 1800s and events associated with the rise of behaviorism in the 1900s.

SETTING THE STAGE FOR THE REEMERGENCE OF THE MIND IN PSYCHOLOGY

Although behaviorism dominated American psychology for many decades, there were some researchers who were not toeing the strict behaviorist line. One of these researchers was Edward Chance Tolman. Tolman, who, from 1918 to 1954 was at the University of California at Berkeley, called himself a behaviorist because his focus was on measuring behavior. But in reality he was one of the early cognitive psychologists, because he used behavior to infer mental processes.

In one of his experiments, Tolman (1938) placed a rat in a maze like the one in ● Figure 1.8. Initially the rat explored the maze, running up and down each of the alleys (Figure 1.8a). After this initial period of exploration, the rat was placed at A and food was placed at B, and the rat quickly learned to turn right at the intersection to obtain the food. This is exactly what the behaviorists would predict, because turning right was rewarded with food (Figure 1.8b). However, when Tolman then placed the rat at C, something interesting happened. At the intersection, the rat turned *left* to reach the food at B (Figure 1.8c). Tolman's explanation of this result was that when the rat initially experienced the maze it was developing a **cognitive map**, a conception of the maze's layout (Tolman, 1948). Thus, even though the rat had previously learned to turn right, when the rat was placed at C, it used its map to turn left at the intersection to reach the food at B. Tolman's use of the word *cognitive*, and the idea that something other than stimulus-response

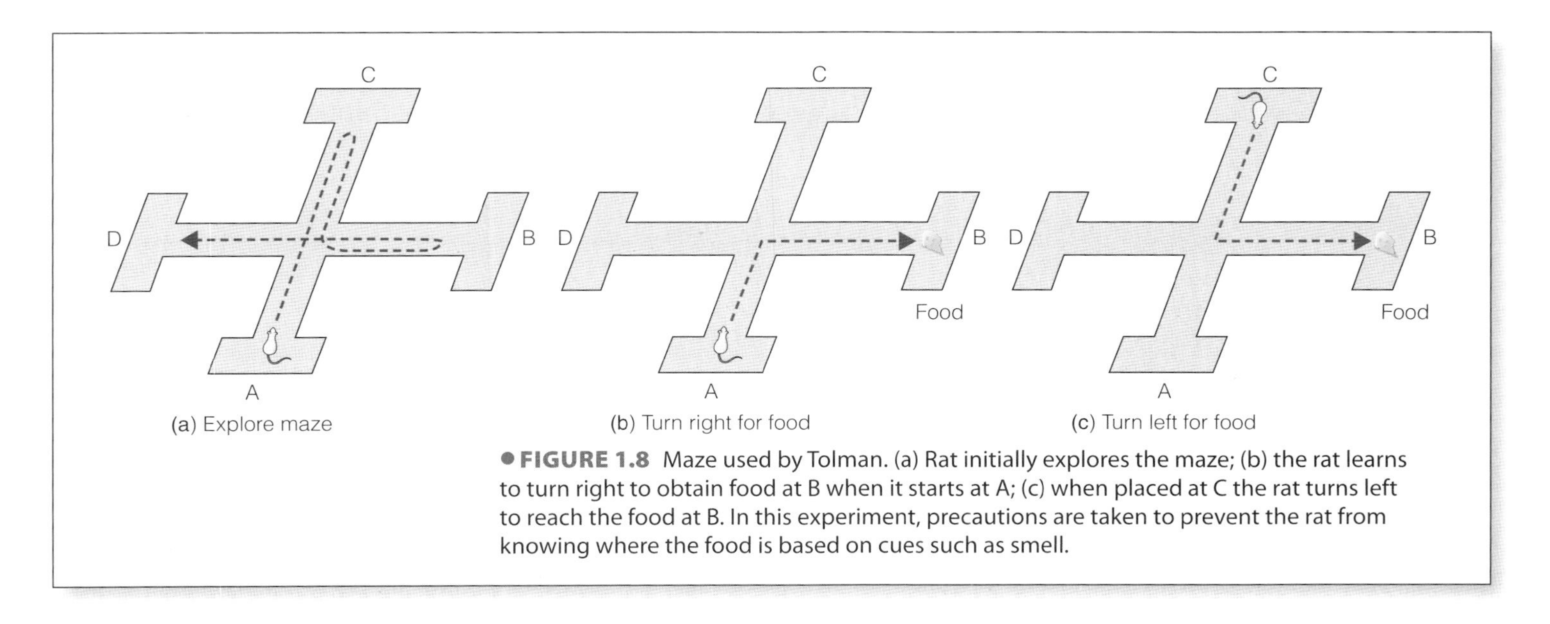

● **FIGURE 1.8** Maze used by Tolman. (a) Rat initially explores the maze; (b) the rat learns to turn right to obtain food at B when it starts at A; (c) when placed at C the rat turns left to reach the food at B. In this experiment, precautions are taken to prevent the rat from knowing where the food is based on cues such as smell.

connections might be occurring in the rat's mind, placed Tolman outside of mainstream behaviorism.

Other researchers were aware of Tolman's work, but for most American psychologists in the 1940s, the use of the term *cognitive* was difficult to accept because it violated the behaviorists' idea that internal processes, such as thinking or maps in the head, were not acceptable topics to study. It wasn't until about a decade after Tolman introduced the idea of cognitive maps that developments occurred that were to lead to a resurgence of the mind in psychology. Ironically, one of these developments was the publication, in 1957, of a book by B. F. Skinner titled *Verbal Behavior*. In this book, Skinner argued that children learn language through operant conditioning. According to this idea, children imitate speech that they hear and repeat correct speech because it is rewarded. But in 1959 Noam Chomsky, a linguist from the Massachusetts Institute of Technology, published a scathing review of Skinner's book, in which he pointed out that children say many sentences that have never been rewarded by parents ("I hate you, Mommy," for example), and that during the normal course of language development, they go through a stage in which they use incorrect grammar, such as "the boy hitted the ball," even though this incorrect grammar may never have been reinforced.

Chomsky saw language development as being determined not by imitation or reinforcement, but by an inborn biological program that holds across cultures. Chomsky's idea that language is a product of the way the mind is constructed, as opposed to being caused by reinforcement, led psychologists to reconsider the idea that language and other complex behaviors, such as problem solving and reasoning, can be explained by operant conditioning. Instead, they began to realize that to understand complex cognitive behaviors, it is necessary not only to measure observable behavior, but also to consider what this behavior tells us about how the mind works.

The Rebirth of the Study of the Mind

The decade of the 1950s is generally recognized as the beginning of the **cognitive revolution**—a shift in psychology from the behaviorist's stimulus-response relationships to an approach whose main thrust was to understand the operation of the mind. Chomsky's critique of Skinner's book was only one of many events in the 1950s that reintroduced the mind to psychology. These events provided a new way to study the mind, called the **information-processing approach**—an approach that traces the sequence of mental operations involved in cognition. One of the events that inspired psychologists to think of the mind in terms of information processing was a newly introduced device called the digital computer.

INTRODUCTION OF THE DIGITAL COMPUTER

The first digital computers, developed in the late 1940s, were huge machines that took up entire buildings, but in 1954 IBM introduced a computer that was available to the general public. These computers were still extremely large compared to the laptops of today, but they found their way into university research laboratories, where they were used both to analyze data and, most important for our purposes, to suggest a new way of thinking about the mind.

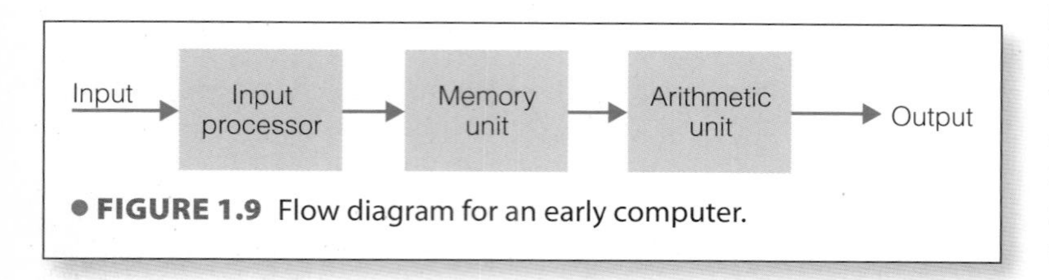

● **FIGURE 1.9** Flow diagram for an early computer.

Flow Diagrams for Digital Computers One of the characteristics of computers that captured the attention of psychologists in the 1950s was that they processed information in stages. For example, the diagram in ● Figure 1.9 shows the layout of a computer in which information is received by an "input processor" and is then stored in a "memory unit" before it is processed by an "arithmetic unit," which then creates the computer's output. Using this stage approach as their inspiration, some psychologists proposed the then-revolutionary idea that the operation of the mind could also be described as occurring in a number of stages. Applying this stage approach to the mind led psychologists to ask new questions and to frame their answers to these questions in new ways. One of the first experiments influenced by this new way of thinking about the mind involved studying how well people are able to pay attention to only some information when a lot of information is being presented at the same time.

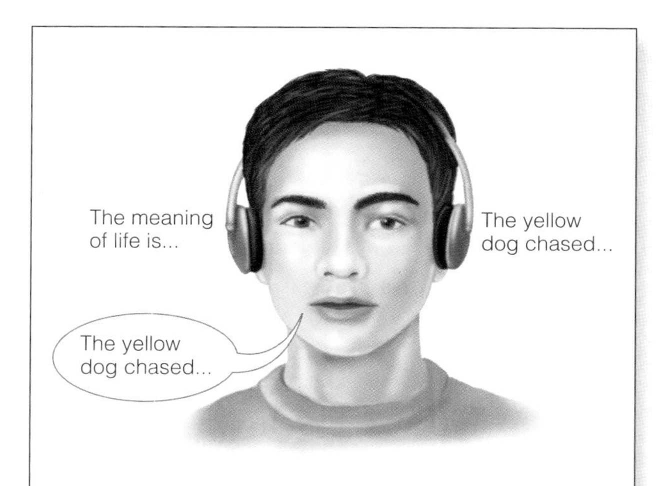

● **FIGURE 1.10** This person in Colin Cherry's (1953) selective attention experiment is listening to the message being presented to his left ear (the attended message) and not to the message presented to his right ear (the unattended message). He repeats the attended message out loud to indicate that he is paying attention to it. The results of experiments such as this were used by Broadbent to create his filter model of attention.

Flow Diagrams for the Mind Beginning in the 1950s, a number of researchers became interested in describing how well the mind can deal with incoming information. One question they were interested in answering was: When a number of auditory messages are presented at once (as might occur at a noisy party, for example), can a person focus on just one of these messages (as when you are having a conversation with one of the people at the party)? In one experiment, by British psychologist Colin Cherry (1953), participants were presented with two messages simultaneously, one to the left ear and one to the right (● Figure 1.10), and were told to focus their attention on one of the messages (called the *attended message*) and to ignore the other one (called the *unattended message*).

The results of this experiment, which we will describe in detail when we discuss attention in Chapter 4, is that people could focus their attention on the message presented to one ear, and when they did, they were aware of little of the message being presented to the other, unattended ear. This result led another British psychologist, Donald Broadbent (1958), to propose the first flow diagram of the mind (● Figure 1.11). This diagram represented what happens in a person's mind as he or she directs attention to one stimulus in the environment. This flow diagram, which we will describe in more detail in Chapter 4, is notable because it was the first to depict the mind as processing information in a sequence of stages. Applied to the attention experiments, "input" would be the sounds entering the person's ears; the "filter" lets through only the part of the input to which the person is attending; and the "detector" records the information that gets through the filter.

Applied to your experience when talking to a friend at a noisy party, the filter lets in your friend's conversation and filters out all of the other conversations and noise. Thus, although you might be aware that there are other people talking, you would not be aware of detailed information, such as what the other people were talking about.

Broadbent's flow diagram provided a way to analyze the operation of the mind in terms of a sequence of processing stages and proposed a **model** that could be tested by further experiments. You will see many more flow diagrams like this throughout this book because they have become one of the standard ways of depicting the operation of the mind.

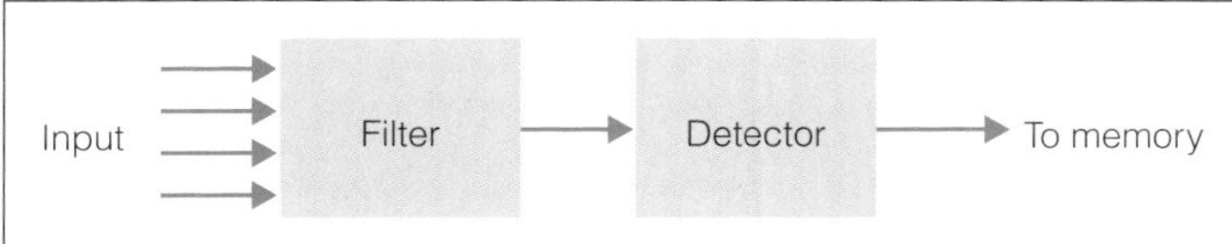

● **FIGURE 1.11** Flow diagram for Broadbent's filter model of attention. This diagram shows that many messages enter a "filter" that selects the message to which the person is attending for further processing by a detector and then storage in memory. We will describe this diagram more fully in Chapter 4.

CONFERENCES ON ARTIFICIAL INTELLIGENCE AND INFORMATION THEORY

In the early 1950s John McCarthy, a young professor of mathematics at Dartmouth College, had an idea. Would it be possible, McCarthy wondered, to program computers to mimic the operation of the human mind? Rather than simply asking the question, McCarthy decided to do something about it by organizing a conference at Dartmouth in the summer of 1956 to provide a forum for researchers to discuss ways that computers could be programmed to carry out intelligent behavior. The title of the conference, Summer

Research Project on Artificial Intelligence, was the first use of the term **artificial intelligence**. McCarthy defined the artificial intelligence approach as "making a machine behave in ways that would be called intelligent if a human were so behaving" (McCarthy et al., 1955).

Researchers from a number of different disciplines—psychologists, mathematicians, computer scientists, linguists, and experts in information theory—attended the conference, which spanned 10 weeks. A number of people attended most of the conference, others dropped in and out, but perhaps the two most important participants of all—Herb Simon and Alan Newell from Carnegie Institute of Technology—were hardly there at all (Boden, 2006). The reason they weren't there is that they were busy trying to create the artificial intelligence machine that McCarthy had envisioned. Simon and Newell's goal was to create a computer program that could create proofs for problems in logic—something that up until then had only been achieved by humans.

Newell and Simon succeeded in creating the program, which they called the **logic theorist**, in time to demonstrate it at the conference. What they demonstrated was revolutionary, because the logic theorist program was able to create proofs of mathematical theorems that involve principles of logic too complex to describe here. This program, although primitive compared to modern artificial intelligence programs, was a real "thinking machine" because it did more than simply process numbers—it used human-like reasoning processes to solve problems.

Shortly after the Dartmouth conference, in September of the same year, another pivotal conference was held, the Massachusetts Institute of Technology Symposium on Information Theory. This conference provided another opportunity for Newell and Simon to demonstrate their logic theorist program, and the attendees also heard George Miller, a Harvard psychologist, present a version of his paper "The Magical Number 7 Plus or Minus 2," which had just been published (Miller, 1956). In that paper, Miller presented the idea that there are limits to the human's ability to process information—that the information processing of the human mind is limited to about 7 items (for example, the length of a telephone number). As we will see when we discuss this idea in Chapter 5, there are ways to increase our ability to take in and remember information (for example, we have little trouble adding an area code to the 7 digits of many telephone numbers). Nonetheless, Miller's basic principle that there are limits to the amount of information we can take in and remember was an important idea, which, you might notice, was similar to the point being made by Broadbent's filter model at about the same time.

The events we have described, Broadbent's filter model and the two conferences in 1956, represented the beginning of a shift in psychology from behaviorism to the study of the mind. This shift has been called the cognitive revolution, but the word *revolution* should not be interpreted as meaning that the shift from behaviorism to the cognitive approach occurred quickly. The scientists attending the conferences in 1956 had no idea that these conferences would, years later, be seen as historic events in the birth of a new way of thinking about the mind or that scientific historians would someday call 1956 "the birthday of cognitive science" (Bechtel et al., 1998; Miller, 2003; Neisser, 1988). In fact, even years after these meetings, a textbook on the history of psychology made no mention of the cognitive approach (Misiak & Sexton, 1966), and it wasn't until 1967 that Ulrich Neisser published a textbook with the title *Cognitive Psychology* (Neisser, 1967).

Neisser's textbook, which coined the term *cognitive psychology* and emphasized the information-processing approach to studying the mind is, in a sense, the grandfather of the book you are now reading. As often happens, each successive generation creates new ways of approaching problems, and cognitive psychology has been no exception. Since the 1956 conferences and the 1967 textbook, many experiments have been carried out, new theories proposed, and new techniques developed; as a result, cognitive psychology, and the information-processing approach to studying the mind, has become one of the dominant approaches in psychology. ● Figure 1.12 shows a timeline illustrating the events that led to the establishment of the field of cognitive psychology.

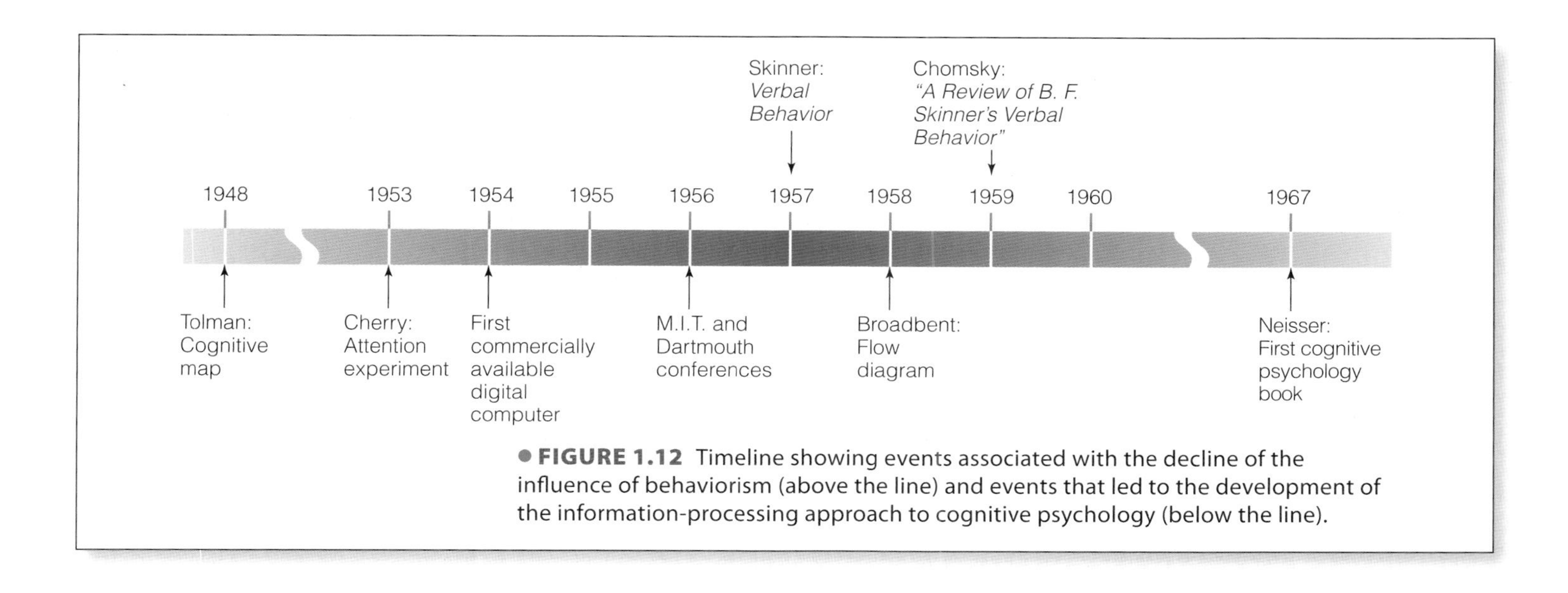

● **FIGURE 1.12** Timeline showing events associated with the decline of the influence of behaviorism (above the line) and events that led to the development of the information-processing approach to cognitive psychology (below the line).

Researching the Mind

How is the mind studied? The basic principle of using behavior to infer mental processes, as Donders did, still guides present-day research. In addition, new technologies have enabled psychologists to expand their research to also study the relation between mental processes and the brain. To illustrate how cognitive psychologists have used both **behavioral** and **physiological approaches** to studying the operation of the mind, we will now describe a few experiments designed to study a phenomenon called *memory consolidation.*

MEMORY CONSOLIDATION FROM A BEHAVIORAL PERSPECTIVE

Recall of first list

1 2 No delay — Test for list 1 — 28%

(a) Immediate group

1 2 (6 minutes) — Test for list 1 — 48%

(b) Delay group

● **FIGURE 1.13** Procedure for Muller and Pilzecker's experiment. (a) In the immediate condition, participants learned the first list (1) and then immediately learned the second list (2). (b) In the delay condition, the second list was learned after a 6-minute delay. Numbers on the right indicate the percentage of items from the first list recalled when memory for that list was tested later.

A football player is running downfield, the ball tucked securely under his arm. Suddenly, his run is unexpectedly cut short by a vicious tackle. His helmet hits the ground, and he lies still for a few moments before slowly getting up and making his way back to the bench. Later, sitting on the bench, he can't remember getting hit, or even taking the handoff from the quarterback at the beginning of the play.

The football player's lack of memory for the events that occurred just before he got hit illustrate that our memory for recent events is fragile. Normally, he would have had no trouble remembering the handoff and run, but the hit he took wiped out his memory for these events. More accurately, the hit prevented the information about the handoff and run from undergoing a process called **memory consolidation**, during which the information about the handoff and run, which was in a fragile state, could become strengthened and transformed into a strong memory that is more resistant to interference by events such as taking a hit to the head.

Research on the phenomenon of memory consolidation dates back to the beginnings of the study of cognition, when the German psychologists Georg Muller and Alfons Pilzecker (1900; also see Deware et al., 2007) had two groups of participants each learn two lists of nonsense syllables. The "immediate" group learned one list and were then asked to immediately learn a second list. The "delay" group learned the first list and then waited for 6 minutes before learning the second list (● Figure 1.13). When recall for the first list was then measured, participants in the delay group remembered 48 percent of the syllables, but participants in the immediate group remembered only 28 percent of the syllables. Apparently, immediately presenting the second list to the immediate group interrupted the forming of a stable memory for the first list—the process that came to be called consolidation.

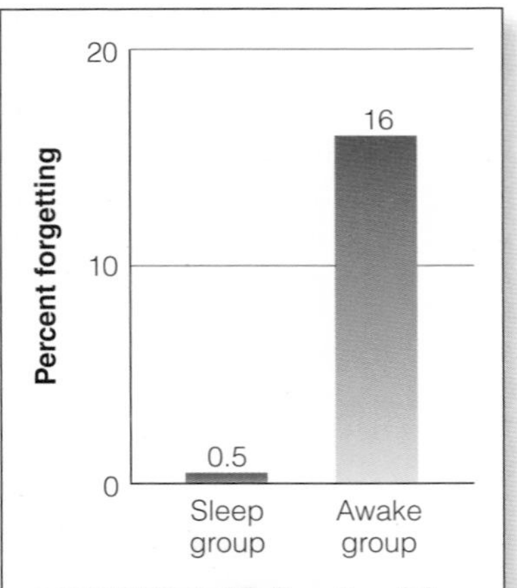

● **FIGURE 1.14** Results of the Gais et al. (2007) experiment in which memory for word pairs was tested for two groups. The sleep group went to sleep shortly after learning a list of word pairs. The awake group stayed awake for quite a while after learning the word pairs. Both groups did get to sleep before testing, so they were equally rested before being tested, but the performance of the sleep group was better.

Many experiments investigating this consolidation process have been done in the more than 100 years since Muller and Pilzecker's experiment. One question that is a topic of current investigation is "How does going to sleep right after learning affect consolidation?" To investigate this question, Steffan Gais and coworkers (2006) had high school students learn a list of 24 pairs of English-German vocabulary words. The "sleep group" studied the words and then went to sleep within 3 hours. The "awake group" studied the words and remained awake for 10 hours before getting a night's sleep. Both groups were tested within 24 to 36 hours after studying the vocabulary lists (The actual experiment involved a number of different sleep and awake groups to control for time of day and other factors we aren't going to consider here.) The results of the experiment, shown in ● Figure 1.14, indicate that students in the sleep group forgot much less material than the students in the awake group.

This result, like Muller and Pilzecker's 100 years earlier, raises its own questions. What is it about going to sleep right away that improves memory? Is sleeping just a way to avoid being exposed to interfering stimuli, or is something special happening during the sleep process that helps strengthen memory? This question is being researched in a number of laboratories. Some results indicate that sleep may just be a way of avoiding interference (Sheth et al., 2009), but research is continuing on this question.

MEMORY CONSOLIDATION FROM A PHYSIOLOGICAL PERSPECTIVE

The two experiments we have just described studied consolidation by measuring behavior. But what brain processes are involved in consolidation? Although early researchers knew that consolidation involved processes in the brain, they had no way of determining what those processes might be. Modern researchers, armed with techniques for measuring physiological processes, have begun to determine these processes. For example Louis Flexner and coworkers (1963) did an experiment in which they showed that injecting a chemical that inhibits the synthesis of proteins in rats eliminates formation of memories. This suggests that interference, such as that experienced by the football player, may disrupt chemical reactions that are necessary for consolidation.

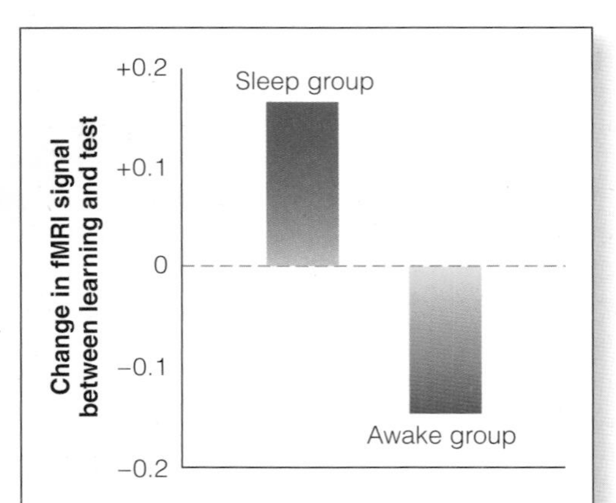

● **FIGURE 1.15** Results of the Gais et al. (2007) experiment in which the brain activity of participants' in the sleep and awake groups was measured as they were initially learning a list of word pairs and as they were remembering the list two days later. Activity in the hippocampus increased for participants in the sleep group, but decreased for participants in the awake group. Also, in data not shown here, the overall level of activity in the hippocampus was greater during testing in the sleep group.

Flexner's study provides information about how consolidation might operate at the molecular level involved in protein synthesis. Cognitive psychologists are also interested in determining which structures in the brain are involved in consolidation. One way to determine this is to use a technique called brain scanning (which we will describe in Chapter 2), which makes it possible to measure the response of different areas of the human brain.

In an extension of the experiment described previously, in which Gais and coworkers (2006) showed that participants in the sleep group had better memory for word pairs than participants in the awake group, Gais and coworkers (2007) carried out another experiment, in which participants learned word pairs and then were tested two days later. As in the previous experiment, participants in the sleep group remembered more word pairs than participants in the awake group. This time, however, in addition to measuring memory, Gais measured brain activity, using a brain imaging technique called fMRI (which we will describe in the next chapter). He measured this activity first as participants were learning the word pairs and again as they were tested two days later.

● Figure 1.15 shows that the activity of the hypothalamus, a structure deep in the brain that is known to be involved in the storage of new memories, increased from learning to test for the sleep group but decreased from learning to test for the awake group. Gais concluded from this result that immediate sleep helps strengthen the memory trace in the hypothalamus.

The purpose of these examples of behavioral and physiological experiments is not to provide an explanation of how consolidation works (we will discuss consolidation further in Chapter 7), but to illustrate how cognitive psychologists use both behavioral and physiological measurements to search for answers. The basic premise of much research in cognitive psychology, and of the approach taken in this book, is that only by studying cognition both behaviorally and physiologically can we completely understand the mechanisms underlying cognition.

Another point that our example of consolidation illustrates is how results of basic research can have practical applications. Even without knowing the mechanisms responsible for consolidation, we can conclude that when studying for an exam it might make sense to go to sleep soon after studying, rather than doing something that might keep all that knowledge from being consolidated (thereby eliminating the "I-knew-it-last-night-but-it-wasn't-there-for-the-exam" phenomenon!). We will be considering how the findings of cognitive psychology research can be applied to real-life situations throughout this book. (See Chapter 7, page 187, for some more "study hints" based on principles of cognitive psychology.)

MODELS OF THE MIND

As you read about cognitive psychology in this book, you will encounter many models of the mind. A model can be a representation of something, as a model car or airplane represents the appearance of a real car or airplane. Similarly, plastic models of the brain are often used to illustrate the locations of different structures of the brain. But models can also illustrate how something works, and in cognitive psychology models are generally used to represent how information is processed by the mind. These models often take the form of flow diagrams, which represent how information flows through various components of the mind. For example, Broadbent's flow diagram in Figure 1.11 is a model of how a person processes information to selectively attend to one message out of many.

One advantage of models is that they often make a complicated system easier to understand. Although the process of selective attention is certainly more complex than the two processing steps in Broadbent's model, this simple model provides a good starting point for seeking further details of how selective attention operates.

One of the ways that models provide this "starting point" is by helping suggest questions to ask. For example, a researcher studying attention might want to ask questions about how the filter in Broadbent's model works. According to Broadbent, the filter lets through attended information (such as the contents of the conversation you are having with a friend at a party) and filters out the unattended information (such as all of the other conversations and noise at the party). But what about the situation that occurs when you hear someone across the room call out your name? Hearing your name means that your name somehow got through the filter, even though you were focusing your attention on the conversation you were having.

Could this mean that perhaps there isn't a filter? Or perhaps there is a filter, but its operation is more complicated than Broadbent's initial proposal. Good models such as Broadbent's are usually stated in a way that suggests further questions, which can be answered by doing further experiments, and the results of these experiments often lead to the proposal of a new, updated model.

Students often wonder whether the boxes in models such as Broadbent's stand for specific areas in the brain. Although in some models each box corresponds to a specific place in the brain, the boxes in most of the models we will be describing do not correspond to one brain area. We will see that a basic principle of the operation of the mind is that activity is distributed across many areas of the brain. Thus, although a model might represent the attentional filter by a single box, the actual filtering may be accomplished by a number of different structures that are located in different parts of the brain.

➔ Something to Consider

LEARNING FROM THIS BOOK

Congratulations! You now know how some researchers began doing cognitive psychology experiments in the 19th century, how the study of the mind was suppressed in the middle of the 20th century, how the study of the mind made a glorious comeback in the 1950s, and that present-day psychologists use both behavioral and physiological techniques to study the mind. One of the purposes of this chapter—to provide you with some background to orient you to the field of cognitive psychology—has been accomplished.

Another purpose of this chapter is to help you get the most out of this book. After all, cognitive psychology is the study of the mind. As you will see as you get further into the book, especially in the chapters on memory, there are things that have been discovered about cognitive psychology that can help you get as much as possible from this book and from the course you are taking. One way to appreciate how cognitive psychology can be applied to studying is to look at pages 187–189 in Chapter 7. It would make sense to skim this material now, rather than waiting. There will be some terms that you may not be familiar with, but these aren't crucial for what you want to accomplish—picking up some hints that will make your studying more efficient and effective. Two terms worth knowing, though, are *encoding*—which is what is happening as you are learning the material—and *retrieval*—what is happening when you are remembering the material. The trick is to encode the material during your studying in a way that will make it easier to retrieve it later. (Also see page xxix in the preface.)

Something else that might help as you learn from this book is to be aware of how it is constructed. As you read the book, you will see that often a basic idea or theory is presented and then it is supported by examples or experiments. Consider our discussion of memory consolidation in this chapter. First the phenomenon was described (memory is initially fragile and so can be disrupted), and then experiments were presented to illustrate it (Muller and Pilzecker: memory is interrupted if a second list is learned immediately; Gais and coworkers: memory is better if sleep occurs shortly after learning).

This way of presenting information breaks the discussion of a particular topic into a series of "mini-stories." Each story begins with an idea or phenomenon and is followed by demonstrations of the phenomenon and usually evidence to support it. Often there is also a connection between one story and the next. For example, once consolidation is described behaviorally, the next story is about how it can be studied physiologically.

What's important about this is that realizing how the story of cognitive psychology is presented can help you remember what you have read. It is easier to remember a number of facts if they are presented as part of a story than if they are presented as separate, unrelated facts. So as you read this book, keep in mind that your main job is to understand the stories, each of which is a basic premise followed by supporting evidence. Thinking about the material in this way will make it more meaningful and therefore easier to remember.

One more thing: Just as specific topics can be described as a number of small stories that are linked together, the field of cognitive psychology as a whole consists of many themes that are related to each other, even if they appear in different chapters. Perception, attention, memory, and other cognitive processes all involve the same nervous system and therefore share many of the same properties. The principles shared by many cognitive processes are part of the larger story of cognition that will unfold as you progress through this book.

TEST YOURSELF 1.1

1. Why could we say that Donders and Ebbinghaus were cognitive psychologists, even though in the 19th century there was no field called cognitive psychology? Describe Donders' experiment and the rationale behind it, and Ebbinghaus's memory experiments. What do Donders' and Ebbinghaus's experiments have in common?
2. When was the first laboratory of scientific psychology founded? How important was the study of mental functioning in psychology at the end of the 19th century and beginning of the 20th?
3. Describe the rise of behaviorism, especially the influence of Watson and Skinner. How did behaviorism affect research on the mind?
4. Describe the events that helped lead to the decline in importance of behaviorism in psychology and the events that led to the "cognitive revolution." Be sure you understand what the information-processing approach is.

5. Describe the behavioral and physiological approaches to the study of cognition. How are they different, and what do they have in common? Give some examples of how both approaches have been used to study the phenomenon of memory consolidation.
6. Why are models important in cognitive psychology? Do the boxes in models like Broadbent's model of memory correspond to structures in the brain?
7. What are two suggestions for improving your ability to learn from this book?

CHAPTER SUMMARY

1. Cognitive psychology is the branch of psychology concerned with the scientific study of the mind.
2. The mind creates and controls mental capacities such as perception, attention, and memory, and creates representations of the world that enable us to function.
3. The work of Donders (simple vs. choice reaction time) and Ebbinghaus (the forgetting curve for nonsense syllables) are examples of early experimental research on the mind.
4. Because the operation of the mind cannot be observed directly, its operation must be inferred from what we can measure, such as behavior or physiological responding. This is one of the basic principles of cognitive psychology.
5. The first laboratory of scientific psychology, founded by Wundt in 1879, was concerned largely with studying the mind. Structuralism was the dominant theoretical approach of this laboratory, and analytic introspection was one of the major methods used to collect data.
6. William James, in the United States, used observations of his own behavior as the basis of his textbook, *Principles of Psychology*.
7. In the first decades of the 20th century, John Watson founded behaviorism, partly in reaction to structuralism and the method of analytic introspection. His procedures were based on classical conditioning. Behaviorism's central tenet was that psychology was properly studied by measuring observable behavior, and that invisible mental processes were not valid topics for the study of psychology.
8. Beginning in the 1930s and '40s, B. F. Skinner's work on operant conditioning assured that behaviorism would be the dominant force in psychology through the 1950s.
9. In the 1950s, a number of events occurred that led to what has been called the cognitive revolution—a decline in the influence of behaviorism and the reemergence of the study of the mind. These events included the following: (a) Chomsky's critique of Skinner's book *Verbal Behavior*; (b) the introduction of the digital computer and the idea that the mind processes information in stages, like computers; (c) Cherry's attention experiments and Broadbent's introduction of flow diagrams to depict the processes involved in attention; and (d) interdisciplinary conferences at Dartmouth and the Massachusetts Institute of Technology.
10. The phenomenon of memory consolidation was used to illustrate how answering one question can lead to many additional questions, and how cognitive psychologists study the mind by using both behavioral and physiological approaches. Using these two approaches together results in a more complete understanding of how the mind operates than using either one alone.
11. Models play an essential role in cognitive psychology, by helping organize data from many experiments. Broadbent's model of attention is an example of one of the early models in cognitive psychology. It is important to realize that models such as this one are constantly being revised in response to new data, and also that the boxes in these models often do not correspond to areas in the brain.
12. Two things that may help in learning the material in this book are to read the study hints in Chapter 7, which are based on some of the things we know about memory research, and to realize that the book is constructed like a story, with basic ideas or principles followed by supporting evidence.

Think ABOUT IT

1. What do you think the "hot topics" of cognitive psychology are, based on what you have seen or heard in the media? Hint: Look for stories such as the following: "Scientists Race to Find Memory Loss Cure"; "Defendant Says He Can't Remember What Happened."
2. The idea that we have something called "the mind" that is responsible for our thoughts and behavior is reflected in the many ways that the word *mind* can be used. A few examples of the use of *mind* in everyday language were cited at the beginning of the chapter. See how many more examples you can think of that illustrate

different uses of the word *mind*, and decide how relevant each is to what you will be studying in cognitive psychology (as indicated by the table of contents of this book).

3. The idea that the operation of the mind can be described as occurring in a number of stages was the central principle of the information-processing approach that was one of the outcomes of the cognitive revolution that began in the 1950s. How can Donders' reaction time experiment from the 1800s be conceptualized in terms of the information-processing approach?

4. Donders compared the results of his simple and choice reaction time experiments to infer how long it took to make the decision as to which button to push, when given a choice. But what about other kinds of decisions? Design an experiment to determine the time it takes to make a more complex decision. Then relate this experiment to the diagram in Figure 1.3.

If You WANT TO KNOW MORE

1. **The birth of cognitive psychology.** To get a feel for the kinds of things cognitive psychologists were concerned with near the beginning of the "cognitive revolution," look at Ulrich Neisser's book, *Cognitive Psychology*. This was the first modern textbook on the subject. Try comparing it to what's in this book. One thing you will notice is that the field of cognitive psychology is far more concerned with physiological processes now than it was at the beginning.

   Neisser, U. (1967). *Cognitive psychology*. New York: Appleton-Century-Crofts.

2. **How the mind works.** An engaging book for the general reader, *How The Mind Works*, is worth checking out for a well-known cognitive psychologist's perspective on the mind. Pinker describes the mind as a natural computer and presents his ideas regarding how the mind has been shaped by the process of natural selection and how its operation is influenced by our modern environment.

   Pinker, S. (1997). *How the mind works*. New York: Norton.

Key TERMS

Media RESOURCES

The *Cognitive Psychology* Book Companion Website

www.cengage.com/international

Prepare for quizzes and exams with online resources—including a glossary, flashcards, tutorial quizzes, crossword puzzles, and more.

2 Brain and Cognition

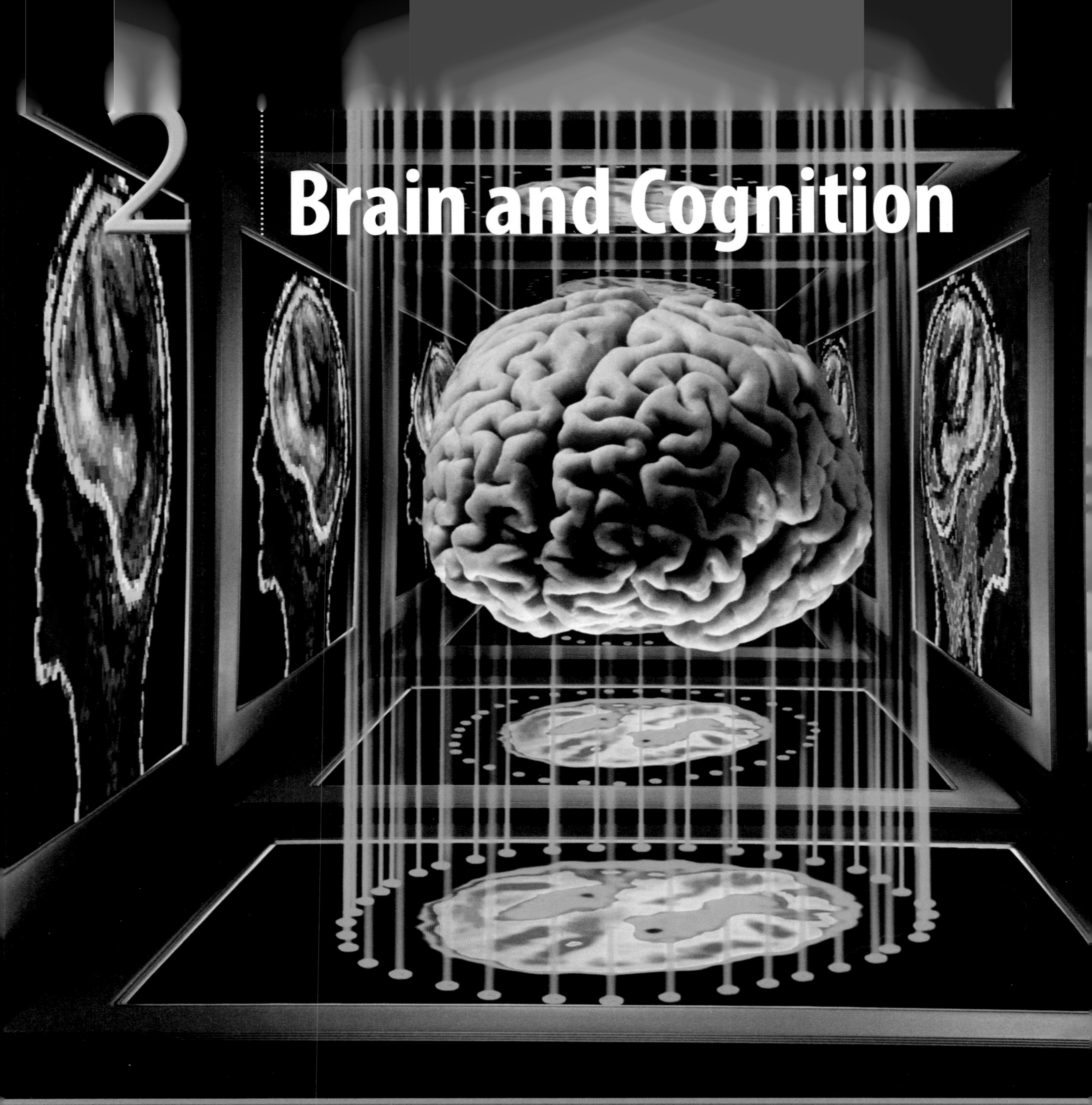

Brain imaging technology has made it possible to visualize both the structure and functioning of different areas of the brain.

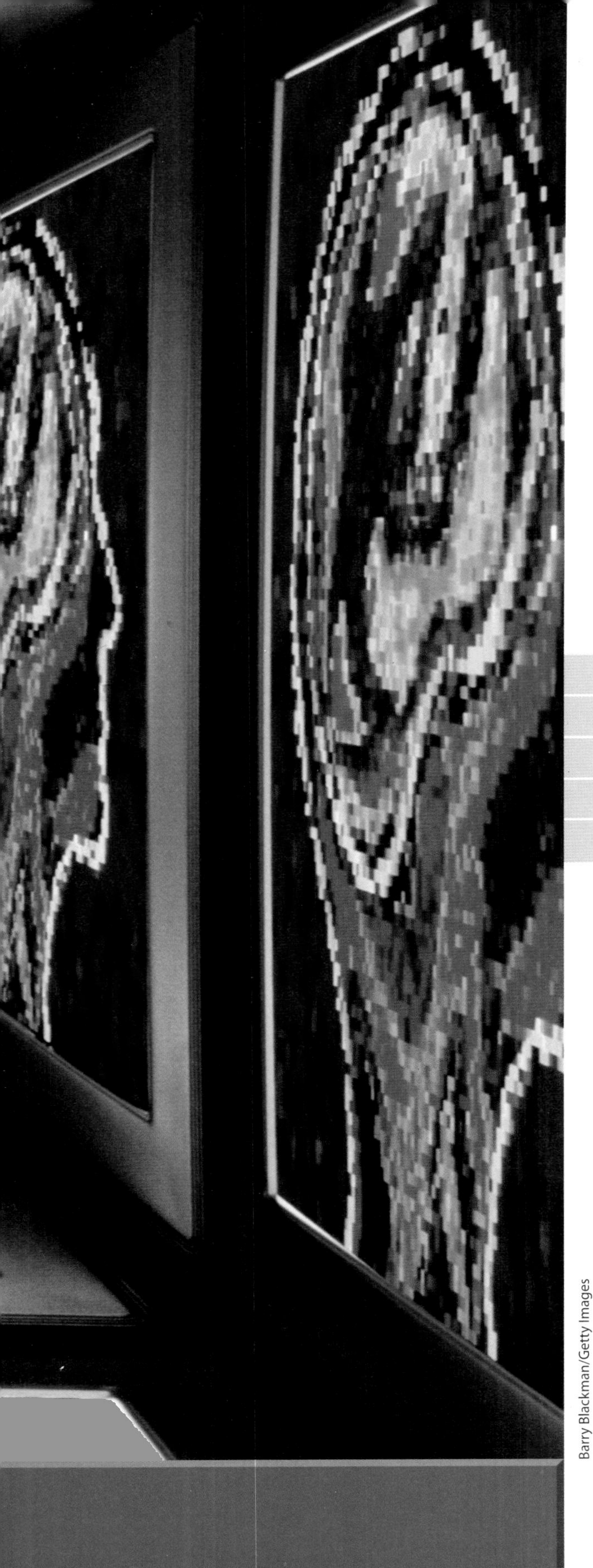

Barry Blackman/Getty Images

Some Questions We Will Consider

- What is cognitive neuroscience, and why is it necessary? (24)
- How is information transmitted from one place to another in the nervous system? (26)
- How are things in the environment, such as faces and trees, represented in the brain? (38)
- Is it possible to read a person's mind by measuring the activity of the person's brain? (41)

At 7:00 a.m., in response to hearing the familiar but irritating sound of his alarm clock, Juan swings his arm in a well-practiced arc, feels the contact of his hand with the snooze button, and in the silence he has created, turns over for 10 more minutes of sleep. How can we explain Juan's behavior in terms of physiology? What is happening inside Juan's brain that makes it possible for him to hear the alarm, take appropriate action to turn it off, and know that he can sleep a little longer and still get to his early morning class on time?

We can give a general answer to this question by considering some of the steps involved in Juan's action of turning off the alarm. The first step in hearing the alarm occurs when sound waves from the alarm enter Juan's ears and stimulate receptors that change the sound energy into electrical signals (● Figure 2.1a). These signals then reach the auditory area of Juan's brain, which causes him to hear the ringing of the bell (Figure 2.1b). Then signals are sent from a number of places in the brain to the motor area, which controls movement. The motor area sends signals to the muscles of Juan's hand and arm (Figure 2.1c), which carry out the movement that turns off the alarm.

But there is more to the story than this sequence of events. For one thing, Juan's decision to hit the snooze button of his alarm is based on his knowledge that this will silence the alarm temporarily, and that the alarm will sound again in 10 minutes. He also knows that if he stays in bed for 10 more minutes, he will still have time to get to his class. A more complete picture of what's happening in Juan's brain when the alarm rings would, therefore, have to include processes involved in retrieving knowledge from memory and making decisions based on that knowledge. Thus, a seemingly simple behavior such as turning off an alarm in the morning involves a complex series of physiological events.

Students often wonder why they need to know about principles of nervous system functioning for a course in cognitive psychology. One answer to this question is that the development of brain scanning technology over the last few decades has placed the brain at the center of much present-day research in cognitive psychology. The study of cognitive psychology today consists of both purely behavioral experiments and experiments that consider links between behavior and the brain.

The purpose of this chapter is to introduce **cognitive neuroscience**, the study of the physiological basis of cognition. This chapter provides the basic background you will need to understand the physiological material on perception, attention, memory, language, decision making, and problem solving that we will be covering in the chapters that follow. We will describe some basic principles of nervous system functioning by first considering the structure and functioning of cells called **neurons**, which are the building blocks and transmission lines of the nervous system. We then focus on the collection of 180 billion of these neurons that form the brain. As we do this, you will see that to understand the brain we need to understand how its neurons are organized and how they signal information about the environment and our actions within the environment.

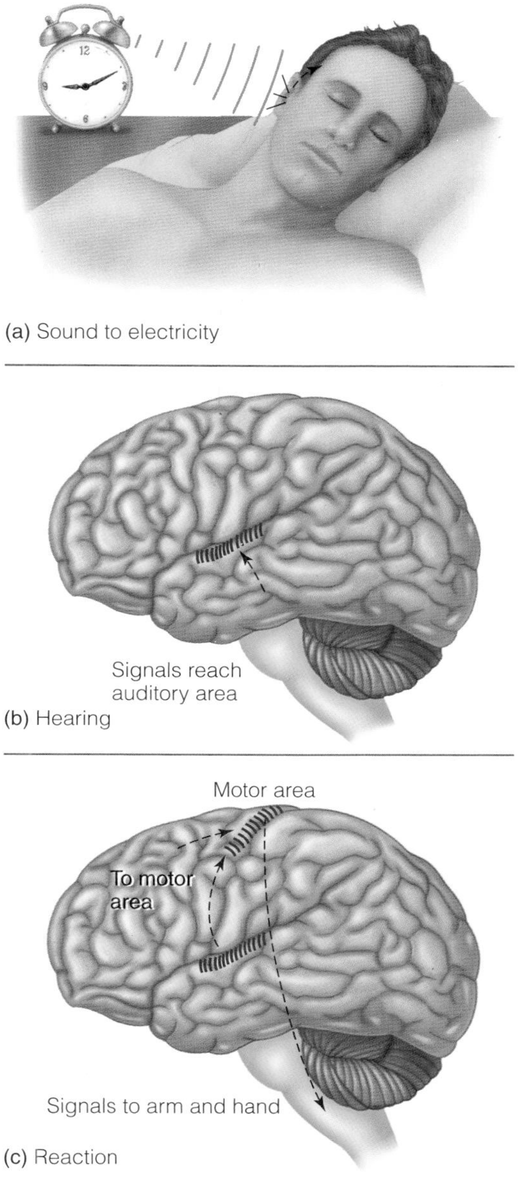

● **FIGURE 2.1** Some of the physiological processes that occur as Juan turns off his alarm. (a) Sound waves are changed to electrical signals in the ear and are sent to the brain. (b) Signals reaching the auditory areas of the brain—which are located inside the brain, under the hatched area—cause Juan to hear the alarm. (c) After Juan hears the alarm, signals are sent to the motor area. The two arrows pointing up symbolize the fact that these signals reach the motor area along a number of different pathways. Signals are then sent from the motor area to muscles in Juan's arm and hand so he can turn off the alarm.

(a) Sound to electricity

(b) Hearing

(c) Reaction

Neurons: The Building Blocks of the Nervous System

How is it possible that the 3.5-pound structure called the brain could be the seat of the mind? It is, after all, just static tissue. It has no moving parts (like the heart). It doesn't expand or contract (like the lungs), and when observed with the naked eye it looks almost solid. As it turns out, to understand the relation between the brain and the mind it is necessary to look within the brain and observe the small units that make up its structure and the electrical signals that travel in these units.

THE MICROSTRUCTURE OF THE BRAIN: NEURONS

For many years, the nature of the brain's tissue was a mystery. Looking at the interior of the brain with the unaided eye gave no indication that it is made up of billions of smaller units. The nature of electrical signals in the brain and the pathways over which they traveled were just beginning to be discovered in the 19th century.

To observe the structure of the brain, 19th-century anatomists applied special stains to the brain tissue, which increased the contrast between different types of tissue within the brain. When they viewed this stained tissue under a microscope, they saw a network they called a **nerve net**. This network was believed to be continuous, like a highway system in which one street connects directly to another, but without stop signs or traffic lights. When visualized in this way, the nerve net provided a complex pathway for conducting signals uninterrupted through the network (● Figure 2.2a).

One reason for describing the microstructure of the brain as a continuously interconnected network was that the staining techniques and microscopes of the time could not resolve small details, and without these details, the nerve net appeared to be continuous. However, in the 1870s, the Italian anatomist Camillo Golgi developed a staining technique that involved immersing a thin slice of brain tissue in a solution of silver nitrate. This technique created pictures like the one in Figure 2.2b, in which individual cells were randomly stained. What made this technique useful was that fewer than 1 percent of the cells were stained, so they stood out from the rest of the tissue. (If all of the cells had been stained, it would be difficult to distinguish one cell from another because the cells are so tightly packed). Also, the cells that were stained were stained completely, so it was possible to see their structure.

This brings us to Ramon y Cajal, a Spanish physiologist who was interested in investigating the nature of the nerve net. Cajal cleverly used two techniques to achieve his goal. First he used the Golgi stain, which stained only some of the cells in a slice of brain tissue. Second, he decided to study tissue from the brains of newborn animals, because the density of cells in the newborn brain is small compared to the density in the adult brain. This property of the newborn brain, combined with the fact that the Golgi stain affects less than 1 percent of the neurons, made it possible for Cajal to clearly see that the Golgi-stained cells were individual units (Kandel, 2006). Cajal's discovery that individual units called neurons were the basic building blocks of the brain was the centerpiece of **neuron doctrine**—the idea that individual cells transmit signals in the nervous system, and that these cells are not continuous with other cells as proposed by nerve net theory.

● Figure 2.3a shows the basic parts of a neuron. The **cell body** contains mechanisms to keep the cell alive. **Dendrites** branch out from the cell body to receive signals from other neurons, and the **axon** or **nerve fiber** transmits signals to other neurons. Thus, the neuron has a receiving end and a transmitting end, and its role, as visualized by Cajal, was to transmit signals.

Cajal also came to some other conclusions about neurons: (1) In addition to neurons in the brain, there are also neurons that pick up information from the environment, such as the neurons in the skin, eye, and ear. These neurons, called **receptors** (Figure 2.3b), are similar to brain neurons in that they have a cell body and axon, but they have specialized

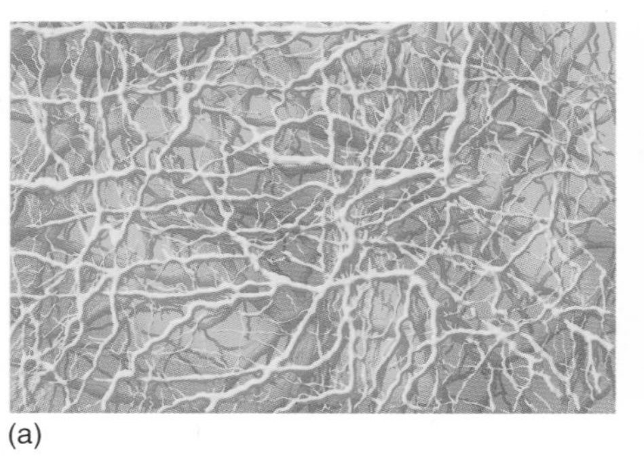

(a)

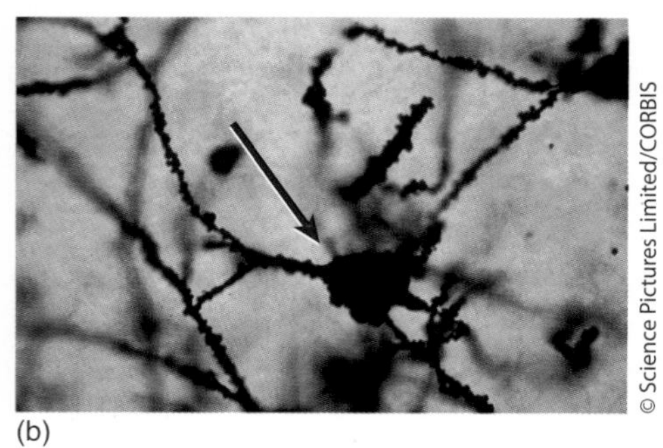

(b)

© Science Pictures Limited/CORBIS

● **FIGURE 2.2** (a) Nerve net theory proposed that signals could be transmitted throughout the net in all directions. (b) A portion of the brain that has been treated with Golgi stain shows the shapes of a few neurons. The arrow points to a neuron's cell body. The thin lines are dendrites or axons (see Figure 2.3).

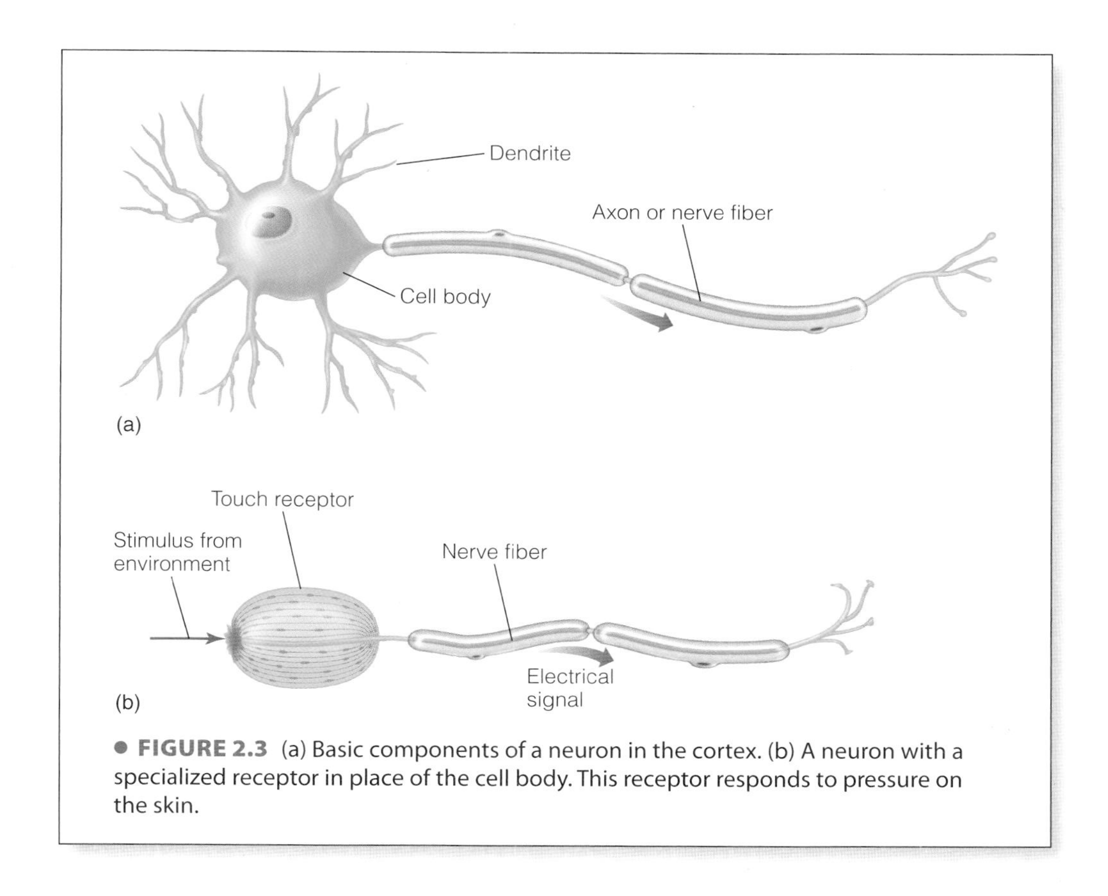

● **FIGURE 2.3** (a) Basic components of a neuron in the cortex. (b) A neuron with a specialized receptor in place of the cell body. This receptor responds to pressure on the skin.

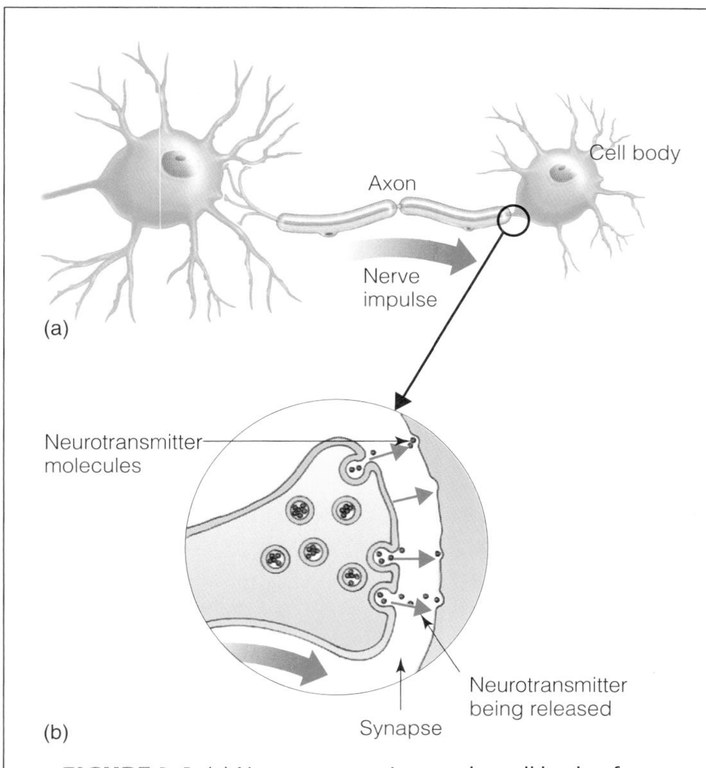

● **FIGURE 2.4** (a) Neuron synapsing on the cell body of another neuron; (b) close-up of the synapse showing the space between the end of one neuron and the cell body of the next neuron, and neurotransmitter being released.

receptors that pick up information from the environment. (2) For all neurons, there is a small gap between the end of the neuron's axon and the dendrites or cell body of another neuron. This gap is called a **synapse** (● Figure 2.4). (3) Neurons are not connected indiscriminately to other neurons, but form connections only to specific neurons. Usually many neurons are connected together to form **neural circuits**.

Cajal's idea of individual neurons that communicate with other neurons to form neural circuits was an enormous leap forward in the understanding of how the nervous system operates. All of the concepts introduced by Cajal—individual neurons, synapses, and neural circuits—are basic principles that today are used to explain how the brain creates cognitions. These discoveries earned Cajal the Nobel Prize in 1906, and today he is recognized as "the person who made this cellular study of mental life possible" (Kandel, 2006, p. 61).

THE SIGNALS THAT TRAVEL IN NEURONS

Cajal succeeded in describing the structure of individual neurons and how they are related to other neurons, and he knew that these neurons transmitted signals. However, determining the exact nature of these signals had to await the development of electronic amplifiers that were powerful enough to make the extremely small electrical signals generated by the neuron visible. In the 1920s, Edgar Adrian was able to record electrical signals from single sensory neurons, an achievement for which he was awarded the Nobel Prize in 1932 (Adrian, 1928, 1932).

METHOD Recording From a Neuron

Adrian recorded electrical signals from single neurons using **microelectrodes**—small shafts of hollow glass filled with a conductive salt solution that can pick up electrical signals at the electrode tip and conduct these signals back to a recording device. Modern physiologists use metal microelectrodes. The electrode is lowered into tissue until the tip of the electrode is positioned near a neuron. This electrode, called the **recording electrode**, is connected to a recording device and to another electrode, called the **reference electrode**, which is located outside of the tissue (● Figure 2.5a).

The key principle for understanding how electrical signals are recorded from neurons is that we are always measuring the *difference in charge* between the recording and reference electrodes. The difference in charge between these two electrodes is displayed on an oscilloscope, which indicates the difference in charge by the vertical position of a small dot that creates a line as it moves across the screen. For example, the record in Figure 2.5b indicates that the difference in charge between the recording and reference electrode is −70 mV (mV = millivolt = 1/1,000 volt) and the dot continues to move along this −70 mV line as long as no electrical signals are being transmitted in the neuron. However, when an electrical signal, called a **nerve impulse** or **action potential**, is transmitted down the axon, the dot is deflected up (as the neuron becomes more positive) and then back down (as the charge returns to its original level), all within 1 millisecond (1/1,000 second), as shown in Figure 2.5c. Figure 2.5d shows action potentials on a compressed time scale, so an action potential like the one in Figure 2.5c appears to be a vertical line. Each line in this record is an action potential, so the series of lines indicates that a number of action potentials are traveling past this electrode. There are other electrical signals in the nervous system, but we will focus here on the action potential, because it is the mechanism by which information is transmitted throughout the nervous system.

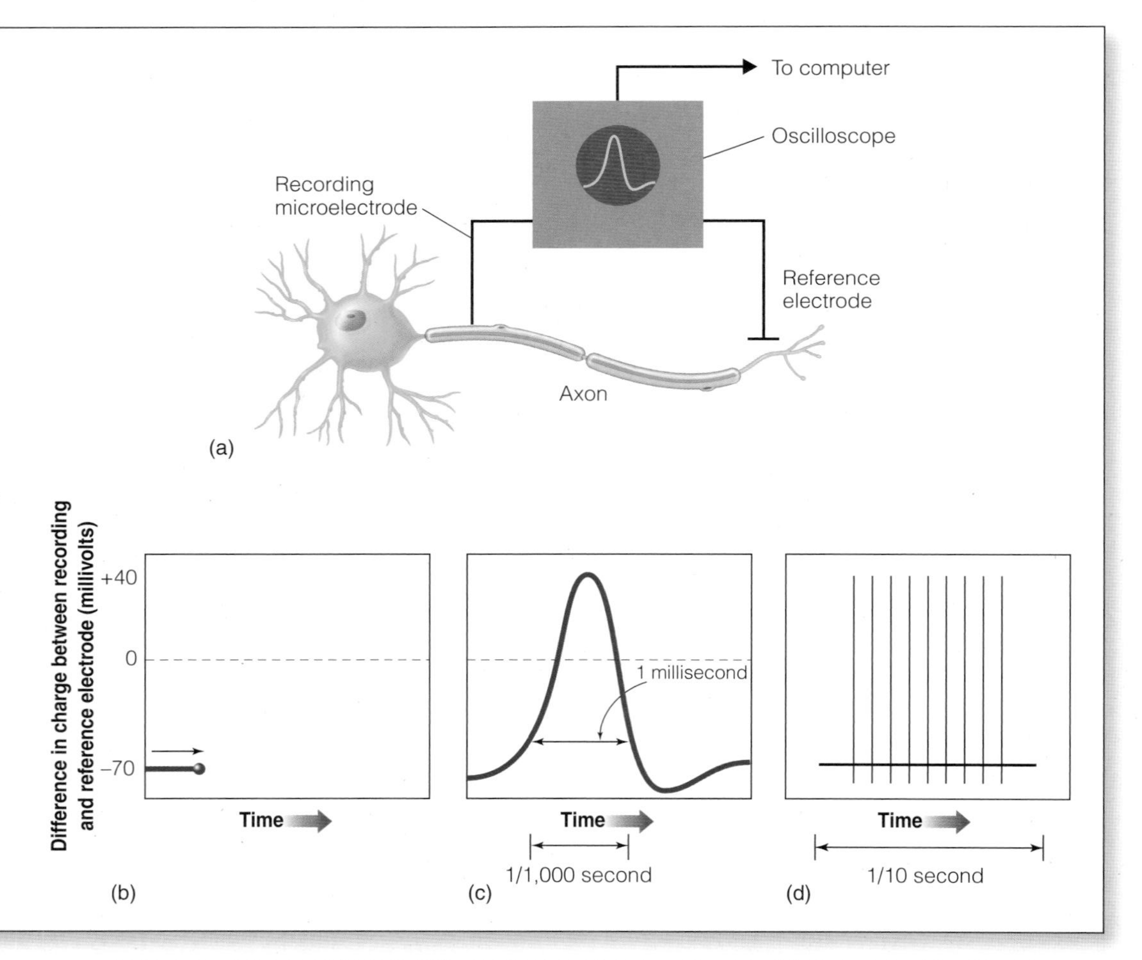

● **FIGURE 2.5** Recording from a single neuron. (a) The difference in charge between the recording and reference electrodes is displayed on the oscilloscope screen. (b) A small dot moves across the screen, which briefly leaves a trail. In this situation, electrical signals are not being transmitted by the axon, so the difference in charge remains at −70 millivolts. (c) When an action potential travels down the axon, it causes a brief positive pulse, like the one shown here, as the potential passes the recording electrode. (d) A number of action potentials are displayed on an expanded time scale, so a single action potential appears as a "spike."

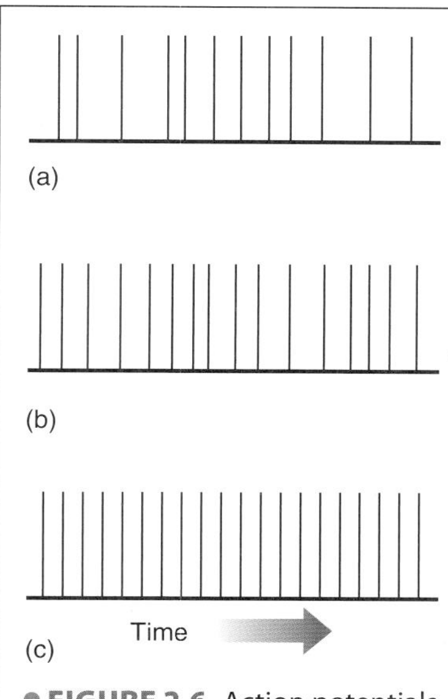

● **FIGURE 2.6** Action potentials recorded from an axon in response to three levels of pressure stimulation on the skin: (a) light; (b) medium; (c) strong. Increasing stimulus intensity causes an increase in the rate of nerve firing.

In addition to recording action potentials from single neurons, Adrian made other discoveries as well. He also found that each action potential travels all the way down the axon without changing its size. This property makes action potentials ideal for sending signals over a distance, because it means that once an action potential is started at one end of an axon, the signal is still the same size when it reaches the other end.

At about the same time Adrian was recording from single neurons, other researchers were showing that when the signals reach the end of the axon, a chemical called a **neurotransmitter** is released that makes it possible for the signal to be transmitted across the synaptic gap that separates the end of the axon from the dendrite or cell body of another neuron (see Figure 2.4).

Although all of these discoveries about the nature of neurons and the signals that travel in them were extremely important (and garnered a number of Nobel prizes for their discoverers), our main interest is not in how axons transmit signals, but in how these signals contribute to the operation of the mind. So far our description of how signals are transmitted is analogous to describing how the Internet transmits electrical signals without describing how the signals are transformed into words and pictures that people can understand. Adrian was acutely aware that it was important to go beyond simply describing nerve signals, so he did a series of experiments to relate nerve signals to stimuli in the environment and therefore to people's experience.

Adrian studied the relation between nerve firing and sensory experience by measuring how the firing of a neuron from a receptor in the skin changed as he applied more pressure to the skin. What he found was that the shape and height of the action potential remained the same as he increased the pressure, but the *rate* of nerve firing—that is, the number of action potentials that travel down the axon per second—increased (● Figure 2.6).

What this means in terms of cognition is that the intensity of a stimulus can be represented by the *rate* of nerve firing. So, for example, increasing the pressure to the skin causes neurons in the touch system to fire more rapidly, and this causes an experience of increased pressure. Or increasing the intensity of light presented to visual receptors in the retina causes more rapid firing of neurons in the visual system and an increased perception of brightness. Thus, the rate of neural firing is related to the intensity of stimulation which, in turn, is related to the magnitude of an experience such as feeling pressure on the skin or experiencing the brightness of a light.

If the *amplitude* of experience—our perception of a 100-watt light as brighter than a 40-watt bulb—is related to the rate of nerve firing, what about the *quality* of experience? For the senses, quality refers to the different experience associated with each of the senses—perceiving light for vision, sound for hearing, smells for olfaction, and so on. We can also ask about quality *within* a particular sense. How do we perceive different shapes, different colors, and various directions of movement, for example?

One way to answer the question of how action potentials determine different qualities is to propose that the action potentials for each quality might look different. However, Adrian ruled out that possibility by determining that all action potentials are basically the same.

If all nerve impulses are basically the same whether they are caused by seeing a red fire engine or remembering what you did last week, how can these impulses stand for different qualities? The answer to this question is that neurons serving different cognitive functions transmit signals to different areas of the brain, a principle called *localization of function*.

Localization of Function

One of the basic principles of brain organization is **localization of function**—specific functions are served by specific areas of the brain. Most of the cognitive functions are served by the **cerebral cortex**, which is a layer of tissue about 3 mm thick that covers the brain (Fischl & Dale, 2000). The cortex is the wrinkled covering you see when you look at an intact brain (● Figure 2.7). Localization of function has been demonstrated for many different cognitive functions. We first consider perception.

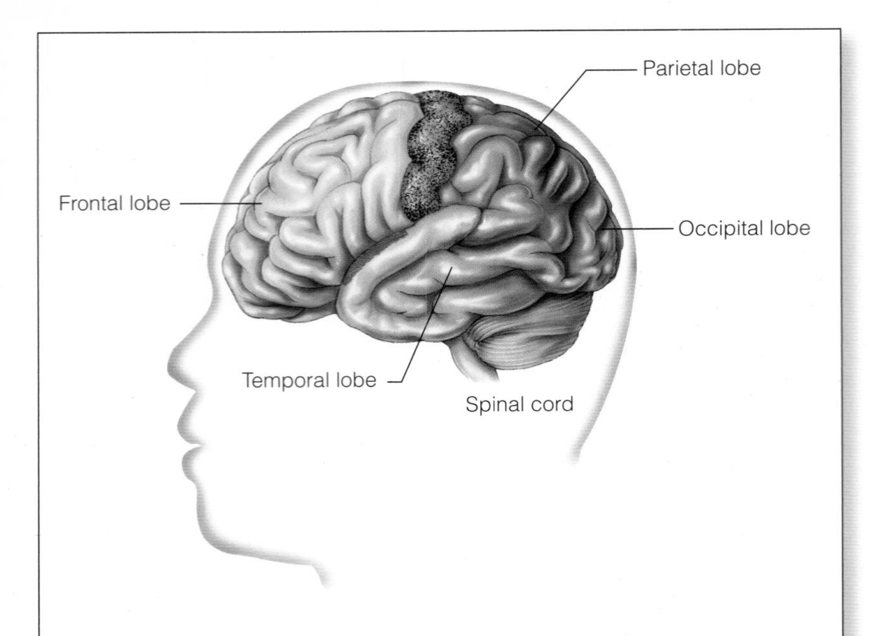

● **FIGURE 2.7** The human brain, showing the locations of the primary receiving areas for the senses: vision = occipital lobe; skin senses = parietal lobe (dotted area); hearing = temporal lobe (located within the temporal lobe, approximately under the hatched area). Areas for taste and smell are not visible. The frontal lobe responds to all of the senses and is involved in higher cognitive functioning.

LOCALIZATION FOR PERCEPTION

One of the most basic demonstrations of localization of function is the **primary receiving areas** for the senses, shown in Figure 2.7. These are the first areas of the cerebral cortex to receive signals from each of the senses. For example, when sound stimulates receptors in the ear, the resulting electrical signals reach the auditory receiving area in the **temporal lobe.**

The primary receiving area for vision occupies most of the **occipital lobe,** and the area for the skin senses—touch, temperature, and pain—is located in the **parietal lobe.** The areas for taste and smell are located on the underside of the temporal lobe (smell) and in a small area within the frontal lobe (taste). The **frontal lobe** receives signals from all of the senses and plays an important role in perceptions that involve the coordination of information received through two or more senses.

The primary receiving areas were initially identified by noting the effects of brain damage. For example, it was noted that damage to the occipital lobe caused by battlefield injuries caused blindness. Another source of brain damage is stroke—disruption of the blood supply to the brain, usually due to a blood clot. As with battlefield injuries, the perceptual effects of strokes are linked to each of the sensory receiving areas.

In addition to the primary receiving areas, other areas also serve specific sensory functions. People who have suffered damage to a certain area in the temporal lobe on the lower right side of the brain (not the auditory area, which is higher up in the temporal lobe) have a condition called **prosopagnosia**—an inability to recognize faces. People with prosopagnosia can tell that a face is a face, but can't recognize whose face it is, even for people they know well such as friends and family members. In some cases, people with prosopagnosia look into a mirror and, seeing their own image, wonder who the stranger is looking back at them! What is special about this condition is that the problem is restricted to using the sense of vision to recognize faces. The person can recognize other objects, can recognize people based on their voices or mannerisms, and have normal memory and general cognitive functioning (Burton et al., 1991; Hecaen & Angelergues, 1962; Parkin, 1996).

Localization of function has also been demonstrated by recording from neurons in different areas of the brains of animals (mainly monkeys). Neurons in the occipital lobe respond to stimulation of the eye with light, neurons in the temporal lobe to sound, neurons in another area in the temporal lobe to faces, and so on. In addition, a technique called brain imaging has been used to demonstrate localization of function in the human cortex.

METHOD Brain Imaging

A widely used technique for measuring brain activity in humans is **brain imaging**, which allows researchers to create images that show which areas of the brain are activated as awake humans carry out various cognitive tasks. One of these techniques, **positron emission tomography (PET)**, was introduced in the 1970s (Hoffman et al., 1976; Ter-Pogossian et al., 1975). PET takes advantage of the fact that blood flow increases in areas of the brain that are activated by a cognitive task. To measure blood flow, a low dose of a radioactive tracer is injected into a person's bloodstream.

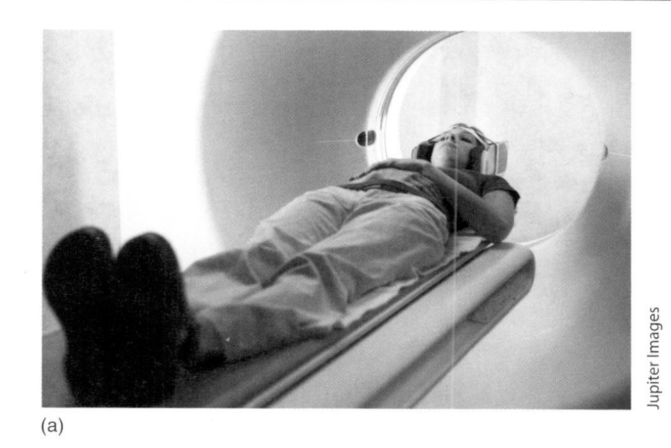

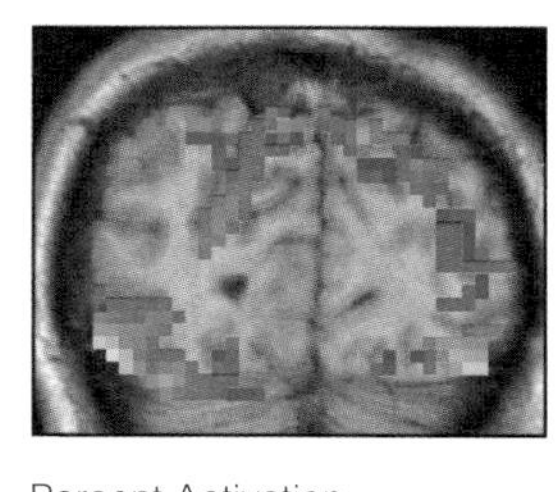

● **FIGURE 2.8** (a) Person in a brain scanner. (b) In this cross section of the brain, areas of the brain that are activated are indicated by the colors. Increases in activation are indicated by red and yellow, decreases by blue and green. (Source: Part b from Alumit Ishai, Leslie G. Ungerleider, Alex Martin, James V. Haxby, "The Representation of Objects in the Human Occipital and Temporal Cortex," *Journal of Cognitive Neuroscience, 12*:2, 2000, pp. 35–51. © 2000 by the Massachusetts Institute of Technology.)

(The dose is low enough that it is not harmful to the person.) The person's brain is then scanned by the PET apparatus, which measures the signal from the tracer at each location in the brain. Higher signals indicate higher levels of brain activity (● Figure 2.8).

PET enabled researchers to track changes in blood flow, and thus to determine which brain areas were being activated. To use this tool, researchers developed the **subtraction technique**. Brain activity is measured first in a "control state," before stimulation is presented, and again while the stimulus is presented. For example, in a study designed to determine which areas of the brain are activated when a person manipulates an object, activity generated by simply placing the object in the hand would be measured first. This is the control state (● Figure 2.9a). Then activity is measured as the person manipulates the object. This is the stimulation state (Figure 2.9b). Finally, the activity due to manipulation is determined by subtracting the control activity from the stimulation activity (Figure 2.9c).

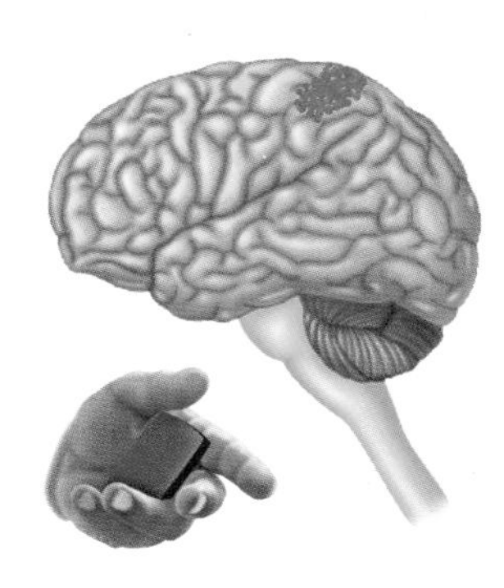
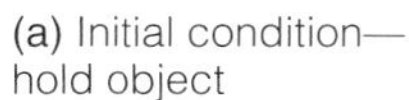

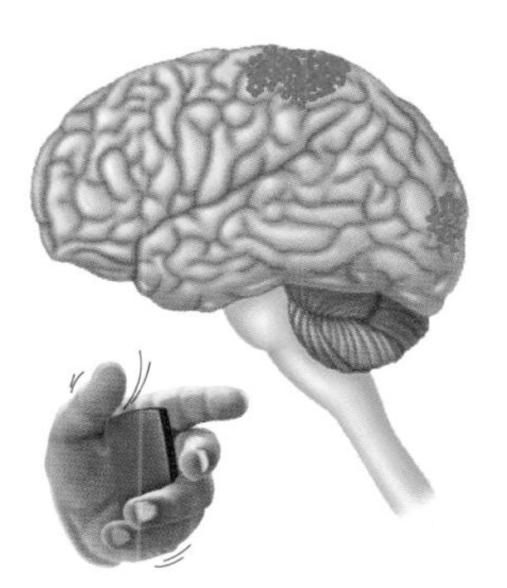

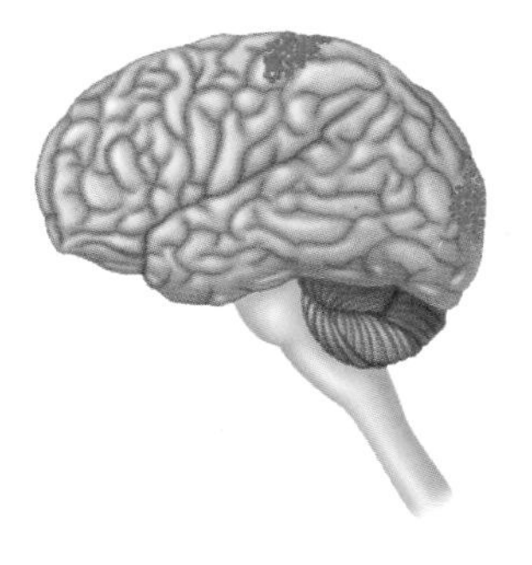

● **FIGURE 2.9** The subtraction technique used to interpret the results of brain imaging experiments. (a) Colored area indicates activation when a person is holding a small object. (b) Colored areas indicate activation when the person begins manipulating the object. (c) Subtracting the activation in (a) from the activation in (b) indicates the activation due to manipulation of the object. (Source: B. Goldstein, *Sensation and Perception*, 8th ed., Fig. 4.16, p. 83. Copyright © 2010, Wadsworth, a part of Cengage Learning. Reproduced with permission. www.cengage.com/permissions.)

Following the introduction of PET, another neuroimaging technique, called **functional magnetic resonance imaging (fMRI)**, was introduced. Like PET, fMRI is based on the measurement of blood flow. An advantage of fMRI is that blood flow can be measured without radioactive tracers. fMRI takes advantage of the fact that hemoglobin, which carries oxygen in the blood, contains a ferrous (iron) molecule and therefore has magnetic properties. If a magnetic field is presented to the brain, the hemoglobin molecules line up, like tiny magnets.

fMRI indicates the presence of brain activity because the hemoglobin molecules in areas of high brain activity lose some of the oxygen they are transporting. This makes the hemoglobin more magnetic, so these molecules respond more strongly to the magnetic field. The fMRI apparatus determines the relative activity of various areas of the brain by detecting changes in the magnetic response of the hemoglobin. The subtraction technique described above for PET is also used for fMRI. Because fMRI doesn't require radioactive tracers and is more accurate, this technique has become the main method for determining which areas of the brain are activated by different cognitive functions.

● Figure 2.10 shows the location of the area in the human brain that responds to faces, as determined by fMRI. This area, which is called the **fusiform face area (FFA)** because it is in the fusiform gyrus on the underside of the temporal lobe, corresponds to the area usually damaged in patients with prosopagnosia (Kanwisher et al., 1997).

In addition to the FFA, two other specialized areas in the temporal cortex have been identified. The **parahippocampal place area (PPA)** is activated by pictures representing indoor and outdoor scenes like those shown in ● Figure 2.11a (Aguirre et al., 1998; R. Epstein et al., 1999). Apparently what is important for this area is information about spatial layout, because increased activation occurs when viewing pictures both of empty rooms and of rooms that are completely furnished (Kanwisher, 2003). The other specialized area, the **extrastriate body area (EBA)**, is activated by pictures of bodies and parts of bodies (but not by faces), as shown in Figure 2.11b (Downing et al., 2001).

As we will see throughout this book, the technique of brain imaging has also identified many other connections between cognitive functioning and specific areas of the brain. In fact, this idea has become so prominent that a new term, *modularity*, is often used to refer to localization. A **module** is an area specialized for a specific function. Using this terminology, we would say that the fusiform face area, extrastriate body area, and parahippocampal place area are modules for perceiving faces, bodies, and places, respectively.

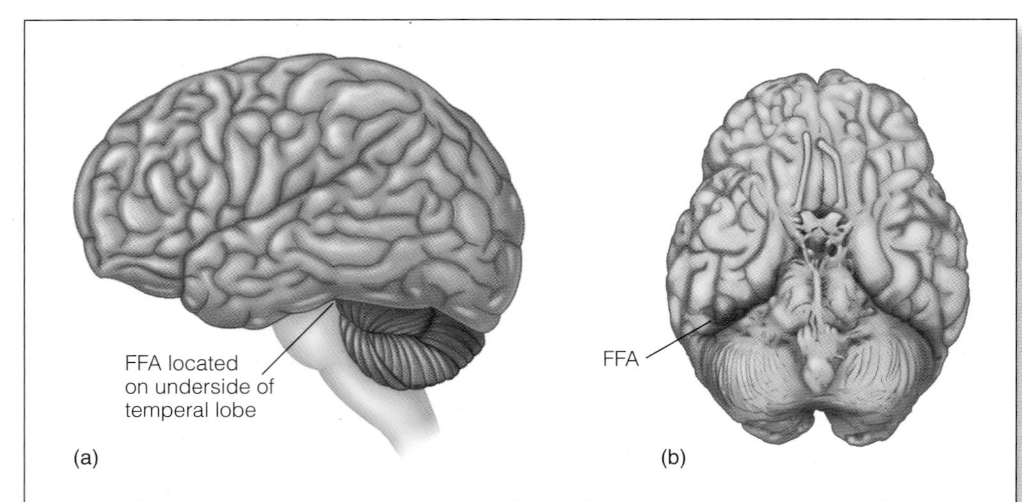

● **FIGURE 2.10** (a) Side view of the brain. The fusiform face area (FFA) is not visible in this view because it is located on the underside of the brain. (b) Underside of the brain, showing location of the FFA. (Source: B. Goldstein, *Sensation and Perception*, 8th ed., Fig. 13.14, p. 323. Copyright © 2010 Wadsworth, a part of Cengage Learning. Reproduced with permission. www.cengage.com/permissions.)

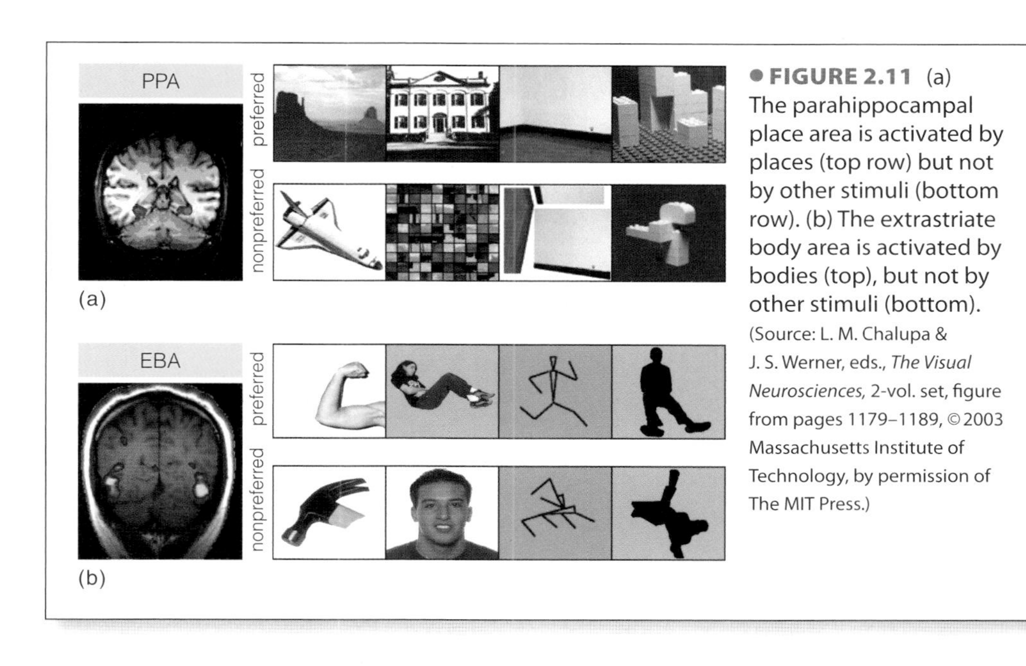

● **FIGURE 2.11** (a) The parahippocampal place area is activated by places (top row) but not by other stimuli (bottom row). (b) The extrastriate body area is activated by bodies (top), but not by other stimuli (bottom). (Source: L. M. Chalupa & J. S. Werner, eds., *The Visual Neurosciences*, 2-vol. set, figure from pages 1179–1189, © 2003 Massachusetts Institute of Technology, by permission of The MIT Press.)

LOCALIZATION FOR LANGUAGE

Early evidence for localization of function was provided by Paul Broca's and Carl Wernicke's studies of patients whose difficulty in producing and understanding language could be traced to damage in different areas of the brain.

In 1861, the French neurologist Paul Broca proposed that there is an area in the frontal lobe that is specialized for producing language. Broca based this idea on his study of patients who had suffered strokes and who produced speech that was slow and labored, often with jumbled sentence structure. Following is an example of the speech of a modern patient with similar symptoms. This person is attempting to describe when he had his stroke, which occurred when he was in a hot tub.

> Alright...Uh...stroke and un...I...huh tawanna guy...H...h...hot tub and...And the...Two days when uh...Hos...uh...Huh hospital and uh...amet...am...ambulance. (From Dick et al., 2001, p. 760)

Although Broca's patients had difficulty expressing themselves, they had no trouble understanding what other people were saying. When patients died, Broca performed autopsies and determined that one specific area in the brain was damaged (● Figure 2.12). This area, in the frontal lobe, came to be called **Broca's area**, and the condition he described was called **Broca's aphasia**.

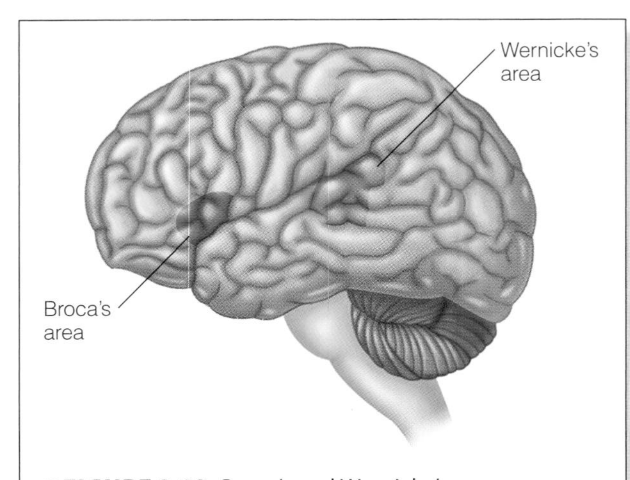

● **FIGURE 2.12** Broca's and Wernicke's areas were identified in early research as being specialized for language production and comprehension. (Source: L. M. Chalupa & J. S. Werner, eds., *The Visual Neurosciences*, 2-vol. set, Fig. 13.14, p. 323. © 2003 Massachusetts Institute of Technology, by permission of The MIT Press.)

In 1879, Carl Wernicke studied another group of patients, who had damage in an area of the temporal lobe now called **Wernicke's area**. Their speech was fluent and grammatically correct, but tended to be incoherent. The following is a modern example of the speech of a patient similar to those Wernicke studied:

> It just suddenly had a feffort and all the feffort had gone with it. It even stepped my horn. They took them from earth you know. They make my favorite nine to severed and now I'm a been habed by the uh stam of fortment of my annulment which is now forever. (From Dick et al., 2001, p. 761)

Patients such as this not only produced meaningless speech, but were unable to understand speech and writing. This condition was called **Wernicke's aphasia**.

The straightforward link between language production and Broca's area and language understanding and Wernicke's area was for many years the accepted model of language processing. But as we described in our introduction of models in Chapter 1 (see page 17), models are often revised in response to new data, and the Broca/Wernicke model is no exception.

Beginning in the 1970s, researchers began providing new evidence about language processing and the brain. One line of evidence shows how important it is to pay close attention to how the behavior of brain-damaged patients is tested. Broca's idea that patients with Broca's aphasia could understand language but had a problem producing it has been challenged by research showing that these patients do, in fact, have problems understanding language. Consider, for example, the following two sentences:

(1) The apple was eaten by the girl.

(2) The boy was pushed by the girl.

Patients with Broca's aphasia have no trouble understanding the first sentence, but have difficulty with the second one. The problem they have with the second sentence is deciding who was doing the pushing and who got pushed. Did the girl push the boy, or did the boy push the girl? While you may think it is obvious that the girl pushed the boy, patients with Broca's aphasia have difficulty processing connecting words such as "was" and "by," and this makes it difficult to determine who was pushed (notice what happens to the sentence when these two words are omitted). In contrast, the first sentence cannot be interpreted in two ways. It is clear that the girl ate the apple, because it is not possible, outside of an unlikely science fiction scenario, for the apple to eat the girl (Dick et al., 2001; Novick et al., 2005).

The fact that Broca's patients do have a problem understanding language indicates that Broca's aphasia is not simply a problem with producing language. The results of many behavioral and physiological experiments have caused some researchers to distinguish not between problems of *production* and *understanding*, but between problems of *form* and *meaning*. Form problems involve difficulties in determining the relation between words in a sentence (like the Broca's aphasia patients' problem with sentence 2, above). Meaning problems involve wider differences in understanding like those experienced by Wernicke's aphasia patients, who would also have difficulty with sentence 1.

A method of recording rapid electrical responses of the human brain, called the *event-related potential (ERP)*, has provided additional evidence for distinguishing between form and meaning in language.

METHOD Event-Related Potential

The **event-related potential (ERP)** is recorded with small disc electrodes placed on a person's scalp, as shown in ● Figure 2.13a. Each electrode picks up signals from groups of neurons that fire together. Figure 2.13b shows an event-related potential recorded as a person listens to the phrase "The cats won't eat." Notice that the signals are very rapid, occurring on a time scale of fractions of a second. This makes the ERP ideal for investigating a process such as understanding a conversation, in which speakers say three words per second, on the average (Levelt, 1999). The rapid response of the ERP contrasts with the slow response of brain imaging techniques such as fMRI, which take seconds to develop. A disadvantage of the ERP is that it is difficult to pinpoint where the response is originating in the brain. There are ways to estimate where an ERP is originating, but it isn't as straightforward as the fMRI, which highlights specific structures that are activated. However, the ability of the ERP to provide a nearly continuous record of what is happening in the brain from moment to moment makes it particularly well suited for studying dynamic processes such as language (Kim & Osterhout, 2005; Osterhout et al., in press).

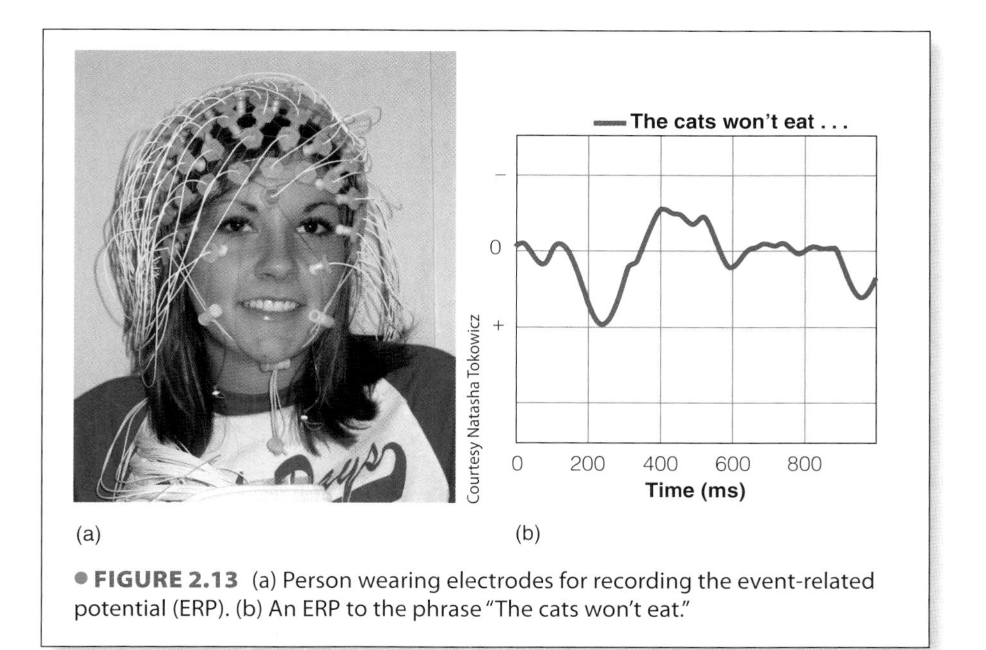

● **FIGURE 2.13** (a) Person wearing electrodes for recording the event-related potential (ERP). (b) An ERP to the phrase "The cats won't eat."

The ERP is useful in distinguishing between form and meaning because the ERP consists of a number of waves that occur at different delays after a stimulus is presented and that can be linked to different functions. Two components that respond to different aspects of language are the N400 component and the P600 component, where N stands for "negative" (note that negative is up in ERP records) and P for "positive." The numbers 400 and 600 stand for the time at which the response peaks, in milliseconds.

● Figure 2.14 shows the response to "The cats won't eat" plus the response to two modified versions of this phrase. In Figure 2.14a, the phrase "The cats won't bake" results in a larger N400 response. This component of the response is sensitive to the meaning of words in a sentence, and is larger when words don't fit the sentence. In Figure 2.14b, the phrase "The cats won't eating" results in a larger P600 response. This response is sensitive to the form of a sentence, and is larger when the form is incorrect.

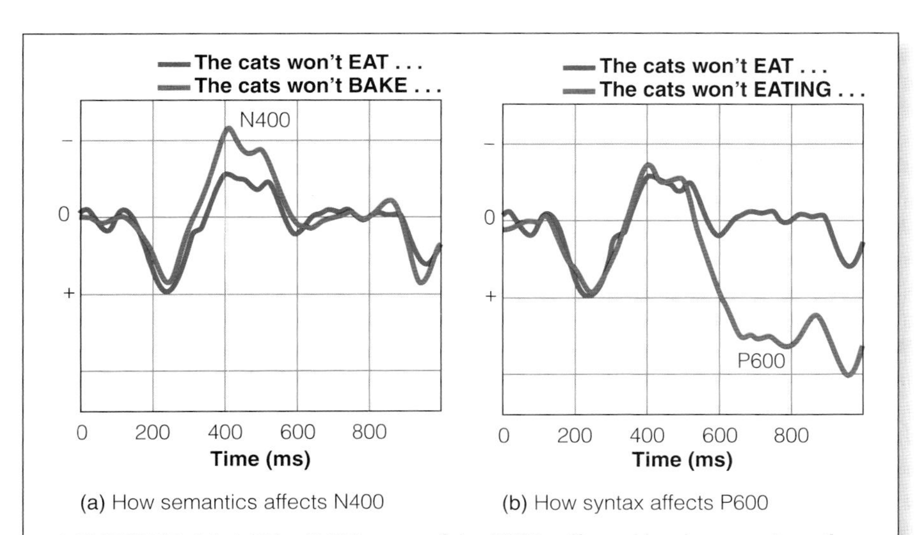

● **FIGURE 2.14** (a) The N400 wave of the ERP is affected by the meaning of the word. It becomes larger (red line) when the meaning of a word does not fit the rest of the sentence. (b) The P600 wave of the ERP is affected by grammar. It becomes larger (red line) when a grammatically incorrect form is used.
(Source: From Osterhout et al., "Event-Related Potentials and Language," in *Trends in Cognitive Sciences,* Volume 1, Issue 6. Copyright © 1997 Elsevier Ltd. Reproduced with permission.)

What is important about these results is that they illustrate different physiological responses to two different aspects of language: form and meaning. Other experiments have shown that the N400 response is associated with structures in the temporal lobe. For example, damage to areas in the temporal lobes reduces the larger N400 response that occurs when meanings don't fit in a sentence. The P600 response is associated with structures in the frontal lobe, more toward the front of the brain. Damage to areas in the frontal lobe reduces the larger P600 response that occurs when the form of a sentence is incorrect (Osterhout et al., in press; Van Petten & Luka, 2006).

The studies of the effects of brain damage and ERP results we have described as examples of modern research related to Broca and Wernicke are only two results out of many. Hundreds of experiments have shown that the physiology of language processing is more complex than proposed by Broca and Wernicke, both because the idea of a strict separation of "production" and "comprehension" is too simple and because many areas in addition to Broca's and Wernicke's areas are involved in language processing (Binder et al., 1997; Dick et al., 2001; Dronkers et al., 2004; Friederici, 2002, 2009; Friederici et al., 2006).

The picture that is emerging from all of this research is that (1) specific language functions are localized in specific brain areas, so that localization of function is an important part of language processing; and (2) language processing is distributed over a large area of the brain. In the next section we will see that this widespread processing across the brain is an important principle that holds not only for language, but for other cognitive functions as well.

TEST YOURSELF 2.1

1. How did early brain researchers describe the brain in terms of a nerve net? How does the idea of individual neurons differ from the idea of a nerve net?
2. Describe the research that led Cajal to propose the neuron doctrine.
3. Describe the structure of a neuron. Describe the synapse and neural circuits.
4. How are action potentials recorded from a neuron? What do these signals look like, and what is the relation between action potentials and stimulus intensity?
5. How has the question of how action potentials indicate different qualities been answered?
6. Describe evidence for localization of function for perception, including the primary receiving areas of the brain and evidence from brain damage and brain imaging. Be sure you understand the principle behind brain imaging.
7. How did Broca and Wernicke use the behavior of patients with brain damage to provide evidence for localization of function?
8. What behavioral evidence caused a modification of the idea of two areas, one for language production and one for language understanding? What is the ERP, and how has it been used to demonstrate different aspects of language functioning? What basic conclusions about localization of function have emerged from research on the physiology of language?

Distributed Processing in the Brain

The idea of **distributed processing** is that specific functions are processed by many different areas in the brain. Although this might at first seem to contradict the ideas of localization of function and modules described above, we will see that these two ideas actually complement each other.

We can describe distributed processing by starting with localization of face perception in the brain. We saw that brain imaging experiments have identified an area called the FFA that is strongly activated by faces and responds more weakly to other types of stimuli. But just because there is an area that is specialized to respond to faces doesn't mean that faces activate *only* that area. Faces strongly activate the FFA, *plus* other areas as well.

What is particularly significant about faces is that while a number of areas of the brain participate in *perception* of a face, other areas also respond to various *reactions* to a face. For example, when you see someone walking down the street, looking at the person's face activates many neurons in your FFA plus neurons in other areas that are responding to the face's form. But your response to that person's face may go beyond simply "That's a person's face." You may also be affected by whether the person is looking at you, how attractive you think the person is, any emotions the face may elicit, and your reactions to the person's facial expression. As it turns out, different areas in the brain are activated by each of these responses to the face (see ● Figure 2.15). Looking at a face thus

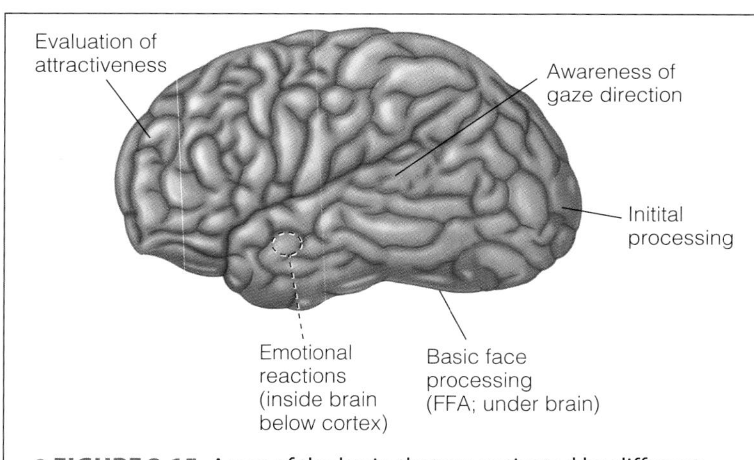

● **FIGURE 2.15** Areas of the brain that are activated by different aspects of faces. (Source: B. Goldstein, *Sensation and Perception,* 8th ed., Fig. 5.45, p. 121. Copyright © 2010 Wadsworth, a part of Cengage Learning. Reproduced with permission. www.cengage.com/permissions.)

activates areas involved in perceiving the face plus areas associated with reactions elicited by the face.

But what about an encounter with a much simpler stimulus—one that doesn't look (or not look) at you, have emotional expressions, or elicit emotional responses? How about perceiving a rolling red ball, as the person is doing in ● Figure 2.16? Even this simple, neutral stimulus causes a wide distribution of activity in the brain, because each of the ball's qualities—color (red), movement (to the right), shape (round), depth, location—is processed in a different area of the brain.

There is an important message in the way that these qualities, which are processed in separate areas of the brain, come together to result in the perception of the rolling red ball. The message is that even simple everyday experiences result in activation of widespread areas of the brain, but that our experience contains little or no evidence of this widely distributed activity. We just see the object! The importance of this observation extends beyond perceiving a rolling red ball to other cognitive functions, such as memory, language, making decisions, and solving problems, all of which involve distributed activity in the brain.

For example, research on the physiology of memory, which we will consider in detail in Chapters 5 and 7, has revealed that multiple areas in every lobe of the brain are involved in storing memories for facts and events and then remembering them later. Recalling a fact or remembering an event not only elicits associations with other facts or events but can also elicit visual, auditory, smell, or taste perceptions associated with the memory, emotions elicited by the memory, and other thought processes as well. Additionally, there are different types of memory—short-term memory, long-term memory, memories about events in a person's life, memories for facts, and so on—all of which activate different, and sometimes partially overlapping, areas of the brain.

The idea that the principle of distributed processing holds for perception, memory, and other cognitive processes reflects the generality of the mechanisms responsible for cognition. Even though this book contains separate chapters on various types of cognitions, this separation does not always occur in the mind or the brain. The mind is, after all, not a textbook; it does not necessarily subdivide our experiences or cognitions into neat categories. Instead, the mind creates cognitive processes that can involve a number of different functions. Just as a symphony is created by many different instruments, all working together in an orchestra to create the harmonies and melodies of a particular composition, cognitive processes are created by many specialized brain areas, all working together to create a distributed pattern of activity that creates all of the different components of that particular cognition.

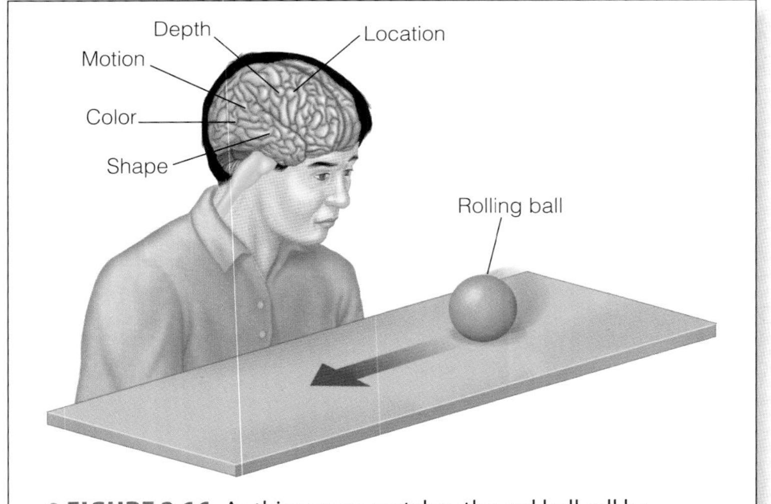

● **FIGURE 2.16** As this person watches the red ball roll by, different properties of the ball activate different areas of his cortex. These areas are in separate locations, although there is communication between them. (Source: B. Goldstein, *Sensation and Perception,* 8th ed., Fig. 6.18, p. 144. Copyright © 2010 Wadsworth, a part of Cengage Learning. Reproduced with permission. www.cengage.com/permissions.)

Representation in the Brain

So far we have explained the connection between physiology and cognition in terms of (1) action potentials, (2) specialized areas of the brain, and (3) distributed activity in the brain. We can describe what happens when you see someone you know as involving activation of your fusiform face area plus other areas, which enables you to recognize and perhaps react to the person. But this description, while correct, is too general. We want to know how you are able to respond "That's Bill," as opposed to identifying the person as Roger or Sally. What is it about the electrical activity in your brain that goes beyond "That's a face" to actually representing a specific face such as Bill's? This is the question of *representation*, and to begin answering it, we will consider what happens when you perceive another stimulus—a tree.

REPRESENTING A TREE: FEATURE DETECTORS

Considering how a tree is represented in the nervous system brings us back to one of the definitions of mind presented in Chapter 1, which stated that *the mind is a system that creates representations of the world, so we can act within it to achieve our goals.* Applied to the brain, the major idea behind this statement is that a tree, and everything else we perceive, is *represented* in the brain. We can appreciate what this means by considering what happens as we look at a tree.

We see the tree because light reflected from the tree enters the eye and an image of the tree is focused onto the **retina**, the layer of neurons that lines the back of the eye (● Figure 2.17). The important word here is *image*, because it is the image created by light reflected by the tree that gets into the eye, not the tree itself. The idea of the tree not getting into the eye may seem silly because it is so obvious, but the point is an important one: What enters the eye is a *representation* of the tree—something that stands for the tree.

One property of this representation is that although it may look like the tree, it is also different from the tree. It is not only smaller, but may be distorted or blurred because of the optics of the eye. This difference between the actual tree and its representation becomes more dramatic about a few thousandths of a seconds later when receptors in the retina transform the tree's image into electrical signals, which then travel through the retina, leave the eye via the optic nerve, and eventually reach the primary visual receiving area of the brain. Our perception of the tree is therefore based not on direct contact with the tree, but on the way the tree is represented by action potentials in the brain. Early research on the nature of this representation led to the proposal that this representation could involve neurons called **feature detectors** that respond to features that make up objects.

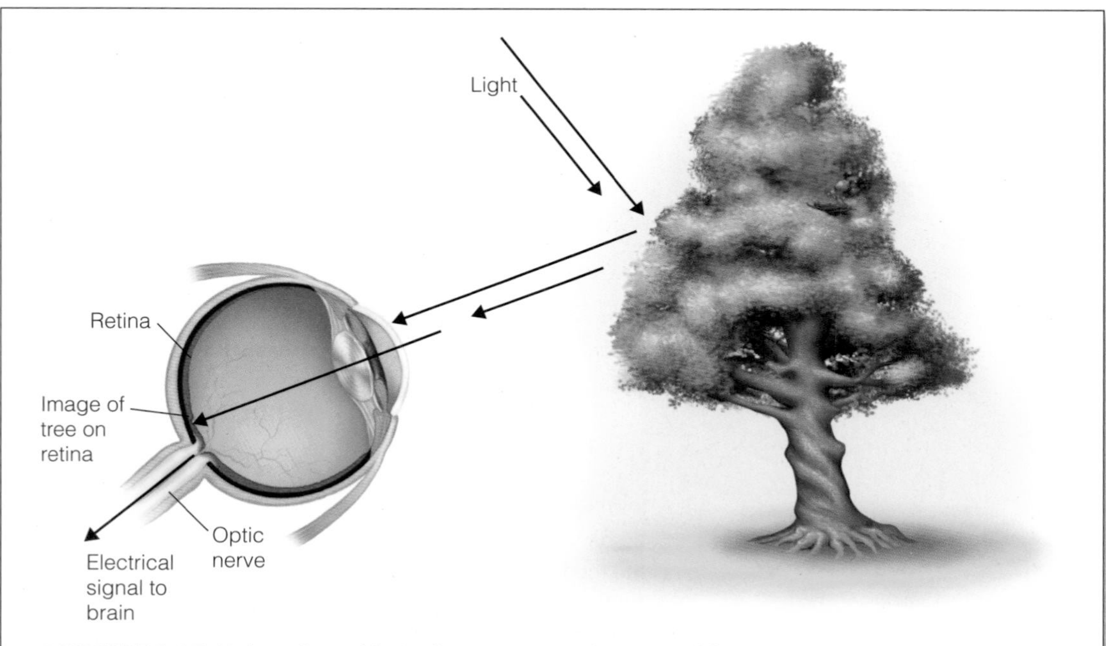

● **FIGURE 2.17** Light reflected from the tree enters the eye and forms an image of the tree on the retina. This image is transformed into electrical signals that travel out the back of the eye along the optic nerve and eventually reach the brain. Our perception of the tree is based on the information contained in these neural signals.

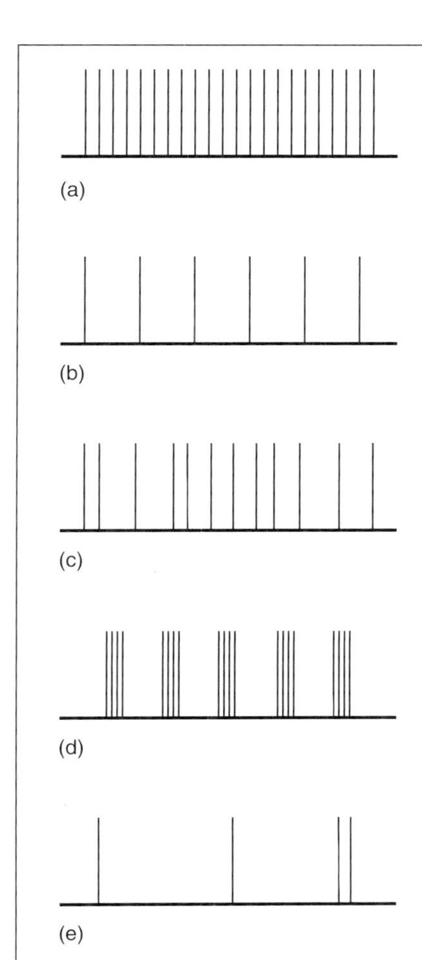

● **FIGURE 2.19** The types of nerve firing patterns that would be recorded from a few of the feature detectors that respond to the tree: (a) rapid, evenly spaced firing; (b) slower, evenly spaced firing; (c) irregular firing; (d) bursts of firing; (e) little or no firing. The overall pattern of firing of these neurons, and the many other neurons that respond to the tree, are the neural representation of the tree.

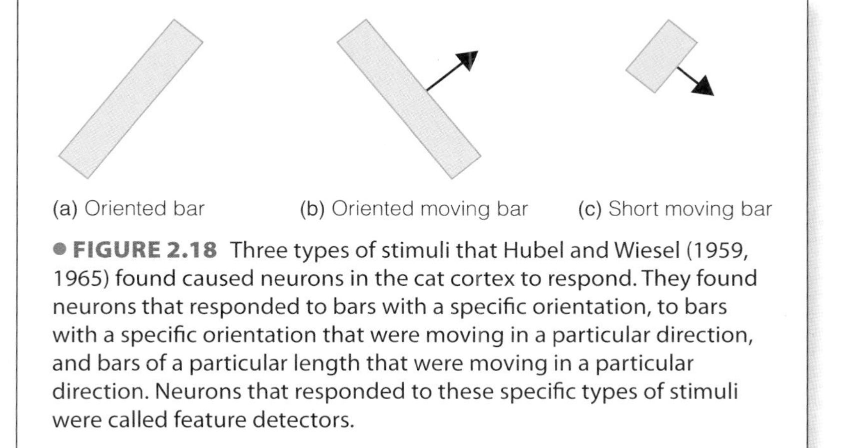

● **FIGURE 2.18** Three types of stimuli that Hubel and Wiesel (1959, 1965) found caused neurons in the cat cortex to respond. They found neurons that responded to bars with a specific orientation, to bars with a specific orientation that were moving in a particular direction, and bars of a particular length that were moving in a particular direction. Neurons that responded to these specific types of stimuli were called feature detectors.

Two researchers who played an important role in describing feature detectors are David Hubel and Thorsten Wiesel, who began their careers at Johns Hopkins University and then established a laboratory at Harvard, where they carried out research on the visual system that earned them a Nobel Prize in 1981. Their tactic was to monitor the signals generated by neurons in the cortex of cats and monkeys (see Method: Recording From a Neuron, p. 28) and determine which visual stimuli caused each neuron to fire. Hubel and Wiesel found that each neuron fired only to a specific type of stimulation presented to a small area of the retina. ● Figure 2.18 shows some of the stimuli that caused neurons in and near the visual receiving area to fire (Hubel, 1982; Hubel & Wiesel, 1959, 1961, 1965).

This knowledge that neurons in the visual system fire to specific types of stimuli led researchers to propose that each of the thousands of neurons that fire when we look at a tree fire to different features of the tree. Some neurons fire to the vertically oriented trunk, others to the variously oriented branches, and some to more complex combinations of a number of features. We could, in fact, describe the firing of all of these neurons together as creating a "chorus" of neural signals, with some neurons firing vigorously (● Figure 2.19a), some slowly (Figure 2.19b), some steadily (Figures 2.19a and b), some irregularly (Figure 2.19c), some in bursts (Figure 2.19d), and some little or not at all (Figure 2.19e). What is important about this "neural chorus" is that it stands for—or represents—the tree. Other objects in the environment create their own, unique choruses of firing. Thus, we can describe the tree we are looking at or other stimuli in the environment, such as the sound of a bird's chirping or the smell of pine needles, as each being represented by a particular pattern of firing in a number of neurons. The way these patterns of neural firing represent environmental stimuli is called the **neural code**.

The discovery of feature detectors in the primary visual receiving area was the first step in determining the neural code. Further research in areas beyond the primary receiving area revealed neurons that respond to stimuli that are more complex than oriented lines. Many researchers, recording from neurons in the temporal lobe, found neurons that responded to complex geometrical objects and some to that now familiar stimulus—the face (● Figure 2.20). Because faces are such a common stimulus, and because of the discovery of neurons sensitive to faces, we will now consider some ideas about the neural code for faces.

CogLab
Receptive Fields

THE NEURAL CODE FOR FACES

How can a particular face be represented by the firing of neurons in the temporal cortex? Although we will use faces as an example, our answer applies to all experiences, not just to seeing faces. One possible way that faces could be represented is by **specificity coding**—the representation of a specific stimulus, such as a particular person's face, by the firing of very specifically tuned neurons that are specialized to respond just to that face. This

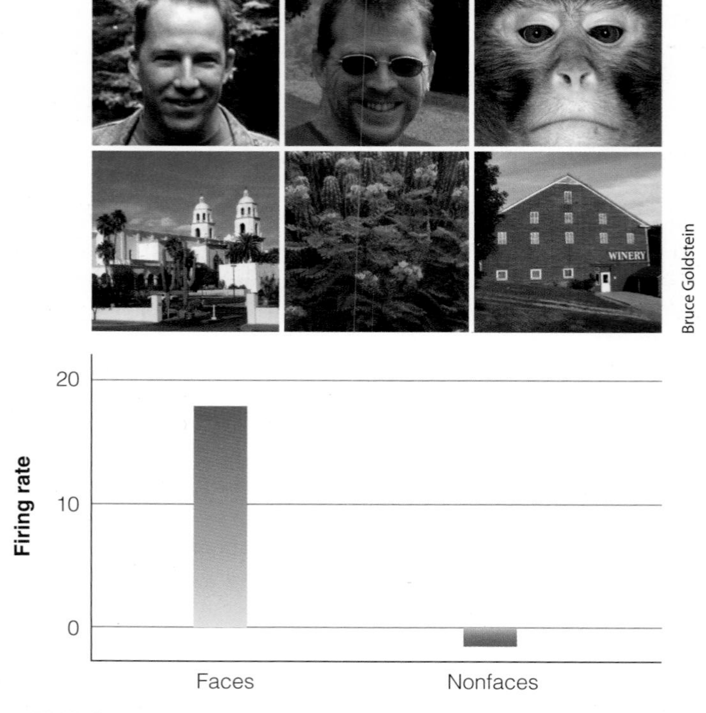

● **FIGURE 2.20** Firing rate, in nerve impulses per second, of a neuron in the monkey's temporal cortex that responds to face stimuli but not to nonface stimuli. (Source: Based on data from Rolls & Tovee, 1995.)

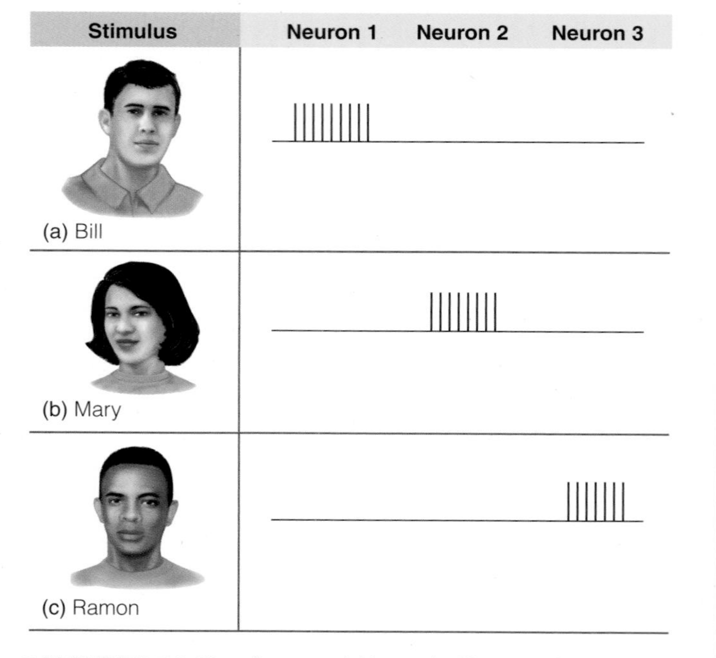

● **FIGURE 2.21** How faces could be coded by specificity coding. Each faces causes one specialized neuron to respond. (Source: B. Goldstein, *Sensation and Perception* 8th ed., Fig. 2.21, p. 36. Copyright © 2010 Wadsworth, a part of Cengage Learning. Reproduced with permission. www.cengage.com/permissions.)

is illustrated in ● Figure 2.21, which shows that Bill's face would be signaled by the firing of neuron 1, which responds only to his face; Mary's face is signaled by the firing of neuron 2; and Ramon's face by the firing of neuron 3. Thus, specificity coding proposes that there are neurons that are tuned to respond just to one specific stimulus.

The idea that there might be single neurons that respond only to specific stimuli was proposed in the 1960s by Jerzy Konorski (1967) and Jerry Lettvin (see Barlow, 1995; Gross, 2002; Rose, 1996). Lettvin coined the term *grandmother cell* to describe this highly specific type of cell. A **grandmother cell**, according to Lettvin, is a neuron that responds only to a specific stimulus. This stimulus could be a specific image, such as a picture of your grandmother; a concept, such as the idea of grandmothers in general; or your real-life grandmother (Gross, 2002).

But there are problems with this idea: (1) There are just too many different faces and other objects in the environment to assign specific neurons to each one; and (2) although there are neurons that respond only to specific types of stimuli, such as faces, even these neurons respond to a number of different faces. Thus, a neuron that responds to Bill's face would also respond to Roger's and Samantha's faces. Because of these problems, the idea of a highly specific grandmother-type neuron has not been accepted by researchers.

The generally accepted solution to the problem of neural coding is that a particular face is represented not by the firing of a single neuron, but by the firing of *groups* of neurons. For example, let's consider how the three neurons in ● Figure 2.22 fire to a number of different faces. Bill's face causes all three neurons to fire, with neuron 1 responding the most and neuron 3 responding the least. Mary's face also causes firing in all three neurons, but the pattern is different, with neuron 3 responding the most and neuron 1 the least. All three neurons also fire to Ramon's and Roger's faces, but with their own individual patterns.

Thus, each face is represented by a pattern of firing across a number of neurons. This solution to the problem of neural coding is basically the same thing as the idea of a "chorus" of neural firing that we described when considering how feature detectors could represent a tree. This is called **distributed coding** because the code that indicates a specific face is *distributed* across a number of neurons. One of the advantages of distributed coding is that the firing of just a few neurons can signal a large number of stimuli. In our example, the firing of three neurons signals four faces, but these three neurons could also signal other faces, which would have their own pattern of firing. (The similarity of the terms *distributed coding* and *distributed processing* might cause some confusion. For our purposes, distributed coding refers to the pattern of firing of a number of individual neurons, and distributed processing refers to the activation of a number of different areas of the brain.)

What all of this means is that our ability to identify and recognize the huge number of different objects in our environment is the end result of distributed cooperation

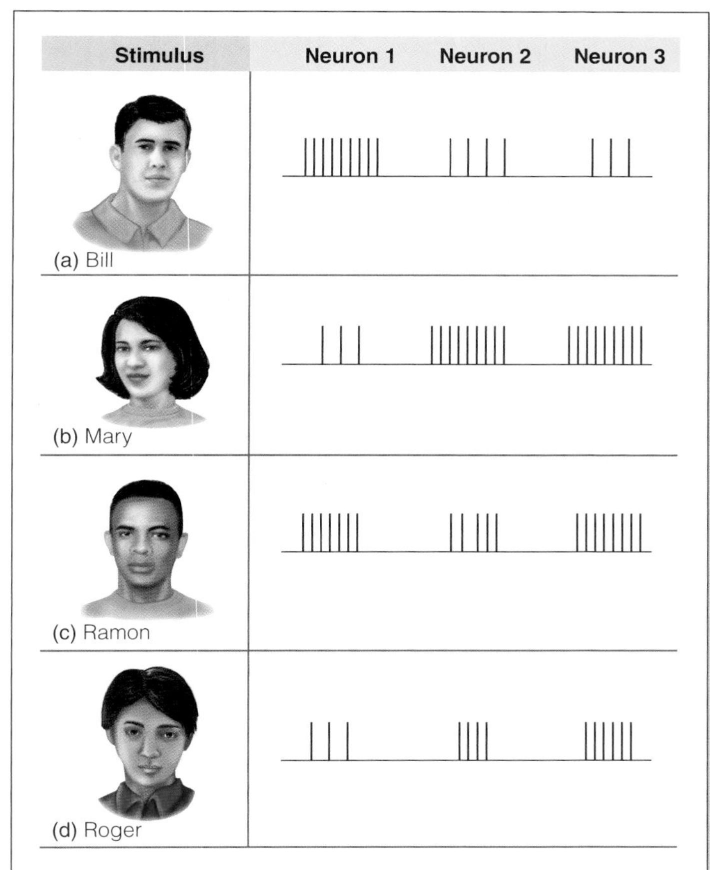

● **FIGURE 2.22** How faces could be coded by distributed coding. Each face causes all the neurons to fire, but the pattern of firing is different for each face. One advantage of this method of coding is that many faces could be represented by the firing of the three neurons. (Source: B. Goldstein, *Sensation and Perception*, 8th ed., Fig. 2.23, p. 38. Copyright © 2010 Wadsworth, a part of Cengage Learning. Reproduced with permission. www.cengage.com/permissions.)

among many neurons. This occurs even for stimuli like faces that are served by specialized neurons that respond just to faces. It may not take many neurons to let you know that you are seeing a face, but it takes a number of neurons working together to signal the presence of one particular face.

THE NEURAL CODE FOR MEMORY

Memories are also represented in the brain, and the same principles hold for memory as for perception—experiences are represented by nerve firing, with different experiences represented by different patterns of firing. Thus, if a few weeks after you look at the tree you remember seeing it, perhaps even visualizing what it looked like, this memory is elicited by a particular pattern of the firing of many neurons in the brain. There is, however, an important difference between the neural firing caused by perception and the neural firing caused by memory.

The neural firing associated with experiencing a perception is caused by stimulation of the sensory receptors. In contrast, the neural firing associated with experiencing a memory is caused by firing in structures that contain information about what happened in the past. Thus, while the firing associated with perception is associated with what is happening as you are looking at the tree, firing associated with memory is associated with information that has been stored in the brain. We know less about the actual form of this stored information for memory, but it is likely that the basic principle of distributed coding also operates for memory, with specific memories being represented by particular patterns of stored information that result in a particular pattern of nerve firing when we experience the memory. We will discuss the physiological processes involved in memory in Chapters 5 and 7.

➔ Something to Consider

"MIND READING" BY MEASURING BRAIN ACTIVITY

The idea that cognitions are represented by distributed activity in the brain raises an interesting question: Is it possible to determine what a person is seeing, thinking, or remembering by measuring the activity of the brain? To achieve this, we would have to know exactly what pattern of activity was associated with every possible object, thought, or memory, and we are far from being able to do this. However, recent research using computer programs that can be trained to recognize the patterns of brain activity associated with seeing and thinking about an object has brought us closer to this goal. Computer programs have recently been developed that can, with a surprising degree of accuracy, identify from a group of objects the specific object a person is seeing.

We will describe an experiment by Svetlana Shinkareva and coworkers (2008). In the first part of the experiment, a computer learned the patterns of neural activity that were associated with different objects. The first step was to have participants look at a series of pictures like the one in ● Figure 2.23. These pictures are line drawings of tools and dwellings. The participants' saw pictures of five different tools and five different dwellings while in a brain scanner, which measured the fMRI response to each

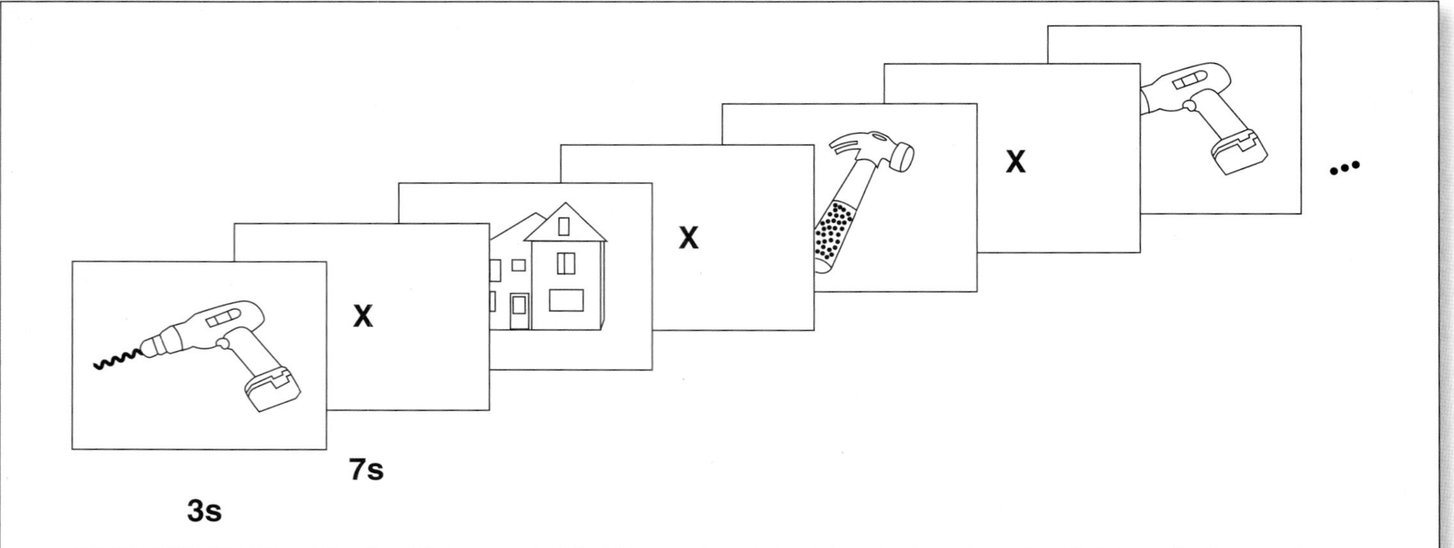

● **FIGURE 2.23** Stimuli for the Shinkareva et al. (2008) experiment. Participants viewed a series of pictures for 3 seconds each, with 7 seconds between pictures, while their brain activity was being measured in an fMRI scanner. (Source: S. V. Shinkareva et al., "Using fMRI Brain Activation to Identify Cognitive States Associated with Perception of Tools and Dwellings," *PLoS One*, Figure 1, p. 2, 2008.)

picture. Participants were asked to think of properties of the object as they looked at the picture. For example, when looking at the drill they might think about drilling holes in a board. Each picture was presented for 3 seconds, followed by a 7-second rest interval. While the participants viewed the pictures, the activity of their cortex was being recorded by the fMRI scanner.

The key to the success of this experiment was the computer program, which analyzed the responses of the brain voxel by voxel, where a voxel is a small cube-shaped area of the brain about 2 or 3 mm on a side. (The size of the voxel depends on the resolution of the fMRI scanner. Scanners are being developed that will be able to resolve volumes smaller than 2 or 3 mm on a side.) By determining which voxels were activated by each picture and how strongly they were activated, the computer created a response profile, or "neural signature," for each object, which included many areas of the brain. Eventually, after collecting patterns from a dozen participants, the computer determined the neural pattern associated with each class of objects (tool vs. dwelling) and with each individual object (hammer, apartment, or screwdriver, for example).

The computer was then tested by having it analyze a person's brain activity as he or she was viewing an object. Based on the pattern, the computer predicted what the person was seeing. When the computer's task was simply to indicate whether the person was looking at a tool or a dwelling, the accuracy for 4 of the 12 participants was 97 percent; for the entire group of 12 participants, it was 87 percent (chance performance being 50 percent because there were two possible answers). The average accuracy for identifying specific objects was 78 percent (chance being 10 percent, because there were 10 different objects).

This is impressive performance, but what is even more impressive is that the computer made accurate predictions even for people whose data had not been previously analyzed. Imagine what this means. You walk into the brain imaging facility for the first time, are placed in the scanner, and view a picture of an apartment building. The computer analyzes your brain activity and concludes that you are looking at a "dwelling," and also predicts "apartment building." Average accuracy for determining the category ("dwelling") is 82 percent. This ability to determine what a particular person is seeing based on the data from other people is possible because patterns of brain activation are similar for different people. In other words, different people have similar neural signatures for specific types of objects. This commonality among people is illustrated in ● Figure 2.24, which shows the

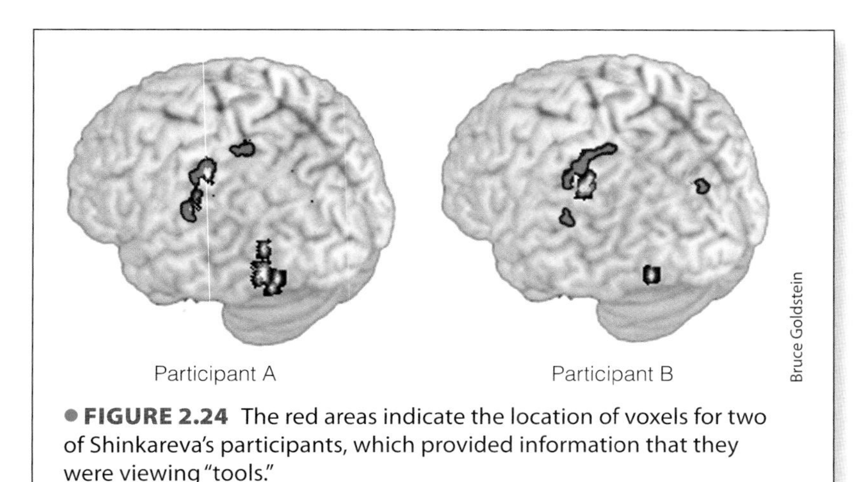

● **FIGURE 2.24** The red areas indicate the location of voxels for two of Shinkareva's participants, which provided information that they were viewing "tools."

location of the voxels that provided information the computer used to determine that two different participants were looking at "tools."

Do these results mean that a computer could determine what you are thinking by analyzing your brain's pattern of activation? At this point, being able to determine whether someone is looking at an apartment or an igloo is far from being able to tell that you are thinking about what you did on your summer vacation. Nonetheless being able to make predictions about what category of object a person is looking at is a huge advance, especially when we consider that just 50 years earlier the state-of-the-art discovery was neurons that respond most vigorously to oriented bars (Figure 2.18).

TEST YOURSELF 2.2

1. What is distributed processing? How was it described in the text, beginning with how information about faces is localized in the brain? What is "particularly significant" about faces?
2. How was distributed processing illustrated by the example of the rolling red ball? The physiology of memory?
3. What does it mean to say that a tree, or other object, is *represented* in the brain? How did early researchers describe this representation in terms of feature detectors?
4. How do current researchers describe the neural code for faces? Be sure you understand specificity coding, grandmother cells, and distributed coding. What is the distinction between distributed coding, as described in this section, and distributed processing that was described earlier?
5. Describe recent experiments that have been able to demonstrate a form of "mind reading" by monitoring brain activity.

CHAPTER SUMMARY

1. Cognitive neuroscience is the study of the physiological basis of cognition.
2. Ramon y Cajal's research resulted in the abandonment of the neural net theory in favor of the neuron doctrine, which states that individual cells called neurons transmit signals in the nervous system.
3. Signals can be recorded from neurons using microelectrodes. Adrian, who recorded the first signals from single neurons, determined that action potentials remain the same size as they travel down an axon and that increasing stimulus intensity increases the rate of nerve firing.
4. The idea of localization of function in perception is supported by the existence of a separate primary receiving area for each sense, by the effects of brain damage on perception (for example, prospoganosia), and by the results of brain imaging experiments.
5. Brain imaging measures brain activation by measuring blood flow in the brain. Functional magnetic resonance imaging (fMRI) is widely used to determine brain activation during cognitive functioning. One result of brain imaging experiments has been the identification of areas in the human brain that respond best to faces, places, and bodies.
6. Research on brain-damaged patients by Broca and Wernicke provided evidence for localization of function for language. Based on the patients' symptoms, they identified two different conditions, Broca's aphasia and Wernicke's aphasia, as involving problems in language production and language understanding, respectively. These two conditions were associated with damage to different areas of the brain.
7. Recent research has resulted in modification of the Broca/Wernicke model. Behavioral research has shown

that patients with Broca's aphasia can, under certain conditions, have difficulty understanding language. Physiological research, involving both studying brain-damaged patients and recording the event-related potential, suggests two processes for language processing, one involving the form of language and the other involving meaning.

8. The idea of distributed processing is that specific functions are processed by many different areas in the brain. This principle is illustrated by the finding that faces activate many areas of the brain and by the simpler example of the rolling red ball, which also activates a number of areas.
9. Distributed processing also occurs for other cognitive functions, such as memory, decision making, and problem solving. A basic principle of cognition is that different cognitive functions often involve similar mechanisms.
10. Objects and properties of the environment are represented by electrical signals in the nervous system.
11. Research indicating that individual neurons in the visual system fire to specific simple stimuli, such as oriented bars, led to the idea of feature detectors. This research suggests that a particular object is represented by the firing of many neurons, creating a unique "chorus" of electrical signals for that object. The pattern of neural firing that represents an environmental stimulus is called the neural code.
12. Among proposals regarding the nature of the neural code are specificity theory, which includes the idea of grandmother cells, and distributed coding. Current evidence favors the idea of distributed coding. Thus, a particular face would be represented by the pattern of firing across a number of neurons. This is similar to the idea of a neural chorus.
13. The idea of a distributed neural code also applies to memory and other cognitive functions. The code for memory involves stored information.
14. Computer programs have recently been developed that can, with a surprising degree of accuracy, use data from brain imaging, collected as a person is observing pictures of different objects, to identify from a group of objects the specific object that a person is seeing.

Think ABOUT IT

1. Some cognitive psychologists have called the brain the mind's computer. What are computers good at, that the brain is not? How do you think the brain and the mind compare in terms of complexity? What advantage does the brain have over a computer?
2. People generally feel that they are experiencing their environment directly, especially when it comes to sensory experiences such as seeing, hearing, or feeling the texture of a surface. However, our knowledge of how the nervous system operates indicates that this is not the case. Why would a physiologist say that all of our experiences are indirect?
3. When brain activity is being measured in an fMRI scanner, the person's head is surrounded by an array of magnets and must be kept perfectly still. In addition, the operation of the machine is very noisy. How do these characteristics of brain scanners limit the types of behaviors that can be studied using brain scanning?
4. It has been argued that we will never be able to fully understand how the brain operates because doing this involves using the brain to study itself. What do you think of this argument?

If You WANT TO KNOW MORE

Brain damage and behavior. There are numerous books that describe fascinating case studies of people whose behavior has been affected by brain damage.

Farah, M. J., & Feinberg, T. E. (2003). *Behavioral neurology and neuropsychology* (2nd ed.). New York: McGraw-Hill.

Ramachandran, V. S., & Blakeslee, S. (1998). *Phantoms of the mind: Probing the mysteries of the human mind.* New York: HarperCollins.

Sacks, O. (1985). *The man who mistook his wife for a hat.* New York: Touchstone.

Key TERMS

Action potential, 28
Axon, 26
Brain imaging, 30
Broca's aphasia, 33
Broca's area, 33
Cell body, 26
Cerebral cortex, 29
Cognitive neuroscience, 24
Dendrites, 26
Distributed coding, 40
Distributed processing, 36
Event-related potential (ERP), 34
Extrastriate body area (EBA), 32
Feature detectors, 38
Frontal lobe, 30
Functional magnetic resonance imaging (fMRI), 32
Fusiform face area (FFA), 32
Grandmother cell, 40
Localization of function, 29
Microelectrode, 28
Module, 32
Nerve fiber, 26
Nerve impulse, 28
Nerve net, 26
Neural circuit, 27
Neural code, 39
Neuron, 26
Neuron doctrine, 26
Neurotransmitter, 29
Occipital lobe, 30
Parahippocampal place area (PPA), 32
Parietal lobe, 30
Positron emission tomography (PET), 30
Primary receiving area, 30
Prosopagnosia, 30
Receptors, 26
Recording electrode, 28
Reference electrode, 28
Retina, 38
Specificity coding, 39
Subtraction technique, 31
Synapse, 27
Temporal lobe, 30
Wernicke's aphasia, 33
Wernicke's area, 33

Media RESOURCES

The *Cognitive Psychology* Book Companion Website

www.cengage.com/international

Prepare for quizzes and exams with online resources—including a glossary, flashcards, tutorial quizzes, crossword puzzles, and more.

CogLab

CogLab

To experience these experiments for yourself, go to coglab.wadsworth.com. Be sure to read each experiment's setup instructions before you go to the experiment itself.Otherwise, you won't know which keys to press.

Primary Lab

Receptive fields A receptive field of a visual neuron is the area on the retina that influences the activity of that neuron. In this lab, you can map the receptive fields of some neurons. (p. 39)

Related Lab

Brain asymmetry How speed of processing for shapes and words may be different in the left and right hemispheres.

3 Perception

Perception occurs when stimulation of the sensory receptors results in experiences such as seeing, hearing, taste, smell, and touch. This chapter describes the mechanisms responsible for creating perceptions. It also considers how perception is involved in guiding actions such as reaching for a coffee cup and negotiating a corner on a bicycle, and how these actions, in turn, can influence perception.

Some Questions We Will Consider

- Why can two different people experience different perceptions in response to exactly the same stimulus? (57)
- How does perception depend on a person's knowledge about characteristics of the environment? (63)
- How does the brain become tuned to respond best to things that are likely to appear in the environment? (66)
- Are there neurons in the visual system that might help us understand other people's actions? (75)

Crystal begins her run along the beach just as the sun is rising over the ocean. She loves this time of day, both because it is cool and because the mist rising from the sand creates a mystical effect. As she looks down the beach, she notices something about 100 yards away that wasn't there yesterday. "What an interesting piece of driftwood," she thinks, although it is difficult to see because of the mist and dim lighting (● Figure 3.1a). As she approaches the object, she begins to doubt her initial perception, and just as she is wondering whether it might not be driftwood, she realizes that it is, in fact, the old beach umbrella that was lying under the lifeguard stand yesterday (Figure 3.1b). When she realizes this, she is amazed at what has happened. "Driftwood transformed into an umbrella, right before my eyes," she thinks.

Continuing down the beach, she passes some tangled rope that appears to be abandoned (Figure 3.1c). She stops to check it out. Grabbing one end, she flips the rope and sees that, as she suspected, it is one continuous strand. But she needs to keep running,

(a) (b) (c)

Bruce Goldstein

● **FIGURE 3.1** (a) Initially Crystal thinks she sees a large piece of driftwood far down the beach. (b) Eventually she realizes she is looking at an umbrella. (c) On her way down the beach, she passes a piece of rope.

because she is supposed to meet a friend at Beach Java, a coffeehouse far down the beach at the end of her run. Later, sitting in the coffeehouse, she tells her friend about the piece of magic driftwood that was transformed into an umbrella.

The Nature of Perception

Crystal's experiences illustrate a number of things about **perception**, which we define as experiences resulting from stimulation of the senses. Her experience illustrates how perceptions can change, based on added information (Crystal's view became better as she got closer to the umbrella), and how perception can involve a process similar to reasoning or problem solving (Crystal figured out what the object was based partially on remembering having seen that umbrella the day before). (Another example of an initially erroneous perception followed by a correction is the tag line "It's a bird. It's a plane. It's Superman!")

Crystal's experience also demonstrates how arriving at a perception can involve a *process*. It took some time for Crystal to realize that what she thought was driftwood was actually an umbrella, so it is possible to describe her perception as involving a "reasoning" process. However, in most cases perception occurs so rapidly and effortlessly that it appears to be automatic. But as we will see in this chapter, perception is far from automatic. It involves complex, and usually invisible, processes that do resemble reasoning, although they occur much more rapidly than Crystal's realization that the driftwood was actually an umbrella.

Finally, Crystal's experience also illustrates how perception occurs in conjunction with action. Crystal is running and perceiving at the same time; later, she easily reaches for her cup of coffee, a process that involves a coordination between seeing the coffee cup, determining its location, physically reaching for it, and grasping its handle. This aspect of Crystal's experiences is just like what happens in everyday perception. We are usually moving, and even when we are just sitting in one place watching TV, a movie, or a sporting event, our eyes are constantly moving as we shift our attention from one thing to another to perceive what is happening. We also grasp and pick up things many times a day, whether it is a cup of coffee, a pen or pencil, or this book. As we will see in this chapter, perception involves dynamic processes that accompany and support our actions.

Before describing these processes, it is important to note that the importance of perception extends beyond identifying objects or helping us take action within our environment. We can appreciate this by remembering that cognitive psychology is about acquiring knowledge, storing this knowledge in memory, and retrieving it later to accomplish various tasks such as remembering events from the past, solving problems, communicating with other people, recognizing someone you met last week, and answering questions on a cognitive psychology exam. Without perception, it is unlikely that these feats of cognition would be possible.

Think about this for a moment. How aware could you be of things that are happening right now, and how well could you accomplish the cognitive skills mentioned above, if you had lost all of your senses and, therefore, your ability to perceive? Considered in this way, perception is the gateway to all of the other cognitions that we will be describing in the other chapters in this book.

The goal of this chapter is to explain the mechanisms responsible for perception. We will do this by first describing how perception begins when receptors are activated by stimuli in the environment. We will then show that other factors, in addition to stimulation of the receptors, are also involved in creating perceptions. As we do this, you will see that although perception appears to occur automatically, it is actually the outcome of complex processes that resemble, to some extent, processes involved in solving problems. Finally, we will describe how perception occurs in conjunction with action, as when Crystal perceives an object as she runs down the beach and as she combines perception and action in reaching for her cup of coffee.

Perception Starts at the Receptors: Bottom-Up Processing

The first step in perception is the stimulation of receptors by stimuli from the environment. Let's first consider the signals generated in Crystal's visual receptors. Crystal sees the umbrella because light reflected from the umbrella enters her eyes, stimulates receptors, and starts electrical signals traveling toward the visual receiving area of the cortex. Processing that begins with stimulation of the receptors is called **bottom-up processing**. All of our sensory experiences, with the exception of situations in which we might imagine something or "see stars" from getting hit on the head, begins with bottom-up processing. We can describe bottom-up processing both physiologically and behaviorally.

BOTTOM-UP PROCESSING: PHYSIOLOGICAL

We can describe the physiological approach to bottom-up processing briefly, because we have already described, in Chapter 2, the sequence of events that occur after light reflected from a tree stimulates the visual receptors in the eye (see page 38). We saw that stimulation of the receptors triggers a series of events in which electrical signals are transmitted from the receptors toward the brain. Perceiving the tree or a bird chirping occurs after electrical signals that start in the receptors reach the brain.

The initial effect of these signals in the cortex has been determined by recording electrical signals from individual neurons. As we described in Chapter 2, neurons in the cortex that respond best to simple shapes like lines or bars with specific orientations are called feature detectors because they respond to simple features.

Perceiving a tree, or any other object, depends on activity beyond the visual cortex, but the feature detectors' response is the first step in the brain's response to objects. Thus, when you look at an object such as a tree, neurons in the visual cortex that respond to specific orientations fire to features of the tree, such as the trunk and branches, as shown in ● Figure 3.2.

(a)

(b)

Bruce Goldstein

● **FIGURE 3.2** A tree such as this one can be created from a number of simple features, such as oriented bars (a few of which are highlighted on the right). When a person looks at the tree, each feature can activate feature detectors in the cortex that respond best to specific orientations. This occurs at an early stage of cortical processing.

BOTTOM-UP PROCESSING: BEHAVIORAL

The idea that neurons fire to individual features of a tree suggests that perhaps our perception of the tree is created by combining the information provided by the firing of many feature detectors. A behavioral approach to this idea that perception can be created by combinations of individual features has been proposed by Irving Biederman (1987). His idea, called **recognition-by-components (RBC)** theory, proposes that we perceive objects by perceiving elementary features like those in ● Figure 3.3a, called **geons**. Geons are perceptual building blocks that can be combined to create objects, as shown in Figure 3.3b.

One of the characteristics of object perception, according to RBC, is that we can recognize an object if we are able to perceive just a few of its geons. For example, Biederman showed that an airplane that has a total of nine geons (● Figure 3.4a) was recognized correctly about 78 percent of the time even if only three geons were present (Figure 3.4b), and 96 percent of the time if six geons were present.

We can also perceive objects even if portions of the geons are obscured, as shown in ● Figure 3.5a. The reason you can tell this is a flashlight, according to RBC, is that you are able to make out its geons. This is an example of the **principle of componential recovery**—if we can recover (see) an object's geons, we can identify the object.

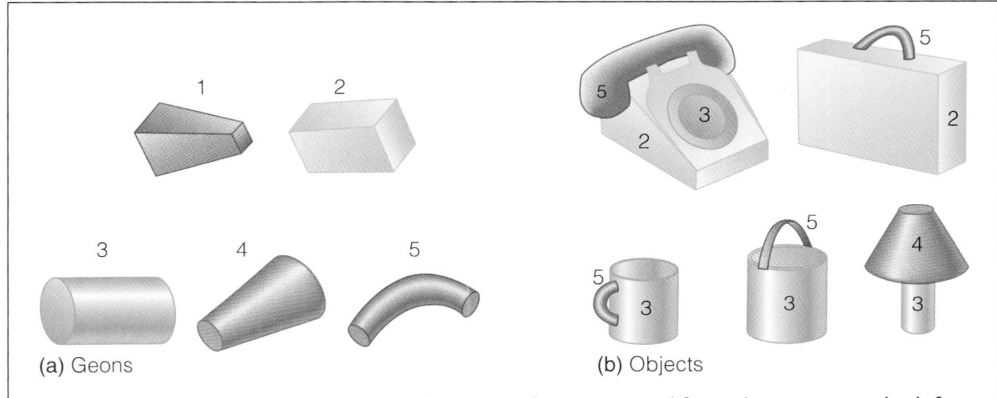

● **FIGURE 3.3** *Left*: Some geons. *Right*: Some objects created from the geons on the left. The numbers on the objects indicate which geons are present. Note that recognizable objects can be formed by combining just two or three geons. Also note that the relations between the geons matter, as illustrated by the cup and the pail. (Source: Adapted from I. Biederman, "Recognition-by-Components: A Theory of Human Image Understanding," *Psychological Review, 24*, 2, 115–147, Figures 3, 6, 7, and 11, Copyright © 1987 by the American Psychological Association. Reprinted by permission.)

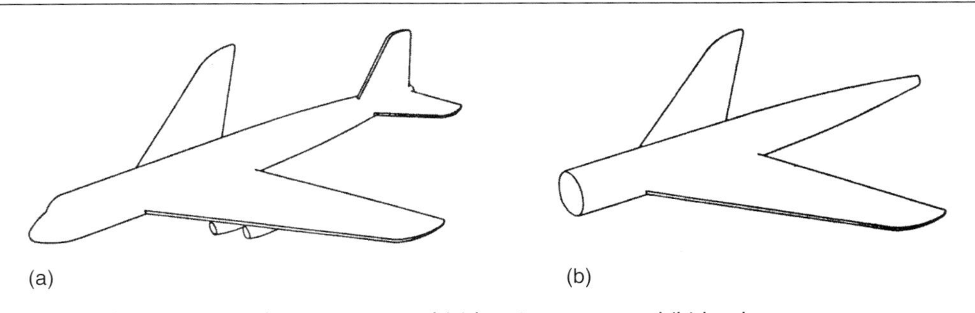

● **FIGURE 3.4** An airplane represented (a) by nine geons and (b) by three geons. (Source: From I. Biederman, *Computer Vision, Graphics and Image Processing*, p. 73. Copyright © 1985 by Irving Biederman. Academic Press, 1985. All rights reserved. Reproduced by permission of Elsevier, Ltd.)

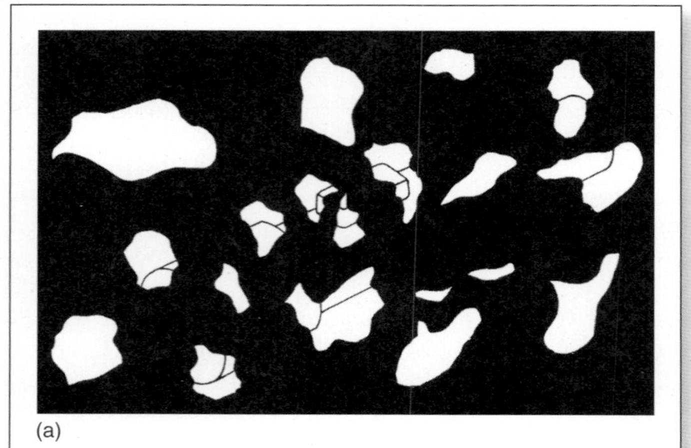

(a)

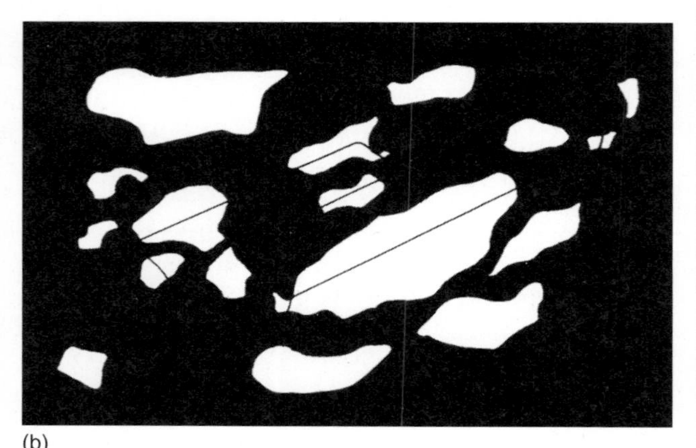

(b)

● **FIGURE 3.5** (a) It is possible to identify this object as a flashlight, even though it is partially obscured, because it is possible to perceive its geons. (b) When the shading is arranged so the geons can't be perceived, it is not possible to recognize the flashlight. (Source: From I. Biederman, *Computer Vision, Graphics and Image Processing*, pp. 29 and 32. Copyright © 1985 by Irving Biederman. Academic Press, 1985. All rights reserved. Reproduced by permission of Elsevier, Ltd.)

Figure 3.5b shows an example in which the corners and intersections of the flashlight's geons are covered, so the geons can't be identified. This is the flip side of the principle of componential recovery—if we *can't* see an object's individual geons, we *can't* recognize the object.

RBC provides an example of bottom-up processing because its basic unit—the geon—is simple and because perceiving simple geometric objects like the ones in Figure 3.3 can be related to patterns of stimulation on the retina. This is similar to how the cortical neurons in Figure 3.2 can be related to stimuli that are presented to the retina. But although perceiving objects begins with stimulation of receptors that leads to the activation of physiologically or behaviorally determined features, there is more to perceiving objects than this.

Beyond Bottom-Up Processing

If perception were determined solely by bottom-up processing, then we could understand perception by considering only the information presented to the receptors. But perception depends on information in addition to that falling on the receptors, including knowledge that a person brings to the situation.

PERCEPTION DEPENDS ON ADDITIONAL INFORMATION

Consider the objects in Figure 3.3b. Although the individual geons that make up these objects may be determined by bottom-up processing, additional processing is involved when the geons are combined to create objects. In fact, the same geons can be combined to create different objects, such as the pail and the cup. We are able to recognize these different objects based on the arrangement of their geons, and to give these objects names like "pail" or "cup," because of knowledge we bring to the situation. Processing that begins with a person's prior knowledge or expectations is called **top-down processing**. Top-down processing is also involved in our ability to recognize objects based on just a few geons, as in Figure 3.4, or when large portions of the object are obscured, as in Figure 3.5. In both of these cases, prior knowledge about airplanes and flashlights probably helps a person perceive these objects.

Another example of how top-down processing is involved in perceiving objects is illustrated in ● Figure 3.6, which is called "the multiple personalities of a blob" (Oliva & Torralba, 2007). The blob shown in (a) is perceived as different objects depending on its orientation and the context within which it is seen. It appears to be an object on a table in (b), a shoe on a person bending down in (c), and a car and a person crossing the street in (d). Even though the blob has the same geons in all of the pictures, we perceive it as different objects because of our knowledge of the kinds of objects that are likely to be found in different types of scenes.

The idea that perception involves more than bottom-up processing also becomes apparent when we return to our discussion of physiology. We saw that signals traveling from the receptors to the brain provide information about an object's basic features. However, as these signals travel to the brain, other signals in addition to those generated by the object's features become involved as well. Some signals provide information about other parts of the scene. For example, signals from the tree (green arrows in ● Figure 3.7) are accompanied by signals from the grass surrounding the tree and from the sky in

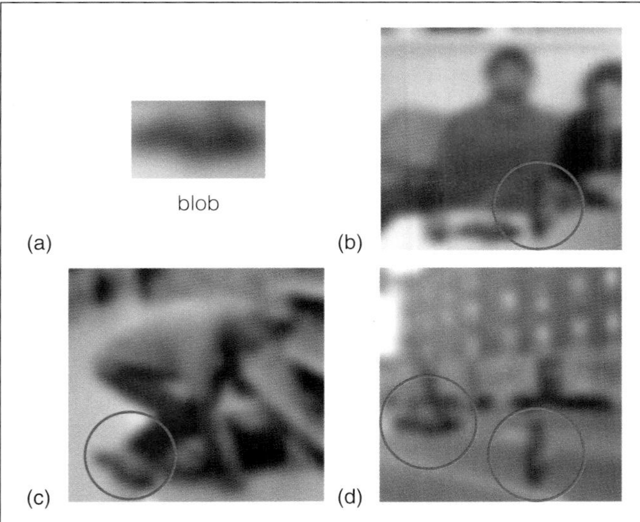

• **FIGURE 3.6** "Multiple personalities of a blob." What we expect to see in different contexts influences our interpretation of the identity of the "blob" inside the circles. (Source: Adapted from A. Oliva & A. Torralba, "The Role of Context in Object Recognition," *Trends in Cognitive Sciences, 11,* Figure 2, 520–527. Copyright © 2007, with permission from Elsevier. Photographs courtesy of Antonio Torralba.)

the background (blue arrows). In addition, other signals, which are associated with a person's knowledge and expectations, are being transmitted down from higher levels in the brain (dashed arrow). Signals such as this, that travel down from higher centers to influence incoming signals, are called **feedback signals** (Di Lollo, 2010).

From the physiological point of view, therefore, perception of an object is based on signals representing the object plus signals representing other aspects of the environment and feedback signals representing prior knowledge or expectations (Figure 3.7). Looking at perception in this way, we can draw an analogy between perception and baking a loaf of bread. The basic ingredients for bread are flour and water, plus extra ingredients such as poppy seeds or salt, depending on the recipe. But if you just mix these ingredients together, the bread doesn't rise. A little yeast is also necessary to make the bread rise. Add the yeast to these other ingredients, bake, and you get a loaf of bread. (Without the yeast, unleavened bread such as matzo, flatbread, or communion wafers results.)

Just as creating a loaf of bread requires the basic ingredients plus yeast, perception depends on information provided by stimulation of receptors plus additional information such as information about the environment and a person's prior knowledge. This information is carried in the additional physiological signals we have described, but we can also use perceptual examples to demonstrate how the perceptual system takes additional information into account. We will do this by describing two different kinds of perceptions: perception of the size of an object and perception of the intensity of an odor.

PERCEIVING SIZE: TAKING DISTANCE INTO ACCOUNT

Imagine that you are walking down some railroad tracks when you suddenly come upon the scene in • Figure 3.8. The small creature near you seems harmless, but you're a little worried about the larger one! You perceive the two creatures to be very different in size, yet they both cover the same distance across your field of view and therefore have the same-sized image on your retina (• Figure 3.9). (Check this out by measuring them!) This means that something in addition to the size of the creature's image on the retina determines your perception of its size.

What other information is available? Perhaps the most obvious is that the creatures are at different distances. A large amount of research has shown that if two objects are perceived to be at different distances but cast the same-sized image on the retina, the perceptual system takes the distance of the farther object into account, so it is perceived as its true, larger size. This makes sense, because in our everyday experience a distant object can result in the same-sized image on the retina as a much smaller object that is closer (see • Figure 3.10), so the way the perceptual system takes depth into account helps us more accurately perceive the size of the faraway object.

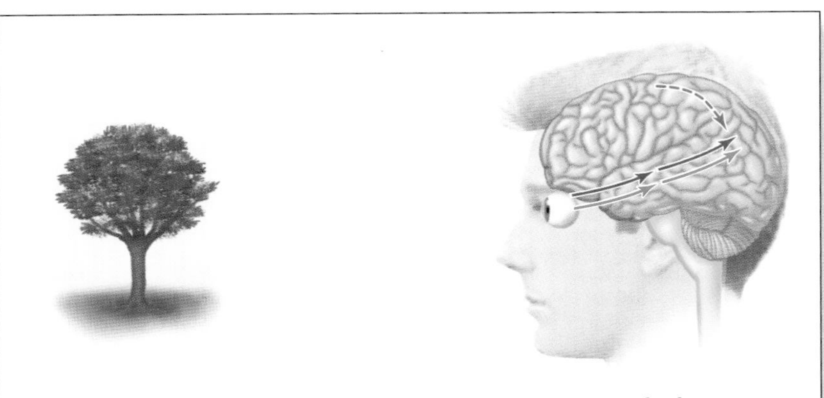

• **FIGURE 3.7** Perception is determined by three sources of information: (1) information originating from stimulation of the receptors (bottom-up = green arrows); (2) additional information such as the context in which an object appears (blue arrows); (3) knowledge or expectations of the perceiver (top-down = dashed arrows). The dashed red arrows represents feedback signals.

In addition to depth, the perceptual system could also be taking into account the size of the object relative to other objects in the environment. Returning to our creatures on the railroad tracks, we can see that the near creature fits within the two tracks with space to spare, while the far one

● **FIGURE 3.8** These two creatures are at different distances, but the farther one is larger. Both creatures cover the same amount of the observer's field of view (measure them!).
(Source: William Vann/www.edupic.net.)

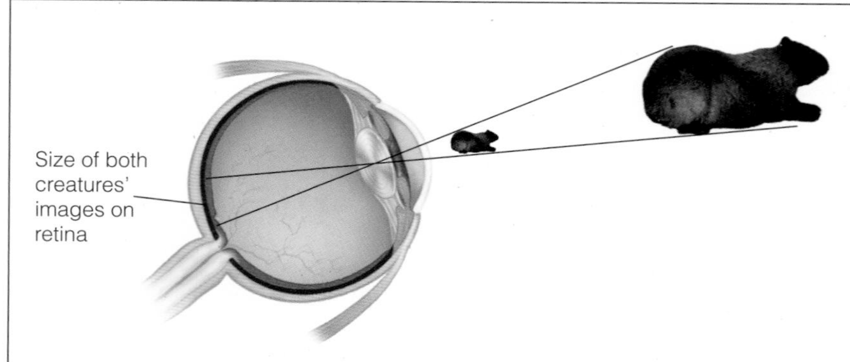

● **FIGURE 3.9** The two creatures on the railroad tracks cover the same area in the field of view and cast the same-sized images on the retina because one is small but close and the other is larger but farther away.

overlaps the tracks. Thus, the relationship of the creatures to the railroad tracks provides information about their relative sizes. The perceptual system's use of information about the creatures' distance and their size relative to the tracks illustrates how information in addition to the size of the image on the retina helps determine the perception of their size.

Here's a demonstration that shows how information provided by the retinal image does not necessarily correspond to what we perceive.

DEMONSTRATION Two Quarters

Hold two quarters as shown in ● Figure 3.11a, with one far away and one closer (at about half the distance). Then close one eye and view the two quarters, keeping them at the same distances and positioning them so their edges appear to be touching (Figure 3.11b). Notice how you perceive the sizes of the two quarters under these conditions. Then open your other eye and view the quarters with both eyes so they no longer appear to be right next to each other. How does that affect your perception of the sizes of the two quarters?

● **FIGURE 3.10** Like the two creatures on the railroad tracks, the top part of the nearby planter and the faraway building are the same size in the observer's field of view.

It is likely that in the first part of the demonstration, when you viewed the quarters next to each other with one eye, the farther quarter appeared smaller. This perception corresponds to the fact that the farther quarter creates a smaller image on the retina (Figure 3.11c). It is also likely that in the second part of the demonstration, with both eyes open, the quarters appeared more similar in size. This occurs because opening both eyes increases your ability to perceive depth, or the relative distance of the two quarters. The perceptual system can then take into account the quarters' distance, and this added information enables you to perceive their sizes more accurately.

Taking distance into account occurs all the time in real life. For example, as a person who is standing near you begins to walk away, he doesn't appear to shrink as his distance increases. A person who appears to be 6 feet tall when he is nearby also appears to be 6 feet tall when he is standing across the room, even though the size of his image on your retinas (as with the far quarter in the demonstration) is much smaller when he is farther away. This phenomenon is called **size constancy**—we tend to perceive objects as remaining the same size even when they move to different distances. All of the examples above, which are summarized in Table 3.1, lead to the same conclusion: Perception of the size of an object does not depend solely on the size of the object's image on the receptors.

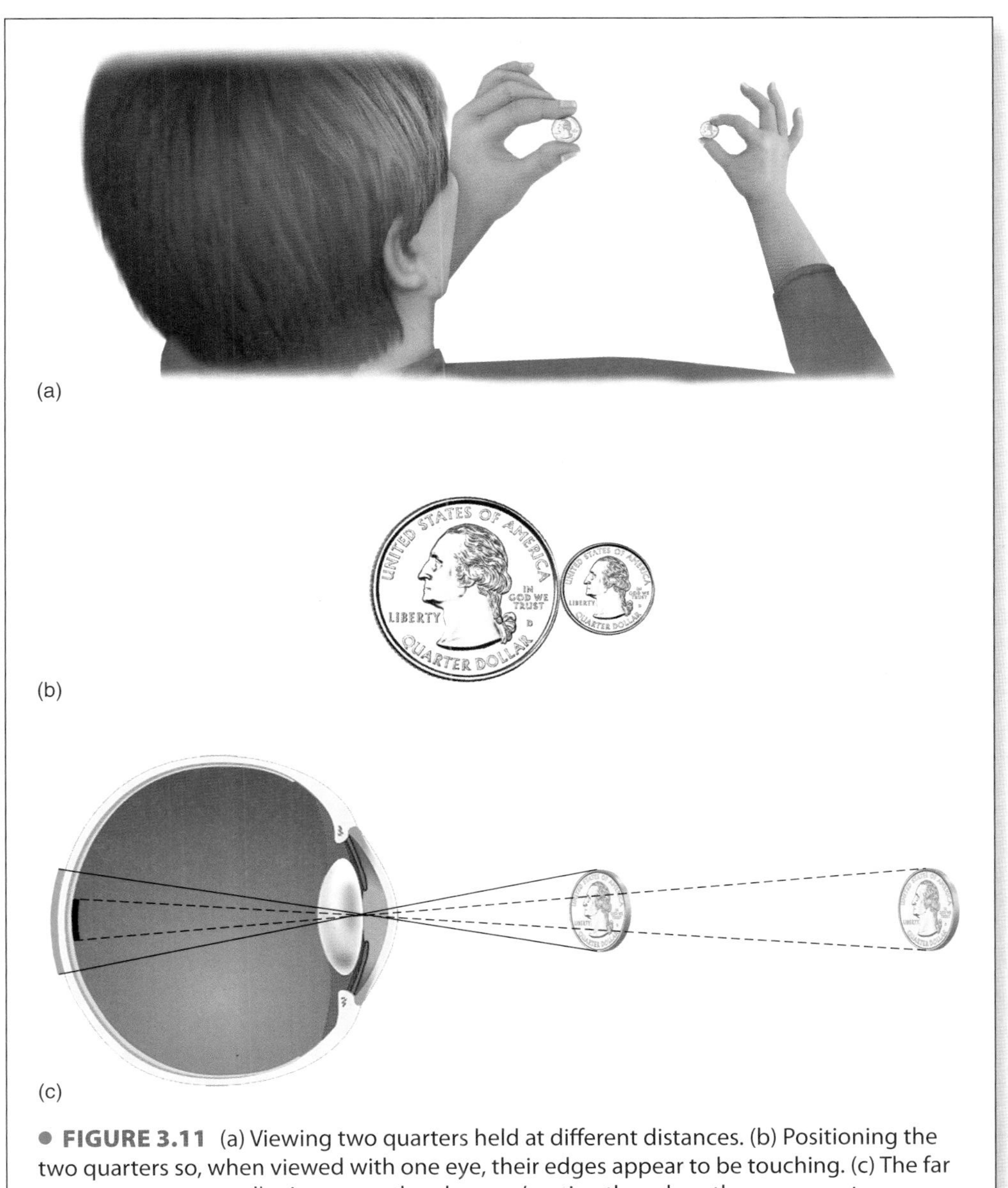

● **FIGURE 3.11** (a) Viewing two quarters held at different distances. (b) Positioning the two quarters so, when viewed with one eye, their edges appear to be touching. (c) The far quarter causes a smaller image on the observer's retina than does the near quarter.

TABLE 3.1 Perception Is Not Completely Determined by the Size of the Image on the Retina

Example	Size of Image on Receptors	Perception
Two creatures on railroad tracks	Image size is the same.	Far creature appears larger.
Two quarters at different distances	Far quarter has smaller image on the receptors.	Two quarters appear about the same size when viewed with two eyes.
Person walking to the other side of the room	Person's image on observer's retina becomes smaller as he walks away.	Person appears the same size when near and farther away.

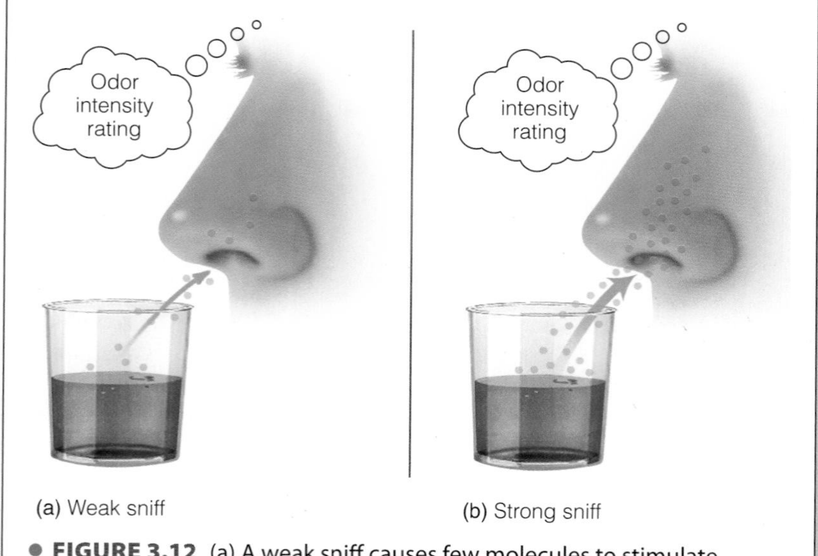

● **FIGURE 3.12** (a) A weak sniff causes few molecules to stimulate receptors inside the nose; (b) a stronger sniff increases the number of molecules reaching the receptors. Even though the receptors are stimulated differently in the two cases, the person's rating of odor intensity does not change.

PERCEIVING ODOR INTENSITY: TAKING SNIFFING INTO ACCOUNT

Imagine that you are given the following instructions: "Your task is to smell this flower and rate the intensity of its odor on a scale of 1 to 10. Flowers with very strong odors, with a fragrance you can smell from a distance, would receive a rating near the high end of the scale. Flowers with more subtle odors, which can be smelled only from very close up, would receive a rating nearer the low end of the scale. The odor of the flower you are going to smell is somewhere between these two extremes." Following these instructions, you bring the flower to your nose and sniff. You begin with a weak sniff, and then sniff more strongly. The question is, Would you rate the flower's odor intensity differently following these two different sniffs?

In a classic experiment, Robert Teghtsoonian and coworkers (1978) asked participants in a laboratory situation to rate the odor intensity of different odorants (chemical solutions with odors) and found that their participants gave almost identical ratings for weak sniffs and for strong sniffs. Think about what this means. Even though stronger sniffing causes more odor molecules to stimulate the receptors, this did not influence the participants' odor intensity ratings (● Figure 3.12). Teghtsoonian and coworkers concluded from this result that their participants were taking the strength of their sniff into account in making their ratings. Does this sound familiar? Just as the perceptual system takes distance and perhaps other factors into account when a person is perceiving size, the perceptual system takes sniff intensity into account when a person is perceiving odor intensity.

It is clear from these two very different examples that while perception may start at the receptors, it depends on additional sources of information as well. The goal of the perceptual system, after all, is to provide accurate information about what is out there in the environment. This is obviously important for survival. For example, we will know to take care when we see a large creature, even if it is far away and so casts a small image on our retinas, and to sniff only very weakly when we might be dealing with a potentially dangerous chemical.

TEST YOURSELF 3.1

1. What does Crystal's run down the beach illustrate about perception? List at least three different characteristics of perception. Why does the importance of perception extend beyond identifying objects?
2. What is bottom-up processing? How can it be described physiologically? Behaviorally? Be sure you understand the basic idea behind recognition-by-components theory, including the role of geons and the principle of componential recovery.
3. Describe how the following indicate that perception involves more than bottom-up processing: (1) naming objects created by geons; (2) multiple personalities of a blob; (3) physiological feedback signals. Following up on this, what is top-down processing, and how can we draw an analogy between perception and baking bread?
4. Describe how the following examples show that perception involves taking into account information in addition to what is on the receptors: (1) perceiving size, including the examples of the creatures on the railroad tracks, the two-quarters demonstration, and perceiving a person at two different distances; (2) perceiving the intensity of smell stimuli with weak and strong sniffs.

Using Knowledge: Top-Down Processing

We will now consider some further examples of how perception depends on more than just stimulation of the receptors. In this section we consider the role of top-down processing, processing that depends on a person's prior knowledge or expectations. We have already described two examples of top-down processing: the naming of objects created by different arrangements of geons, and the blob with the multiple personalities.

Another example of top-down processing is illustrated by something that happens when, as I channel-surf on TV, I stop at Telemundo, a channel that often has dramatic programs in which the action seems extremely interesting. My problem, however, is that Telemundo is a Spanish-language station and I don't understand Spanish. So while the people on the program understand each other, to me the dialogue often sounds like an unbroken string of sound, except occasionally when a familiar word like *gracias* pops out. My perception reflects the fact that the sound signal for speech is generally continuous, and when there are breaks in the sound, they do not necessarily occur between words. You can see this in ● Figure 3.13 by comparing the place where each word in the sentence begins with the pattern of the sound signal.

But when my Spanish-speaking acquaintances watch Telemundo, they perceive this unbroken string of sound as individual, meaningful words. Because of their knowledge of the language, they are able to tell when one word ends and the next one begins, a phenomenon called **speech segmentation**. The fact that a listener familiar only with English and another listener familiar with Spanish can receive *identical sound stimuli* but experience *different perceptions* means that each listener's experience with language (or lack of it!) is influencing his or her perception.

This example illustrates how knowledge that a person brings to the situation can influence perception. In our example, this knowledge is prior knowledge of Spanish, which makes it possible to perceive the individual words and therefore identify where one word ends and the other begins. The idea that perception depends on knowledge is not a new one. The 19th-century physicist and physiologist Hermann von Helmholtz (1866/1911) proposed a theory based on this idea.

HELMHOLTZ'S THEORY OF UNCONSCIOUS INFERENCE

Helmholtz proposed a principle called the **theory of unconscious inference**, which states that some of our perceptions are the result of unconscious assumptions that we

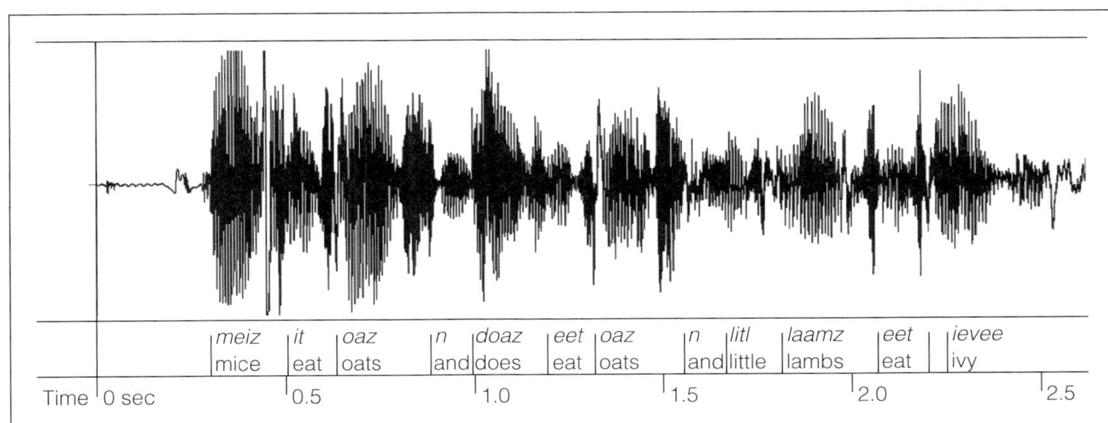

● **FIGURE 3.13** Sound energy for the sentence "Mice eat oats and does eat oats and little lambs eat ivy." The italicized words just below the sound record indicate how this sentence was pronounced by the speaker. The vertical lines next to the words indicate where each word begins. Note that it is difficult or impossible to tell from the sound record where one word ends and the other begins. (Source: Speech signal courtesy of Peter Howell.)

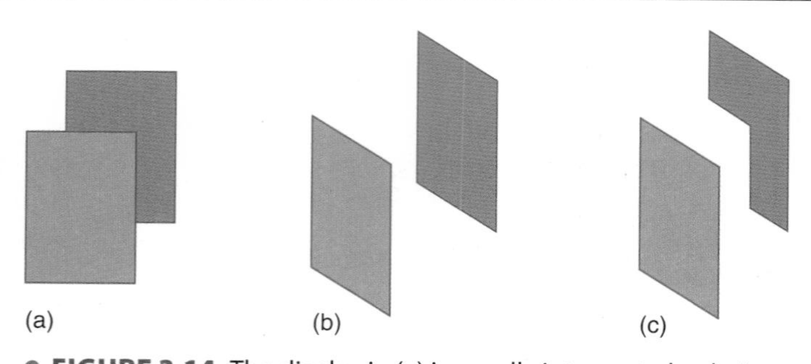

• **FIGURE 3.14** The display in (a) is usually interpreted as being (b) a blue rectangle in front of a red rectangle. It could, however, be (c) a blue rectangle and an appropriately positioned six-sided red figure.

make about the environment. This theory was proposed to account for our ability to create perceptions from stimulus information that can be seen in more than one way. For example, what do you see in the display in • Figure 3.14a? Most people perceive a blue rectangle in front of a red rectangle, as shown in Figure 3.14b. But as Figure 3.14c indicates, this display could have been caused by a six-sided red shape positioned either in front of or behind the blue rectangle.

The theory of unconscious inference includes the **likelihood principle**, which states that we perceive the object that is *most likely* to have caused the pattern of stimuli we have received. Thus, we infer that it is likely that Figure 3.14a is a rectangle covering another rectangle because of experiences we have had with similar situations in the past. Helmholtz therefore described the process of perception as being similar to the process involved in solving a problem. For perception, the problem is to determine which object has caused a particular pattern of stimulation, and this problem is solved by a process in which the observer applies his or her knowledge of the environment in order to infer what the object might be. In cases such as the overlapping shapes in Figure 3.14, this process is unconscious, hence the term *unconscious inference*. (See Rock, 1983, for a modern version of this idea.)

We can apply this idea that perception involves a process similar to solving a problem to Crystal's attempts to identify the faraway shape on the beach. Based on what she saw at first, she hypothesized "driftwood" based on the image on her receptors and her knowledge of which objects are often found on the beach. But as she got closer, she decided it was more likely that the image was caused by the umbrella she had seen the day before. Although in this example Crystal used a conscious reasoning process that was much slower than Helmholtz's unconscious inference, the basic principle is similar to his proposal that perception involves an inferential process that resembles the process involved in solving a problem.

THE GESTALT LAWS OF ORGANIZATION

About 30 years after Helmholtz proposed his theory of unconscious inference, a group called the **Gestalt psychologists** proposed another approach. The goal of this approach was the same as Helmholtz's—to explain how we perceive objects—but the emphasis was different. The Gestalt psychologists were concerned with **perceptual organization**, the way elements are grouped together to create larger objects. For example, in • Figure 3.15, some of the black areas become grouped to form a Dalmatian and others are seen as shadows in the background. The Gestalt psychologists proposed a number of **laws of perceptual organization** that indicate how elements in the environment are organized, or grouped together.

The starting points for the Gestalt laws are things that usually occur in the environment. Consider, for example, the rope in • Figure 3.16a that Crystal saw as she was running down the beach (Figure 3.1c). Remember that when she grabbed one end of the rope and flipped it, it didn't surprise her that it was one continuous strand (page 48). The reason this didn't surprise her is that even though there were many places where one part of the rope overlapped another part, she didn't perceive the rope as consisting of a number of separate pieces, but perceived the rope as continuous. She perceived it this way because when one object overlaps another in the environment, the overlapped (underneath) object usually continues unbroken beneath the object on top. This is illustrated by the highlighted segment of the rope in Figure 3.16b.

Observations such as this led the Gestalt psychologists to propose the **law of good continuation**, which states: *Points that, when connected, result in straight or smoothly curving lines are seen as belonging together, and the lines tend to be seen in such a way*

● **FIGURE 3.15** Some black and white shapes. Some of these shapes become perceptually organized into a Dalmatian.

● **FIGURE 3.16** (a) Rope on the beach. (b) Good continuation helps us perceive the rope as a single strand.

as to follow the smoothest path. Also, objects that are overlapped by other objects are perceived as continuing behind the overlapping object. The Celtic knot pattern in ● Figure 3.17 illustrates this overlap effect, in which good continuation assures that we see a continuous interwoven pattern that does not appear to be broken into little pieces every time one strand overlaps another.

The rationale behind the law of good continuation bears repeating: It predicts that what we perceive is based on what usually happens in the environment. This means that if perception follows the Gestalt laws, it is likely that the resulting perception will

• **FIGURE 3.17** Because of good continuation, we perceive this pattern as a continuous interwoven strand.

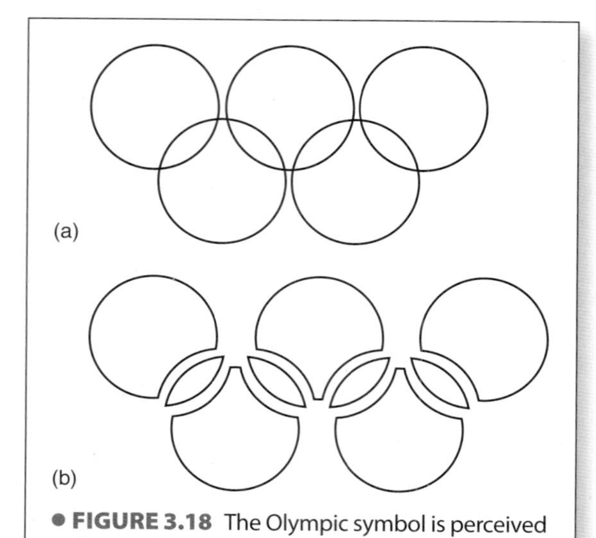

• **FIGURE 3.18** The Olympic symbol is perceived as five circles (a), not as the nine shapes in (b).

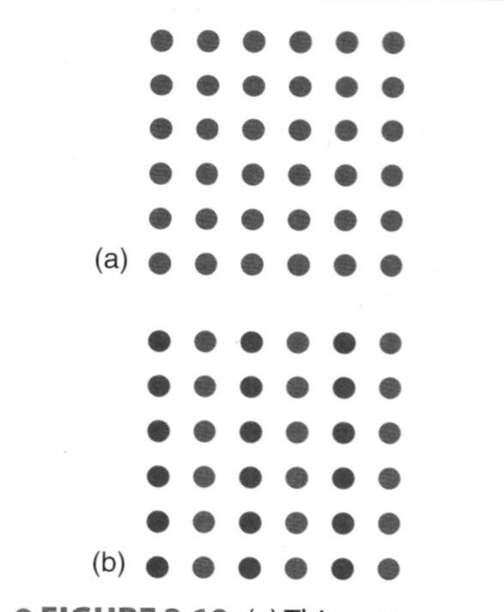

• **FIGURE 3.19** (a) This pattern of dots is perceived as horizontal rows, vertical columns, or both. (b) This pattern of dots is perceived as vertical columns. (Source: From E. B. Goldstein, *Sensation and Perception,* 8th ed., Fig. 5.14, p. 106. Copyright © 2010 Wadsworth, a part of Cengage Learning. Reproduced with permission. www .cengage.com/permissions.)

accurately reflect what is happening in the environment. This is similar to Helmholtz's likelihood principle: Our perception corresponds to the object that is most likely to have caused the pattern of stimulation we have received. Here are some other Gestalt laws that make additional predictions about our perception based on what usually happens in the environment.

Pragnanz *Pragnanz,* roughly translated from the German, means "good figure." The **law of pragnanz,** also called the **law of good figure** or the **law of simplicity,** states: *Every stimulus pattern is seen in such a way that the resulting structure is as simple as possible.* The familiar Olympic symbol in • Figure 3.18a is an example of the law of simplicity at work. We see this display as five circles and not as a larger number of more complicated shapes such as the ones in Figure 3.18b. (The law of good continuation also contributes to perceiving the five circles. Can you see why this is so?)

Similarity Most people perceive • Figure 3.19a as either horizontal rows of circles, vertical columns of circles, or both. But when we change the color of some of the columns, as in Figure 3.19b, most people perceive vertical columns of circles. This perception illustrates the **law of similarity:** *Similar things appear to be grouped together.* The law of similarity causes us to perceive a number in • Figure 3.20, and in environmental scenes helps define individual objects.

To understand how similarity helps define objects, look at the environmental scene in • Figure 3.21. Pick a point on the scene (such as A), then move slightly away from that point to B. If the color at this second point is the same as the color at A, then it is likely that these two points are on the same object. If, however, you move to a point that is a different color, like point C, then it is likely that you have crossed over a contour to another object. While you are looking at this scene, see if you can also find examples of good continuation and good figure.

Meaningfulness or Familiarity According to the **law of familiarity,** *things that form patterns that are familiar or meaningful are likely to be grouped together* (Helson, 1933; Hochberg, 1971). This is illustrated by the Dalmatian picture in Figure 3.15 and by the following demonstration.

DEMONSTRATION Finding Faces in a Landscape

Consider the picture in • Figure 3.22. At first glance this scene appears to contain mainly trees, rocks, and water. On closer inspection, however, you can see some faces in the trees in the background, and if you look more closely, you can see that a number of faces are formed by various groups of rocks. See if you can find all 13 faces hidden in this picture.

Some people find it difficult to perceive the faces at first, but then suddenly they succeed. The change in perception from "rocks in a stream" or "trees in a forest" to "faces" is a change in the perceptual organization of the rocks and the trees. The two shapes that you at first perceive as two separate rocks in the stream become perceptually grouped together when they become the left and right eyes of a face. In fact, once you perceive a particular grouping of rocks as a face, it is often difficult *not* to perceive them in this way—they have become permanently organized into a face. This is similar to the process we observed for the Dalmatian. Once we see the Dalmatian, it is difficult not to perceive it. Although it is unlikely that elements in an actual scene would be arranged to create so many faces, arrangements do occur in the environment that

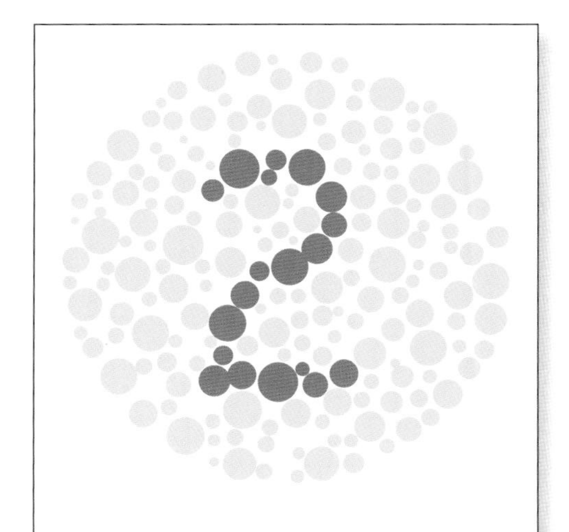

● **FIGURE 3.20** Perception of a number reflects the law of similarity, because dots of the same color are grouped together.

Bruce Goldstein

● **FIGURE 3.21** This scene illustrates a number of Gestalt principles. See text for details.

become perceptually organized into "objects." Consider, for example, the pattern in ● Figure 3.23. When the blue area just over the mountain is perceived as a bird's head facing to the right, the small white cloud becomes the bird's eye and so becomes perceptually grouped with the head.

● **FIGURE 3.22** *The Forest Has Eyes* by Bev Doolittle (1984). Can you find 13 faces in this picture? E-mail the author at bruceg@email.arizona.edu for the solution. (Source: "The Forest Has Eyes" © 1984 Bev Doolittle, courtesy of The Greenwich Workshop, Inc.)

Bruce Goldstein

• **FIGURE 3.23** Clouds over a mountain. Can you see a bird?

THE GESTALT "LAWS" ARE "HEURISTICS"

Although the Gestalt psychologists called their principles *laws* of perceptual organization, they fall short of being laws because they don't always accurately predict what is in the environment. For example, consider the following situation in which the Gestalt laws might cause an incorrect perception: As you are hiking in the woods, you stop cold in your tracks because not too far ahead you see what appears to be an animal lurking behind a tree (• Figure 3.24a). The Gestalt laws of organization play a role in creating this perception. You see the two shapes to the left and right of the tree as a single object because of the Gestalt law of similarity (because both shapes are the same color, it is likely that they are part of the same object). Also, good continuation links these two parts into one because the line along the top of the object extends smoothly from one side of the tree to another. Finally, the image resembles animals you've seen before. For all of these reasons, it is not surprising that you perceive the two objects as part of one animal.

Because you fear that the animal might be dangerous, you take a different path. As your detour takes you around the tree, you notice that the dark shapes aren't an animal after all, but are two oddly shaped tree stumps (Figure 3.24b). In this case, the Gestalt laws have misled you. Notice, however, that the reason the Gestalt laws didn't "work" was because of an unusual arrangement of objects that would normally occur only rarely in the environment.

The fact that the Gestalt laws can sometimes lead to incorrect perceptions means that it is more accurate to call them **heuristics**—rules of thumb that provide a best-guess solution to a problem. We can understand what heuristics are by comparing them to another way of solving a problem, called algorithms.

An **algorithm** is a procedure that is *guaranteed* to solve a problem. An example of an algorithm is the procedures we learn for addition, subtraction, and long division. If we apply these procedures correctly, we get the right answer every time. In contrast, a heuristic may not result in a correct solution every time. For example, suppose that you want to find your keys that you have misplaced somewhere in the house. An algorithm for doing this would be to systematically search every room in the house. If you do this, looking everywhere in each room, you will eventually find the keys, although it may take a while. A heuristic for finding the keys would be to first look in the places where you usually leave your keys and in the places you went right after you used the keys to unlock the front door. This may not always lead to finding the keys, but if it does, it has the advantage of usually being faster than the algorithm.

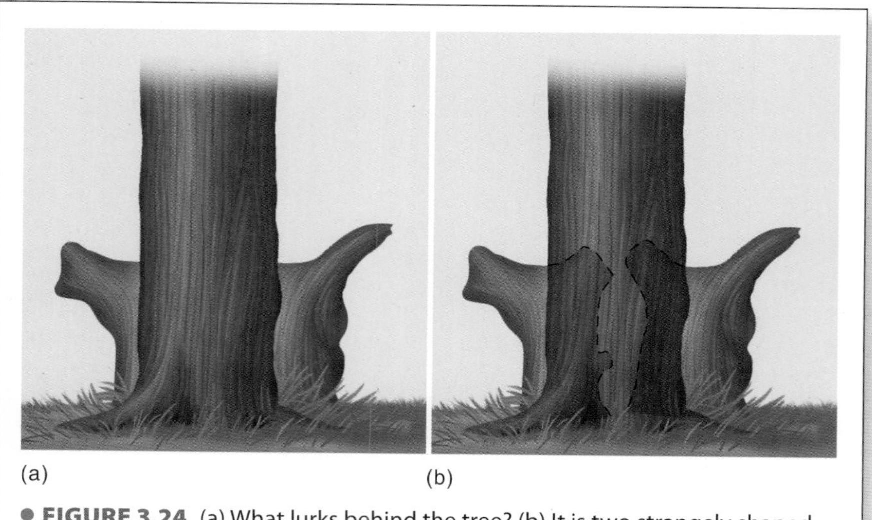

• **FIGURE 3.24** (a) What lurks behind the tree? (b) It is two strangely shaped tree stumps, not an animal!

We say the Gestalt principles are heuristics because they are best-guess rules, based on how the environment is organized, that work *most* of the time, but not necessarily all of the time. The fact that heuristics are usually faster than algorithms helps explain why the perceptual system is designed to operate in a way that sometimes produces errors. Consider, for example, what the algorithm would be for determining what the shape in Figure 3.24a really is. It would involve walking around the tree so you can see it from different angles and perhaps taking a closer look at the objects behind the tree. Although this may result in an accurate perception, it is potentially slow and therefore risky (what if the object actually *is* a dangerous animal?).

The idea of describing the operation of Gestalt principles as heuristics surprises some people, because heuristics are most often associated with reasoning, solving problems, and making decisions. In fact, many books don't discuss heuristics until the chapter on problem solving. But doing that would miss a chance to introduce one of the main messages of this book, which is that different types of cognition, such as perception, attention, memory, language, reasoning, problem solving, and decision making, involve similar mechanisms.

Because all of these cognitions share the same nervous system and are outcomes of the operation of the same mind, it shouldn't be surprising that they have some operating principles in common. We will see, for example, when we discuss long-term memory in Chapter 8, that knowledge gained from past experiences can influence memory. Thus, when a person is asked to remember a written passage describing a familiar situation, such as visiting a dentist's office, the memory report is often influenced by earlier experiences the person has had in visiting the dentist. Sometimes these experiences aid memory, and sometimes they result in errors, just as occurred in our perceptual example when the forms in Figure 3.24 were mistaken for a creature.

In Chapters 7 and 8 we will have more to say about how our prior knowledge affects memory. To continue our discussion of the role of knowledge in perception, we now consider the idea that perception is influenced by *regularities in the environment*.

TAKING REGULARITIES IN THE ENVIRONMENT INTO ACCOUNT

Modern perceptual psychologists have introduced the idea that perception is influenced by our knowledge of regularities in the environment—characteristics of the environment that occur frequently. For example, blue is associated with open sky, landscapes are often green and smooth, and verticals and horizontals are often associated with buildings. We can distinguish two types of regularities, *physical regularities* and *semantic regularities*.

Physical Regularities Physical regularities are regularly occurring physical properties of the environment. For example, there are more vertical and horizontal orientations in the environment than oblique (angled) orientations. This occurs in human-made environments (for example, buildings contain lots of horizontals and verticals) and also in natural environments (trees and plants are more likely to be vertical or horizontal than slanted) (Coppola et al., 1998). It is therefore no coincidence that people can perceive horizontals and verticals more easily than other orientations, an effect called the **oblique effect** (Appelle, 1972; Campbell et al., 1966; Orban et al., 1984). Another example of a physical regularity is that when one object partially covers another one, the contour of the partially covered object "comes out the other side," as occurs for the rope in Figure 3.16 and the Celtic knot in Figure 3.17.

Another physical regularity is illustrated by the following demonstration.

DEMONSTRATION Shape From Shading

What do you perceive in ● Figure 3.25a? Do some of the discs look as though they are sticking out, like parts of three-dimensional spheres, and others appear to be indentations? If you do see the discs in this way, notice that the ones that appear to be sticking out are arranged in a square. After observing this, rotate the page so the small dot is below the discs. Does this change your perception?

Figures 3.25b and c show that if we assume that light is coming from above (which is usually the case in the environment), then patterns like the circles that are light-colored on the top would be created by an object that bulges out, as illustrated in Figure 3.25b,

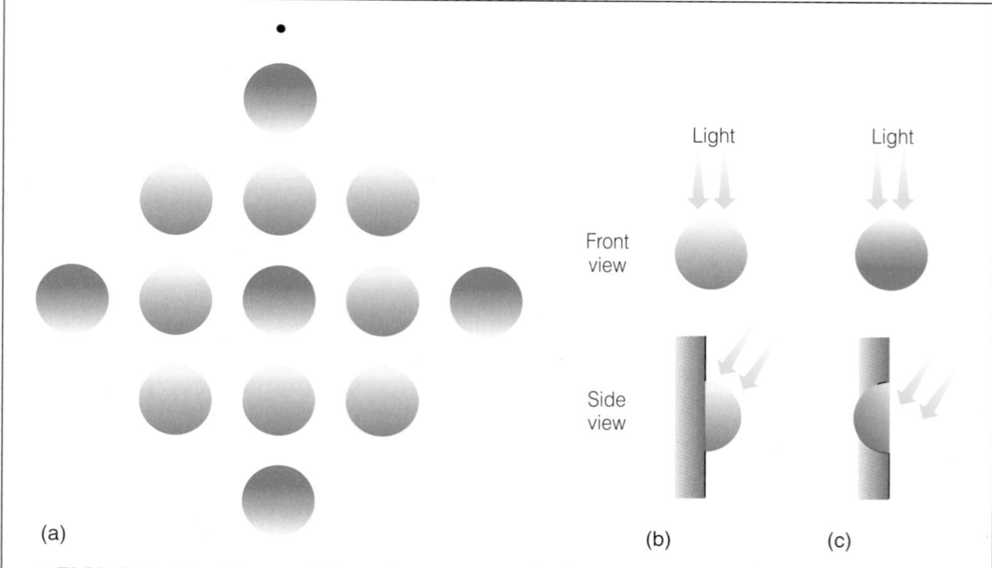

• **FIGURE 3.25** a) Some of these discs are perceived as jutting out, and some are perceived as indentations. The explanation for this perception is that light coming from above will illuminate (b) the top of a shape that is jutting out and (c) the bottom of an indentation.

but a pattern like the circles that are light on the bottom would be created by an indentation in a surface (see Figure 3.25c). The assumption that light is coming from above has been called the **light-from-above heuristic** (Kleffner & Ramachandran, 1992). Apparently, people make the light-from-above assumption because most light in our environment comes from above. This is true of the sun, as well as most artificial light sources.

Another example of the light-from-above heuristic at work is provided by the two pictures in • Figure 3.26. Figure 3.26a shows indentations created by people walking in the sand. But when we turn this picture upside down, as shown in Figure 3.26b, the indentations in the sand become rounded mounds.

Thus, one reason we are able to perceive and recognize objects and scenes is because of our knowledge of physical characteristics of our environment. We also have knowledge about regularities of the environment that indicate what types of objects typically occur in specific types of scenes.

Semantic Regularities In language, *semantics* refers to the meanings of words or sentences. Applied to perceiving scenes, *semantics* refers to the meaning of a scene. This

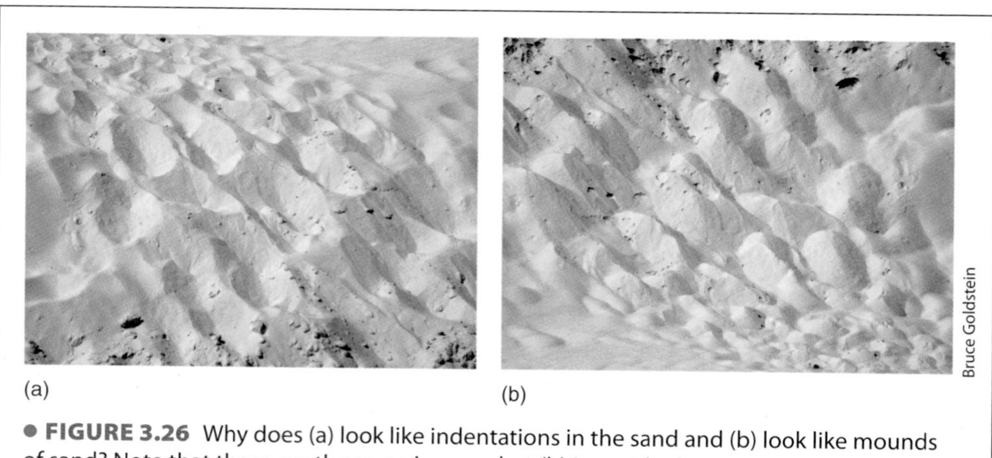

• **FIGURE 3.26** Why does (a) look like indentations in the sand and (b) look like mounds of sand? Note that these are the same images, but (b) is upside down.

meaning is often related to what happens within a scene. For example, food preparation, cooking, and perhaps eating occur in a kitchen; waiting around, buying tickets, checking luggage, and going through security checkpoints happen in airports. **Semantic regularities** are the characteristics associated with the functions carried out in different types of scenes.

One way to demonstrate that people are aware of semantic regularities is simply to ask them to imagine a particular type of scene or object, as in the following demonstration.

DEMONSTRATION Visualizing Scenes and Objects

Your task in this demonstration is simple. Close your eyes and then visualize or simply think about the following scenes and objects:

1. An office
2. The clothing section of a department store
3. A microscope
4. A lion

Most people who have grown up in modern society have little trouble visualizing an office or the clothing section of a department store. What is important about this ability, for our purposes, is that part of this visualization involves details within these scenes. Most people see an office as having a desk with a computer on it, bookshelves, and a chair. The department store scene contains racks of clothes, a changing room, and perhaps a cash register.

What did you see when you visualized the microscope or the lion? Many people report seeing not just a single object, but an object within a setting. Perhaps you perceived the microscope sitting on a lab bench or in a laboratory and the lion in a forest, on a savannah, or in a zoo. Knowledge of semantic regularities were probably at work when Crystal used her knowledge of the things that are usually found on beaches when she first perceived "driftwood" and then "beach umbrella."

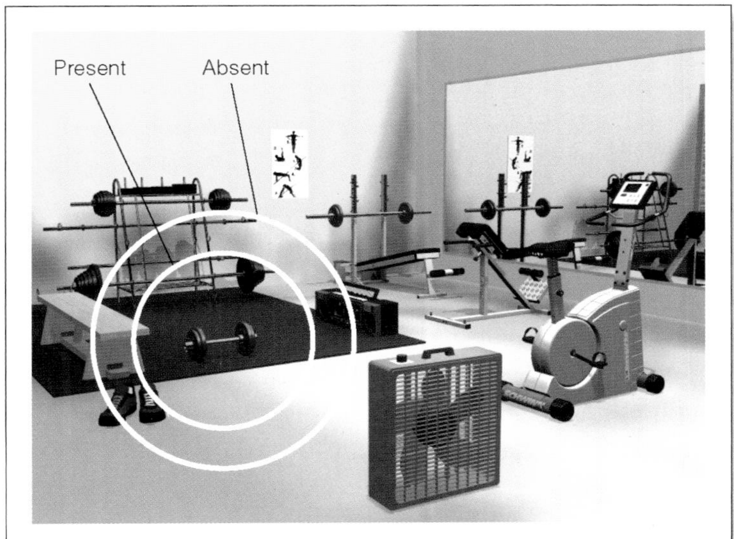

• **FIGURE 3.27** Hollingworth's (2005) observers saw scenes like this one (without the circles). In this scene, the target object is the barbell, although observers do not know this when they are viewing the scene. "Non-target" scenes are the same but do not include the target. The circles indicate the average error of observers' judgments of the position of the target object for trials in which they had seen the object in the scene (small circle) and trials in which the object had not appeared in the scene (larger circle). (Source: A. Hollingworth, "Memory for Object Position in Natural Scenes," *Visual Cognition, 12,* 1003–1016, 2005. Reprinted by permission of the publisher, Taylor & Francis Ltd, http://www.tandf.co.uk/journals.)

An example of the knowledge we have of things that typically belong in certain scenes is provided by an experiment in which Andrew Hollingworth (2005) had observers study for 20 seconds a scene, such as the picture of the gym in • Figure 3.27, that contained a target object, such as the barbell on the mat, or the same scene but without the target object. Observers then saw a picture of the target object alone in the center of the screen followed by a blank screen, and were asked to move a cursor on the blank screen to the place where the target object was in the scene they had just seen (if they had seen the picture of the scene containing the target object) or where they would *expect* to see the target object in the scene (if they had seen the picture of the scene but without the target object).

The results, which included the averaged data for many different objects and scenes, indicated that observers who saw the target objects located their positions accurately in the scene (small circle), but observers who had not seen the target objects were still able to predict where they would be (larger circle). What this means for the gym scene is that observers were apparently able to predict where the barbell would appear based on their prior experience in seeing objects in gyms.

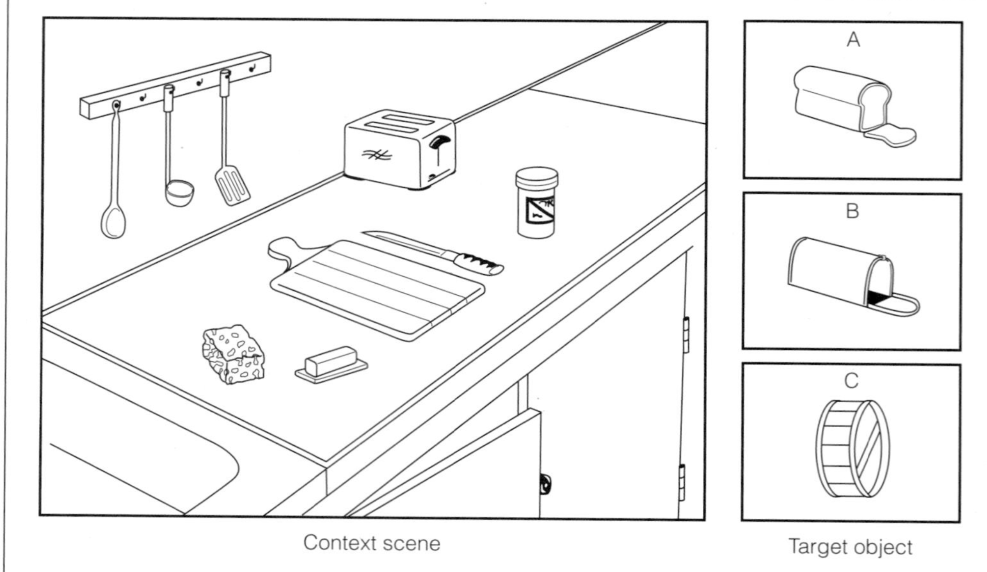

● **FIGURE 3.28** Stimuli used in Palmer's (1975) experiment. The scene at the left is presented first, and the observer is then asked to identify one of the objects on the right. (Source: S. E. Palmer, "The Effects of Contextual Scenes on the Identification of Objects," *Memory and Cognition, 3*, 519–526, 1975. Reprinted by permission of the Psychonomic Society, Inc.)

This effect of semantic knowledge on our ability to perceive was illustrated in an experiment by Stephen Palmer (1975), using stimuli like the picture in ● Figure 3.28. Palmer first presented a context scene such as the one on the left and then briefly flashed one of the target pictures on the right. When Palmer asked observers to identify the object in the target picture, they correctly identified an object like the loaf of bread (which is appropriate to the kitchen scene) 80 percent of the time, but correctly identified the mailbox or the drum (two objects that don't fit into the scene) only 40 percent of the time. Apparently Palmer's observers were using their knowledge about kitchens to help them perceive the briefly flashed loaf of bread. The effect of semantic regularities is also illustrated by the "multiple personalities of a blob" illustration in Figure 3.6, because our perception of the blob depends on our knowledge of what is usually found in different types of scenes.

TEST YOURSELF 3.2

1. What is speech segmentation? How does the author's description of his Telemundo experience illustrate how perception is influenced by knowledge?
2. Describe Helmholtz's theory of unconscious inference. What does it say about the role of knowledge in determining perception?
3. Describe the Gestalt laws of perceptual organization. Why do we say that these laws are based on what usually occurs in the environment? What is the relation between these laws and Helmholtz's likelihood principle? Why can the Gestalt laws be called "heuristics"?
4. What are regularities in the environment? Describe physical regularities and semantic regularities. Be sure you understand the following concepts and experiments: oblique effect; light-from-above heuristic; Hollingworth gym experiment; Palmer kitchen experiment; multiple personalities of a blob.

Neurons and Knowledge About the Environment

Our discussion of how perception is linked to the perceiver's knowledge of the environment has so far focused on behavioral examples. But there is neural activity behind every behavior, and research has demonstrated connections between neural activity, the nature of the environment, and perception by showing that there are neurons that are tuned to respond best to things that occur regularly in the environment. We can understand why this is important by considering the problem of designing a machine that can perceive.

DESIGNING A PERCEIVING MACHINE

Imagine that you are given the assignment of designing a computer-based system that could scan a room and determine its layout. Luckily, you have at your disposal a powerful computer, an expert computer programmer, and an array of high-technology sensing devices.

One approach to this problem would be to have the sensors scan the environment, determining the patterns of light and dark within a room, and have the computer analyze this information to determine the layout of the room. But since we know that it helps to have some knowledge of the environment, it would make sense to design your computer program to be able to recognize elements that frequently appear inside rooms. One of the first things to do would be to be sure the program was designed to pick up verticals and horizontals. These are features that are usually found in rooms; they are associated with the borders between the walls, ceilings, and the floor. It would also make sense to program the computer to be able to sense flat surfaces, such as floors, ceilings, and walls. In other words, your computer-based seeing system would operate more efficiently if it were programmed to be especially sensitive to features that occur frequently in rooms. This principle for designing a perceiving machine is the same principle used by the "computer" for the human "perceiving machine"—the brain.

THE HUMAN "PERCEIVING MACHINE"

One of the basic operating principles of the human brain is that it contains some neurons that respond best to things that occur regularly in the environment. When we described physical regularities in the environment, we mentioned that horizontals and verticals are common features of the environment, and behavioral experiments have shown that people are more sensitive to these orientations than to other orientations that are not as common (the *oblique effect*, see page 63). It is not a coincidence, therefore, that when researchers have recorded the activity of single neurons in the visual cortex of monkeys and ferrets, they have found more neurons that respond best to horizontals and verticals compared to neurons that respond best to other orientations, such as slants (Coppola et al., 1998; DeValois et al., 1992). There is evidence from brain scanning experiments that this occurs in humans as well (Furmanski & Engel, 2000).

Why are there more neurons that respond to horizontals and verticals? One possible answer is that through the process of evolution the brain has evolved to respond best to situations or stimuli that are commonly found in the environment. According to the **theory of natural selection**, genetically based characteristics that enhance an animal's ability to survive, and therefore reproduce, will be passed on to future generations. A person whose visual system contains neurons that fire to important things in the environment (such as verticals and horizontals, which would occur frequently in the forest, for example) will be more likely to survive and pass on his or her characteristics than will a person whose visual system does not contain these specialized neurons. Through this evolutionary process, the visual system may have been shaped to contain neurons that respond to things that are found frequently in the environment.

Although there is no question that perceptual functioning has been shaped by evolution, it is difficult to prove whether a particular capacity is, in fact, "built in" by evolution or acquired by learning (Kanwisher, 2003). There is, however, a great deal of evidence that learning can shape the response properties of neurons through a process called *experience-dependent plasticity*.

EXPERIENCE-DEPENDENT PLASTICITY

The brain is changed, or "shaped," by its exposure to the environment so it can perceive the environment more efficiently. The mechanism through which the structure of the brain is changed by experience, called **experience-dependent plasticity**, has been demonstrated in many experiments on animals. These experiments have shown that if an animal is reared in a particular environment, neurons in the animal's brain change so they become tuned to respond more strongly to specific aspects of that environment. For example, when a kitten is born, its visual cortex contains orientation-selective neurons that fire to oriented bars like the ones in Figure 3.2b. Normally the kitten's brain contains neurons that respond to all orientations, ranging from horizontal to slanted to vertical, but Colin Blakemore and Graham Cooper (1970) found that rearing a kitten in an environment consisting only of verticals (● Figure 3.29a) reshaped the kitten's visual cortex so it eventually contained neurons that responded mainly to verticals (Figure 3.29b). Similarly, kittens reared in an environment consisting only of horizontals ended up with a visual cortex that contained neurons that responded mainly to horizontals. Thus, the kitten's brain had been shaped to respond best to the environment to which the kitten had been exposed.

Experience-dependent plasticity has also been demonstrated in humans, using the brain imaging technique of fMRI (see Method: Brain Imaging, page 30). The starting point for this research is the finding that there is an area in the temporal lobe called the fusiform face area (FFA) that contains many neurons that respond best to faces (see Chapter 2, page 32). Isabel Gauthier and coworkers (1999) determined whether this response to faces might be due to experience-dependent plasticity by measuring the level of activity in the FFA in response to faces and to objects called Greebles (● Figure 3.30). Greebles are families of computer-generated "beings" that all have the same basic configuration but differ in the shapes of their parts (just like faces). The bars and the brain scans in ● Figure 3.31a show that for "Greeble novices" (people who have had little experience in perceiving Greebles), the faces cause more activity than the Greebles in the FFA. This is also evident in the brain cross section, in which the white areas indicate higher activity.

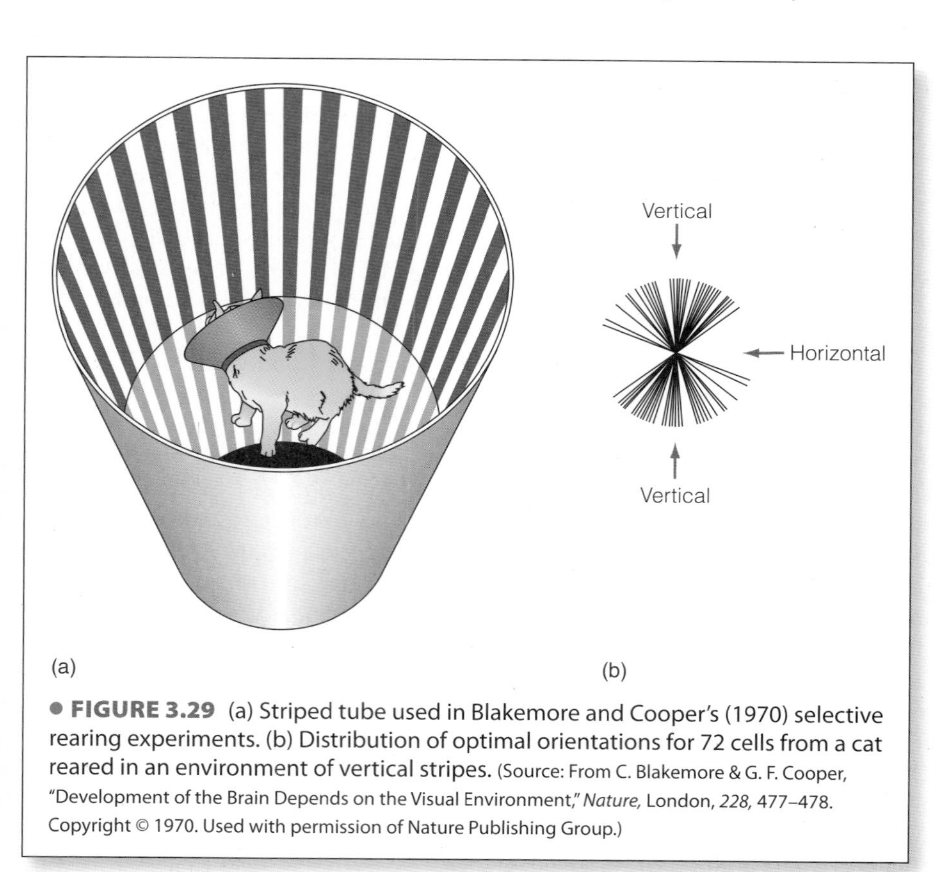

● FIGURE 3.29 (a) Striped tube used in Blakemore and Cooper's (1970) selective rearing experiments. (b) Distribution of optimal orientations for 72 cells from a cat reared in an environment of vertical stripes. (Source: From C. Blakemore & G. F. Cooper, "Development of the Brain Depends on the Visual Environment," *Nature*, London, *228*, 477–478. Copyright © 1970. Used with permission of Nature Publishing Group.)

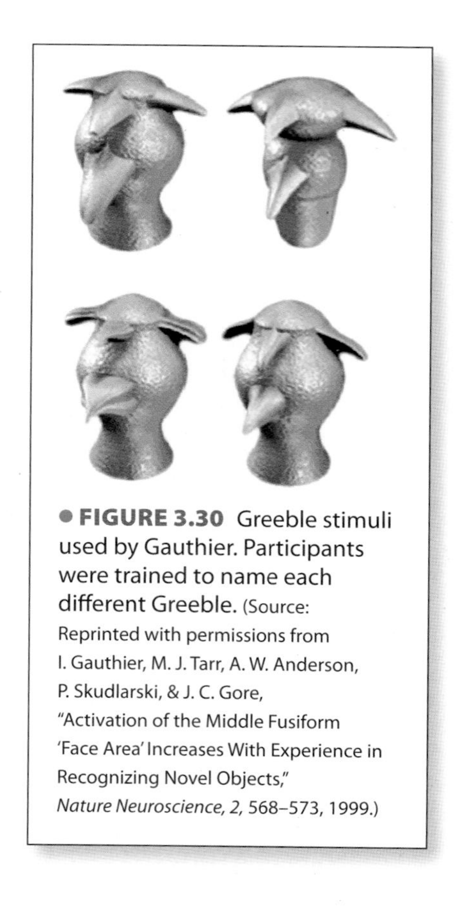

● FIGURE 3.30 Greeble stimuli used by Gauthier. Participants were trained to name each different Greeble. (Source: Reprinted with permissions from I. Gauthier, M. J. Tarr, A. W. Anderson, P. Skudlarski, & J. C. Gore, "Activation of the Middle Fusiform 'Face Area' Increases With Experience in Recognizing Novel Objects," *Nature Neuroscience*, *2*, 568–573, 1999.)

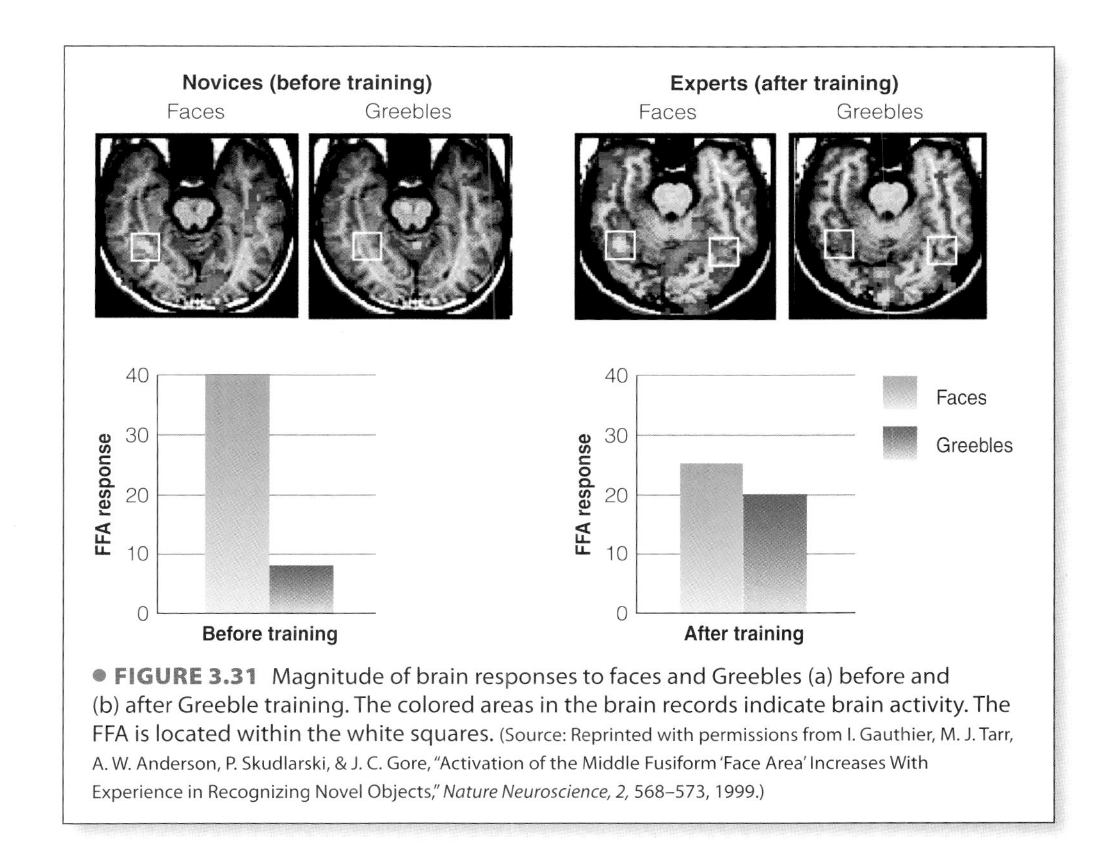

● **FIGURE 3.31** Magnitude of brain responses to faces and Greebles (a) before and (b) after Greeble training. The colored areas in the brain records indicate brain activity. The FFA is located within the white squares. (Source: Reprinted with permissions from I. Gauthier, M. J. Tarr, A. W. Anderson, P. Skudlarski, & J. C. Gore, "Activation of the Middle Fusiform 'Face Area' Increases With Experience in Recognizing Novel Objects," *Nature Neuroscience, 2,* 568–573, 1999.)

Gauthier then gave her participants extensive training over a 4-day period in "Greeble recognition." These training sessions, which required that each configuration of Greeble be labeled with a specific name, turned the participants into "Greeble experts." The bars and brain pictures in Figure 3.31b show that after the training, the FFA responded almost as well to Greebles as to faces. Apparently, the FFA contains neurons that respond not just to faces, but to other complex objects as well. The particular objects to which the neurons respond best are established by experience with the objects. In fact, Gauthier has also shown that neurons in the FFA of people who are experts in recognizing cars and birds respond well not only to human faces, but to cars (for the car experts) and to birds (for the bird experts) (Gauthier et al., 2000).

These demonstrations of experience-dependent plasticity in kittens and humans show that the brain's functioning can be "tuned" to operate best within a specific environment. Thus, continued exposure to things that occur regularly in the environment can cause neurons to become adapted to respond best to these regularities. Looked at in this way, it is not unreasonable to say that neurons can reflect knowledge about properties of the environment.

Reaching for a Cup: The Interaction Between Perceiving and Taking Action

Our discussion so far has considered the relationship between stimuli and what we perceive. This approach has yielded valuable information about how perception works, but it could be called the "sitting in a chair" way of studying perception—all of the situations we have described could occur as a person sits in a chair viewing various stimuli. In fact, that is probably what you are doing as you read this book—reading words, looking at pictures, doing "demonstrations," all while sitting still. We will now

● **FIGURE 3.32** Three views of a "horse." Moving around an object can reveal its true shape.

consider how movement helps us perceive, and how movement and perception interact with one another.

MOVEMENT FACILITATES PERCEPTION

Although movement adds a complexity to perception that isn't there when we are sitting in one place, movement also helps us perceive objects in the environment more accurately. One reason this occurs is that moving reveals aspects of objects that are not apparent from a single viewpoint. For example, consider the "horse" in ● Figure 3.32. From one viewpoint this object looks like a metal sculpture of a fairly normal horse (Figure 3.32a). However, it walking around the horse reveals that it isn't as normal as it first appeared (Figures 3.32b and c). Thus, seeing an object from different viewpoints provides added information that results in more accurate perception, especially for objects that are out of the ordinary, such as the distorted horse.

THE INTERACTION OF PERCEPTION AND ACTION

Our concern with movement extends beyond noting that it helps us perceive objects by revealing additional information about them. Movement is also important because of the coordination that is continually occurring between perceiving stimuli and taking action toward these stimuli. Consider, for example, what happens when Crystal reaches out and picks up her coffee cup (● Figure 3.33). She first identifies the coffee cup among

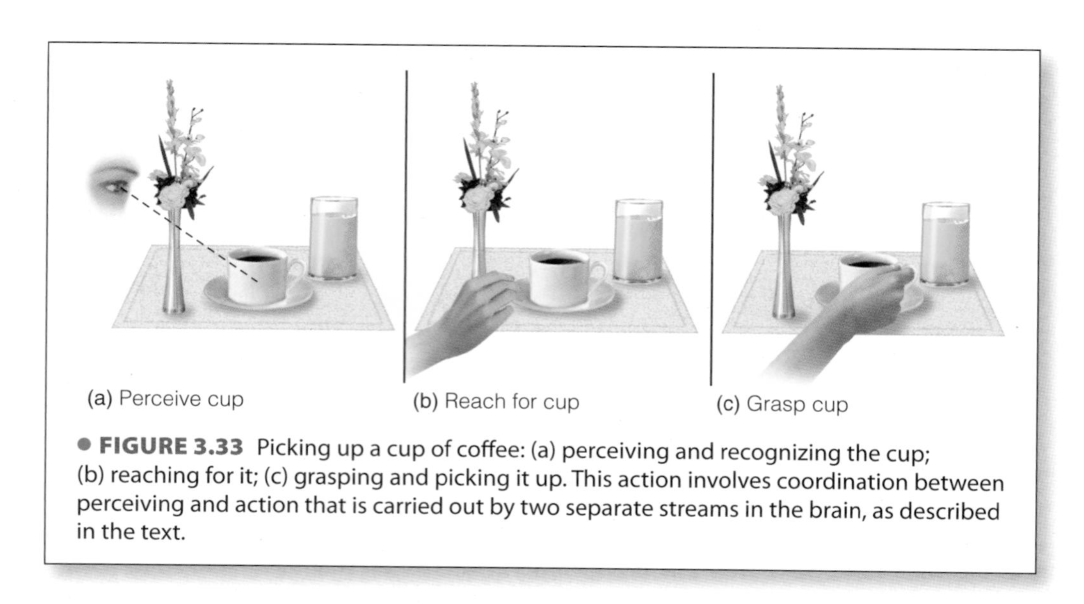

● **FIGURE 3.33** Picking up a cup of coffee: (a) perceiving and recognizing the cup; (b) reaching for it; (c) grasping and picking it up. This action involves coordination between perceiving and action that is carried out by two separate streams in the brain, as described in the text.

the flowers and other objects on the table (Figure 3.33a). Once the coffee cup is perceived, she reaches for it, taking into account its location on the table (Figure 3.33b). As she reaches, avoiding the flowers, she positions her fingers to grasp the cup, taking into account her perception of the cup's handle (Figure 3.33c); then she lifts the cup with just the right amount of force, taking into account her estimate of how heavy it is based on her perception of its fullness. This simple action requires continually perceiving the position of the cup, and her hand and fingers relative to the cup, while calibrating her actions in order to accurately grasp the cup and then pick it up without spilling any coffee (Goodale, 2010). All this just to pick up a cup of coffee!! What's amazing about this sequence is that it happens almost automatically, without much effort at all. But as with everything else about perception, this ease and apparent simplicity are achieved with the aid of complex underlying mechanisms. We will now describe the physiology behind these mechanisms.

THE PHYSIOLOGY OF PERCEPTION AND ACTION

Psychologists have long realized the close connection between perceiving objects and interacting with them, but the details of this link between perception and action have become clearer as a result of physiological research that began in the 1980s. This research has shown that there are two processing streams in the brain—one involved with perceiving objects, and the other involved with locating and taking action toward these objects. In describing this physiological research, we will introduce two methods: *brain ablation*—the study of the effect of removing parts of the brain in animals, and *neuropsychology*—the study of the behavior of people with brain damage. Both of these methods demonstrate how studying the functioning of animals and humans with brain damage can reveal important principles about the functioning of the normal (intact) brain. Later in the book we will see that both brain ablation and neuropsychology have also been applied to the study of other cognitive processes—notably, memory and language.

***What* and *Where* Streams** In a classic experiment, Leslie Ungerleider and Mortimer Mishkin (1982) studied how removing part of a monkey's brain affected its ability to identify an object and to determine the object's location. This experiment used a technique called brain ablation—removing part of the brain.

METHOD Brain Ablation

The goal of a brain ablation experiment is to determine the function of a particular area of the brain. This is accomplished by first determining an animal's capacity by testing it behaviorally. Most ablation experiments studying perception have used monkeys because of the similarity of its visual system to that of humans and because monkeys can be trained to determine perceptual capacities such as acuity, color vision, depth perception, and object perception.

Once the animal's perception has been measured, a particular area of the brain is ablated (removed or destroyed), either by surgery or by injecting a chemical in the area to be removed. Ideally, one particular area is removed and the rest of the brain remains intact. After ablation, the monkey is tested to determine which perceptual capacities remain and which have been affected by the ablation.[1]

[1]Because a great deal of physiological research has been done on cats and monkeys, students often express concerns about how these animals are treated. All animal research in the United States follows strict guidelines for the care of animals established by organizations such as the American Psychological Association and the Society for Neuroscience. The central tenet of these guidelines is that every effort should be made to ensure that animals are not subjected to pain or distress. Research on animals has provided essential information for developing aids to help people with sensory disabilities such as blindness and deafness, for helping develop techniques to ease severe pain, and for improving our understanding of deficits such as amnesia and blindness that are caused by damage to the brain.

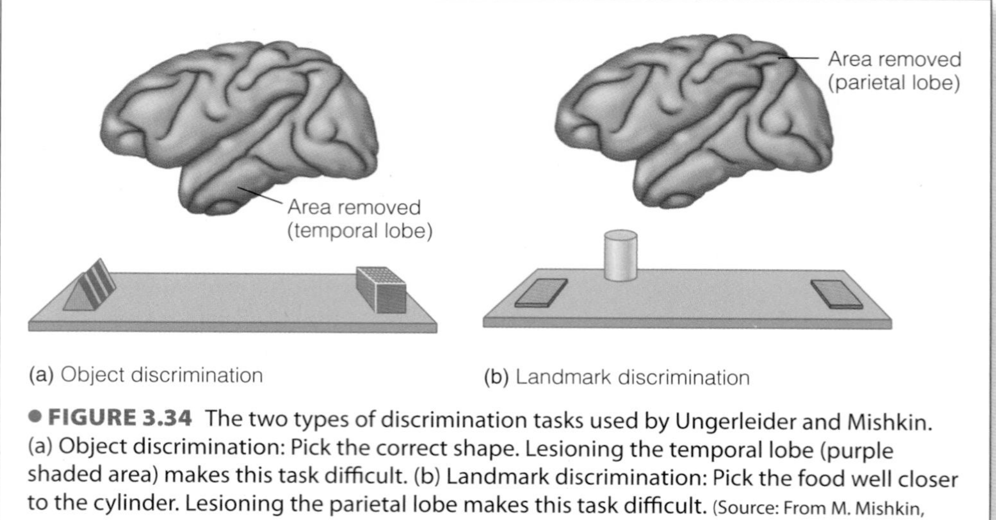

● **FIGURE 3.34** The two types of discrimination tasks used by Ungerleider and Mishkin. (a) Object discrimination: Pick the correct shape. Lesioning the temporal lobe (purple shaded area) makes this task difficult. (b) Landmark discrimination: Pick the food well closer to the cylinder. Lesioning the parietal lobe makes this task difficult. (Source: From M. Mishkin, L. G. Ungerleider, & K. A. Makco, "Object Vision and Spatial Vision: Two Central Pathways," Trends in *Neuroscience, 6,* 414-417, Figure 2. Copyright © 1983 Elsevier Science Publishers B.V. Reprinted by permission.)

Ungerleider and Mishkin presented monkeys with two tasks: (1) an object discrimination problem and (2) a landmark discrimination problem. In the **object discrimination problem**, a monkey was shown one object, such as a rectangular solid, and was then presented with a two-choice task like the one shown in ● Figure 3.34a, which included the "target" object (the rectangular solid) and another stimulus, such as the triangular solid. If the monkey pushed aside the target object, it received the food reward that was hidden in a well under the object. The **landmark discrimination problem** is shown in ● Figure 3.34b. Here, the monkey's task is to remove the food well cover that is closer to the tall cylinder.

In the ablation part of the experiment, part of the temporal lobe was removed in some monkeys. Behavioral testing showed that the object discrimination problem was very difficult for monkeys with their temporal lobes removed. This result indicates that the pathway that reaches the temporal lobes is responsible for determining an object's identity. Ungerleider and Mishkin therefore called the pathway leading from the striate cortex to the temporal lobe the ***what* pathway** (● Figure 3.35).

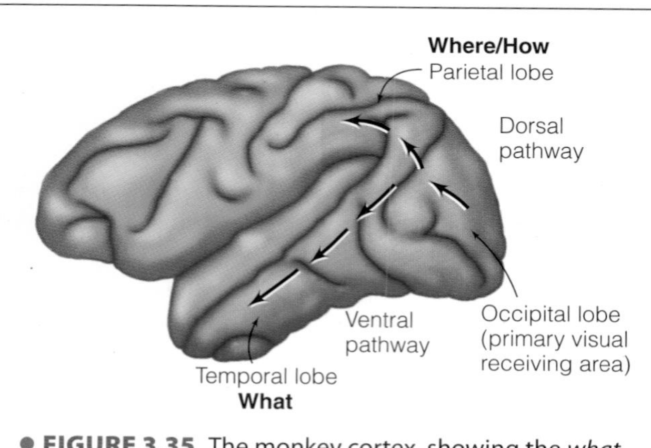

● **FIGURE 3.35** The monkey cortex, showing the *what* or *perception* pathway from the occipital lobe to the temporal lobe, and the *where* or *action* pathway from the occipital lobe to the parietal lobe. (Source: From E. B. Goldstein, *Sensation and Perception,* 8th ed., Fig. 4.27, p. 88. Copyright © 2010 Wadsworth, a part of Cengage Learning. Reproduced with permission. www.cengage.com/permissions. Adapted from Mishkin, Ungerleider, & Macko, 1983.)

Other monkeys, which had their parietal lobes removed, had difficulty solving the landmark discrimination problem. This result indicates that the pathway that leads to the parietal lobe is responsible for determining an object's location. Ungerleider and Mishkin therefore called the pathway leading from the striate cortex to the parietal lobe the ***where* pathway**.

Applying this idea of *what* and *where* pathways to our example of a person picking up a cup of coffee, the *what* pathway would be involved in the initial perception of the cup and the *where* pathway in determining its location—important information if we are going to carry out the action of reaching for the cup. In the next section we consider another physiological approach to studying perception and action, describing how the study of the behavior of a person with brain damage provides further insights into what is happening in the brain as a person reaches for an object.

Perception and Action Streams Another approach that has revealed two streams, one involving the temporal lobe and the

	Name object	Accurately reach for object
(a) **Alice**	No	Yes
(b) **Bert**	Yes	No

● **FIGURE 3.36** (a) Alice can't name objects but can accurately reach for them; (b) Bert can name objects, but has trouble accurately reaching for them. Alice and Bert together illustrate a double dissociation.

other involving the parietal lobe, is **neuropsychology**—studying the behavior of people with brain damage. One of the central procedures in neuropsychology is determining *dissociations*.

METHOD Dissociations in Neuropsychology

One of the basic principles of neuropsychology is that we can understand the effects of brain damage by studying **dissociations**—situations in which one function is absent while another function is present. There are two kinds of dissociations: **single dissociations**, which can be studied in one person, and **double dissociations**, which require two or more people.

To illustrate a single dissociation, let's consider a woman, Alice, who has suffered damage to her temporal lobe. She is shown an object, then asked to name the object and indicate where it is on the table by pointing to it. When given this task, Alice can't name the object, but she can reach to where it is located on the table (● Figure 3.36a). Alice demonstrates a single dissociation—one function is absent (naming objects) and another is present (locating objects). From a single dissociation such as this, in which one function is lost while another function remains, we can conclude that the two functions (in this example, naming and locating objects) involve different mechanisms, although they may not operate totally independently of one another.

We can illustrate a double dissociation by finding another person who has one function present and another absent, but in a way opposite to Alice. For example, Bert, who has parietal lobe damage, can identify objects but can't tell exactly where they are located (Figure 3.36b). The key to understanding the cases of Alice and Bert is that they are both given the same two tasks, but Alice can do one task (reaching) and not the other (naming) while the opposite result occurs for Bert. The cases of Alice and Bert, taken together, represent a double dissociation. Establishing a double dissociation enables us to conclude that two functions are served by different mechanisms *and* that these mechanisms operate independently of one another.

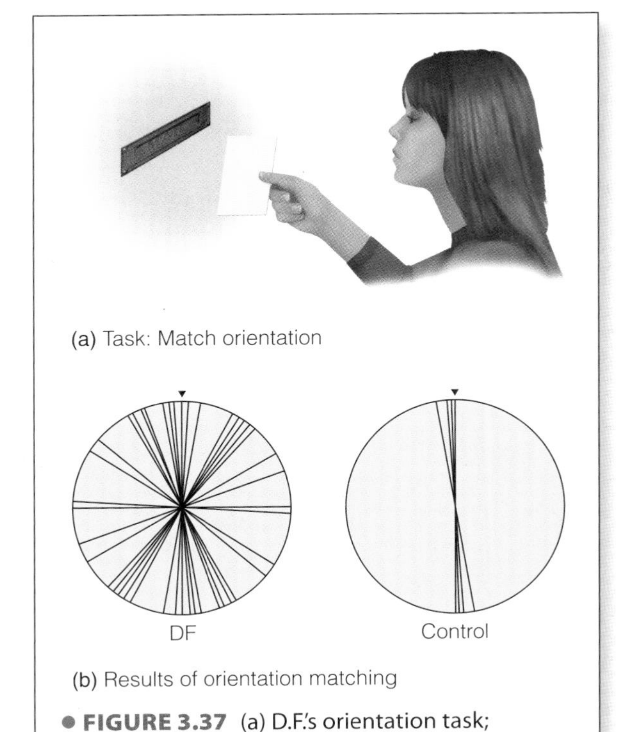

● **FIGURE 3.37** (a) D.F.'s orientation task; (b) results for the orientation task.

The method of determining dissociations was used by Milner and Goodale (1995) to study D.F., a 34-year-old woman who suffered damage to her temporal lobe from carbon monoxide poisoning caused by a gas leak in her home. One result of the brain damage was revealed when D.F. was asked to match the orientation of a card held in her hand to different orientations of a slot (● Figure 3.37a). She was unable to do this, as shown in the left circle in Figure 3.37b. Each line in the circle indicates how D.F. adjusted the card's orientation. Perfect matching performance would be indicated by a vertical line for each trial, but D.F.'s responses are widely scattered. The right circle shows the accurate performance of the normal controls.

Because D.F. had trouble orienting a card to match the orientation of the slot, it would seem reasonable that she would also have trouble *placing* the card through the slot because to do this she would have to turn the card so that it was lined up with the slot. But when D.F. was asked to "mail" the card through the slot (● Figure 3.38a), she could do it, as indicated by the results in Figure 3.38b. Even though D.F. could not turn the card to match the slot's orientation, *once she started moving the card toward the slot*, she began rotating it to match the orientation of the slot. Thus, D.F. performed poorly in the static orientation-matching task but did well as soon as *action* was involved (Murphy, Racicot, & Goodale, 1996). Milner and Goodale interpreted D.F.'s behavior as showing that there is one mechanism for judging orientation and another for coordinating vision and action.

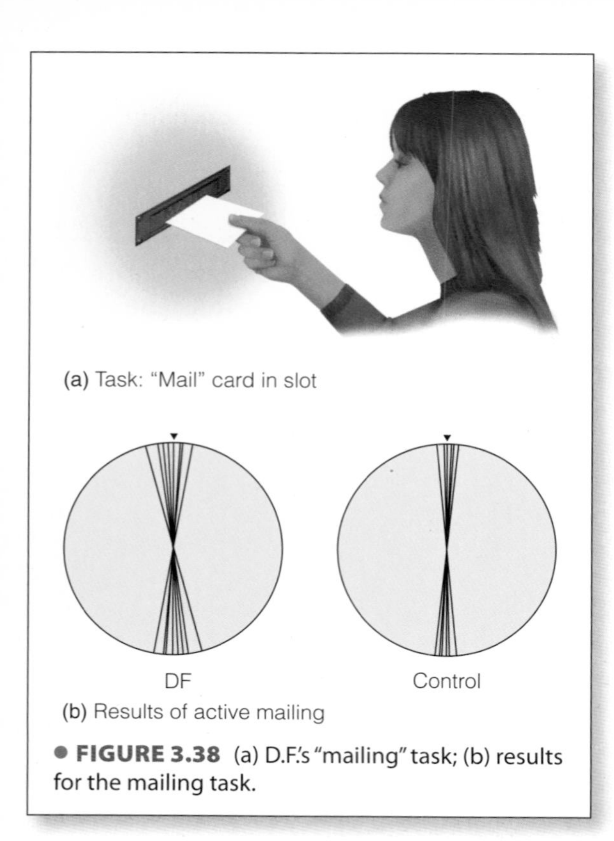

• **FIGURE 3.38** (a) D.F.'s "mailing" task; (b) results for the mailing task.

These results for D.F. demonstrate a single dissociation, which indicates that judging orientation and coordinating vision and action involve different mechanisms. To show that these two functions are not only served by different mechanisms but are also *independent* of one another, we have to demonstrate a double dissociation. As we saw in the example of Alice and Bert, this involves finding a person whose symptoms are the opposite of D.F.'s, and such people do, in fact, exist. These people can judge visual orientation, but they can't accomplish the task that combines vision and action. As we would expect, whereas D.F.'s temporal lobe is damaged, these other people have damage to their parietal lobe.

Based on these results, Milner and Goodale suggested that the pathway from the visual cortex to the temporal lobe (which was damaged in D.F.'s brain) be called the **perception pathway** and the pathway from the visual cortex to the parietal lobe (which was intact in D.F.'s brain) be called the **action pathway**. The perception pathway corresponds to the *what* pathway we described in conjunction with the monkey experiments, and the action pathway corresponds to the *where* pathway. Thus, some researchers refer to *what* and *where* pathways and some to perception and action pathways. But whatever the terminology, this research demonstrates that perception and action are processed in two separate pathways in the brain.

PICKING UP A COFFEE CUP AND OTHER BEHAVIORS

With our knowledge that perception and action involve two separate mechanisms, we can add physiological notations to our description of picking up the coffee cup, as follows:

> The first step in the process of picking up the cup is to identify the coffee cup among the vase of flowers and the glass of orange juice on the table (*perception pathway*). Once the coffee cup is perceived, we reach for the cup (*action pathway*), taking into account its location on the table. As we reach, avoiding the flowers and orange juice, we position our fingers to grasp the cup (*action pathway*), taking into account our perception of the cup's handle (*perception pathway*), and we lift the cup with just the right amount of force (*action pathway*), taking into account our estimate of how heavy it is based on our perception of the fullness of the cup (*perception pathway*).

Thus, even a simple action like picking up a coffee cup involves a number of areas of the brain, which coordinate their activity to create perceptions and behaviors. A similar coordination between different areas of the brain also occurs for the sense of hearing. Thus, hearing someone call your name and then turning to see who it is activates two separate pathways in the auditory system—one that enables you to hear and identify the sound (the auditory *what* pathway) and another that helps you locate where the sound is coming from (the auditory *where* pathway) (Lomber & Malhotra, 2008).

The discovery of different pathways for perceiving, determining location, and taking action illustrates how studying the physiology of perception has helped broaden our conception far beyond the old "sitting in the chair" approach. These physiological findings, combined with behavioral experiments that have focused on active aspects of perception (Gibson, 1979), mean that we can call perception "dynamic" not only because it involves processes such as inference and taking knowledge into account, but also because of how closely perception is linked to action. In the next section we show how this idea has been carried even further, by describing neurons that fire not only when a person takes action, but also when a person watches someone else take action.

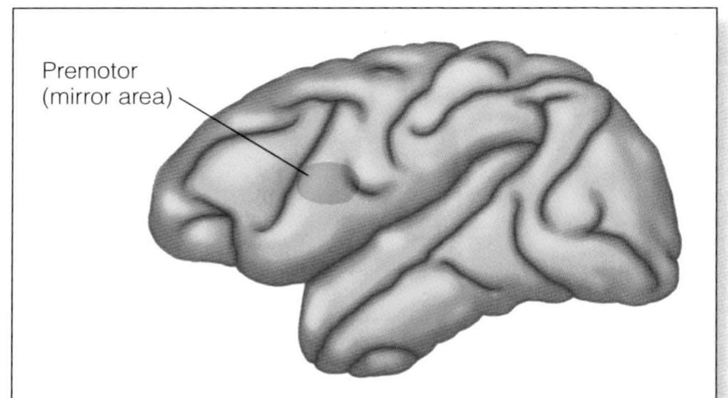

• **FIGURE 3.39** The green shaded area indicates the location of the premotor cortex, which is where mirror neurons are found. (Source: From E. B. Goldstein, *Sensation and Perception,* 8th ed., Fig. 7.8, p. 161. Copyright © 2010 Wadsworth, a part of Cengage Learning. Reproduced with permission. www.cengage.com/permissions.)

➔ Something to Consider

Mirror Neurons

We not only take action ourselves, but we regularly watch other people take action. This "watching others act" is most obvious when we watch other people's actions on TV or in a movie, but it also occurs any time we are around someone else who is doing something. One of the most exciting outcomes of research studying the link between perception and action has been the discovery of neurons in the premotor cortex (• Figure 3.39) called *mirror neurons.*

In the early 1990s, Giacomo Rizzolatti and coworkers (2006; also see di Pellegrino et al., 1992; Gallese et al., 1996) were investigating how neurons in the monkey's premotor cortex fired as the monkey performed actions such as picking up a toy or a piece of food. Their goal was to determine how neurons fired as the monkey carried out specific actions, but they observed something they didn't expect. They found neurons in the monkey's premotor cortex that fired not only when the monkey picked up a piece of food, but also when the monkey observed the experimenter picking up a piece of food.

This initial observation, followed by many additional experiments, led to the discovery of **mirror neurons**—neurons that respond both when a monkey observes someone else (usually the experimenter) grasping an object, such as food on a tray (• Figure 3.40a), and when the monkey itself grasps the food (Figure 3.40b) (Rizzolatti et al., 1996). These neurons are called *mirror neurons* because the neuron's response to watching the experimenter grasp an object is similar to the response that would occur if the monkey were performing the action. Just looking at the food causes no response, and watching the experimenter grasp the food with a pair of pliers instead of his hands, as in Figure 3.40c, causes only a small response (Gallese et al., 1996; Rizzolatti et al., 2000).

Most mirror neurons are specialized to respond to only one type of action, such as grasping or placing an object somewhere. Although you might think that perhaps the monkey was responding to the anticipation of receiving food, the type of object made little difference. The neurons responded just as well when the monkey observed the experimenter pick up an object that was not food.

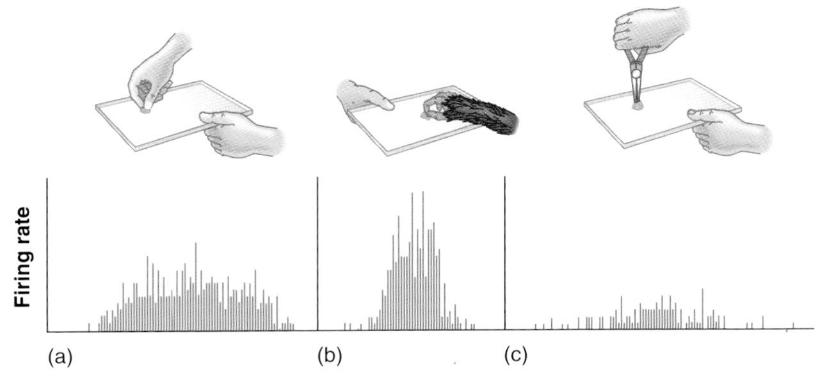

Consider what is happening when a mirror neuron fires in response to seeing someone else perform an action. This firing provides information about the characteristics of the action, because the neuron's response to watching someone else perform the action is the same as the response that occurs when the observer performs the action. This means that one function of the mirror neurons might be to help understand another person's actions and react appropriately to them (Rizzolatti & Arbib, 1998; Rizzolatti et al., 2000, 2006).

• **FIGURE 3.40** Response of a mirror neuron when (a) the monkey watches the experimenter grasp food on the tray; (b) the monkey grasps the food; (c) the monkey watches the experimenter pick up food with a pair of pliers. (Source: Reprinted from G. Rizzolatti et al., "Premotor Cortex and the Recognition of Motor Actions," *Cognitive Brain Research, 3,* 131–141, Copyright © 2000, with permission from Elsevier.)

What is the evidence that these neurons are actually involved in helping "understand" an action? The fact that a strong response occurs when the experimenter picks up the food with his hand but not when the experimenter uses pliers argues that the neuron is not just responding to the pattern of motion. Other evidence that mirror neurons are doing more than just responding to a particular pattern of stimulation is that neurons have been discovered that

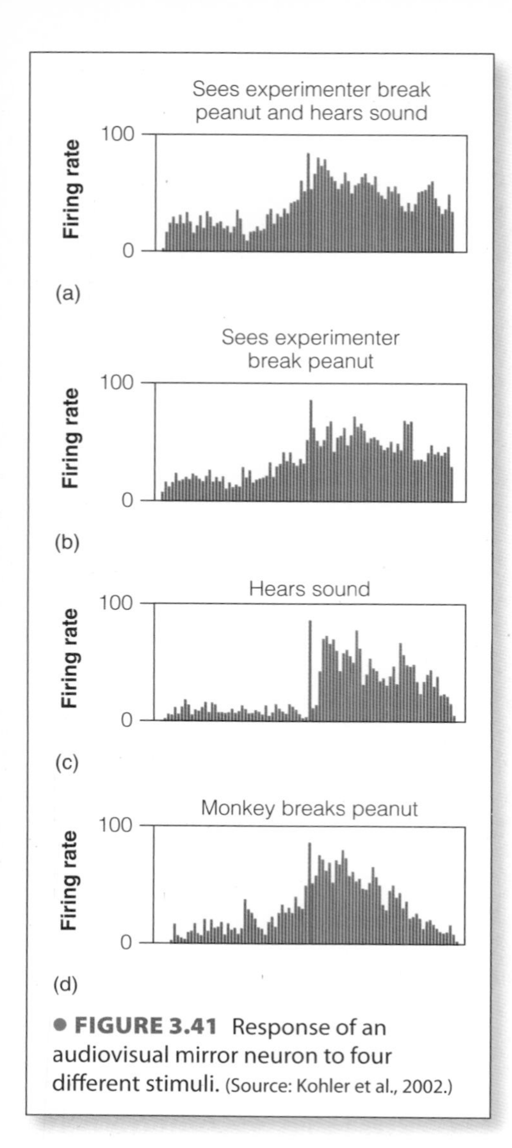

● **FIGURE 3.41** Response of an audiovisual mirror neuron to four different stimuli. (Source: Kohler et al., 2002.)

respond to sounds that are *associated with* actions. These neurons, also in the premotor cortex, called **audiovisual mirror neurons**, respond when a monkey performs a hand action *and* when it hears the sound associated with this action (Kohler et al., 2002). For example, the results in ● Figure 3.41 show the response of a neuron that fires (a) when the monkey sees and hears the experimenter break a peanut, (b) when the monkey just sees the experimenter break the peanut, (c) when the monkey just hears the sound of the breaking peanut, and (d) when the *monkey* breaks the peanut. What this means is that just *hearing* a peanut breaking or just *seeing* a peanut being broken causes activity that is also associated with the perceiver's *action* of breaking a peanut. These neurons are, therefore, responding to the characteristics of observed actions—in this case, what the action of breaking a peanut looks like and what it sounds like.

Since the first descriptions of mirror neurons in the 1990s, a great deal of research has confirmed the existence of these neurons in both monkeys and humans. Researchers have proposed other functions in addition to understanding another person's actions, including understanding language (Rizzolatti & Arbib, 1998), imitation (Iacoboni, 2009), deficits in autism (Dapretto et al., 2006), and determining another person's intentions (Iacoboni et al., 2005). Not all researchers agree with all of the functions that have been attributed to mirror neurons, but there is no question that mirror neurons provide an impressive example of the link between perception and action.

Although we have described many different principles and experiments in this chapter, we can summarize the chapter by noting that perception is the outcome of processes that are also involved in other cognitive functions. In common with memory, problem solving, and decision making, perception involves underlying "intelligent" processes such as inference, taking into account multiple factors, and making use of prior knowledge. Like memory, it is sometimes fallible, but often correct and highly adaptive. But sharing properties with other cognitive processes is only part of the story. The other part is that perception and all cognitive processes interact with each other. This interaction will be apparent in the next chapter, when we see that what we perceive is often determined by how we pay attention, and how we pay attention is influenced by perceptual qualities of the environment.

TEST YOURSELF 3.3

1. What is experience-dependent plasticity? Describe the kitten-in-the tube experiment and the Greeble experiment. What is behind the idea that neurons can reflect knowledge about properties of the environment?
2. Describe the link between perception and action in everyday perception, by giving a specific example and describing the interaction between perceiving and taking action.
3. Describe the Ungerleider and Mishkin experiment. How did they use the procedure of brain ablation to demonstrate *what* and *where* streams in the cortex?
4. Describe the dissociation procedure used in neuropsychology and how it was used to determine the presence of two processing streams in patient D.F. How do the results obtained from D.F. compare to the results of the Ungerleider and Mishkin monkey experiment?
5. Describe how the perception and action pathways both play a role in an action such as walking on a crowded sidewalk.
6. What is a mirror neuron? What are some potential functions of mirror neurons?

CHAPTER SUMMARY

1. The example of Crystal running on the beach and having coffee later illustrates how perception can change based on new information, that perception is a process, and how perception and action are connected.
2. Perception starts with bottom-up processing, which involves receptors. Signals from these receptors cause neurons in the cortex to respond to specific types of stimuli.
3. Recognition-by-components theory, which provides a behavioral example of bottom-up processing, proposes that recognizing objects is based on building blocks called geons.
4. Examples of situations in which perception can't be explained only in terms of the information on the receptors include (1) recognizing different arrangements of geons; (2) recognizing a "blob" shape in different contexts; (3) the effect of physiological feedback signals; (4) size constancy; and (5) perceiving odors following different intensities of sniffing.
5. An example of top-down processing is that knowledge of a language makes it possible to perceive individual words in a conversation even though the sound signal for speech is often continuous.
6. The idea that perception depends on knowledge was proposed by Helmholtz's theory of unconscious inference.
7. The Gestalt approach to perception proposed a number of laws of perceptual organization, which were based on how stimuli usually occur in the environment. These laws provide best-guess predictions of how we will perceive stimuli in the environment. The laws are therefore best described as "heuristics," because they are rules of thumb that are usually, but not always, correct.
8. Regularities in the environment are characteristics of the environment that occur frequently. We take both physical regularities and semantic regularities into account when perceiving.
9. One of the basic operating principles of the brain is that it contains some neurons that respond best to things that occur regularly in the environment.
10. Experience-dependent plasticity is one of the mechanisms responsible for creating neurons that are tuned to respond to specific things in the environment. The experiments in which kittens were reared in vertical or horizontal environments and in which people's brain activity was measured as they learned about Greebles support this idea.
11. Perceiving and taking action are linked. Movement of an observer relative to an object provides information about the object. Also, there is a constant coordination between perceiving an object (such as a cup) and taking action toward the object (such as picking up the cup).
12. Research involving brain ablation in monkeys and neuropsychological studies of the behavior of people with brain damage have revealed two processing pathways in the cortex: a pathway from the occipital lobe to the temporal lobe responsible for perceiving objects, and a pathway from the occipital lobe to the parietal lobe responsible for controlling actions toward objects. These pathways work together to coordinate perception and action.
13. Mirror neurons are neurons that respond both to carrying out an action and to observing someone else carry out the same action. Mirror neurons may help people understand other people's actions; other functions have also been proposed.

Think ABOUT IT

1. Describe a situation in which you initially thought you saw or heard something, but then realized that your initial perception was in error. (Two examples: misperceiving an object under low-visibility conditions; mishearing song lyrics.) What was the role of bottom-up and top-down processing in this process of first having an incorrect perception and then realizing what was actually there?
2. Look at the picture in • Figure 3.42. Is this a huge giant's hand getting ready to pick up a horse, a normal-size hand picking up a tiny plastic horse, or something else? Explain, based on some of the things we take into account in addition to the image that this scene creates on the retina, why it is unlikely that this picture shows either a giant hand or a tiny horse. How does your answer relate to top-down processing?
3. In the section on experience-dependent plasticity, it was stated that neurons can reflect knowledge about properties of the environment. Would it be valid to suggest that the response of these neurons represents top-down processing? Why or why not?
4. Try observing the world as though there were no such thing as top-down processing. For example, without the aid of top-down processing, seeing a restaurant's restroom sign that says "Employees must wash hands" could be taken to mean that we should wait for an employee to wash our hands! If you try this exercise, be warned that it is extremely difficult because top-down processing is so pervasive in our environment that we usually take it for granted.

• **FIGURE 3.42** Is a giant hand about to pick up the horse?

Kristin Durr

If You WANT TO KNOW MORE

1. **"Top-down" processing in the visual cortex.** Some research has shown that the responding of neurons in the visual receiving area of the cortex can be affected by factors such as attention, which suggests that top-down processing can influence responding in this area of the cortex.

Mehta, A. D., Ulbert, I., & Schroeder, C. E. (2000). Intermodal selective attention in monkeys: I. Distribution and timing of effects across visual areas. *Cerebral Cortex, 10*, 343–358.

2. **Gestalt psychology.** The ideas of the Gestalt psychologists dominated the field of perception in the mid-20th century and are still important today. Wolfgang Kohler was one of the founders of the Gestalt school.

Kohler, W. (1929). *Gestalt psychology.* New York: Liveright.

3. **Organization in hearing.** The process of perceptual organization is usually illustrated using visual examples, but it occurs in hearing as well.

Bregman, A. S. (1990). *Auditory scene analysis.* Cambridge, MA: MIT Press.

Deutsch, D. (1996). The perception of auditory patterns. In W. Prinz & B. Bridgeman (Eds.), *Handbook of perception and action* (Vol. 1, pp. 253–296). San Diego, CA: Academic Press.

4. **Perception as problem solving.** A number of modern researchers have proposed that perceptual mechanisms are similar to the mechanisms involved in cognitive processes like thinking and problem solving.

Ramachandran, V. S., & Anstis, S. M. (1986, May). The perception of apparent motion. *Scientific American*, pp. 102–109.

Rock, I. (1983). *The logic of perception.* Cambridge, MA: MIT Press.

5. **Interactive activation model of word recognition.** A model of word recognition, proposed in the 1980s, proposed that recognizing words is based on activation of feature-detector-like units that are arranged in layers. Units that respond to simple features, such as line orientation or combinations of lines, are in lower layers, and units that respond to words are in the upper layer.

Goldstein, E. B. (2008). *Cognitive psychology* (2nd ed., pp. 61–66). Belmont, CA: Wadsworth.

McClelland, J. L., & Rumelhart, D. E. (1981). An interactive activation model of context effects in letter perception: Part 1. An account of basic findings. *Psychological Review, 88*, 375–405.

Rumelhart, D. E., & McClelland, J. L. (1982). An interactive activation model of context effects in letter perception: Part 2. The contextual enhancement effect and some tests and extensions of the model. *Psychological Review, 89*, 60–94.

Key TERMS

Action pathway, 74
Algorithm, 62
Audiovisual mirror neuron, 76
Bottom-up processing, 50
Brain ablation, 71
Componential recovery, principle of, 51
Dissociation, 73
Double dissociation, 73
Experience-dependent plasticity, 68
Familiarity, law of, 60
Feedback signal, 53
Geon, 51
Gestalt psychologists, 58
Good continuation, law of, 58
Good figure, law of, 60
Heuristic, 62
Landmark discrimination problem, 72
Light-from-above heuristic, 64
Likelihood principle, 58
Mirror neuron, 75
Natural selection, theory of, 67
Neuropsychology, 73
Object discrimination problem, 72
Oblique effect, 63
Perception, 49
Perception pathway, 74
Perceptual organization, 58
Perceptual organization, laws of, 58
Physical regularities, 63
Pragnanz, law of, 60
Recognition-by-components (RBC) theory, 51
Regularities in the environment, 63
Semantic regularities, 65
Similarity, law of, 60
Simplicity, law of, 60
Single dissociation, 73
Size constancy, 54
Speech segmentation, 57
Top-down processing, 52
Unconscious inference, theory of, 57
What pathway, 72
Where pathway, 72

Media RESOURCES

The *Cognitive Psychology* Book Companion Website

www.cengage.com/international

Prepare for quizzes and exams with online resources—including a glossary, flashcards, tutorial quizzes, crossword puzzles, and more.

CogLab

To experience these experiments for yourself, go to coglab.wadsworth.com. Be sure to read each experiment's setup instructions before you go to the experiment itself. Otherwise, you won't know which keys to press.

Related Labs

Apparent motion How flashing two dots one after another can result in an illusion of motion.

Blind spot Map the blind spot in your visual field that is caused by the fact that there are no receptors where the optic nerve leaves the eye.

Metacontrast masking How presentation of one stimulus can impair perception of another stimulus.

Muller-Lyer illusion Measure the size of a visual illusion.

Signal detection Collect data that demonstrate the principle behind the theory of signal detection, which explains the processes behind detecting hard-to-detect stimuli.

Visual search Visual searching for targets that are accompanied by different numbers of distractors.

Garner interference An experiment about making perceptual judgments based on different dimensions of a stimulus.

4 Attention

Our environment contains countless stimuli that are competing for our attention. We pay attention to some of these stimuli and ignore others. In this airplane cockpit there are multiple stimuli competing for attention, including the instruments, the controls, the visual scene out the window, and messages from the control tower. It is crucial that pilots pay attention to each of these sources of information.

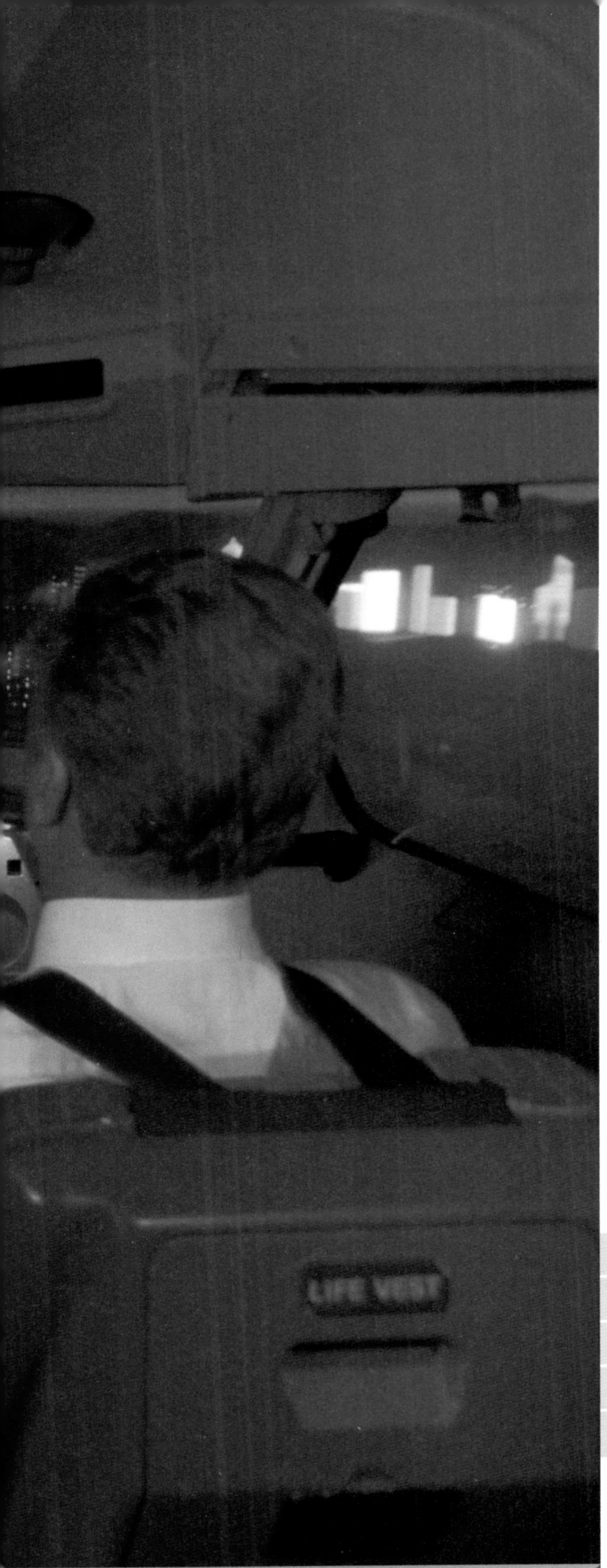

Frederic Pitchal/Sygma/Corbis

Some Questions We Will Consider

- Is it possible to focus attention on just one thing, even when there are lots of other things going on at the same time? (83)
- Under what conditions can we pay attention to more than one thing at a time? (91)
- What does attention research tell us about the effect of talking on cell phones while driving a car? (94)
- Is it true that we are not paying attention to a large fraction of the things that are happening in our environment? (96)

To begin this chapter, let's revisit Crystal who we sent off on a run down the beach in Chapter 3. The reason for following Crystal's run was to introduce some perceptual phenomena. Perceiving something initially as a piece of driftwood and then realizing it was an umbrella illustrated the creative, problem-solving nature of perception. Perceiving the rope as continuous illustrated perceptual organization. Picking up the coffee cup later illustrated the connection between perception and action.

But Crystal could not have achieved her feats of perception without another cognitive mechanism, **attention**—the ability to focus on specific stimuli or locations. This idea of focusing is most often associated with **selective attention**—the focusing of attention on one specific location, object, or message. This is what Crystal was doing when she was looking at the umbrella, and it is what we are constantly doing as we make our way through the environment, because we can only deal with a small fraction of the objects and events that surround us. Think, for example, of all of the stimuli that are present as you walk down a city street or across campus. There are people, buildings, perhaps birds, signs, cars, various sounds, and maybe even a few hundred ants whose universe is inside a crack in the sidewalk beneath your feet. Because it would be overwhelming to try to take in all of these stimuli, you focus on what is important at a particular time and shift where you are looking from one place, object, or sound source to another.

In the case of visual attention, the process of shifting attention from one place to another by moving the eyes is called *overt attention* because the movements of the eyes provide observable signals of how attention is changing over time. There are other types of attention as well. There is *covert attention*, which occurs when attention is shifted without moving the eyes, commonly referred to as seeing something "out of the corner of the eye" (as you might do while trying to check someone out without looking directly at him or her); and **divided attention**, attending to two or more things at once, as Crystal might be doing as she looks at the umbrella while also being careful not to step on any of the rocks that dot the beach. Divided attention can be overt, covert, or a combination of the two. Looking back and forth between two objects or events (both overt) would be divided attention; paying attention to something you are looking at (overt) while at the same time paying attention to something off to the side (covert) would also be divided attention (● Figure 4.1).

As we discuss these aspects of attention in this chapter, it will become clear that attention is not just one process. We will show this both with behavioral examples and by considering the physiology of attention, which involves many different processes distributed throughout the brain.

We begin the story of attention by focusing on selective attention. We start with selective attention because this aspect of attention was the primary concern of early researchers, who, at the beginning of the cognitive revolution that we described in Chapter 1 (see page 12), did experiments on selective attention to demonstrate how the information-processing approach can be used to study the operation of the mind.

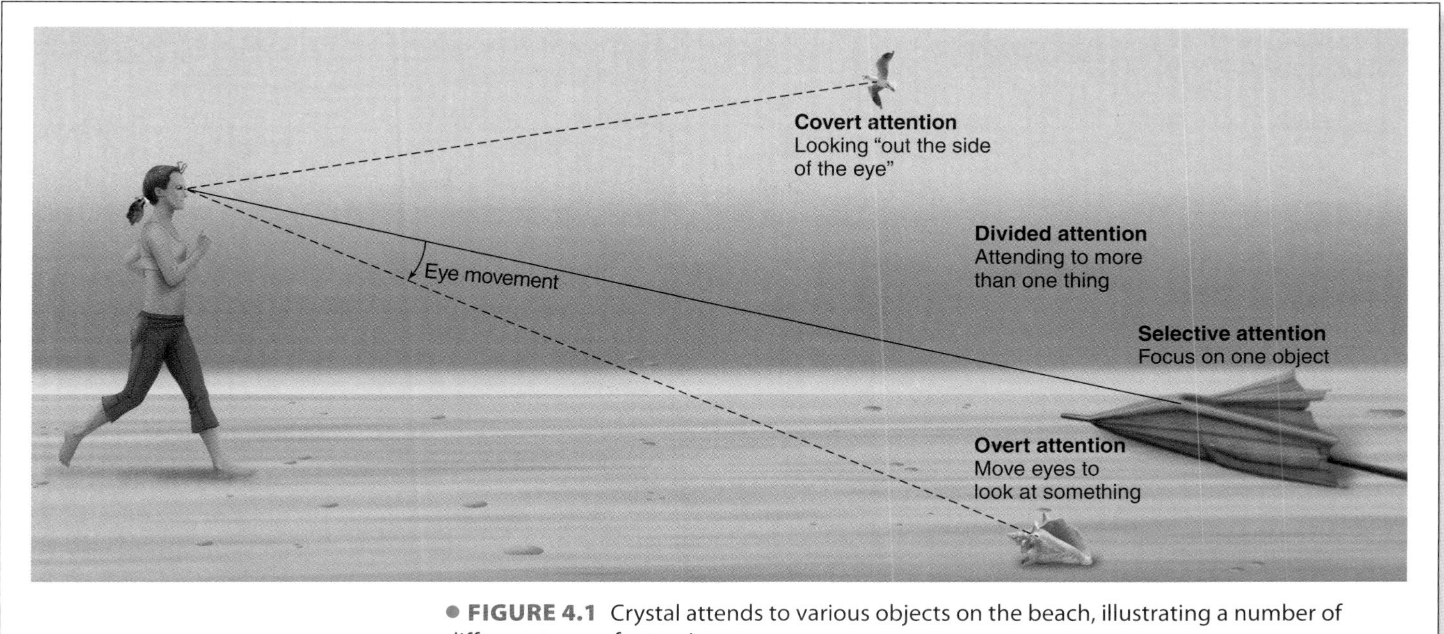

● **FIGURE 4.1** Crystal attends to various objects on the beach, illustrating a number of different types of attention.

Selective Attention

Psychologists' early interest in selective attention is vividly illustrated by the following statement in William James' (1890) textbook, *Principles of Psychology*:

> Millions of items...are present to my senses which never properly enter my experience. Why? Because they have no interest for me. My experience is what I agree to attend to.... Everyone knows what attention is. It is the taking possession by the mind, in clear and vivid form, of one out of what seem several simultaneously possible objects or trains of thought.... It implies withdrawal from some things in order to deal effectively with others.

Thus, according to James, we focus on some things to the exclusion of others. As you walk down the street, the things that you pay attention to—a classmate you recognize, the "Don't Walk" sign at a busy intersection, and the fact that just about everyone except you seems to be carrying an umbrella—stand out more than many other things in the environment.

According to this idea, selective attention not only highlights whatever is being attended, but also keeps us from perceiving whatever isn't being attended. Early researchers found that this idea is generally correct, but that it needed to be revised to account for the fact that some nonattended information is sometimes perceived. The goal in these early experiments was to describe how humans process incoming information.

SELECTIVE ATTENTION AS FILTERING

Many of the early experiments involved the idea of a "filter" that acted on incoming information, keeping some information out and letting some information in for further processing. These early experiments used mainly auditory stimuli. Later research also included visual stimuli like the examples from Crystal's run. The following demonstration illustrates how auditory stimuli were used in one of the early selective attention experiments.

DEMONSTRATION Focusing on One Message

Enlist the help of two people. Select two books on different topics that you have not read before and have both people read passages aloud simultaneously. Your task is to focus on just one of the passages. As you do this, notice (1) how well you are able to take in information in the "attended" passage and (2) whether you are taking in anything from the "unattended" passage. Try this with two male readers and with one male and one female reader, and note whether this influences your ability to focus on just one of the messages.

Your task in this demonstration—focusing on one message—is similar to the task in classic experiments done by Colin Cherry (1953), who used a procedure called *dichotic listening*.

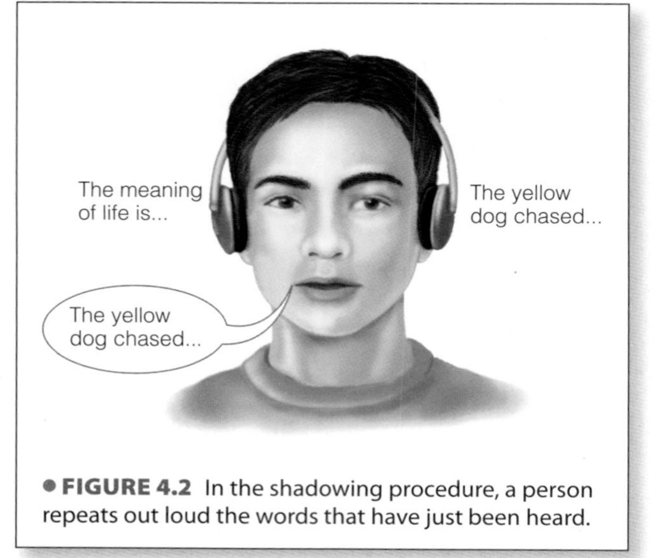

● **FIGURE 4.2** In the shadowing procedure, a person repeats out loud the words that have just been heard.

METHOD Dichotic Listening

In a **dichotic listening** experiment, different messages are presented to the two ears. In a selective attention experiment, participants are instructed to pay attention to the message presented to one ear (the attended message), repeating it out loud as they are hearing it, and to ignore the message presented to the other ear (the unattended message). Participants are usually able to accomplish this task easily, repeating the message with a delay of a few seconds between hearing a word and saying it. This procedure of repeating a message out loud is called **shadowing** (● Figure 4.2). The shadowing procedure is used to ensure that participants are focusing their attention on the attended message.

As Cherry's participants shadowed the attended message, the other message was stimulating auditory receptors within the unattended ear. However, when asked what they had heard in the unattended ear, participants could say only that they could tell there was a message and could identify it as a male or female voice. They could not report the content of the message. Other dichotic listening experiments have confirmed this lack of awareness of most of the information being presented to the unattended ear. For example, Neville Moray (1959) showed that participants were unaware of a word that had been repeated 35 times in the unattended ear.

Cherry showed that a listener can attend to just one message, and Donald Broadbent (1958) created a model of attention to explain how this selective attention is achieved. This **early selection model**, which introduced the flow diagram to cognitive psychology (see page 13), proposed that information passes through the following stages (● Figure 4.3):

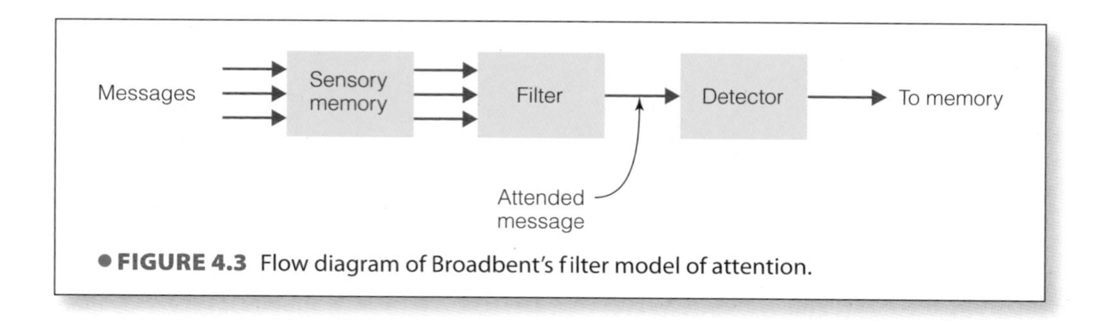

● **FIGURE 4.3** Flow diagram of Broadbent's filter model of attention.

1. *Sensory memory* holds all of the incoming information for a fraction of a second and then transfers all of it to the next stage. We will discuss sensory memory in more detail in Chapter 5.
2. The *filter* identifies the attended message based on its physical characteristics—things like the speaker's tone of voice, pitch, speed of talking, and accent—and lets only this message pass through to the detector in the next stage. All other messages are filtered out.
3. The *detector* processes information to determine higher-level characteristics of the message, such as its meaning. Because only the important, attended information has been let through the filter, the detector processes all of the information that enters it.
4. *Short-term memory* receives the output of the detector. Short-term memory holds information for 10–15 seconds and also transfers information into long-term memory, which can hold information indefinitely. We will describe short- and long-term memory in Chapters 5–8.

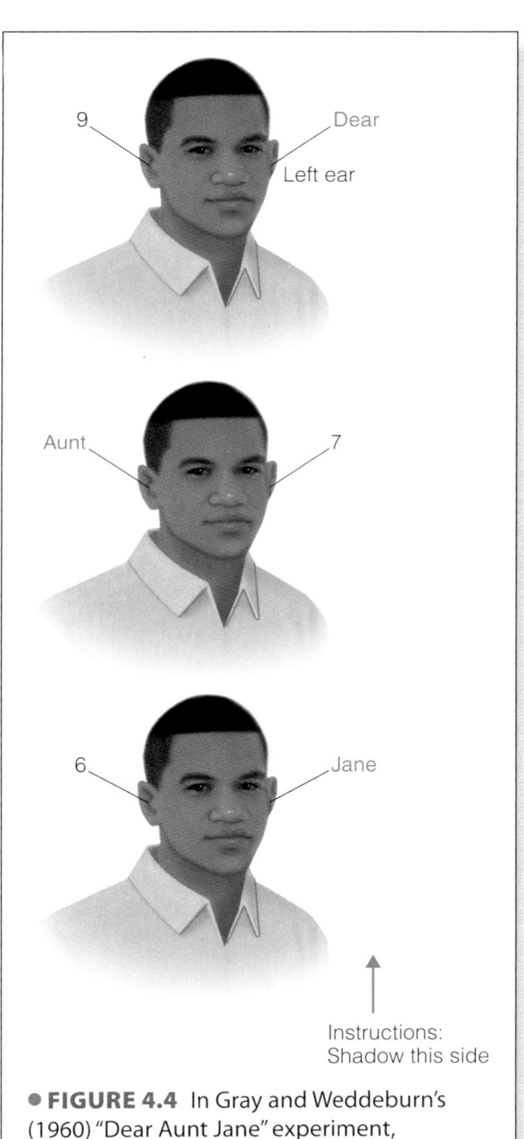

● **FIGURE 4.4** In Gray and Weddeburn's (1960) "Dear Aunt Jane" experiment, participants were told to shadow the message presented to the left ear. But they reported hearing the message "Dear Aunt Jane," which starts in the left ear, jumps to the right ear, and then goes back to the left.

Broadbent's model has been called a **bottleneck model** because the filter restricts information flow, much as the neck of a bottle restricts the flow of liquid. When one pours liquid from a bottle, the narrow neck restricts the flow, so the liquid escapes only slowly even though there is a large amount in the bottle. Applying this analogy to information, Broadbent proposed that the filter restricts the large amount of information available to a person so that only some of this information gets through to the detector. But unlike the neck of a bottle, which lets through the liquid closest to the neck, Broadbent's filter lets information through based on specific physical characteristics of the information, such as the rate of speaking or the pitch of the speaker's voice.

Broadbent's model provided testable predictions about selective attention, some of which turned out not to be correct. For example, according to Broadbent's model, information in the unattended message should not be accessible to consciousness. However, Neville Moray (1959) did an experiment in which his participants shadowed the message presented to one ear and ignored the message presented to the other ear. But when Moray presented the listener's name to the other, unattended ear, about a third of the participants detected it (also see Wood & Cowan, 1995). This phenomenon, in which a person is selectively listening to one message among many yet hears his or her name or some other distinctive message such as "Fire!" that is not being attended, is called the **cocktail party effect**.

Moray's participants had recognized their names even though, according to Broadbent's theory, the filter is supposed to let through only one message, based on its physical characteristics. Clearly, the person's name had not been filtered out and, most important, it had been analyzed enough to determine its meaning. You may have had an experience similar to Moray's laboratory demonstration if, as you were talking to someone in a noisy room, you suddenly heard someone else saying your name.

Following Moray's lead, other experimenters showed that information presented to the unattended ear is processed enough to provide the listener with some awareness of its meaning. For example, J. A. Gray and A. I. Wedderburn (1960), while undergraduates at the University of Oxford, did the following experiment, sometimes called the "Dear Aunt Jane" experiment. As in Cherry's dichotic listening experiment, the participants were told to shadow the message presented to one ear. As you can see in ● Figure 4.4, the attended (shadowed) ear received the message "Dear 7 Jane," and the unattended ear received the message "9 Aunt 6." However, rather than reporting the "Dear 7 Jane" message that was presented to the attended ear, participants reported hearing "Dear Aunt Jane."

Switching to the unattended channel to say "Aunt" means that the participant's attention had jumped from one ear to the other and then back again.

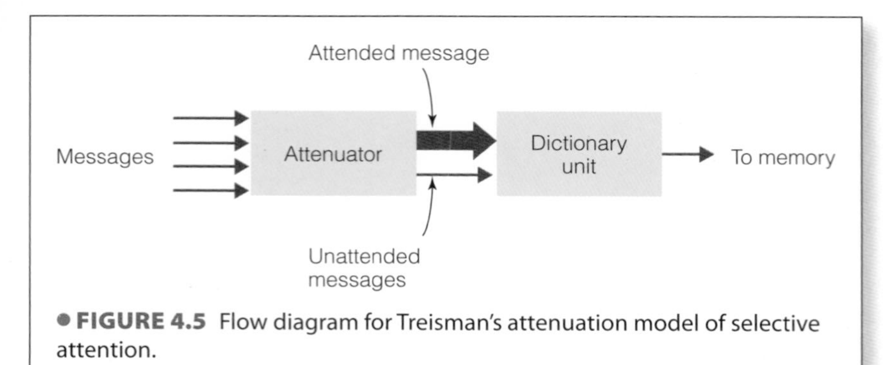

• **FIGURE 4.5** Flow diagram for Treisman's attenuation model of selective attention.

This occurred because they were taking the *meaning* of the words into account. (An example of top-down processing! See page 52.) Because of results such as these, Anne Treisman (1964) proposed a modification of Broadbent's theory.

Treisman proposed that selection occurs in two stages, and she replaced Broadbent's filter with an *attenuator* (• Figure 4.5). The **attenuator** analyzes the incoming message in terms of (1) its physical characteristics—whether it is high-pitched or low-pitched, fast or slow; (2) its language—how the message groups into syllables or words; and (3) its meaning—how sequences of words create meaningful phrases. Note that this is similar to what Broadbent proposed, but in Treisman's **attenuation theory of attention**, language and meaning can also be used to separate the messages. Treisman proposed, however, that the analysis of the message proceeds only as far as is necessary to identify the attended message. For example, if there are two messages, one in a male voice and one in a female voice, then analysis at the physical level is adequate to separate the low-pitched male voice from the higher-pitched female voice. If, however, the voices are similar, then it might be necessary to use meaning to separate the two messages.

Once the attended and unattended messages have been identified, both messages are let through the attenuator, but the attended message emerges at full strength and the unattended messages are attenuated—they are still present, but are weaker than the attended message. Because at least some of the unattended message gets through the attenuator, Treisman's model has been called a "leaky filter" model.

The final output of the system is determined in the second stage, when the message is analyzed by the **dictionary unit**. The dictionary unit contains stored words, each of which has a threshold for being activated (• Figure 4.6). A threshold is the smallest signal strength that can barely be detected. Thus, a word with a low threshold might be detected even when it is presented softly or is obscured by other words.

According to Treisman, words that are common or especially important, such as the listener's name, have low thresholds, so even a weak signal in the unattended channel can activate that word, and we hear our name from across the room. Uncommon words or words that are unimportant to the listener have higher thresholds, so it takes the strong signal of the attended message to activate these words. Thus, according to Treisman, the attended message gets through, *plus* some parts of the weaker unattended message.

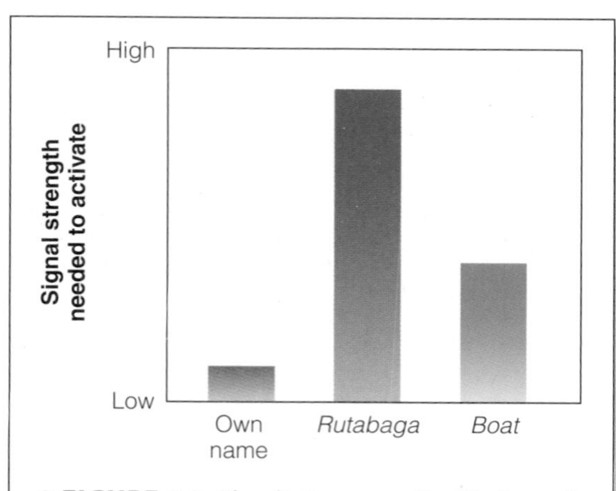

• **FIGURE 4.6** The dictionary unit of Treisman's model contains words, each of which has a threshold for being detected. This graph shows the thresholds that might exist for three words. The person's name has a low threshold, so it will be easily detected. The thresholds for the words *rutabaga* and *boat* are higher, because they are used less or are less important to this particular listener.

The research we have been describing so far was extremely important, not only because it defined some of the important phenomena of attention, but also because it demonstrated how an aspect of cognition could be conceptualized as a problem of information processing, in which the flow of information from the environment is followed through various stages of processing. Theories like Broadbent's and Treisman's are sometimes called *early selection theories* of selective attention because they propose a filter that operates at an early stage in the flow of information, in many cases eliminating information based only on physical characteristics of the stimulus.

Other theories were also proposed to take into account the results of experiments that showed that messages can be selected at a later stage of processing, based primarily on their meaning. For example, participants in an experiment by Donald MacKay (1973) listened to ambiguous sentences, such as "They were throwing stones at the bank," that could be taken more than one way. (In this example, "bank" can refer to a riverbank or to a financial institution.) These ambiguous sentences were presented to the attended ear, while biasing words were presented to the other, unattended ear. For example, as the participants were shadowing "They were throwing stones at the bank," either the word "river" or the word "money" was being presented to the unattended ear.

After hearing a number of the ambiguous sentences, participants were presented with pairs of sentences such as the following:

- They threw stones toward the side of the river yesterday.
- They threw stones at the savings and loan association yesterday.

When they indicated which of these two sentences was closest in meaning to one of the sentences they had heard previously, MacKay found that the meaning of the biasing word affected the participants' choice. For example, if the biasing word was "money," participants were more likely to pick the second sentence. This occurred even though participants reported that they were unaware of the biasing words that had been presented to the unattended ear.

Because the meaning of the unattended word ("money") was affecting the participant's judgment, this word must have been processed to the level of meaning. Results such as this led McKay and other theorists to propose **late selection models** of attention, which proposed that most of the incoming information is processed to the level of meaning before the message to be processed is selected (Deutsch & Deutsch, 1963; Norman, 1968).

The selective attention research we have been describing centered around when selective attention occurs (early or late) and what types of information are used for the selection (physical characteristics or meaning). But as research in selective attention has progressed, researchers have realized that there is no one answer to what had been called the "early-late" controversy. Early selection can be demonstrated under some conditions and later selection under others, depending on the observer's task and the type of stimuli presented. Thus, researchers began focusing instead on simply understanding the many different factors that control attention. Two of these factors are *cognitive resources* and *cognitive load.*

COGNITIVE RESOURCES, COGNITIVE LOAD, AND TASK-IRRELEVANT STIMULI

Cognitive resources refers to the idea that a person has a certain cognitive capacity, which can be used for carrying out various tasks. **Cognitive load** is the amount of a person's cognitive resources needed to carry out a particular cognitive task. Some tasks, especially easy, well-practiced ones, have low cognitive loads; these **low-load tasks** use up only a small amount of the person's cognitive resources. Other tasks, those that are difficult and perhaps not as well practiced, are **high-load tasks** and use more of a person's cognitive resources.

One thing that has been studied about cognitive resources and cognitive load is the relation between (1) the amount of a person's cognitive resources that are used by a primary task or stimulus and (2) how this affects the person's ability to avoid attending to other, task-irrelevant, stimuli. Nilli Lavie (1995, 2005) has proposed that the amount of cognitive resources that remain as a person is carrying out a primary task determines how well the person can avoid attending to task-irrelevant stimuli.

This idea is illustrated in ● Figure 4.7. The circle in this figure represents a person's total cognitive resources, and the shading represents the portion that is used up by a primary task. In Figure 4.7a, only part of the person's resources are being used by a low-load primary task, leaving resources

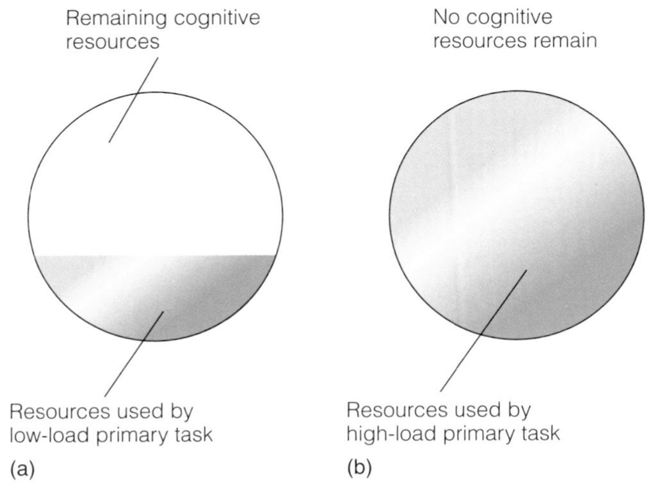

Remaining cognitive resources
Resources used by low-load primary task
(a)
No cognitive resources remain
Resources used by high-load primary task
(b)

● **FIGURE 4.7** The rationale for the idea that (a) low-load tasks that use few cognitive resources may leave resources available for processing task-irrelevant stimuli, whereas (b) high-load tasks that use all of a person's cognitive resources don't leave any resources to process task-irrelevant stimuli.

available for processing other stimuli that may be present. This can occur even if the person does not intend to process these other stimuli. For example, a person is sitting in her dorm room listening to music, which uses only a portion of her cognitive resources, so the voices of people talking in the hall intrude even though the person would rather not hear them. Stimuli such as talking in the hall are task-irrelevant stimuli that have made use of some of the person's remaining cognitive resources.

Figure 4.7b shows a situation in which all of a person's cognitive resources are being used by a high-load primary task. When this occurs, no resources remain to process other stimuli, so these stimuli can't be processed. This means that the person's attention is totally focused on the primary task. Such a situation might occur when a person is sitting in his dorm room concentrating intensely on a particularly difficult homework problem. The person is concentrating so hard that he is devoting all of his cognitive resources to the task, so he is only vaguely aware of the people talking in the hall.

We will now describe a laboratory test of these ideas, which involves a task called the *flanker compatibility task*.

METHOD Flanker Compatibility Task

The **flanker compatibility task** is a task in which participants are told to carry out a task that requires them to focus their attention on specific stimuli and to ignore other stimuli (Eriksen & Eriksen, 1974). An example is shown in ● Figure 4.8, in which the task is to selectively attend to the target in the center position (A in this example) and to press the "z" key if A or B is presented in the center and the "m" key if C or D is presented. They are told to ignore the "flanker" stimuli that are presented on either side because these are task-irrelevant stimuli that aren't needed for the primary task. One target stimulus is presented in the central position on each trial, and this target is flanked on either side by A, B, C, D, or X.

In Figure 4.8a, the flankers are associated with the same response as the target (pushing the z key is the response for both). These flankers (B's) are therefore called **compatible flankers**. In Figure 4.8b, the flankers (C's) are associated with a different response (pushing the m key) than the target; these are called **incompatible flankers**. In Figure 4.8c, the flankers (X) are neutral; they aren't associated with any response.

Because pushing a key in response to an easily visible target is easy, this task wouldn't use all of a person's cognitive resources, so some cognitive resources would remain available, as in Figure 4.7a. If this is so, we would expect that the flanker stimuli will be processed even if the participant doesn't intend to process them.

Typical results for a flanker compatibility experiment, shown in the right column, indicate that this is the case. When participants try to respond to the target as quickly as possible, they typically respond more slowly when incompatible flankers are present (as in b) than when neutral flankers (c) or compatible flankers (a) are present. This occurs because the incompatible flanker elicits a response that is different from the one that is required for the target and therefore competes with the response that the participant is supposed to make to the target. The fact that the flanker has this effect demonstrates that even though participants were told to ignore the flankers, they still processed information from them.

STIMULUS	FLANKERS	TYPICAL RESULT
(a) **B A B**	Compatible	Fastest response to target
(b) **C A C**	Incompatible	Slowest response to target
(c) **X A X** (↑ Target)	Neutral	Intermediate response to target

● **FIGURE 4.8** Stimuli for flanker compatibility tasks. A is the target in these examples. (a) A task with compatible flankers (like B) results in a fast response to A. (b) Incompatible flankers (like C) result in the slowest response time to A. (c) Neutral flankers (like X) result in an intermediate response speed.

We will now consider an experiment similar to the one above, but in which the load of the task is varied (Lavie, 2005; Lavie & Cox, 1997). In this experiment, a target stimulus appears somewhere in a ring of six

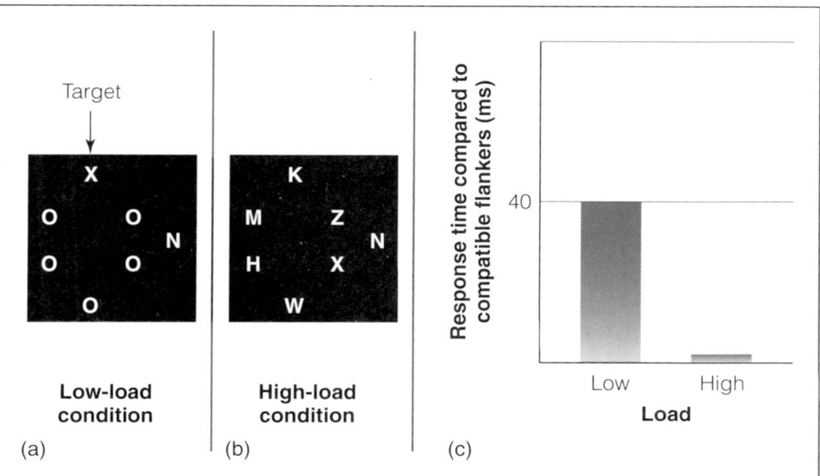

● **FIGURE 4.9** Stimuli for a flanker compatibility task in which the load is increased by adding additional stimuli to the display. In this example, X is the target and N is the flanker. The response to the flanker, N, is incompatible with the response to the target, X, in both (a) the easy task (low-load) condition and (b) the hard task (high-load) condition. (c) Results of this experiment indicate that the incompatible flanker N slowed responding in the low-load condition compared to responding when the flanker was compatible, but did not slow responding in the high-load condition (Lavie, 2005).

stimuli. The flanker stimulus is presented off to the side. In the examples shown in ● Figure 4.9, the X is the target and the N is the flanker. Participants are told to respond to the target stimulus. When the X is the target (as in this example), participants are told to press one key; when the N is the target, they are to press a different key. Because the X and N are associated with different responses, the N is an incompatible flanker when the X is the target.

In Figure 4.9a, the task of responding to the X is easy (low-load condition) because it is easy to see the X among the O's. In Figure 4.9b, the task of responding to the X is more difficult (high-load condition) because it is harder to find among the other letters. The results of experiments for these two conditions, shown in Figure 4.9c, indicate that the incompatible flanker causes a slower response in the low-load condition (like the result for the letter display in Figure 4.8b) but has no effect in the high-load condition.

These results correspond to the two conditions in Figures 4.7a and b. The low-load condition corresponds to Figure 4.7a. Because cognitive resources are available, the incompatible flankers intrude and cause slower responding. The high-load condition corresponds to Figure 4.7b. Because no cognitive resources are available, the incompatible flankers have no effect. This means that when you are involved in a low-load task, such as driving on a familiar road, you are able to process additional information; in fact, you might do so even if you don't intend to. In contrast, if you are involved in a high-load task, such as driving in a construction zone, potentially distracting stimuli are more easily ignored.

The ability to ignore task-irrelevant stimuli is a function not only of the load of the task you are trying to do, but also of how powerful the task-irrelevant stimulus is. For example, while focusing on solving a math problem you may be able to ignore a conversation in the hallway, but a loud siren, indicating fire, would probably attract your attention. An example of a situation in which task-irrelevant stimuli are difficult to ignore is provided by the *Stroop effect*, described in the following demonstration.

CogLab
Stroop Effect

DEMONSTRATION The Stroop Effect

Look at ● Figure 4.10. Your task is to name, as quickly as possible, the *color of ink* used to print each of the shapes. For example, starting in the upper left corner, and going across, you would say, "red, blue,..." and so on. Time yourself (or a friend you have enlisted to do this task), and determine how many seconds it takes to report the colors of all of the shapes. Then repeat the same task for ● Figure 4.11, remembering that your task is to specify the color of the *ink*, not the color name that is spelled out.

If you found it harder to name the colors of the words than the colors of the shapes, then you were experiencing the Stroop effect, which was first described by J. R. Stroop in 1935. This effect occurs because the names of the words cause a competing response (just as in the incompatible condition in the flanker compatibility task) and therefore slow responding to the target—the color of the ink. In the Stroop effect the task-irrelevant stimuli are extremely powerful, because reading words is highly practiced and has become so automatic that it is difficult *not* to read them (Stroop, 1935).

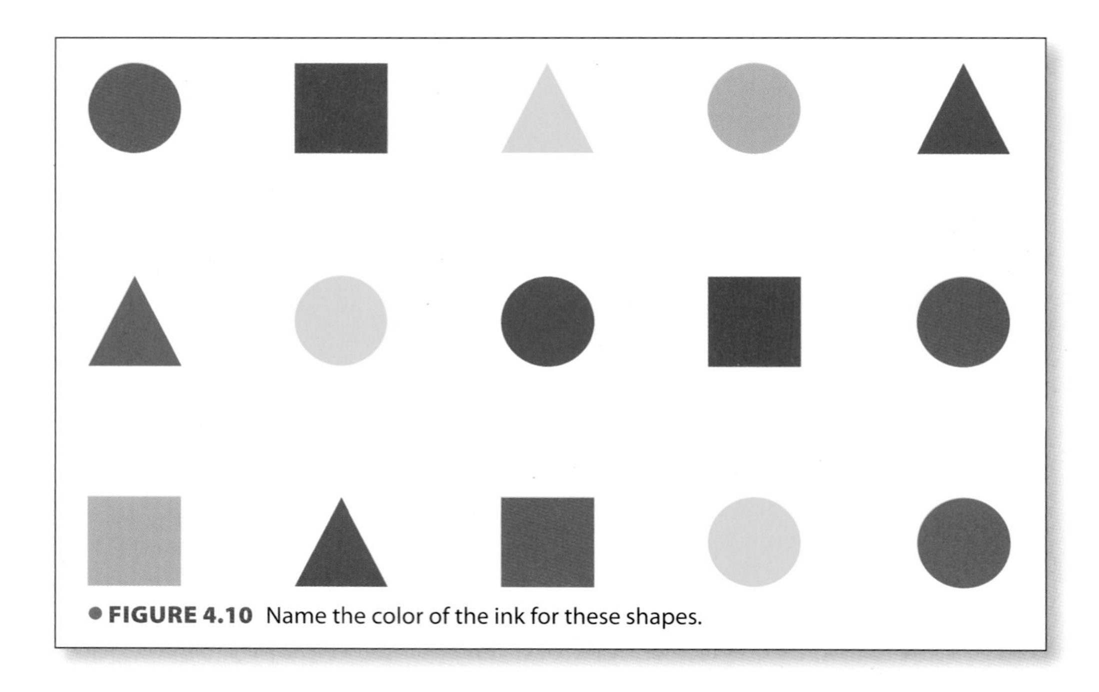

● **FIGURE 4.10** Name the color of the ink for these shapes.

YELLOW RED BLUE PURPLE GREEN

ORANGE YELLOW GREEN BLUE RED

GREEN PURPLE ORANGE RED BLUE

● **FIGURE 4.11** Name the color of the ink for these words.

TEST YOURSELF 4.1

1. How was the dichotic listening procedure used to determine how well people can focus on the attended message and how much information can be taken in from the unattended message? What is the cocktail party effect, and what does it demonstrate?
2. Describe Broadbent's model of selective attention. Why is it called an early selection model?
3. What were the results of experiments by Moray (words in the unattended ear) and Gray and Wedderburn ("Dear Aunt Jane")? Why are the results of these experiments difficult to explain based on Broadbent's filter model of attention?
4. Describe Treisman's attenuation theory. First indicate why she proposed the theory, then how she modified Broadbent's model to explain some results that Broadbent's model couldn't explain.
5. Describe MacKay's "bank" experiment. Why does his result provide evidence for late selection?
6. What is the flanker compatibility task? How have experiments using this task shown how attention is affected by load and by the nature of task-irrelevant

stimuli? Be sure you understand the explanation for the relation between load, cognitive capacity, and whether task-irrelevant stimuli are processed.

7. What is the Stroop effect? What does this demonstrate about how the nature of a task-irrelevant stimulus can affect attention?

Divided Attention

Our emphasis so far has been on attention as a mechanism for focusing on one task. We have seen that sometimes we take in information from an "unattended" task, even when we are trying to focus on one task, as in the low-load condition in the flanker compatibility experiments and the Stroop effect. But what if you want to purposely distribute your attention among a few tasks? Is it possible to pay attention to more than one thing at a time? Although you might be tempted to answer "no," based on the difficulty of listening to two conversations at once, there are many situations in which *divided attention*—the distribution of attention among two or more tasks—can occur. For example, Crystal is able to look at the umbrella while simultaneously being sure she doesn't step on any rocks. Also, people can simultaneously drive, have conversations, listen to music, and think about what they're going to be doing later that day. As we will see, the ability to divide attention depends on a number of factors, including practice and the difficulty of the task.

DIVIDED ATTENTION CAN BE ACHIEVED WITH PRACTICE: AUTOMATIC PROCESSING

We are going to describe some experiments by Walter Schneider and Robert Shiffrin (1977) that involve divided attention because they require the participant to carry out two tasks simultaneously: (1) holding information about target stimuli in memory and (2) paying attention to a series of "distractor" stimuli and determining if one of the target stimuli is present among these distractor stimuli. ● Figure 4.12 illustrates the procedure. The participant was shown a *memory set* like the one in Figure 4.12a, consisting of one to four characters called *target stimuli*. The memory set was followed by rapid presentation of 20 "test frames," each of which contained *distractors*. On half of the trials, one of the frames contained a target stimulus from the memory set. A new memory set was presented on each trial, so the targets changed from trial to trial, followed by new test frames. In this example, there is one target stimulus in the memory set, there are four stimuli in each frame, and the target stimulus *3* appears in one of the frames.

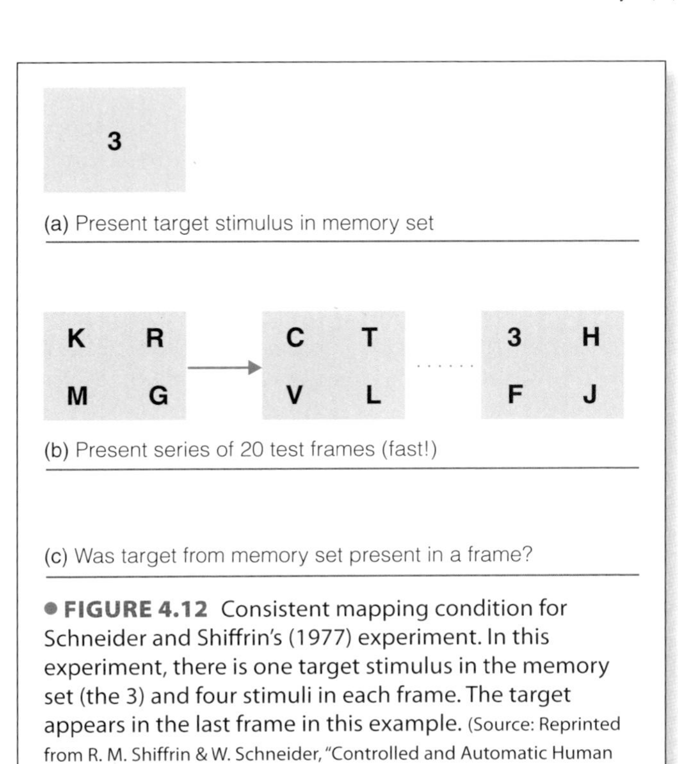

● **FIGURE 4.12** Consistent mapping condition for Schneider and Shiffrin's (1977) experiment. In this experiment, there is one target stimulus in the memory set (the 3) and four stimuli in each frame. The target appears in the last frame in this example. (Source: Reprinted from R. M. Shiffrin & W. Schneider, "Controlled and Automatic Human Information Processing: Perceptual Learning, Automatic Attending, and a General Theory," *Psychological Review, 84,* 127–190. Copyright © 1977 with permission of the American Psychological Association.)

The targets and distractors were always from different categories, so if the targets were numbers, as in our example, the distractors were always letters. Schneider and Shiffrin called this way of presenting stimuli the *consistent mapping condition* because even though the targets changed from trial to trial, the participants always knew that the target would be numbers and the distractors would be letters.

At the beginning of the experiment, the participants' performance was only 55 percent correct, and it took 900 trials for performance to reach 90 percent (● Figure 4.13). Participants reported that for the first 600 trials, they had to keep repeating the target items in each memory set in order to remember them. (Although targets were always numbers and distractors letters, remember that the actual targets and distractors changed from trial to trial.) However, participants reported that after about 600 trials, the task had become automatic: The frames appeared and

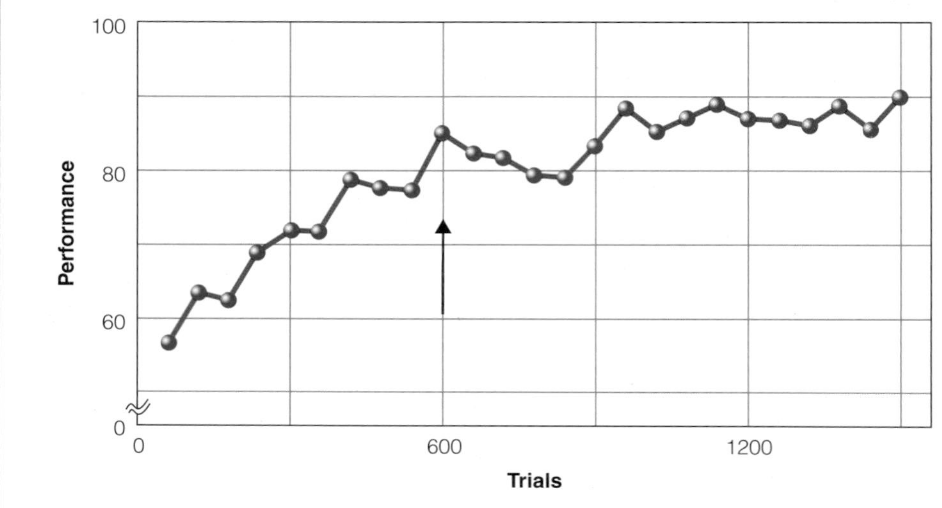

● **FIGURE 4.13** Improvement in performance with practice in Schneider and Schiffrin's (1977) experiment. The arrow indicates the point at which participants reported that the task had become automatic. This is the result of experiments in which there were four target stimuli in the memory set, and two stimuli in each frame. (Source: Reprinted from R. M. Shiffrin & W. Schneider, "Controlled and Automatic Human Information Processing: Perceptual Learning, Automatic Attending, and a General Theory," *Psychological Review, 84,* 127–190. Copyright © 1977 with permission of the American Psychological Association.)

participants responded without consciously thinking about it. They would do this even when as many as four targets had been presented.

What this means, according to Schneider and Shiffrin, is that practice made it possible for participants to divide their attention to deal with all of the target and test items simultaneously. Furthermore, the many trials of practice resulted in **automatic processing**, a type of processing that occurs (1) without intention (it happens automatically without the person intending to do it) and (2) at a cost of only some of a person's cognitive resources.

Real-life experiences are filled with examples of automatic processing because there are many things that we have been practicing for years. For example, have you ever wondered, after leaving home, whether you had locked the door, and then returned to find that you had? Locking the door has, for many people, become such an automatic response that they do it without paying attention. Another example of automatic processing (which is sometimes scary) occurs when you have driven somewhere and can't remember the trip once you get to your destination. In many cases this involves being "lost in thought" about something else, yet driving has become so automatic that it seems to take care of itself (at least until a traffic "situation" occurs, such as road construction or another car cutting in front of you). Finally, you may carry out many motor skills, such as touch-typing or texting, automatically, without attention. Try paying attention to what your fingers are doing while typing and notice what happens to your performance. Concert pianists have reported that if they start paying attention to their fingers while they are playing, their performance falls apart.

Having demonstrated that practice leads to automatic processing in the consistent mapping condition, Schneider and Shiffrin made the task more difficult by changing the way the test and distractor stimuli were presented.

DIVIDED ATTENTION WHEN TASKS ARE HARDER: CONTROLLED PROCESSING

To get a feel for the modified experiment, try the following demonstration.

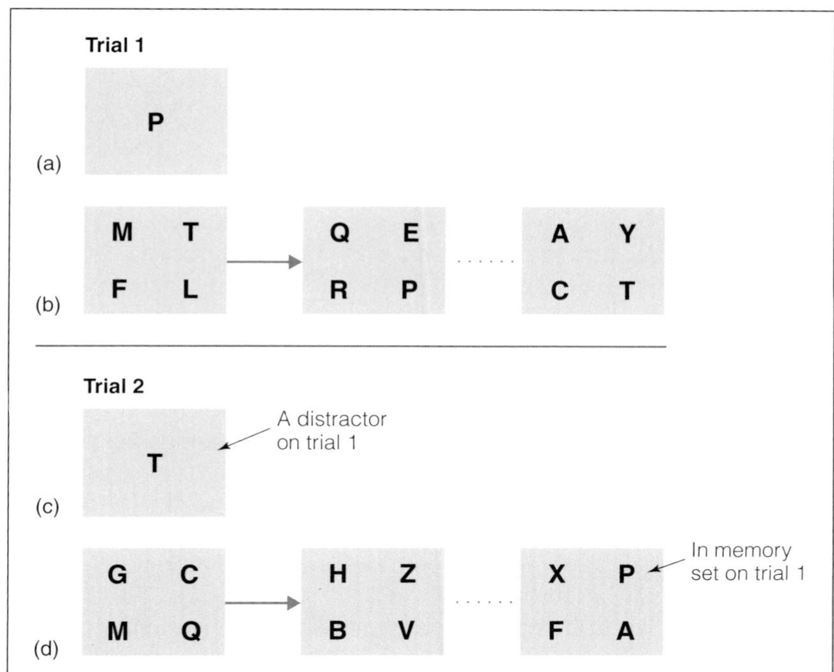

● **FIGURE 4.14** Varied mapping condition for Schneider and Shiffrin's (1977) experiment. This is more difficult than the consistent mapping condition because all the characters are letters and also because a character that was a distractor on one trial (like the T) can become a target on another trial, and a character that was a target on one trial (like the P) can become a distractor on another trial. (Source: Reprinted from R. M. Shiffrin & W. Schneider, "Controlled and Automatic Human Information Processing: Perceptual Learning, Automatic Attending, and a General Theory," *Psychological Review, 84,* 127–190. Copyright © 1977 with permission of the American Psychological Association.)

DEMONSTRATION Detecting a Target

Cover ● Figure 4.14b, c, and d. Note the target stimulus in (a). Then uncover (b) and determine if the target stimulus is present in the sequence of frames in Figure 4.14b, scanning from left to right. Now repeat this procedure for the new target stimulus in (c) and the frames in (d).

This is the same procedure as in the previous experiment, but with the following modifications that make it more difficult: (1) The targets in the memory set and the distractors are both letters. In the previous experiment, the targets were numbers and the distractors were letters. (2) Just as in Schneider and Shiffrin's previous experiment (Figure 4.12), the targets and distractors are changed on each trial. However, for this new task, a target on one trial can be a distractor on the next trial. For example, target stimulus P on trial 1 becomes a distractor on trial 2. Also, the target stimulus T on trial 2 was a distractor on trial 1. This is called the *varied mapping condition* because the rules keep changing from trial to trial.

● Figure 4.15 shows that performance was worse in the varied mapping condition than in the consistent mapping condition. Each data point is the maximum performance achieved after many trials of practice, when there was one target stimulus and four stimuli in each test frame. The duration that each frame was visible is plotted on the horizontal axis.

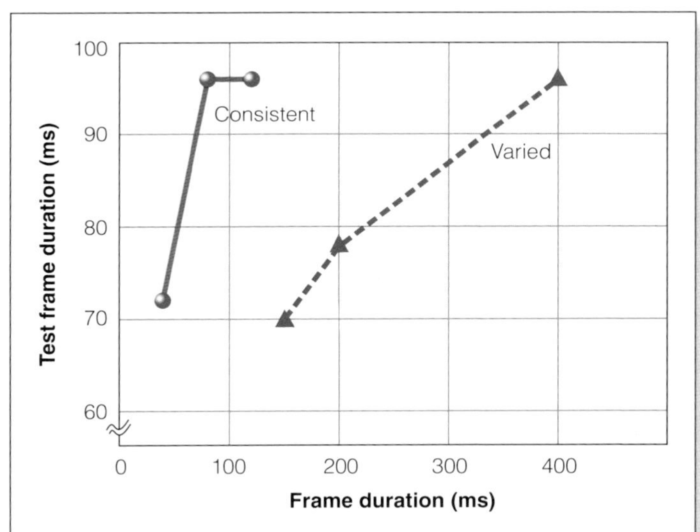

● **FIGURE 4.15** Comparing performance on the consistent and varied mapping tasks. Note that the horizontal axis indicates the duration of each test frame. These graphs show that frames must be presented for longer durations to achieve good performance in the varied mapping condition. (Source: Based on data from R. M. Shiffrin & W. Schneider, "Controlled and Automatic Human Information Processing: Perceptual Learning, Automatic Attending, and a General Theory," *Psychological Review, 84,* 127–190. Copyright © 1977 with permission of the American Psychological Association.)

First look at the consistent mapping condition. Performance reaches above 90 percent correct when the test frame duration is only 80 ms. This speed is too fast for varied mapping, so the presentation has to be slowed down by increasing frame duration. When this is done, performance doesn't exceed 90 percent until each test frame is presented for 400 ms. Clearly, the varied mapping condition is much more difficult.

Another important outcome of varied mapping is that participants never achieved automatic processing. Schneider and Shiffrin describe the processing used in the varied mapping condition as **controlled processing**, because the participants had to pay close attention at all times and had to search for the target among the distractors in a much more focused and controlled way than in the consistent mapping condition.

Let's summarize the results of the experiments we have discussed in this section. Divided attention is possible and can become automatic if tasks are easy or well-practiced. Divided attention becomes difficult and can require controlled processing when the task is made too hard (also see Schneider & Chein, 2003). For example, you may find it easy to drive and talk at the same time if traffic is light on a familiar road. But as traffic increases, you see a flashing "Construction Ahead" sign, and the road suddenly becomes rutted, you might have to stop your conversation to devote all of your cognitive resources to driving. Because of the importance of driving in our society and the recent phenomenon of people talking on cell phones while driving, researchers have begun to investigate the consequences of attempting to divide attention between driving and talking on a cell phone.

DISTRACTIONS WHILE DRIVING

Driving is one of those tasks that demand constant attention. Not paying attention due to drowsiness or involvement in other tasks can have disastrous consequences. The seriousness of driver inattention has recently been verified by a research project called the 100-Car Naturalistic Driving Study (Dingus et al., 2006). In this study, video recorders in 100 vehicles created records of both what the drivers were doing and the view out the front and rear windows.

These recordings documented 82 crashes and 771 near crashes in more than 2 million miles of driving. In 80 percent of the crashes and 67 percent of the near crashes, the driver was inattentive in some way 3 seconds beforehand. One man kept glancing down and to the right, apparently sorting through papers in a stop-and-go driving situation, until he slammed into an SUV. A woman eating a hamburger dropped her head below the dashboard just before she hit the car in front of her. One of the most distracting activities was pushing buttons on a cell phone or similar device. More than 22 percent of near crashes involved that kind of distraction.

This naturalistic research confirms earlier findings, which demonstrated a connection between cell phone use and traffic accidents. A survey of accidents and cell phone use in Toronto showed that the risk of a collision was four times higher when using a cell phone than when a cell phone was not being used (Redelmeier & Tibshirani, 1997). Perhaps the most significant result of the Toronto study is that hands-free cell phone units offered no safety advantage.

In a laboratory experiment on the effects of cell phones, David Strayer and William Johnston (2001) placed participants in a simulated driving task that required them to apply the brakes as quickly as possible in response to a red light. Doing this task while talking on a cell phone caused participants to miss twice as many of the red lights as when they weren't talking on the phone (● Figure 4.16a) and also increased the time it took them to apply the brakes (Figure 4.16b). In agreement with the results of the Toronto study, the same decrease in performance occurred regardless of whether participants used a "hands-free" cell phone device or a handheld model. Strayer and Johnston concluded from this result that talking on the phone uses cognitive resources that would otherwise be used for driving the car (also see Haigney & Westerman, 2001; Lamble et al., 1999; Spence & Read, 2003; Violanti, 1998). This idea that the problem posed by cell phone use during driving is related to the use of cognitive resources is an important one. The problem isn't driving with one hand. It is driving with fewer cognitive resources available to focus attention on driving.

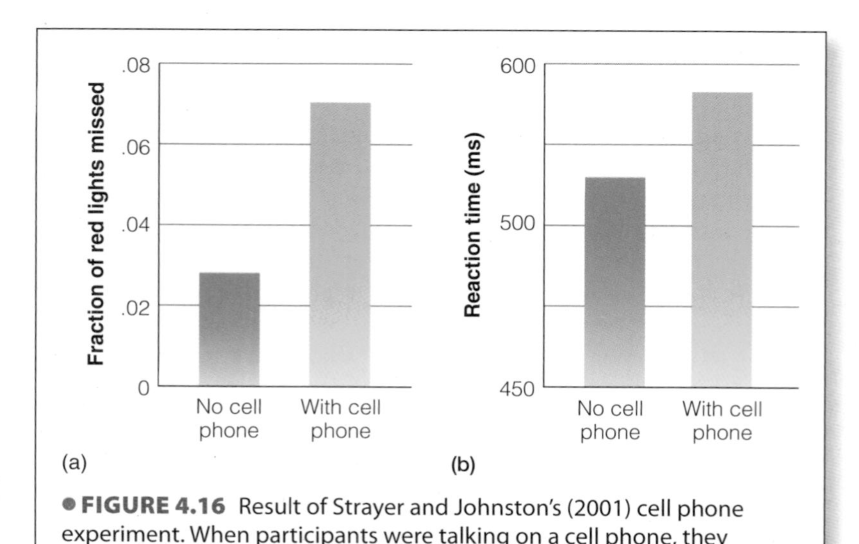

● **FIGURE 4.16** Result of Strayer and Johnston's (2001) cell phone experiment. When participants were talking on a cell phone, they (a) missed more red lights and (b) took longer to apply the brakes.

Students often react to results such as this by asking what the difference is between talking on a hands-free cell phone and having a conversation with a passenger in the car. It is possible, of course, that having a conversation with a passenger could have an adverse effect on driving, but it seems likely that this effect—if it exists—would not be as large as the cell phone effect.

One way to appreciate the difference between talking on a cell phone and talking to a passenger is to imagine the situation in which you are sitting down (not in a car) and you place a call to your friend's cell phone. Your friend answers and you start talking. As far as you are concerned, you are just having a phone conversation. But unbeknownst to you, the person you called is in the process of negotiating his way through heavy traffic, or is perhaps reacting to a car that has just cut in front of him, traveling 70 miles per hour on the highway. The question to ask yourself is, would you be having the same conversation if you were a passenger sitting next to the driver? As a passenger, you would be aware of the traffic situation and would be able to react by pausing the conversation or perhaps warn the driver of upcoming hazards (This is sometimes called "backseat driving"!). It is also relevant to consider the social demands of phone conversations. Because it is generally considered poor form to suddenly stop talking or to pause for long periods, the person talking on the phone while driving might continue talking even when driving is becoming challenging.

An interesting phenomenon related to cell phone use is revealed by the results of a 2008 survey by Nationwide Mutual Insurance, which found that even though an overwhelming majority of people who talk on cell phones while driving consider themselves safe drivers, 45 percent of them reported that they had been hit or nearly hit by another driver talking on a cell phone. Thus, people identify talking on cell phones while driving as risky, but they think others are dangerous, not themselves (Nationwide Insurance, 2008).

The main message here is that the distraction of attention associated with talking on a cell phone can degrade driving performance. And cell phones aren't the only attention-grabbing device found in cars. An article in the *New York Times* titled "Hi, I'm Your Car. Don't Let Me Distract You," notes that many new cars have distraction-producing devices such as GPS navigation systems and menu screens for high-tech computer controls (Peters, 2004). Because these devices require attention and time (an average of 5.4 seconds to read and process electronic maps, for example), these distractions could, like cell phone use, also be contributing to unsafe driving by causing drivers to glance away from the road. Recently, with more people beginning to send text messages while driving, a study by the Virginia Tech Transportation Institute found that truck drivers who send text messages while driving are 23 times more likely to cause a crash or near crash than truckers who are not texting (Hanowski et al., 2009).

Attention and Visual Perception

It is clear that attention is an important component of many of the tasks we carry out routinely every day. In this section we take this idea a step farther by describing experiments that show that attention is so important that, without it, we may fail to perceive things that are clearly visible in our field of view.

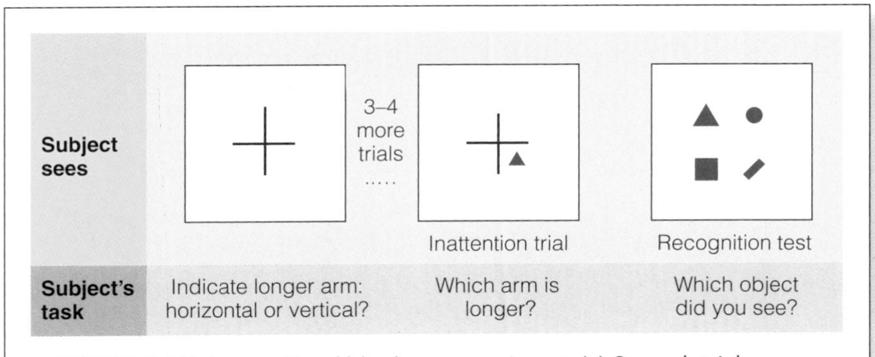

● **FIGURE 4.17** Inattentional blindness experiment. (a) On each trial, participants judge whether the horizontal or vertical arm is longer. (b) After a few trials, the inattention trial occurs, in which a geometric object is flashed along with the arms. (c) In the recognition test, the participant is asked to indicate which geometric object was presented. (Source: From E. B. Goldstein, *Sensation and Perception*, 8th ed., Fig. 6.9, p. 139. Copyright © 2010 Wadsworth, a part of Cengage Learning. Reproduced with permission. www.cengage.com/permissions.)

INATTENTIONAL BLINDNESS

One way to demonstrate the importance of attention for perception is to create a situation in which a person's attention is focused on one task and then determining whether the person perceived an easily visible nearby stimulus. Arien Mack and Irvin Rock (1998) used this procedure, as shown in ● Figure 4.17. The observer's task was to indicate which arm of the cross was longer, the horizontal arm or the vertical arm. Then, on one trial, a small test object, which was within the observer's field of clear vision, was added to the display. When observers were then given a recognition test in which they are asked to pick the object that had been presented, they were unable to do so. Paying attention to the vertical and horizontal arms apparently made observers "blind" to the unattended test object. This effect is called **inattentional blindness**.

Mack and Rock demonstrated inattentional blindness using rapidly flashed geometric test stimuli. But other research has shown that similar effects can be achieved using more naturalistic stimuli that are presented for longer periods of time. Imagine looking at a display in a department store window. When you focus your attention on the display, you will probably fail to notice the reflections on the surface of the window. Shift your attention to the reflections, and you become less aware of the display inside the window.

● **FIGURE 4.18** Frame from the film shown by Simons and Chablis in which a person in a gorilla suit walked through the "basketball" game. (Source: D. J. Simons & C. F. Chabris, "Gorillas in Our Midst: Sustained Inattentional Blindness for Dynamic Events," *Perception, 28,* 1059–1074, 1999. Figure provided by Daniel Simons.)

Daniel Simons and Christopher Chabris (1999) created a situation like the department store window, in which one part of a scene is attended and the other is not. They created a 75-second film that showed two teams of three players each. The team that was dressed in white was passing a basketball around, and the other, dressed in black, was not handling the ball. Observers were told to count the number of passes, a task that focused their attention on the team in white. After about 45 seconds, an event that took 5 seconds occurred. One of these events was a person dressed in a gorilla suit, walking through the scene (● Figure 4.18).

After seeing the video, observers were asked whether they had seen anything unusual happen or whether they had seen anything other than the six players. Nearly half—46 percent—of the observers failed to report having seen the event, even though it was clearly visible. These experiments demonstrate that when observers are attending to one sequence of events, they can fail to notice another event, even when it is right in front of them (also see Goldstein & Fink, 1981; Neisser & Becklen, 1975).

CogLab
Change Detection

CHANGE DETECTION

Following in the footsteps of the experiments in which observers were given a distracting task, researchers developed another way to demonstrate how a lack of attention can affect perception. Instead of presenting a task that distracted attention from a test stimulus, they presented first one picture, then another slightly different picture, and asked observers to indicate whether they saw any difference between the two pictures. To appreciate how this works, try the following demonstration.

DEMONSTRATION Change Detection

Look at the picture on the left (● Figure 4.19) for just a moment; then cover the picture and see whether you can determine what is different in ● Figure 4.20. If you don't see the difference, repeat the procedure. Do this now, before reading further.

● **FIGURE 4.19** Look at this picture for about a second, cover it, and look at Figure 4.20 (at the top of the next page).

Were you able to see what was different in the second picture? People often have trouble detecting the change even though it is obvious when you know where to look. (Try again, paying attention to the sign near the lower left portion of the picture.) Ronald Rensink and coworkers (1997) did a similar experiment in which they presented

Bruce Goldstein

● **FIGURE 4.20** What is different in this picture?

one picture, followed by a blank field, followed by the same picture but with an item missing, followed by the blank field, and so on. The pictures were alternated in this way until observers were able to determine what was different about the two pictures. Rensink found that the pictures had to be alternated back and forth a number of times before the difference was detected.

This difficulty in detecting changes in scenes is called **change blindness** (Rensink, 2002). The importance of attention (or lack of it) in determining change blindness is demonstrated by the fact that when Rensink added a cue indicating which part of a scene had been changed, participants detected the changes much more quickly (also see Henderson & Hollingworth, 2003; Rensink, 2002).

Change blindness has also been demonstrated by having observers view films. ● Figure 4.21 shows successive frames from a video of a brief conversation between two women. The noteworthy aspect of this video is that changes take place in each new shot. In shot B, the woman's scarf has disappeared; in shot C, the other woman's hand is on her chin, although immediately after, in shot D, both arms are on the table. Also, the paper plates change color from red in the initial views to white in shot D.

Although participants who viewed this video were told to pay close attention, only 1 of 10 participants claimed to notice any changes. Even when the participants were shown the video again and were warned that there would be changes in "objects, body position, or clothing," they noticed fewer than a quarter of the changes that occurred (Levin & Simons, 1997).

(a)

(b)

(c)

(d)

● **FIGURE 4.21** Frames from the video shown in the Levin and Simons' (1997) experiment. Note that the woman on the right is wearing a scarf around her neck in shots A, C, and D, but not in shot B. Also, the color of the plates changes from red in the first three frames to white in frame D, and the hand position of the woman on the left changes between shots C and D. (Source: From D. Levin & D. Simons, "Failure to Detect Changes in Attended Objects in Motion Pictures," *Psychonomic Bulletin and Review, 209,* 1997.)

This blindness to change in films is not just a laboratory phenomenon. It occurs regularly in popular films, in which some aspect of the scene, which should remain the same, changes from one shot to the next, just as objects changed in the film shots in Figure 4.21. These changes in films, which are called *continuity errors*, are spotted by viewers who are looking for them, usually by viewing the film multiple times, but are usually missed by viewers in theaters who are not looking for these errors. For example, in the film *Oceans 11* (2001), Rusty, the character played by Brad Pitt, is talking to Linus, the character played by Matt Damon. In one shot, Rusty is holding a cocktail glass full of shrimp in his hand, but in the next shot, which moves in closer and is from a slightly different angle, the glass has turned into a plate of fruit, and then in the next shot the plate changes back to the cocktail glass! If you are interested in exploring continuity errors further, you can find websites devoted to them by searching for "continuity errors in movies."

All of the experiments we have described—both the ones in which a distracting task kept people from noticing a test stimulus and the ones in which small, but easily visible, changes in pictures are not perceived—demonstrate that attention is necessary for perception. This has implications for perception that occurs in our everyday experience, because there are usually so many stimuli present in the environment that we are able to pay attention to only a small fraction of these stimuli at any point in time. This means that we are constantly missing stimuli in the environment.

Before you conclude that missing some of the things in the environment is a serious problem, let's return to a cognitive capacity we discussed in Chapter 3—the cognitive system's ability to "fill in" the blanks because of our knowledge of regularities in the environment (see Chapter 3, page 63). As you approach an intersection with four-way stop signs, you may not be aware of the exact kind of car that is approaching from the left, or that it has a Florida license plate, but you do know that a car is approaching and have had enough experience driving to know that you need to check to see if the other car is slowing down and to be ready for the possibility that the other car might not stop. Thus, your knowledge of things that normally occur in the environment enable you to predict what is likely to be happening "off to the side" without being aware of every detail of the situation.

Another factor that helps you deal with unattended stimuli in the environment is that potentially dangerous stimuli, such as traffic, other people, or a dog running across your path, often move or produce sound. This movement or sound causes you to direct your attention to the stimulus, so you can react to it.

Reacting to movement or sound is often an automatic process. Something moves off to the side and, without thinking, you automatically look toward it. A car backfires, and you turn your head to determine where the sound came from. Automatic attraction of attention by a sudden visual or auditory stimulus is called **exogenous attention.** This is different from the type of attention that occurs when you consciously decide to scan the environment, perhaps to find a specific stimulus or just to keep track of what is going on. This consciously determined attention is called **endogenous attention.** Both types of attention can involve *overt attention*, shifting attention by moving the eyes (Carrasco, 2010; Henderson, 2003).

TEST YOURSELF 4.2

1. Describe the Schneider and Shiffrin divided attention experiments. Compare the stimulus conditions for consistent and varied mapping conditions, and how these different conditions result in automatic or controlled processing.
2. What conclusions can be reached from the results of experiments testing the ability to drive while talking on a cell phone? What are some of the differences between a driver talking to a passenger and a driver talking on a cell phone?
3. Describe the following evidence that attention is necessary for perception: inattentional blindness experiment; "basketball" experiment; change detection experiments. Be sure you understand what is preventing attention from being directed to parts of a display or scene in each of these experiments.

Overt Attention: Attending by Moving Our Eyes

The shifts of attention that occur in **overt attention** are accompanied by eye movements. Why do we need to move our eyes to shift attention? We began answering this question in the previous section in which we described inattentional blindness and change detection. Both of these cases indicate that we miss objects or changes in the environment that we are not paying attention to, but when people are told where to look in a scene, they can detect the objects or changes they had previously missed.

Inattentional blindness and change blindness are therefore situations in which attention and perception are closely linked. We can perceive things we pay attention to, and we miss things we don't pay attention to. This section continues this theme by specifically considering the connection between eye movements, attention, and perception.

EYE MOVEMENTS, ATTENTION, AND PERCEPTION

The link between eye movements, attention, and perception is illustrated by the following demonstration.

Michael Ochs Archives/Getty Images

● **FIGURE 4.22** Find Bob Dylan's face in this group.

DEMONSTRATION Looking for a Face in the Crowd

Your task in this demonstration is to find Bob Dylan's face in the crowd pictured in ● Figure 4.22. Time yourself to see how rapidly you can accomplish this task.

You may have located Dylan's face right away if you just happened to look right at him, but it is more likely that it took a while, because it was necessary to move your eyes from face to face to see each one clearly. This shifting of the eyes can be measured using a device called an **eye tracker**, which creates records like the one in ● Figure 4.23. This example shows a person's eye movements when looking at a picture of a fountain. The small dots indicate **fixations**, places where the eyes briefly paused, and the lines indicate **saccadic eye movements**—movements of the eye from one fixation to the next. Typically, people make about three fixations per second when viewing an unfamiliar scene. Eye movement records like this one indicate the parts of the scene that are attracting the person's attention.

We will now consider two factors that determine how people shift their attention by moving their eyes: *bottom-up*, based primarily on physical characteristics of the stimulus; and *top-down*, based on the relation between the observer and the scene—what the person knows about the scene and the demands of a task that involves objects in the scene.

● **FIGURE 4.23** Scan path of a person viewing a fountain in Bordeaux, France.

BOTTOM-UP DETERMINANTS OF EYE MOVEMENTS

Attention can be influenced by **stimulus salience**—the physical properties of the stimulus, such as color, contrast, or movement. Capturing attention by stimulus salience is a bottom-up process because it depends solely on the pattern of light and dark, color and contrast in a stimulus. For example, the task of finding the people wearing yellow hats in Figure 4.22 would involve bottom-up processing because it involves responding to the physical property of color, without considering the meaning of the image (Parkhurst et al., 2002).

But where we look is not determined only by the bottom-up processes triggered by stimulus salience. We can see that this is true by checking the eye movements caused by the fountain in Figure 4.23. Notice that the person never looks at the fence in the foreground, even though it is very salient because of its high contrast and its position near the front of the scene. Instead, the person focuses on aspects of the fountain that are more interesting, such as the horses. In this example, it is the *meaning* of the horses that attracts attention.

TOP-DOWN DETERMINANTS OF EYE MOVEMENTS

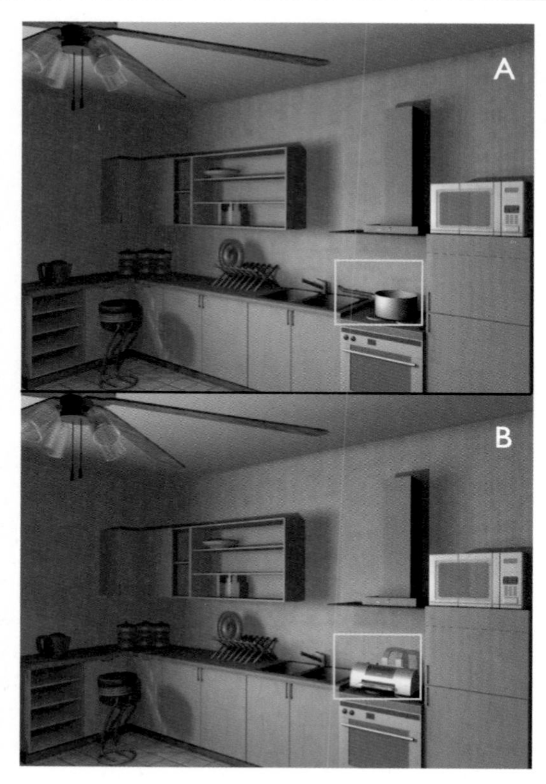

● **FIGURE 4.24** Stimuli used by Vo and Henderson (2009). Observers spent more time looking at the printer (in B) than at the pot (in A), shown inside the yellow rectangles (which were not visible to the observers). (Source: M. L. Vo & J. M. Henderson, "Does Gravity Matter? Effects of Semantic and Syntactic Inconsistencies on the Allocation of Attention During Scene Perception," *Journal of Vision, 9,* 3, Article 24, Figure 1A & B, 1–15, 2009.)

Top-down processing is also associated with **scene schemas**—an observer's knowledge about what is contained in typical scenes (remember "environmental regularities" from Chapter 3, page 63). Thus, when Melissa Vo and John Henderson showed observers pictures like the ones in ● Figure 4.24, observers looked longer at the printer in Figure 4.24b than the pan in Figure 4.24a because a printer is less likely to be found in a kitchen.

The fact that people look longer at things that seem out of place in a scene means that attention is being affected by their knowledge of what is usually found in the scene. Consider, for example where the person looked when presented with the baseball scene in ● Figure 4.25. The person's attention appears to have been initially captured by the bright yellow band (perhaps an example of stimulus salience at work), but the person's gaze immediately shifts to the field, fixating on the various players. It seems probable that the person's knowledge of the layout of the bases and positions of players played a role in determining where he or she looked.

The way the person scanned the baseball scene also suggests that attention is influenced by a particular person's knowledge and interests. This person appears to be interested in baseball and have some knowledge about it. Where do you think a person with little interest in baseball but a great deal of interest in architecture might have looked? Most likely the person would be more interested in, and therefore pay more attention to, the buildings in the upper part of the scene.

Attention occurs not only as we view static scenes, but as we carry out actions. The development of portable eye trackers like the one in ● Figure 4.26 makes it possible to track people's eye movements as they perform tasks. This research shows that when a person is carrying out a task, the demands of the task override factors such as stimulus saliency. ● Figure 4.27 shows the fixations and eye movements that occurred as a person was making a peanut butter sandwich. The process of making the sandwich begins with the movement of a slice of bread from the bag to the plate. Notice that this operation is accompanied by an eye

● **FIGURE 4.25** Pattern of eye movements to this picture of a baseball game in PNC Park in Pittsburgh. The person looks at the yellow stripe first.

● **FIGURE 4.26** A wearable eye tracker. (a) The scene camera and eye camera are mounted on a lightweight glasses frame. The backpack carries a battery and a video camera, which tracks eye position relative to the scene the person is observing. (b) Image of a scene from the head-mounted video camera while the participant makes a peanut butter and jelly sandwich. Fixations are indicated by the yellow circles. Circle diameters reflect the duration of the fixation. (Source: M. F. Land & M. Hayhoe, "In What Ways Do Eye Movements Contribute to Everyday Activities?" *Vision Research, 41,* 3559–3565, 2001. Figure b courtesy C. A. Rothkopf & J. B. Pelz, "Head Movement Estimation for Wearable Eye Tracker," *Proceedings ACM SIGCHI Eye Tracking Research & Applications Symposium,* San Antonio, Texas, 123–130, 2004.)

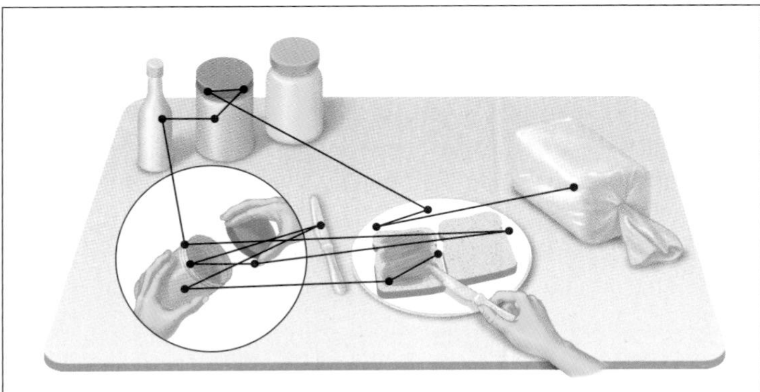

● **FIGURE 4.27** Sequence of fixations of a person making a peanut butter sandwich. The first fixation is on the loaf of bread. (Source: M. F. Land, N. Mennie, & J. Rusted, "The Roles of Vision and Eye Movements in the Control of Activities of Daily Living," *Perception, 28,* 11, Figure 2 and Figure 8, 1311–1328, 1999. Copyright © 1999 by Pion Limited, London. All rights reserved. Reproduced by permission.)

movement from the bread to the plate. The peanut butter jar is then fixated on, lifted, and moved to the front as its lid is removed. The knife is then fixated on, picked up, and used to scoop the peanut butter, which is then spread on the bread (Land & Hayhoe, 2001).

The key finding of these measurements, and also of another experiment in which eye movements were measured as a person prepared tea (Land et al., 1999), is that the person's eye movements were determined primarily by the task. Participants did not look at objects or areas that were irrelevant to the task. Furthermore, the eye movement usually preceded a motor action by a fraction of a second, as when the person first fixated the peanut butter jar and then reached over to pick it up. This is an example of the "just in time" strategy—eye movements occur just before we need the information they will provide.

Although eye movements often indicate where a person is directing attention, it is possible to be looking directly at something without paying attention to it. You may have experienced this if you have been reading a book and then suddenly realized that although you had been moving your eyes across the page, looking at the words, you had no idea what you had read, because you were thinking about something else. This is an example of looking without paying attention.

Another reason looking at something doesn't always mean we are paying attention to it is that it is possible to direct attention off to the side from where we are looking. For example, consider a basketball player who dribbles down court while paying attention to a teammate off to the side, just before she throws a dead-on pass without looking. Attention that is not associated with eye movements is called *covert attention*.

Covert Attention: Directing Attention Without Eye Movements

CogLab
Spatial Cueing

Covert attention has been studied using a procedure called **precueing**, in which the participant is presented with a "cue" that indicates where a stimulus is most likely to appear. Precuing has been used to study **location-based attention**—how attention is directed to a specific location or place, and **object-based attention**—attention that is directed to a specific object (Behrman & Shomstein, 2010; Shomstein, 2010).

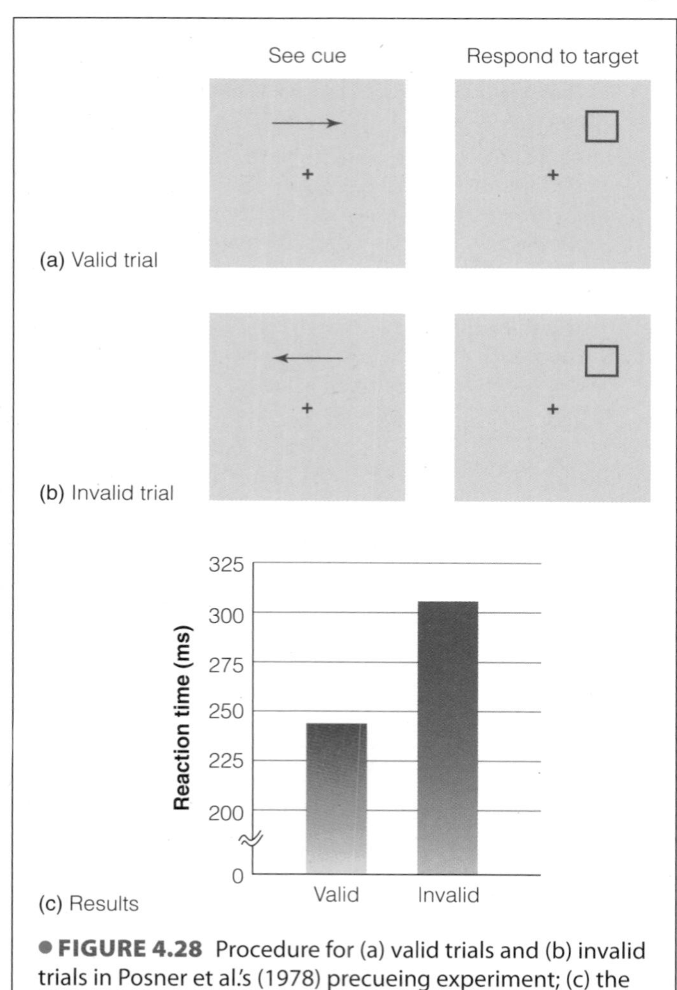

● **FIGURE 4.28** Procedure for (a) valid trials and (b) invalid trials in Posner et al.'s (1978) precueing experiment; (c) the results of the experiment. The average reaction time was 245 ms for valid trials but 305 ms for invalid trials.
(Source: M. I. Posner, M. J. Nissen, & W. C. Ogden, *Modes of Perceiving and Processing Information*. Copyright © 1978 by Taylor & Francis Group LLC–Books. Reproduced with permission of Taylor & Francis Group LLC.)

LOCATION-BASED ATTENTION

Michael Posner and coworkers (1978) were interested in answering the following question: Does attention to a specific location improve our ability to respond rapidly to a stimulus presented at that location? To answer this question, Posner used the *precuing* procedure, as shown in ● Figure 4.28.

METHOD Precueing

The general principle behind a precuing experiment is to determine whether presenting a cue indicating where a test stimulus will appear enhances the processing of the test stimulus. The participants in Posner and coworkers' (1978) experiment kept their eyes stationary throughout the experiment, always looking at the +. They first saw an arrow cue indicating on which side of the target a stimulus was likely to appear (left panel). In Figure 4.28a, the cue indicates that they should focus their attention to the right. (Remember, they do this without moving their eyes.) The participant's task was to press a key as rapidly as possible when a target square was presented off to the side (right panel). The trial shown in Figure 4.28a is a *valid trial* because the square appears on the side indicated by the cue arrow. The location indicated by the arrow was valid 80 percent of the time. Figure 4.28b shows an *invalid trial*. The cue arrow indicates that the observer should attend to the left, but the target is presented on the right.

The results of this experiment, shown in Figure 4.28c, indicate that observers reacted more rapidly on valid trials than on invalid trials. Posner interpreted this result as showing that information processing is more effective *at the place where attention is directed*. This result and others like it gave rise to the idea that attention is like a spotlight or zoom lens that improves processing when directed toward a particular location

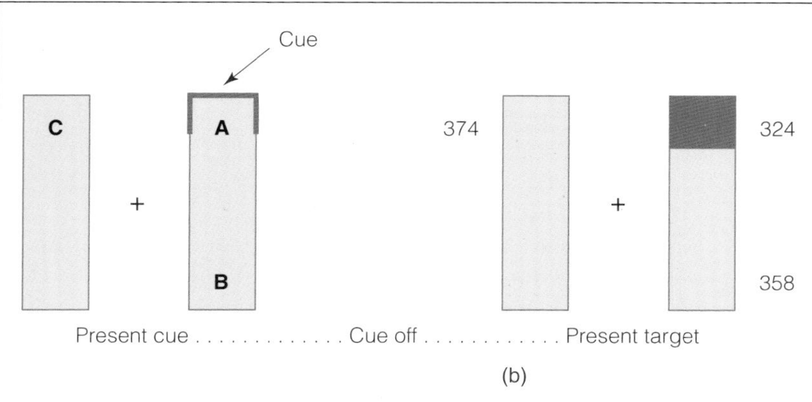

● **FIGURE 4.29** Stimuli for Egly et al.'s (1994) object-based attention experiment. (a) The cue signal, darkened lines, appears at the top or bottom of one of the rectangles to indicate where the target will probably appear. The letters were not present in the display viewed by participants. (b) The target, a darkened square, appears at one end of one of the rectangles. Numbers indicate how long it took, in milliseconds, to respond to targets presented at positions A, B, and C when the cue had appeared at position A.

(Marino & Scholl, 2005). Although experiments have shown that the spotlight idea is a useful way to think about the way attention enhances processing, directing covert attention is more complicated than this. One complication becomes apparent when considering what happens when attention is directed to specific objects.

OBJECT-BASED ATTENTION

Studies of attention using the precueing procedure consider how people move their attention from one location to another. But other experiments have used precueing to show that attention can also be associated with specific objects. Experiments studying *object-based attention* have shown that when attention is directed to one place on an object, the enhancing effect of this attention spreads throughout the object.

Consider, for example, the experiment diagrammed in ● Figure 4.29 (Egly et al., 1994). As participants were instructed to keep their eyes on the +, one end of the rectangle was briefly highlighted (Figure 4.29a). This was the cue signal that indicated where a target, a dark square (Figure 4.29b), would probably appear. In this example, the cue indicates that the target is likely to appear in the upper part of the right rectangle. The participants' task was to press a button when the target appeared anywhere in the display (Figure 4.29b). Reaction times were fastest when the target appeared where the cue signal predicted it would appear (at A in this example; note that the letters were not present in the actual experiment) and slower at other locations. However, the most important result of this experiment is that participants responded faster when the target appeared within the same rectangular object at location B than when it appeared in the other object at location C. Note that B and C are the same distance from A. However, participants respond more rapidly when the target was presented at B, which is in the same object as A. Apparently, the enhancing effect of attention had spread within the rectangle on the right, so even though the cue was at A, some enhancement occurred at B as well. This result is called **same-object advantage** (Marino & Scholl, 2005).

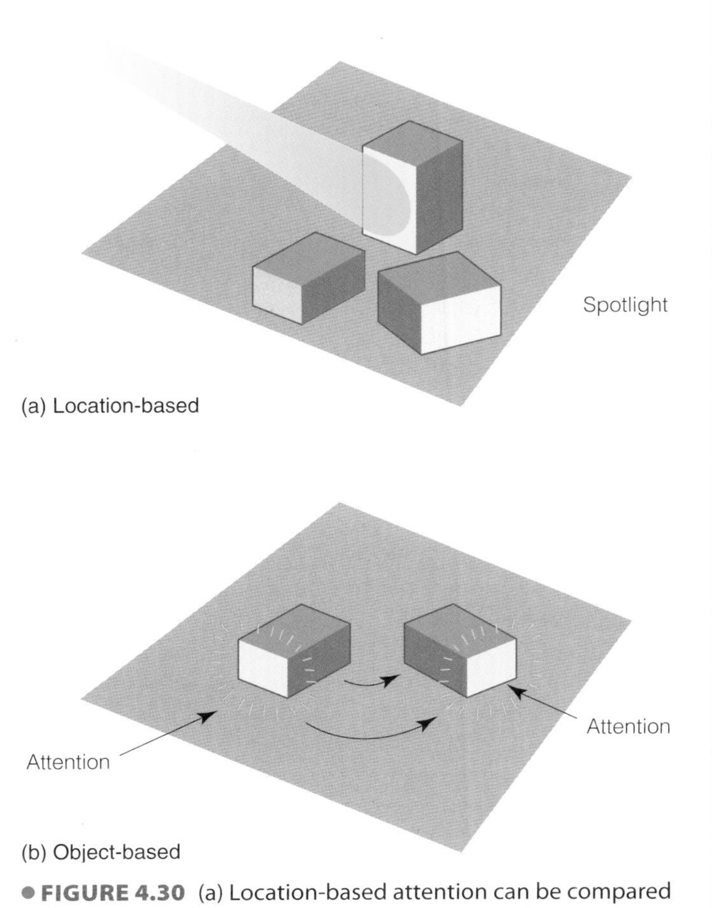

We have seen that attention can be based both on where a person is looking *in the environment* (location-based attention) and on where a person is looking *on a specific object* (object-based attention). We can think of these two modes of visual attention as involving two different mechanisms that operate under different conditions. For static scenes or scenes that contain few objects, location-based visual attention can be likened to a spotlight that scans different locations (● Figure 4.30a). In dynamic environments, object-based visual attention can involve a mechanism that locks onto objects and follows them as they move (Figure 4.30b; Behrmann & Tipper, 1999; Luck & Vecera, 2002). Recent physiological evidence has

Spotlight

(a) Location-based

Attention

Attention

(b) Object-based

● **FIGURE 4.30** (a) Location-based attention can be compared to a spotlight that scans a scene. (b) Object-based attention involves focusing attention on specific objects. These objects can be stationary or moving.

shown that location-based and object-based attention activate different areas of the brain. This result supports the idea that location-based attention and object-based attention involve different mechanisms (Shomstein & Behrmann, 2006).

Feature Integration Theory

So far we have described a number of ways that attention contributes to our awareness. When we selectively attend, we focus our awareness on one thing among many; when we divide our attention, we spread our awareness or carry out multiple tasks; when we scan a scene, we direct awareness to different parts of a display or scene.

Now we are going to consider another function of attention, which is notable because we are unaware of its operation. This property of attention, which operates in the background outside of our awareness, enables us to perceive an object's visual features as belonging together. To appreciate why it is necessary to propose a mechanism that enables us to perceive an object's features as belonging together, think back to Chapter 2 (page 37), where we introduced a person observing a rolling red ball, shown again in ● Figure 4.31. Remember that the ball's features—color (red), shape (round), movement (to the right) —are processed in different parts of the person's brain, so the ball's features are separated physiologically. The point of this example was that even though observing the ball activates separate areas in the brain, we perceive one object, a red ball, moving to the right.

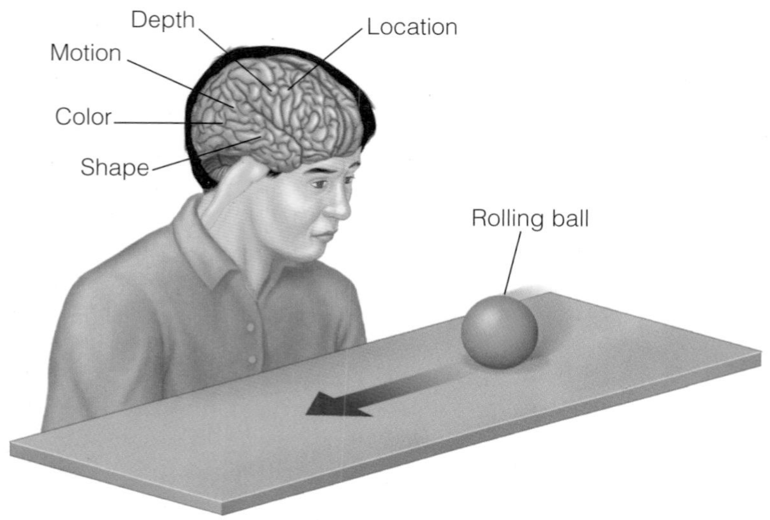

● **FIGURE 4.31** As this person watches the red ball roll by, different areas of his cortex are activated by different properties of the ball. These areas are in separated locations in the cortex, although there is communication between them. (Source: From E. B. Goldstein, *Sensation and Perception,* 8th ed., Fig. 6.18.

Anne Treisman (1986, 1998) proposed a theory, called **feature integration theory**, to explain how we perceive these initially separated features as part of the same object. In her theory, the first step in processing an image of an object is the **preattentive stage** (the first box in the flow diagram in ● Figure 4.32). In the preattentive stage, objects are analyzed into separate features. For example, the rolling red ball would be analyzed into the features color (red), shape (round), and movement (to the right). Because each of these features is processed in a separate area of the brain, they exist independently of one another at this stage of processing.

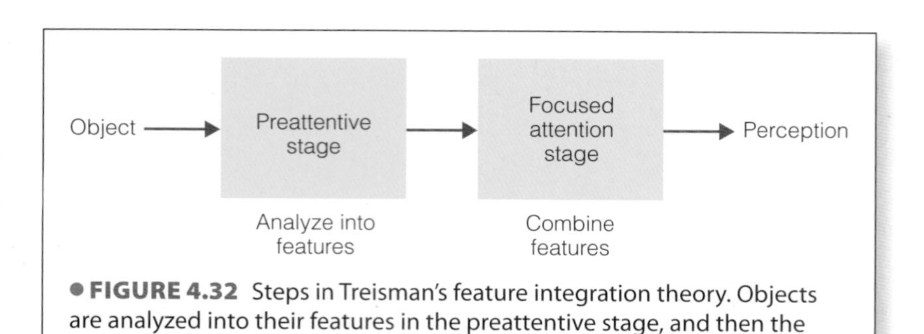

● **FIGURE 4.32** Steps in Treisman's feature integration theory. Objects are analyzed into their features in the preattentive stage, and then the features are combined later with the aid of attention.

The idea that an object is automatically broken into features may seem counterintuitive because when we look at an object, we see the whole object, not an object that has been divided into its individual features. The reason we aren't aware of this process of feature analysis is that it occurs early in the perceptual process, before we have become conscious of the object. Thus, when you see this book, you are conscious of its rectangular shape, but you are not aware that before you saw this rectangular shape, your perceptual system

● **FIGURE 4.33** Stimuli for illusory conjunction experiment. (Source: Reprinted from A. Treisman & H. Schmidt, "Illusory Conjunctions in the Perception of Objects," *Cognitive Psychology, 14,* 107–141, 1982, with permission from Elsevier.)

analyzed the book into individual features such as lines with different orientations.

To provide some perceptual evidence that objects are, in fact, analyzed into features, Anne Treisman and H. Schmidt (1982) did an ingenious experiment to show that early in the perceptual process, features may exist independently of one another. Treisman and Schmidt's display consisted of four objects flanked by two black numbers (● Figure 4.33). They flashed this display onto a screen for one-fifth of a second, followed by a random-dot masking field designed to eliminate any residual perception that might remain after the stimuli were turned off. Participants were told to report the black numbers first and then to report what they saw at each of the four locations where the shapes had been.

In 18 percent of the trials, participants reported seeing objects that were made up of a combination of features from two different stimuli. For example, after being presented with the display in Figure 4.33, in which the small triangle was red and the small circle was green, they might report seeing a small red circle and a small green triangle. These combinations of features from different stimuli are called **illusory conjunctions.** Illusory conjunctions can occur even if the stimuli differ greatly in shape and size. For example, a small blue circle and a large green square might be seen as a large blue square and a small green circle.

Although illusory conjunctions are usually demonstrated in laboratory experiments, they can occur in other situations as well. Recently I ran a class demonstration to illustrate that observers sometimes make errors in eyewitness testimony. In the demonstration, a male wearing a green shirt burst into the class, grabbed a yellow purse that was sitting on a desk (the owner of the purse was in on the demonstration!) and left the room. This event happened very rapidly and was a surprise to students in the class. Their task was to describe what had happened as eyewitnesses to a "crime." Interestingly enough, one of the students reported that a male wearing a yellow shirt grabbed a green purse from the desk! Interchanging the colors of these objects is an example of illusory conjunctions (Treisman, 2005).

According to Treisman, illusory conjunctions occur because at the beginning of the perceptual process each feature exists independently of the others. That is, features such as "redness," "curvature," or "tilted line" are, at this early stage of processing, not associated with a specific object. They are, in Treisman's (1986) words, "free floating," as shown in ● Figure 4.34, and can therefore be incorrectly combined if there is more than one object, especially in laboratory situations when briefly flashed stimuli are followed by a masking field.

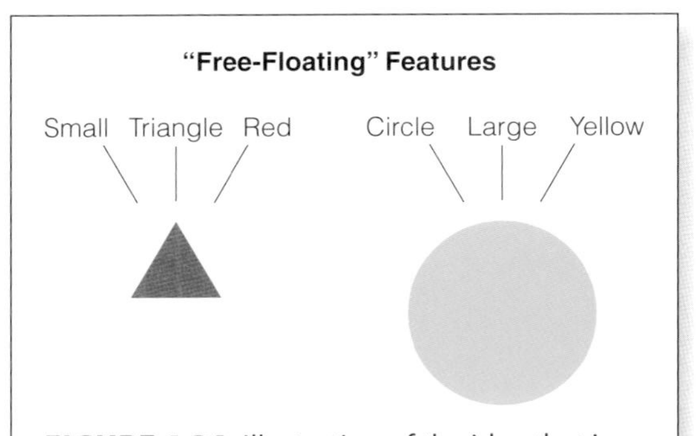

FIGURE 4.34 Illustration of the idea that in the preattentive stage an object's features are "free floating." Because they are not attached to a particular object, they can potentially become associated with any object in a display. When this happens, an illusory conjunction is created. (Source: Reprinted from A. Treisman & H. Schmidt, "Illusory Conjunctions in the Perception of Objects," *Cognitive Psychology, 14,* 107–141, 1982, with permission from Elsevier.)

You can think of these features as components of a visual "alphabet." At the very beginning of the process, perceptions of each of these components exist independently of one another, just as the letter tiles in a game of Scrabble exist as individual units when the tiles are scattered at the beginning of the game. However, just as the individual Scrabble tiles are combined to form words, the individual features combine to form perceptions of whole objects. According to Treisman's model, these features are combined in the second stage, called the **focused attention stage** (Figure 4.32). Once the features have been combined in this stage, we perceive the object.

During the focused attention stage, the observer's attention plays an important role in combining the features to create the perception of whole objects. To illustrate the importance of attention for combining the features, Treisman repeated the illusory conjunction experiment using the stimuli in Figure 4.33, but this time she instructed her participants to ignore the black numbers and to focus all of their attention on the four target items. This focusing of attention eliminated illusory conjunctions so that all of the shapes were paired with their correct colors.

• FIGURE 4.35 Stimuli used to show that top-down processing can reduce illusory conjunctions. (Source: Reprinted from A. Treisman & H. Schmidt, "Illusory Conjunctions in the Perception of Objects," *Cognitive Psychology, 14*, 107–141, 1982, with permission from Elsevier.)

When I describe this process in class, some students aren't convinced. One student said, "I think that when people look at an object, they don't break it into parts. They just see what they see." To convince this student (and the many others who, at the beginning of the course, are not comfortable with the idea that cognition sometimes involves rapid processes we aren't aware of), I describe the case of R.M., a patient who had parietal lobe damage that resulted in a condition called **Balint's syndrome.** The crucial characteristic of Balint's syndrome is an inability to focus attention on individual objects.

According to feature integration theory, lack of focused attention would make it difficult for R.M. to combine features correctly, and this is exactly what happened. When R.M. was presented with two different letters of different colors, such as a red T and a blue O, he reported illusory conjunctions such as "blue T" on 23 percent of the trials, even when he was able to view the letters for as long as 10 seconds (Friedman-Hill et al., 1995; Robertson et al., 1997). The case of R.M. illustrates how a breakdown in the brain can reveal processes that are not obvious when the brain is functioning normally.

The feature analysis approach involves mostly bottom-up processing because knowledge is usually not involved. In some situations, however, top-down processing can come into play. For example, when Treisman did an illusory conjunction experiment using stimuli such as the ones in • Figure 4.35 and asked participants to identify the objects, the usual illusory conjunctions occurred; the orange triangle, for example, would sometimes be perceived to be black. However, when she told participants that they were being shown a carrot, a lake, and a tire, illusory conjunctions were less likely to occur, and participants were more likely to perceive the triangular "carrot" as being orange. In this situation, the participants' knowledge of the usual colors of objects influenced their ability to correctly combine the features of each object. In our everyday experience, in which we are often perceiving familiar objects, top-down processing combines with feature analysis to help us perceive things accurately.

The Physiology of Attention

A great deal of research has studied the physiological mechanisms of attention. Two important results are that (1) attention enhances neural responding, and (2) attentional processing is distributed across a large number of areas in the brain.

COVERT ATTENTION ENHANCES NEURAL RESPONDING

Most research investigating how attention affects neural responding has studied how neural responding is affected by shifting attention covertly—that is, without eye movements. The reason for using covert tasks when studying how attention affects neural responding is that the eye movements that accompany overt attention cause a change in the image on the retina, which can cause a neural response. Thus, to be sure that any neural responses are caused not by changes in the image on the retina but by changes in attention, researchers use a covert attention procedure in which the eyes remain stationary.

In a covert attention experiment on monkeys, Carol Colby and coworkers (1995) trained a monkey to keep its eyes fixated on a dot (see • Figure 4.36) while a peripheral light was flashed at a location off to the right. In the "fixation only" condition (Figure 4.36a), the monkey's task was to continue looking at the fixation light and to release its hand from a bar when the *fixation* light dimmed. In the "fixation and attention" condition (Figure 4.36b), the monkey also kept looking at the fixation light but released the bar when the *peripheral stimulus* light dimmed. Thus, in the fixation and attention condition, the monkey had to pay attention to what was happening off to the side.

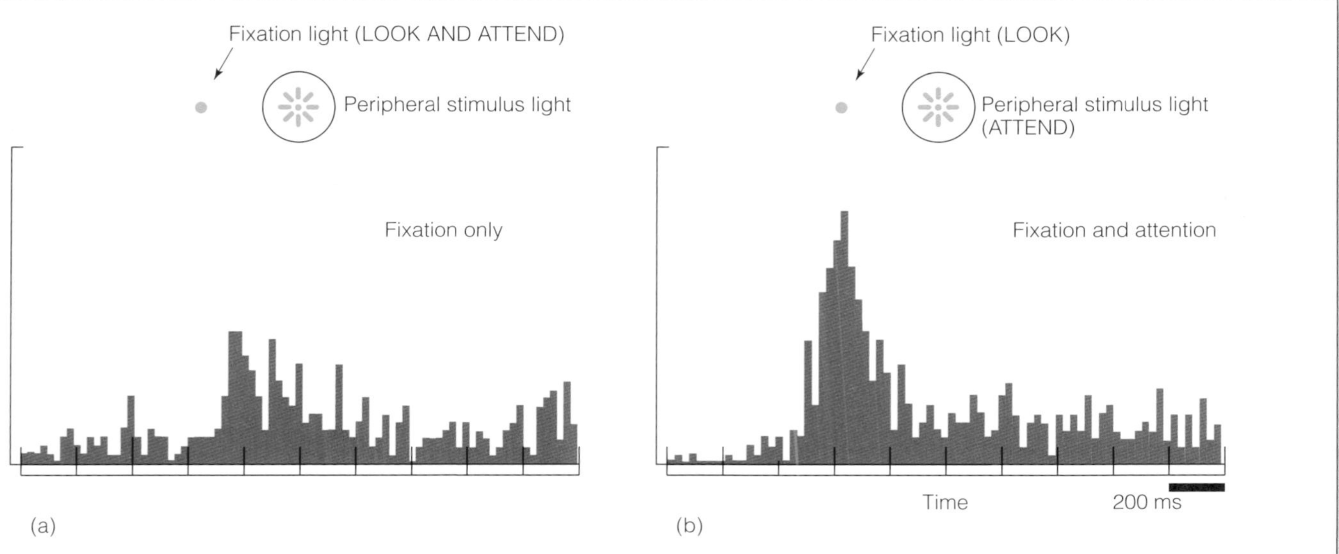

● **FIGURE 4.36** *Top*: Stimuli for Colby et al.'s (1995) selective attention experiment. The monkey always looked at the fixation light on the left. A peripheral stimulus light was flashed inside the circle on the right. *Below*: (a) Nerve firing when the monkey was looking at the fixation light but was not paying attention to the peripheral light; (b) firing when the monkey was looking at the fixation light and was paying attention to the peripheral light. (Source: C. L. Colby, J. R. Duhamel, & M. E. Goldberg, "Oculocentric Spatial Representation in Parietal Cortex," *Cerebral Cortex, 5,* 470–481, 1995. Copyright © 1995 Oxford University Press. Reprinted with permission from Oxford University Press.)

As the monkey was performing these tasks, Colby recorded from a neuron in the parietal cortex that fired to the peripheral light. The records in Figure 4.36 show that this neuron responded poorly when the monkey was not paying attention to the light but that the response increased when the monkey shifted its attention off to the side—even though it was still looking directly at the fixation light. Because the image of the light on the monkey's retina was always the same, the greater response when the monkey was paying attention to the peripheral light must have been caused by the monkey's attention to the light (also see Desimone & Duncan, 1995; McAdams & Reid, 2005; Moran & Desimone, 1985). This result means that a neuron's response can be affected not just by which receptors are stimulated but also by other factors, such as whether the observer is interested in the stimulus or whether the stimulus is important for carrying out a task.

This larger response due to attention to a stimulus has also been demonstrated in humans using fMRI. We will now describe an experiment that shows both that attention enhances responding and that this attentional enhancement occurs in many areas in the visual system.

ATTENTIONAL PROCESSING IS DISTRIBUTED ACROSS THE CORTEX

Gordon Shulman and coworkers (1999) showed that attention to a particular direction of motion increases activity in a number of brain structures. Using fMRI, they measured participants' brain activity while participants performed a task in which they paid attention to a specific direction of motion. Participants saw either (1) a cue that alerted them to pay attention to a particular direction of motion or (2) a cue indicating that they should just passively observe the display on the screen (● Figure 4.37a). Following the cue, participants saw *random motion*, which was created by a field of dots that were moving in random directions (like the snow on a TV set that isn't tuned to a channel). After about a second, some of the dots started moving in the cued direction of motion, a condition called *coherent motion* because a number of dots were moving in the same direction. If the participants had seen

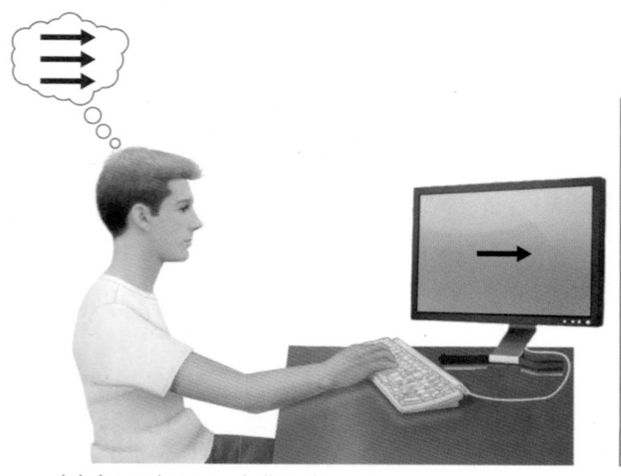

● **FIGURE 4.37** (a) Participants in Shulman and coworkers' (1999) experiment saw either a cue indicating which direction of a moving dot display they should attend to (the arrow shown here) or a cue indicating that they should passively observe the moving dot display. (b) After seeing random dot movement for about a second, participants saw coherent movement in a particular direction. Participants in the attention condition pressed a key when they saw coherent motion. Participants in the passive group continued to observe the display.

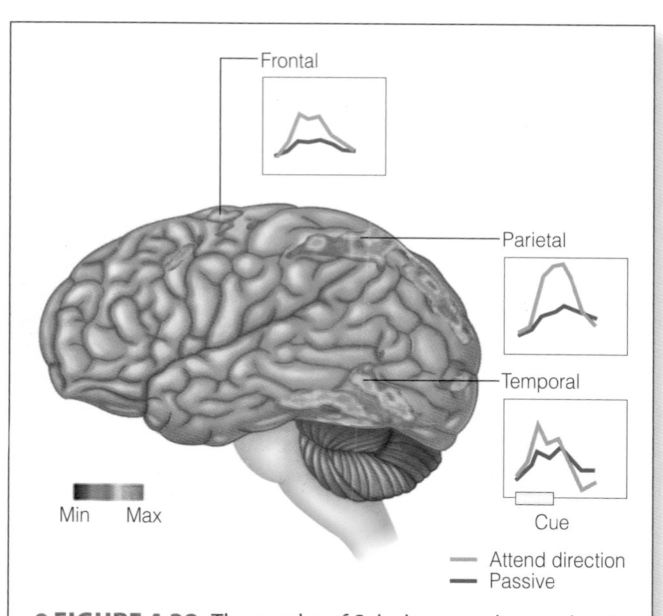

● **FIGURE 4.38** The results of Schulman and coworkers' (1999) experiment, showing some of the brain areas that were activated by viewing the moving dots. The graphs indicate the amount of brain activity when participants were cued to pay attention to a particular direction of movement (orange lines) and when they were cued to just passively view the moving dots (green lines).

(Source: From M. Corbetta & G. L. Shulman, "Control of Goal-Directed and Stimulus Driven Attention in the Brain," *Nature Reviews Neuroscience, 3,* 201–215, Figure 2, p. 203, 2002. Reprinted by permission of Macmillan Publishers Ltd.)

the direction cue, their task was to press a key when they saw the coherent motion (● Figure 4.37b). If they had seen the other cue, they were to continue passively observing the display. Brain activity was measured during and after the cue was presented, but before the coherent motion.

The orange lines in ● Figure 4.38 indicate that attention to an expected direction of motion caused brain activity to increase in a number of brain areas. The green lines indicate brain activity for the passive condition. The main significance of this result is that attention increases activity throughout the brain.

Widespread attentional effects have been demonstrated in many other experiments as well. ● Figure 4.39 shows locations of areas that Michael Posner and Mary Rothbart (2007) have identified as being involved in three different types of attentional processing: (1) *Alerting* is achieving a high sensitivity to incoming stimuli, like that achieved by air traffic controllers who must be continually vigilant. (2) *Orienting* is focusing attention where visual targets may appear. This occurs in both overt attention, when the person shifts attention by making an eye movement, and covert attention, when attention shifts without eye movements, as in the precueing task. (3) *Executive* control of attention occurs for tasks that involve conflict, such as the Stroop task or flanker compatibility task.

For our purposes, the names of the specific brain structures aren't important; what is important is that so many different areas of the brain are involved. However, it is worth noting that executive functions, which involve resolving conflicts between responses caused by different stimuli, are served by areas in the frontal lobe, which is also the site of high-level thinking, such as solving problems and making decisions.

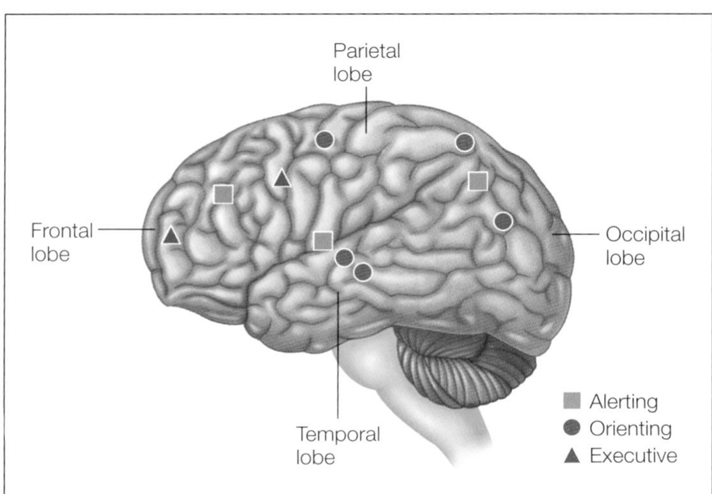

● **FIGURE 4.39** Areas that are associated with different kinds of attention. (Source: From M. I. Posner & M. K. Rothbart, "Research on Attention Networks as a Model for the Integration of Psychological Science," *Annual Review of Psychology, 58,* 1–23, Figure 2, p. 6, 2007. Reprinted by permission.)

Something to Consider

Attention in Social Situations—The Case of Autism

Attention is a crucial component of social situations. We pay attention not only to what others are saying, but also to facial expressions and body language that provide information about the person's thoughts, emotions, and feelings. Recent research has shown, for example, that the direction of another person's gaze is a determinant of attention. When Alan Kingstone and coworkers (2003) presented pictures of eyes looking in different directions, participants shifted their attention toward the direction the eyes were looking. Eyes, according to Kingstone, influence attention because the perception of someone else's eye movements is a powerful social signal.

The link between attention and social interactions becomes especially evident when we consider a situation in which that link is disturbed, as occurs in people with **autism.** Autism is a serious developmental disorder in which one of the major symptoms is withdrawal of contact from other people. People with autism typically do not make eye contact with others and have difficulty telling what emotions others are experiencing in social situations.

Research has revealed many differences in both behavior and brain processes between autistic and nonautistic people (Grelotti et al., 2002). Ami Klin and coworkers (2003) point out the following paradox: Even though people with autism can often solve reasoning problems that involve social situations, they cannot function when placed in an actual social situation. One possible reason for this involves differences in the way autistic people observe what is happening. Klin and coworkers demonstrated this by comparing eye fixations of autistic and nonautistic people as they watched the film *Who's Afraid of Virginia Woolf?*

● Figure 4.40 shows fixations on a shot of George Segal's and Sandy Dennis's faces. The shot occurs just after another character in the film, played by Richard Burton, has smashed a bottle. The nonautistic observers fixated on Segal's eyes in order to access his emotional reaction, but the autistic observers looked near Sandy Dennis's mouth or off to the side.

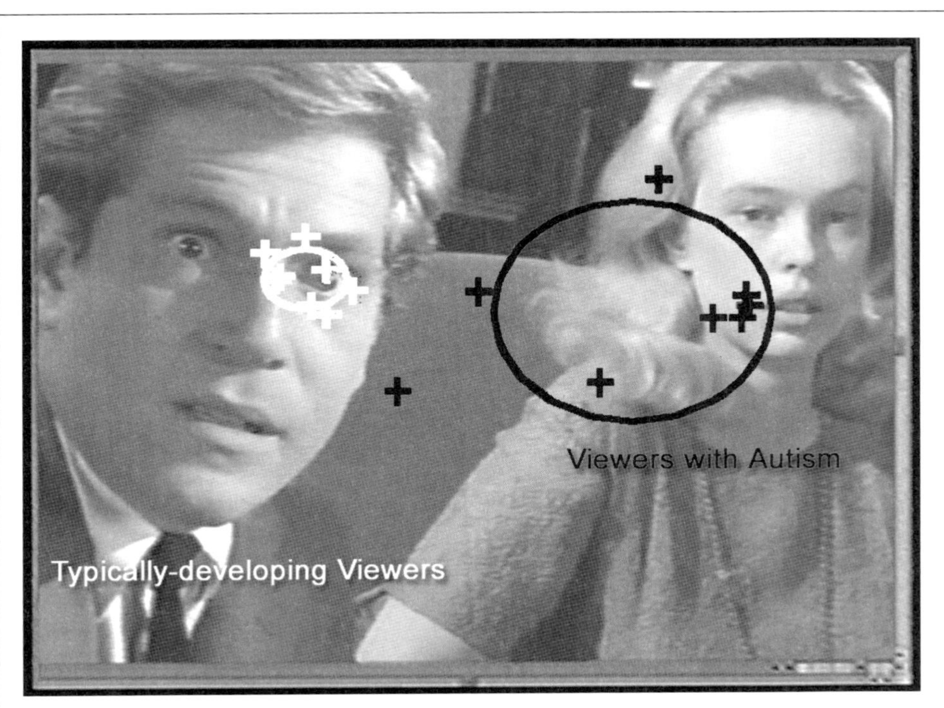

● **FIGURE 4.40** Where people look when viewing this image from the film *Who's Afraid of Virginia Woolf?* Nonautistic viewers: white crosses; autistic viewers: black crosses. (Source: A. Klin, W. Jones, R. Schultz, & F. Volkmar, "The Enactive Mind, or From Actions to Cognition: Lessons From Autism." The Royal Society, 2003. Published online.)

Another difference between how autistic and nonautistic observers direct their attention is related to the tendency to direct their eyes to the place where a person is pointing. ● Figure 4.41 compares the fixations of a nonautistic person (shown in white) and an autistic person (shown in black). In this scene,

• FIGURE 4.41 Scan paths for nonautistic viewers (white path) and autistic viewers (black path) in response to the picture and dialogue while viewing this shot from *Whose Afraid of Virginia Woolf?* (Source: A. Klin, W. Jones, R. Schultz, & F. Volkmar, "The Enactive Mind, or From Actions to Cognition: Lessons From Autism." The Royal Society, 2003. Published online.)

Segal points to the painting and asks Burton's character, "Who did the painting?" The nonautistic person follows the pointing movement from Segal's finger to the painting to Burton's face to await a reply. In contrast, the autistic observer looks elsewhere first, then back and forth between the pictures.

All of these results indicate that because of the way autistic people attend or don't attend to events as they unfold in a social situation, they see different things in the environment than nonautistic observers. People with autism look more at things, whereas nonautistic observers look at other people's actions and especially at their faces and eyes. Autistic observers therefore create a mental representation of a situation that does not include much of the information that nonautistic observers usually use in interacting with others.

The eye movement patterns we have described are probably not the *cause* of difficulties in social situations for people with autism. Their difficulties may have more to do with negative emotional reactions they experience when looking at or interacting with other people. These negative emotions influence where they look, which influences how well they can understand what is happening, which in turn makes it even more difficult to function in social situations. Our understanding of autism is still far from complete, however, and a great deal of research is currently in progress to determine the physiological and behavioral mechanisms involved in autism.

TEST YOURSELF 4.3

1. What is overt attention? What is the relation between overt attention and eye movements?
2. How are eye movements determined by bottom-up processes, such as physical characteristics of the stimuli? How are eye movements determined by top-down processes, such as people's knowledge about characteristics of the environment, their interests, and the type of task?
3. What is covert attention? Location-based attention? Describe the precueing procedure used by Posner. What does the result of Posner's experiment indicate about the effect of attention on information processing?
4. Describe the Egly precueing experiment. What is the same-object advantage, and how was it demonstrated by Egly's experiment?
5. Describe Treisman's feature integration theory. What does the theory seek to explain about perceiving objects? What are the stages of the theory, and at what point does attention become involved?
6. What are illusory conjunctions, and what do they demonstrate about feature analysis? How have illusory conjunction experiments supported the role of attention in feature analysis? How do experiments with Balint's syndrome patients support feature integration theory?

7. Describe physiological research on how covert attention influences neural responding in monkeys and in humans. What is the evidence that attentional processing is distributed throughout the brain?
8. How do eye movements of autistic and normally developing people compare?

CHAPTER SUMMARY

1. Selective attention, the ability to focus on one message while ignoring all others, has been demonstrated using the dichotic listening procedure.
2. A number of models have been proposed to explain the process of selective attention. Broadbent's filter model proposes that the attended message is separated from the incoming signal early in the analysis of the signal. Treisman's model proposes later separation and adds a dictionary unit to explain how the unattended message can sometimes get through. Late selection models propose that selection doesn't occur until messages are processed enough to determine their meaning.
3. The flanker compatibility task has been used to determine how cognitive load affects attention. Generally, when the load is low, task-irrelevant stimuli are processed even if the observer is focusing attention on another stimulus. However, when the load is high, task-irrelevant stimuli are not processed.
4. The Stroop effect demonstrates how a powerful task-irrelevant stimulus, such as meaningful words that result in a response that competes with the observer's task, can capture attention.
5. Divided attention is possible for easy tasks, or for highly practiced difficult tasks. In these situations, automatic processing is possible. Divided attention for highly demanding tasks requires controlled processing.
6. Driver inattention is one of the major causes of automobile accidents. There is evidence that using cell phones during driving is associated with increases in traffic accidents and decreases in performance of driving-related tasks.
7. Inattentional blindness and change blindness experiments provide evidence that without attention we may fail to perceive things that are clearly visible in the field of view.
8. Eye movements are mechanisms of overt attention. Overt attention is determined by bottom-up processes such as stimulus salience and by top-down processes such as scene schemas and task demands, which influence how eye movements are directed to parts of a scene.
9. Visual attention can be directed to different places in a scene even without eye movements, a process called covert attention. The effect of covert attention has been demonstrated by precueing experiments, which have shown that covert attention to a location enhances processing at that location. This is called location-based attention.
10. Object-based attention occurs when attention is directed toward specific objects. The enhancing effects of attention spread throughout an object; this is called the same-object advantage.
11. Feature integration theory proposes two stages of processing: preattentive processing and focused attention. The basic idea is that objects are analyzed into their features and attention is necessary to combine these features to create perception of an object.
12. Covert attention enhances responding in single neurons in the monkey brain and increases activity in a number of areas of the human brain. fMRI experiments have shown that attention causes distributed activity across the cortex.
13. People with autism do not direct their attention in social situations in the same way as nonautistic observers. Autistic people attend to things, where nonautistic people attend more to other people.

Think ABOUT IT

1. Pick two items from the following list, and decide how difficult it would be to do both at the same time. Some things are difficult to do simultaneously because of physical limitations. For example, it would be extremely difficult to dance while rock climbing! Others things are difficult to do simultaneously because of cognitive limitations. For each pair of activities that you pick, decide why it would be easy or difficult to do them simultaneously. Be sure to take the idea of cognitive load into account.

Driving a car
Reading a book for pleasure
Doing math problems
Talking to a friend
Thinking about tomorrow
Rock climbing
Talking on a cell phone
Flying a kite
Walking in the woods
Listening to a story
Writing a paper for class
Dancing

2. Find someone who is willing to participate in a brief "observation exercise." Cover a picture (preferably one that contains a number of objects or details) with a piece of paper. Tell the person that you are going to uncover the picture and that the task is to report everything that he or she sees. Then uncover the picture very briefly (less than a second), and have the person write down, or tell you, what he or she saw. Then repeat this procedure, increasing the exposure of the picture to a few seconds, so the person can direct his or her attention to different parts of the picture. Perhaps try this a third time, allowing even more time to observe the picture. From the person's responses, what can you conclude about the role of attention in determining what people are aware of in their environment?
3. Art composition books often state that it is possible to arrange elements in a painting in a way that controls both *what* a person looks at in a picture and the *order* in which a person looks at things. What would the results of research on visual attention have to say about this idea?
4. How does the attention involved in carrying out actions in the environment differ from the attention involved in scanning a picture for details, as in the previous "observation exercise"?
5. As you sit in a stadium watching a football game, there is a lot going on in the game, in the stands, and on the sidelines. Which things that you might look at would involve object-based attention, and which would involve location-based attention?
6. As the quarterback steps back to pass, the offensive line blocks out the defense, so the quarterback has plenty of time to check out what is happening downfield and hits an open receiver. Later in the game, two 300-pound linemen get through to the quarterback. While he scrambles for safety, he fails to see the open receiver downfield and instead throws a pass toward another receiver that is almost intercepted. How can these two situations be related to the way selective attention is affected by task load?
7. Given the mounting evidence that talking on cell phones (even hands-free) while driving increases the chances of having an accident, it could be argued that laws should be passed making all cell phone use illegal while driving. What would be your reaction if this occurred? Why?

If You WANT TO KNOW MORE

1. **Losing a sense.** Loss of one sense can cause changes both in a person's ability to perceive with the other senses and in the physiological mechanisms of the remaining senses.

Proksch, J., & Bavelier, D. (2002). Changes in the spatial distribution of visual attention after early deafness. *Journal of Cognitive Neuroscience, 14*, 687–701.

2. **Video games.** It has been shown that practice with video games can improve a person's ability to process visual information.

Green, C. S., & Bavelier, D. (2003). Action video game modifies visual selective attention. *Nature, 423*, 534–537.

Green, C. S., & Bavelier, D. (2006). Effect of action video games on the spatial distribution of visuo-spatial attention. *Journal of Experimental Psychology: Human Perception & Performance, 32*, 1465–1478.

3. **Visual neglect.** An effect of brain damage called visual neglect causes people to pay attention to only half of their visual field.

Behrmann, M., & Tipper, S. P. (1999). Attention accesses multiple reference frames: Evidence from visual neglect. *Journal of Experimental Psychology: Human Perception and Performance, 25*, 83–101.

Halligan, P. W., Fink, G. R., Marshall, J. C., & Vallar, G. (2003). Spatial cognition: Evidence from visual neglect. *Trends in Cognitive Sciences, 7*, 125–133.

Tipper, S. P., & Behrmann, M. (1996). Object-centered not scene-based visual neglect. *Journal of Experimental Psychology: Human Perception and Performance, 22*, 1261–1278.

4. **Attention and memory.** A connection has been demonstrated between attention and our ability to hold information in memory.

Awh, E., Vogel, E. K., & Oh, S.-H. (2006). Interactions between attention and working memory. *Neuroscience, 139*, 201–206.

Conway, A. R. A, Cowan, N., & Bunting, M. F. (2001). The cocktail party phenomenon revisited: The importance of working memory capacity. *Psychonomic Bulletin and Review, 8*, 331–335.

Key TERMS

Attention, 82
Attenuation theory of attention, 86
Attenuator, 86
Autism, 109
Automatic processing, 92
Balint's syndrome, 106
Bottleneck model, 85
Change blindness, 97
Cocktail party effect, 85
Cognitive load, 87
Cognitive resources, 87
Compatible flanker, 88

Controlled processing, 93
Covert attention, 102
Dichotic listening, 84
Dictionary unit, 86
Divided attention, 82
Early selection model, 84
Endogenous attention, 98
Exogenous attention, 98
Eye tracker, 99
Feature integration theory, 104
Fixation, 99
Flanker compatibility task, 88
Focused attention stage, 105
High-load tasks, 87
Illusory conjunctions, 105
Inattentional blindness, 96
Incompatible flanker, 88
Late selection model, 87
Location-based attention, 102
Low-load tasks, 87
Object-based attention, 102
Overt attention, 98
Preattentive stage, 104
Precueing, 102
Saccadic eye movements, 99
Same-object advantage, 103
Scene schema, 100
Selective attention, 82
Shadowing, 84
Stimulus salience, 100
Stroop effect, 89

Media RESOURCES

The Cognitive Psychology Book Companion Website

www.cengage.com/international

Prepare for quizzes and exams with online resources—including a glossary, flashcards, tutorial quizzes, crossword puzzles, and more.

CogLab

To experience these experiments for yourself, go to coglab.wadsworth.com. Be sure to read each experiment's setup instructions before you go to the experiment itself. Otherwise, you won't know which keys to press.

Primary Labs

Stroop effect How reaction time to naming font colors is affected by the presence of conflicting information from words. (p. 89)

Change detection A task involving detecting changes in alternating scenes. (p. 96)

Spatial cueing How cueing attention affects reaction time to the cued area. Evidence for the spotlight model of attention. (p. 102)

Related Labs

Attentional blink How paying attention to one stimulus affects the ability to attend to a subsequent stimulus.

Simon effect How speed and accuracy of responding is affected by the location of the response to a stimulus.

Von Restorff effect How the distinctiveness of a stimulus can influence memory.

5 Introduction to Memory

Experienced chess players have stored a large number of game situations in their memories, as well as knowledge about how past games have unfolded. Research has shown that experienced chess players are much better at remembering the arrangements of pieces on a chessboard than are inexperienced chess players. This finding has implications for basic mechanisms of memory.

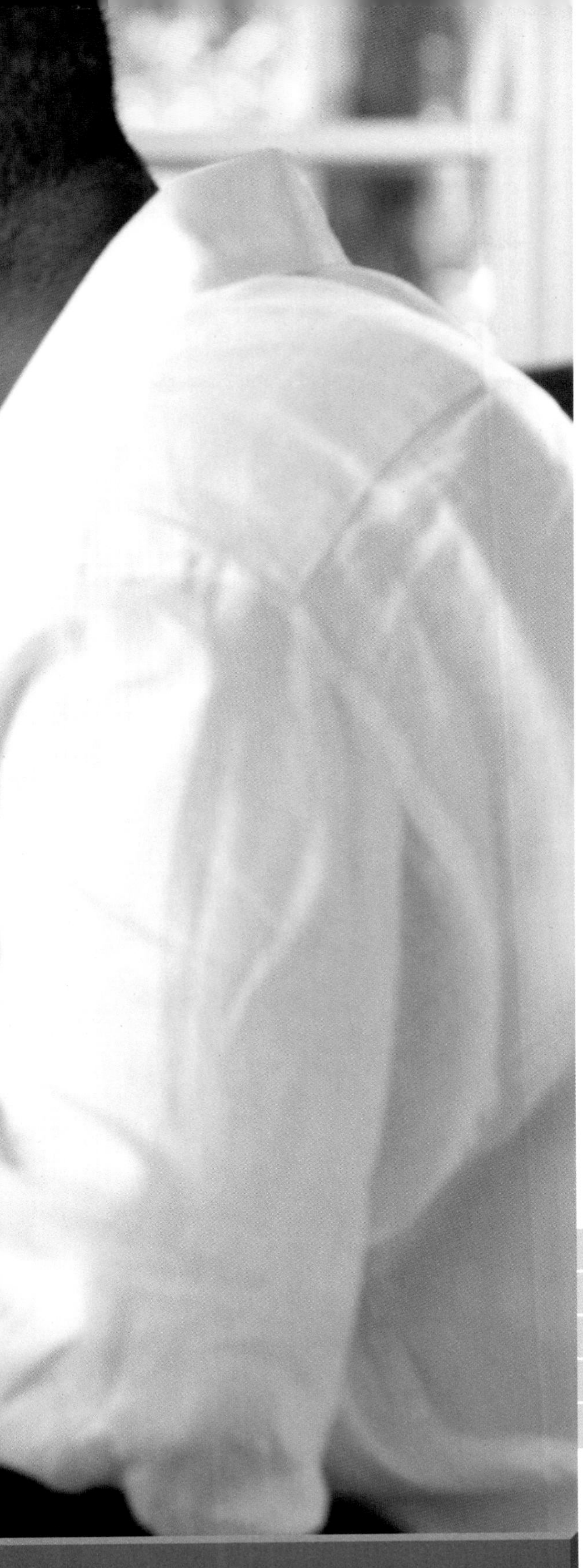

Some Questions We Will Consider

▶ Why can we remember a telephone number long enough to place a call, but then we forget it almost immediately? (123)

▶ How is memory involved in processes such as doing math problems? (131)

▶ Do we use the same memory system to remember things we have seen and things we have heard? (132)

▶ Is there a relationship between memory capacity and intelligence? (141)

"Has it ever struck you...that life is all memory, except for the one present moment that goes by so quickly you hardly catch it going? It's really all memory...except for each passing moment."

Tennessee Williams, *The Milk Train Doesn't Stop Here Anymore*

What you will read in this chapter and the three chapters that follow supports the idea, stated above, that "life is all memory." We will see how our memory of the past not only provides a record of a lifetime of events we have experienced and knowledge we have learned, but also even affects "each passing moment" by enabling us to do things that are happening "right now," such as having conversations, solving problems, and making decisions.

The Importance of Memory in Our Lives

The definition of memory provides the first indication of its importance in our lives: **Memory** is *the processes involved in retaining, retrieving, and using information about stimuli, images, events, ideas, and skills after the original information is no longer present.* The fact that memory retains information that is no longer present means that we can use our memory as a "time machine" to go back just a moment—to the words you read at the beginning of this sentence—or many years—to events as early as a childhood birthday party. This "mental time travel" afforded by memory can place you back in a situation, so you feel as though you are reliving it, even to the extent of experiencing feelings that occurred long ago. But memory goes beyond reexperiencing events. We also use memory to remember what we need to do later in the day, to remember facts we have learned, and to use skills we have acquired.

If you were asked to create a "Top 10" list of what you use memory for, what would you include? When I ask my students to do this, most of their items relate to day-to-day activities. The top five items on their list involved remembering the following things:

1. Material for exams
2. Their daily schedule
3. Names
4. Phone numbers
5. Directions to places

Remembering material for exams is probably high on most students' lists, but it is likely that other people, such as business executives, construction workers, homemakers, or politicians, would create lists that differ from the ones created by college students in ways that reflect the demands of their particular lives. A construction worker's list would not be likely to include remembering the material that will be on the next cognitive psychology exam, but might include remembering the procedure for framing a house.

One reason I ask students to create a "memory list" is to get them to think about how important memory is in their day-to-day lives. But the main reason is to make them aware of the things they *don't* include on their lists, because they take them for granted. A few of these things include labeling familiar objects (you know you are reading a "book" because of your past experience with books), having conversations (you need memory to keep track of the flow of a conversation), knowing what to do in a restaurant (you need to remember a sequence of events, starting with being seated and ending with paying the check), and finding your way to class (you need to remember where your class is and the spatial layout of part of the campus).

● **FIGURE 5.1** Clive Wearing's diary looked like this. Sometimes he would cross out previous entries because he could only remember writing the most recent entry.

The list of things that depend on memory is an extremely long one because just about everything we do depends on remembering what we have experienced in the past. Perhaps the most powerful way to demonstrate the importance of memory is to consider what happens to people's lives when they lose their memory. Consider, for example, the case of Clive Wearing (Annenberg, 2000; D. Wearing, 2005).

Wearing was a highly respected musician and choral director in England who, in his 40s, contracted viral encephalitis, which destroyed parts of his temporal lobe that are important for forming new memories. Because of his brain damage, Wearing lives totally within the most recent one or two minutes of his life. He remembers what just happened and forgets everything else. When he meets someone, and the person leaves the room and returns three minutes later, Wearing reacts as if he hadn't met the person earlier. Because of his inability to form new memories, he constantly feels he has just become conscious for the first time.

This feeling is made poignantly clear by Wearing's diary, which contains hundreds of entries like "I have woken up for the first time" and "I am alive" (● Figure 5.1). But Wearing has no memory of ever writing anything except for the sentence he has just written. When questioned about previous entries, Wearing acknowledges that they are in his handwriting, but because he has no memory of writing them, he denies that they are his. It is no wonder that he is confused, and not surprising that he describes his life as being "like death." His loss of memory has robbed him of his ability to participate in life in any meaningful way, and he needs to be constantly cared for by others.

Studying Memory

What kinds of things do we want to know about memory? Here are a few of the questions that occur to me:

1. Why am I unable to remember some things, like where my keys are and what happened during my 10th birthday party?
2. Why is it that when I describe to my wife what I remember about something we both experienced, her memory of the event is different from mine?
3. What is the best way to get things into memory, especially remembering people's names?
4. Why is it that sometimes I know that I know something, but I just can't remember it, then later it pops into my head?
5. What is happening in my brain that causes all of the above things to happen?

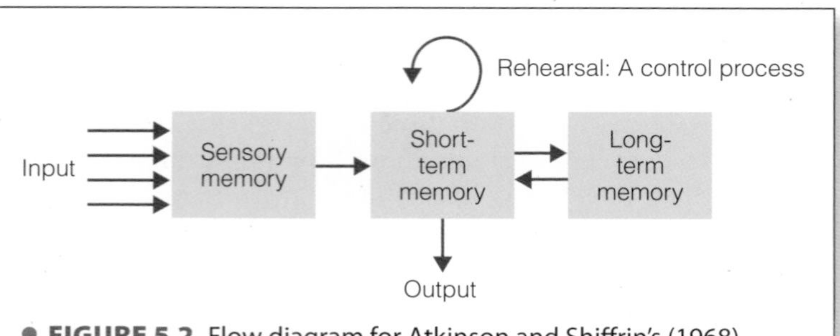

• **FIGURE 5.2** Flow diagram for Atkinson and Shiffrin's (1968) model of memory. This model, which is described in the text, is called the modal model because it contained features of many of the memory models that were being proposed in the 1960s.

You may have wondered about questions similar to these, as well as others that apply to your life. Any explanation of how memory works needs to be able to answer these kinds of questions. But what is the best way to go about discovering how memory works? One tactic cognitive psychologists have used is to create models like Donald Broadbent's filter model in Figure 4.3, that propose a series of processing stages to explain how people can selectively attend to one message out of many. One of the advantages of models is that they help organize what we know about an area. They can also help suggest questions to ask. For example, we saw in Chapter 4 that attention researchers did many experiments designed to determine how the filter in Broadbent's model works.

Models have played a large role in memory research. We begin our discussion of memory by describing a model proposed by Richard Atkinson and Richard Shiffrin (1968). This model, shown in • Figure 5.2, is called the **modal model of memory** because it included many of the features of memory models that were being proposed in the 1960s. This model became extremely influential and shaped research on memory for many years. The stages in the model are called the **structural features** of the model. There are three major structural features:

1. *Sensory memory* is an initial stage that holds all incoming information for seconds or fractions of a second.
2. *Short-term memory (STM)* holds 5–7 items for about 15–30 seconds. We will describe the characteristics of short-term memory in this chapter.
3. *Long-term memory (LTM)* can hold a large amount of information for years or even decades. We will describe long-term memory in Chapters 6, 7, and 8.

Atkinson and Shiffrin also described the memory system as including **control processes**, which are active processes that can be controlled by the person and may differ from one task to another. An example of a control process is **rehearsal**—repeating a stimulus over and over, as you might repeat a telephone number in order to hold it in your mind after looking it up in the phone book or on the Internet. Other examples of control processes are (1) strategies you might use to help make a stimulus more memorable, such as relating the numbers in a phone number to a familiar date in history, and (2) strategies of attention that help you focus on information that is particularly important or interesting.

To illustrate how the structural features and control processes operate, let's consider what happens as Rachel looks up the number for Mineo's Pizza on the Internet (• Figure 5.3). When she first looks at the screen, all of the information that enters her eyes is registered in sensory memory (Figure 5.3a). Rachel uses the control process of selective attention to focus on the number for Mineo's, so the number enters short-term memory (Figure 5.3b), and she uses the control process of rehearsal to keep it there (Figure 5.3c).

Rachel knows she will want to use the number again later, so she decides that in addition to storing the number in her cell phone, she is going to memorize the number so it will also be stored in her mind. The process she uses to memorize the number, which involves control processes we will discuss in Chapter 6, transfers the number into long-term memory, where it is stored (Figure 5.3d). The process of storing the number in long-term memory is called **encoding**. A few days later, when Rachel's urge for pizza returns, she remembers the number. This process of remembering information that is stored in long-term memory is called **retrieval** (Figure 5.3e).

One thing that becomes apparent from our example is that the components of memory do not act in isolation. Long-term memory is essential for storing information, but before we can become *aware* of this stored information, it must be moved back into STM. We will now consider each component of the model, beginning with sensory memory.

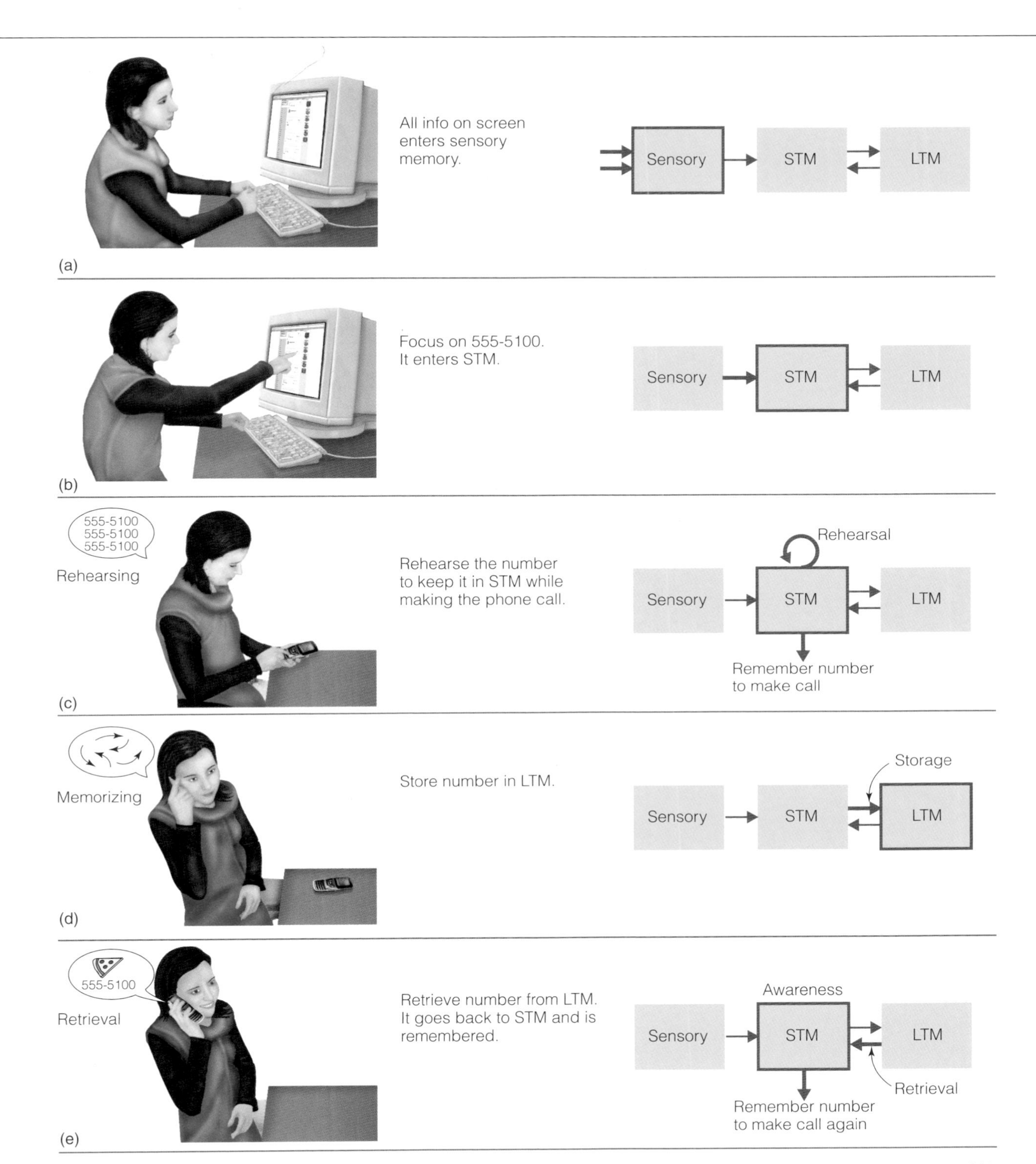

● FIGURE 5.3 What happens in different parts of Rachel's memory as she is (a and b) looking up the phone number, (c) calling the pizza shop, and (d) memorizing the number. A few days later, (e) she retrieves the number from long-term memory to order pizza again. The parts of the modal model that are outlined in red indicate which processes are activated for each action that Rachel takes.

Sensory Memory

Sensory memory is the retention, for brief periods of time, of the effects of sensory stimulation. We can demonstrate this brief retention for the effects of visual stimulation with two familiar examples: the trail left by a moving sparkler and the experience of seeing a film.

THE SPARKLER'S TRAIL AND THE PROJECTOR'S SHUTTER

It is dark, sometime around the Fourth of July, and you put a match to the tip of a sparkler. As sparks begin radiating from the hot spot at the tip, you sweep the sparkler through the air, creating a trail of light (● Figure 5.4). Although it appears that this trail is created by light left by the sparkler as you wave it through the air, there is, in fact, no light along this trail. The lighted trail is a creation of your mind, which retains a perception of the sparkler's light for a fraction of a second. This retention of the perception of light in your mind is called the **persistence of vision**.

Something similar happens while you are watching a film in a darkened movie theater. You may see actions moving smoothly across the screen, but what is actually projected is quite different. We can appreciate what is happening on the screen by considering the sequence of events that occur as a film is projected. First, a single film frame is positioned in front of the projector lens, and when the projector's shutter opens, the image on the film frame flashes onto the screen. The shutter then closes, so the film can move to the next frame without causing a blurred image, and during that time, the screen is dark. When the next frame has arrived in front of the lens, the shutter reopens, flashing the next image onto the screen. This process is repeated rapidly, 24 times per second, so 24 still images are flashed on the screen every second, with each image separated by a brief period of darkness (see Table 5.1).

A person viewing the film doesn't see the dark intervals between the images because the persistence of vision fills in the darkness by retaining the image of the previous frame. If the period between the images is too long, the mind can't fill in the darkness completely, and the intensity of the image appears to flicker. This is what happened in the early movies when the projectors flashed images more slowly, causing longer dark

Perceptual trail

BAZUKI MUHAMMAD/Reuters/Corbis

● **FIGURE 5.4** (a) A sparkler can cause a trail of light when it is moved rapidly. (b) This trail occurs because the perception of the light is briefly held in the mind.

TABLE 5.1 Persistence of Vision in Film

What Happens?	What Is on the Screen?	What Do You Perceive?
Film frame 1 is projected.	Picture 1	Picture 1
Shutter closes and film moves to the next frame.	Darkness	Picture 1 (persistence of vision)
Shutter opens and film frame 2 is projected.	Picture 2	Picture 2*

*Note that the images appear so rapidly (24 per second) that you don't see individual images, but see a moving image created by the rapid sequence of images. This illusion of movement is called *apparent movement* (see Goldstein, 2010).

intervals. This is why these early films were called "flickers," a term that remains today, when we talk about going to the "flicks."

SPERLING'S EXPERIMENT: MEASURING THE CAPACITY AND DURATION OF THE SENSORY STORE

The persistence of vision effect that adds a trail to our perception of moving sparklers and fills in the dark spaces between frames in a film has been known since the early days of psychology (Boring, 1942). But George Sperling (1960) wondered how much *information* people can take in from briefly presented stimuli. He determined this in a famous experiment in which he flashed an array of letters, like the one in ● Figure 5.5a, on the screen for 50 milliseconds (50/1000 second) and asked his participants to report as many of the letters as possible. This part of the experiment used the **whole report method**; that is, participants were asked to report as many letters as possible from the whole matrix. Given this task, they were able to report an average of 4.5 out of the 12 letters.

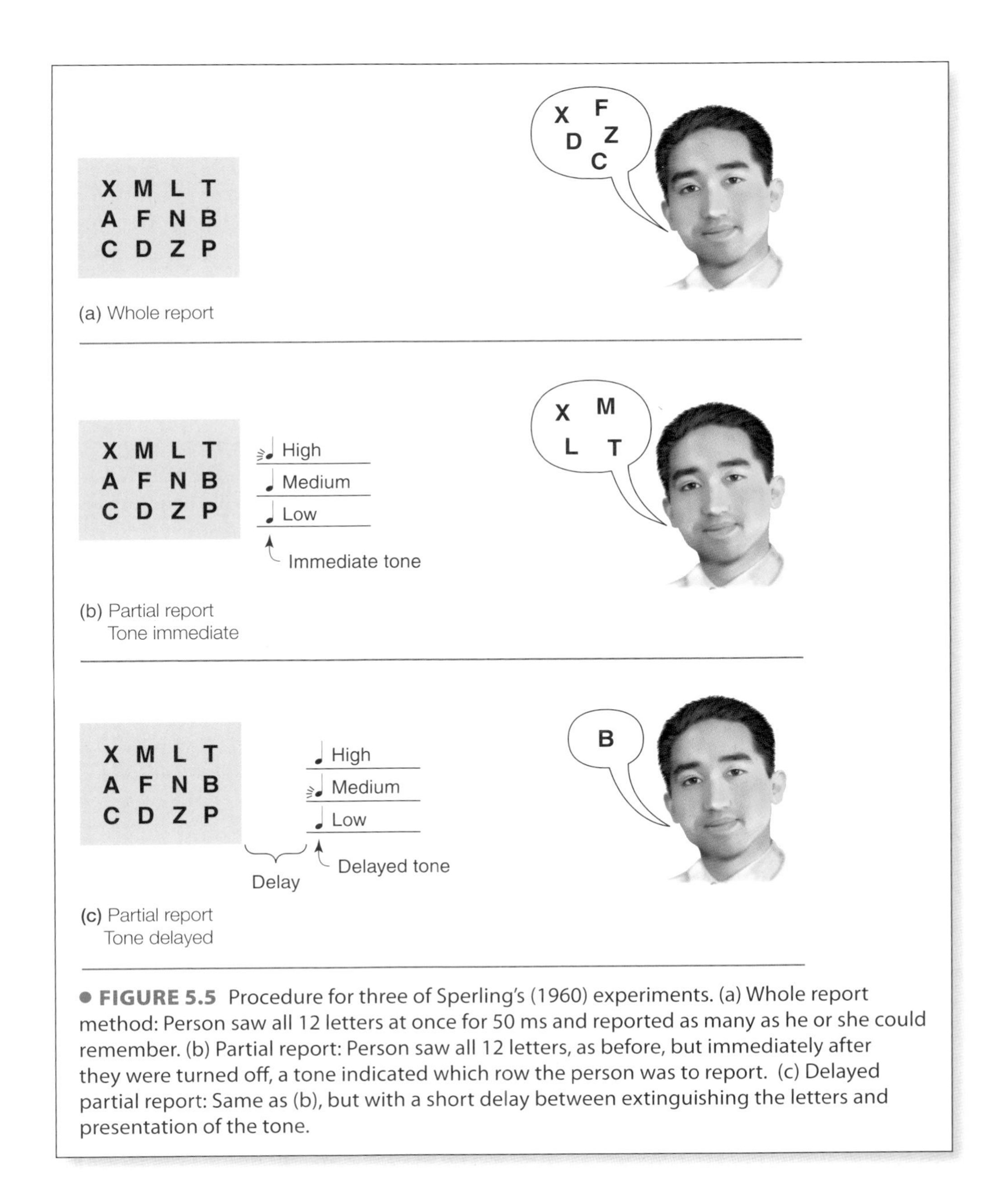

● **FIGURE 5.5** Procedure for three of Sperling's (1960) experiments. (a) Whole report method: Person saw all 12 letters at once for 50 ms and reported as many as he or she could remember. (b) Partial report: Person saw all 12 letters, as before, but immediately after they were turned off, a tone indicated which row the person was to report. (c) Delayed partial report: Same as (b), but with a short delay between extinguishing the letters and presentation of the tone.

At this point Sperling could have concluded that because the exposure was brief, participants saw only an average of 4.5 of the 12 letters. However, there is another possibility: Perhaps participants saw most of the letters immediately after they were presented, but their perception faded rapidly as they were reporting the letters, so by the time they had reported 4–5 letters, they could no longer see the matrix or remember what had been there.

Sperling devised the **partial report method** to determine which of these two possibilities is correct. In this technique, he flashed the matrix for 50 ms, as before, but immediately after it was flashed, he sounded one of the following cue tones, to indicate which row of letters the participants were to report (Figure 5.5b):

High-pitched: Top row
Medium-pitched: Middle row
Low-pitched: Bottom row

Note that because the tones were presented *after* the letters were turned off, the participant's attention was directed not to the actual letters, which were no longer present, but to whatever trace remained in the participant's mind after the letters were turned off.

CogLab
Partial Report

When the cue tones directed participants to focus their attention on one of the rows, they correctly reported an average of about 3.3 of the 4 letters (82 percent) in that row. Because participants saw an average of 82 percent of the letters no matter which row was cued, Sperling concluded that the correct description of what was happening was that immediately after the display was presented, participants saw an average of 82 percent of the letters in the whole display, but were not able to report all of these letters because they rapidly faded as the initial letters were being reported.

Sperling then did an additional experiment to determine the time course of this fading. For this experiment, Sperling devised a **delayed partial report method** in which the presentation of cue tones was delayed for a fraction of a second after the letters were extinguished (Figure 5.5c).

The result of the delayed partial report experiments was that when the cue tones were delayed for 1 second after the flash, participants were able to report only slightly more than 1 letter in a row, the equivalent of about 4 letters for all three rows—the same number of letters they reported using the whole report method. • Figure 5.6 plots this result, showing the percentage of letters available to the participants from the entire display as a function of time following presentation of the display. This graph indicates that immediately after a stimulus is presented, all or most of the stimulus is available for perception. This is sensory memory. Then, over the next second, sensory memory fades, until by 1 second, the number of letters is about the same as the number of letters that were reported using the whole report method.

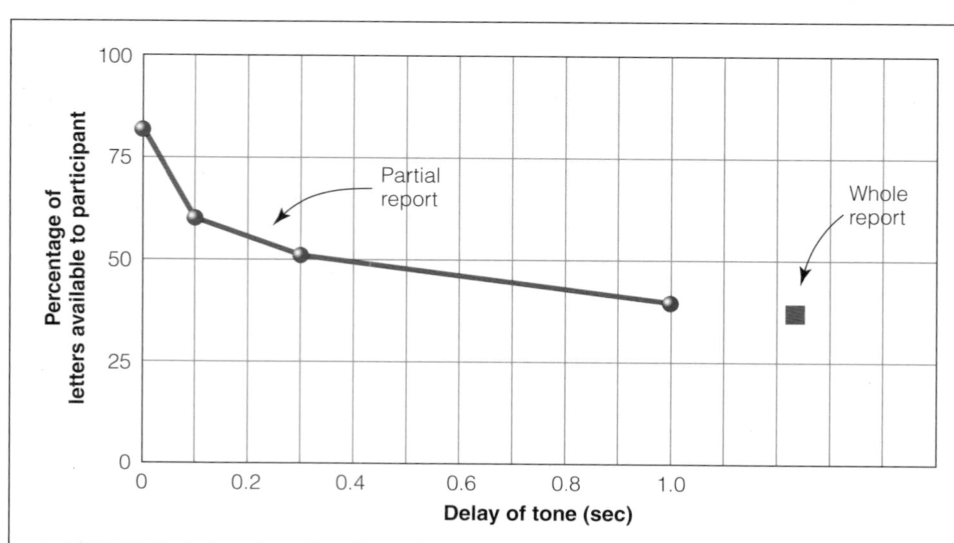

• **FIGURE 5.6** Results of Sperling's (1960) partial report experiments. The decrease in performance is due to the rapid decay of iconic memory (sensory memory in the modal model).

Sperling concluded from these results that a short-lived sensory memory registers all or most of the information that hits our visual receptors, but that this information decays within less than a second. This brief sensory memory for visual stimuli is called **iconic memory** or the **visual icon** (icon means "image"), and corresponds to the sensory memory stage of Atkinson and Shiffrin's model. Other research, using auditory stimuli, has shown that sounds also persist in the mind. This persistence of sound, which is called **echoic memory**, lasts for a few seconds after presentation of the original stimulus (Darwin et al., 1972).

Thus, sensory memory can register huge amounts of information (perhaps all of the information that reaches the receptors), but it retains this information for only seconds or fractions of a second. There has been some debate regarding the purpose of this large but rapidly fading store (Haber, 1983), but many cognitive psychologists believe that the sensory store is important for (1) collecting information to be processed, (2) holding the information briefly while initial processing is going on, and (3) filling in the blanks when stimulation is intermittent.

Sperling's experiment is important not only because it reveals the capacity of sensory memory (large) and its duration (brief), but also because it provides yet another demonstration of how clever experimentation can reveal extremely rapid cognitive processes that we are usually unaware of. In the next section we consider the second stage of the modal model, short-term memory, which also holds information briefly, but for much longer than sensory memory.

Short-Term Memory

Short-term memory (STM) is the system involved in storing small amounts of information for a brief period of time (Baddeley et al., 2009). Thus, whatever you are thinking about right now, or remember from what you have just read, is in your short-term memory. As we will see below, most of this information is eventually lost, and only some of it reaches the more permanent store of long-term memory (LTM). Because of the brief duration of STM, it is easy to downplay its importance compared to LTM. In my class survey of the uses of memory, my students focused almost entirely on how memory enables them to hold information for long periods, such as remembering directions, people's names, or material that might appear on an exam.

Certainly, our ability to store information for long periods is important, as attested by cases such as Clive Wearing's, whose inability to form LTMs makes it impossible for him to function independently. But, as we will see, STM (and working memory, a short-term component of memory that we will describe later) is responsible for a great deal of our mental life. Everything we think about or know at a particular moment in time involves STM because short-term memory is our window on the present. (Remember from Figure 5.3e that Rachel became aware of the pizzeria's phone number by transferring it from LTM to STM.) We will now describe some early research on STM that focused on answering the following two questions: (1) What is the duration of STM? (2) How much information can STM hold? These questions were answered in experiments that used the method of *recall* to test memory.

METHOD Recall

Most of the experiments we will be describing in this chapter use a **recall test**, in which participants are presented with stimuli and then, after a delay, are asked to remember as many of the stimuli as possible. Memory performance can be measured as a percentage of the stimuli that are remembered. (For example, studying a list of 10 words and later recalling 3 of them is 30 percent recall.) Participants' responses can also be analyzed to determine if there is a pattern to the way items are recalled. (For example, if participants are given a list consisting of types of fruits and models of cars, their recall can be analyzed to determine whether they grouped cars together and fruits together as they were recalling them.) Recall is also involved when a person is asked to recollect life events, such as graduating from high school, or to recall facts they have learned, such as the capital of Nebraska.

Measuring *recall* contrasts with measuring *recognition*, in which people are asked to pick an item they have previously seen or heard from a number of other items that they have not seen or heard, as occurs for multiple-choice questions on an exam. Recognition tests can also be used to test STM, but we will consider recognition tests in more detail in Chapter 6, when we discuss some recognition memory experiments used to test long-term memory.

WHAT IS THE DURATION OF SHORT-TERM MEMORY?

John Brown (1958) in England and Lloyd Peterson and Margaret Peterson (1959) in the United States used the method of recall to determine the duration of STM. In their experiments, participants were given a task similar to the one in the following demonstration.

DEMONSTRATION Remembering Three Letters

CogLab
Brown-Peterson

You will need another person to serve as a participant in this experiment. Read the following instructions to the person:

> I will say some letters and then a number. Your task will be to remember the letters. When you hear the number, repeat it and begin counting backwards by 3s from that number. For example, if I say ABC 309, then you say 309, 306, 303, and so on, until I say "Recall." When I say "Recall," stop counting immediately and say the three letters you heard just before the number.

Start with the letters and number in trial 1 below. It is important that the person count out loud because this prevents the person from rehearsing the letters. Once the person starts counting, time 20 seconds, and say "recall." Note how accurately the person recalled the three letters and continue to the next trial, noting the person's accuracy for each trial.

Trial 1: F Z L 45
Trial 2: B H M 87
Trial 3: X C G 98
Trial 4: Y N F 37
Trial 5: M J T 54
Trial 6: Q B S 73
Trial 7: K D P 66
Trial 8: R X M 44
Trial 9: B Y N 68
Trial 10: N T L 39

We will return to your results in a moment. First let's consider what Peterson and Peterson found when they did a similar experiment in which they varied the time between when they said the number and when the participant began recalling the letters. Peterson and Peterson found that their participants were able to remember about 80 percent of the letters after counting for 3 seconds but could remember an average of only 12 percent of the three-letter groups after counting for 18 seconds (● Figure 5.7a). They interpreted this result as demonstrating that participants forgot the letters because of **decay**. That is, their memory trace decayed because of the passage of time after hearing the letters. However, when G. Keppel and Benton Underwood (1962) looked closely at Peterson and Peterson's results, they found that if they considered the participants' performance *on just the first trial*, there was little falloff between the 3-second and the 18-second delay (Figure 5.7b). How does this compare to your results? Did performance become worse on later trials? Apparently, the poor memory at 18 seconds reported by Peterson and Peterson was caused by a drop-off in performance after the first few trials.

Why would memory become worse after a few trials? Keppel and Underwood suggested that the drop-off in memory was due not to decay of the memory trace, as Peterson and Peterson had proposed, but to **proactive interference (PI)**—interference

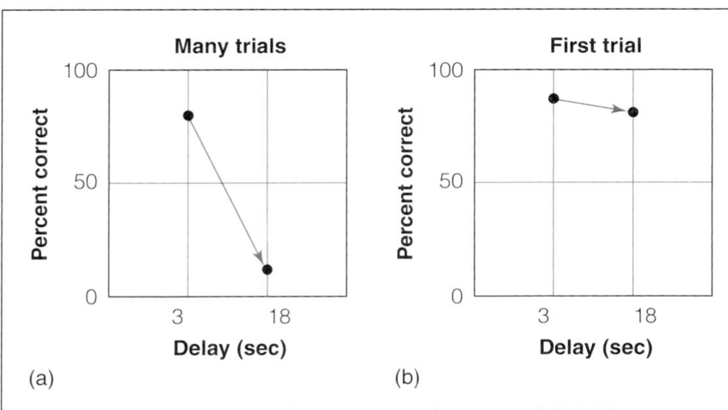

● **FIGURE 5.7** Results of Peterson and Peterson's (1959) duration of STM experiment. (a) The result originally presented by Peterson and Peterson, showing a large drop in memory for letters with a delay of 18 seconds between presentation and test. These data are based on the average performance over many trials. (b) Analysis of Peterson and Peterson's results by Keppel and Underwood, showing little decrease in performance if only the first trial is included.

that occurs when information that was learned previously interferes with learning new information.

The effect of proactive interference is illustrated by what might happen when a frequently used phone number is changed. Consider, for example, what might happen when Rachel calls the number she has memorized for Mineo's Pizza, 521-5100, only to get a recording saying that the phone number has been changed to 522-4100. Although Rachel tries to remember the new number, she makes mistakes at first because proactive interference is causing her memory for the old number to interfere with her memory for the new number. The fact that the new number is similar to the old one adds to the interference and makes it harder to remember the new number.

Keppel and Underwood proposed that proactive interference is what caused the decrease in memory observed in the later trials of Peterson and Peterson's experiment. Thus, recalling the early letters in the list created interference that made it more difficult to remember the later letters in the list.

What does it mean that the reason for the decrease in short-term memory is proactive interference? From the point of view of our everyday life experience, it is easy to see that interference is happening constantly as one event follows the next, and as we pay attention to one thing after another. The outcome of this constant interference is that the effective duration of STM, when rehearsal is prevented, is about 15–20 seconds.

WHAT IS THE CAPACITY OF SHORT-TERM MEMORY?

CogLab
Memory Span

Not only is information lost rapidly from STM, but there is a limit to how much information can be held there. As we will see, estimates for how many items can be held in STM range from four to nine.

Digit Span One measure of the capacity of STM is provided by the **digit span**—the number of digits a person can remember. You can determine your digit span by doing the following demonstration.

DEMONSTRATION Digit Span

Using an index card or piece of paper, cover all of the numbers below. Move the card down to uncover the first string of numbers. Read the numbers, cover them up, and then write them down in the correct order. Then move the card to the next string, and repeat this procedure until you begin making errors. The longest string you are able to reproduce without error is your digit span.

2 1 4 9
3 9 6 7 8
6 4 9 7 8 4
7 3 8 2 0 1 5
8 4 2 6 4 1 3 2
4 8 2 3 9 2 8 0 7
5 8 5 2 9 8 4 6 3 7

If you succeeded in remembering the longest string of digits, you have a digit span of 10 or perhaps more. The typical span is between 5 and 8 digits.

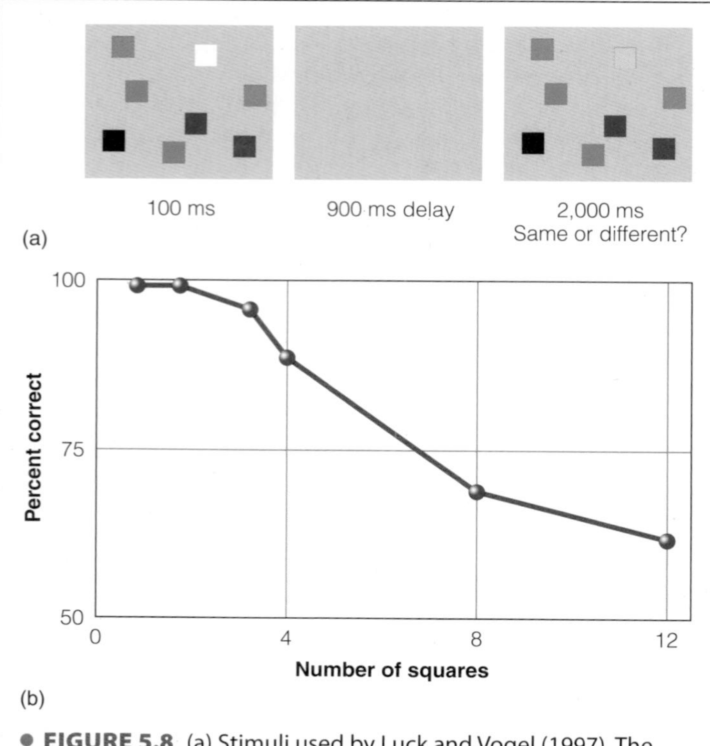

• **FIGURE 5.8** (a) Stimuli used by Luck and Vogel (1997). The participant sees the first display and then indicates whether the second display is the same or different. In this example, the color of one square is changed in the second display. (b) Result of the experiment, showing that performance began to decrease once there were 4 squares in the display. (Source: Adapted from E. K. Vogel, A. W. McCollough, & M. G. Machizawa, "Neural Measures Reveal Individual Differences in Controlling Access to Working Memory," *Nature 438,* 500–503, 2005.)

According to measurements of digit span, the average capacity of STM is about 5 to 9 items—about the length of a phone number. This idea that the limit of STM is somewhere between 5 and 9 was suggested by George Miller (1956) in a famous paper titled "The Magical Number Seven, Plus or Minus Two." In that paper, Miller summarized evidence suggesting that STM can hold 5 to 9 items.

More recent measures of STM capacity have set the capacity at about 4 items (Cowan, 2001). This conclusion is based on the results of experiments like the one by Steven Luck and Edward Vogel (1997), which measured the capacity of STM by flashing two arrays of colored squares separated by a brief delay (• Figure 5.8a). The participants' task was to indicate whether the second array was the same as or different from the first array. On trials in which the second array was different, the color of one square was changed, as shown in Figure 5.8a.

The result of this experiment, shown in Figure 5.8b, shows that performance was almost perfect when there were 1 to 3 squares in the arrays, but that performance began decreasing when there were 4 or more squares. Luck and Vogel concluded from this result that participants were able to retain about 4 items in their short-term memory. Other experiments, using verbal materials, have come to the same conclusion (Cowan, 2001).

These estimates of either 4 items or 5 to 9 items set rather low limits on the capacity of STM. If our ability to hold items in memory is so limited, how is it possible to hold many more items in memory in some situations, as when words are arranged in a sentence? The answer to this question was proposed by Miller, who introduced the idea of *chunking* in his 7-plus-or-minus-2 paper.

Chunking Miller (1956) introduced the concept of **chunking** to describe the fact that small units (like words) can be combined into larger meaningful units, like phrases, or even larger units, like sentences, paragraphs, or stories. Consider, for example, trying to remember the following words: *monkey, child, wildly, zoo, jumped, city, ringtail, young.* How many units are there in this list? There are 8 words, but if we group them differently, they can form the following 4 pairs: *ringtail monkey, jumped wildly, young child, city zoo.* We can take this one step further by arranging these groups of words into one sentence: The *ringtail monkey jumped wildly* for the *young child* at the *city zoo.*

A **chunk** has been defined as a collection of elements that are strongly associated with one another but are weakly associated with elements in other chunks (Cowan, 2001; Gobet et al., 2001). In our example, the word *ringtail* is strongly associated with the word *monkey* but is not as strongly associated with the other words, such as *child* or *city.*

Thus, chunking in terms of meaning increases our ability to hold information in STM. We can recall a sequence of 5 to 8 unrelated words, but arranging the words to form a meaningful sentence so that the words become more strongly associated with one another increases the memory span to 20 words or more (Butterworth et al., 1990). Chunking of a series of letters is illustrated by the following demonstration.

DEMONSTRATION Remembering Letters

Read the string of letters below at a rate of about 1 letter every 2 seconds, and then cover the letters and write down as many as you can, in the correct order:

B C I F N C C A S I C B

How did you do? This task isn't easy, because it involves remembering a series of 12 individual letters, which is larger than the usual letter span of 5 to 9.

Now try remembering the following sequence of letters in order:

C I A F B I N B C C B S

How did your performance on this list compare to the one above?

Although the second list has the same letters as the first group, it was easier to remember if you realized that this sequence consists of the names of four familiar organizations. You can therefore create four chunks, each of which is meaningful, and therefore easy to remember.

K. Anders Ericsson and coworkers (1980) demonstrated an effect of chunking by showing how a college student with average memory ability was able to achieve amazing feats of memory. Their participant, S.F., was asked to repeat strings of random digits that were read to him. Although S.F. had a typical memory span of 7 digits, after extensive training (230 one-hour sessions), he was able to repeat sequences of up to 79 digits without error. How did he do it? S.F. used chunking to recode the digits into larger units that formed meaningful sequences. For example, 3492 became "3 minutes and 49 point 2 seconds, near world-record mile time," and 893 became "89 point 3, very old man." This example illustrates an interaction between STM and LTM, because S.F., who was a runner, created some of his chunks based on his knowledge of running times that were stored in LTM.

Another example of chunking that is based on an interaction between STM and LTM is provided by an experiment by William Chase and Herbert Simon (1973a, 1973b) in which they showed chess players arrangements of chess pieces taken from actual games, for 5 seconds. The chess players were then asked to reproduce the positions they had seen. Chase and Simon compared the performance of a chess master who had played or studied chess for more than 10,000 hours to the performance of a beginner who had less than 100 hours of experience. The results, shown in • Figure 5.9a, show that the chess master placed 16 pieces out of 24 correctly on his first try, compared to just 4 out of 24 for the beginner. Moreover, the master required only four trials to reproduce all of the positions exactly, whereas even after seven trials the beginner was still making errors.

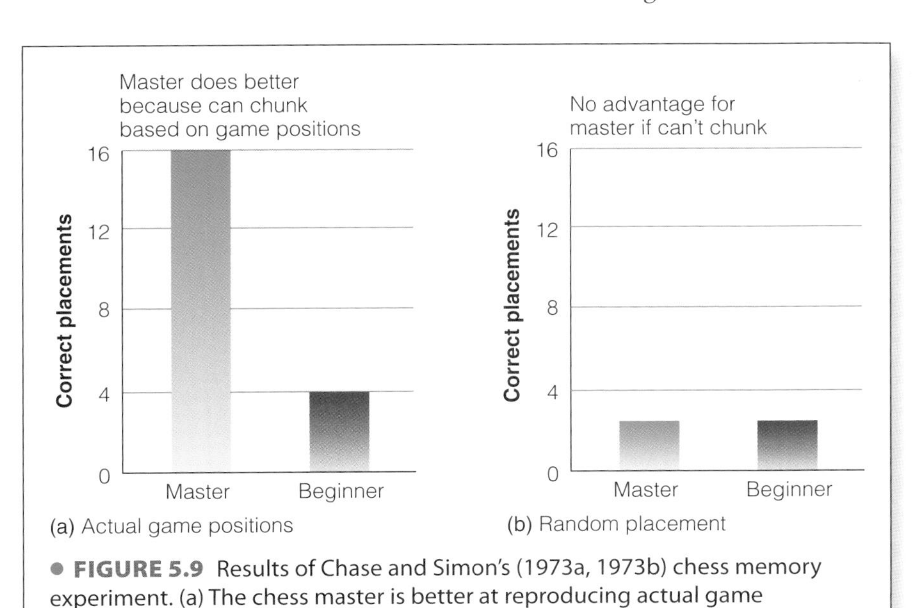

• **FIGURE 5.9** Results of Chase and Simon's (1973a, 1973b) chess memory experiment. (a) The chess master is better at reproducing actual game positions. (b) The master's performance drops to the level of the beginner's when the pieces are arranged randomly. (Source: Based on W. G. Chase & H. A. Simon, "Perception in Chess," *Cognitive Psychology, 4,* 55–81, 1973.)

Does this result mean that chess masters have a more highly developed short-term memory than the beginners? Chase and Simon answered this question by testing the ability of masters and beginners to remember random arrangements of the chess pieces. Under these conditions, the chess master performed as poorly as the beginner (Figure 5.9b). Chase and Simon concluded that the chess master's advantage was due not to a more highly developed short-term memory, but to his ability to group the chess pieces into meaningful chunks. Because the chess master had stored many of the patterns that occur in real chess games in LTM, he saw the layout of chess pieces not in terms of individual pieces but in terms of 4 to 6 chunks, each made up of a group of pieces that formed familiar, meaningful patterns. When the pieces were arranged randomly, the familiar patterns were destroyed, and the chess master's advantage vanished (also see DeGroot, 1965; Gobet et al., 2001).

Chunking enables the limited-capacity STM system to deal with the large amount of information involved in many of the tasks we perform every day, such as chunking letters into words as you read this, remembering the first three numbers of familiar telephone exchanges as a unit, and transforming long conversations into smaller units of meaning.

HOW IS INFORMATION CODED IN SHORT-TERM MEMORY?

Coding refers to the way information is represented. Remember, for example, our discussion in Chapter 2 of how a person's face can be represented by the pattern of firing of a number of neurons. Determining how a stimulus is represented by the firing of neurons is a **physiological approach to coding**. We can also take a **mental approach to coding** by asking how a stimulus or an experience is represented in the mind. For example, imagine that you have just finished listening to your cognitive psychology professor give a lecture. We can describe different kinds of mental coding that occur for this experience by considering some of the ways you might remember what happened in class.

Remembering the sound of your professor's voice is an example of *auditory coding*. Imagining what your professor looks like, perhaps by conjuring up an image in your mind, is an example of *visual coding*. Finally, remembering what your professor was talking about is an example of coding in terms of meaning, which is called *semantic coding* (see Table 5.2).

TABLE 5.2 Types of Coding.

Type of Coding	Example
Auditory	Sound of the person's voice
Visual	Image of a person
Semantic	Meaning of what the person is saying

Auditory Coding **Auditory coding** involves representing items in STM based on their sound. One of the early experiments that investigated coding in STM was done by R. Conrad in 1964. In Conrad's experiment, participants saw a number of target letters flashed briefly on a screen and were told to write down the letters in the order they were presented. Conrad found that when participants made errors, they were most likely to misidentify the target letter as another letter that *sounded like* the target. For example, "F" was most often misidentified as "S" or "X," two letters that sound similar to "F," but it was not as likely to be confused with letters like "E," that *look like* the target. Thus, even though the participants *saw* the letters, the mistakes they made were based on the letters' *sounds.*

From these results Conrad concluded that the code for STM is auditory (based on the *sound* of the stimulus), rather than visual (based on the *visual appearance* of the stimulus). This conclusion fits with our common experience with telephone numbers. Even though our contact with them is often visual, we usually remember them by repeating their sound over and over rather than by visualizing what the numbers looked like on the computer screen (also see Wickelgren, 1965).

Visual Coding **Visual coding** involves representing items visually, as would occur when remembering the details of a floor plan or the layout of streets on a map (Kroll, 1970; Posner & Keele, 1967; Shepard & Metzler, 1971). This use of visual codes in STM was demonstrated in an experiment by Sergio Della Sala and coworkers (1999), in which participants were presented with a task like the one in the following demonstration.

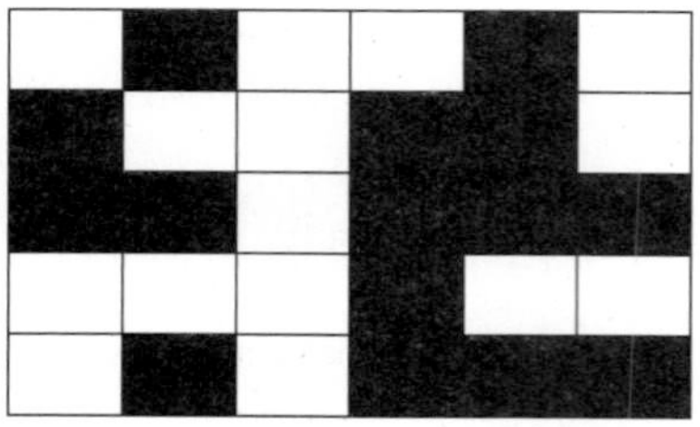

DEMONSTRATION Recalling Visual Patterns

Look a the pattern in • Figure 5.10 for 3 seconds. Then turn the page and indicate which of the squares in • Figure 5.13 on page 130 need to be filled in to duplicate this pattern.

• **FIGURE 5.10** Test pattern for visual recall test. After looking at this for 3 seconds, turn the page.

The task in the demonstration involves visual coding in STM because the patterns are difficult to code verbally, so completing the pattern depends on visual memory. Della Sala presented his participants with patterns ranging from small (a 2 × 2 matrix with

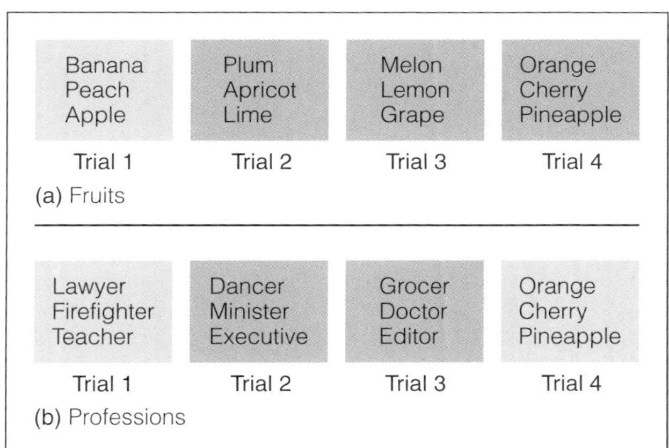

● **FIGURE 5.11** Stimuli for the Wickens et al. (1976) experiment. Participants in the fruit group are presented with the names of three fruits on each trial. Participants in the professions group are presented with the names of three professions on trials 1, 2, and 3, and with the names of three fruits on trial 4. Proactive interference based on meaning could occur on trials indicated by the blue rectangles. (Source: Based on D. D. Wickens, R. E. Dalezman, & F. T. Eggemeier, "Multiple Encoding of Word Attributes in Memory," *Memory & Cognition, 4,* 307–310, 1976.)

2 shaded squares) to large (a 5 × 6 matrix with 15 shaded squares), with half of the squares being shaded in each pattern. He found that participants were able to complete patterns consisting of an average of 9 shaded squares before making mistakes.

The fact that it is possible to remember the patterns in Della Sala's matrix illustrates visual coding. But how come the participants could remember patterns consisting of as many as 9 squares? This number is at the high end of Miller's range of 5 to 9 and is far above the lower estimate of 4 items from Luck and Vogel's experiment (Figure 5.8). Try answering this question. (For a possible answer, see the footnote at the bottom of this page.*)

Semantic Coding Semantic coding is representing items in terms of their meaning. An example of semantic coding in STM is provided by an experiment by Delos Wickens and coworkers (1976). ● Figure 5.11 shows the experimental design for Wickens' experiment. On each trial, participants were presented with words related to either (a) fruits (the "fruit group") or (b) professions (the "professions group"). Participants in each group listened to three words (for example, *banana, peach, apple* for the fruit group), counted backward for 15 seconds, and then attempted to recall the three words. They did this for a total of four trials, with different words presented on each trial.

The basic idea behind this experiment was to create *proactive interference*, the decrease in memory that occurs due to prior learning (see page 124), by presenting words in a series of trials from the same category. For example, for the fruit group, *banana, peach, and apple* were presented on trial 1 and *plum, apricot, and lime* were presented on trial 2.

Let's consider the results for the fruit group, shown in ● Figure 5.12a. On the first trial the average percent recalled was 86 percent, but performance dropped on trials 2, 3, and 4 as additional names of fruits were presented. The blue data points indicate the presence of proactive interference caused by repeated presentation of the names of fruits.

Evidence that this interference can be attributed to the *meanings* of the words (all of the words were fruits) is provided by the results for the professions group, shown in Figure 5.12b. As with the fruits group, performance is high on trial 1 and then drops on trials 2 and 3 because all of the words are names of professions. But on trial 4, the names of fruits are presented. Because these are from a different category, proactive interference is reduced, which results in an increase in performance on trial 4. This effect is called **release from proactive interference.**

What does release from proactive interference tell us about coding in STM? The key to answering this question is to realize that the release from PI that occurs in the Wickens experiment depends on the words' *categories* (fruits, professions). Because placing words into categories involves the *meanings* of the words, the results of the Wickens experiment demonstrate the operation of *semantic coding* in STM.

TEST YOURSELF 5.1

1. The beginning of the chapter makes the claim that "life is all memory." How has this claim been supported by considering what memory does for people with the ability to remember and what happens when this ability is lost, as in cases like that of Clive Wearing?
2. Describe Atkinson and Shiffrin's modal model of memory, in terms of both its structure (the boxes connected by arrows) and the control processes. Then describe how each part of the model comes into play when you decide you want to order pizza but can't remember the pizzeria's phone number.

---

*With patterns such as the ones in Figure 5.10, it is possible to combine individual squares into subpatterns. This is an example of chunking, which could increase the number of squares remembered, much as Chase and Simon's expert chess players remembered the patterns of chess pieces (page 127).

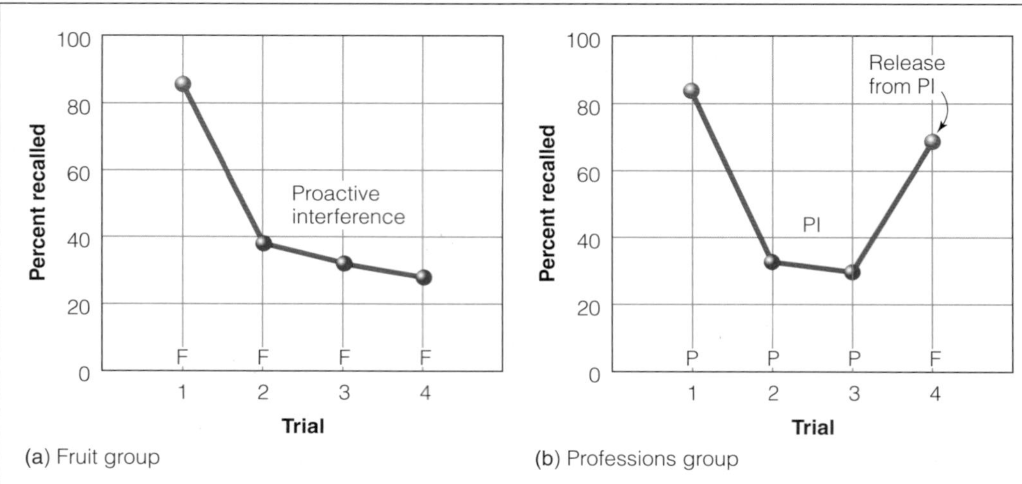

● **FIGURE 5.12** Results of Wickens et al.'s (1976) proactive inhibition experiment. (a) Fruit group, showing reduced performance on trials 2, 3, and 4 caused at least partially by proactive interference (indicated by blue points). (b) Professions group, showing reduced performance on trials 2 and 3 but improved performance on trial 4. The increase in performance on trial 4 represents a release from proactive interference caused by the change of category from professions to fruits. (Source: Based on D. D. Wickens, R. E. Dalezman, & F. T. Eggemeier, "Multiple Encoding of Word Attributes in Memory," *Memory & Cognition, 4,* 307–310, 1976.)

3. Describe sensory memory and Sperling's experiment in which he briefly flashed an array of letters to measure the capacity and duration of sensory memory.
4. Is memory lost from STM by decay or by interference? Be sure you understand the Peterson and Peterson experiment and Keppel and Underwood's interpretation of it. What is the time span of STM?
5. What is the capacity of STM, and how is it influenced by chunking?
6. Describe evidence supporting the following types of coding in STM: auditory (Conrad letter memory experiment); visual (Della Sala matrix experiment); and semantic coding (Wickens fruits and professions experiment).

Working Memory

The modal model stimulated a great deal of research on short-term memory. But as research on STM progressed, it became apparent that the concept of STM as presented in the modal model was too narrow to explain many research findings. The problem was that STM was described mainly as a short-term storage mechanism. But as we saw in our description of Rachel ordering a pizza, memorizing a phone number involves transferring the number from STM into LTM, and remembering it then involves transferring it from LTM back into STM. Thus, the role of STM extends beyond storage. It is also involved in the transfer of information to and from LTM. We can take this idea further by listening in on Rachel's conversation with the pizza shop:

RACHEL: "I'd like to order a large pizza with broccoli and mushrooms."
REPLY: "I'm sorry, but we're out of mushrooms. Would you like to substitute spinach instead?

● **FIGURE 5.13** Answer matrix for the visual recall test. Put a check in each square that was darkened in the pattern you just looked at.

Rachel was able to understand the pizza shop's reply by holding the first sentence, "I'm sorry, but we're out of mushrooms," in her memory while listening to the second sentence and then making the connection between the two. If she had remembered only

"Would you like to substitute spinach instead?" she wouldn't know whether it was being substituted for the broccoli or for the mushrooms. Thus, short-term processes are needed not only for storage, but also for active processes like understanding conversations. Another example of an active process occurs when we solve even simple math problems, such as "Multiply 43 times 6 in your head." Stop for a moment and try this while being aware of what you are doing in your head.

One way to solve this problem involves the following steps:

(1) Visualize: $\begin{array}{r} 43 \\ \underline{\times 6} \end{array}$

(2) Multiply 3 × 6 = 18.

(3) Hold 8 in memory, while carrying the 1 over to the 4.

(4) Multiply 6 × 4 = 24.

(5) Add the carried 1 to the 24.

(6) Place the result, 25, next to the 8.

(7) The answer is 258.

It is easy to see that this calculation involves both storage (holding the 8 in memory; remembering the 6 and 4 for the next multiplication step) and active processes (carrying the 1, multiplying 6 × 4) at the same time. If only storage were involved, the problem could not be solved. There are other ways to carry out this calculation, but whatever method you chose involves both holding information in memory and processing information.

The fact that STM and the modal model do not consider dynamic processes that unfold over time led Baddeley to begin considering alternatives to the modal model. In addition, Baddeley noticed something else that was not explained by the modal model: Under certain conditions it is possible to carry out two tasks simultaneously, as illustrated in the following demonstration.

DEMONSTRATION Reading Text and Remembering Numbers

Keep the numbers 7, 1, 4, and 9 in your mind as you read the following passage:

> Baddeley reasoned that if STM had a limited storage capacity of about the length of a telephone number, filling up the storage capacity should make it difficult to do other tasks that depend on STM. But he found that participants could hold a short string of numbers in their memory while carrying out another task, such as reading or even solving a simple word problem. How are you doing with this task? What are the numbers? What is the gist of what you have just read?

According to the modal model, it should only be possible to perform one of these tasks, which should occupy the entire STM. But when Baddeley did experiments involving tasks similar to those in the previous demonstration, he found that participants were able to read while simultaneously remembering numbers.

What kind of model can take into account both (1) the dynamic processes involved in cognitions such as understanding language and doing math problems and (2) the fact that people can carry out two tasks simultaneously? Baddeley concluded that the short-term process must be dynamic and must also consist of a number of components that can function separately. According to this idea, the digit span task in the demonstration (holding numbers in your memory) would be handled by one component while comprehending the paragraph would be handled by another component.

The model Baddeley proposed was first described in a paper with Graham Hitch (Baddeley & Hitch, 1974) and, as we will see, was later modified to explain new findings. In this model, the short-term component of memory is called *working memory.* **Working memory** is defined as *a limited-capacity system for temporary storage and manipulation*

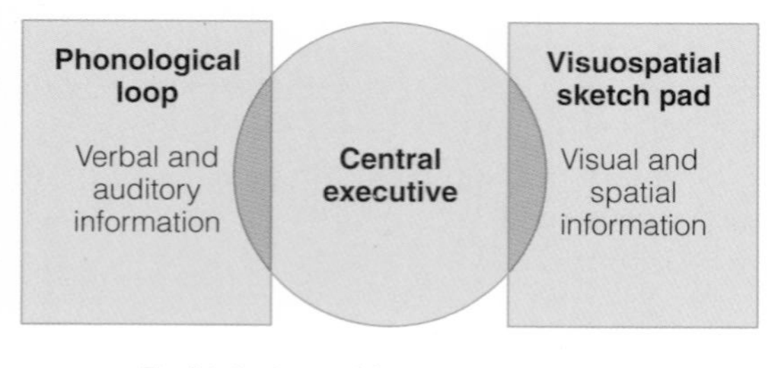

Baddeley's working memory model

● **FIGURE 5.14** Diagram of the three main components of Baddeley and Hitch's (1974; Baddeley, 2000a, 2000b) model of working memory: the phonological loop, the visuospatial sketch pad, and the central executive.

of information for complex tasks such as comprehension, learning, and reasoning. From this definition we can see that working memory differs from STM in two ways:

1. Short-term memory is concerned mainly with *storing information* for a brief period of time (for example, remembering a phone number), whereas working memory is concerned with the *manipulation of information* that occurs during complex cognition (for example, remembering numbers while reading a paragraph).
2. Short-term memory consists of a *single component*, whereas working memory consists of a *number of components*.

Thus, working memory is concerned not just with how information is stored, but with how information is manipulated in the service of various forms of cognition (Baddeley, 2000b). Working memory accomplishes the manipulation of information through the action of three components: the *phonological loop,* the *visuospatial sketch pad,* and the *central executive* (● Figure 5.14).

- The **phonological loop** consists of two components: the **phonological store**, which has a limited capacity and holds information for only a few seconds; and the **articulatory rehearsal process**, which is responsible for rehearsal that can keep items in the phonological store from decaying. The phonological loop holds verbal and auditory information. Thus, when you are trying to remember a telephone number or a person's name, or to understand what your cognitive psychology professor is talking about, you are using your phonological loop.
- The **visuospatial sketch pad** holds visual and spatial information. When you form a picture in your mind or do tasks like solving a puzzle or finding your way around campus, you are using your visuospatial sketch pad. As you can see from the diagram, the phonological loop and the visuospatial sketch pad are attached to the central executive.
- The **central executive** is where the major work of working memory occurs. The central executive pulls information from long-term memory and coordinates the activity of the phonological loop and visuospatial sketch pad by focusing on specific parts of a task and switching attention from one part to another. One of the main jobs of the central executive is to decide how to divide attention between different tasks. Looked at in this way, we can describe the central executive as the "traffic cop" of the working memory system. For example, imagine you are driving in a strange city, and a friend in the passenger seat is reading you directions to a restaurant while the news is being broadcast on the car radio. As your phonological loop takes in the verbal directions, your sketch pad is helping you visualize a map of the streets leading to the restaurant (● Figure 5.15), and the central executive is coordinating and combining these two kinds of information. In addition, the central executive might be helping you ignore the messages from the radio, so you can focus your attention on the directions.

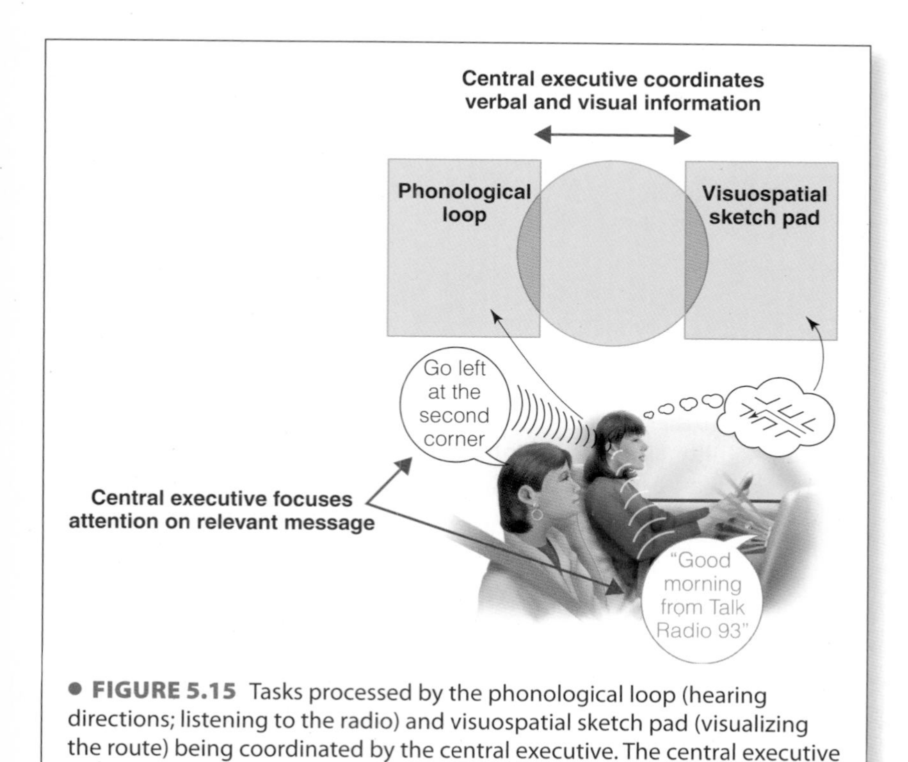

● **FIGURE 5.15** Tasks processed by the phonological loop (hearing directions; listening to the radio) and visuospatial sketch pad (visualizing the route) being coordinated by the central executive. The central executive also helps the person ignore the messages from the radio, so attention can be focused on hearing the directions.

We will now describe a number of phenomena that illustrate how the different components of working memory operate in different situations.

THE PHONOLOGICAL LOOP

We will describe three phenomena that support the idea of a system specialized for language: the phonological similarity effect, the word length effect, and articulatory suppression.

CogLab
Phonological Similarity Effect

Phonological Similarity Effect The **phonological similarity effect** is the confusion of letters or words that sound similar. Remember Conrad's experiment, described on page 128, in which he showed that in a memory test people often confuse similar-sounding letters, such as "F" and "S." Conrad interpreted this result to support the idea of auditory coding in STM. In present-day terminology, Conrad's result would be described as a demonstration of the phonological similarity effect, which occurs when words are processed in the phonological store part of the phonological loop. Memory suffers for similar items because they are confused with one another.

Word Length Effect The **word length effect** occurs when memory for lists of words is better for short words than for long words.

DEMONSTRATION Word Length Effect

Task 1: Read the following words, look away, and then write down the words you remember.

beast, bronze, wife, golf, inn, limp, dirt, star

Task 2: Now do the same thing for the following list.

alcohol, property, amplifier, officer, gallery, mosquito, orchestra, bricklayer

Each list in the demonstration contains eight words, but according to the word length effect, the second list will be more difficult to remember because the words are longer. Results of an experiment by Baddeley and coworkers (1984) that illustrate this advantage for short words are shown in ● Figure 5.16. The word length effect occurs because it takes longer to rehearse the long words and to produce them during recall.

In another study of memory for verbal material, Baddeley and coworkers (1975) found that people are able to remember the number of items that they can pronounce in about 1.5–2.0 seconds (also see Schweickert & Boruff, 1986). Try counting out loud, as fast as you can, for 2 seconds. According to Baddeley, the number of words you can say should be close to your digit span. (Note, however, that some researchers have proposed that the word length effect does not occur under some conditions; see Lovatt et al., 2000, 2002).

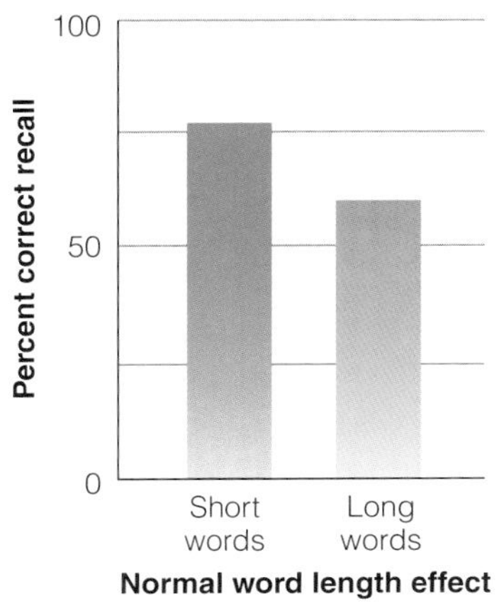

Percent correct recall: 100, 50, 0
Short words | Long words
Normal word length effect

● **FIGURE 5.16** How word length affects memory, showing that recall is better for short words (Baddeley et al., 1984).

Articulatory Suppression One way that the operation of the phonological loop has been studied is by determining what happens when its operation is disrupted. This occurs when a person is prevented from rehearsing items to be remembered by repeating an irrelevant sound, such as "the, the, the..." (Baddeley, 2000b; Baddeley et al., 1984; Murray, 1968).

This repetition of an irrelevant sound results in a phenomenon called **articulatory suppression**, which reduces memory because speaking interferes with rehearsal. The following demonstration, which is based on an experiment by Baddeley and coworkers (1984), illustrates this effect of articulatory suppression.

DEMONSTRATION Articulatory Suppression

Task 1: Read the following list. Then turn away and recall as many words as you can.

dishwasher, hummingbird, engineering, hospital, homelessness, reasoning

Task 2: Read the following list while repeating "the, the, the..." out loud. Then turn away and recall as many words as you can.

automobile, apartment, basketball, mathematics, gymnasium, Catholicism

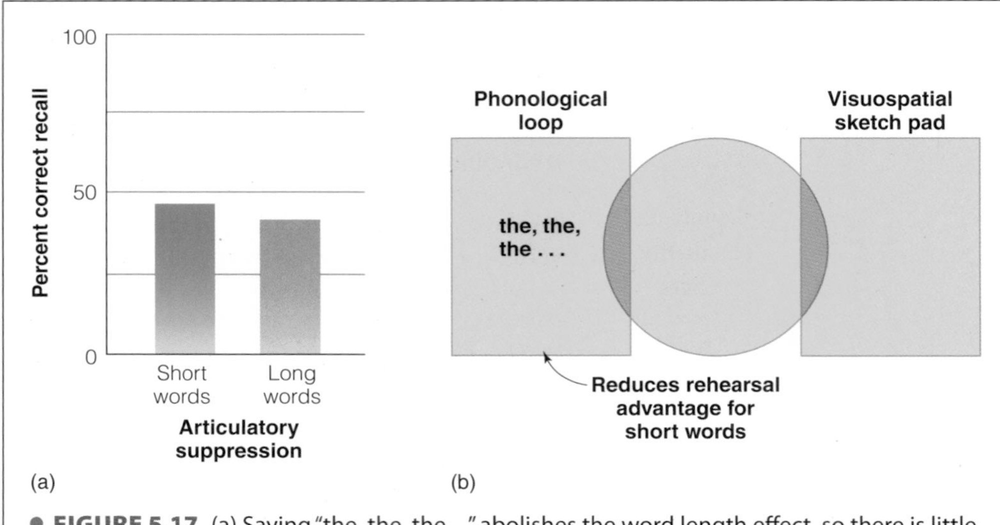

● **FIGURE 5.17** (a) Saying "the, the, the..." abolishes the word length effect, so there is little difference in performance for short words and long words (Baddeley et al., 1984). Saying "the, the, the..." causes this effect by reducing rehearsal in the phonological loop.

Articulatory suppression occurs when remembering the second list becomes harder because repeating "the, the, the..." overloads the phonological loop.

Baddeley and coworkers (1984) found that repeating "the, the, the..." not only reduces the ability to remember a list of words, but also eliminates the word length effect (● Figure 5.17a). According to the word length effect, a list of one-syllable words should be easier to recall than a list of longer words because the shorter words leave more space in the phonological loop for rehearsal. However, eliminating rehearsal by saying "the, the, the..." eliminates this advantage for short words, so both short and long words are lost from the phonological store (Figure 5.17b).

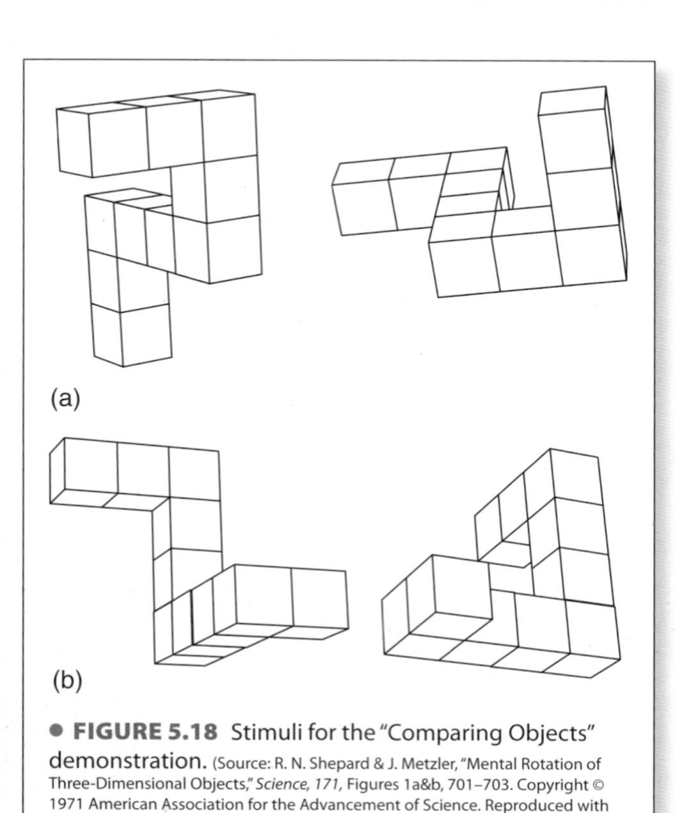

● **FIGURE 5.18** Stimuli for the "Comparing Objects" demonstration. (Source: R. N. Shepard & J. Metzler, "Mental Rotation of Three-Dimensional Objects," *Science, 171,* Figures 1a&b, 701–703. Copyright © 1971 American Association for the Advancement of Science. Reproduced with permission.)

THE VISUOSPATIAL SKETCH PAD

The visuospatial sketch pad handles visual and spatial information and is therefore involved in the process of **visual imagery**—the creation of visual images in the mind in the absence of a physical visual stimulus. The following demonstration illustrates an early visual imagery experiment by Roger Shepard and J. Metzler (1971).

DEMONSTRATION Comparing Objects

Look at the two pictures in ● Figure 5.18a and decide, as quickly as possible, whether they represent two different views of the same object ("same") or two different objects ("different"). Also make the same judgment for the two objects in Figure 5.18b.

When Shepard and Metzler measured participants' reaction time to decide whether pairs of objects were the same or different, they obtained the relationship shown in ● Figure 5.19 for objects that were the same. From this function, we can see that when two shapes were separated by an orientation difference of 40 degrees

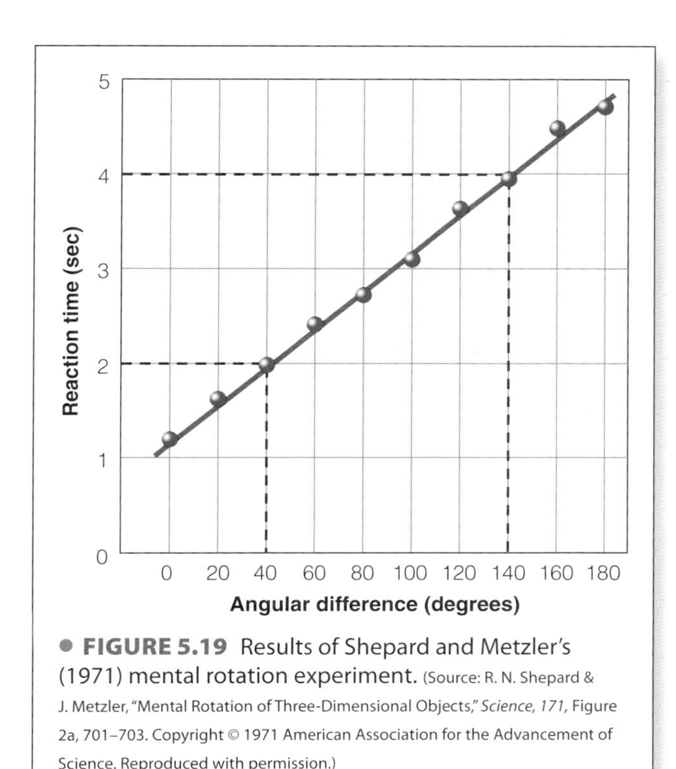

● **FIGURE 5.19** Results of Shepard and Metzler's (1971) mental rotation experiment. (Source: R. N. Shepard & J. Metzler, "Mental Rotation of Three-Dimensional Objects," *Science, 171*, Figure 2a, 701–703. Copyright © 1971 American Association for the Advancement of Science. Reproduced with permission.)

(like Figure 5.18a), it took 2 seconds to decide that a pair was the same shape, but for a difference of 140 degrees (like Figure 5.18b), it took 4 seconds. Based on this finding that reaction times were longer for greater differences in orientation, Shepard and Metzler inferred that participants were solving the problem by rotating an image of one of the objects in their mind, a phenomenon called **mental rotation.** This mental rotation is an example of the operation of the visuospatial sketch pad because it involves visual rotation through space.

Just as the operation of the phonological loop is disrupted by interference (articulatory suppression, see page 133), so is the visuospatial sketch pad. Lee Brooks (1968) did some experiments in which he demonstrated how interference can affect the operation of the visuospatial sketch pad. The following demonstration is based on one of Brooks's tasks.

DEMONSTRATION Holding a Spatial Stimulus in the Mind

Task 1: Visualize the *F* in ● Figure 5.20. Then cover the F and while visualizing it in your mind, start at the upper left corner (the one marked with the *) and, moving around the outline of the F in a clockwise direction in your mind, point to "Out" in ● Figure 5.21 for an outside corner (like the one marked with the *), and "In" for an inside corner (like the one marked with the ●). Move your response down one level in Figure 5.21 for each new corner.

Task 2: Visualize the F again, but this time, as you move around the outline of the F in a clockwise direction in your mind, say "Out" if the corner is an outside corner or "In" if it is an inside corner.

Which was easier, *pointing* to "Out" or "In" or *saying* "Out" or "In"?

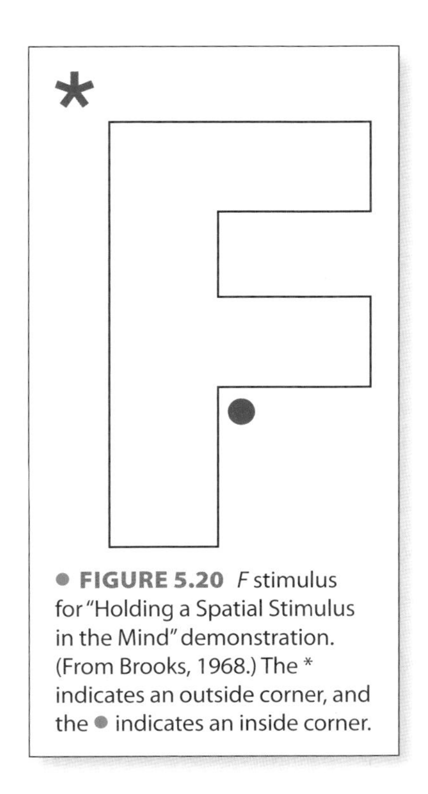

● **FIGURE 5.20** *F* stimulus for "Holding a Spatial Stimulus in the Mind" demonstration. (From Brooks, 1968.) The * indicates an outside corner, and the ● indicates an inside corner.

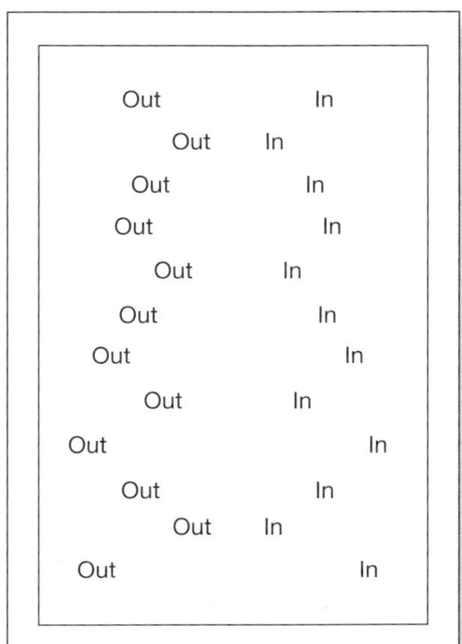

● **FIGURE 5.21** Response matrix for the "Holding a Spatial Stimulus in the Mind" demonstration. (From Brooks, 1968.)

Most people find that the pointing task is more difficult. The reason is that holding the image of the letter and pointing are both visuospatial tasks, so the visuospatial sketch pad becomes overloaded. In contrast, saying "Out" or "In" is an articulatory task that is handled by the phonological loop, so speaking didn't interfere with visualizing the F.

THE CENTRAL EXECUTIVE

The central executive is the component that makes working memory "working," because it is the control center of the working memory system. Its mission is not to store information, but to coordinate how information is used by the phonological loop and visuospatial sketch pad (Baddeley, 1996).

Baddeley describes the central executive as being an *attention controller.* It determines how attention is focused on a specific task, how it is divided between two tasks, and how it is switched between tasks. The central executive is therefore essential in situations such as the ones described in Chapter 4, when a person is attempting to simultaneously drive and use a cell phone. In this example, the executive would be controlling a phonological loop process (talking on the phone; understanding the conversation) and a sketchpad process (visualizing landmarks and the layout of the streets; navigating the car).

One of the ways the central executive has been studied is by assessing the behavior of patients with brain damage. As we will see later in the chapter, the frontal lobe plays a central role in working memory. It is not surprising, therefore, that patients with frontal lobe damage have problems controlling their attention. A typical behavior of frontal lobe patients is **perseveration**—repeatedly performing the same behavior even if it is not achieving the desired goal.

Consider, for example, a problem that can be easily solved by following a particular rule ("Pick the red object"). A person with frontal lobe damage might be responding correctly on each trial, as long as the rule stays the same. However, when the rule is switched ("Now pick the blue object"), the person continues following the old rule, even when given feedback that his or her responding is now incorrect. This perseveration represents a breakdown in the central executive's ability to control attention.

Another example of how the central executive controls attention is provided by situations in which a person is supposed to focus attention on "relevant" stimuli and ignore other, "irrelevant" stimuli. Some people are better at focusing attention than others. When we describe these individual differences in the "Something to Consider" section, we will see that these differences may be one of the reasons that some people perform better than others on tests of comprehension and reasoning ability.

THE EPISODIC BUFFER

We have seen that Baddeley's three-component model can explain a number of results. However, research has shown that there are some things the model can't explain. One of those things is that working memory can hold more than would be expected based on just the phonological loop or visuospatial sketch pad. For example, people can remember long sentences consisting of as many as 15 to 20 words. The ability to do this is related to chunking, in which meaningful units are grouped together (page 126) and it is also related to long-term memory, which is involved in knowing the meanings of words in the sentence and in relating parts of the sentence to each other based on the rules of grammar.

These ideas are nothing new. It had long been known that the capacity of working memory can be increased by chunking and that there is an interchange of information between working memory and long-term memory. But Baddeley decided it was necessary to propose an additional component of working memory to address these abilities. This new component, which he called the **episodic buffer**, is shown in Baddeley's new model of working memory in ● Figure 5.22. The episodic buffer can store information

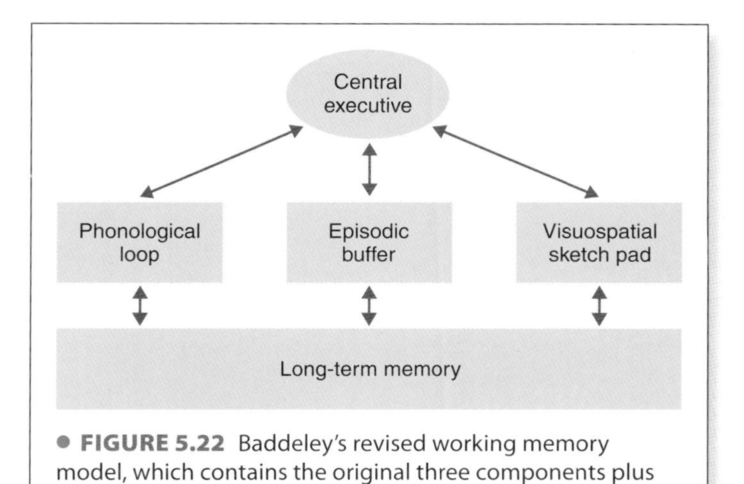

● **FIGURE 5.22** Baddeley's revised working memory model, which contains the original three components plus the episodic buffer.

(thereby providing extra capacity) and is connected to LTM (thereby making interchange between working memory and LTM possible). Notice that this model also shows that the visuospatial sketch pad and phonological loop are linked to long-term memory.

The proposal of the episodic buffer represents another step in the evolution of Baddeley's model, which has been stimulating research on working memory for more than 30 years since it was first proposed. If the exact functioning of the episodic buffer seems a little vague, it is because it is a "work in progress." Even Baddeley (Baddeley et al., 2009) states that "the concept of an episodic buffer is still at a very early stage of development" (p. 57). The main "take-home message" about the episodic buffer is that it represents a way of increasing storage capacity and communicating with LTM.

Although we have been focusing on Baddeley's model because of the large amount of research it has generated, his is not the only model of working memory. For example, a model proposed by Nelson Cowan (1988, 1999, 2005) has focused on how working memory is related to attention and suggests that working memory and attention are essentially the same mechanism. This idea is supported by the finding that the same areas of the brain are activated by attention and by working memory tasks (Awh & Vogel, 2008).

TEST YOURSELF 5.2

1. Describe two findings that led Baddeley to begin considering alternatives to the modal model.
2. What are the differences between STM and working memory?
3. Describe Baddeley's three-component model of working memory.
4. Describe the phonological similarity effect, the word length effect, and the effect of articulatory suppression. What do these effects indicate about the phonological loop?
5. Describe the visuospatial sketch pad, the Shepard and Meltzger mental rotation task, and Brooks's "F" task. Be sure you understand what each task indicates about the visuospatial sketch pad.
6. What is the central executive? What happens when executive function is lost because of damage to the frontal lobe?
7. What is the episodic buffer? Why was it proposed, and what are its functions?

Working Memory and the Brain

We have seen from previous chapters that cognitive psychologists have a number of tools at their disposal to determine the connection between cognitive functioning and the brain. The major methods are (1) analysis of behavior after brain damage, either animal (Method: Brain Ablation, Chapter 3, page 71) or human (Method: Dissociations in Neuropsychology, Chapter 3, page 73); (2) recording from single neurons in animals (Method: Recording From a Neuron, Chapter 2, page 28); and (3) recording electrical signals from the human brain (Method: Event-Related Potential, Chapter 2, page 34) and measuring activity of the human brain (Method: Brain Imaging, Chapter 2, page 30).

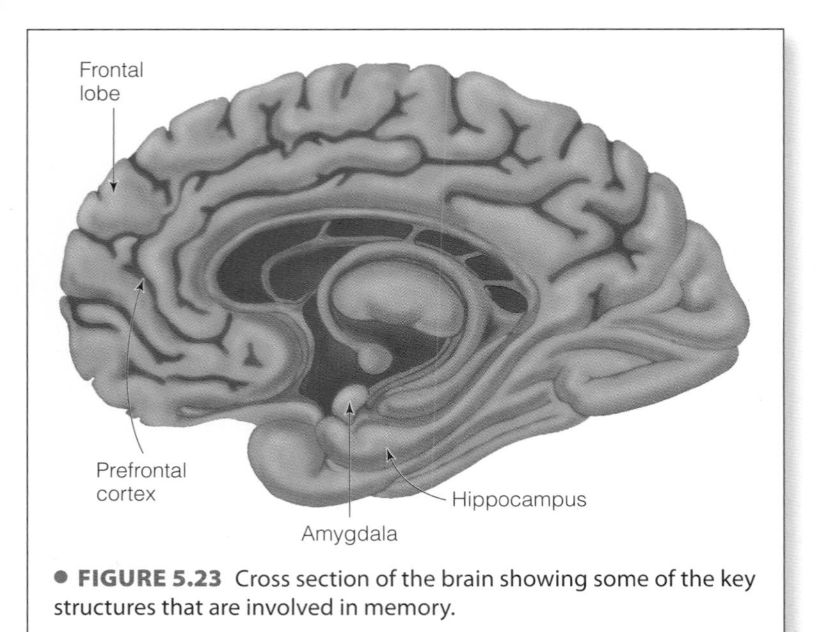

• **FIGURE 5.23** Cross section of the brain showing some of the key structures that are involved in memory.

What are the researchers who use these methods to study working memory and the brain trying to explain? To answer this question, we have only to look back at this chapter to appreciate that an important characteristic of memory is that it involves *delay* or *waiting*. Something happens, followed by a delay, which is brief for working memory; then, if memory is successful, the person remembers what has happened. Researchers, therefore, have looked for physiological mechanisms that hold information about events after they are over.

We will describe the following research, which is designed to determine where and how this information is held in the brain (• Figure 5.23): (1) brain damage—how damage to or removal of the prefrontal cortex affects the ability to remember for short periods of time; (2) neurons—how neurons in the monkey prefrontal cortex hold onto information during a brief delay; and (3) brain activity—areas of the brain that are activated by working memory tasks, and how the brains of people with good and poor working memory respond to a working memory task.

THE EFFECT OF DAMAGE TO THE PREFRONTAL CORTEX

We have already seen that damage to the frontal lobe (see Figure 5.23) in humans causes problems in controlling attention, which is an important function of the central executive (page 136). Early research on the frontal lobe and memory was carried out in monkeys using a task called the **delayed-response task**, which required a monkey to hold information in working memory during a delay period (Goldman-Rakic, 1992). • Figure 5.24 shows the setup for this task. The monkey sees a food reward in one of two food wells. Both wells are then covered, a screen is lowered, and then there is a delay before the screen is raised again. When the screen is raised, the monkey must remember which well had the food and uncover the correct food well to obtain a reward. Monkeys can be trained to accomplish this task. However, if their prefrontal cortex is removed, their performance drops to chance level, so they pick the correct food well only about half of the time.

This result supports the idea that the prefrontal (PF) cortex is important for holding information for brief periods of time. In fact, it has been suggested that one reason we can describe the memory behavior of very young infants (younger than about 8 months of age) as "out of sight, out of mind" (when an object that the infant can see

• **FIGURE 5.24** The delayed-response task being administered to a monkey.

is then hidden from view, the infant behaves as if the object no longer exists) is that their frontal and prefrontal cortex does not become adequately developed until about 8 months of age (Goldman-Rakic, 1992).

PREFRONTAL NEURONS THAT HOLD INFORMATION

The idea that the PF cortex is important for working memory is also supported by experiments that have looked at how some neurons in the PF cortex are able to hold information after the original stimulus is no longer present, by continuing to respond during a brief delay. Shintaro Funahashi and coworkers (1989) conducted an experiment in which they recorded from neurons in a monkey's PF cortex while the monkey carried out a delayed-response task. For the task, the monkey first looked steadily at a fixation point, X, while a square was flashed at one position on the screen (● Figure 5.25a). In this example, the square was flashed in the upper left corner (on the other trials, the square was flashed at different positions on the screen). This causes a small response in the neuron.

After the square went off, there was a delay of a few seconds. The nerve firing records in Figure 5.25b show that the neuron was firing during this delay. This firing is the neural record of the monkey's working memory for the position of the square. After the delay, the fixation X went off. This was a signal for the monkey to move its eyes to where the square had been flashed (Figure 5.25c). The monkey's ability to do this provides behavioral evidence that it had, in fact, remembered the location of the square.

The key result of this experiment was that Funahashi found neurons that responded only when the square was flashed in a *particular location* and that these neurons continued responding during the delay. For example, some neurons responded only when the square was flashed in the upper right corner and then during the delay; other neurons responded only when the square was presented at other positions on the screen and then during the delay. The firing of these neurons indicates that an object was presented

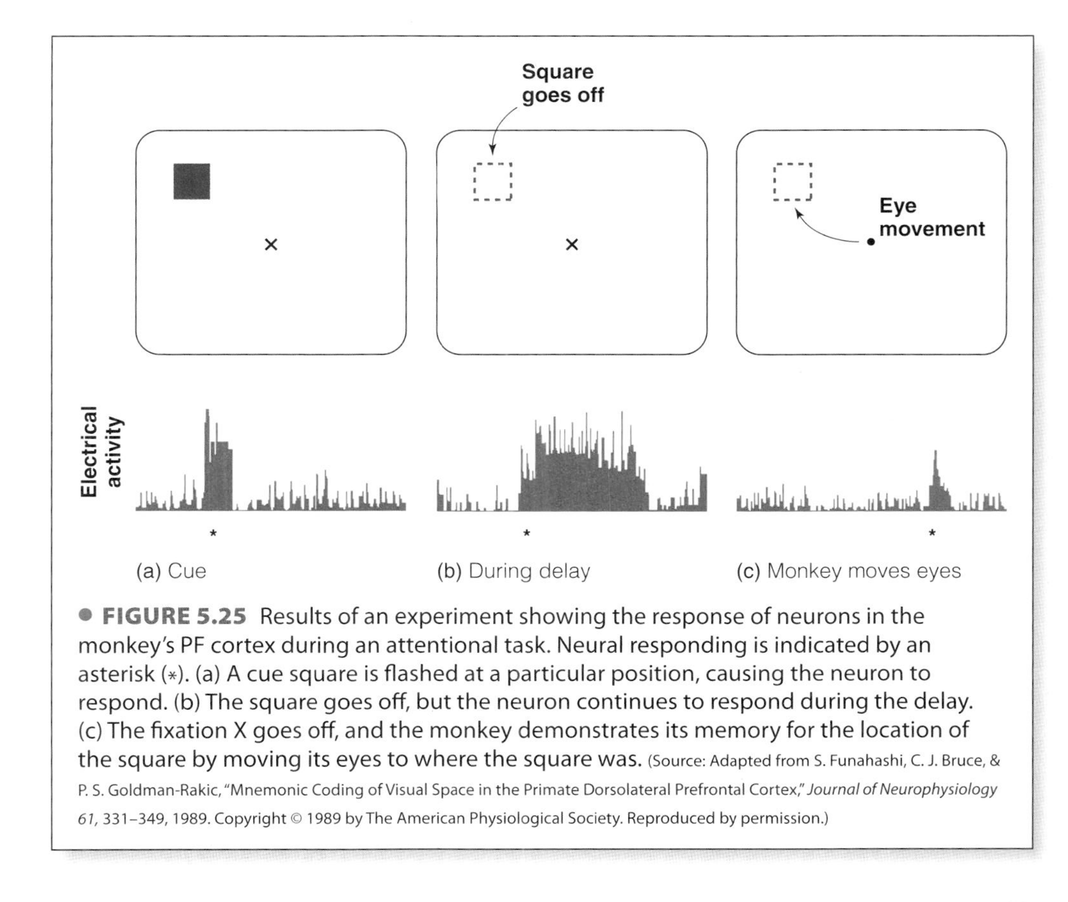

● **FIGURE 5.25** Results of an experiment showing the response of neurons in the monkey's PF cortex during an attentional task. Neural responding is indicated by an asterisk (*). (a) A cue square is flashed at a particular position, causing the neuron to respond. (b) The square goes off, but the neuron continues to respond during the delay. (c) The fixation X goes off, and the monkey demonstrates its memory for the location of the square by moving its eyes to where the square was. (Source: Adapted from S. Funahashi, C. J. Bruce, & P. S. Goldman-Rakic, "Mnemonic Coding of Visual Space in the Primate Dorsolateral Prefrontal Cortex," *Journal of Neurophysiology 61*, 331–349, 1989. Copyright © 1989 by The American Physiological Society. Reproduced by permission.)

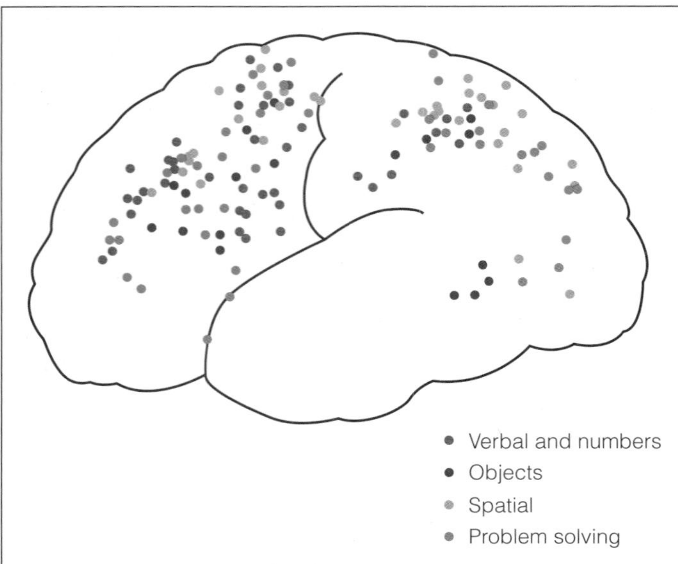

● **FIGURE 5.26** Some of the areas in the cortex that have been shown by brain imaging research to be involved in working memory. The colored dots represent the results of more than 60 experiments that tested working memory for words and numbers (red), objects (blue), spatial location (orange), and problem solving (green). (Source: R. Cabeza & L. Nyberg, "Imaging Cognition II: An Empirical Review of 275 PET and fMRI Studies," *Journal of Cognitive Neuroscience, 12,* 1–47, 2000.)

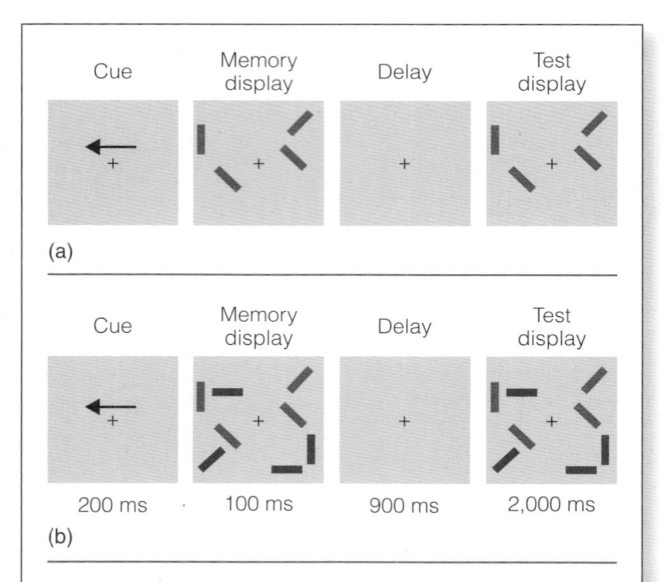

● **FIGURE 5.27** Sequence for the Vogel et. al (2005) task. The arrow in this example tells the participant to pay attention to the left side of the memory and test displays. The task is to indicate if the red rectangles on the attended side are the same or different in the two displays. (a) Display with two red rectangles on each side of the display. (b) Display with two blue rectangles added to each side. The participant is told to ignore the blue rectangles. (Source: Based on E. K. Vogel, A. W. McCollough, & M. G. Machizawa, "Neural Measures Reveal Individual Differences in Controlling Access to Working Memory," *Nature 438,* 500–503, 2005.)

at a particular place, and this information about where the object was remains available for as long as these neurons continue firing (also see Funahashi, 2006).

Research has also found neurons that are involved with working memory in other areas of the brain, including the primary visual cortex, which is the first area of the brain to receive visual signals (Super et al., 2001), and the temporal and parietal areas, where visual information is transmitted from the primary visual cortex (Jonides et al., 2005). Thus, although the PF cortex may be the brain area that is most closely associated with working memory, other areas are also involved. This idea that a number of areas of the brain are involved in working memory is another example of distributed processing (see Chapter 2, page 36) that we described for perception (Chapter 2, page 37) and attention (Chapter 4, page 107).

BRAIN ACTIVATION IN HUMANS

The conclusion that many brain areas are involved in working memory has been confirmed by research using imaging techniques such as PET and fMRI to measure brain activity in humans. These studies show that as a person carries out a working memory task, activity occurs in the prefrontal cortex (Courtney et al., 1998) and in other areas as well (Fiez, 2001; Olesen et al., 2004). ● Figure 5.26, which summarizes the data from many experiments, shows that in addition to the prefrontal cortex, other areas in the frontal lobe and also areas in the parietal lobe and the cerebellum are involved in working memory (Cabeza & Nyberg, 2000).

In addition to determining which areas of the brain are involved in working memory, researchers have also been concerned with determining how the brain is involved in the "workings" of working memory. For example, one of the functions of the central executive is to focus attention on items that are important for a task and to ignore items that are not relevant to the task.

Edward Vogel and coworkers (2005) did an experiment on the allocation of attention by measuring a component of the event-related potential (ERP) in humans, recorded during a working memory task. (See Method: Event-Related Potential, Chapter 2, page 34.) The response they measured was related to encoding items in working memory, so a larger ERP response indicated that more space was used in working memory.

What makes Vogel and coworkers' experiment interesting is that they separated participants into two groups based on their performance on a test of working memory. Participants in the *high memory capacity group* were able to hold a number of items in working memory; participants in the *low memory capacity group* were able to hold fewer items in working memory. Both groups viewed the stimuli shown in ● Figure 5.27. They first saw a cue indicating whether to direct their attention to the red rectangles on the left side or the red rectangles on the right side of the displays that followed. They then saw a memory display for one-tenth of a second, followed by a brief blank screen and then a test display. On some trials, two red rectangles were presented on the left and right sides of the display, as shown in Figure 5.27a. On other trials, two red rectangles and two blue rectangles (which the participants were told to ignore) were presented (Figure 5.27b).

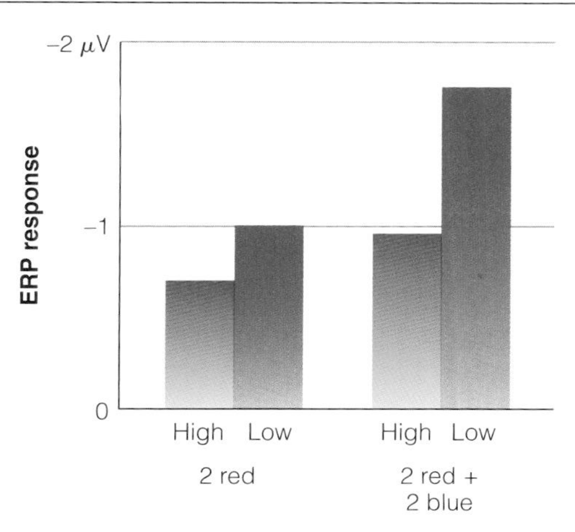

● **FIGURE 5.28** Results of the Vogel et al. (2005) experiment. The key finding is that performance is about the same for high- and low-capacity participants when only the red rectangles are present (left pair of bars), but although adding the two blue rectangles has little effect for the high-capacity participants, it causes an increase in the response for the low-capacity participants (right pair of bars). (Source: Based on E. K. Vogel, A. W. McCollough, & M. G. Machizawa, "Neural Measures Reveal Individual Differences in Controlling Access to Working Memory," *Nature 438*, 500–503, 2005.)

The participants' task was to respond to the test display by indicating whether the orientations of the red rectangles in the cued side of the test display was the same as or different from the orientations of the red rectangles on the cued side of the memory display. In the examples in Figure 5.27, the answers would be "same."

The results in ● Figure 5.28 show the size of the ERP responses for both groups. The left pair of bars in Figure 5.28 show that the ERP response when just red rectangles were presented was similar for the high-capacity and low-capacity participants. However, the right pair of bars indicate that adding blue rectangles had little effect on the response of the high-capacity group, but caused an increase in the response of the low-capacity group.

The fact that adding the two blue rectangles had little effect on the response of the high-capacity group means that these participants were very efficient at ignoring the distractors, so the irrelevant blue stimuli did not take up any space in working memory. Because allocating attention is a function of the central executive, this means that the central executive was functioning well for these participants.

The fact that adding the two blue rectangles caused a large increase in the response of the low-capacity group means that these participants were not able to ignore the irrelevant blue stimuli, and the blue rectangles were therefore taking up space in working memory. The central executive of these participants is not operating as efficiently as the central executives of the high-capacity participants. Vogel and coworkers concluded from these results that some people's central executives are better at allocating attention than others'. The reason this is important is that other experiments have shown that people with more efficient working memories are more likely to perform well on tests of reading and reasoning ability and on tests designed to measure intelligence.

➔ Something to Consider

THE ADVANTAGES OF HAVING A MORE EFFICIENT WORKING MEMORY

At the beginning of a chapter on individual differences in working memory, Andrew Conway and coworkers (2007, p. 3) state:

> The ability to mentally maintain information in an active and readily accessible state, while concurrently and selectively processing new information, is one of the greatest accomplishments of the human mind; it makes possible planning, reasoning, problem solving, reading, and abstraction. *Of course some minds accomplish these goals with more success than others.* (italics added)

The chapter goes on to describe research that has shown that people who have a large-capacity working memory are often better at cognitive processes such as reading and reasoning, and that this is also reflected in higher scores on intelligence tests.

One of the pioneering studies linking working memory and cognitive processes is a study of reading by Meredyth Daneman and Patricia Carpenter (1980). The reason Daneman and Carpenter's experiment is considered a "classic" is because of their insight that tests such as the digit span test used to measure the capacity of STM (see page 125) are not useful for measuring the capacity of working memory. They reasoned that any test of working memory capacity has to involve a dynamic process more like what goes on in everyday cognitions such as reading and solving problems.

Operation Span

The test they developed, called **reading span**, was designed to measure both the storage *and* processing functions of working memory. It accomplishes this by measuring the maximum number of sentences that a person can read while simultaneously holding the last word in each sentence in memory. This method is illustrated in the following Methods section.

METHOD Reading Span

Reading span is measured as follows (try it!). Read the first sentence below *out loud* (important!), then cover the sentence and remember the last word in the sentence. Then read the second sentence out loud, cover it, remember the last word, and finally read the third sentence. After reading the third sentence, indicate what the three last words in the sentences were, in order.

> When at last his eyes opened, there was no gleam of triumph, no shade of anger.
>
> The taxi turned up Michigan Avenue, where they had a clear view of the lake.
>
> After he got out of the car, he began walking rapidly toward the bus station.

In Daneman and Carpenter's experiment, reading span was measured by determining how many sentences a person could read and then successfully repeat the last words in order.

Daneman and Carpenter measured reading spans for 20 participants and also presented a comprehension test in which participants answered a question about a paragraph they had read. When they compared reading spans and performance on the comprehension test, they found that participants with larger reading spans performed better on the comprehension test. The five readers with a reading span of 2 correctly answered an average of 13.6 out of 24 questions, but the six readers with spans of 4 and 5 answered 19.7 of the 24 questions. Reading span was also related to the participants' verbal SAT scores, with larger spans being associated with higher scores.

Many other experiments have obtained similar results, showing that better working memory scores are associated with better comprehension and also with better reasoning ability and higher intelligence (Conway et al., 2003). One idea about what this means is that people with better working memory capacity score better on these tests because there is more space in their working memory to hold and manipulate information. But another idea is that a person's working memory capacity reflects not only how many items can be stored, but how efficiently the person can focus attention on relevant information and filter out irrelevant information (Awh & Vogel, 2008; McNab & Klingberg, 2008). If this sounds familiar, it is because this is the result of the Vogel et al. (2005) event-related potential experiment we described earlier (see Figure 5.28).

Thus, we end this chapter with the message that opened our discussion of working memory on page 130: The important characteristic of working memory is not just how much space there is in it, but how it manipulates information. The relation between memory and our interactions in the world is captured best by considering the dynamic properties of memory. In the three chapters that follow, we will see that this is also true for long-term memory.

TEST YOURSELF 5.3

1. The physiology of working memory has been studied using (a) brain lesions in monkeys, (b) neural recording from monkeys, and (c) brain imaging and event-related potential recording experiments in humans. What do the results of each of these procedures tell us about working memory and the brain?
2. What is the reading span task? Why is it a better test of working memory than the digit span task?
3. What is the evidence supporting the idea that better comprehension, reasoning, and intelligence are related to having a larger and more efficient working memory?

CHAPTER SUMMARY

1. Memory is the process involved in retaining, retrieving, and using information about stimuli, images, events, ideas, and skills after the original information is no longer present. It is important for dealing with day-to-day events, and cases such as Clive Wearing's illustrate the importance of memory for normal functioning.
2. Atkinson and Shiffrin's modal model of memory consists of three structural features—sensory memory, short-term memory, and long-term memory. Another feature of the model is control process such as rehearsal and attentional strategies.
3. Sperling used two methods, whole report and partial report, to determine the capacity and time course of visual sensory memory. The duration of visual sensory memory (iconic memory) is less than 1 second, and of auditory sensory memory (echoic memory) about 2–4 seconds.
4. Short-term memory is our window on the present. Brown, and Peterson and Peterson, determined that the duration of STM is about 15–20 seconds. They interpreted the short duration of STM as being caused by decay, but a later reanalysis of their data indicated it was due to proactive interference.
5. According to George Miller's classic seven plus or minus two paper, the capacity of STM is 5 to 9 items. According to more recent experiments, the capacity is about 4 items. The amount of information held in STM can be expanded by chunking—combining small units into larger, more meaningful ones. Examples of chunking are the memory performance of the runner S.F. and how chess masters use their knowledge of chess to remember chess piece positions.
6. Information can be coded in STM in terms of sound (auditory coding), vision (visual coding), and meaning (semantic coding). Auditory coding was illustrated by Conrad's experiment that analyzed the type of errors made in memory for letters. Visual coding was illustrated by Della Sala's recalling visual patterns experiment, and semantic coding by Wickens' release from proactive interference experiment.
7. The short-term memory component of the modal model was revised by Baddeley to deal with results that couldn't be explained by a single short-term process. In this new model, working memory replaces STM.
8. Working memory is a limited-capacity system for storage and manipulation of information in complex tasks. It consists of three components: the phonological loop, which holds auditory or verbal information; the visuospatial sketch pad, which holds visual and spatial information; and the central executive, which coordinates the action of the phonological loop and visuospatial sketch pad.
9. The following effects can be explained in terms of operation of the phonological loop: (a) phonological similarity effect; (b) word length effect; and (c) articulatory suppression.
10. Shepard and Metzler's mental rotation experiment illustrates visual imagery, which is one of the functions of the visuospatial sketch pad. Brooks's "F" experiment showed that two tasks can be handled simultaneously if one involves the visuospatial sketch pad and the other involves the phonological loop. Performance decreases if one component of working memory is called on to deal with two tasks simultaneously.
11. The central executive coordinates how information is used by the phonological loop and visuospatial sketch pad, and can therefore be thought of as an attention controller. Patients with frontal lobe damage have trouble controlling their attention, as illustrated by the phenomenon of perseveration.
12. The working memory model has been updated to include an additional component called the episodic buffer, which helps connect working memory with LTM and which has a greater capacity and can hold information longer than the phonological loop or visuospatial sketch pad.
13. Behaviors that depend on working memory can be disrupted by damage to the prefrontal cortex. This has been demonstrated by testing monkeys on the delayed-response task.
14. There are neurons in the prefrontal cortex that fire to presentation of a stimulus and continue firing as this stimulus is held in memory.
15. Brain imaging experiments in humans reveal that a large number of brain areas are involved in working memory. Event-related potential (ERP) studies have provided physiological evidence supporting the idea that a more efficient working memory is associated with the ability to focus on relevant information and filter out irrelevant information.
16. There is a great deal of evidence that having a larger or more efficient working memory is associated with better comprehension, reasoning ability, and intelligence.

Think ABOUT IT

1. Analyze the following in terms of how the various stages of the modal model are activated, using Rachel's pizza-ordering experience in Figure 5.3 as a guide: (1) listening to a lecture in class, taking notes, or reviewing the notes later as you study for an exam; (2) watching a scene in a James Bond movie in which Bond captures the female enemy agent whom he slept with the night before.
2. Adam has just tested a woman who has brain damage, and he is having difficulty understanding the results. She can't remember any words from a list when she is tested immediately after hearing the words, but her memory gets better when she is tested after a delay. Interestingly enough, when the woman reads the list herself, she remembers well at first, so in that case the delay is not necessary. Can you explain these observations using the modal model? The working memory model? Can you think of a new model that might explain this result better than those two?

If You WANT TO KNOW MORE

1. **Physiology of visual working memory.** Recent physiological research has studied how long visual information is held in working memory, individual differences in visual working memory capacity, and where different types of stimuli are processed in the brain.

Cowan, N., & Morey, C. C. (2006). Visual working memory depends on attentional filtering. *Trends in Cognitive Sciences, 10*, 139–141.

Mecklinger, A., Gruenwald, C., Besson, M., Magnie, M., & Von Cramon, D. Y. (2002). Separable neuronal circuits for manipulable and non-manipulable objects in working memory. *Cerebral Cortex, 12*, 1115–1123.

Todd, J. J., & Marios, R. (2004). Capacity limit of visual short-term memory in human posterior parietal cortex. *Nature, 428*, 751–754.

2. **Working memory and language.** Working memory is important for many language functions, including reading ability and second language learning.

Bayliss, D. M., Jarrold, C., Baddeley, A. D., & Leigh, E. (2005). Differential constraints on the working memory and reading abilities of individuals with learning difficulties and typically developing children. *Journal of Experimental Child Psychology, 92*, 76–99.

Perani, D. (2005). The neural basis of language talent in bilinguals. *Trends in Cognitive Sciences, 9*, 211–213.

3. **Cognitive neuroscience of working memory.** A special issue of the journal *Neuroscience* contains 35 papers that survey current knowledge about the neuroscience of working memory. The paper below leads off the issue.

Repovs, G., & Bresjanac, M. (2006). Cognitive neuroscience of working memory. *Neuroscience, 139*, 1–3.

Key TERMS

Media RESOURCES

The *Cognitive Psychology* Book Companion Website

www.cengage.com/international

Prepare for quizzes and exams with online resources—including a glossary, flashcards, tutorial quizzes, crossword puzzles, and more.

CogLab

To experience these experiments for yourself, go to coglab.wadsworth.com. Be sure to read each experiment's setup instructions before you go to the experiment itself. Otherwise, you won't know which keys to press.

Primary Labs

Partial report The partial report condition of Sperling's iconic memory experiment (p. 122).

Brown-Peterson How memory for trigrams fades (p. 124).

Memory span How memory span depends on the nature of stimuli that are presented (p. 125).

Phonological similarity effect How recall for items on a list is affected by how similar the items sound (p. 133).

Operation span Measuring the operation-word span, a measure of working memory (p. 141).

Related Labs

Apparent movement How the perception of movement can be achieved by flashing still images (p. 120).

Irrelevant speech effect How recall for items on a list is affected by the presence of irrelevant speech.

Modality effect How memory for the last one or two items in a list depends on whether the list is heard or read.

Position error What happens when trying to remember the order of a series of letters.

Sternberg search A method to determine how information is retrieved from short-term memory.

6 Structure of Long-Term Memory

In this scene from *Slumdog Millionaire*, the character Jamal Malik is challenged to come up with the answer to a question on the Indian version of the quiz show *Who Wants to Be a Millionaire?* To answer this question, Jamal will have to access his semantic memory, which is his storehouse of memory for facts. This chapter describes semantic memory and contrasts it with episodic memory, which is memory for personal experiences.

SOME QUESTIONS WE WILL CONSIDER

- How does damage to the brain affect the ability to remember what has happened in the past and the ability to form new memories of ongoing experiences? (148)
- How are memories for personal experiences, like what you did last summer, different from memories for facts, like the capital of your state? (157)
- How do the different types of memory interact in our everyday experience? (159)
- How has memory loss been depicted in popular films? (165)

JIMMY G. HAD BEEN ADMITTED TO THE HOME FOR THE AGED, ACCOMPANIED BY A transfer note that described him as "helpless, demented, confused, and disoriented." As neurologist Oliver Sacks talked with Jimmy about events of his childhood, his experiences in school, and his days in the Navy, Sacks noticed that Jimmy was talking as if he were still in the Navy, even though he had been discharged 10 years earlier. Sacks (1985) recounts the rest of his conversation with Jimmy as follows:

> "What year is this, Mr. G?" I asked, concealing my perplexity under a casual manner.
>
> "Forty-five, man. What do you mean?" He went on, "We've won the war, FDR's dead, Truman's at the helm. There are great times ahead."
>
> "And you, Jimmy, how old would you be?" Oddly, uncertainly, he hesitated a moment, as if engaged in calculation. "Why, I guess I'm nineteen, Doc. I'll be twenty next birthday." Looking at the gray-haired man before me, I had an impulse for which I have never forgiven myself—it was, or would have been, the height of cruelty had there been any possibility of Jimmy's remembering it.
>
> "Here," I said, and thrust a mirror toward him. "Look in the mirror and tell me what you see. Is that a nineteen-year-old looking out from the mirror?"
>
> He suddenly turned ashen and gripped the sides of the chair. "Jesus Christ," he whispered. "Christ, what's going on? What's happened to me? Is this a nightmare? Am I crazy? Is this a joke?"—and he became frantic, panicky.
>
> "It's okay, Jim," I said soothingly. "It's just a mistake. Nothing to worry about. Hey!" I took him to the window. "Isn't this a lovely spring day. See the kids there playing baseball?" He regained his color and started to smile, and I stole away, taking the hateful mirror with me.
>
> Two minutes later I reentered the room. Jimmy was still standing by the window, gazing with pleasure at the kids playing baseball below. He wheeled around as I opened the door, and his face assumed a cheery expression.
>
> "Hiya, Doc!" he said. "Nice morning! You want to talk to me—do I take this chair here?" There was no sign of recognition on his frank, open face.
>
> "Haven't we met before, Mr. G?" I said casually.
>
> "No, I can't say we have. Quite a beard you got there. I wouldn't forget you, Doc!"
>
> . . .
>
> "You remember telling me about your childhood, growing up in Pennsylvania, working as a radio operator in a submarine? And how your brother is engaged to a girl from California?"
>
> "Hey, you're right. But I didn't tell you that. I never met you before in my life. You must have read all about me in my chart."
>
> "Okay," I said. "I'll tell you a story. A man went to his doctor complaining of memory lapses. The doctor asked him some routine questions, and then said, 'These lapses. What about them?' 'What lapses?' the patient replied."
>
> "So that's my problem," Jimmy laughed. "I kinda thought it was. I do find myself forgetting things, once in a while things that have just happened. The past is clear, though." (Sacks, 1985, p. 14)

Jimmy G. suffers from **Korsakoff's syndrome**, a condition caused by a prolonged deficiency of vitamin B1, usually as a result of chronic alcoholism. The deficiency leads to the destruction of areas in the frontal and temporal lobes, which causes severe and permanent impairments in memory. The damage to Jimmy G.'s memory has resulted in **anterograde amnesia**, the loss of the ability to assimilate or retain new knowledge. He cannot recognize people he has just met, follow a story in a book, find his way to the corner drugstore, or solve problems that take more than a few moments to figure out. Jimmy also suffers from some **retrograde amnesia**, the loss of memory for events that have happened in the past. Jimmy's problem is similar to Clive Wearing's, from Chapter 5. He has forgotten much of his past and is unable to form new long-term memories. His reality therefore consists of a few memories from long ago plus what has happened within the last 30–60 seconds.

The severe disabilities suffered by Jimmy G. and Clive Wearing illustrate the importance of being able to retain information about what has happened in the past. The purpose of this chapter is to introduce long-term memory by describing how it interacts with short-term memory (STM) and working memory (WM), and how it differs from STM/WM. We then describe two types of long-term memory to lay the groundwork for Chapter 7, in which we will consider how information becomes stored in long-term memory and how it is retrieved when we need it.

Distinguishing Between Long-Term Memory and Short-Term Memory

Long-term memory (LTM) is the system that is responsible for storing information for long periods of time. One way to describe LTM is as an "archive" of information about past events in our lives and knowledge we have learned. What is particularly amazing about this storage is how it stretches from just a few moments ago to as far back as we can remember.

LONG-TERM AND SHORT-TERM PROCESSES

The long time span of LTM is illustrated in ● Figure 6.1, which shows what a student who has just taken a seat in class might be remembering about events that have occurred at various times in the past. His first recollection—that he has just sat down—would be

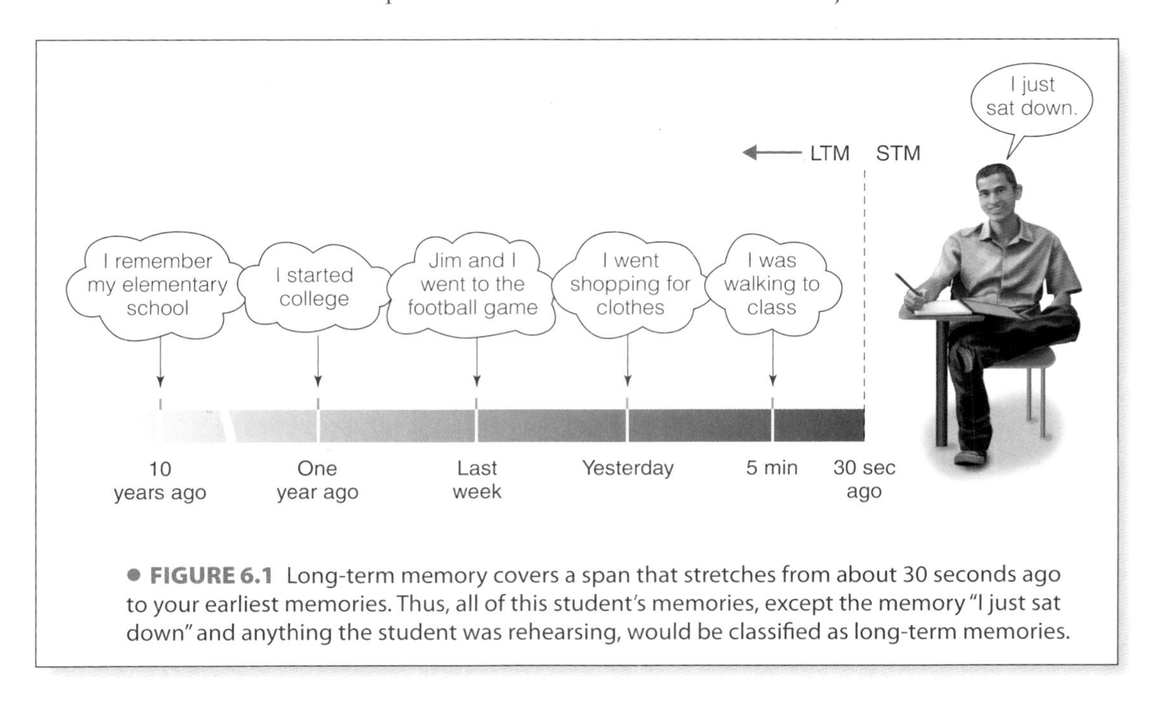

● **FIGURE 6.1** Long-term memory covers a span that stretches from about 30 seconds ago to your earliest memories. Thus, all of this student's memories, except the memory "I just sat down" and anything the student was rehearsing, would be classified as long-term memories.

in his working memory because it has happened within the last 30 seconds. But everything before that—from his recent memory that 5 minutes ago he was walking to class, to a memory from 10 years earlier of the elementary school he attended in the third grade—is part of long-term memory.

Although all of these memories are contained in LTM, recent memories tend to be more detailed, and much of this detail and often the specific memories themselves fade with the passage of time and as other experiences accumulate. Thus, on October 1, 2010, this person would probably not remember the details of what happened while walking to class on October 1, 2009, but would remember some of the general experiences from around that time. One of the things that we will be concerned with in this chapter and the next is why we retain some information and lose other information.

Our goal in this chapter is to introduce long-term memory by first showing how it can be distinguished from STM/WM in ways that go beyond the basic facts about duration (LTM = long; STM/WM = very short) and capacity (LTM = very large; STM/WM = very limited). After contrasting LTM and STM/WM, the rest of the chapter describes the various types of LTM, which include memories for personal experiences (what you did last summer), memories for knowledge or facts (the identity of the third president of the United States), and how to do things (your ability to ride a bike or drive a car).

Our starting point for comparing LTM and STM/WM takes us back to our discussion of STM, in which we noted that most of the research on STM emphasized its storage function—how much information it can hold and for how long. This led to the proposal of working memory, with its emphasis on dynamic processes that are needed to explain complex cognitions such as understanding language, solving problems, and making decisions.

A similar situation exists for LTM. Although retaining information about the past is an important characteristic of LTM, we also need to understand how this information is used. We can do this by focusing on the dynamic aspects of how LTM operates, including how it interacts with working memory to create our ongoing experience.

Consider, for example, what happens when Tony's friend Cindy says, "Jim and I saw the new James Bond movie last night" (● Figure 6.2). As Tony's working memory is holding the exact wording of that statement in his mind, it is simultaneously accessing

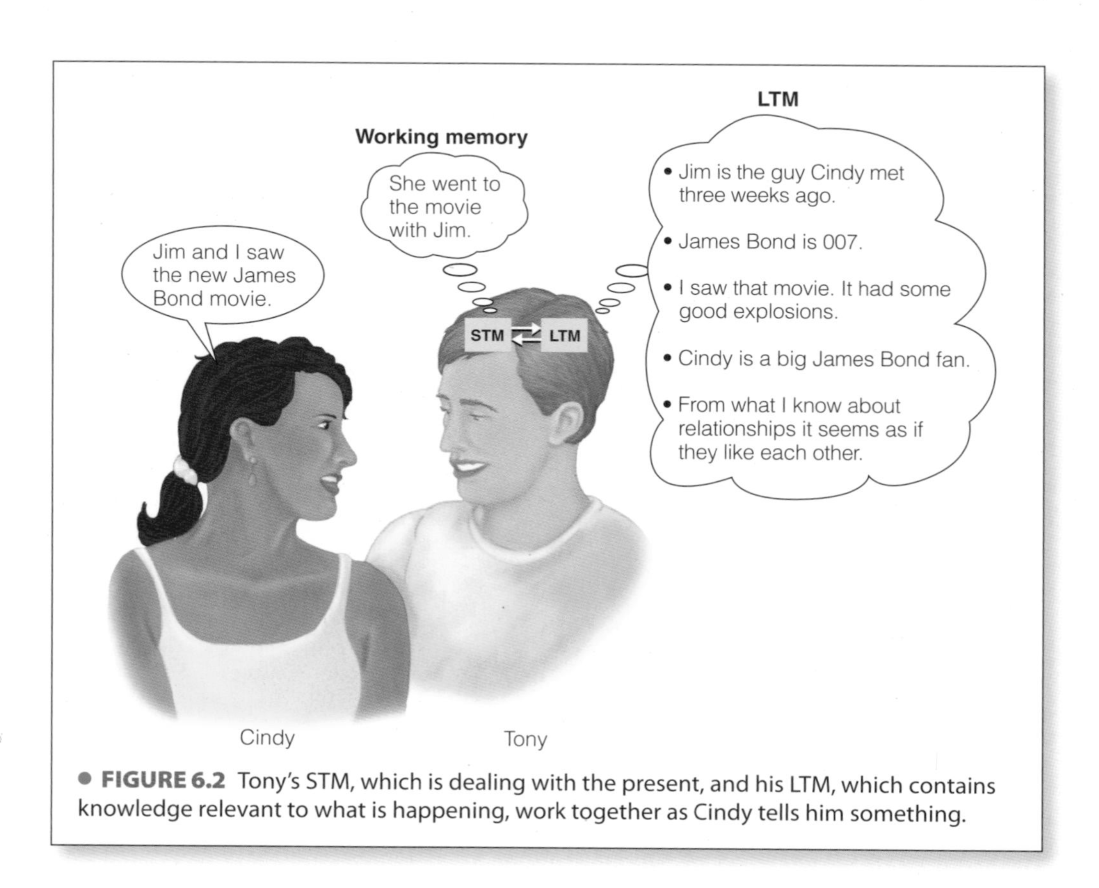

● **FIGURE 6.2** Tony's STM, which is dealing with the present, and his LTM, which contains knowledge relevant to what is happening, work together as Cindy tells him something.

the meaning of words from LTM, which helps him understand the meaning of each of the words that make up the sentence.

Tony's LTM also contains a great deal of additional information about movies, James Bond, and Cindy. Although Tony might not consciously think about all of this information (after all, he has to pay attention to the next thing that Cindy is going to tell him), it is all there in his LTM and adds to his understanding of what he is hearing and his interpretation of what it might mean. LTM therefore provides both an archive that we can refer to when we want to remember events from the past, and a wealth of background information that we are constantly consulting as we use working memory to make contact with what is happening at a particular moment.

The interplay between what is happening in the present and information from the past, which we described in the interaction between Tony and Cindy, is based on the distinction between STM/WM and LTM. Beginning in the 1960s, a great deal of research was conducted that was designed to distinguish between short-term and long-term processes. In describing these experiments, we will identify the short-term process as short-term memory (STM) for the early experiments that used that term, and as working memory for more recent experiments that focused on working memory.

The distinction between STM and LTM was studied in a classic experiment by B. B. Murdoch, Jr. (1962), which is illustrated by the following demonstration.

CogLab
Serial Position

DEMONSTRATION Serial Position

Read the stimulus list below (omitting the numbers) to another person at a rate of about one word every 2 seconds. At the end of the list, tell the person to write down all of the words he or she can remember, in any order. This is the recall procedure we introduced in Chapter 5 (page 123).

1. barricade
2. children
3. diet
4. gourd
5. folio
6. meter
7. journey
8. mohair
9. phoenix
10. crossbow
11. doorbell
12. muffler
13. mouse
14. menu
15. airplane

Analyze your results by noting how many words the person remembered from the first five entries on the list, the middle five, and the last five. Did they remember more words from the first or last five than from the middle? Individual results vary widely, but when Murdoch did this experiment on a large number of participants and plotted the percentage recall for each word against the word's position on the list, he obtained a function called the **serial position curve**.

SERIAL POSITION CURVE

Murdoch's serial position curve, shown in ● Figure 6.3, indicates that memory is better for words at the beginning of the list and at the end of the list than for words in the middle. Superior memory for stimuli presented at the beginning of a sequence is called the **primacy effect**. A possible explanation of the primacy effect is that participants had time to rehearse these words and transfer them to LTM. According to this idea, participants begin rehearsing the first word right after it is presented; because no other words have been presented, it receives 100 percent of the person's attention. When the second word is presented, attention becomes spread over two words, and so on; as additional words are presented, less rehearsal is possible for later words.

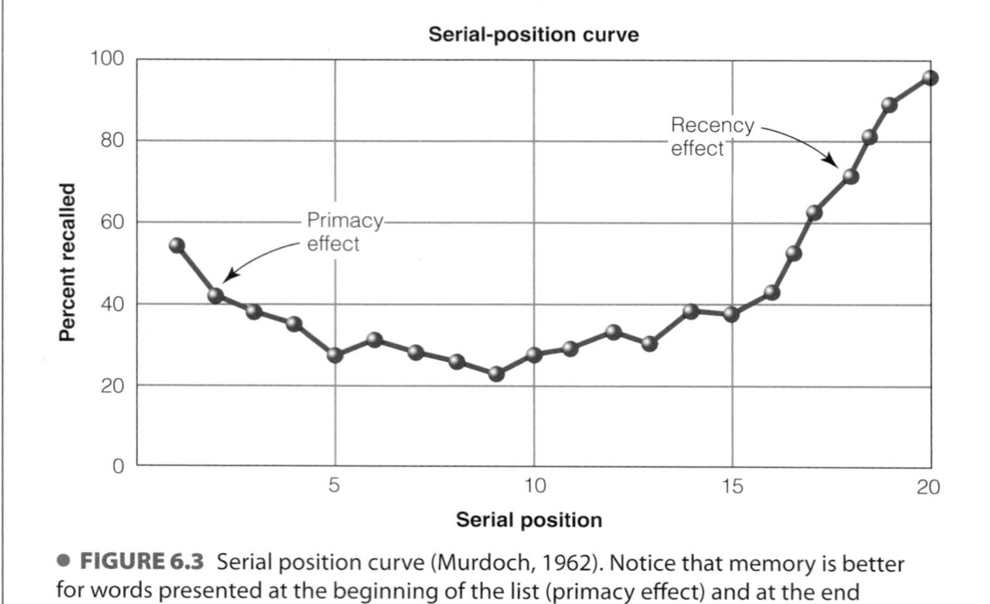

• **FIGURE 6.3** Serial position curve (Murdoch, 1962). Notice that memory is better for words presented at the beginning of the list (primacy effect) and at the end (recency effect). (Source: B. B. Murdoch, Jr., "The Serial Position Effect in Free Recall," *Journal of Experimental Psychology, 64,* 482–488.)

The idea that the primacy effect occurs because participants have more time to rehearse earlier words on the list was tested by Dewey Rundus (1971). Rundus derived a serial position curve by presenting a list of 20 words at a rate of 1 word every 5 seconds and then asking his participants to write down all of the words they could remember. The resulting serial position curve, which is the red curve in • Figure 6.4, demonstrates the same primacy and recency effects as Murdoch's curve in Figure 6.3. But Rundus added a further twist to his experiment by asking his

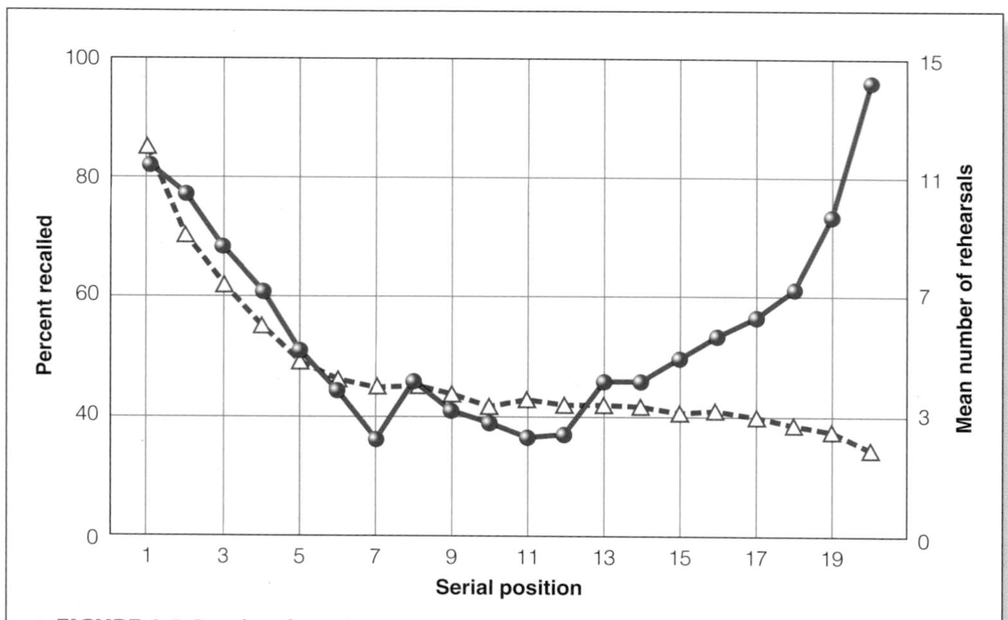

• **FIGURE 6.4** Results of Rundus's (1971) experiment. The solid red line is the usual serial position curve. The dashed blue line indicates how many times the participant rehearsed (said out loud) each word on the list. Note how closely the rehearsal curve matches the initial part of the serial position curve. (Source: D. Rundus, "Analysis of Rehearsal Processes in Free Recall," *Journal of Experimental Psychology, 89,* 63–77, Figure 1, p. 66. Copyright © 1971 by the American Psychological Association. Reprinted by permission.)

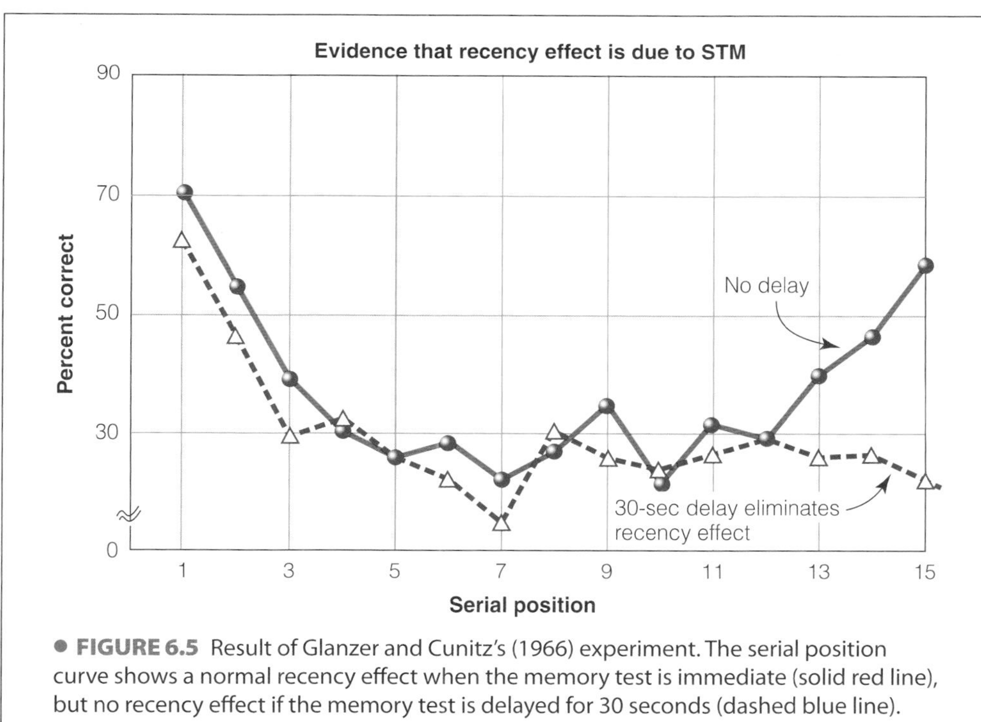

● **FIGURE 6.5** Result of Glanzer and Cunitz's (1966) experiment. The serial position curve shows a normal recency effect when the memory test is immediate (solid red line), but no recency effect if the memory test is delayed for 30 seconds (dashed blue line). (Source: M. Glanzer & A. R. Cunitz, "Two Storage Mechanisms in Free Recall," *Journal of Verbal learning and Verbal Behavior, 5,* Figures 1 & 2, 351–360. Copyright © 1966 Elsevier Ltd. Republished with permission.)

participants to study the list as it was being presented by repeating the words out loud during the 5-second intervals between words. They were not told which words to repeat—just that they should keep repeating words during the 5-second intervals between words. The dashed curve, which indicates how many times each word was repeated, bears a striking resemblance to the first half of the serial position curve. Words presented early in the list were rehearsed more, and they were more likely to be remembered later. This result supports the idea that the primacy effect is related to the longer rehearsal time available for the earlier words on the list.

Superior memory for stimuli presented at the end of a sequence is called the **recency effect**. One possible explanation for the better memory for words at the end of the list is that the most recently presented words are still in STM. To test this idea, Murray Glanzer and Anita Cunitz (1966) first derived a serial position curve in the usual way (red curve in ● Figure 6.5). Then, in another experiment, they measured the curve after having their participants count backward for 30 seconds right after hearing the last word of the list. This counting prevented rehearsal and allowed time for information to be lost from STM. The result, shown in the blue dashed curve in Figure 6.5, was what we would predict: The delay caused by the counting eliminated the recency effect. Glanzer and Cunitz therefore concluded that the recency effect is due to storage of recently presented items in STM.

CODING IN LONG-TERM MEMORY

We can also distinguish between STM and LTM by comparing the way information is coded by the two systems. In Chapter 5 we saw that auditory, visual, and semantic coding can occur for STM (with auditory and visual coding being the most prominent). LTM can also involve each of these types of coding. For example, you use visual coding in LTM when you recognize someone based on his or her appearance, auditory coding when you recognize a person based on the sound of his or her voice, and semantic coding when you remember the general gist or meaning of something that happened in the past.

Although all three types of coding can occur in LTM, semantic coding is the *predominant* type of coding in LTM. Semantic encoding is illustrated by the kinds of errors that people make in tasks that involve LTM. For example, misremembering the word *tree* as *bush* would indicate that the meaning of the word *tree* (rather than its visual appearance or the sound of saying "tree") is what was registered in LTM.

A study by Jacqueline Sachs (1967) demonstrated the importance of meaning in LTM. Sachs had participants listen to a tape recording of a passage and then measured their recognition memory to determine whether they remembered the exact wording of sentences in the passage or the general meaning of the passage.

METHOD Recognition Memory

Recognition memory is the identification of a stimulus that was encountered earlier. The procedure for measuring recognition memory is to present a stimulus during a study period and later to present the same stimulus plus others that were not presented. For example, in the study period a list of words might be presented that includes the word *house*. Later, in the test, a series of words is presented that includes *house* plus some other words that were not presented, such as *table* and *money*. The participant's task is to answer "Yes" if the word was presented previously (the word *house* in this example) and "No" if it wasn't presented (the words *table* and *money*). Notice how this method is different from testing for *recall* (see Method: Recall, Chapter 5, page 123). In a recall test, the person must *produce* the item to be recalled. An example of a recall test is a fill-in-the-blanks exam question. In contrast, an example of recognition is a multiple-choice exam, in which the task is to pick the correct answer from a number of alternatives. The way Sachs applied recognition to the study of coding in long-term memory is illustrated in the next demonstration.

DEMONSTRATION Reading a Passage

Read the following passage:

> There is an interesting story about the telescope. In Holland, a man named Lippershey was an eyeglass maker. One day his children were playing with some lenses. They discovered that things seemed very close if two lenses were held about a foot apart. Lippershey began experimenting, and his "spyglass" attracted much attention. He sent a letter about it to Galileo, the great Italian scientist. Galileo at once realized the importance of the discovery and set about building an instrument of his own.

Now cover up the passage and indicate which of the following sentences is identical to a sentence in the passage and which sentences are changed.

1. He sent a letter about it to Galileo, the great Italian scientist.
2. Galileo, the great Italian scientist, sent him a letter about it.
3. A letter about it was sent to Galileo, the great Italian scientist.
4. He sent Galileo, the great Italian scientist, a letter about it.

Which sentence did you pick? Sentence 1 is the only one that is identical to one in the passage. Many of Sachs's participants (who heard a passage about twice as long as the one you read) correctly identified (1) as being identical and knew that (2) was changed. However, a number of people identified (3) and (4) as matching one in the passage, even though the wording was different. These participants apparently remembered the sentence's meaning and not its exact wording. The finding that specific wording is forgotten but the general meaning can be remembered for a long time has been confirmed in many experiments.

LOCATING SHORT- AND LONG-TERM MEMORY IN THE BRAIN

We introduced the physiology of working memory at the end of Chapter 5 (see page 137), and we will be describing the physiology behind how long-term memories are established in Chapter 7. Our goal here is to describe some experiments that compare where STM/WM and LTM are represented in the brain. We will see that there is evidence that STM and LTM are separated in the brain, but also that there is some evidence for overlap. The strongest evidence for separation is provided by neuropsychological studies.

Neuropsychological Studies In Chapter 3 we introduced the technique of determining dissociations, which is used to draw conclusions from case studies of brain-damaged patients (see Method: Dissociations in Neuropsychology, page 73). This technique has been used in memory research to differentiate between STM and LTM by studying people with brain damage that has affected one of these functions while sparing the other. We will see that studies of patients have established a double dissociation between STM and LTM. That is, there are some patients with functioning STM who can't form new LTMs and other patients who have poor STM but functioning LTM. Taken together, these two types of patients establish a double dissociation, which indicates that STM and LTM operate independently and are served by different mechanisms.

In Chapter 5 we described Clive Wearing, the musician who lost his memory as a result of viral encephalitis. He has a functioning STM, as indicated by his ability to remember what has happened to him for the most recent 30 seconds, but is unable to form new LTMs. Another case of functioning STM but absent LTM is the case of H.M., who became one of the most famous cases in neuropsychology when surgeons removed his hippocampus on both sides of the brain (see Figure 5.23) in an attempt to eliminate epileptic seizures that had not responded to other treatments (Scoville & Milner, 1957).

The operation eliminated H.M.'s seizures, but unfortunately also eliminated his ability to form new LTMs. Thus, the outcome of H.M.'s case is similar to that of Clive Wearing and Mr. G, except that Clive Wearing's brain damage was caused by disease, Mr. G's by vitamin deficiency, and H.M.'s by surgery.

H.M.'s unfortunate situation occurred because in 1953 the surgeons did not realize that the hippocampus is crucial for the formation of LTMs. Once they realized the devastating effects of removing the hippocampus on both sides of the brain, H.M.'s operation was never repeated. However, research on H.M. over the 55 years between 1953 and his death at the age of 82 in 2008 taught memory researchers a great deal about memory. The case of H.M. clearly demonstrated that it is possible to lose the ability to form new LTMs while still retaining STM. (We will return to H.M. shortly.)

There are also people, such as patient K.F., with the opposite problem: normal LTM but poor STM. K.F.'s problem with STM was indicated by a reduced digit span—the number of digits she could remember (see page 125; Shallice & Warrington, 1970). Whereas the typical span is between 5 and 8 digits, K.F. had a digit span of 2; in addition, the recency effect in her serial position curve, which is associated with STM, was reduced. Even though K.F.'s STM was greatly impaired, she had a functioning LTM, as indicated by her ability to form and hold new memories of events in her life. (See Think About It on page 168 for more on K.F.)

Table 6.1, which indicates which aspects of memory are impaired and which are intact for Clive Wearing, H.M., and K.F., demonstrates that a double dissociation exists for STM and LTM. This evidence supports the idea that STM and LTM are caused by different mechanisms, which can act independently.

TABLE 6.1 A Double Dissociation for STM and LTM

	STM	LTM
Clive Wearing and H.M.	OK	Impaired
K.F.	Impaired	OK

Brain Imaging Some brain imaging experiments have demonstrated activation of different areas of the brain for STM and LTM. For example, Deborah Talmi and coworkers (2005) measured the fMRI response to tasks involving STM and LTM. They first presented a list of words to participants, as is done to determine a serial position curve. But instead of asking participants to recall the words, they presented a single "probe" word. The probe was either (1) a word from near the beginning of the list, (2) a word from near the end of the list, or (3) a new word that hadn't been presented earlier. The participants' task was to indicate whether the word had been presented before. Their brain activity was measured with fMRI after the probe was presented and as they were preparing to respond.

The results indicated that probe words that were from the beginning of the list (which, if remembered, would therefore represent long-term memory) activated areas of the brain associated with both long-term memory and short-term memory. It would be expected that both areas would be activated because words at the beginning of the list would be in long-term memory (primacy effect, see page 151) and would then be transferred into STM when they were being recalled. In contrast, probe words from the end of the list only activated areas of the brain associated with short-term memory. This would be expected because the recently presented words would be recalled directly from short-term memory (recency effect, see page 153).

Although Talmi's experiment demonstrated activation of different areas for STM and LTM, the results of other brain imaging experiments have not been as clear-cut. Some of these experiments have shown that tasks that involve either STM or LTM can activate the same areas of the brain (Jonides et al., 2008). One possible reason for this overlap is the constant interplay that occurs between STM and LTM. Another reason is that STM and LTM may share some of the same mechanisms.

TYPES OF LONG-TERM MEMORY

There are a number of different types of long-term memory. ● Figure 6.6 indicates that the two main divisions of LTM are *explicit memory* and *implicit memory*. **Explicit memory** (also called *conscious memory* or *declarative memory*), on the left of the figure, consists of **episodic memory**, memory for personal experiences, and **semantic memory**, stored knowledge and memory for facts. Episodic and semantic memories are illustrated by two memories that Cliff, the student shown in ● Figure 6.7, is experiencing. When he remembers talking with Gail yesterday about meeting to study for the cognitive psychology exam, he is having an episodic memory. When he remembers some facts about theories of attention that he learned in his cognitive psychology class, he is having a semantic memory. Both of these types of memory are called *explicit*, because their contents can be described or reported (Smith & Grossman, 2008).

The other division of long-term memory, implicit memory, is shown at the right of ● Figure 6.6. **Implicit memories** (also called **nondeclarative memory** or *unconscious memory*) are memories that are used without awareness, so the contents of implicit memories cannot be reported (Smith & Grossman, 2008). One type of implicit memories that has influenced Cliff's behavior is **priming**—a change in response to a stimulus caused by the previous presentation of the same or a similar stimulus. An example of priming would be finding it easier to recognize

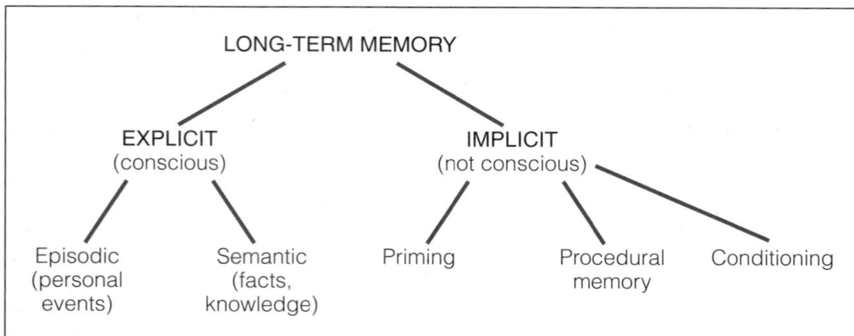

● **FIGURE 6.6** Long-term memory can be divided into explicit memory and implicit memory. We can also distinguish between two types of explicit memory, episodic and semantic. There are a number of different types of implicit memory. Three of the main types are priming, procedural memory, and conditioning.

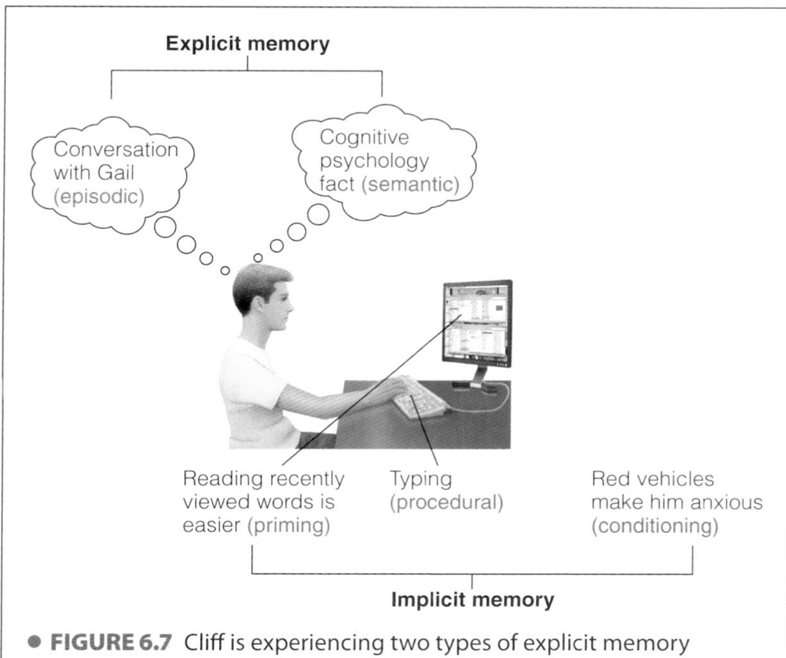

● **FIGURE 6.7** Cliff is experiencing two types of explicit memory (episodic and semantic), and his behavior is being influenced by three types of implicit memory (priming, procedural, and conditioning).

words that are familiar or that he has recently seen compared to words that he has rarely encountered.

Another type of implicit memory is **procedural memory**, also called *skill memory*, which is memory for doing things. When Cliff is typing notes into his computer, his ability to type is procedural memory. Finally, **classical conditioning** is another form of implicit memory. As we described in Chapter 1 (see page 10), classical conditioning occurs when pairing an initially neutral stimulus with another stimulus results in the neutral stimulus taking on new properties. For example, about a week ago Cliff had a frightening accident in which a red SUV smashed into his car. He escaped without serious injury, but was emotionally shaken. Now, when he sees a red SUV or even red cars, he begins to feel anxious, just as he felt immediately after the accident. Because of classical conditioning, the previously neutral cars have taken on new properties.

The different types of long-term memory are the topic of the rest of this chapter. Starting with the definitions above, we will elaborate on and provide further examples for each of these types of long-term memory.

TEST YOURSELF 6.1

1. What was Jimmy G.'s problem, and why did it occur?
2. Describe the "time scale" of short-term and long-term memory. Are all long-term memories created equal?
3. How does the example of Tony and Cindy show how LTM and WM work together? (Hint: James Bond movie)
4. Describe how differences between STM/WM and LTM have been demonstrated based on (a) the serial position curve, (b) neuropsychological evidence, and (c) differences in coding.
5. Describe the method of recognition, including how it differs from recall and how this method was used in the Sachs experiment involving the passage about Galileo.
6. What is the difference between explicit memory and implicit memory? What are the two types of explicit memory? The three types of implicit memory?

Episodic and Semantic Memory (Explicit)

In our introduction to types of memory, we saw that episodic and semantic memory are types of explicit memory because we are conscious of them and can describe or report their contents. We now consider in more detail how these two types of explicit memory are distinguished, how they have been separated physiologically, and how they interact with one another.

DISTINGUISHING BETWEEN EPISODIC AND SEMANTIC MEMORY

When we say that episodic memory is memory for events and semantic memory is memory for facts, we are distinguishing between these two types of memory based on the types of *information* remembered. Endel Tulving (1985) has suggested, however, that episodic and semantic memory can also be distinguished based on the type of *experience* associated with each (also see Gardiner, 2001; Wheeler et al., 1997).

According to Tulving, the defining property of the experience of episodic memory is that it involves **mental time travel**—the experience of traveling back in time to reconnect with events that happened in the past. For example, I can travel back in my mind to 1996 to remember cresting the top of a mountain near the California coast and seeing the Pacific Ocean far below, stretching into the distance. I remember sitting in the car, seeing the ocean, saying "Wow!" to my wife who was sitting next to me, and some of the emotions I was experiencing. Tulving describes this experience of mental time travel/episodic memory as *self-knowing* or *remembering*. Note, however, that putting oneself back in a situation through mental time travel does not guarantee that the memory is accurate. As we will see in Chapter 8, memories of events from our past do not always correspond to what actually happened.

In contrast to the mental time travel property of episodic memory, the experience of semantic memory involves accessing knowledge about the world that does not have to be tied to remembering a personal experience. This knowledge can be things like facts, vocabulary, numbers, and concepts. When we *experience* semantic memory, we are not traveling back to a specific event from our past, but we are accessing things we are familiar with and know about. For example, I know many facts about the Pacific Ocean—where it is located, that it is big, that if you travel west from San Francisco you end up in Japan—but I can't remember exactly when I learned these things. All of these things are semantic memories. Tulving describes the experience of semantic memory as *knowing*, with the idea that knowing does not involve mental time travel. We will now consider the evidence that supports the idea that episodic and semantic memories are served by different mechanisms.

THE SEPARATION OF EPISODIC AND SEMANTIC MEMORIES

It is possible to classify some memories as episodic and others as semantic, but is there any evidence to support the idea that these two types of long-term memory are served by different mechanisms? Neuropsychological research on people with different kinds of brain damage provides evidence for differences.

Neuropsychological Evidence We first consider the case of K.C., who at the age of 30 rode his motorcycle off a freeway exit ramp and suffered severe damage to his hippocampus and surrounding structures (Rosenbaum et al., 2005). As a result of this injury, K.C. lost his episodic memory—he can no longer relive any of the events of his past. He does, however, know that certain things happened, which would correspond to semantic memory. He is aware of the fact that his brother died two years ago, but is not aware of things related to his brother's death that he previously experienced, such as hearing about the circumstances of his brother's death, where he was when he heard about it, or what he experienced at the funeral. K.C. also remembers facts like where the eating utensils are located in the kitchen and the difference between a strike and a spare in bowling. Thus, K.C. has lost the episodic part of his memory, but his semantic memory is largely intact.

A person whose brain damage resulted in symptoms opposite to those experienced by K.C. is an Italian woman who was in normal health until she suffered an attack of encephalitis at the age of 44 (DeRenzi et al., 1987). The first signs of a problem were headaches and a fever, which were later followed by hallucinations lasting for 5 days. When she returned home after a 6-week stay in the hospital, she had difficulty recognizing familiar people; she had trouble shopping because she couldn't remember the meaning of words on the shopping list or where things were in the store; and she could no longer recognize famous people or recall facts such as the identity of Beethoven or the fact that Italy was involved in World War II. All of these are semantic memories.

TABLE 6.2 Dissociations of Episodic and Semantic Memory

	Semantic	Episodic
K.C.	OK	Poor
Italian woman	Poor	OK

Despite this severe impairment of memory for semantic information, she was still able to remember events in her life. She could remember what she had done during the day and things that had happened weeks or months before. Thus, although she had lost semantic memories, she was still able to form new episodic memories. Table 6.2 summarizes the two cases we have described. These cases, taken together, demonstrate a double dissociation between episodic and semantic memory, which supports the idea that memory for these two different types of information probably involves different mechanisms.

Although the double dissociation shown in Table 6.2 supports the idea of separate mechanisms for semantic and episodic memory, interpretation of the results of studies of brain-damaged patients is often tricky because the extent of brain damage often differs from patient to patient. In addition, the method of testing patients may differ in different studies. It is important, therefore, to supplement the results of neuropsychological research with other kinds of evidence. This additional evidence is provided by brain imaging experiments. (See Squire & Zola-Morgan, 1998, and Tulving & Markowitsch, 1998, for further discussion of the neuropsychology of episodic and semantic memory.)

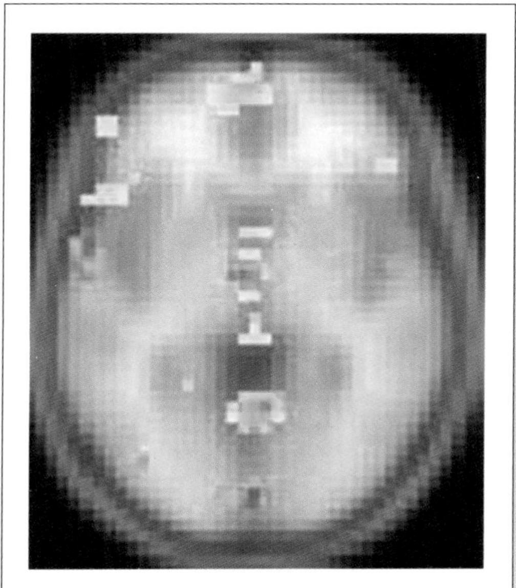

● **FIGURE 6.8** Brain showing areas activated by episodic and semantic memories. The yellow areas represent brain regions associated with episodic memories; the blue areas are regions associated with semantic memories. (Source: B. Levine et al., "The Functional Neuroanatomy of Episodic and Semantic Autobiographical Remembering: A Prospective Functional MRI Study," *Journal of Cognitive Neuroscience, 16,* 1633–1646, 2004 , MIT Press Journals.)

Brain Imaging Evidence Evidence for separate mechanisms has also been provided by the results of brain imaging experiments. Brian Levine and coworkers (2004) had participants keep diaries on audiotape describing everyday personal events (example: "It was the last night of our Salsa dance class.... People were dancing all different styles of Salsa...."), and facts drawn from their semantic knowledge ("By 1947, there were 5,000 Japanese Canadians living in Toronto").

When the participants later listened to these audiotaped descriptions while in an MRI scanner, the recordings of everyday events elicited detailed episodic autobiographical memories (people remembered their experiences), while the other recordings simply reminded people of semantic facts. ● Figure 6.8 shows a cross section of the brain. The yellow areas represent brain regions associated with episodic memories; the blue areas are brain regions associated with semantic, factual knowledge (personal and nonpersonal). These results and others indicate that while there is overlap between activation caused by episodic and semantic memories, there are major differences. Other research has also found differences between the areas activated by episodic and semantic memory (Cabeza & Nyberg, 2000; Duzel et al., 1999; Nyberg et al., 1996).

CONNECTIONS BETWEEN EPISODIC AND SEMANTIC MEMORIES

The distinctions between episodic and semantic memories have been extremely useful for understanding memory mechanisms. But although we can distinguish between episodic and semantic memory, we can also show that they are connected in various ways. For example, when we are learning facts (potential semantic memories), we are usually simultaneously having a personal experience, such as sitting in class or studying in the library (a potential episodic memory, if remembered later). Here are some examples of these connections between episodic and semantic memory.

Episodic Memories Can Be Lost, Leaving Only Semantic Memories Consider how we acquire the knowledge that makes up our semantic memories. Sitting in the sixth grade, you learn that the legislative branch of the U.S. government consists of the Senate and the House of Representatives. If, a few weeks later, you remember what was going on in class as you were learning these facts, you are having an episodic memory, and if you remember the facts about the House and Senate, you are having a semantic memory.

Many years later, in college, you probably still know the difference between the Senate and the House of Representatives (your semantic memory is still present), but it is unlikely that you remember what was happening on the specific day you were sitting in class in the sixth grade learning about the U.S. government (your episodic memory for that event has been lost). As this example illustrates, the knowledge that makes up semantic memories is initially attained through a personal experience that could be the basis of an episodic memory, but memory for this experience often fades, leaving only semantic memory.

Another example of "morphing" from episodic plus semantic to only semantic memory is provided by important personal experiences such as graduating from high school. This is an important event in many people's lives, and one that they may remember for many years. It is likely that many readers of this book can clearly place themselves at their high school graduation and so still have episodic memories for this event. However, memory for many of the details of this event may fade over the years, until many years later, not enough of the details remain to achieve the mental time travel required for episodic memory (as in the case of your author, who graduated from high school earlier in the last century!). Nonetheless, semantic memory remains if people know the year they graduated, the high school they graduated from, and other *facts* associated with their graduation.

Semantic Memory Can Be Enhanced If Associated With Episodic Memory Another connection between semantic and episodic memories is that semantic memories that have personal significance are easier to remember than semantic memories that are not personally significant. For example, knowledge about the facts associated with your high school graduation would be personally significant semantic memories because your high school graduation has personal significance for you. Robyn Westmacott and Morris Moscovitch (2003) showed that participants have better recall for names of public figures, such as actors, singers, and politicians, whom they associate with personal experiences. For example, you would be more likely to recall the name of a popular singer in a memory test if you had attended one of his or her concerts than if you had just read about the singer in magazines.

Semantic Memory Can Influence Our Experience by Influencing Attention Consider this situation: Steven and Troy are watching a football game. The quarterback takes the snap, is rushed hard, and flips the ball over the oncoming linemen for a completion. Later, Troy remembers the details of the play, which was a pass over the left side, but the play doesn't stand out for Steven. Troy remembers the play because his semantic memory, which contains a large amount of knowledge about football, caused him to direct his attention to what various players were doing as the play unfolded. Thus, Troy's detailed semantic memory about the various types of plays in football helped direct his attention, and he formed memories about specific plays. In contrast, Steven observed the game differently because of his sparse knowledge of football, so he just remembers that there were running plays and passing plays (● Figure 6.9).

The research on chess experts described in Chapter 5 (see page 127) also illustrates how semantic memory can influence how people allocate their attention. Remember that the experts had better memory for the positions of chess pieces because of their ability to group pieces together in *chunks* based on the experts' semantic memory for the

Semantic knowledge can influence formation of episodic memory

They both saw the same game!

● **FIGURE 6.9** A person's knowledge can influence episodic memory. Even though two people have seen the same football game, they remember different things about it because of their differing knowledge of football.

positions of chess pieces in other games. The experts' attention would therefore be directed toward identifying these groups. The nonexperts, who did not have this knowledge, were likely to focus their attention differently, looking at the chess pieces individually rather than as groups.

Priming, Procedural Memory, and Conditioning (Implicit)

CogLab
Implicit Learning

When we access explicit memory, we are conscious of doing so. We know we are thinking back to relive an earlier experience (episodic memory—Tulving's "self-knowing" or "remembering") or that we are retrieving knowledge about past events or about facts we have learned (semantic memory—Tulving's "knowing"). The defining characteristic of implicit memory, in contrast, is that we are not conscious we are using it (see the right side of Figure 6.6). Implicit memory occurs when some previous experience influences our performance on a task, even though we do not consciously remember the previous experience. We may not even be aware of exactly how we are accomplishing a particular task. We just do it! (Roediger, 1990; Schacter, 1987; Tulving, 1985). Tulving describes implicit memory as *nonknowing*.

PRIMING

Priming occurs when the presentation of one stimulus (the priming stimulus) changes the response to a subsequent test stimulus (the test stimulus), either positively (*positive priming*, which causes an increase in speed or accuracy of the response to the test stimulus) or negatively (*negative priming*, which causes a decrease in the speed or accuracy of response to the test stimulus). We will focus on positive priming because most research has studied this type of priming.

One type of positive priming, **repetition priming**, occurs when the test stimulus is the same as or resembles the priming stimulus. For example, seeing the word *bird* may cause you to respond more quickly to another presentation of the word *bird* than to a word you had not seen, even though you may not remember seeing *bird* earlier. **Conceptual priming** occurs when the enhancement caused by the priming stimulus is based on the meaning of the stimulus. For example, presentation of the word *furniture* might cause you to respond faster to a later presentation of the word *chair*.

Repetition priming and conceptual priming are both considered to be implicit memory because their effects can occur even though participants may not remember the original presentation of the priming stimulus when they are responding to the test stimulus.

You may wonder how we can be sure that a person isn't remembering the priming stimulus when responding to the test stimulus. After all, if we present the word *bird*, and then later measure how fast a person reacts to another presentation of the word *bird*, couldn't that happen because the person remembers the first time *bird* was presented? If the person did remember the initial presentation of *bird*, then this would be an example of explicit memory, not implicit memory. Researchers have used a number of methods to reduce the chances that a person in a priming experiment will remember the original presentation of the priming stimulus.

METHOD Avoiding Explicit Remembering in a Priming Experiment

One way to minimize the chances that a person will remember the presentation of the priming stimulus is to present the priming stimulus in a task that does not appear to be a memory task. For example, if the priming stimuli are the names of animals, participants could be presented with the names and asked to indicate whether the animals would stand more than 2 feet high.

In addition to disguising the purpose of the priming stimulus, researchers have devised tests that do not directly test memory. An example of such a test is the word completion task, in which the participant's task is to create a word from a fragment. For example, the priming stimulus could be the word *parrot*, and the test stimulus could be the fragment *par*. The participant's task is to add letters to create a word. If repetition priming occurs, the participant will be more likely to complete the fragment to form the priming stimulus then he or she would be if the stimulus had not been presented earlier. In this example, creating the word *parrot*, rather than other possibilities such as *parent* or *party*, would illustrate an effect of priming.

Another example of a test used in repetition priming experiments involves measuring how accurately or quickly the participant responds to a stimulus. For example, participants could be tested by presenting a list of words and asking them to press a key every time they see a word that has four letters. Priming would be indicated by faster or more accurate responding to four-letter words that corresponded to priming stimuli that had been presented earlier. The key characteristic of this test is speed. Requiring a rapid response decreases the chances that the participant will take the time to consciously recollect whether or not they have previously seen the word.

Many experiments have been done in which researchers have demonstrated implicit memory using techniques like the ones described above (Roediger, 1990). But the definite proof that priming involves implicit memory is provided by neuropsychology experiments on people with amnesia like Jimmy G., whom we described at the beginning of the chapter, who cannot remember events that have just happened to them.

An example is provided by an experiment by Peter Graf and coworkers (1985), who tested three groups of participants: (1) eight amnesia patients with Korsakoff's syndrome and two patients with another form of amnesia; (2) patients without amnesia who were under treatment for alcoholism; and (3) patients without amnesia who had no history of alcoholism.

Graf and coworkers presented lists of words to their participants and asked them to rate each word on a scale of 1 to 5 based on how much they liked each word (1 = like extremely; 5 = dislike extremely). This caused participants to focus on rating the words rather than on committing the words to memory. Immediately after rating the words in the lists, participants were tested in one of two ways: (1) a test of explicit memory, in which they were asked to recall the words they had seen; or (2) a test of implicit memory, in which they were presented with three-letter fragments and were asked to add a few letters to create the first word that came into their mind.

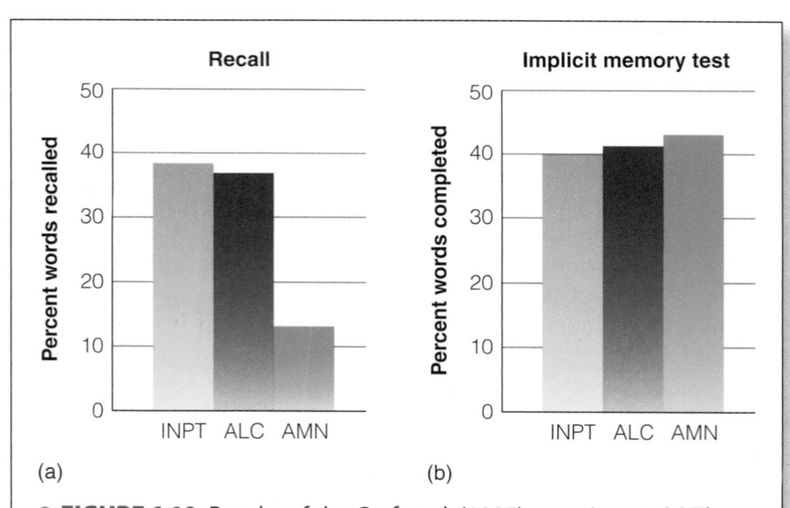

• **FIGURE 6.10** Results of the Graf et al. (1985) experiment. (a) The results of the recall test indicate that the amnesic patients (AMN) did poorly on the test compared to the medical inpatients (INPT) and the alcoholic controls (ALC). (b) The results of the implicit memory test, in which the task was to complete three-letter word stems, shows that the amnesic patients performed as well as the other patients. (Source: P. Graf, A. P. Shimamura, & L. R. Squire, "Priming Across Modalities and Priming Across Category Levels: Extending the Domain of Preserved Function in Amnesia," *Journal of Experimental Psychology: Learning, Memory, and Cognition, 11*, 386–396, 1985.)

The results of the recall experiment, shown in • Figure 6.10a, show that the amnesia patients had poor recall compared to the two control groups. This poor recall confirms the poor explicit memory associated with their amnesia. But the result of the implicit memory test, in Figure 6.10b, tells a different story. These results, which indicate the percentage of primed words that were created in the word completion test, demonstrates that the amnesia patient performed just as well as the controls. This shows that priming can occur even when there is little explicit memory for the words.

Another example of repetition priming in a person with brain damage is an experiment in which Elizabeth Warrington and Lawrence Weiskrantz (1968) tested five patients with Korsakoff's syndrome. The researchers presented incomplete pictures, such as the ones in • Figure 6.11 (Gollin, 1960), and the participant's task was to identify the picture. The fragmented version in

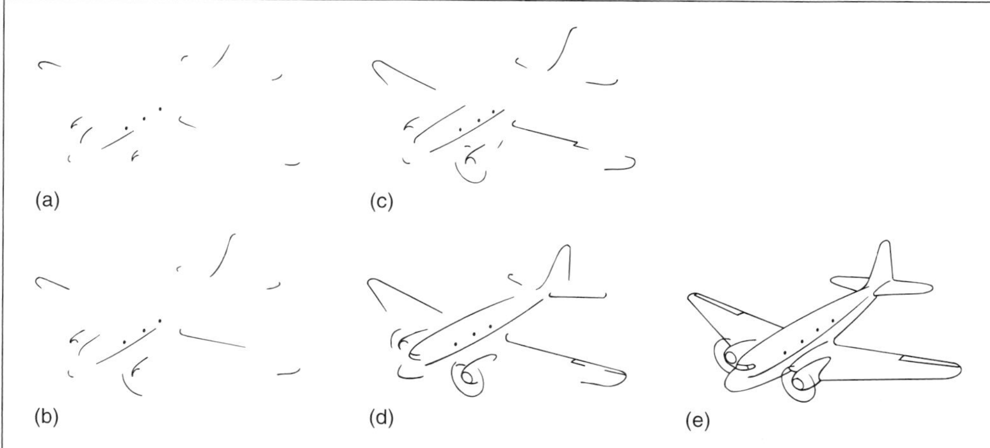

• **FIGURE 6.11** Incomplete pictures developed by Gollin (1960) that were used by Warrington and Weiskrantz (1968) to study implicit memory in patients with amnesia. (Source: E. K. Warrington & L. Weiskrantz, "New Method of Testing Long-Term Retention With Special Reference to Amnesic Patients," *Nature, London, 217,* March 9, 1968, 972–974, Figure 1. Copyright © 1968 Nature Publishing Group. Republished with permission.)

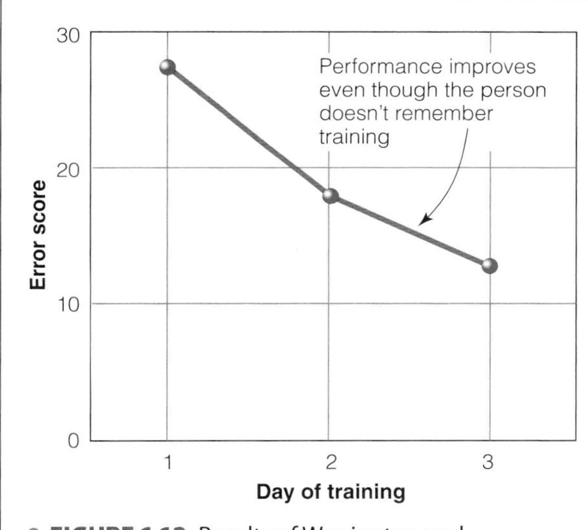

• **FIGURE 6.12** Results of Warrington and Weiskrantz's (1968) experiment. (Source: Based on E. K. Warrington & L. Weiskrantz, "New Method of Testing Long-Term Retention With Special Reference to Amnesic Patients," *Nature, 217,* 972–974, March 9, 1968.)

Figure 6.11a was presented first, and then participants were shown more and more complete versions (b, c, d, and e) until they were able to identify the picture.

The results, shown in • Figure 6.12, indicate that by the third day of testing these participants made fewer errors before identifying the pictures than they did at the beginning of training, even though they had no memory for any of the previous day's training. The improvement of performance represents an effect of implicit memory because the patients learned from experience even though they couldn't remember having had the experience.

Implicit memory is not simply a laboratory phenomenon, but also occurs in everyday experience. An example of a situation in which implicit memory may affect our behavior without our awareness is when we are exposed to advertisements that extol the virtues of a product or perhaps just present the product's name. Although we may believe that we are unaffected by some advertisements, they can have an effect just because we are exposed to them.

This idea is supported by the results of an experiment by T. J. Perfect and C. Askew (1994), who had participants scan articles in a magazine. Each page of print was faced by an advertisement, but participants were not told to pay attention to the advertisements. When they were later asked to rate a number of advertisements on various dimensions, such as how appealing, eye-catching, distinctive, and memorable they were, they gave higher ratings to the ones they had been exposed to than to other advertisements that they had never seen. This result qualifies as an effect of implicit memory because when the participants were asked to indicate which advertisements had been presented at the beginning of the experiment, they recognized only an average of 2.8 of the original 25 advertisements.

This result is related to the propaganda effect, in which participants are more likely to rate statements they have read or heard before as being true, simply because they have been exposed to them before. This effect can occur even when the person is told that the statements are false when they first read or hear them (Begg et al., 1992). The propaganda effect involves implicit memory because it can operate even when people are not aware that they have heard or seen a statement before, and may even have thought it was false when they first heard it.

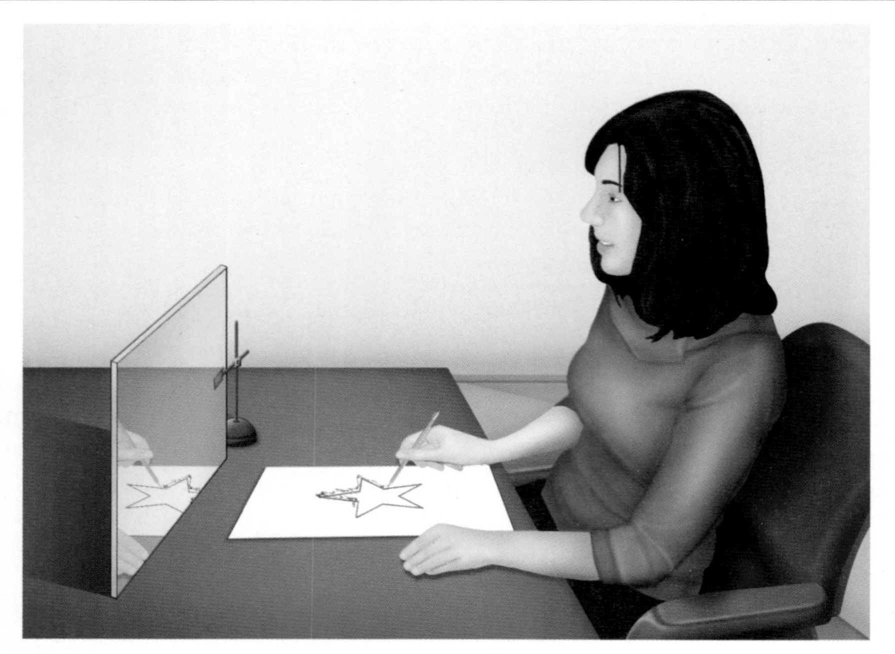

● **FIGURE 6.13** Mirror drawing. The task is to trace the outline of the star while looking at its image in the mirror.

Later in our discussion of LTM, especially in Chapter 8, we will see how implicit memory can lead to memory errors. We will see, for example, that eyewitnesses to crimes have identified people as having been at the crime scene not because they were actually there, but because the eyewitnesses had seen them somewhere else at another time, so they seemed familiar.

PROCEDURAL MEMORY

Procedural memory is also called *skill memory* because it is memory for doing things that usually require action. The implicit nature of procedural memory has been demonstrated in amnesia patients who can master a skill without remembering any of the practice that led to this mastery (like the improvement in the picture completion task in Figure 6.11). For example, H.M., whose amnesia was caused by having his hippocampus removed (see page 138), practiced a task called *mirror drawing*, which involves copying a picture that is seen in a mirror (● Figure 6.13). You can appreciate this task by doing the following demonstration.

DEMONSTRATION Mirror Drawing

Draw a star like the one in Figure 6.13 on a piece of paper. Place a mirror or some other reflective surface (some cell phone screens work) about an inch or two from the star, so that the reflection of the star is visible. Then, while looking at the reflection, trace the outline of the star on the paper (no fair looking at the actual drawing on the paper!). You will probably find that the task is difficult at first, but becomes easier with practice.

After a number of days of practice, H.M. became quite good at mirror drawing, but each time he did it, he thought he was practicing it for the first time. H.M.'s ability to trace the star in the mirror, even though he couldn't remember having done it before, illustrates procedural memory.

Other amnesia patients also demonstrate procedural memory. Jimmy G. could still tie his shoes, and Clive Wearing, who was a professional musician, was able to play the piano. In fact, people who can't form new long-term memories can still learn new skills. K.C., who had lost his episodic memory because of a motorcycle accident (see page 158), learned how to sort and stack books in the library after his injury. Even though he doesn't remember learning to do this, he can still do it, and his performance can improve with practice. The fact that people with amnesia can retain skills from the past and learn new ones has led to an approach to rehabilitating patients with amnesia by teaching them tasks, such as sorting mail or repetitive computer-based tasks, that they can become expert at, even though they can't remember their training (Bolognani et al., 2000; Clare & Jones, 2008).

We can also understand the implicit nature of procedural memory from our own experience. We do not remember where or when we learned many of our basic skills; nonetheless, we usually have little trouble doing them. Also, people can do things without being consciously aware of *how* they do them. For example, can you explain how you keep your balance when riding a bike? What about tying your shoes? Tying shoes is so easy for most people that they do it without even thinking about it. If you think you are aware of how you do it, describe which lace you loop over the other one, and then what you do next. Most people have to either tie their shoes or visualize tying their shoes before they can answer this question.

Riding a bike and tying your shoes are both motor skills that involve movement and muscle action. You have also developed many purely cognitive skills that qualify as involving procedural memory. Consider, for example, your ability to read the sentences in this book. Can you describe the rules you are following for creating sentences from the words and creating meaningful thoughts from the sentences? Unless you've studied linguistics, you probably don't know these rules, but that doesn't stop you from being a skilled reader.

Finally, consider the plight of the concert pianist who, when he tried to become conscious of how he was moving his fingers as he played a difficult passage, found that he was no longer able to play the passage. For many skills, the best practice is to disengage the mind and let implicit procedural memory take over!

CLASSICAL CONDITIONING

Classical conditioning occurs when the following two stimuli are paired: (1) a neutral stimulus that initially does not result in a response and (2) a conditioning stimulus that does result in a response (see page 10). An example of classical conditioning from the laboratory is presenting a tone to a person followed by a puff or air to the eye that causes the person to blink. The tone initially does not cause an eyeblink, but after a number of pairings with the puff of air, the tone alone causes an eyeblink. This is implicit memory because it can occur even if the person has forgotten about the original pairing of the tone and air puff. The example we cited for Cliff on page 157 involved a situation in which the neutral stimulus was red cars and the conditioning stimulus was the accident that caused an emotional reaction. Having an emotional reaction to the previous neutral cars is an effect of classical conditioning. Conditioned emotional responses similar to what Cliff experienced can cause people to have emotional reactions to people, places, or events, even when they are unaware of the reasons for their reactions.

We have described a number of different types of long-term memory, ranging from vivid memories of personal experiences (episodic, explicit) to the ability to ride a bicycle (procedural, implicit). Each of these types of long-term memories has been the subject of a great deal of research devoted to discovering how events can leave an imprint in the mind that later results in an experience (a memory) or a behavior (a skill or reaction to a specific stimulus). In addition to being the subject of research, which we will discuss further in Chapters 7 and 8, memory has also been the subject of many movies over the years, most often stories in which a main character has suffered a loss of memory.

Something to Consider

MEMORY LOSS IN THE MOVIES

Countless movies have featured a character with memory loss. The accuracy of these depictions, compared to actual cases, ranges from depictions that resemble types of memory loss that actually occur to completely fictional types of memory loss that have never occurred. Sometimes, even when the memory loss in a movie resembles actual cases, it is described using incorrect terminology. We will describe some examples of fact-based memory loss, fictional memory loss, and the use of incorrect terminology in movies.

In some movies, characters lose their memory for everything in their past, including their identity, but are able to form new memories. This is what happened to Jason Bourne, the character played by Matt Damon in *The Bourne Identity* (2002). In this film, the unconscious and badly wounded Bourne is plucked out of the water by a fishing boat. When he regains consciousness, he has no memory of his identity. As he searches for his previous identity, he realizes people are out to kill him, but, because of his memory loss, he doesn't know why. Although Bourne has lost his episodic memories of his past, his semantic memory appears to be intact, and, most interesting of all, he has lost none of his procedural memories from his training as a CIA agent, including ways to outsmart, outrun, and eliminate his adversaries.

Bourne's situation is related to a rare condition called *psychogenic fugue*. Symptoms of this condition include traveling away from where the person lives and a lack of memory for the past, especially personal information such as name, relationships, place of residence, and occupation. In the few cases that have been reported, a person vanishes from his or her normal life situation, often travels far away, and takes on a new identity unrelated to the previous one (Coons & Milstein, 1992; Loewenstein, 1991).

A number of other movies revolve around a central character who loses his or her identity or takes on a new one. In *Who Am I?* (1998), Jackie Chan, a top secret soldier, loses his memory in a helicopter crash, triggering a quest to recover his identity. In *Dead Again* (1991), a mystery woman played by Emma Thompson can't remember anything about her life. In *The Long Kiss Goodnight* (1996), Geena Davis plays a suburban homemaker who begins remembering events from her previous life as a secret agent after suffering a blow to her head.

© Keline Howard/Sygma/Corbis

● **FIGURE 6.14** Guy Pearce's character, Lenny, from the film *Memento*. To deal with his memory problem, he had key facts he wanted to remember tattooed on his body.

In other movies, the main character has trouble forming new memories. For example, Lenny, the character played by Guy Pearce in *Memento* (2000), continually forgets what has just happened to him. This situation is based on cases such as those of Clive Wearing and Jimmy G., who were unable to form new memories and were therefore only able to remember the current one or two minutes of their lives. Lenny's problem is apparently not as debilitating as in these real-life cases, because he is able to function in the outside world, although with some difficulty. To compensate for his inability to form new memories, Lenny records his experiences with a Polaroid camera and has key facts tattooed on his body (● Figure 6.14).

The use of terminology in movies that is not the same as that used by psychologists is seen in *Memento*, where Lenny's problem is identified as a loss of short-term memory. This reflects a common belief (at least among those who have not taken a cognitive psychology course) that forgetting things that have happened within the last few minutes or hours is a breakdown in short-term memory. Cognitive psychologists, in contrast, identify short-term memory as memory for what has happened in the last 15–30 seconds (or longer, if the events are rehearsed). According to that definition, Lennie's short-term memory was fine, because he could remember what had just happened to him. His problem was that he couldn't form new long-term memories, so, like Clive Wearing and Jimmy G., he forgot everything that had happened more than a few minutes previously.

Although some movies, like the ones already mentioned, are based at least loosely on actual memory disorders, some stray farther into fiction. Douglas Quaid, the character played by Arnold Schwarzenegger in *Total Recall* (1990), lives in a future world in which it is possible to implant memories. Quaid makes the mistake of having an artificial memory of a holiday on Mars implanted, which triggers a series of nightmarish events.

The reverse of *creating* specific memories is selectively *forgetting* specific events. This occasionally occurs, as when memories for particularly traumatic events are lost (although sometimes the opposite happens, so traumatic events stand out in memory; Porter & Birt, 2001). But the characters in *The Eternal Sunshine of the Spotless Mind* (2004) take the idea of selective forgetting to an extreme, by purposely undergoing a high-tech procedure to selectively eliminate their memory for a previous relationship.

First Clementine, played by Kate Winslet, has her memory for her ex-boyfriend, Joel, played by Jim Carrey, erased. When Joel discovers she has done this, he decides to undergo the same procedure to have Clementine erased from his memory. The aftermath of this procedure is both thought provoking and entertaining!

The movie *50 First Dates* (2004) is an example of a memory movie based on a condition that exists only in the imagination of the filmmaker. Lucy, played by Drew Barrymore, remembers what is happening to her on a given day (so her short-term and long-term memory are fine during the day), but every morning she contracts a case of retrograde amnesia, which has wiped out her memory for what happened the day before. The fact that her memory "resets" every morning seems not to bother Henry, played by Adam Sandler, who falls in love with her. Strangely enough, even though Lucy wakes up every morning with no memory for the previous day, and therefore shouldn't remember Henry, she develops a fondness for him. This behavior—responding positively to Henry without remembering him—is an example of implicit memory.

All of the movies we have described are fictional and so can take liberties with the facts for the purposes of entertainment. However, knowing about how memory actually works can help us sort out what might be at least somewhat plausible from what is wildly fictional.

TEST YOURSELF 6.2

1. How are episodic and semantic memory distinguished from each other?
2. Describe the following evidence for the idea that semantic and episodic memories involve different mechanisms: (a) neuropsychological evidence; (b) brain imaging evidence.
3. What are the connections between episodic and semantic memory?
4. What is priming, and why is it called a type of implicit memory? What precautions are taken to be sure episodic memory is not accessed in an implicit memory experiment? What is repetition priming? Conceptual priming?
5. Describe the Graf and the Warrington and Weiskrantz priming experiments. How do these experiments demonstrate that their participants are not aware of the initial priming stimuli?
6. What is the propaganda effect, and why could it be considered a form of priming?
7. What is procedural memory? Describe the mirror drawing experiment and other examples from the chapter. Why is procedural memory considered a form of implicit memory?
8. What is classical conditioning? Why is it a form of implicit memory?
9. Describe how memory loss is depicted in movies. How accurate are these depictions?

CHAPTER SUMMARY

1. Long-term memory is an "archive" of information about past experiences in our lives and knowledge we have learned, but it is important to consider the dynamic qualities as well, such as how LTM coordinates with working memory to help create our ongoing experience.
2. The primacy and recency effects that occur in the serial position curve have been linked to long-term memory and short-term memory, respectively.
3. The following evidence supports the idea that STM and LTM are two separate processes: (a) differences in the primary mode of coding, with LTM more likely than STM to be coded semantically; (b) neuropsychological studies that demonstrate dissociations between STM and LTM; and (c) brain imaging studies that demonstrate different patterns of activity for STM and LTM.
4. Explicit memory is our conscious recollection of events we have experienced or facts we have learned. There are

two types of explicit memory: Episodic memory is memory for personal events in our lives; semantic memory is memory for facts and knowledge.

5. Implicit memories are memories used without awareness. Types of implicit memory are priming, procedural memory, and classical conditioning.
6. According to Tulving, the defining property of the experience of episodic memory is that it involves mental time travel (self-knowing or remembering). The experience of semantic memory (knowing) does not involve mental time travel.
7. The following evidence supports the idea that episodic and semantic memory involve different mechanisms: (a) double dissociation of episodic and semantic memory in patients with brain damage; (b) brain imaging, which indicates that overlapping but different areas are activated by episodic and semantic memories.
8. Even though episodic and semantic memories are served by different mechanisms, they are connected in the following ways: (a) Episodic memories can be lost, leaving semantic memory; (b) semantic memory can be enhanced by association with episodic memory; (c) semantic memory can influence attention, and therefore what information we take in and potentially remember later.
9. Implicit memory occurs when previous experience improves our performance on a task, even though we do not remember the experience. Tulving calls implicit memory nonknowing.
10. Priming occurs when the presentation of a stimulus affects a person's response to the same or a related stimulus when it is presented later. There are two main types of priming: repetition priming and conceptual priming.
11. The demonstration of implicit memory depends on showing that a particular change in behavior has occurred without participants' consulting their episodic memory (because then the memory would not be unconscious, as required if it is an implicit memory). Various techniques can be used to achieve this; the most effective is to use amnesiac patients as participants.
12. Implicit memory is not just a laboratory phenomenon, but also occurs in real life. The propaganda effect is one example of real-life implicit memory.
13. Procedural memory, also called skill memory, has been studied in amnesiac patients. They are able to learn new skills, although they do not remember learning them. Procedural memory is a common component of many of the skills we have learned.
14. Classical conditioning occurs when a neutral stimulus is paired with a stimulus that elicits a response, so that the neutral stimulus than elicits the response. Classically conditioned emotions occur in everyday experience.
15. Memory loss has been depicted in movies in a number of ways, some of which bear at least a resemblance to actual cases of amnesia, and some of which are totally fictional conditions.

Think ABOUT IT

1. What do you remember about the last 5 minutes? How much of what you are remembering is in your STM while you are remembering it? Were any of these memories ever in LTM?
2. On page 155, we described the case of K.F., who had normal LTM but poor STM. What problem does K.F.'s condition pose for the modal model of memory? Can you think of a way to modify the model that would handle K.F.'s condition?
3. Not all long-term memories are alike. There is a difference between remembering what you did 10 minutes ago, 1 year ago, and 10 years ago, even though all of these memories are called "long-term memories." What kinds of investigations could you carry out to demonstrate the properties of these different long-term memories?
4. Rent movies like *Memento, 50 First Dates,* or others that depict memory loss. (Search the Internet for "Movies amnesia" for films in addition to those listed in the book.) Describe the memory loss depicted in these movies, and compare the problem depicted with the cases of memory loss described in this chapter. Determine how accurately depictions of memory loss in movies correspond to memory loss that occurs in actual cases of trauma or brain damage. You may have to do some additional research on memory loss to answer this question.

If You WANT TO KNOW MORE

1. **Top-down processing and the suffix effect.** The suffix effect occurs when a sound presented at the end of a list of words decreases the recency effect in the serial position curve. This effect can depend on the participant's interpretation of the meaning of the sound, which means that top-down processing can be involved in this effect.

Neath, I., Surprenant, A. M., & Crowder, R. G. (1993). The context-dependent stimulus suffix effect. *Journal of Experimental Psychology: Learning, Memory and Cognition, 19*, 698–703.

2. **The "unitary" view of memory.** Not all researchers accept the idea that short-term memory and long-term memory are separate processes. There are other theories, supported by evidence, that propose one system, centered on long-term memory, and propose that a great deal of what is called short-term memory occurs when information is retrieved from long-term memory.

Cowan, N. (2000). The magical number 4 in short-term memory: A reconsideration of mental storage capacity. *Behavioral and Brain Sciences, 24*, 87–185.

Jonides, J., Lewis, R. L., Nee, D. E., Lustig, C. A., Berman, G, & Moore, K. S. (2008). The mind and brain of short-term memory. *Annual Review of Psychology, 59*, 193–224.

3. **Memory loss in Alzheimer's disease.** Patients with Alzheimer's disease experience progressive loss of memory as different structures are attacked by the disease.

Fleischman, D. A., & Gabrieli, J. (1999). Long-term memory in Alzheimer's disease. *Current Opinion in Neurobiology, 9*, 240–244.

Fleischman, D. A., Wilson, R. S., Gabrieli, J. D. E., Schneider, J. A., Bienias, J. L., & Bennett, D. A. (2005). Implicit memory and Alzheimer's disease: Neuropathology. *Brain, 128*, 2006–2015.

Gilboa, A., Ramirex, J., Kohler, S., Westmacott, R., Black, S. E., & Moscovitch, M. (2005). Retrieval of autobiographical memory in Alzheimer's disease: Relation to volumes of medial temporal lobe and other structures. *Hippocampus, 15*, 535–550.

4. **Mental time travel in animals.** Experiments with scrub jays, rats, and nonhuman primates have demonstrated parallels in their behavior to behaviors associated with mental time travel in humans.

Roberts, W. A., & Feeney, M. C. (2009). The comparative study of mental time travel. *Trends in Cognitive Science, 13*, 271–277.

Key TERMS

Media RESOURCES

The *Cognitive Psychology* Book Companion Website

www.cengage.com/international

Prepare for quizzes and exams with online resources—including a glossary, flashcards, tutorial quizzes, crossword puzzles, and more.

CogLab

CogLab

To experience these experiments for yourself, go to coglab.wadsworth.com. Be sure to read each experiment's setup instructions before you go to the experiment itself. Otherwise, you won't know which keys to press.

Primary Labs

Serial position How memory for a list depends on an item's position on the list (p. 151).

Implicit learning How we can learn something without being aware of the learning (p. 161).

Related Lab

Suffix effect How adding an irrelevant item to the end of a list affects recall for the final items on a list in a serial position experiment.

7 Encoding and Retrieval

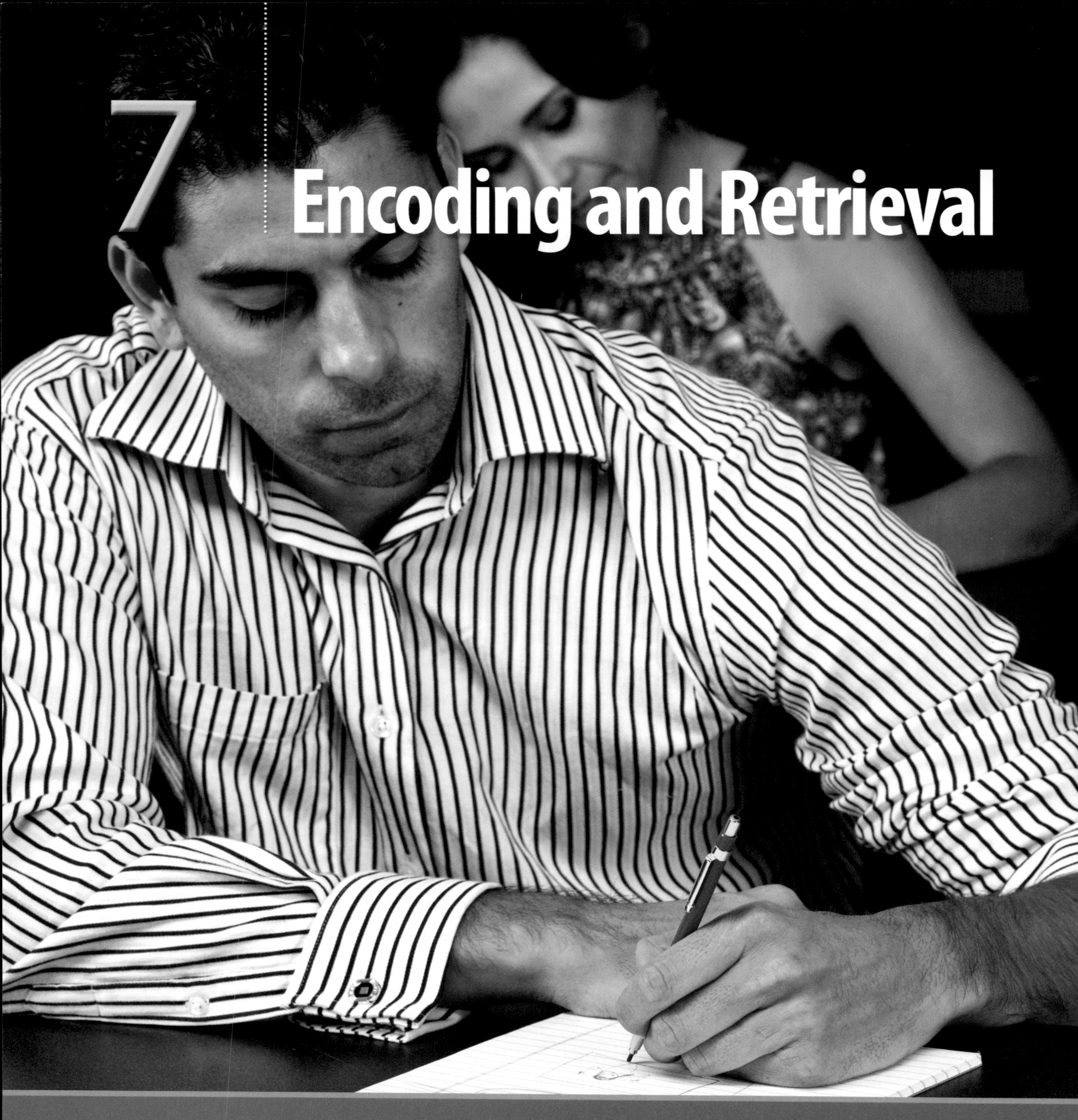

What is the best way to put information into your memory through studying, and then to access this information later when you need to remember it for the test? The answer to this question involves basic principles of memory that are described in this chapter.

Some Questions We Will Consider

- What is the best way to store information in long-term memory? (173)
- What are some techniques we can use to help us get information out of long-term memory when we need it? (181)
- How can the results of memory research be used to create more effective study techniques? (187)
- How is it possible that a lifetime of experiences and accumulated knowledge can be stored in neurons? (190)

When I asked students in my class to write Top 10 lists of "What I use memory for," "Remembering material for exams" was at the top of the class's list (see Chapter 5, page 116). This is, of course, important (your grade depends on it!), and students have therefore devised numerous ways to get the information they need to know into memory. In the previous edition of this book, I invited students to send, by e-mail, their favorite study techniques. Here are excepts from a few of the responses I received:

STUDENT #1: The main technique I use to study is to make up a story in my mind, basically a fake memory, the type a person would use to create an effective lie, in order to remember material. An example of this strategy is how I studied for our first cognitive psych exam this semester. "Jo changed his name to Hermann Helmholtz today. Jo has always been an odd one. He always infers things are there that aren't. Like the time he liked that girl Amygdala. Speaking of Amygdala, she was an emotional girl." When I tell this story to myself I create an image, much like a memory to associate with what I am trying to remember. That way when I take the test an entire sequence of events is recalled so that I am better able to remember the information. (Elizabeth Eowyn Waibel, University of Wisconsin)

STUDENT #2: I like to go to class early and study in the classroom. To remember, I need to take notes from the book as I read. For certain harder classes, I remember better if I do this before class. Then during class I just add to my previous notes. This lets me listen more during class instead of being busy writing.... I like to start conversations with my parents or friends about what I've learned in class. They have usually learned something about it too, and remind me of details I may have forgotten. (Kristin Eddinger, Florida Atlantic University)

STUDENT #3: A technique I've used has been to find someone unsuspecting, perhaps a friend or family member, and teach them what I've learnt. I did this to a mate about 5 years ago, taught him about the structure of the tooth. To this day he remembers it and always reminds me of the time I jumped him with this "random" information! (Brigitte Dunbar, Massey University, Auckland, New Zealand)

STUDENT #4: My tactic is to go through my textbook (and lecture notes) and to create a sort of "tabbed" set of notes, where sub-concepts are tabbed underneath larger concepts. This follows the organization of textbooks to a degree ... so I get something like Declarative Memory–Episodic–About events in our lives–Semantic–About facts.... After reading a few paragraphs, I write down what I learned, but first I have to figure out the major and minor points. But the most important part about this is it acts as a way to test myself. I can just throw a piece of paper over my notes and slowly move it down the page, and I try to recall what is "inside" a certain heading (and explain it to myself), and then I go down it line by line to check (if I missed a sub-heading, I try to recall what's under it, if anything). (Taylor Murphy, University of Alberta)

STUDENT #5: I read each chapter, take notes (sometimes word for word, or by shorthand) on my computer where I can organize them in a way that makes sense to me. Finally, I make note cards and study these. (Natalie Tyler, Georgia State University)

Each of the techniques suggested by these students is based on one or more basic principles behind the operation of long-term memory. In this chapter we begin by describing these principles and then show how the principles can be applied to the student examples and to studying in general. One of the goals of studying is to get information into LTM. We saw in Chapter 5, when we described Rachel ordering pizza, that the process of acquiring information and transferring it into LTM is called encoding.

Notice that the term *encoding* is similar to the term *coding* that we discussed in relation to STM in Chapter 5 and LTM in Chapter 6. Some authors use these terms interchangeably. We will use the term *coding* to refer to the *form* in which information is represented. For example, a word can be coded visually or by its sound or by its meaning. We will use the term *encoding* to refer to the *process* used to get information into LTM. For example, a word can be encoded by repeating it over and over, by thinking of other words that rhyme with it, or by using it in a sentence. One of the main messages in this chapter is that some methods of encoding are more effective than others.

Imagine that you've just finished studying for an exam and are pretty sure that you have encoded the material that is likely to be on the exam into your LTM. But the moment of truth occurs when you are in the exam and you have to remember some of this information to answer a question. This remembering involves accessing some of the information that you've encoded and transferring it from LTM into working memory, to become consciously aware of it. This process of transferring information from LTM to working memory is called retrieval. It is, of course, essential to your success on the exam, because even if information is in LTM, it doesn't help you answer the exam question if you can't retrieve it. One of the main factors that determines whether you can retrieve information from LTM is the way that information was encoded when you learned it. In the next section we will focus on how information is encoded into LTM. We will then consider retrieval and how it relates to encoding.

Encoding: Getting Information Into Long-Term Memory

There are a number of ways to get information into memory, some more effective than others. You can mindlessly read something, or take in its deeper meaning; you can consider a topic by repeating its individual points, or you can become aware of how a topic is organized by noting how the individual points relate to each other. We begin describing methods of getting information into memory by discussing the process of rehearsal—repeating information over and over.

MAINTENANCE REHEARSAL AND ELABORATIVE REHEARSAL

One of the central concerns of early cognitive psychologists was determining the relationship between encoding and rehearsal. We saw in Chapter 5 that rehearsal can be used to keep information in STM/working memory, as when you repeat a phone number you have just looked up in the phone book. Although rehearsal can keep information in working memory, rehearsal doesn't guarantee that information will be transferred into LTM. You know this from your experience in rehearsing a telephone number and then forgetting it right after you place the call. When you rehearse a telephone number in this way, you are usually just repeating the numbers without any consideration of meaning or making connections with other information. This kind of rehearsal, called maintenance rehearsal, helps *maintain* information in STM/WM, but it is not an effective way of *transferring* information into long-term memory.

Another kind of rehearsal, elaborative rehearsal, is more effective at transferring information into LTM; it occurs when you think about the meaning of an item or make connections between the item and something you know. We can demonstrate that elaborative rehearsal is a good way to establish long-term memories by describing an approach to memory called *levels-of-processing theory*.

LEVELS-OF-PROCESSING THEORY

In 1972 Fergus Craik and Robert Lockhart proposed the idea of **levels of processing** (LOP). According to **levels-of-processing theory**, memory depends on how information is encoded, with "deeper" processing resulting in better encoding and retrieval than "shallow" processing. In other words, memory depends on how information is programmed into the mind.

CogLab
Levels of Processing

The Basics of Levels of Processing According to levels-of-processing theory, depth of processing is determined by the nature of the task during encoding. The following demonstration illustrates how different tasks affects memory for a list of words.

DEMONSTRATION Remembering Lists

Part 1. Cover the list below and then uncover each word one by one. Your task is to count the number of vowels in each word and then go right on to the next one. Once you get to the end of the list, cover it and follow the instructions at the end of the list.

chair
mathematics
elephant
lamp
car
elevator
thoughtful
cactus

Instructions: Count backward by 3s from 100. When you get to 76, write down the words you remember. Do that now.

Part 2. Cover the list below and uncover each word one by one as you did in the previous part. This time, visualize how useful the item might be if you were stranded on an uninhabited island. When you get to the end of the list, follow the instructions.

umbrella
exercise
forgiveness
rock
hamburger
sunlight
coffee
bottle

Instructions: Count backward by 3s from 99. When you reach 75, write down the words you remember. Do that now.

Which procedure resulted in better memory, counting the number of vowels or visualizing an item's function? Most of the experiments that have asked this kind of question have found that memory is superior when a meaningful connection has been made between an item and something else. Thus, memory for words is better when the words are processed by relating them to other knowledge, such as how useful an object might be on an uninhabited island, than when processed based on a nonmeaningful characteristic such as the number of vowels. Craik and Lockhart's levels-of-processing theory states that memory depends on the **depth of processing** that an item receives. They describe depth of processing by distinguishing between *shallow processing* and *deep processing*.

Shallow processing involves little attention to meaning. Shallow processing occurs when attention is focused on physical features, such as whether a word is printed in lowercase or capital letters, or the number of vowels in a word, as was done in Part 1 of the "Remembering Lists" demonstration. Shallow processing also occurs during maintenance rehearsal, in which an item is repeated to keep it in memory but without considering its meaning or its connection with anything else.

Deep processing involves close attention, focusing on an item's meaning and relating it to something else. Considering how an item might be useful in a particular situation, as was done in Part 2 of the demonstration, or creating an image of the item in relation to another item would create deep processing. This way of processing an item occurs during elaborative rehearsal and, according to levels-of-processing theory, results in better memory than shallow processing.

The previous demonstration illustrated one way of varying depth of processing. The following Method, which corresponds to the method used in an experiment by Fergus Craik and Endel Tulving (1975), illustrates how depth of processing can be varied by asking different kinds of questions about a word.

METHOD Varying Depth of Processing

The procedure for the Craik and Tulving experiment is diagrammed in ● Figure 7.1a. A question was presented, followed by a word, and then the participant responded. Shallow processing was achieved by asking questions about the word's physical characteristics; deeper processing was achieved by asking about the word's sound; and the deepest processing was achieved by a task that involved the word's meaning. The following examples are similar to those used in Craik and Tulving's experiment.

1. Shallow processing: A question about physical features of the word
   Question: Is the word printed in capital letters?
   Word: *bird*
2. Deeper processing: A question about rhyming
   Question: Does the word rhyme with *train*?
   Word: *pain*
3. Deepest processing: A fill-in-the-blanks question
   Question: Does the word fit into the sentence "He saw a ____________ on the street"?
   Word: *car*

After participants responded to questions like the ones above, they were given a memory test to see how well they recalled the words. The results, shown in Figure 7.1b, indicate that deeper processing is associated with better memory.

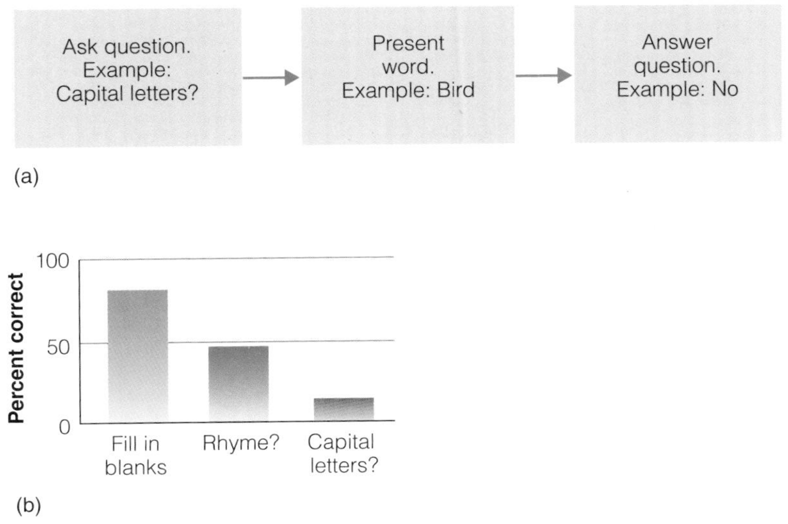

● **FIGURE 7.1** (a) Sequence of events in Craik and Tulving's (1975) experiment. (b) Results of this experiment. Deeper processing (fill-in-the-blanks question) is associated with better memory.

The idea of levels of processing motivated a great deal of research that investigated how the way a stimulus is encoded affects the ability to retrieve it later. However, the levels-of-processing theory and the idea of depth of processing became less important to memory researchers when it became apparent that it was difficult to define exactly what depth of processing is.

The Difficulty in Defining Depth of Processing

The way we have described depth of processing is based mainly on common sense: It seems obvious that paying attention to how a word is used in a sentence would be "deeper" than

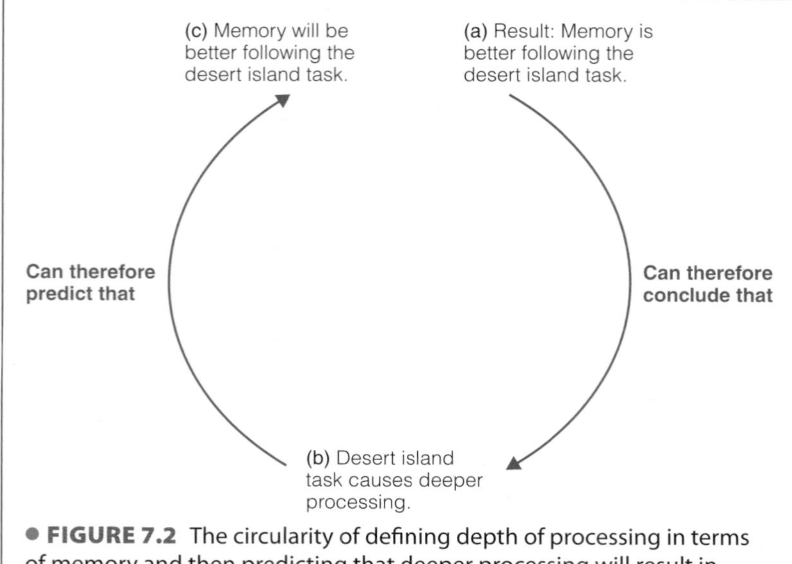

• **FIGURE 7.2** The circularity of defining depth of processing in terms of memory and then predicting that deeper processing will result in better memory. See text for details.

noting if the word is printed in capital letters. But let's consider a more difficult problem. What about using a word in a sentence (as in the Craik and Tulving experiment) versus deciding how useful an object might be on a desert island (as in the Demonstration). Which of these results in deeper processing? Unfortunately, levels-of-processing theory does not offer a way to answer this question.

One possibility that might be worth trying is to pit these two procedures against each other in a memory experiment. If, in our hypothetical experiment, participants in the desert island condition remember more than participants in the fill-in-the-blanks condition, then couldn't we conclude that the desert island condition resulted in deeper processing? Although this may sound logical, a little reflection indicates that this procedure does not really solve the problem. We can appreciate why by considering the reasoning behind the memory experiment more closely.

We started by asking whether the desert island task causes *deeper* or *shallower* processing than the fill-in-the-blanks task. To answer this question, we ran a memory experiment and determined that the desert island task resulted in better memory (• Figure 7.2a). From this, we concluded that the desert island task results in deeper processing (Figure 7.2b). This seems to have solved the problem, but not so fast! Once we have determined that the desert island task results in deeper processing, we can predict from this that memory will be better for the desert island task (Figure 7.2c). This is called *circular reasoning*, and it occurs because depth of processing has not been defined *independently* of memory performance. We can't use memory performance to determine depth of processing and then turn around and use depth of processing to predict memory performance.

Because no procedure was offered to define depth of processing independently of memory performance, levels-of-processing theory became less popular with memory researchers. But the main conclusion of levels-of-processing theory—that memory retrieval is affected by how items are encoded—is still widely accepted, and a great deal of research has been done that demonstrates this relationship.

RESEARCH SHOWING THAT ENCODING INFLUENCES RETRIEVAL

A number of different procedures have been used to show that encoding can affect retrieval. The basic idea in all of these experiments is to vary encoding and measure how retrieval (memory performance) is affected. We will show how this has been done in experiments that involve (1) placing words to be remembered in complex sentences; (2) forming visual images based on words; (3) forming links between words and personal characteristics; (4) generating information; (5) organizing information; and (6) testing.

Placing Words in a Complex Sentence If you were given the task of remembering the word *chicken*, which sentence do you think would result in better memory?

1. She cooked the chicken.
2. The great bird swooped down and carried off the struggling chicken.

Craik and Tulving (1975) found that memory for a word is much better when the word is presented in a complex sentence. Their explanation for this result is that the complex sentence creates more connections between the word to be remembered and other things, and these other things act as *cues* that help us retrieve the word when we are trying to remember it. Consider, for example, your response to each of the sentences about the chicken. If reading them resulted in images in your mind, which image was more vivid—a woman cooking, or a giant bird carrying a struggling chicken?

Apparently, most of the participants in Craik and Tulving's experiment found the giant-bird sentence to be more memorable. This wasn't true for one student in my class, however, who reported that because her mother cooks a lot of chicken, she thought of her mother when reading the shorter sentence. Thus, for this student, the image of her mother cooking formed a stronger connection than the image of the swooping bird.

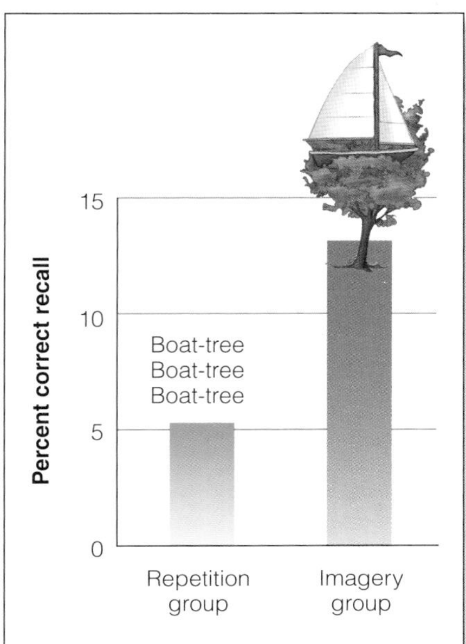

● **FIGURE 7.3** Results of the Bower and Winzenz (1970) experiment. Participants in the repetition group repeated word pairs. Participants in the imagery group formed images representing the pairs.

Forming Visual Images Gordon Bower and David Winzenz (1970) decided to test whether using visual imagery—"images in the head" that connect words visually—can create connections that enhance memory. They used a procedure called paired-associate learning, in which a list of word pairs is presented. Later, the first word of each pair is presented, and the participant's task is to remember the word it was paired with.

Bower and Winzenz presented a list of 15 pairs of nouns, such as *boat–tree*, to participants for 5 seconds each. One group was told to silently repeat the pairs as they were presented, and another group was told to form a mental picture in which the two items were interacting. When participants were later given the first word and were asked to recall the second one for each pair, the participants who had created images remembered more than twice as many words as the participants who had just repeated the word pairs (● Figure 7.3).

Linking Words to Yourself Another example of how memory is improved by encoding is the self-reference effect: Memory is better if you are asked to relate a word to yourself. T. B. Rogers and coworkers (1977) demonstrated this by using the same procedure Craik and Tulving had used in their depth-of-processing experiment. The design of Rogers' experiment is shown in ● Figure 7.4a. Participants were presented with a question for 3 seconds followed by a brief pause and then a word. The task was to answer the question "yes" or "no" after seeing the word. Here are examples of the four types of questions:

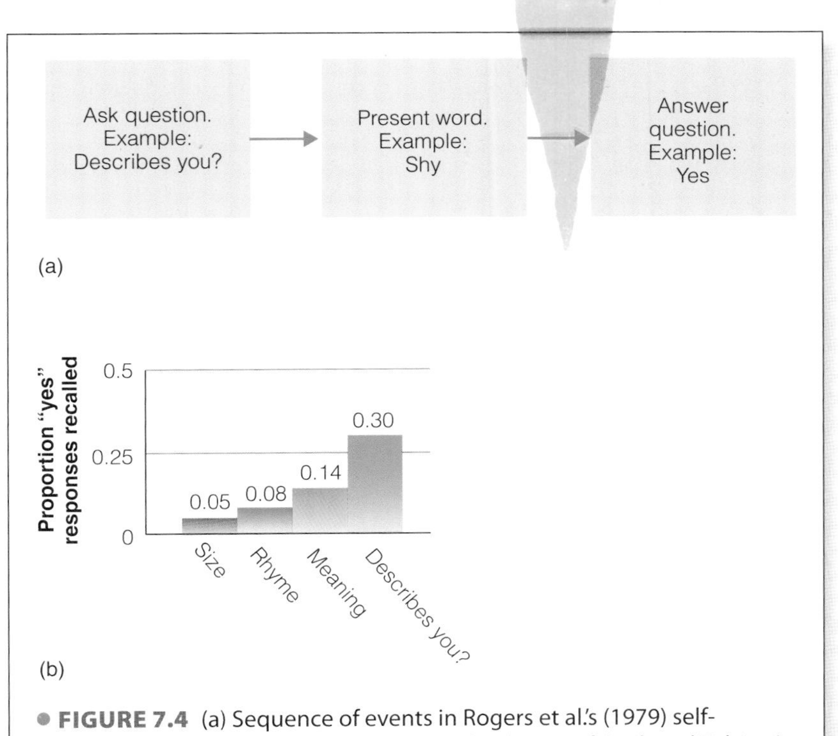

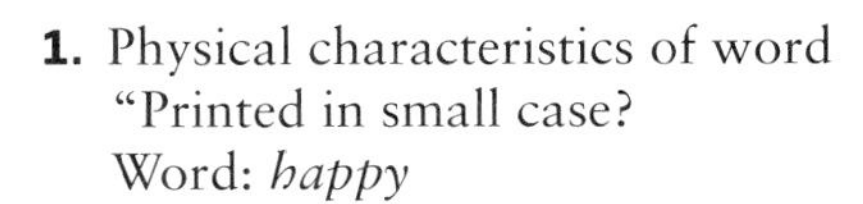

● **FIGURE 7.4** (a) Sequence of events in Rogers et al.'s (1979) self-reference experiment. This is the same as the design of Craik and Tulving's (1975) experiment shown in Figure 7.1, but some of the questions refer to the person being tested. (b) Results of the experiment. (Source: T. B. Rogers, N. A. Kuiper, & W. S. Kirker, "Self-Reference and the Encoding of Personal Information," *Journal of Personality and Social Psychology, 35*, 677–688, 1977.)

1. Physical characteristics of word
   "Printed in small case?
   Word: *happy*
2. Rhyming
   "Rhymes with *happy*?"
   Word: *snappy*
3. Meaning
   "Means the same as *happy*?"
   Word: *upbeat*
4. Self-reference
   "Describes you?"
   Word: *happy*

When Rogers then tested his participants' recall, he obtained the results shown in Figure 7.4b for words that resulted in a "yes" response. Participants were more likely to remember words that they rated as describing themselves.

Why are participants more likely to remember words they connect to themselves? One possible explanation is that the words become linked to something the participants know well—themselves. This is similar to the example in which the information provided by the giant swooping bird provided a link that helped participants remember the word *chicken*. Generally, statements that result in richer, more detailed representations in a person's mind result in better memory.

Generating Information Generating material yourself, rather than passively receiving it, enhances learning and retention. Norman Slameka and Peter Graf (1978) demonstrated this effect, called the **generation effect**, by having participants study a list of word pairs in two different ways:

1. *Read* group: Read these pairs of related words.
   king–crown; horse–saddle; lamp–shade; etc.
2. *Generate* group: Fill in the blank with a word that is related to the first word.
   king–cr_____ ; horse–sa_____ ; lamp–sh_____ ; etc.

After either reading or generating the list of word pairs, they were presented with the first word in each pair and were told to indicate the word that went with it. Participants who had *generated* the second word in each pair were able to reproduce 28 percent more word pairs than participants who had just *read* the word pairs. You might guess that this finding has some important implications for studying for exams. We will return to this idea later in the chapter.

Organizing Information Folders on your computer's desktop, computerized library catalogs, and tabs that separate different subjects in your notebook are all designed to organize information so it can be accessed more efficiently. The memory system also uses organization to access information. This has been shown in a number of ways.

DEMONSTRATION Reading a List

Get paper and pen ready. Read the following words, then cover them and write down as many as you can.

apple, desk, shoe, sofa, plum, chair, cherry, coat, lamp, pants, grape, hat, melon, table, gloves

STOP! Do the demonstration now, before reading further.

Look at the list you created and notice whether similar items (for example, *apple, plum, cherry*; *shoe, coat, pants*) are grouped together. If they are, your result is similar to the result of research that shows that participants spontaneously organize items as they recall them (Jenkins & Russell, 1952). One reason for this result is that remembering words in a particular category may serve as a **retrieval cue**—a word or other stimulus that helps a person remember information stored in memory—for other words in that category. So, remembering the word *apple* is a retrieval cue for other fruits, such as *grape* or *plum*, and therefore creates a recall list that is more organized than the original list that you read.

If words presented randomly become organized in the mind, what happens when words are presented in an organized way from the beginning, during encoding? Gordon Bower and coworkers (1969) answered this question by presenting material to be learned in an "organizational tree," which organized a number of words according to categories. For example, one tree organized the names of different minerals by grouping together precious stones, rare metals, and so on (• Figure 7.5).

One group of participants studied four separate trees for minerals, animals, clothing, and transportation for 1 minute each and were then asked to recall as many words as they could from all four trees. In the recall test, participants tended to organize their responses in the same way the trees were organized, first saying "minerals," then "metals," then "common," and so on. Participants in this group recalled an average of 73 words from all four trees.

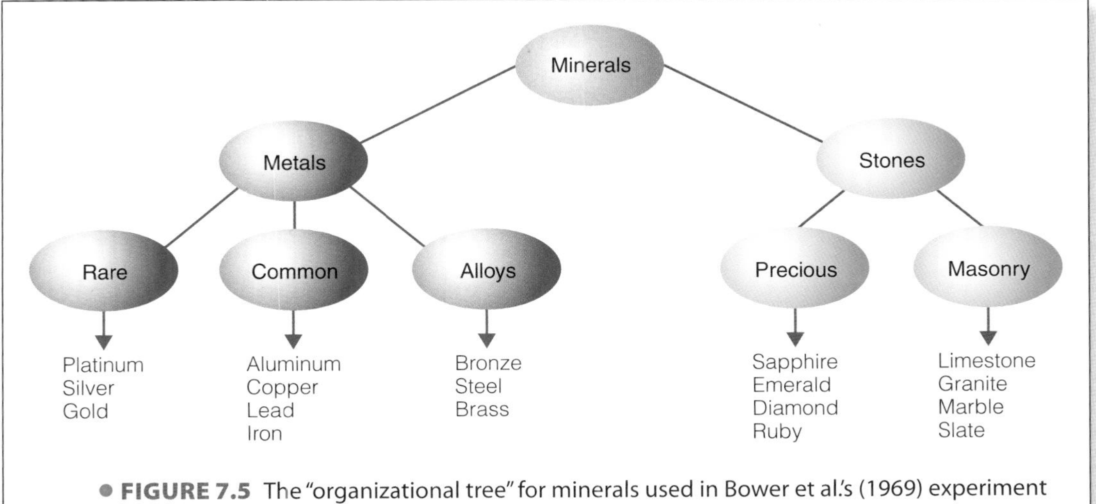

● **FIGURE 7.5** The "organizational tree" for minerals used in Bower et al.'s (1969) experiment on the effect of organization on memory. (Source: G. H. Bower et al., "Hierarchical Retrieval Schemes in Recall of Categorized Word Lists," *Journal of Verbal Learning and Verbal Behavior, 8,* Figure 1, 323–343. Copyright © 1969 Elsevier Ltd. Republished with permission.)

Another group of participants also saw four trees, but the words were randomized, so that each tree contained a random assortment of minerals, animals, clothing, and transportation. These participants were able to remember only 21 words from all four trees. Thus, organizing material to be remembered results in substantially better recall. Perhaps this is something to keep in mind when creating study materials for an exam. You might, for example, find it useful to organize material you are studying for your cognitive psychology exam in trees like the one in ● Figure 7.6.

If presenting material in an organized way improves memory, we might expect that *preventing* organization from happening would *reduce* the ability to remember. Read the passage below and try to figure out what it is about, before turning the page.

> If the balloons popped, the sound wouldn't be able to carry since everything would be too far away from the correct floor. A closed window would also prevent the sound from carrying, since most buildings tend to be well insulated. Since the whole operation depends on the steady flow of electricity, a break in the middle of the wire would also cause problems. Of course, the fellow could shout, but the human voice is not loud enough to carry that far. An additional problem is that the string could break on the instrument. Then there would be no accompaniment to the message. It is clear that the best situation would involve less distance. Then there would be fewer potential problems. With face to face contact, the least number of things could go wrong. (p. 719)

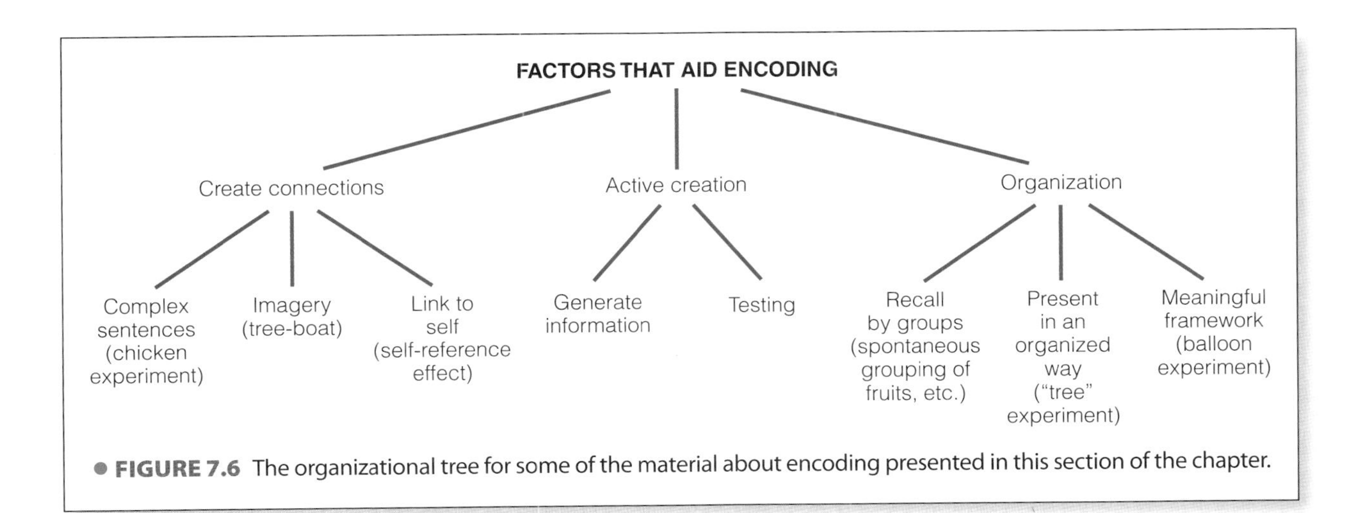

● **FIGURE 7.6** The organizational tree for some of the material about encoding presented in this section of the chapter.

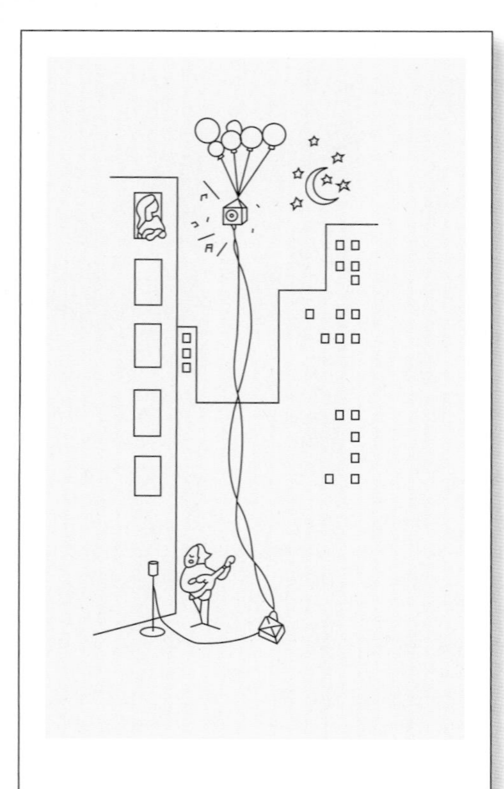

● **FIGURE 7.7** Picture used by Bransford and Johnson (1972) to illustrate the effect of organization on memory. (Source: J. D. Bransford & M. K. Johnson, "Contextual Prerequisites for Understanding: Some Investigations of Comprehension and Recall," *Journal of Verbal Learning and Verbal Behavior, 11,* Figure 1, 717–726. Copyright © 1972 Elsevier Ltd. Republished with permission.)

If you had a problem understanding the passage, you're not alone, because so did participants who read the passage in an experiment done by John Bransford and Marcia Johnson (1972). More important, their participants also found it extremely difficult to *remember* this passage.

To make sense of this passage, look at ● Figure 7.7 and then reread the passage. When you do this, the passage makes more sense. Bransford and Johnson's (1972) participants who saw this picture *before* they read the passage remembered twice as much from the passage as participants who did not see the picture or participants who saw the picture *after* they read the passage. The key here is organization. The picture provides a mental framework that helps the reader link one sentence to the next to create a meaningful story. The resulting organization makes this passage easier to comprehend and much easier to remember later. This example illustrates once again that the ability to remember material depends on how that material is programmed into the mind.

Testing A survey of student study techniques reveals that rereading the material to be learned is the predominant method used for studying (Karpicke et al., 2009). However, recent research shows that being tested on the material to be remembered results in better memory than rereading it.

Henry Roediger and Jeffrey Karpicke (2006) demonstrated the advantages of testing using the experimental design in ● Figure 7.8. In the first phase of the experiment, college students read prose passages for 7 minutes followed by a 2-minute break during which they solved math problems. Then one group (the testing group) took a 7-minute recall test in which the were asked to write down as much of the passage as they could remember, in no particular order. The other group (the rereading group) were given 7 minutes to reread the material.

In the second phase of the experiment, which occurred after a delay of either 5 minutes, 2 days, or 1 week, participants were given the recall test in which they wrote down what they remembered from the passage. The results, in ● Figure 7.9, show that there was little difference between the rereading and testing groups after the 5-minute delay. However, when performance for both groups dropped during the 2-day and 1-week delays, the performance of the testing group dropped much less, so the testing group's performance was much better after the delay. This enhanced performance due to testing is called the **testing effect.** It has been demonstrated in a large number of experiments, both in the laboratory and in classroom settings (Karpicke et al., 2009). For example, testing resulted in better performance than rereading for eighth-grade students' performance on a history test (Carpenter et al., 2009) and for college students' performance on an exam in a brain and behavior course (McDaniel et al., 2007).

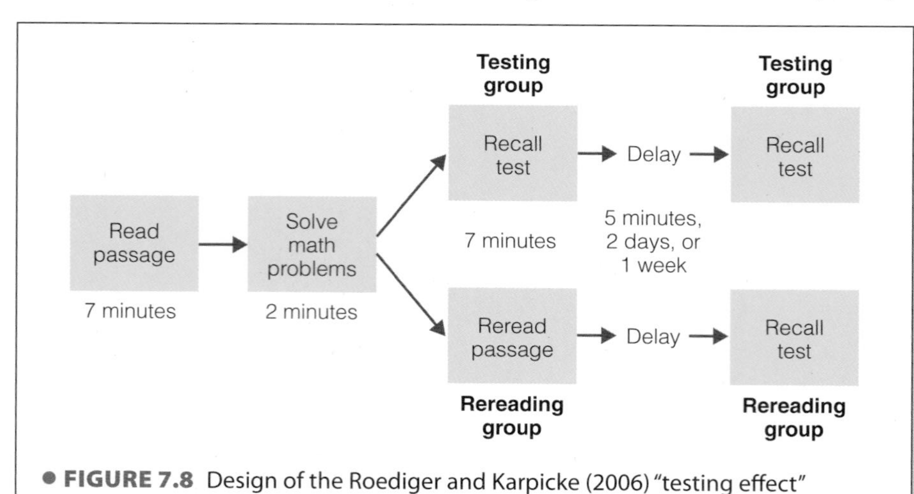

● **FIGURE 7.8** Design of the Roediger and Karpicke (2006) "testing effect" experiment.

Table 7.1 lists all of the examples we have described of methods of encoding that increase memory. What do these procedures have in common? The testing and generation effects both involve actively creating material. Similarities between the other procedures are not as obvious, but it is probably accurate to say that each, in its own way, increases the richness of representation in memory by providing connections between the material to be remembered and other material in memory. For example, when material is organized, it become easier to form links between items (such as *apple*, *grape*, and *plum*) in a list. What all this means is that there is a close relationship

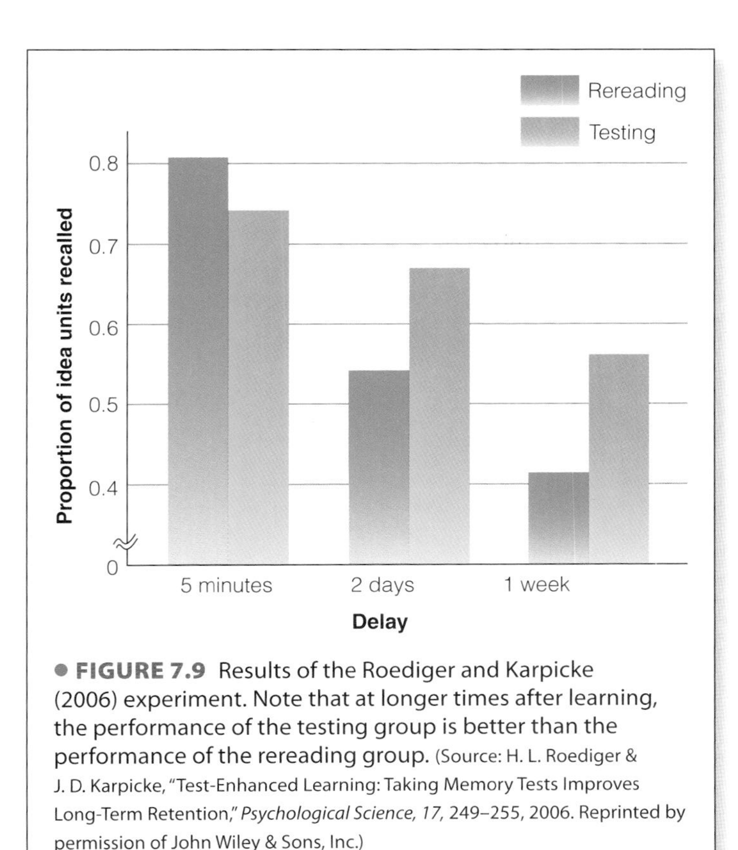

● **FIGURE 7.9** Results of the Roediger and Karpicke (2006) experiment. Note that at longer times after learning, the performance of the testing group is better than the performance of the rereading group. (Source: H. L. Roediger & J. D. Karpicke, "Test-Enhanced Learning: Taking Memory Tests Improves Long-Term Retention," *Psychological Science, 17,* 249–255, 2006. Reprinted by permission of John Wiley & Sons, Inc.)

TABLE 7.1 Encoding Procedures That Affect Retrieval

Condition	Experiment/Result
Word in complex sentence	Better memory for a word ("chicken") used in a complex sentence (more detailed description of the word)
Forming visual image	Pairs of words remembered better if images formed (compared to just reading word pairs)
Linking to self	Words associated with self are remembered better (self-reference effect)
Generating information	Memory better if second word of a word pair is generated by the person, compared to just being presented with the word (generation effect)
Organizing information	Studying information that is organized, as in a "tree," results in better memory; presenting information so organization is difficult ("balloon" story) results in poor memory
Testing	Testing following learning results in better memory than rereading material after learning (testing effect)

between encoding and retrieval. We will consider further evidence for this connection as we discuss retrieval in the next section.

TEST YOURSELF 7.1

1. What is encoding? Retrieval? Why is each necessary for successful memory?
2. What is the difference between elaborative rehearsal and maintenance rehearsal, in terms of (a) the procedures associated with each type of rehearsal and (b) their effectiveness for creating long-term memories?
3. What is levels-of-processing theory? Be sure you understand depth of processing, shallow processing, and deep processing. What would LOP theory say about the difference between maintenance rehearsal and elaborative rehearsal?
4. What does it mean to say that LOP theory does not define depth of processing independently of memory? Why is this a problem for LOP theory?
5. Give examples of how memory for a word can be increased by (a) using it in a sentence, (b) forming visual images, (c) linking words to yourself, (d) generating the word during acquisition, (e) organizing information, and (f) testing. What do these procedures have in common?
6. What do the results of the procedures in #5 indicate about the relationship between encoding and retrieval?

Retrieval: Getting Information Out of Memory

Before material that has been encoded can be used, it must be retrieved. The process of retrieval is extremely important because most of our failures of memory are failures of retrieval. These retrieval failures occur when the information is "in there," but we can't get it out. For example, you've studied hard for an exam but can't come up with the answer when you're taking the exam, only to remember it later when the exam is over. Or when you unexpectedly meet someone you have previously met, you can't recall the person's name, but it suddenly comes to you as you are talking (or worse, after the person leaves). In both of these examples, the information you needed had been encoded, but you couldn't retrieve it when you needed it.

RETRIEVAL CUES

When we discussed how remembering the word *apple* might serve as a retrieval cue for *grape* (page 178), we defined *retrieval cues* as words or other stimuli that help us remember information stored in our memory. As we now consider these cues in more detail, we will see that these cues can be provided by a number of different sources.

An experience I had as I was preparing to leave home to go to class illustrates how *location* can serve as a retrieval cue. While I was in my office at home, I made a mental note to be sure to take the DVD on amnesia to school for my cognitive psychology class. A short while later, as I was leaving the house, I had a nagging feeling that I was forgetting something, but I couldn't remember what it was. This wasn't the first time I'd had this problem, so I knew exactly what to do. I returned to my office, and as soon as I got there I remembered that I was supposed to take the DVD. Returning to the place where I had originally thought about taking the disk helped me to retrieve my original thought. My office served as a retrieval cue for remembering what I wanted to take to class.

You may have had similar experiences in which returning to a particular place stimulated memories associated with that place. The following description by one of my students illustrates retrieval of memories of childhood experiences.

> When I was 8 years old, both of my grandparents passed away. Their house was sold, and that chapter of my life was closed. Since then I can remember general things about being there as a child, but not the details. One day I decided to go for a drive. I went to my grandparents' old house and I pulled around to the alley and parked. As I sat there and stared at the house, the most amazing thing happened. I experienced a vivid recollection. All of a sudden, I was 8 years old again. I could see myself in the backyard, learning to ride a bike for the first time. I could see the inside of the house. I remembered exactly what every detail looked like. I could even remember the distinct smell. So many times I tried to remember these things, but never so vividly did I remember such detail. (Angela Paidousis)

My experience in my office and Angela's experience outside her grandparents' house are examples of retrieval cues that are provided by returning to the location where memories were initially formed. Many other things besides location can provide retrieval cues. Hearing a particular song can bring back memories for events you might not have thought about for years. Or consider smell. I once experienced a musty smell like the stairwell of my grandparents' house and was instantly transported back many decades to the experience of climbing those stairs as a child. The operation of retrieval cues has also been demonstrated in the laboratory using a technique called *cued recall*, which is illustrated in the following Method section.

METHOD Cued Recall

We can distinguish two types of recall procedures. In **free recall**, a participant is simply asked to recall stimuli. These stimuli could be words previously presented by the experimenter or events experienced earlier in the participant's life. We have seen how this has been used in many experiments, such as the testing effect experiment described on page 180. In **cued recall**, the participant is presented with retrieval cues to aid in recall of the previously experienced stimuli. These cues are typically words or phrases. For example, Endel Tulving and Zena Pearlstone (1966) did an experiment in which they presented participants with a list of words

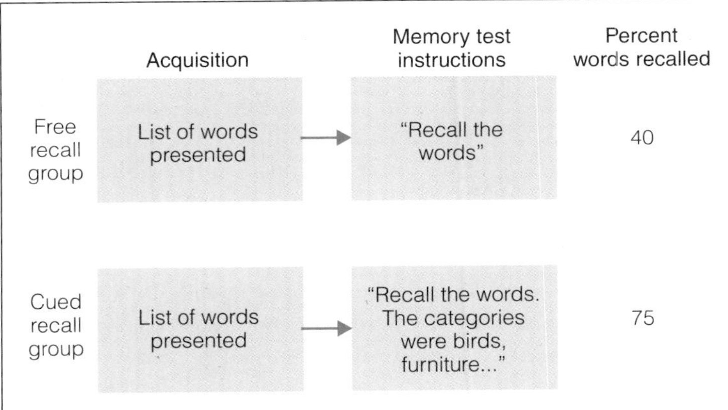

● **FIGURE 7.10** Design of the Tulving and Pearlstone (1966) experiment. The memory performance for each group is shown on the right.

to remember. The words were drawn from specific categories such as birds (*pigeon, sparrow*), furniture (*chair, dresser*), and professions (*engineer, lawyer*), although the categories were not specifically indicated in the original list. For the memory test, participants in the free recall group were asked to write down as many words as they could. Participants in the cued recall group were also asked to recall the words, but were provided with the names of the categories, "birds," "furniture," and "professions" (● Figure 7.10).

The results of Tulving and Pearlstone's experiment demonstrate that retrieval cues aid memory. Participants in the free recall group recalled 40 percent of the words, whereas participants in the cued recall group recalled 75 percent of the words.

One of the most impressive demonstrations of the power of retrieval cues was provided by Timo Mantyla (1986), who presented his participants with a list of 600 nouns, such as *banana*, *freedom*, and *tree*. During learning, the participants were told to write down three words they associated with each noun. For example, three words for *banana* might be *yellow*, *bunches*, and *edible*. When the participants took a surprise memory test, in which they were presented with the three words they had created and were asked to produce the original word, they were able to remember 90 percent of the 600 words (top bar in ● Figure 7.11).

Mantyla ran another group of participants who did not create the three cues on their own. For each noun, they were provided with three cues that had been generated by someone else. When participants in this condition were later presented with the three cue words, they were able to remember 55 percent of the nouns (second bar in Figure 7.11). You might think it would be possible to guess *banana* from the three properties *yellow, bunches*, and *edible*, even if you had never been presented with the word *banana*. But when Mantyla ran another control group in which he presented the cue words generated by someone else to participants who had never seen the original nouns, these participants were able to determine only 17 percent of the nouns. The results of this experiment demonstrate that retrieval cues (the three words) provide extremely effective information for retrieving memories, but that *retrieval cues are significantly more effective when they are created by the person whose memory is being tested*. (Also see Wagenaar, 1986, for a description of a study in which Wagenaar was able to remember almost all of 2,400 diary entries he kept over a 6-year period by using retrieval cues.)

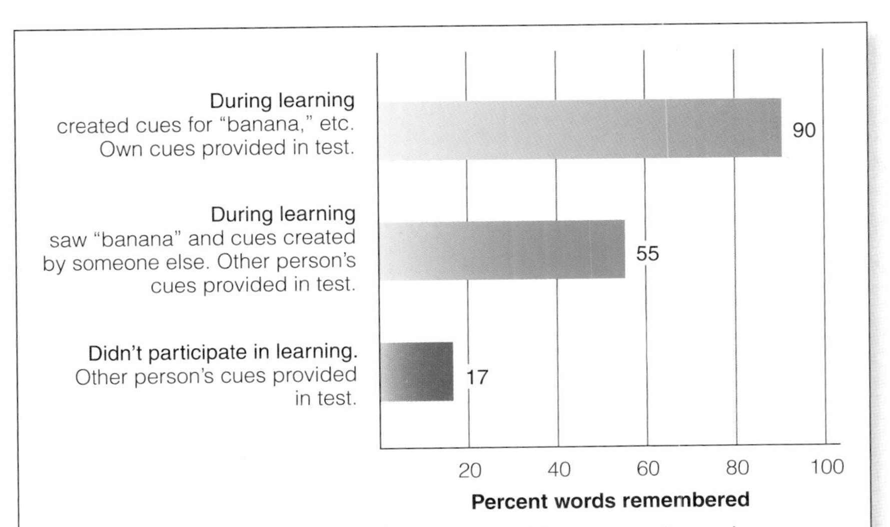

● **FIGURE 7.11** Mantyla's (1986) experiment. Memory was best when retrieval cues were created by the participant (top bar) and not as good when retrieval cues were created by someone else (middle bar). Participants guessed a small percentage of the words if they had not seen the words and saw only cues created by someone else (bottom bar).

MATCHING CONDITIONS OF ENCODING AND RETRIEVAL

The retrieval cues in the two experiments we just described were verbal "hints"—category names like "furniture" in the Tulving and Pearlstone experiment, and three-word descriptions created by the participants in the Mantyla experiment. But we have also seen another kind of "hint" that can help with retrieval: returning to a specific location, such as Angela's grandparents' house or my office.

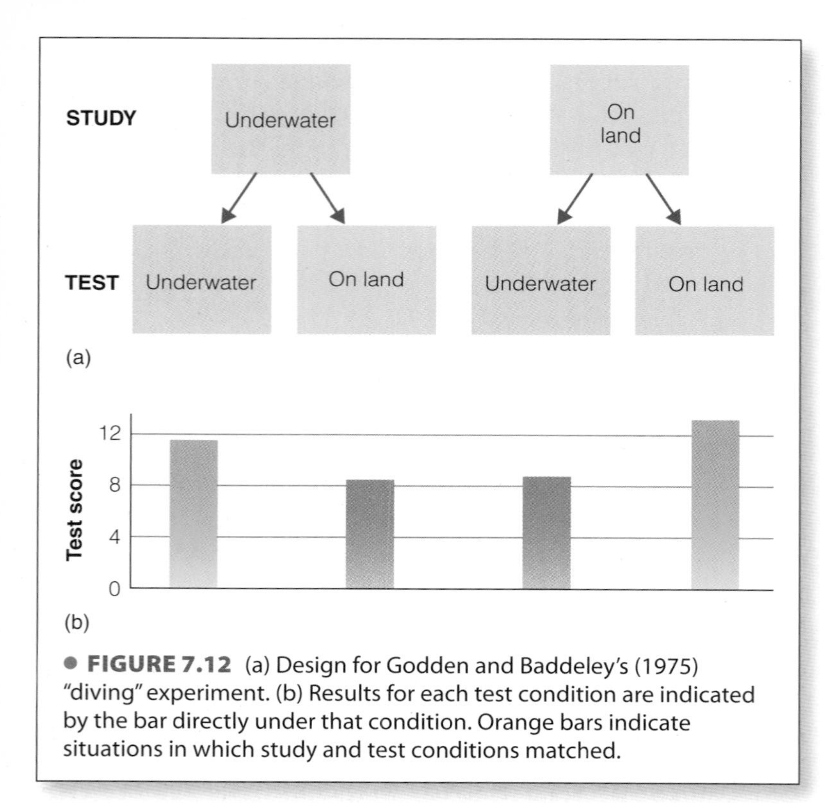

• **FIGURE 7.12** (a) Design for Godden and Baddeley's (1975) "diving" experiment. (b) Results for each test condition are indicated by the bar directly under that condition. Orange bars indicate situations in which study and test conditions matched.

Let's consider what happened in the office example, in which I needed to return to my office to retrieve my thought about taking a DVD to class. The key to remembering the DVD was that I retrieved the thought "Bring the DVD" by returning to the place where I had originally encoded that thought. This example illustrates the following basic principle: *Retrieval can be increased by matching the conditions at retrieval to the conditions that existed at encoding.*

We will now describe three specific situations in which retrieval is increased by matching conditions at retrieval to conditions at encoding. These different ways to achieve matching are (1) encoding specificity—matching the *context* in which encoding and retrieval occur; (2) state-dependent learning—matching the *internal mood* present during encoding and retrieval; and (3) transfer-appropriate processing—matching the *task* involved in encoding and retrieval.

Encoding Specificity The principle of encoding specificity states that we encode information along with its context. For example, Angela encoded many experiences within the context of her grandparents' house. When she reinstated this context by returning to the house many years later, she remembered many of these experiences.

CogLab
Encoding Specificity

A classic experiment that demonstrates encoding specificity is D. R. Godden and Alan Baddeley's (1975) "diving experiment." In this experiment, one group of participants put on diving equipment and studied a list of words underwater, and another group studied the words on land (• Figure 7.12a). These groups were then divided, so half of the participants in the land and water groups were tested for recall on land and half were tested underwater. The results, shown in Figure 7.12b, indicate that the best recall occurred when encoding and retrieval occurred in the same location.

The results of the diving study, and many others, suggest that a good strategy for test taking would be to study in an environment similar to the environment in which you will be tested. Although this doesn't mean you necessarily have to do all of your studying in the classroom where you will be taking the exam, you might want to duplicate, in your study situation, some of the conditions that will occur during the exam.

This conclusion about studying is supported by an experiment by Harry Grant and coworkers (1998), using the design in • Figure 7.13a. Participants read an article on psychoimmunology while wearing headphones. The participants in the "silent" condition heard nothing in the headphones. Participants in the "noisy" condition heard a tape of background noise recorded during lunchtime in a university cafeteria (which they were told to ignore). Half the participants in each group were then given a short-answer test on the article under the silent condition, and the other half were tested under the noisy condition.

The results, shown in Figure 7.13b, indicate that participants did better when the testing condition matched the study condition. Because your next cognitive psychology exam will take place under silent

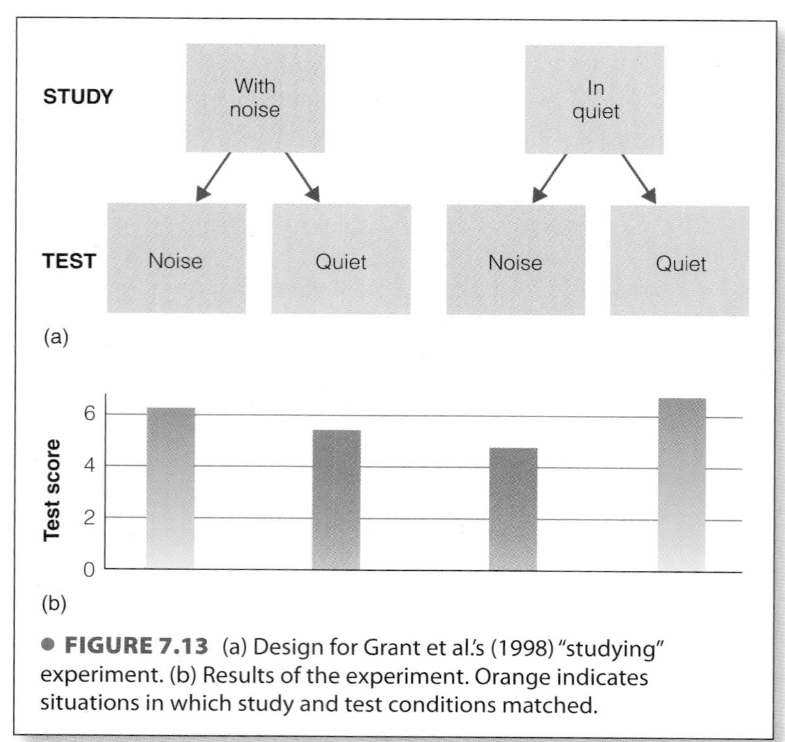

• **FIGURE 7.13** (a) Design for Grant et al.'s (1998) "studying" experiment. (b) Results of the experiment. Orange indicates situations in which study and test conditions matched.

conditions, it might make sense to study under silent conditions. (Interestingly, a number of my students report that having outside stimulation such as music or television present helps them study. This idea clearly violates the principle of encoding specificity. Can you think of some reasons that students might nonetheless say this?)

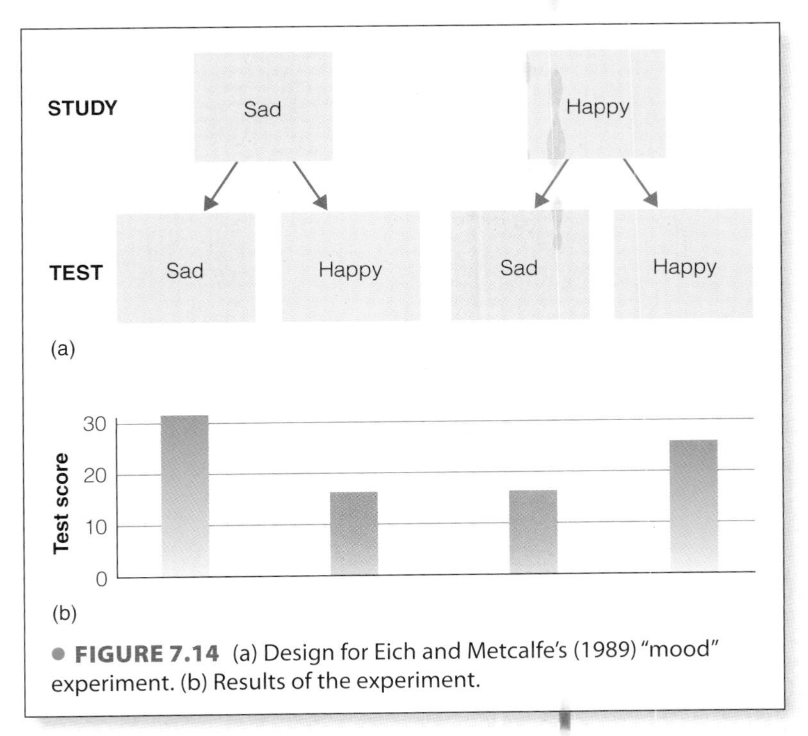

● **FIGURE 7.14** (a) Design for Eich and Metcalfe's (1989) "mood" experiment. (b) Results of the experiment.

State-Dependent Learning Another example of how matching the conditions at encoding and retrieval can influence memory is **state-dependent learning**—learning that is associated with a particular *internal state*, such as mood or state of awareness. According to the principle of state-dependent learning, memory will be better when a person's internal state during retrieval matches his or her internal state during encoding. For example, Eric Eich and Janet Metcalfe (1989) demonstrated that memory is better when a person's mood during retrieval matches his or her mood during encoding. They did this by asking participants to think positive thoughts while listening to "merry" music or depressing thoughts while listening to "melancholic" music (● Figure 7.14a). Participants rated their mood while listening to the music, and the encoding part of the experiment began when their rating reached "very pleasant" or "very unpleasant." Once this occurred, usually within 15–20 minutes, participants studied lists of words while in their positive or negative mood.

After the study session ended, the participants were told to return in 2 days (although those in the sad group stayed in the lab a little longer, snacking on cookies and chatting with the experimenter while happy music played in the background, so they wouldn't leave the laboratory in a bad mood). Two days later, the participants returned, and the same procedure was used to put them in a positive or negative mood. When they reached the mood, they were given a memory test for the words they had studied 2 days earlier. The results, shown in Figure 7.14b, indicate that they did better when their mood at retrieval matched their mood during encoding (also see Eich, 1995).

The two ways of matching encoding and retrieval that we have described so far have involved matching the physical situation (encoding specificity) or an internal feeling (state-dependent learning). Our next example of matching is not quite as obvious, because it involves matching the type of processing that is going on in a person's head. This type of matching is called transfer-appropriate processing.

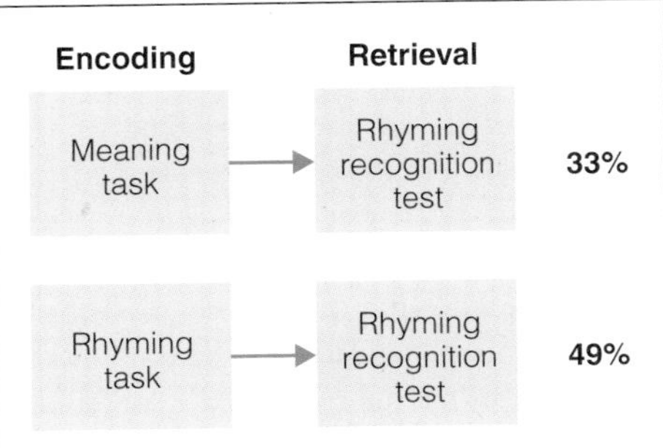

● **FIGURE 7.15** Design and results for the Morris et al. (1977) transfer-appropriate processing experiment. Participants who did a rhyming-based encoding task did better on the rhyming test than participants who did a meaning-based encoding task. This result would not be predicted by levels-of-processing theory, but is predicted by the principle that better retrieval occurs if the encoding and retrieval tasks are matched.

Transfer-Appropriate Processing The phenomenon of **transfer-appropriate processing** shows that memory performance is enhanced if the type of task at encoding matches the type of task at retrieval. A transfer-appropriate processing experiment varies the type of task used for encoding and the task used for retrieval. We can understand what this means by considering two of the groups of participants in an experiment by Donald Morris and coworkers (1977).

Morris's experiment had two parts: encoding and retrieval. The encoding part of the experiment had two conditions: (1) the *meaning condition*, in which the task focused on the meaning of a word, and (2) the *rhyming condition*, in which the task focused on the sound of a word (● Figure 7.15). Participants in both conditions heard a sentence with one word replaced by the word "blank"; 2 seconds later, they heard a target word. The task for the memory group was to answer "yes" or "no" based on the meaning of the sentence created by replacing "blank" with the target word. The task for the rhyming group was to answer "yes" or "no" based on the rhyme created by replacing "blank" with the target word. Here are examples from the encoding part of the experiment for each condition. Note that participants in both conditions heard the same set of target words.

Examples From the Meaning Condition

1. Sentence: The *blank* had a silver engine.

   Target word: *train*

   Correct answer: "yes"

2. Sentence: The *blank* walked down the street.

   Target word: *building*

   Correct answer: "no"

Examples From the Rhyming Condition

1. Sentence: *Blank* rhymes with pain.

   Target word: *train*

   Correct answer: "yes"

2. Sentence: *Blank* rhymes with car.

   Target word: *Building*

   Correct answer: "no"

In the retrieval part of the experiment, participants from both the meaning group and the rhyming were given a rhyming recognition test. (There were other retrieval conditions in this experiment, but we are going to focus just on the results for the rhyming test.) For the rhyming test, participants were presented with 32 words that rhymed with one of the target words presented during encoding, and 32 words that did not rhyme. The rhyming words presented in this test were always different from the target word and the rhyming word (if any) presented during encoding. For example, the target word *train* was the rhyme for *pain* in encoding, as above, but the word presented in the rhyming test was *rain*.

The participants' task was to indicate whether each word presented during retrieval rhymed with one of the target words they had heard during learning. Thus, when presented with the word *rain* the participant would answer "yes" if he or she remembered *train* from before.

The percentage correct for target words that received a correct "yes" response during encoding is indicated on the right in Figure 7.15. These results show that participants who were in the rhyming group during encoding remembered more words than participants who were in the meaning group during encoding. The key to the better performance of the rhyming group was that they experienced the same type of task (rhyming) during both encoding and retrieval. This result is an example of transfer-appropriate processing, because for the rhyming group both encoding and retrieval were based on sound.

This result is related not just to the idea of matching encoding and retrieval, but also to levels-of-processing theory. Remember that the main idea behind LOP theory is that deeper processing leads to better encoding and, therefore, better retrieval. LOP theory would predict that participants who were in the meaning group during encoding would experience "deeper" processing, so they should perform better. Instead, the rhyming group performed better. Thus, Morris's experiment makes two important points: First, deeper processing at encoding does not always result in better retrieval, as LOP proposes. Second, matching the encoding and retrieval tasks results in better retrieval.

TEST YOURSELF 7.2

1. Retrieval cues are a powerful way to improve the chances of remembering something. Why can we say that memory performance is better when you use a word in a sentence, create an image, or relate it to yourself, all techniques involving retrieval cues?
2. What is cued recall? Compare it to free recall.

3. Describe the Tulving and Pearlstone cued recall experiment and Mantyla's experiment in which he presented 600 words to his participants. What were the procedure and results of each experiment, and what does each tell us about retrieval?
4. What is encoding specificity? Describe Godden and Baddeley's "diving" experiment and Grant's studying experiment. What does each one illustrate about encoding specificity? About cued recall?
5. What is state-dependent learning? Describe Eich's experiment.
6. What is transfer-appropriate processing? Describe Morris's transfer-appropriate processing experiment. What implications do the results of this experiment have for matching encoding and retrieval? For levels-of-processing theory?

How to Study More Effectively

How can you apply the principles we have been describing to help remember material for your next exam? Many of the principles that have been discovered in the laboratory work outside the laboratory as well, and you can use some of them to increase the effectiveness of your studying.

The ideas in this section are presented as suggestions for you to consider. I say this because people's learning styles differ, and what might work for one person might be impractical or ineffective for another. Also, different types of material may require different techniques. One method of studying may work best for memorizing lists or definitions, and another method may be better for learning concepts or basic principles. We will discuss the following six ways of increasing the effectiveness of your studying:

1. Elaborate
2. Generate and test
3. Organize
4. Take breaks
5. Match learning and testing conditions
6. Avoid "illusions of learning"

ELABORATE

Because elaboration is one of the themes of this chapter, it should be no surprise that elaboration is an important part of effective studying. The step that helps transfer the material you are reading into long-term memory is elaboration—thinking about what you are reading and giving it meaning by relating it to other things that you know. This becomes easier as you learn more because your prior learning creates a structure on which to hang new information.

Techniques based on association, such as creating images that link two things, as in Figure 7.3, often prove useful for learning individual words or definitions. For example, when I was first learning the difference between proactive interference (old information interferes with learning new information; see page 124) and retroactive interference (new information interferes with remembering old information), I thought of a "pro" football player smashing everything in his path as he runs forward in time. I no longer need this image to remember what proactive interference is, but it was helpful when I was first learning this concept.

This principle of association is involved in the study technique of Student #1, described on page 172 at the beginning of the chapter, in which she makes up a story, thereby linking principles to characters in the storyline and also creating images that she can later call up to help remember the material.

GENERATE AND TEST

The results of research on the generation effect (page 178) and the testing effect (page 180) indicate that creating situations in which it is necessary to take an active role in creating material is a powerful way to create strong encoding and good long-term retrieval. Generation is used by Students 2 and 3, when they explain the material they want to learn to friends and family members (page 172). Another student wrote that she studies by explaining what she learns by talking out loud, even pretending that she is the professor teaching a class. The method of talking out loud may seem strange (do it where no one will hear you!), but its advantage is that you don't have to find a friend or family member to explain things to. In fact, some instructors (including the author of this book) use this "talking out loud" technique to practice material to be presented in lecture.

Testing is actually a form of generation, because it requires active involvement with the material. Although the first step in studying might be to read over the material in your book or lecture notes, research shows that following this initial reading, testing may be a more effective way to strengthen encoding and retrieval than rereading the material. But if you were going to test yourself, where would you get the test questions? One place could be questions that are sometimes provided, such as the Test Yourself questions in this book, or print or electronic study guides. Another way is to make up questions yourself, as Student #4 does by using headings in his outline to stimulate questions. Because making up the questions involves active engagement with the material, it strengthens encoding of the material. Research has shown that students who read a text with the idea of *making up* questions did as well on an exam as students who read a text with the idea of *answering* questions later, and both groups did better than a group who did not create or answer questions (Frase, 1975).

Research has shown, however, that many students believe that reviewing the material is more effective than testing themselves on it; when they do test themselves, it is to determine how they are doing, not as a tool to increase learning (Kornell & Son, 2009). As it turns out, self-testing accomplishes two things. It indicates what you know *and* increases your ability to remember what you know later.

ORGANIZE

Student #5 suggests taking notes and organizing them in a way that makes sense to her. Student #4 also mentions using the organization of the textbook to create an outline. However you organize, creating a framework that helps relate some information to other information makes the material more meaningful and therefore strengthens encoding. Organization can be achieved by making "trees," as in Figure 7.6, or outlines or lists that group similar facts or principles together.

Organization also helps reduce the load on your memory. We can illustrate this by looking at a perceptual example. If you see the black and white pattern in Figure 3.15 as unrelated black and white areas, it is extremely difficult to describe what it is. However, once you've seen this pattern as a Dalmatian, it becomes meaningful and becomes much easier to describe and to remember (Wiseman & Neisser, 1974). Organization relates to the phenomenon of chunking that we discussed in Chapter 5. Grouping small elements into larger, more meaningful ones increases memory. Organizing material is one way to achieve this.

TAKE BREAKS

Saying "Take breaks" is another way of saying, "Study in a number of shorter study sessions rather than trying to learn everything at once," or "Don't cram." There are good reasons to say these things. Research has shown that memory is better when studying is broken into a number of short sessions, with breaks in between, than concentrated in one long session, even if the total study time is the same. This advantage for short study sessions is called the **spacing effect** (Reder & Anderson, 1982; Smith & Rothkopf, 1984).

Another angle on taking breaks is provided by research that shows that memory performance is enhanced if sleep follows learning (review page 16 in Chapter 1). One student who sent me his study technique said he took naps while studying. He would study for a while, take a short nap when he felt tired, and then go right back to studying after the nap. Although one reaction to this technique might be that the student is lazy, the experiments described in Chapter 1 indicate that material studied just before going to sleep is remembered better than material studied long before going to sleep. Thus, one of the most effective breaks you can take from studying involves going to sleep (of course, getting up to finish studying is helpful as well!).

MATCH LEARNING AND TESTING CONDITIONS

From what we know about encoding specificity and state-dependent learning, memory should be better when study (encoding) and testing (retrieval) conditions match as closely as possible. Student #2 takes advantage of this by studying in the classroom. To strictly follow this procedure, you would have to do all of your studying in the classroom in which you will be taking the exam. This might be an impractical strategy, however, not only because of the logistics involved in studying in a room where there are other classes, but also because your classroom might not be a comfortable place to study, and you might not be highly motivated to spend even more time in your classroom. A solution to this problem is to study in a number of different places. Research has shown that people remember material better when they have learned it in a number of different locations, compared to spending the same amount of time studying in one location (Smith et al., 1978). The use of different locations prevents learning from being associated with just one place.

AVOID "ILLUSIONS OF LEARNING"

One of the conclusions of both basic memory research and research on specific study techniques is that some study techniques favored by students may *appear* to be more effective than they actually are. For example, rereading material is the predominant study method for most students (Karpicke et al., 2009). One reason for the popularity of rereading is that it can create the illusion that learning is occurring. This happens because reading and rereading material results in greater *fluency*—that is, repetition causes the reading to become easier and easier. But although this enhanced ease of reading creates the illusion that the material is being learned, increased fluency doesn't necessarily translate into better memory for the material.

Another mechanism that creates the illusion of learning is the *familiarity effect*. Rereading causes material to become familiar, so when you encounter it a second or third time, there is a tendency to interpret this familiarity as indicating that you know the material. Unfortunately, recognizing material that is right in front of you doesn't necessarily mean that you will be able to remember it later.

Finally, beware of highlighting. A survey by S. W. Peterson (1992) found that 82 percent of students highlight, and most of them do so while they are reading the material for the first time. The problem with highlighting is that it seems like elaborative processing (you're taking an active role in your reading by highlighting important points), but it often becomes automatic behavior that involves moving the hand, but little deep thinking about the material.

When Peterson compared comprehension for a group who highlighted and a group who didn't, he found no difference between the performance of the two groups when they were tested on the material. Highlighting may be a good first step for some people, but it is usually important to go back over what you highlighted using techniques such as elaborative rehearsal or generating questions in order to get that information into your memory.

Looking at all of these techniques, we can see that many of them involve using more effective encoding strategies. Elaborating, generating, testing, and organizing all encourage deeper processing of the material you are trying to learn; making up questions about the material and answering these questions incorporates retrieval into studying.

Do you have a study technique that isn't mentioned here—one that works for you and that you can relate to the memory principles discussed in this chapter? If so, I invite you to send a description of your technique to me at bruceg@email.arizona.edu.

Memory and the Brain

When you use your memory to travel back in time to earlier this morning, or last New Year's Eve, or your early days in grade school, you are accessing information about these events that is stored in your brain. This has to be true, but is nonetheless amazing. How can something that happened to you in grade school be represented somewhere in your brain? The answer to that question is extremely complex and is still the topic of a great deal of research. We will consider a few important principles about how memory is represented in the brain, beginning by considering how our experiences affect what happens at synapses.

EXPERIENCES CAUSE CHANGES AT THE SYNAPSE

Remember from Chapter 2 that synapses are the small spaces between the end of one neuron and the cell body or dendrite of another neuron (Figure 2.4), and that when signals reach the end of a neuron, they cause neurotransmitters to be released onto the next neuron. It is here, at the synapse, that the physiology of memory begins, according to an idea first proposed by the Canadian psychologist Donald Hebb.

Hebb (1948) introduced the idea that learning and memory are represented in the brain by physiological changes that take place at the synapse. Let's assume that a particular experience causes nerve impulses to travel down the axon of neuron A in • Figure 7.16a, and when these impulses reach the synapse, neurotransmitter is released onto neuron B. Hebb's idea was that this activity strengthens the synapse by causing structural changes, greater transmitter release, and increased firing (Figures 7.16b and c). Hebb also proposed that changes that occur in the hundreds or thousands of synapses that are activated by a particular experience provide a neural record of the experience. Your New Year's Eve experience, according to this idea, is represented by the pattern of structural changes that occur at many synapses.

Hebb's proposal that synaptic changes provide a record of experiences became the starting point for modern research on the physiology of memory. Researchers who followed Hebb's lead determined that activity at the synapse causes a sequence of chemical reactions, which result in the synthesis of new proteins that cause structural changes at the synapse like those shown in Figure 7.16c (Kida et al., 2002; Chklovskii et al., 2004).

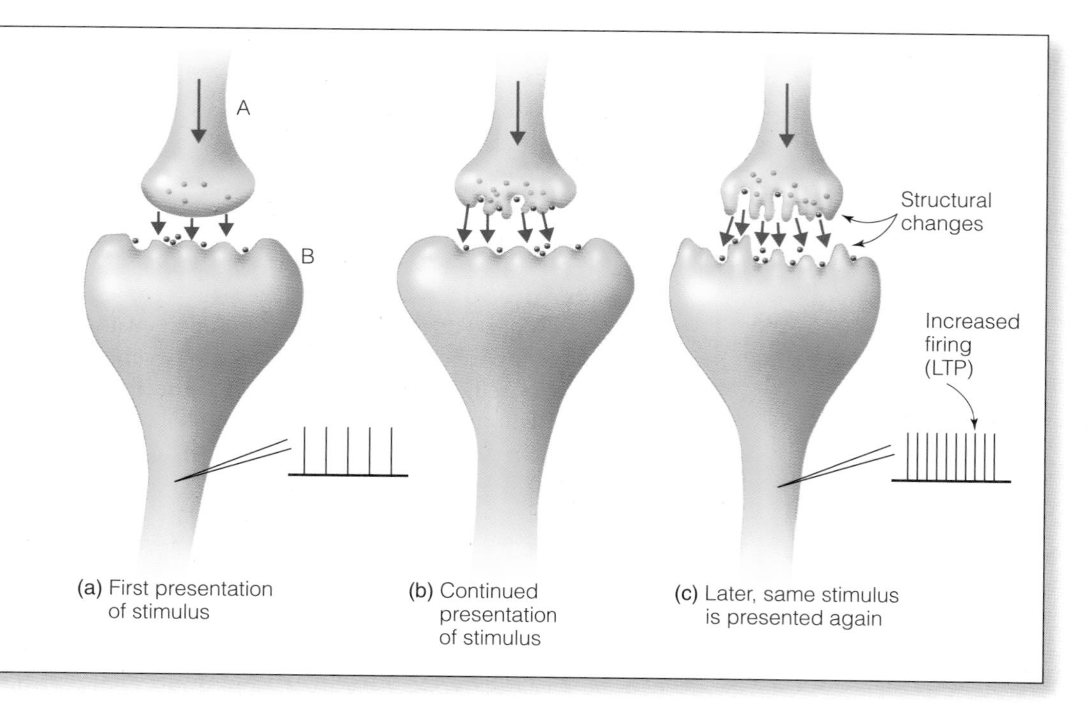

• **FIGURE 7.16** (a) What happens at a synapse as a stimulus is first presented. The record next to the electrode indicates the rate of firing recorded from the axon of neuron B. (b) As the stimulus is repeated, structural changes are beginning to occur. (c) After many repetitions, more complex connections have developed between the two neurons, which causes an increase in the firing rate, even though the stimulus is the same one that was presented in (a).

One outcome of these changes at the synapse is a phenomenon called **long-term potentiation** (LTP)—enhanced firing of neurons after repeated stimulation (Bliss & Lomo, 1973; Bliss et al., 2003; Kandel, 2001). Long-term potentiation is illustrated by the firing records in Figure 7.16. The first time neuron A is stimulated, neuron B fires slowly (Figure 7.16a). However, after repeated stimulation (Figure 7.16b), B fires much more rapidly to the same stimulus (Figure 7.16c). LTP is important because it shows that repeated stimulation causes not only structural changes but also enhanced responding.

Results such as these indicate how experiences can cause changes at the synapse. Memories for a particular experience cause changes in many thousands of synapses, and a particular experience is probably represented by the pattern of firing across this group of neurons. This idea of memories being represented by a pattern of firing is similar to the idea of distributed coding we introduced in Chapter 2 (see page 40).

WHERE DOES MEMORY OCCUR IN THE BRAIN?

So far we have been focusing on synapses. But zooming out from these synapses to look at the brain as a whole provides another way of considering the connection between memory and the brain. One question we can ask is which areas in the brain are involved in memory. The first answer we can give to that question is that memory does not occur in one specific place. Just as perception and attention are distributed across many different areas, so is memory.

We have already seen that the frontal cortex is important for working memory (see Chapter 5, page 138), but that many other areas are involved as well. A similar situation occurs for LTM, with many different areas being involved. We begin with the **medial temporal lobe** (MTL), which contains the structures shown in • Figure 7.17. One of the most clearly established facts about memory and the brain is that the hippocampus, one of the structures in the MTL, is crucial for forming new LTMs. We know this from the case of H.M., who lost his ability to form new memories (anterograde amnesia) and also lost much of his old memory (retrograde amnesia) after his hippocampus was removed (see Chapter 6, page 155).

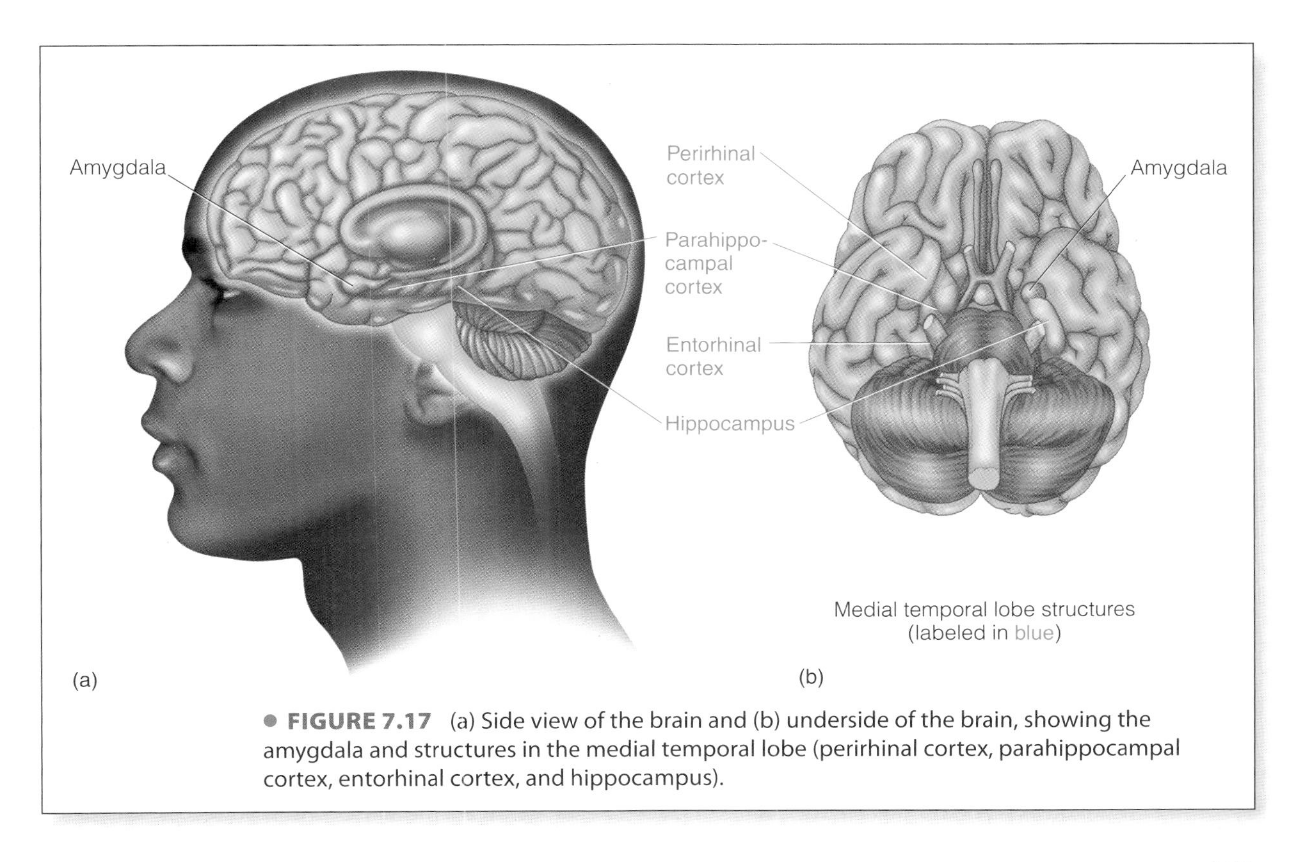

• **FIGURE 7.17** (a) Side view of the brain and (b) underside of the brain, showing the amygdala and structures in the medial temporal lobe (perirhinal cortex, parahippocampal cortex, entorhinal cortex, and hippocampus).

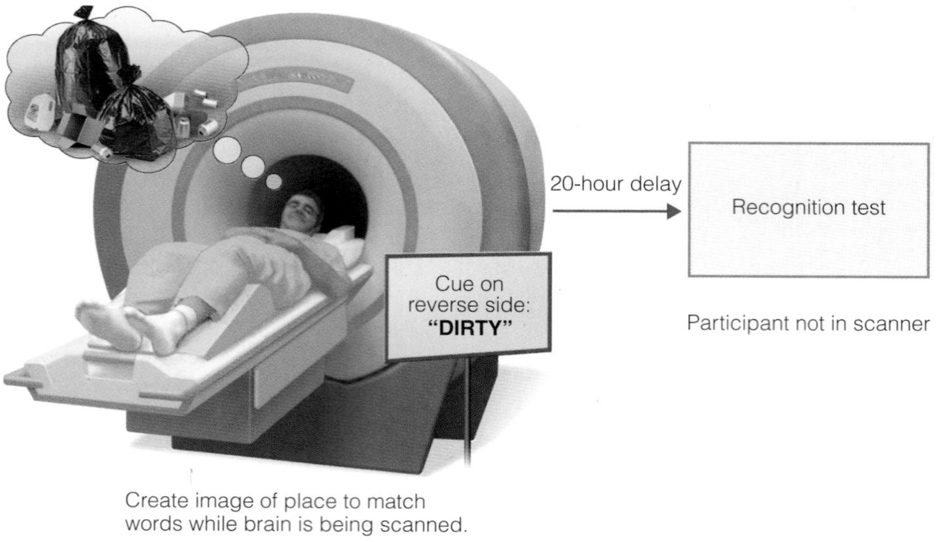

● FIGURE 7.18 Design of Davachi's experiment. During encoding, participants in a scanner created images in their mind in response to words. During retrieval 20 hours later, the participants' task was to recognize the words they had seen.

Other structures in the MTL are also important. Let's consider, for example, the perirhinal cortex, which was studied along with the hippocampus in an experiment by Lila Davachi and coworkers (2003). The study was designed to determine how these structures responded as the names of objects were presented in the encoding part of a memory experiment.

The procedure for this experiment is shown in ● Figure 7.18. Participants, who were in a brain scanner, viewed a series of 200 words. They were instructed to create an image of a specific place that went with each word. For example, if the word was *dirty*, they could create an image of a garbage dump.

Twenty hours later, the participants were presented with a recognition test in which they saw the same 200 words they had seen earlier, along with a new set of 200 words. During this part of the experiment, they were not in the brain scanner. Their task was to indicate which of the words they had seen before, so a correct answer would be "old" when an old word was presented, and "new" when a new one was presented (see Method: Recognition Memory, Chapter 6, page 154). Davachi found that participants remembered 54 percent of the old words (they said "yes" to an old word) and forgot the remaining 46 percent (they said "no" to an old word).

Davachi then determined whether there was any difference between the brain activity that had been recorded in the scanner during encoding for the remembered and forgotten words. The results, shown in ● Figure 7.19a, indicate that activity in the perirhinal cortex was greater for the remembered words than for the forgotten words. Thus, in the perirhinal cortex, words that generated more activity *during encoding* were more likely to be familiar to the participants during the recognition test ("I saw that word before"). This result confirms physiologically what we have seen behaviorally: What happens during encoding affects the chances that memory will occur during retrieval.

Notice that this difference between remembered and forgotten words did not occur in the hippocampus (Figure 7.19b). This doesn't mean that the hippocampus isn't involved in memory. As we have seen from the case of H.M., the hippocampus is crucial for memory. Other experiments have shown that the hippocampus is important for aspects of memory other than recognition, such as remembering the context within which an object appears (Davachi et al., 2003). In addition, as we will see in the next section, the hippocampus plays a crucial role in forming new memories.

Other structures in the MTL are also involved in memory. The parahippocampal area is important for remembering spatial information (in Chapter 2, page 32, we saw

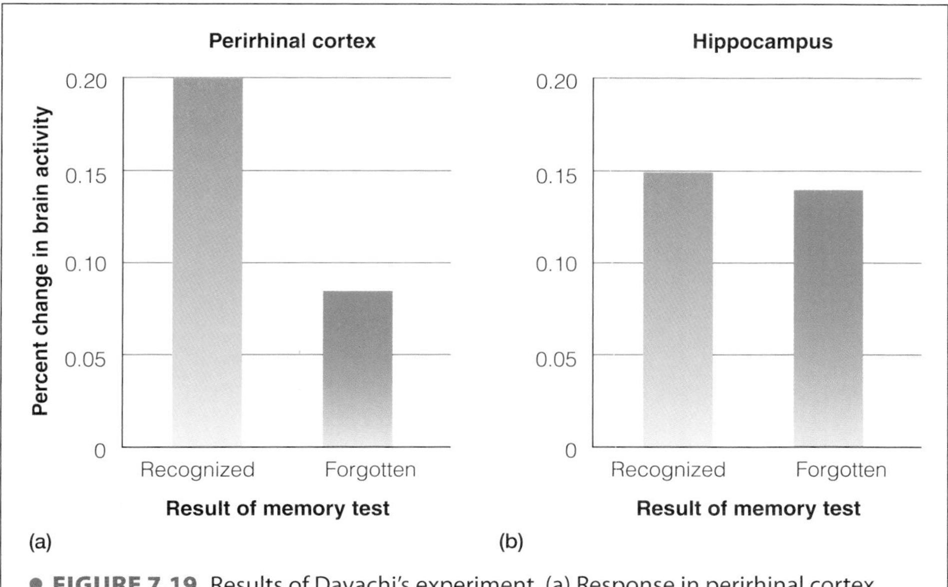

● **FIGURE 7.19** Results of Davachi's experiment. (a) Response in perirhinal cortex measured during encoding for items that were recognized and forgotten in the retrieval test. (b) Response of the hippocampus for recognized and forgotten items.

that the parahippocampal area responds to places, such as pictures of buildings or rooms), and the enthorhinal area, like the perirhinal area, is involved with recognition memory. But LTM extends beyond the MTL, to other areas in the parietal and frontal lobes, as well as to the amygdala (see Figure 7.17) which is important for emotional memories. We will return to the amygdala in Chapter 8 when we consider memory for emotional events such as the terrorist attacks of 9/11.

What's important about the widely distributed nature of memory in the brain is that although specific areas may have specific functions, different areas interact and communicate with each other. One aspect of memory that involves this interaction between areas is *consolidation*, the process that transforms newly formed memories from a fragile state to a more permanent state.

FORMING MEMORIES IN THE BRAIN: THE PROCESS OF CONSOLIDATION

Every experience creates the potential for a new memory. But new memories are fragile and can therefore be easily disrupted.

New Memories Are Fragile but Become Stabilized by Consolidation A well-known observation is that very recent memories can be eliminated by trauma to the head. Examples are easy to find in football. A recent instance occurred on September 26, 2009, when Tim Tebow, the Heisman Trophy quarterback from the University of Florida, suffered a concussion when his head hit another player's knee as he was being sacked. Upon regaining consciousness, the first words he said to his coach were "Did I hold onto the ball?" Typically, players suffering a concussion not only are unaware of what happened during and right after the concussion, but also don't remember events that occurred just prior to the concussion (see Chapter 1, page 15).

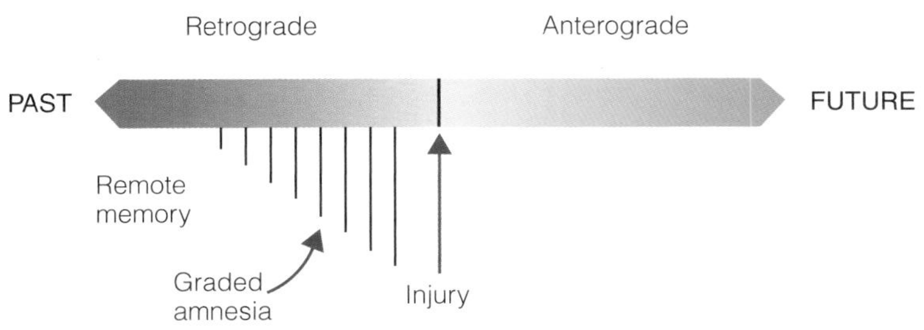

Amnesia caused by trauma or brain damage can affect both the ability to form new memories (*anterograde amnesia*, see page 149) and the ability to remember events that occurred prior to the injury (*retrograde amnesia*). Retrograde amnesia due to concussions is typically less severe for **remote memories**—memory for events that occurred long ago (Frankland & Bontempi, 2005). This effect, which occurs because memory for recent events is more fragile than memory for remote events, is called **graded amnesia** (● Figure 7.20). As time passes after an event, a process called *consolidation* stabilizes memory for the event so it is less likely to be affected by trauma.

● **FIGURE 7.20** Anterograde amnesia is amnesia for events that occur after an injury (the inability to form new memories). Retrograde amnesia is amnesia for events that happened before the injury (the inability to remember information from the past). The vertical lines, which symbolize the amount of retrograde amnesia, indicate that amnesia is more severe for events or learning that was closer in time to the injury. This is the graded nature of retrograde amnesia.

Consolidation is the process that transforms new memories from a fragile state, in which they can be disrupted, to a more permanent state, in which they are resistant to disruption (Frankland & Bontempi,

2005). This process involves a reorganization in the nervous system, which occurs at two levels. **Synaptic consolidation** occurs at synapses and happens rapidly, over a period of minutes. The structural changes shown in Figure 7.16 are an example of synaptic consolidation. **Systems consolidation** involves the gradual reorganization of circuits within brain regions and takes place on a longer time scale, lasting weeks, months, or even years.

Early research, inspired by Hebb's pioneering work on the role of the synapse in memory, focused on synaptic consolidation. More recent research has focused on systems consolidation, investigating the role of different brain areas in consolidation. The case of H.M., who lost his ability to form new memories after his hippocampus was removed, indicates the importance of the hippocampus in consolidation. The hippocampus plays a central role in the *standard model of consolidation.*

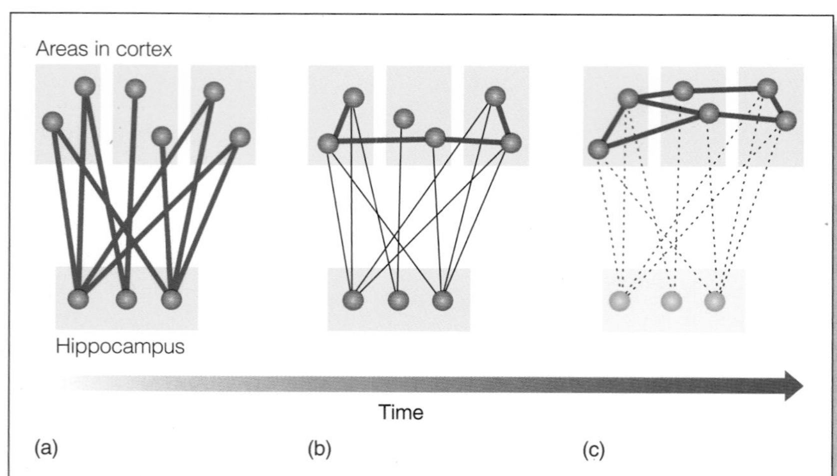

● **FIGURE 7.21** Sequence of events that occur in consolidation. Connections between the cortex and the hippocampus are initially strong but weaken as connections within the cortex are established. (Adapted from Frankland & Bontempi, 2005.)

The Standard Model of Consolidation The graded property of retrograde amnesia, in which amnesia is worse for experiences that occurred just before the brain injury, plus other evidence, led to the proposal of the **standard model of consolidation**. The standard model proposes that memory retrieval depends on the hippocampus during consolidation, but that once consolidation is complete, retrieval no longer depends on the hippocampus.

● Figure 7.21 shows the steps in the process of consolidation, as described by the standard model (Frankland & Bontempi, 2005; Nadel & Moscovitch, 1997). Incoming information activates a number of areas in the cortex (Figure 7.21a). Activation is distributed across the cortex because memories typically involve many sensory and cognitive areas. For example, your memory for last New Year's Eve could include sights, sounds, and possibly smells, as well as emotions you were feeling and thoughts you were thinking at the stroke of midnight. To deal with the fact that the activity resulting from this experience is distributed across many cortical areas, the cortex communicates with the hippocampus, as indicated by the blue lines in Figure 7.21a. The hippocampus coordinates the activity of the different cortical areas, which, at this point, are not yet connected in the cortex.

The major mechanism of consolidation is **reactivation**, a process during which the hippocampus replays the neural activity associated with a memory. During reactivation, activity occurs in the network connecting the hippocampus and the cortex. This activity results in the formation of connections between the cortical areas (Figure 7.21b). This reactivation process occurs during sleep (see Chapter 1, page 16, and this chapter, page 188) or during periods of relaxed wakefulness, and can also be enhanced by conscious rehearsing of a memory (Frankland & Bontempi, 2005; Huber et al., 2004; Nadel & Moscovitch, 1997; Peigneux et al., 2004).

Eventually, the cortical connections become strong enough so that the different sites in the cortex become directly linked, and the hippocampus is no longer necessary (Figure 7.21c). Thus, according to the standard model of consolidation, the hippocampus is strongly active when memories are first formed (● Figure 7.22a), but become less active as memories are consolidated, until eventually only cortical activity is necessary to retrieve remote memories (Figure 7.22b).

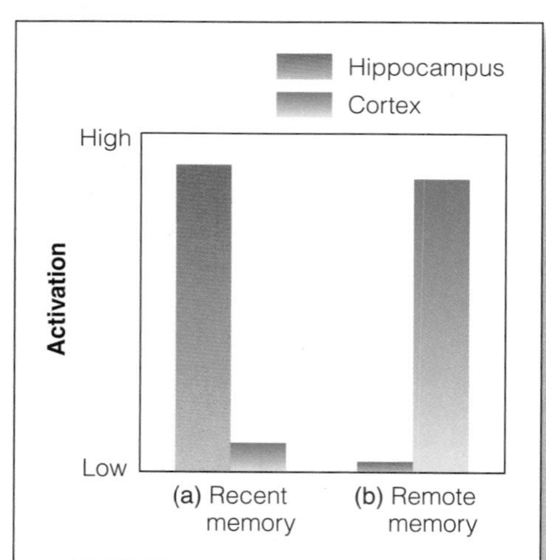

● **FIGURE 7.22** (a) According to the standard model of consolidation, retrieval of recent memories depends on the hippocampus; cortical connections have not yet formed. Thus, for retrieval of recent memories, hippocampal activation is high and cortical activation is low. (b) Once consolidation has occurred, cortical connections have formed, and the hippocampus is no longer needed. Thus, for retrieval of remote memories, cortical activation is high, and there is no hippocampal activation.

The Multiple Trace Hypothesis Most researchers accept that both the hippocampus and the cortex are involved in consolidation. There is, however, some disagreement regarding whether the hippocampus is important only at the beginning of consolidation, as depicted in Figure 7.22, or the hippocampus continues to be important, even for remote memories. According to the **multiple trace hypothesis**, the hippocampus is involved in retrieval of remote memories, especially episodic memories (Nadel & Moskovitch, 1997). Evidence for this idea comes from experiments like one by Asaf Gilboa and coworkers (2004), who elicited recent and remote episodic memories by showing participants photographs of themselves engaging in various activities that were taken at times ranging from very recently to when they were 5 years old. The results of this experiment showed that the hippocampus was activated during retrieval of both recent and remote memories.

The fact that there is evidence supporting both the standard model of consolidation and the multiple trace hypothesis has led to a great deal of discussion among memory researchers regarding whether or not the hippocampus is involved in remote memories (Jadhav & Frank, 2009; Moscovitch et al., 2005). One thing that can be stated, however, is that memories are not simply "stamped in." They involve changes at the synapse and a consolidation process involving both the hippocampus and the cortex. Although there is no question that consolidation makes memories more stable, recent research, described next, opens the possibility that even memories that are consolidated can be modified or eliminated.

Something to Consider

Are Memories Ever "Permanent"?

"These are exciting times in memory research. What once seemed simple and settled now seems complex and open to new ideas" (Nadel & Land, 2000). The "simple and settled" part of memory research that Lynn Nadel and Cantey Land are referring to are the following two ideas, which we have just discussed:

1. Memory is initially fragile, so a disrupting event that occurs shortly after a memory is formed can disrupt formation of the memory.
2. Once consolidation has occurred, then the same disrupting event cannot affect the memory.

New experiments have caused many memory researchers to question the idea that once memory is consolidated, it cannot be disrupted (Lewis & Maher, 1965; Sara & Hars, 2006). These experiments have led to the proposal of a process called *reconsolidation* that can occur after a memory is initially consolidated. This process, which occurs after a memory has been retrieved, was demonstrated in the rat by Karim Nader and coworkers (2000a). Nader used classical conditioning (see Chapter 6, page 165) on a rat to create a fear response of "freezing"(not moving) to presentation of a tone. This was achieved by pairing the tone with a shock. Although the tone initially caused no response, pairing it with the shock caused the tone to take on properties of the shock, so the rat froze in place when the tone was presented alone.

The design of the experiment is shown in ● Figure 7.23. In each condition, the rat receives a tone-shock pairing and is injected with *anisomycin*, an antibiotic that inhibits protein synthesis and so prevents changes at the synapse that are responsible for the formation of new memories. The key to this experiment is *when* the anisomycin is injected. The first two conditions indicate the effect of normal memory consolidation that we have described.

In Condition 1, the rat receives the pairing of the tone and shock on Day 1. It receives anisomycin on Day 2, and then freezes to the tone when tested on Day 3 (Figure 7.23a). This is exactly what we would expect, because conditioning occurs on Day 1 and the drug isn't injected until Day 2, after consolidation has occurred, so the rat still fears the tone on Day 3.

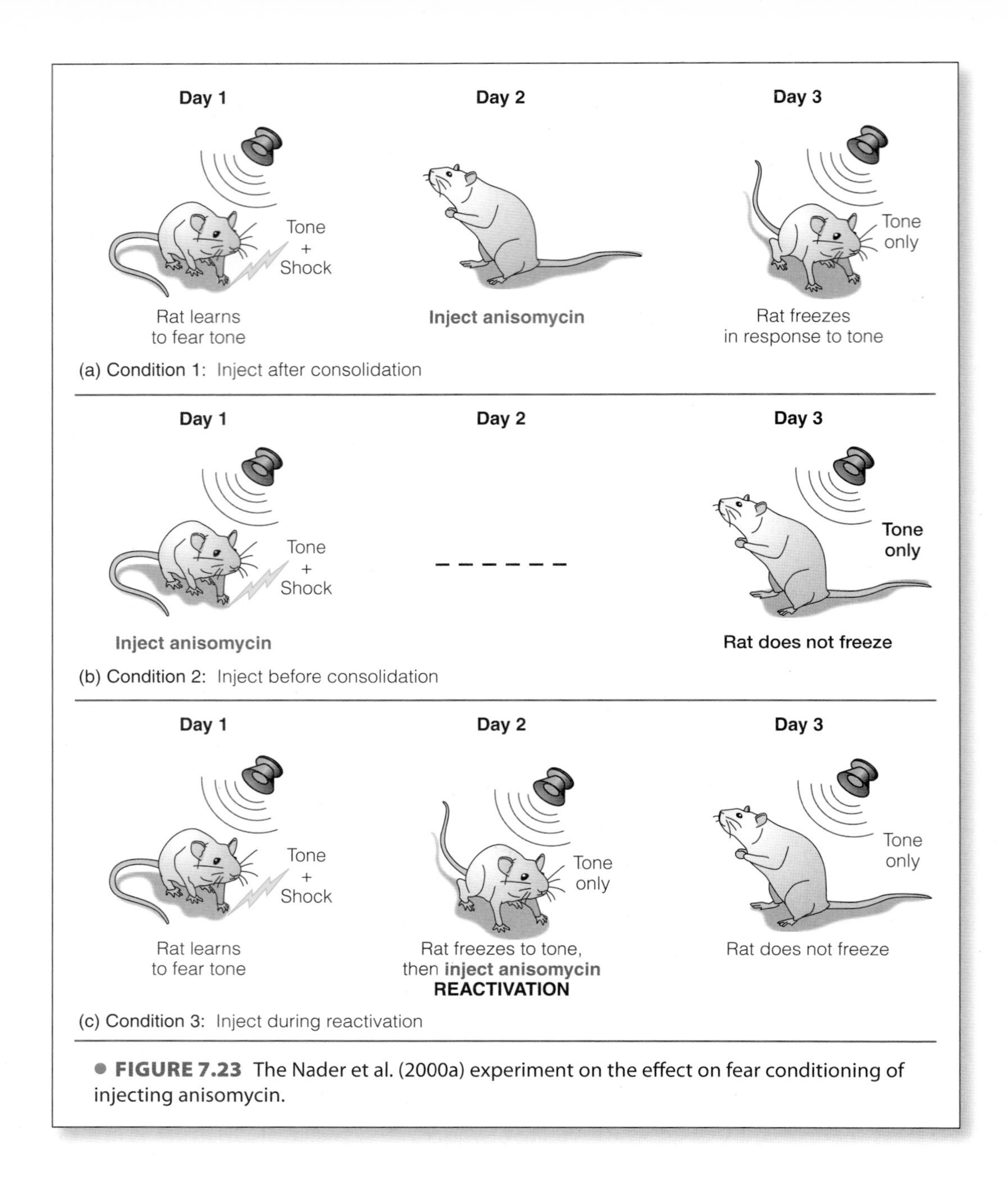

● **FIGURE 7.23** The Nader et al. (2000a) experiment on the effect on fear conditioning of injecting anisomycin.

In Condition 2, the rat receives the pairing of the tone and shock on Day 1, but the drug is injected right away, before consolidation has occurred (Figure 7.23b). The fact that the drug has blocked consolidation is confirmed when the rat does not freeze to the tone on Day 3. The rat behaves as if it never received the tone-shock pairing, because the possibility of forming a stable memory was wiped out by the drug.

Condition 3 is the crucial condition (Figure 7.23c). The procedure on Day 1 is the same as in Condition 1—the rat receives a pairing of tone and shock. On Day 2, the tone is presented again, and the rat freezes because of the conditioning on Day 1. This response to the tone is *reactivation*—eliciting a memory after the initial event. Immediately after the reactivation, the drug is injected. When the rat is tested on Day 3 by presenting the tone again, the rat doesn't freeze. By reactivating the memory on Day 2, Nader set up a situation in which the memory became vulnerable to disruption, and injecting the drug eliminated the memory for the tone-shock pairing.

The result in Condition 3 shows that when a memory is reactivated, it becomes fragile, just as it was immediately after it was first formed. Nader and other researchers have proposed that after a memory is reactivated, it must undergo **reconsolidation**, which is similar to the consolidation that occurred after the initial learning but apparently occurs more rapidly (Dudai, 2006; Dudai & Eisenberg, 2004; Nadel & Land, 2000; Nader, 2003; Sara, 2000). Just as the original memory is fragile until it is consolidated for the first time, a reactivated memory becomes fragile until it is reconsolidated.

Looked at in this way, memory becomes susceptible to being changed or disrupted every time it is retrieved. You might think that this is not a good thing. After all, putting your memory at risk for disruption every time you use it doesn't sound particularly useful. However, everyday memory retrieval isn't usually accompanied by injection with a protein synthesis inhibitor, as in Nader's experiment, or getting hit on the head, as happens with football players, which would eliminate the memory. It is therefore unlikely that, in everyday experience, reactivation and subsequent reconsolidation will eliminate or selectively change memories after they have been retrieved.

Reconsolidation might, however, provide an opportunity for reinforcing or updating memories. For example, consider an animal that returns to the location of a food source and finds that the food has been moved to a new location nearby. Returning to the original location reactivates the original memory, new information about the change in location updates the memory, and the updated memory is then reconsolidated. Looked at in this way, reactivation and reconsolidation makes memory a more dynamic and adaptable process. Rather than being fixed, memories can evolve to deal with new situations.

Does this process of reconsolidation occur in humans? There is some evidence that it does (Nader, 2003). For example, in an experiment by Almut Hupbach and coworkers (2007), participants learned a list of words (List 1) on Day 1. On Day 2, one group (the no-reminder group) learned a new list of words (List 2). Another group (the reminder group) also learned the new list on Day 2, but just before learning the list, they were asked to remember their Day 1 training session (without actually recalling the List 1 words), thus reminding them of their learning.

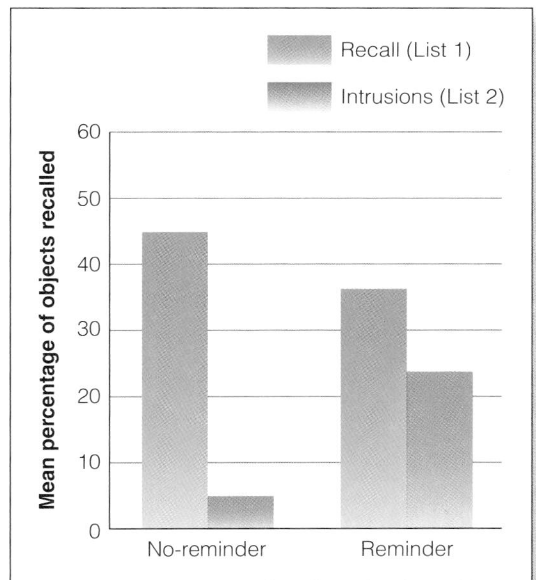

● **FIGURE 7.24** Results of Hupbach et al.'s (2007) experiment. These results support the idea that reactivation and reconsolidation can affect human memory. (Source: Based on A. Hupbach, R. Gomez, O. Hardt, & L. Nadel, "Reconsolidation of Episodic Memories: A Subtle Reminder Triggers Integration of New Information," *Learning and Memory, 14,* 47–53, 2007.)

● Figure 7.24 shows what happened on Day 3, when these two groups were asked to remember List 1. The left pair of bars indicates that the no-reminder group recalled 45 percent of the words from List 1 and mistakenly recalled only 5 percent of the words from List 2. (Remember that their task was to only remember the words from List 1).

The right pair of bars shows that something quite different happened for the reminder group. They recalled 36 percent of the words from List 1, but in addition mistakenly recalled 24 percent of the words from List 2. According to Hupbach and coworkers, what happened was that the reminder on Day 2 reactivated the memory for List 1, making it vulnerable to being changed. Because participants immediately learned List 2, some of the words from List 2 became integrated into the participants' memory for List 1. Another way to express this idea is to say that the reminder reactivated memory for List 1 and "opened the door" for changes to occur in the participants' memory for that list.

One practical outcome of research on reconsolidation is a possible treatment for posttraumatic stress disorder (PTSD), a condition that occurs when, following a traumatic experience, a person experiences "flashbacks" of the experience, often accompanied by extreme anxiety and physical symptoms. The clinical psychologist Alain Brunet (2008) has tested the idea that reactivation of a memory followed by reconsolidation can provide a way to help alleviate these symptoms. The basis of his idea is to reactivate the person's memory for the traumatic event and then administer the drug *probanolol.* This drug blocks production of a stress hormone in the amygdala, a part of the brain important for determining the emotional components of memory. This procedure is equivalent to the administration of *anisomycin* on Day 2 in Condition 3 of Nader's experiment (Figure 7.23c).

Brunet ran two groups. One group of PTSD patients listened to a 30-second recording describing the circumstances of their traumatic experience and received *probanolol.* Another group listened to the recording describing their experience but received a placebo, which had no active ingredients.

One week later, both groups were told to imagine their traumatic experience, while again listening to the 30-second recording. To determine their reaction to imagining their experience, Brunet measured their blood pressure and skin conductance. He found that the *probanolol* group experienced much smaller increases in heart rate and skin conductance than the placebo group. Apparently, presenting *probanolol* when the memory was reactivated a week earlier blocked the stress response in the amygdala, and this reduced the emotional reaction associated with remembering the trauma. Brunet has used this procedure to treat patients with PTSD, and many of the patients report significant reductions in their symptoms, even months after the treatment (Singer, 2009).

Research on reconsolidation and its potential applications is just in its infancy, but from what researchers have learned so far, it appears that our memory is not static or fixed. Rather, it is a "work in progress" that is constantly being constructed and remodeled in response to new learning and changing conditions. We will be describing this aspect of memory in detail in the next chapter, when we consider the creative, constructive properties of memory.

TEST YOURSELF 7.3

1. Describe the following six ways of improving the effectiveness of studying: (1) elaborate; (2) generate and test; (3) organize; (4) take breaks; (5) match learning and testing conditions; (6) avoid "illusions of learning." Be sure you understand how each technique relates to experimental findings about encoding and retrieval.
2. What is the idea behind the statement "Memories are stored at synapses"? What evidence supports this idea?
3. Why is it not correct to say that there is a single "memory center" in the brain?
4. Describe evidence for the idea that memory is distributed. Be sure you understand Davachi's experiment and what it means.
5. Why can we say that new memories are "fragile"? Relate this idea to types of amnesia.
6. What is the standard model of consolidation? How does it describe the process of systems consolidation?
7. What is the multiple trace theory of consolidation? How is it different from the standard model?
8. What is reconsolidation? What are the implications of the results of experiments that demonstrate reconsolidation?

CHAPTER SUMMARY

1. The process of acquiring information and transferring it into long-term memory (LTM) is called encoding. The process of transferring information from LTM into working memory is called retrieval.
2. Some mechanisms of encoding are more effective than others in transferring information into LTM. Maintenance rehearsal helps maintain information in STM but is not an effective way of transferring information into LTM. Elaborative rehearsal is a good way to establish LTMs.
3. Levels-of-processing theory states that memory depends on how information is encoded or programmed into the mind. According to this theory, shallow processing is not as effective as deep processing. An experiment by Craik

and Tulving showed that memory was better following deep processing than following shallow processing.

4. The idea of levels of processing, while influential, suffered from the problem of circularity, because it is difficult to define depth of processing independently of memory.
5. Evidence that encoding influences retrieval includes research looking at the effect of (a) placing a word in a complex sentence; (b) forming visual images; (c) linking words to yourself; (d) generating information (the generation effect); (e) organizing information; (f) testing (the testing effect).
6. Retrieving long-term memories is aided by retrieval cues. This has been determined by cued recall experiments and experiments in which participants created retrieval cues that later helped them retrieve memories.
7. Retrieval can be increased by matching conditions at retrieval to conditions that existed at encoding. This is illustrated by encoding specificity, state-dependent learning, and transfer-appropriate processing.
8. The principle of encoding specificity states that we learn information along with its context. Godden and Baddeley's "diving experiment" and Grant's studying experiment illustrate the effectiveness of encoding and retrieving information under the same conditions.
9. According to the principle of state-dependent learning, a person's memory will be better when his or her internal state during retrieval matches the state during encoding. Eich's mood experiment supports this idea.
10. Transfer-appropriate processing refers to the finding that memory performance is enhanced when the type of coding that occurs during acquisition matches the type of retrieval that occurs during a memory test. The results of an experiment by Morris support this idea.
11. Six memory principles that can be applied to studying are (1) elaborate, (2) generate and test, (3) organize, (4) take breaks, (5) match learning and testing conditions, and (6) avoid "illusions of learning."
12. Research on the physiological basis of memory indicates that the formation of memories is associated with structural changes at the synapse. These structural changes are then translated into enhanced nerve firing, as indicated by long-term potentiation.
13. The medial temporal lobe (MTL) is an important brain area for LTM. The MTL contains the hippocampus and other structures.
14. The hippocampus is crucial for forming new LTMs. Davachi's fMRI experiment shows that the perirhinal cortex is involved in recognizing a stimulus as having been experienced earlier, whereas the hippocampus has other functions. Other areas involved in memory include parts of the frontal and parietal lobes, and the amygdala.
15. Concussions can cause retrograde amnesia. This retrograde amnesia is graded, so that memory loss is greatest for events that happened closest in time to the trauma. This indicates that newly formed memories are fragile.
16. Consolidation transforms new memories into a state in which they are more resistant to disruption. Synaptic consolidation occurs at synapses and is rapid. Systems consolidation involves the reorganization of cortical circuits and is slower.
17. The standard model of consolidation proposes that memory retrieval depends on the hippocampus during consolidation but that after consolidation is complete, retrieval involves the cortex and the hippocampus is no longer involved.
18. The multiple trace hypothesis states that the hippocampus is involved both when memories are being established and during the retrieval of remote episodic memories.
19. There is evidence supporting the standard model, and also evidence supporting the idea that retrieval of episodic memories can involve the hippocampus.
20. Recent research indicates that memories can become susceptible to disruption when they are reactivated by retrieval. After reactivation, these memories must be reconsolidated. This process may be a mechanism for refining and updating memories. Recent experiments have provided evidence for reconsolidation in humans and for the usefulness of reconsolidation therapy in treating conditions such as posttraumatic stress disorder.

Think ABOUT IT

1. Describe an experience in which retrieval cues led you to remember something. This experience could include things like returning to a place where your memory was initially formed, being somewhere that reminds you of an experience you had in the past, having someone else provide a "hint" to help you remember something, or reading about something that triggers a memory.
2. How do you study? Which study techniques that you use should be effective, according to the results of memory research? How could you improve your study techniques by taking into account the results of memory research? (Also see Preface to Students, pages xxix–xxx.)

If You WANT TO KNOW MORE

1. **Cognitive changes in normal aging.** Cognitive changes normally occur as people age. Some of these changes have been related to changes in the brain.

Cabeza, R., Anderson, N. D., Locantore, J. K., & McIntosh, A. R. (2002). Aging gracefully: Compensatory brain activity in high-performing older adults. *Neuroimage, 17*, 1394–1402.

Hedden, T., & Gabrieli, J. D. E. (2004). Insights into the ageing mind: A view from cognitive neuroscience. *Nature Reviews Neuroscience, 5*, 87–97.

2. **Tip-of-the-tongue phenomenon.** The tip-of-the-tongue (TOT) experience occurs when a person can't retrieve a memory but has a strong feeling that he or she will be able to retrieve it sooner or later.

Brown, R., & McNeil, D. (1966). The "tip of the tongue" phenomenon. *Journal of Verbal Learning and Verbal Behavior, 5*, 325–337.

Schwartz, B. I., Travis, D. M., Castro, A. M., & Smith, S. S. (2000). The phenomenology of real and illusory tip-of-the-tongue states. *Memory & Cognition, 28*, 18–27.

3. **Superior memory.** What distinguishes people who have superior memory capabilities from people with "normal" memory capabilities? Apparently, in some cases, the answer has to do with the strategies that these people use.

Maguire, E. A., Valentine, E. R., Wilding, J. M., & Kapur, N. (2003). Routes to remembering: The brains behind superior memory. *Nature Neuroscience, 6*, 90–95.

Wilding, J., & Valentine, E. R. (1997). *Superior memory*. Hove, UK: Psychology Press.

4. **Adaptive memory.** It has been proposed that because the main function of memory is to ensure survival, tasks that involve processing information for its relevance to survival result in the best memory. An example of using such a task to remember a list of words is rating how relevant each word is for survival if stranded in the grasslands of a foreign country.

Nairne, J. S., & Pandeirada, J. N. S. (2008). Adaptive memory: Remembering with a stone-age brain. *Current Directions in Psychological Science, 17*, 239–243.

Weinstein, Y., Bugg, J. M., & Roediger, H. L. (2008). Can the survival recall advantage be explained by basic memory processes? *Memory & Cognition, 36*, 913–919.

5. **How memory for the past affects the ability to imagine the future.** Patients with amnesia due to brain damage have trouble both remembering the past and imagining events that might occur in the future. This result, plus the results of brain imaging experiments, has led to the *constructive episodic simulation hypothesis*, which states that imagining the future involves some of the same mechanisms involved in remembering the past.

Addis, D. R., Wong, A. T., & Schacter, D. L. (2007). Remembering the past and imagining the future: Common and distinct neural substrates during event construction and elaboration. *Neuropsychologia, 45*, 1363–1377.

Schacter, D. L., Addis, D. R., & Buckner, R. L. (2007). Remembering the past to imagine the future: The prospective brain. *Nature Reviews Neuroscience, 8*, 657–661.

Key TERMS

Media RESOURCES

The *Cognitive Psychology* Book Companion Website

www.cengage.com/international

Prepare for quizzes and exams with online resources—including a glossary, flashcards, tutorial quizzes, crossword puzzles, and more.

CogLab

To experience these experiments for yourself, go to coglab.wadsworth.com. Be sure to read each experiment's setup instructions before you go to the experiment itself. Otherwise, you won't know which keys to press.

Primary Labs

Levels of processing How memory is influenced by depth of processing (p. 174).

Encoding specificity How memory is affected by conditions at both encoding and retrieval, and the relation between them (p. 184).

Related Lab

Von Restorff effect How the distinctiveness of a stimulus can influence memory.

8 Everyday Memory

Our memories for the events that make up our lives are called autobiographical memories. This multigenerational picture of three women looking at a photo album along with the pictures on the wall behind them represent the many things that people experience over their lifetimes. Research shows that people tend to remember certain life events and forget others.

Some Questions We Will Consider

- What kinds of events from their lives are people most likely to remember? (206)
- Is there something special about memory for extraordinary events like the 9/11 terrorist attacks? (208)
- What properties of the memory system make it both highly functional and also prone to error? (213)
- Why is eyewitness testimony often cited as the cause of wrongful convictions? (227)

What would it be like to be able to think of a specific date from years before and automatically have the events of that day unfold in your mind? Not special days like holidays or your birthday, but a day on which nothing "special" happened. How about March 4, 2003? (If that's your birthday, pick another date.)

You get the point. This is a difficult, if not impossible, task. However, a woman we will call A.J. can remember what happened on each day of her life, from the age of 11 on. She came to the attention of psychologists by sending an e-mail to James McGaugh, a memory researcher at UCLA. Her letter, and the results of the many tests that she subsequently underwent at UCLA, are reported in a paper by Elizabeth Parker, Larry Cahill, and McGaugh (2006). A.J.'s e-mail read, in part:

> I am 34 years old and since I was eleven I have had this unbelievable ability to recall my past.... I can take a date between 1974 and today, and tell you what day it falls on, what I was doing that day and if anything of great importance... occurred on that day I can describe that to you as well.... Whenever I see a date flash on the television (or anywhere else for that matter) I automatically go back to that day and remember where I was, what I was doing, what day it fell on and on and on and on and on. It is non-stop, uncontrollable and totally exhausting.... I run my entire life through my head every day and it drives me crazy!!!

A.J. describes her memories as happening automatically and not being under her conscious control. When given a date she would, within seconds, relate personal experiences and also special events that occurred on that day, and these recollections proved to be accurate when checked against a diary of daily events that A.J. had been keeping for 24 years (Parker et al., 2006).

A.J.'s memories cause her distress because she has trouble turning off the "movie" of her life, and it troubles her that she is unable to forget negative events from the past. She does, however, find happy memories soothing, commenting that "happy memories hold my head together."

What is special about A.J. is that her exceptional memory is for personal experiences—things that make up what is called *autobiographical memory.* Other reports of people with "super memory" are rare, but those who have been studied can perform memory feats such as remembering long strings of digits or playing many chess games simultaneously. These feats are achieved by using special memory tricks such as chunking and creating images. A.J., in contrast, automatically remembers events in her life.

We will return to A.J. later in this chapter when we discuss some of the advantages and disadvantages of having a memory that far outstrips a typical person's memory. Our goal in this chapter is to describe what we know about memory for everyday events, focusing on the autobiographical events that A.J. is so good at remembering.

Our main focus will be to ask why we remember certain things, and why what we remember sometimes does not correspond to what actually happened. Studying the errors we make when remembering leads to the conclusion that what we remember is determined by creative mental processes. This creativity is a gift that helps us determine what happened when we have incomplete information, but it can also affect the accuracy of our memory.

Autobiographical Memory: What Has Happened in My Life

Autobiographical memory (AM) has been defined as recollected events that belong to a person's past (Rubin, 2005). When we remember the events that make up the stories of our life by using "mental time travel" to place ourselves back into a specific situation, we are experiencing AM. As we saw in Chapter 6, experiencing a memory by using mental time travel is episodic memory. However, autobiographical memories can also contain semantic components. For example, an AM of a childhood birthday party might include images of the cake, people at the party, and games being played (episodic memory); it might also include knowledge about when the party occurred, where your family was living at the time, and your general knowledge about what usually happens at birthday parties (semantic memory) (Cabeza & St. Jacques, 2007).

One of the factors that determines the relative proportions of episodic and semantic components in AM is how long ago the event to be remembered occurred. Memories of recent events that are rich in perceptual details and emotional content are dominated by episodic memory. However, as we mentioned in Chapter 6 (page 159), episodic memories can fade with time, leaving semantic memory. Thus, memories for more distant events become more semantic. For example, I only vaguely remember learning to read, and I have no memory of elementary school teachers and fellow students before the fourth grade. I do, however, remember what school I went to, where my family lived, that I was in about the second grade when I was learning to read, and that the two main characters in my reading book were Dick and Jane. My AM of these events, such as learning to read, that extend far back in time is mainly semantic. Given this interplay of episodic and semantic memory, we can define AM as episodic memory for events in our lives *plus* personal semantic memories of facts about our lives.

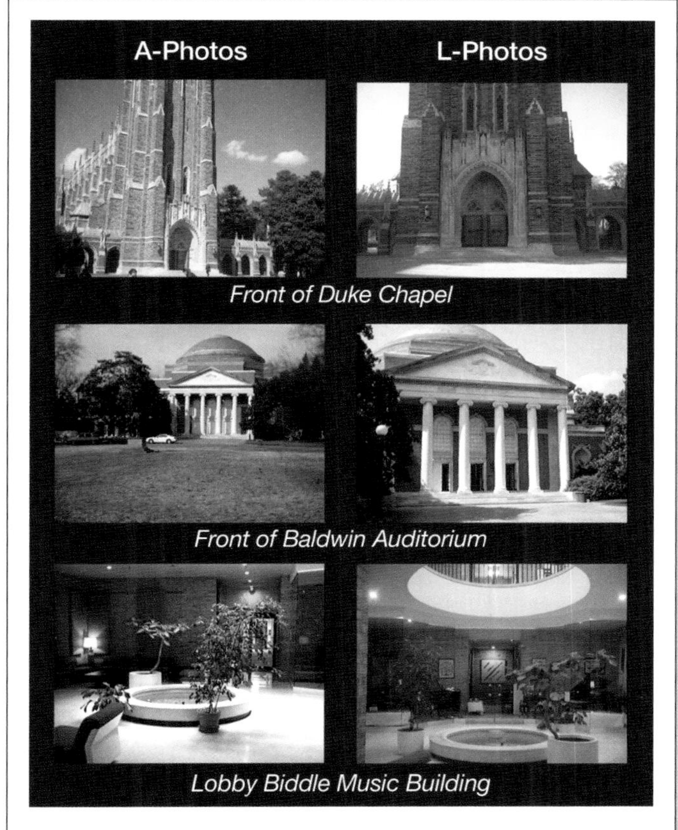

● **FIGURE 8.1** Photographs from Cabeza and coworkers' (2004) experiment. A-photos ("autobiographical photographs") were taken by the participant; L-photos ("laboratory photographs") were taken by someone else. (Source: R. Cabeza et al., "Brain Activity During Episodic Retrieval of Autobiographical and Laboratory Events: An fMRI Study Using a Novel Photo Paradigm," *Journal of Cognitive Neuroscience, 16,* 1583–1594, 2004.)

THE MULTIDIMENSIONAL NATURE OF AM

Autobiographical memories are far more complex than memory that might be measured in the laboratory by asking a person to remember a list of words. Autobiographical memories are multidimensional because they consist of spatial, emotional, and sensory components. The memory of patients who have suffered brain damage that causes a loss of visual memory, but without causing blindness, illustrates the importance of the sensory component of AM. Daniel Greenberg and David Rubin (2003) found that patients who had lost their ability to recognize objects or to visualize objects, because of damage to visual areas of the cortex, also experienced a loss of AM. This may have occurred because visual stimuli were not available to serve as retrieval cues for memories. But even memories not based on visual information are lost in these patients. Apparently, visual experience plays an important role in forming autobiographical memories. (It would seem reasonable that for blind people, auditory experience might take over this role.)

A brain scanning study that illustrates a difference between AM and laboratory memory was done by Roberto Cabeza and coworkers (2004). Cabeza measured the brain activation caused by two sets of stimulus photographs—one set that the participant took and another set that was taken by someone else (● Figure 8.1). We will call the photos taken by the participant A-photos, for "autobiographical photographs," and the ones taken by someone else L-photos, for "laboratory photographs."

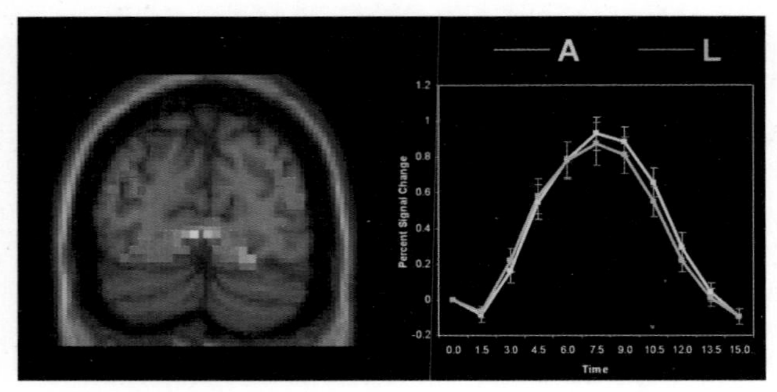

(a) Parietal cortex

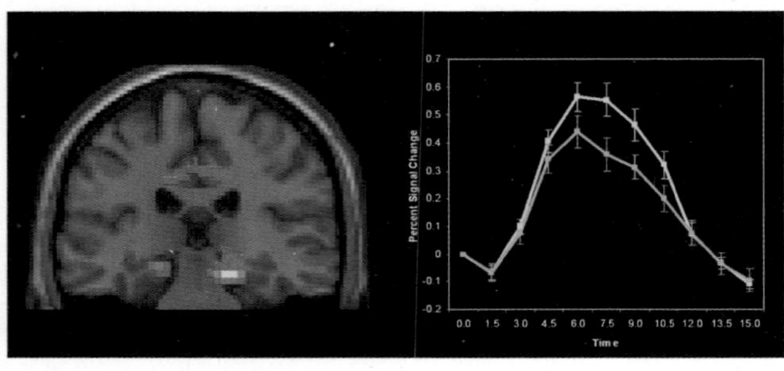

(b) Hippocampus

A photos = more activation

● **FIGURE 8.2** (a) fMRI response of an area in the parietal cortex showing areas activated by both the A-photos and the L-photos during the memory test. The graph on the right indicates that activation was the same for A-photos and L-photos. (b) Hippocampus activation (red areas at bottom) by the A-photos and the L-photos. The graph indicates that in this area of the brain, activation was greater for the A-photos. (Source: R. Cabeza et al., "Brain Activity During Episodic Retrieval of Autobiographical and Laboratory Events: An fMRI Study Using a Novel Photo Paradigm," *Journal of Cognitive Neuroscience*, 16, 1583–1594, 2004.)

The stimulus photographs were created by giving 12 Duke University students digital cameras and telling them to take pictures of 40 specified campus locations over a 10-day period. After taking the photographs, each participant was shown his or her own photos (A-photos) and photos taken by other participants (L-photos). A few days later, they saw their own photos, the L-photos they had seen before, and some new L-photos they had never seen. As participants indicated whether each stimulus was an A-photo, an L-photo they had seen before, or a new L-photo, their brain activity was measured in an MRI scanner.

The brain scans showed that A-photos and L-photos activated many of the same structures in the brain—mainly ones like the MTL that are associated with episodic memory, as well as an area in the parietal cortex that is involved in processing scenes ● Figure 8.2a). However, the A-photos also activated regions associated with processing information about the self, with memory for visual space, and with recollection (memory associated with "mental time travel" that we discussed in Chapter 6). Figure 8.2b shows the greater A-photo activation compared to L-photo activation in the hippocampus. Thus, the pictures of a particular location that people took themselves elicited memories associated with taking the picture, and therefore activated a more extensive network of brain areas, than pictures of the same location that were taken by someone else. This activation reflects the richness of experiencing autobiographical memories, as compared to laboratory memories. Autobiographical memories can also elicit emotions, which activates another area of the brain (which we will describe shortly) called the amygdala.

MEMORY OVER THE LIFE SPAN

What determines which particular life events we will remember years later? Personal milestones such as graduating from college or receiving a marriage proposal stand out, as do highly emotional events such as surviving a car accident (Pillemer, 1998). Events that become significant parts of a person's life tend to be remembered well. For example, going out to dinner with someone for the first time might stand out if you ended up having a long-term relationship with that person, but the same dinner date might be far less memorable if you never saw the person again.

Transition points in people's lives appear to be particularly memorable. This is illustrated by what Wellesley College juniors and seniors said when they were asked to recall the most influential event during their freshman year. Most responses were descriptions of events that occurred in September. When alumni were asked the same question, they remembered more events from September of their freshman year *and* from the end of their senior year—another transition point (Pillemer et al., 1996).

A particularly interesting result occurs when participants over 40 are asked to remember events in their lives. For these participants, memory is high for recent events and for events experienced in adolescence and early adulthood (between 10 and 30 years of age; ● Figure 8.3; Conway, 1996; Rubin et al., 1998). This enhanced memory for adolescence and young adulthood found in people over 40 is called the **reminiscence bump**. Why are adolescence and young adulthood special times for encoding memories? We will describe three hypotheses, all based on the idea that special life events are happening during adolescence and young adulthood.

Clare Rathbone and coworkers (2008) propose that memory is enhanced for events that occur as a person's self-image or life identity is being formed. We will call this idea the **self-image hypothesis** of the reminiscence bump. Rathborne and coworkers base this idea on the results of an experiment in which a group of participants with an average

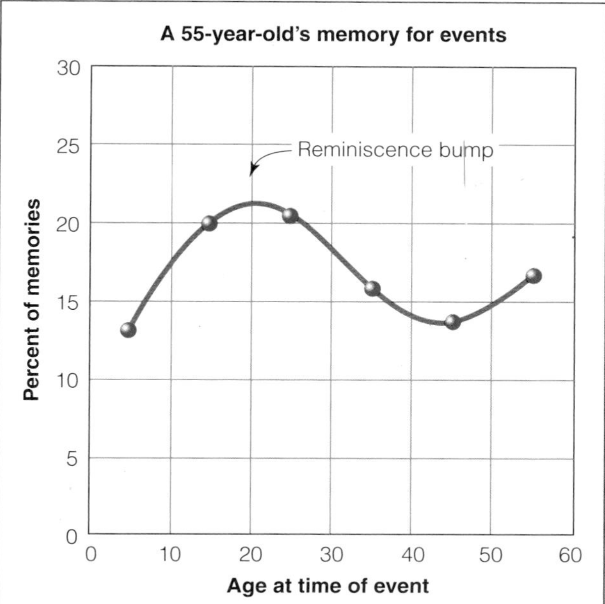

● **FIGURE 8.3** Percentage of memories from different ages, recalled by a 55-year-old, showing the reminiscence bump. (Source: R. W. Schrauf & D. C. Rubin, "Bilingual Autobiographical Memory in Older Adult Immigrants: A Test of Cognitive Explanations of the Reminiscence Bump and the Linguistic Encoding of Memories," *Journal of Memory and Language, 39*, 437–445, Fig. 1. Copyright © 1998 Elsevier Ltd. Republished with permission.)

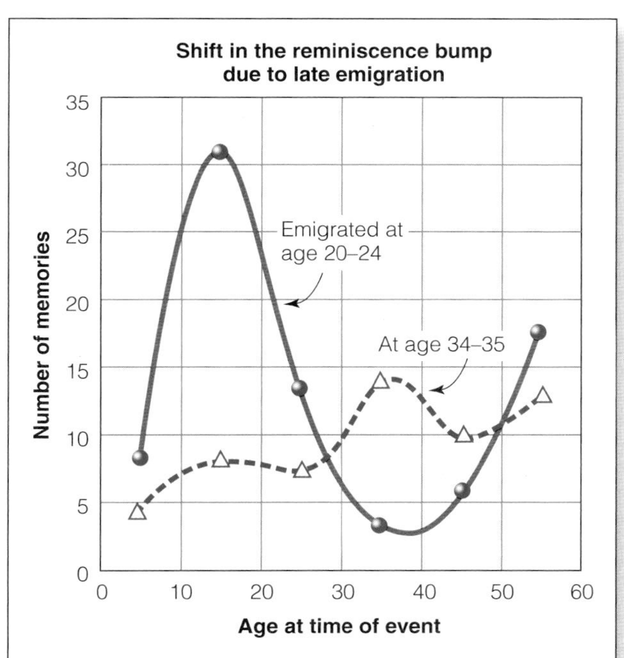

● **FIGURE 8.4** The reminiscence bump for people who emigrated at age 34 to 35 is shifted toward older ages, compared to the bump for people who emigrated between the ages of 20 to 24. (Source: R. W. Schrauf & D. C. Rubin, "Bilingual Autobiographical Memory in Older Adult Immigrants: A Test of Cognitive Explanations of the Reminiscence Bump and the Linguistic Encoding of Memories," *Journal of Memory and Language, 39*, 437–445, Fig. 1. Copyright © 1998 Elsevier Ltd. Republished with permission.)

age of 54 created "I am" statements, such as "I am a mother" or "I am a psychologist," that they felt defined them as a person. They were then asked when each statement had become a significant part of their identity. The average age participants assigned to the origin of these statements was 25 years, which is within the span of the reminiscence bump. When participants then listed events that were connected with each statement (such as "I gave birth to my first child" or "I started graduate school in psychology"), most occurred during the time span associated with the reminiscence bump. Development of the self-image therefore brings with it numerous memorable events, most of which happen during adolescence or young adulthood.

Another explanation for the reminiscence bump, called the **cognitive hypothesis**, proposes that periods of rapid change that are followed by stability cause stronger encoding of memories. Adolescence and young adulthood fit this description because the rapid changes that occur during these periods are followed by the relative stability of adult life. One way this hypothesis has been tested is by finding people who have experienced rapid changes in their lives that occurred at a time later than adolescence or young adulthood. The cognitive hypothesis would predict that the reminiscence bump should occur later for these people. To test this idea, Robert Schrauf and David Rubin (1998) determined the recollections of people who had emigrated to the United States either in their 20s or in their mid-30s. ● Figure 8.4, which shows the memory curves for two groups of immigrants, indicates that the reminiscence bump occurs at the normal age for people who emigrated early, but is shifted to 15 years later for those who emigrated later, just as the cognitive hypothesis would predict.

Finally, another explanation is the **cultural life script hypothesis**. This explanation distinguishes between a person's life story, which is all of the events that have occurred in a person's life, and a **cultural life script**, which are culturally expected events that occur at a particular time in the left span. For example, when Dorthe Berntsen and David Rubin (2004) asked people to list when important events in a typical person's life usually occur, some of the more common responses were falling in love (16 years), college (22 years), marriage (27 years), and having children (28 years). Interestingly, a large number of the most commonly mentioned events occur during the period associated with the reminiscence bump. This doesn't mean that events in a *specific* person's life always occur at those times, but according to the cultural life script hypothesis, events in a person's life story become easier to recall when they fit the cultural life script for that person's culture.

The reminiscence bump is a good example of a phenomenon that has generated a number of explanations, many of them plausible and supported by evidence. It isn't surprising that the crucial factors proposed by each explanation—formation of self-identity, rapid changes followed by stability, and culturally expected events—all occur during the reminiscence bump, because that is what they are trying to explain. It is likely that each of the explanations we have described makes some contribution to creating the reminiscence bump. (See Table 8.1.)

TABLE 8.1 Explanations for the Reminiscence Bump

Explanation	Basic Characteristic
Self-image	Period of assuming person's self-image.
Cognitive	Encoding is better during periods of rapid change.
Cultural life script	Culturally shared expectations structure recall.

Memory for "Exceptional" Events

It is clear that some events in a person's life are more likely to be remembered than others. So far we have been asking *when* these events occur, but we can also ask *what kinds of events* are most likely to be remembered. A characteristic of most memorable events is that they are significant and important to the person and, in many cases, are associated with emotions. For example, studies of what students remember from their freshman year of college have found that many of the events that stand out were associated with strong emotions (Pillemer, 1998; Pillemer et al., 1996; Talarico, 2009).

MEMORY AND EMOTION

Emotions are often associated with events that are more easily remembered. Personal events, such as beginning or ending relationships, or events experienced by many people simultaneously, like the 9/11 terrorist attacks, seem to be remembered more easily and vividly than less emotionally charged events. This feeling that emotionally charged events are easier to remember has been confirmed by laboratory research. For example, when Kevin LaBar and Elizabeth Phelps (1998) tested participants' ability to recall arousing words (for example, profanity and sexually explicit words) and neutral words (such as *street* and *store*) immediately after they were presented, they observed better memory for the arousing words (● Figure 8.5a). Florin Dolcos and coworkers (2005) tested participants' ability to recognize emotional and neutral pictures 1 year after they were initially presented and observed better memory for the emotional pictures (Figure 8.5b).

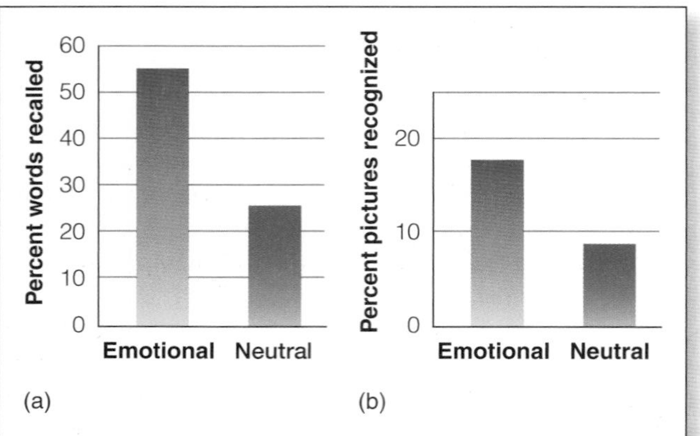

● **FIGURE 8.5** (a) Percent of emotional and neutral words recalled immediately after reading a list of words (based on data from LaBar & Phelps, 1998, Fig. 2, p. 490). (b) Percent of emotional and neutral pictures recognized 1 year after viewing the pictures (adapted from Dolcos et al., 2005, Fig. 1, p. 2628).

When we look at what is happening physiologically, one structure stands out—the **amygdala** (see Figure 7.17). The importance of the amygdala has been demonstrated in a number of ways. For example, in the experiment by Dolcos and coworkers described above, fMRI brain scans, measured as people were remembering, revealed that amygdala activity was higher for the emotional words (also see Cahill et al., 1996; Hamann et al., 1999).

The link between emotions and the amygdala has also been demonstrated by testing a patient, B.P., who had suffered damage to his amygdala. When participants without brain damage viewed a slide show about a boy and his mother in which the boy is injured halfway through the story, these participants had enhanced memory for the emotional part of the story (when the boy is injured). B.P.'s memory was the same as that of the non-brain-damaged participants for the first part of the story, but it was not enhanced for the emotional part (Cahill et al., 1995). It appears, therefore, that emotions may trigger mechanisms in the amygdala that help us remember events that are associated with the emotions.

● **FIGURE 8.6** Posters like this one are just one of the many reminders of the terrorist attacks of September 11, 2001.

FLASHBULB MEMORIES

What about special, highly memorable, or significant events? You may have memories of the terrorist attacks of September 11, 2001 (● Figure 8.6). Do you remember when you first heard about the attacks? How you found out? Where you were? Your initial reaction? What you did next? I remember walking into the psychology department office and hearing from a secretary that someone had crashed a plane into the World Trade Center. At the time, I pictured a small private plane that had gone off course, but a short while later, when I called my wife, she told me that the first tower of the World Trade Center had just collapsed. Shortly after that, in my cognitive psychology class, my students and I discussed what we knew about the situation and decided to cancel class for the day.

The memories I have described about how I heard about the 9/11 attack, and the people and events directly associated with finding out about the attack, are still vivid in my mind more than 8 years later. Is there something special about memories that are associated with unexpected, emotionally charged events? According to Roger Brown and James Kulik (1977), there is. They proposed that memories for the circumstances surrounding learning about events such as 9/11 are special. Their proposal was based on an earlier event—the assassination of President John F. Kennedy on November 22, 1963.

In referring to the day Kennedy's assassination occurred, Brown and Kulik stated that "for an instant, the entire nation and perhaps much of the world stopped still to have its picture taken." This description, which likened the process of forming a memory to the taking of a photograph, led them to coin the term **flashbulb memory** to refer to a person's memory for the circumstances surrounding hearing about shocking, highly charged events. It is important to emphasize that the term *flashbulb memory* refers to memory for the circumstances surrounding how a person *heard about* an event, not memory for the event itself. Thus, a flashbulb memory for 9/11 would be memory for where you were and what you were doing when you found out about the terrorist attack.

Brown and Kulik argue that there is something special about the mechanisms responsible for flashbulb memories. Not only do they occur under highly emotional circumstances, but they are remembered for long periods of time and are especially vivid and detailed. Brown and Kulik describe the mechanism responsible for these vivid and detailed memories as a "Now Print" mechanism, as if these memories are like a photograph that resists fading.

Brown and Kulik's idea that flashbulb memories are like a photograph was based on people's descriptions of what they remembered about how they had heard about events like the assassinations of John F. Kennedy and Martin Luther King, Jr. From these descriptions, Brown and Kulik concluded that people could often describe in some detail what they were doing when they heard about these highly emotional events. But the procedure Brown and Kulik used was flawed because the only data they collected were what people remembered years after the events had occurred. The problem with this procedure is that there was no way to determine whether the reported memories were accurate. The only way to check for accuracy is to compare the person's memory to what actually happened or to memory reports collected immediately after the event. The technique of comparing later memories to memories collected immediately after the event is called **repeated recall**.

METHOD Repeated Recall

The idea behind repeated recall is to determine whether memory changes over time, by testing participants a number of times after an event. The person's memory is first measured immediately after a stimulus is presented or something happens. Even though there is some possibility for errors or omissions immediately after the event, this report is taken as being the most accurate representation of what happened and is used as a baseline. Days, months, or years later, when participants are asked to remember what happened, their reports are compared to this baseline. This use of a baseline provides a way to check the accuracy of later reports.

● **FIGURE 8.7** Neisser and Harsch (1992) studied people's memories for the day they heard about the explosion of the space shuttle *Challenger.*

Over the years since Brown and Kulik's "Now Print" proposal, research using the repeated recall task has shown that flashbulb memories are not like photographs. Unlike photographs, which remain the same for many years, people's memories for how they heard about flashbulb events change over time. In fact, one of the main findings of research on flashbulb memories is that although people report that memories surrounding flashbulb events are especially vivid, they are often inaccurate or lacking in detail. For example, Ulric Neisser and N. Harsch (1992) did a study in which they asked participants how they had heard about the explosion of the space shuttle *Challenger* (● Figure 8.7). The *Challenger* broke apart 77 seconds after blasting off from Cape Canaveral on January 28, 1986, killing the crew of seven, which included Christa McAuliffe, a New Hampshire high school teacher, who was the first member of NASA's Teacher in Space project.

Participants in Neisser and Harsh's experiment filled out a questionnaire within a day after the explosion, and then filled out the same questionnaire 2 1/2 to 3 years later. One participant's response, a day after the explosion, indicated that she had heard about it in class:

> I was in my religion class and some people walked in and started talking about [it]. I didn't know any details except that it had exploded and the schoolteacher's students had all been watching, which I thought was so sad. Then after class I went to my room and watched the TV program talking about it, and I got all the details from that.

Two and a half years later, her memory had changed to the following:

> When I first heard about the explosion I was sitting in my freshman dorm room with my roommate, and we were watching TV. It came on a news flash, and we were both totally shocked. I was really upset, and I went upstairs to talk to a friend of mine, and then I called my parents.

Responses like these, in which participants first reported hearing about the explosion in one place, such as a classroom, and then later remembered that they first heard about it on TV, were common. Right after the explosion, 21 percent of the participants indicated that they had first heard about it on TV, but 2 1/2 years later, 45 percent of the participants reported that they had first heard about it on TV. Reasons for the increase in TV memories could be that the TV reports become more memorable through repetition and that TV is a major source of news. Thus, memory for hearing about the *Challenger* explosion had a property that is also a characteristic of memory for less dramatic, everyday events: It was affected by people's experiences following the event (people may have seen accounts of the explosion) and their general knowledge (before the Internet existed, people often first heard about important news on TV).

The large number of inaccurate responses in the *Challenger* study suggests that perhaps memories that are supposed to be flashbulb memories decay just like regular memories. In fact, many flashbulb memory researchers have expressed doubt that flashbulb memories are much different from regular memories (Schmolck et al., 2000). This conclusion is supported by an experiment in which a group of college students was asked a number of questions on September 12, 2001, the day after the terrorist attacks on the World Trade Center and the Pentagon (Talarico & Rubin, 2003). Some of these questions were about the terrorist attacks ("When did you first hear the news?"). Others were similar questions about an everyday event in the person's life that occurred in the days just preceding the attacks. After picking the everyday event, the participant created a two- or three-word description that could serve as a cue for that event in the future. Some participants were retested 1 week later, some 6 weeks later, and some 32 weeks later by asking them the same questions about the attack and the everyday event.

One result of this experiment was that the participants remembered fewer details and made more errors at longer intervals after the events, with little difference between

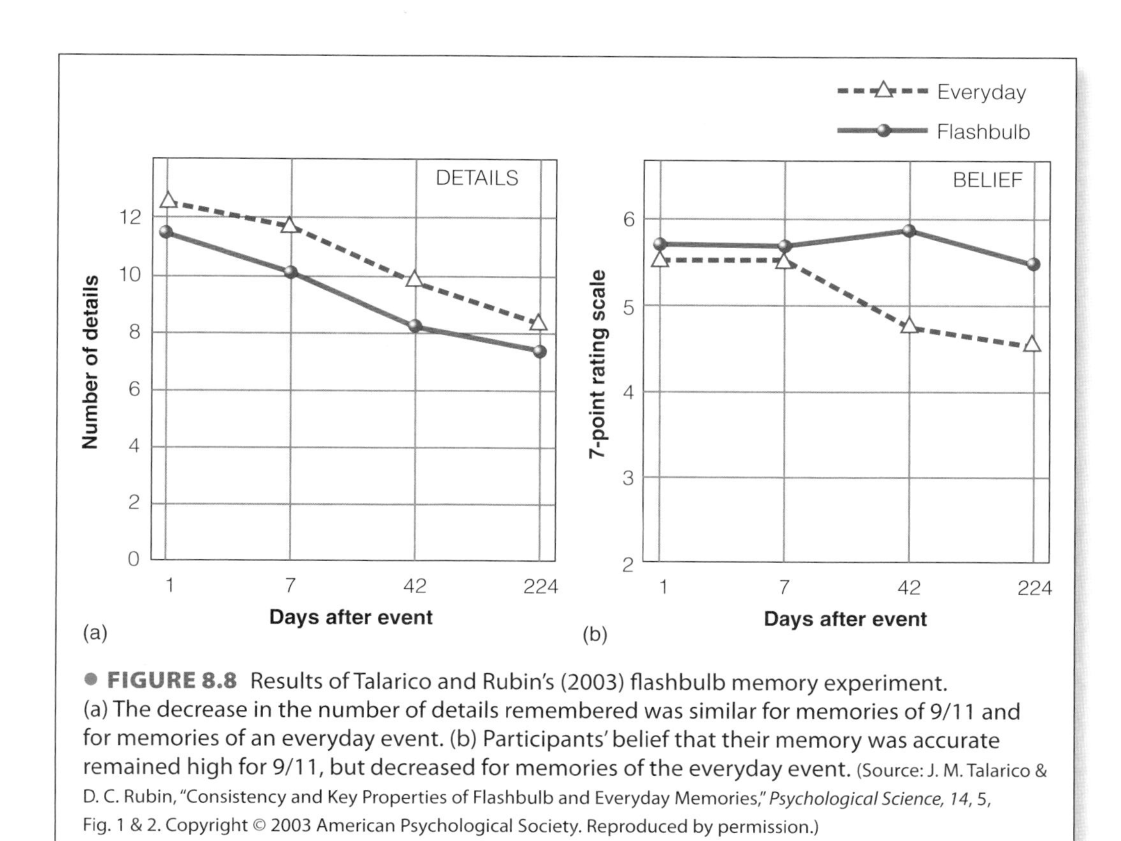

● **FIGURE 8.8** Results of Talarico and Rubin's (2003) flashbulb memory experiment. (a) The decrease in the number of details remembered was similar for memories of 9/11 and for memories of an everyday event. (b) Participants' belief that their memory was accurate remained high for 9/11, but decreased for memories of the everyday event. (Source: J. M. Talarico & D. C. Rubin, "Consistency and Key Properties of Flashbulb and Everyday Memories," *Psychological Science, 14*, 5, Fig. 1 & 2. Copyright © 2003 American Psychological Society. Reproduced by permission.)

the results for the flashbulb and everyday memories (● Figure 8.8a). This result supports the idea that there is nothing special about flashbulb memories. However, another result, shown in Figure 8.8b, did indicate a difference between flashbulb and everyday memories: People's *belief* that their memories were accurate stayed high over the entire 32-week period for the flashbulb memories, but dropped for the everyday memories. Ratings of vividness and how well they could "relive" the events also stayed high and constant for the flashbulb memories but dropped for the everyday memories. Thus, the idea that flashbulb memories are special appears to be based at least partially on the fact that people *think* the memories are stronger and more accurate; however, this study found that *in reality* there was little or no difference between flashbulb and everyday memories in terms of the amount remembered and the accuracy of what is remembered.

Although Talarico and Rubin found that people's memories for hearing about 9/11 decreased in accuracy in the same way as memories for everyday events, another experiment found that memories for events associated with hearing about 9/11 were more resistant to fading than memories for other events that took place at about the same time. Shortly after the 9/11 attacks, Patrick Davidson and coworkers (2006) asked participants questions such as "How did you hear the news?" "Where were you when you heard about the attack?" and "Who was present?" They also had the participants answer the same questions for an everyday event—the most interesting event (as picked by the participant) that had occurred in the few days preceding 9/11.

One year later, the participants were contacted for a surprise memory test in which they were asked the same questions as before. If they weren't able to remember the everyday event, they were given a cue, such as "party" or "movie," to help them remember the event. The participants' response to each question was scored by assigning 0 points if they couldn't remember or remembered it very inaccurately, 1 point if their memory was partially correct or less specific than the original memory, and 2 points if their memory was very similar to their original report. The resulting "congruence score" was determined by adding the points for all of the questions and scaling the total so that 1.0 was the maximum possible. Congruence for 9/11 memories was fairly high 1 year later (0.77), but the score for the everyday events was much lower

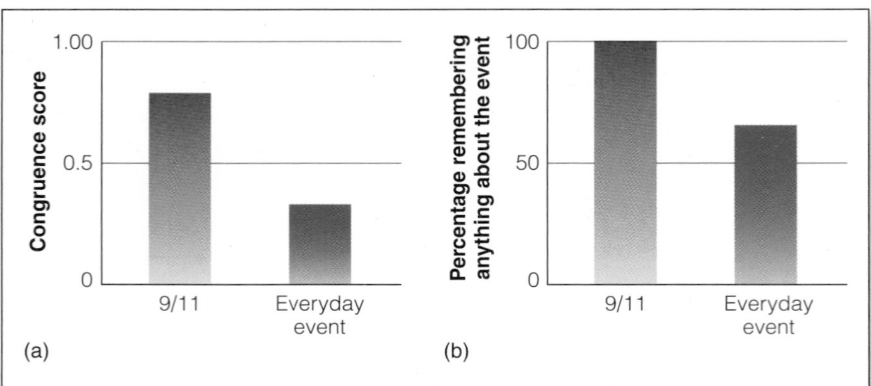

• **FIGURE 8.9** Results of Davidson et al.'s (2006) flashbulb memory experiment. (a) Congruence score for 9/11 memories and memories for the everyday event, measured 1 year after the events. (b) Percent of participants who were able to remember at least something about the 9/11 and everyday events. Note that 35 percent of the participants could not remember anything about the everyday event. (Based on data from Davidson et al., 2006, and personal communication.)

(0.33; • Figure 8.9a). A particularly striking difference between memory for the two events was that whereas all of the participants had no trouble remembering 9/11, only 65 percent of the participants were able to remember what the everyday event was, even after being prompted with a cue (Figure 8.9b).

The results of both the Talarico and Rubin (2003) and Davidson and coworkers (2006) experiments showed that memory for the flashbulb event declined over time. These results support the idea that a "flashbulb memory" is not like a photograph. However, Davidson and coworkers' participants found it more difficult to remember their everyday event. It is not clear why this occurred, but possible reasons are that Davidson's participants were not aware they would be tested later (the 1-year test was a surprise) and the retrieval cues they were given may not have been as effective as those provided to Talarico and Rubin's participants.

We can understand why the retrieval cues may have differed in effectiveness by returning to the results of Timo Mantyla's experiment that we described in Chapter 7 (page 183). The results of that experiment showed that retrieval cues are more effective when they are created by the participant than when they are created by someone else. The fact that Talarico and Rubin's participants created their own retrieval cues, whereas Davidson's participants did not, may explain why Davidson's participants remembered less about their everyday events, and why the results of this experiment demonstrated a large difference in the memories associated with flashbulb and everyday events.

Better memory for 9/11 is probably due to two characteristics of memories surrounding flashbulb events. First, they involve high emotions. Most people associate finding out about 9/11 not just with the event itself but also with intense emotions such as surprise, disbelief, anger, and fear. We know that high emotions trigger responses in the amygdala that are associated with better memory for emotional events (see page 208). It would not be surprising, therefore, if memory for hearing about flashbulb events was somewhat better than memory for less emotional, "everyday" events (Davidson & Glisky, 2002).

A second factor that can potentially enhance memory for flashbulb events is added rehearsal. Ulric Neisser and coworkers (1996) argue we may remember events like those that happened on 9/11 not because of a special mechanism, but because we rehearse these events after they occur. This idea is called the **narrative rehearsal hypothesis**.

The narrative rehearsal hypothesis makes sense when we consider the events that followed 9/11. Pictures of the planes crashing into the World Trade Center were replayed endlessly on TV, and the event and its aftermath were covered extensively for months afterwards in the media. Neisser argues that if rehearsal is the reason for our memories of significant events, then the "flashbulb" analogy is misleading. Remember that the memory we are concerned with is the characteristics surrounding how you *first heard about* 9/11, but much of the "rehearsal" associated with this event was rehearsal for events that occurred *after* hearing about it. Seeing TV replays of the planes crashing into the towers, for example, might result in people focusing more on that than on who told them about the event or where they were. This would explain the intrusion of the TV errors that occurred in the *Challenger* study.

This effect of rehearsal through watching TV coverage of an event is also illustrated by the media coverage following the death of Michael Jackson on June 25, 2009. Although as I write this it is only a little over a month since this event happened, I have seen, read, and heard so much about Michael Jackson that it is difficult to sort out when I first heard about the event from all of my other exposure to it.

The exact mechanism responsible for memory of flashbulb events is still being discussed by memory researchers (Berntsen, 2009; Luminet & Curci, 2009; Talarico &

Rubin, 2009). However, whatever mechanism is involved, perhaps the most important outcome of the flashbulb memory research is what it tells us about memory in general. It confirms that the specific context surrounding an event can influence memory. Both the emotional context of an event and things that happened after the event can potentially affect later reports about the event. The idea that people's memories for an event are determined by the event context and by things in addition to what happened at the time has led many researchers to propose that what people remember is a "construction" that is based on what actually happened plus additional influences. We will discuss this idea in the next section.

TEST YOURSELF 8.1

1. What is autobiographical memory? What does it mean to say that it includes both episodic and semantic components?
2. What does it mean to say that autobiographical memories are "multidimensional"? How did Cabeza's "photography" experiment provide evidence for this idea?
3. What types of events are often the most memorable? What would a plot of "events remembered" versus "age" look like for a 50-year-old person? What theories have been proposed to explain the peak that occurs in this function?
4. What is the evidence that emotionally charged events are easier to remember than nonemotional events? Describe the role of the amygdala in emotional memory, including brain scan (fMRI) and neuropsychological (patient B.P.) evidence linking the amygdala and memory.
5. The idea of flashbulb memories has been debated by psychologists. What is behind the idea that some memories are "special" and are therefore labeled as "flashbulb" memories? What evidence indicates that memories for flashbulb experiences are not long-lived like photographs? What evidence suggests that there may, in fact, be something special about memory for flashbulb events?

The Constructive Nature of Memory

We have seen that we remember certain things better than others because of their special significance or because of when they happened in our lives. But we have also seen that what people remember may not match what actually happened. When people report memories for past events, they may not only omit things, but also distort or change things that happened, and in some cases even report things that never happened at all.

These characteristics of memory reflect the **constructive nature of memory**—what people report as memories are constructed by the person based on what actually happened plus additional factors, such as the person's knowledge, experiences, and expectations. This approach to memory is called *constructive* because the mind *constructs* memories based on a number of sources of information.[1] One of the first experiments to suggest that memory is constructive was Bartlett's "War of the Ghosts" experiment.

BARTLETT'S "WAR OF THE GHOSTS" EXPERIMENT

The British psychologist Fredrick Bartlett conducted a classic study of the constructive nature of memory, known as the "War of the Ghosts" experiment. In this experiment, which Bartlett ran before World War I and published in 1932, his participants read the following story from Canadian Indian Folklore.

---

[1]Some researchers use the term *constructive memory* to refer to constructive processes that influence memory during encoding and *reconstructive memory* to refer to constructive processes that influence memory during retrieval. The distinction between these two terms is, however, often subtle. Both refer to the idea that our memory reports are the result of processes in which we create memories based on what actually happened plus other factors, including inferences based on our previous experiences and knowledge of the world. In this book, therefore, we will follow the lead of those who use only the general term *constructive* (see Schacter et al., 1998).

THE WAR OF THE GHOSTS

One night two young men from Egulac went down to the river to hunt seals, and while they were there it became foggy and calm. Then they heard war cries, and they thought: "Maybe this is a war party." They escaped to the shore and hid behind a log. Now canoes came up, and they heard the noise of paddles and saw one canoe coming up to them. There were five men in the canoe, and they said:

"What do you think? We wish to take you along. We are going up the river to make war on the people."

One of the young men said: "I have no arrows." "Arrows are in the canoe," they said. "I will not go along. I might be killed. My relatives do not know where I have gone. But you," he said, turning to the other, "may go with them."

So one of the young men went, but the other returned home. And the warriors went on up the river to a town on the other side of Kalama. The people came down to the water, and they began to fight, and many were killed. But presently the young man heard one of the warriors say: "Quick, let us go home; that Indian has been hit." Now he thought: "Oh, they are ghosts." He did not feel sick, but they said he had been shot.

So the canoes went back to Egulac, and the young man went ashore to his house and made a fire. And he told everybody and said: "Behold I accompanied the ghosts, and we went to fight. Many of our fellows were killed, and many of those who attacked us were killed. They said I was hit, and I did not feel sick."

He told it all, and then he became quiet. When the sun rose, he fell down. Something black came out of his mouth. His face became contorted. The people jumped up and cried. He was dead. (Bartlett, 1932, p. 65)

After his participants read this story, Bartlett asked them to recall it as accurately as possible. He then used the technique of **repeated reproduction**, in which the same participants came back a number of times to try to remember the story at longer and longer intervals after they first read it. This is similar to the repeated recall technique used in the flashbulb memory experiments (see Method: Repeated Recall, page 209).

Bartlett's experiment is considered important because it was one of the first to use the repeated reproduction technique. But the main reason the "War of the Ghosts" experiment is considered important is the nature of the errors Bartlett's participants made. At longer times after reading the story, participants forgot much of the information in the story. Most participants' reproductions of the story were shorter than the original and contained many omissions and inaccuracies.

But what was most significant about the remembered stories is that they tended to reflect the participant's own culture. The original story, which came from Canadian folklore, was transformed by many of Bartlett's participants to make it more consistent with the culture of Edwardian England that they belonged to. For example, one participant remembered the two men who were out hunting seals as being involved in a sailing expedition, the "canoes" as "boats," and the man who joined the war party as a fighter that any good Englishman would be proud of—ignoring his wounds, he continued fighting and won the admiration of the natives.

One way to think about what happened in Bartlett's experiment is that his participants created their memories from two sources. One source was the original story, and the other was what they knew about stories in their own culture. As time passed, the participants used information from both sources, so their reproductions became more like what would happen in Edwardian England. This idea that memories can be influenced by the sources of information involves a phenomenon called *source monitoring*, which is at the heart of the constructive approach to memory.

SOURCE MONITORING AND SOURCE MONITORING ERRORS

CogLab
Remember/Know

"Did you hear about the mob scene at the movie theater for the opening of the new Harry Potter movie?"

"Yes, I heard about it on the evening news."

"Really? I heard about it from Bernita, who loves Harry Potter, or was it Susan? I can't remember."

Source monitoring is the process of determining the origins of our memories, knowledge, or beliefs (Johnson et al., 1993). In the conversation above, one person identified the evening news as his source of information about the movie; the other person seemed unsure of his source, thinking it was either Bernita or Susan. If he thought it was Bernita, but it turned out to be Susan, he would be committing a **source monitoring error**—misidentifying the source of a memory. Source monitoring errors are also called **source misattributions** because the memory is attributed to the wrong source. Source monitoring provides an example of the constructive nature of memory because when we remember something, we usually retrieve the memory first ("I heard about the scene at the Harry Potter movie") and then use a decision process to determine where that memory came from ("It was either Bernita or Susan, because I talked to them recently. But it's more likely to be Bernita, because I know she really likes Harry Potter") (Mitchell & Johnson, 2000).

Source monitoring errors are common, and we are often unaware of them (as was probably the case for Bartlett's participants). Perhaps you have had the experience of remembering that one person told you about something, but later realized you had heard it from someone else—or the experience of claiming you had said something you had only thought ("I'll be home late for dinner") (Henkel, 2004). President Ronald Regan famously related a story about a heroic act by a U.S. pilot, only to have it revealed later that his story was almost identical to a scene from a 1940s war movie, *A Wing and a Prayer* (Johnson, 2006; Rogin, 1987). Apparently the source of the president's memory was the film rather than an actual event.

Some of the more sensational examples of source monitoring errors are cases of **cryptomnesia**, unconscious plagiarism of the work of others. For example, Beatle George Harrison was sued for appropriating the melody from the song *He's So Fine* (originally recorded by the 1960s group *The Chiffons*) for his song *My Sweet Lord*. Although Harrison had used the tune unconsciously, he was successfully sued by the publisher of the original song. Harrison's problem was that he thought he was the source of the melody, when the actual source was someone else.

Source monitoring errors are important because the mechanisms responsible for them are also involved in creating memories in general. Marcia Johnson (2006) describes memory as a process that makes use of a number of types of information. The primary source of information for memory is information from the actual event, including perceptual experiences, emotions, and thoughts that were occurring at the time. Additional sources of information that influence memory include people's knowledge of the world, and things that happened before or after the event that might become confused with the event.

Later in the chapter we will describe a number of experiments that illustrate how what people know about the world can cause them to misremember material presented earlier. We will also describe experiments in which experimenters provide misleading information after an event that causes participants to make errors when attempting to remember the event. Source monitoring is a factor in these situations because participants are using this additional information, rather than information provided by the actual event, as a source for their memory. We will now describe two experiments that provide examples of how source monitoring errors can influence a person's memory.

The "Becoming Famous Overnight" Experiment: Source Monitoring and Familiarity

An experiment by Larry Jacoby and coworkers (1989) demonstrates an effect of source monitoring errors by testing participants' ability to distinguish between famous and nonfamous names. In the acquisition part of the experiment, Jacoby had participants read a number of made-up nonfamous names like Sebastian Weissdorf and Valerie Marsh (● Figure 8.10). In the *immediate test*, which was presented right after the participants saw the list of nonfamous names, participants were told to pick out the names of famous people from a list containing (1) the nonfamous names they had just seen, (2) new nonfamous names that they had never seen before, and (3) famous names, like Minnie Pearl (a country singer) or Roger Bannister (the first person to run a 4-minute mile), that many people might have recognized in 1988, when the experiment was done. Just before this

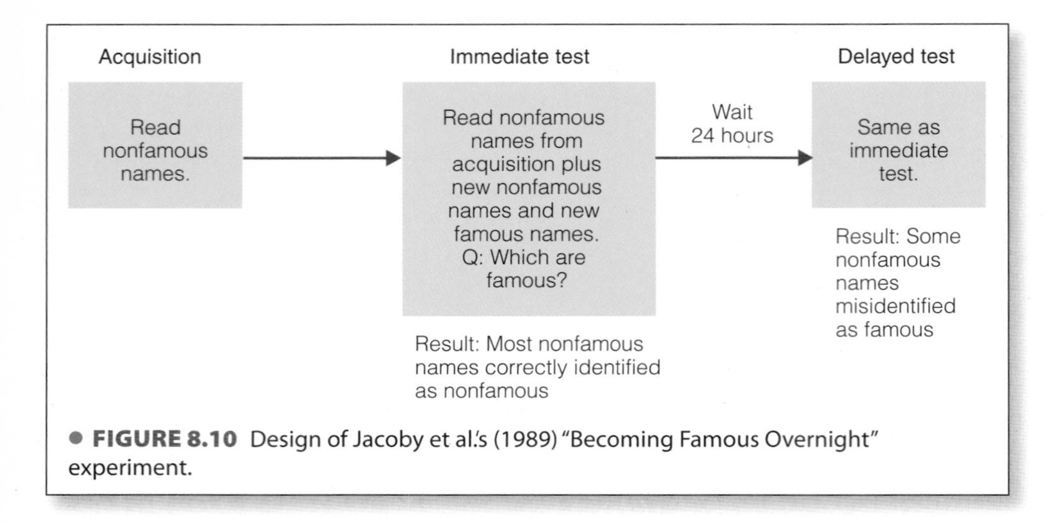

• **FIGURE 8.10** Design of Jacoby et al.'s (1989) "Becoming Famous Overnight" experiment.

test, participants were told that all of the names they had seen in the first part of the experiment were nonfamous. Because the test was given shortly after the participants had seen the first list of nonfamous names, they correctly identified most of the old nonfamous names (like Sebastian Weissdorf and Valerie Marsh) as being nonfamous.

The interesting result occurred in the *delayed test*, which happened 24 hours later. When tested on the same list of names a day later, participants were more likely to identify the old nonfamous names as being famous. Thus, even though they may have identified Sebastian Weissdorf as not being famous in the immediate test, his name was more likely to be labeled as famous 24 hours later. Because of this result, Jacoby's paper is titled "Becoming Famous Overnight."

How did Sebastian Weissdorf become famous overnight? To answer this question, put yourself in the place of one of Jacoby's participants. It is 24 hours since you saw the first list of nonfamous names, and you now have to decide whether Sebastian Weissdorf is famous or nonfamous. How do you make your decision? Sebastian Weissdorf doesn't pop out as someone you know of, but the name is familiar. You ask yourself the question: "Why is this name familiar?" This is a source monitoring problem, because to answer this question you need to determine the source of your familiarity. Are you familiar with the name Sebastian Weissdorf because you saw it 24 hours earlier, or because it is the name of a famous person? Apparently, some of Jacoby's participants decided that the familiarity was caused by fame, so the previously unknown Sebastian Weissdorf became famous!

Later in the chapter, when we consider some of the issues involved in determining the accuracy of eyewitness testimony, we will see that situations that create a sense of familiarity can lead to source monitoring errors, such as identifying the wrong person as having been at the scene of a crime.

Remembering Who Said What: Source Monitoring and Gender Stereotypes When in doubt about what we remember, we often make use of what we know about the world, and often we do this unconsciously. An example is provided by an experiment by Richard Marsh and coworkers (2006), which showed that people's performance on a source monitoring task can be influenced by gender stereotypes. They used the following method to test for source monitoring.

METHOD Testing for Source Monitoring

In a typical memory experiment, items such as words, pictures, or statements are presented, and the participant's task in a later test session is to either recall or recognize as many of the previously presented items as possible. In a source monitoring experiment, items are presented that originate from specific sources, and the participant's task in the later test session is to indicate which *source* was associated with each item. For example, participants can be presented with a number of statements, such as "'I went to the party today,' John said," or "'I have a feeling that the Mets are going to win tonight,' Sally said. " Later, in the source memory test, participants are presented with each statement, but without the speaker's name, and are asked to indicate who the speaker was. Source monitoring errors occur when the statement is attributed to the wrong person. Thus, the key result in a source memory experiment is not what proportion of items were remembered (although those data can be collected in the experiment), but what proportion of items were paired with the correct source.

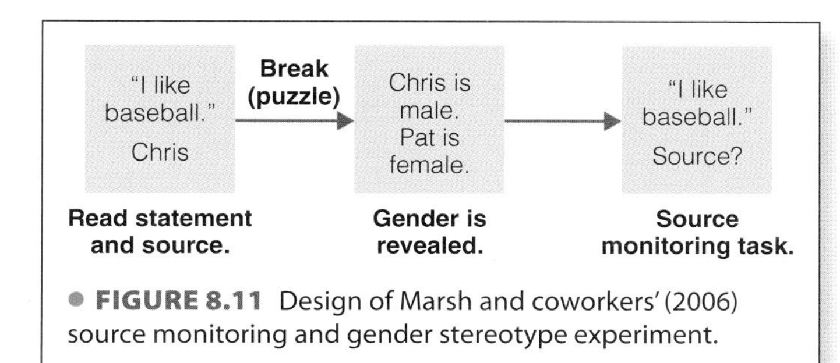

● **FIGURE 8.11** Design of Marsh and coworkers' (2006) source monitoring and gender stereotype experiment.

The experimental design of Marsh's experiment is shown in ● Figure 8.11. Participants read a series of statements presented one at a time on a computer screen for 5 seconds each. Some statements were associated with the stereotype for males ("I swore at the guy who insulted me"), some with the stereotype for females ("I made a centerpiece for the dining table"), and some were neutral ("I am very easygoing"). Each statement was presented with a name, either Chris or Pat, and participants were told to remember the statement and the person who said it.

After seeing all of the statement-name pairs, the participants did a puzzle for 5 minutes and were then told that Chris was a heterosexual male and Pat was a heterosexual female. It is important to remember that the participants did not know Chris's or Pat's gender when they first read the statements. Once they knew the genders, they were given the source monitoring task, which was to read the statements they had originally seen and indicate whether they were said by Chris or by Pat.

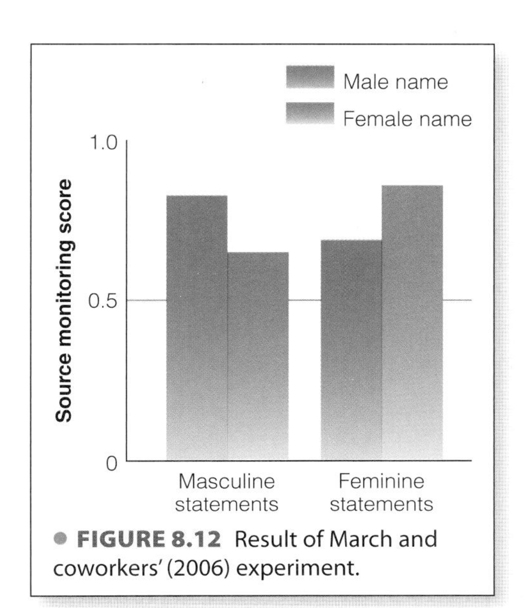

● **FIGURE 8.12** Result of March and coworkers' (2006) experiment.

The results, shown in ● Figure 8.12, indicate that the gender labels affected the participants' memory judgments. The graph plots the source monitoring score. A score of 1.0 would be perfect source monitoring, with each statement linked to the correct name. The left pair of bars indicates that 83 percent of the masculine statements associated with the male (Chris) were correctly assigned to him, but only 65 percent of the masculine statements associated with the female (Pat) were correctly assigned to her. The right pair of bars indicates a similar result for feminine statements, which were more likely to be correctly attributed to the female (Pat) than to the male (Chris).

What this result means, according to Marsh, is that if participants didn't have a strong memory for who made a particular statement, their memory retrieval was biased by their knowledge of what "typical" males and females would say. The influence of real-world knowledge therefore resulted in source monitoring errors. In the next section we will describe a number of additional experiments that illustrate how real-world knowledge can cause memory errors. As with the experiments we have just described, many of these experiments can be related to source monitoring.

HOW REAL-WORLD KNOWLEDGE AFFECTS MEMORY

The effects of creating familiarity and of gender stereotypes on source monitoring illustrate how factors in addition to what actually happened can affect memory. We will now describe some more examples, focusing on how our knowledge of the world can affect memory.

Making Inferences Memory reports can be influenced by inferences that people make based on their experiences and knowledge. In this section, we will consider this idea further. But first, do this demonstration.

DEMONSTRATION Reading Sentences

For this demonstration, read the following sentences, pausing for a few seconds after each one.

1. The children's snowman vanished when the temperature reached 80.
2. The flimsy shelf weakened under the weight of the books.
3. The absent-minded professor didn't have his car keys.
4. The karate champion hit the cinder block.
5. The new baby stayed awake all night.

Now that you have read the sentences, turn to the "Reading Sentences" demonstration on page 237 at the end of the chapter, and follow the directions.

How do your answers from the fill-in-the-blank exercise on page 237 compare to the words in the sentences that you originally read above? William Brewer (1977) and Kathleen McDermott and Jason Chan (2006) presented participants with a similar task, involving many sentences, and found that errors occurred for about a third of the sentences. For the sentences above, the most common errors were as follows: (1) *vanished* became *melted*; (2) *weakened* became *collapsed*; (3) *didn't have* became *lost*; (4) *hit* became *broke* or *smashed*; and (5) *stayed awake* became *cried*.

These wording changes illustrate a process called **pragmatic inference**, which occurs when reading a sentence leads a person to expect something that is not explicitly stated or necessarily implied by the sentence (Brewer, 1977). These inferences are based on knowledge gained through experience. Thus, although reading that a baby stayed awake all night does not include any information about crying, knowledge about babies might lead a person to infer that the baby was crying (Chan & McDermott, 2006).

In a classic experiment that demonstrated how inference can affect memory, John Bransford and Marcia Johnson (1973) had participants read a number of action statements in the acquisition part of the experiment and then tested their memory for the statements later. Statement 1 below is one of the action statements that was read during acquisition by participants in the experimental group, and Statement 2 is one of the action statements read by participants in the control group (● Figure 8.13).

1. *Experimental Group:* John was trying to fix the birdhouse. He was pounding the nail when his father came out to watch him and help him do the work.
2. *Control Group:* John was trying to fix the birdhouse. He was looking for the nail when his father came out to watch him and help him do the work.

Both groups were then tested by presenting a number of statements that they had not seen and asking them to indicate whether they had seen them before. Statement 3 below is a test statement that went with Statements 1 and 2. Notice that this statement contains the word *hammer*, which did not appear in either of the original statements.

3. *Experimental and Control Groups:* John was using a hammer to fix the birdhouse when his father came out to watch him and help him do the work.

Participants in the experimental group said they had previously seen 57 percent of the test statements, but participants in the control group said they had previously seen only 20 percent of the test statements (remember that in reality they hadn't seen any of the test statements). In the example above, participants in the experimental group, who had read the sentence that mentioned *pounding* the nail, were more likely to be misled into thinking that the original sentence had contained the word *hammer* than

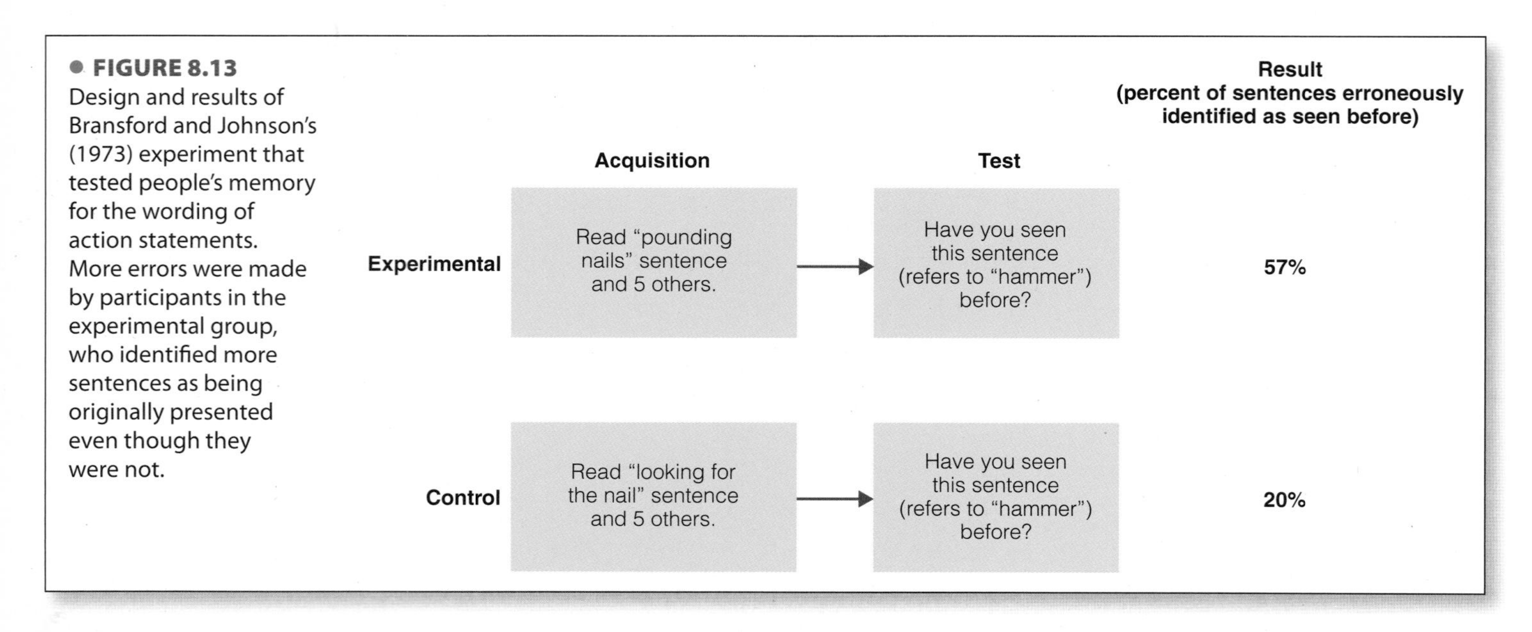

● FIGURE 8.13 Design and results of Bransford and Johnson's (1973) experiment that tested people's memory for the wording of action statements. More errors were made by participants in the experimental group, who identified more sentences as being originally presented even though they were not.

participants in the control group, who had read that John was *looking for* the nail. Apparently, the participants in the experimental group inferred, from the use of the word *pounding*, that a hammer had been used, even though it was never mentioned. This makes sense because we usually pound nails with hammers, but in this case the participant's inference has caused an error of memory (also see McDermott & Chan, 2006).

Here is the scenario used in another memory experiment, which was designed specifically to elicit inferences based on the participants' past experiences (Arkes & Freedman, 1984):

> In a baseball game, the score is tied 1 to 1. The home team has runners on first and third, with one out. A ground ball is hit to the shortstop. The shortstop throws to second base, attempting a double play. The runner who was on third scores, so it is now 2–1 in favor of the home team.

After hearing a story similar to this one, participants were asked to indicate whether the sentence "The batter was safe at first" was part of the passage. From looking at the story, you can see that this sentence was never presented, and most of the participants who didn't know much about baseball answered correctly. However, participants who knew the rules of baseball were more likely to say that the sentence had been presented. They based this judgment on their knowledge that if the runner on third had scored, then the double play must have failed, which means that the batter safely reached first. Knowledge, in this example, resulted in a correct inference about what probably happened in the ball game, but an incorrect inference about the sentence that was presented in the passage.

Scripts and Schemas The examples above illustrate how people's memory reports can be influenced by their knowledge. A schema is a person's knowledge about some aspect of the environment. For example, a person's schema of a post office might include what a post office building usually looks like from the outside, what is inside the post office, and the services it provides. We develop schemas through our experiences in different situations, such as visiting a post office, going to a ball game, or listening to lectures in a classroom.

• **FIGURE 8.14** Office in which Brewer and Treyens' (1981) participants waited before being tested on their memory for what was present in the office. (Source: Reprinted from W. F. Brewer & J. C. Treyens, "Role of Schemata in Memory for Places," *Cognitive Psychology, 13,* 207–230. Copyright 1981, with permission from Elsevier.)

In an experiment that studied how memory is influenced by people's schemas about offices, participants were seated in an office waiting to be in an experiment (• Figure 8.14). When the participants were called into another room, they were told that the experiment was actually a memory experiment, and their task was to write down what they had seen while they were sitting in the office (Brewer & Treyens, 1981). The participants responded by writing down many of the things they remembered seeing, but they also included some things that were not there but that fit into their "office schema." For example, although there were no books in the office, 30 percent of the participants reported having seen books. Thus, the information in schemas can provide a guide for making inferences about what we remember. In this particular example, the inference turned out to be wrong. Other examples of how schemas have led to erroneous decisions in memory experiments have made use of a type of schema called a script.

A script is our conception of the *sequence of actions* that usually occur during a particular experience. For example, your script for visiting a post office might include waiting in line, filling out forms if you want to send the letter by registered or certified mail, giving your letter to the post office employee, watching the employee weigh the letter and determine the postage, paying for the postage, perhaps buying some stamps for future use, and then leaving the post office.

Scripts can influence our memory by setting up expectations about what usually happens in a particular situation. To test the influence of scripts, Gordon Bower and coworkers (1979) did an experiment in which participants were asked to remember short passages like the following:

THE DENTIST

> Bill had a bad toothache. It seemed like forever before he finally arrived at the dentist's office. Bill looked around at the various dental posters on the wall. Finally the dental hygienist checked and x-rayed his teeth. He wondered what the dentist was doing. The dentist said that Bill had a lot of cavities. As soon as he'd made another appointment, he left the dentist's office.

The participants read a number of passages like this one, all of which were about familiar activities such as going to the dentist, going swimming, or going to a party. After a delay period, the participants were given the titles of the stories they had read and were told to write down what they remembered about each story as accurately as possible. The participants created stories that included much material that matched the original stories, but they also included material that wasn't presented in the original story but is part of the script for the activity described. For example, for the dentist story, some participants reported reading that "Bill checked in with the dentist's receptionist." This statement is part of most people's "going to the dentist" script, but it was not included in the original story. Thus, knowledge of the dentist script caused the participants to add information that wasn't originally presented. Another example of a link between knowledge and memory is provided by the demonstration in the next section.

CogLab
False Memory

False Recall and Recognition Try the following demonstration.

DEMONSTRATION Memory for a List

Read the following list at a rate of about one item per second, and then cover the list and write down as many of the words as possible. In order for this demonstration to work, it is important that you cover the words and write down the words you remember before reading past the demonstration.

bed, rest, awake, tired, dream
wake, night, blanket, doze, slumber
snore, pillow, peace, yawn, drowsy

Does your list of remembered words include any words that are not on the list above? This experiment was introduced by James Deese (1959) and studied further by Henry Roediger and Kathleen McDermott (1995). When I present this list to my class, there are always a substantial number of students who report that they remember the word "sleep." Remembering *sleep* is a false memory because it isn't on the list. This false memory occurs because people associate *sleep* with other words on the list. This is similar to the effect of schemas, in which people create false memories for office furnishings that aren't present because they associate these office furnishings with what is usually found in offices. Again, constructive processes have created an error in memory.

The crucial thing to take away from all of these examples is that false memories arise from the same constructive process that produces true memories. Memory, as we have seen, is not a camera or a tape recorder that creates a perfect, unchanging record of everything that happens. This constructive property of memory may actually serve us well in most situations, as described next, but it may not be such a good thing in situations such as testifying in court, which we will describe after the Test Yourself questions.

TAKING STOCK: THE PLUSES AND MINUSES OF CONSTRUCTION

The constructive property of memory reflects the creative nature of our mental processes, which enables us to do things like understand language, solve problems, and make decisions. This creativity also helps us "fill in the blanks" when there is incomplete information. For example, remember the experiment in which some participants inferred that John was using a hammer after reading that he was pounding a nail. Imagine how tiresome it would be if we had to explain everything in excruciating detail in order to know what was happening. After all, John *could* be pounding the nail into the birdhouse with a rock! Luckily, we know that a hammer is the tool that is usually used to pound nails.

Even though this creativity serves a good purpose, it sometimes results in errors of memory. These errors, plus the fact that we forget many of the things we have experienced, have led many people to wish that their memory were better—an idea that most students would agree with, especially around exam time. However, the case of the Russian memory expert Shereshevskii (S.) shows that perhaps almost-perfect memory may not be advantageous after all. After extensively studying S., the Russian psychologist Alexandria Luria (1968) concluded that S.'s memory was "virtually limitless" (though Wilding & Valentine, 1997, point out that he did occasionally make mistakes).

Although S.'s impressive memory enabled him to make a living by demonstrating his memory powers on stage, it did not seem to be very helpful in other aspects of his life. Luria described S.'s personal life as "in a haze." And when S. performed a memory feat, he had trouble forgetting what he had just remembered. His mind was like a blackboard on which everything that happened was written and couldn't be erased. Many things flit through our minds briefly, and then we don't need them again. Unfortunately for S., these things stayed there even when he wished they would go away.

S. also was not good at reasoning that involved drawing inferences or "filling in the blanks" based on partial information. We do this so often that we take it for granted, but S.'s ability to record massive amounts of information, and his inability to erase it, may have hindered his ability to do this.

A.J.'s excellent memory for personal experiences, which we described at the beginning of the chapter, differed from S.'s in that the contents that she couldn't erase were not numbers or names from memory performances, but the details of her personal life. This was both positive (recalling happy events) and negative (recalling unhappy or disturbing events). But was her memory *useful* to her in areas other than remembering life events? Apparently, she was not able to apply her powers to help her remember material for exams, as she was an average student. And testing revealed that she had impaired performance on tests that involved organizing material, thinking abstractly, and working with concepts—skills that are important for thinking creatively.

What the cases of S. and A.J. illustrate is that it is not necessarily an advantage to be able to remember everything; in fact, the mechanisms that result in superior powers of memory may work against the constructive processes that are an important characteristic not only of memory, but of our ability to think creatively. Moreover, storing everything that is experienced is an inefficient way for a system to operate because storing everything can overload the system. To avoid this "overload," our memory system is designed to selectively remember things that are particularly important to us or that occur often in our environment (Anderson & Schooler, 1991). Although the resulting system does not record everything we experience, it does operate well enough to have enabled humans to survive as a species.

One way to appreciate the survival value of the memory system is to remember our discussion in Chapter 3 of why we may erroneously perceive the object in Figure 3.24a (repeated here as ● Figure 8.15) as an animal lurking behind a tree. Our perceptual system, like our memory system, is designed to use partial information to arrive at a "best guess" solution to a perceptual problem, which is correct most of the time. Occasionally, this system comes up with an erroneous perception (see Figure 3.24b), but most of the time it provides the correct answer. The few errors we may experience are more than compensated for by a feature of our perceptual system that is

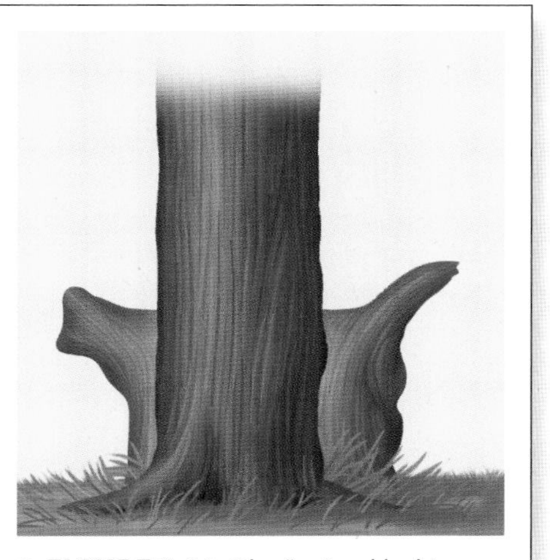

● **FIGURE 8.15** The "animal lurking behind a tree" picture from Chapter 3. This looks like an animal, but maybe it isn't one.

essential for our survival—its great speed even when faced with incomplete information. Our memory system works the same way. Although it may not come up with the correct answers every time, it usually provides us with what we need to know to function rapidly and efficiently, even though we may not always have complete information.

Memory is clearly a highly functional system that serves us well. However, sometimes the requirements of modern life create situations that humans have not been designed to handle. Consider, for example, driving a car. Evolution has not equipped our perceptual and motor systems to deal with weaving in and out of heavy traffic or driving at high rates of speed. Of course, we do these things anyway, but accidents happen. Similarly, our perceptual and memory systems have not evolved to handle demands such as providing eyewitness testimony in court. In a situation such as this, memory should ideally be perfect. After all, another person's freedom or life might be at stake. And just as car accidents happen, memory accidents happen as well. We will shortly consider what can happen when memory is put to the test in the courtroom, but first we will consider another aspect of memory that can potentially result in memory errors.

TEST YOURSELF 8.2

1. Source monitoring errors provide an example of the constructive nature of memory. Describe what source monitoring and source monitoring errors are and why they are considered "constructive." How does Bartlett's "War of the Ghosts" experiment provide an example of source monitoring errors?
2. Describe the following examples of situations that involved source monitoring errors: (a) familiarity (becoming famous experiment); (b) world knowledge (gender stereotype experiment). Be sure you can describe the experiments related to each example.
3. Describe the following examples of how memory errors can occur because of a person's knowledge of the world: (a) making inferences (pragmatic inference; "birdhouse" experiment; baseball experiment); (b) schemas and scripts (office experiment; dentist experiment); (c) false recall and recognition ("sleep" experiment).
4. What is the evidence from clinical case studies that "super memory" may have some disadvantages? What are some advantages of constructive memory?
5. Why can we say that memory is highly functional but that it may not be perfectly suited to all situations?

Memory Can Be Modified or Created by Suggestion

People are suggestible. Advertisements pitching the virtues of different products influence what people purchase. Arguments put forth by politicians, opinion makers, and friends influence how people vote. Advertisements and political arguments are examples of things that might influence a person's attitudes, beliefs, or behaviors. We will now see that information presented by others can also influence a person's memory for past events. We first consider a phenomenon called the *misinformation effect*, in which a person's memory for an event is modified by things that happen after the event has occurred.

THE MISINFORMATION EFFECT

In a typical memory experiment, a person sees or hears some stimulus, such as words, letters, or sentences, or observes pictures or a film of an event, and is asked to report what he or she experienced. But what if the experimenter were to add information that went beyond simply asking the person what he or she remembered? This is the question that Elizabeth Loftus and coworkers (1978) asked in a series of pioneering experiments that established the **misinformation effect**—misleading information presented after a person witnesses an event can change how the person describes that event later. This misleading information is referred to as **misleading postevent information**, or MPI.

METHOD Presenting Misleading Postevent Information

The usual procedure in an experiment in which misleading postevent information (MPI) is presented is to first present the stimulus to be remembered. For example, this stimulus could be a list of words or a film of an event. The MPI is then presented to one group of participants before their memory is tested and is not presented to a control group. As you will see below, MPI is often presented in a way that seems natural, so it does not occur to participants that they are being misled. We will also see, however, that even when participants are told that postevent information may be incorrect, presenting this information can still affect their memory reports. The effect of MPI is determined by comparing the memory reports of participants who received this misleading information to the memory reports of participants who did not receive it.

An experiment by Elizabeth Loftus and coworkers (1978) illustrates a typical MPI procedure. Participants saw a series of slides in which a car stops at a stop sign and then turns the corner and hits a pedestrian. Some of the participants then answered a number of questions, including "Did another car pass the red Datsun while it was stopped at the stop sign?" For another group of participants (the MPI group), the words "yield sign" replaced "stop sign" in the stop sign question. Participants were then shown pictures from the slide show plus some pictures they had never seen. Those in the MPI group were more likely to say they had seen the picture of the car stopped at the yield sign (which, in actuality, they had never seen) than were participants who had not been exposed to MPI. This shift in memory caused by MPI demonstrates the misinformation effect.

Presentation of MPI can alter not only what participants report they saw, but their conclusions about other characteristics of the situation. For example, Loftus and Steven Palmer (1974) showed participants films of a car crash (● Figure 8.16) and then asked either (1) "How fast were the cars going when they *smashed* into each other?" or (2) "How fast were the cars going when they *hit* each other?" Although both groups saw the same event, the average speed estimate by participants who heard the word "smashed" was 41 miles per hour, whereas the estimates for participants who heard "hit" was 34 miles per hour. Even more interesting for the study of memory are the participants' responses to the question "Did you see any broken glass?" which Loftus asked 1 week after they had seen the slide show. Although there was no broken glass in the original presentation, 32 percent of the participants who heard "smashed" before estimating the speed reported seeing broken glass, whereas only 14 percent of the participants who heard "hit" reported seeing the glass (see Loftus, 1993, 1998).

● **FIGURE 8.16** Participants in the Loftus and Palmer (1974) experiment saw a film of a car crash, with scenes similar to the picture shown here, and were then asked leading questions about the crash.

The misinformation effect shows not only that false memories can be created by suggestion but also provides an example of how different researchers can interpret the same data in different ways. Remember that the goal of cognitive psychology is to study mental processes, but that these mental processes must be inferred from the results of behavioral or physiological experiments. The question posed by the misinformation effect is "What is happening that changes the participants' memory reports?" Different researchers have proposed different answers to this question. We will now describe three explanations, one of which proposes that MPI replaces old memories, another that emphasizes the role of interference, and another that is based on source monitoring.

MPI as Replacing the Original Memory Loftus explains the misinformation effect by proposing the memory trace replacement hypothesis, which states that MPI impairs or replaces memories that were formed during the original experiencing of an event. According to this idea, seeing a stop sign creates a memory trace for a stop sign, but presentation of MPI that a yield sign was present causes the memory for the stop sign to be replaced by a new memory for a yield sign. The process of reconsolidation, which we described in Chapter 7 (page 197), could provide a physiological mechanism for this replacement. According to the idea of reconsolidation, reactivating a memory can create the potential for forming new memory traces.

MPI as Causing Interference Another explanation proposes that the original information is forgotten because of retroactive interference, which occurs when more recent learning (the misinformation in this example) interferes with memory for something that happened in the past (the actual event). For example, retroactive interference would be involved if studying for your Spanish exam made it more difficult to remember some of the vocabulary words you had studied for your French exam earlier in the day. This explanation is similar to the memory trace replacement hypothesis in that the new information affects the old information. However, in this case, the old information isn't eliminated; it is simply interfered with.

MPI as Causing Source Monitoring Errors Another explanation for the misinformation effect is based on the idea of source monitoring, which we discussed earlier. According to source monitoring, a person incorrectly concludes that the source of his or her memory for the incorrect event (yield sign) was the slide show, even though the actual source was the experimenter's statement after the slide show. The following experiment by Stephen Lindsay (1990) investigated source monitoring and MPI by asking whether participants who are exposed to MPI really believe they saw something that was only suggested to them. The answer to this question would be "yes" if the participant is making a source monitoring error.

Lindsay's participants first saw a sequence of slides showing a maintenance man stealing money and a computer. This slide presentation was narrated by a female speaker, who simply described what was happening as the slides were being shown. Two days later, participants returned to the lab for a memory test. Just before the test, they listened to a story, without slides, by the same female speaker. This story was similar to the one they had heard and seen 2 days earlier, but with a few details changed. For example, a pack of Marlboro cigarettes in the original became Winstons in the retelling of the story, and a can of Maxwell House coffee became Folgers.

Before the participants heard the second telling of the story, they were informed that there were some incorrect details in it, so they should ignore what they heard in the second story when taking the memory test. In the memory test, participants were asked questions such as "The man had a pack of cigarettes. What brand of cigarette was shown in the slides?" Three of the questions were about misled items, for which they had received incorrect information in the second story, and three were about control items, for which they had received correct information.

The results, shown in • Figure 8.17a, indicate that for the misled items, 27 percent of the responses corresponded to the incorrect information in the second story. This compares to only 9 percent of incorrect responses for the control items. These responses to the misled items would be source monitoring errors if the participants were confusing the information from the second story with the information from the first story.

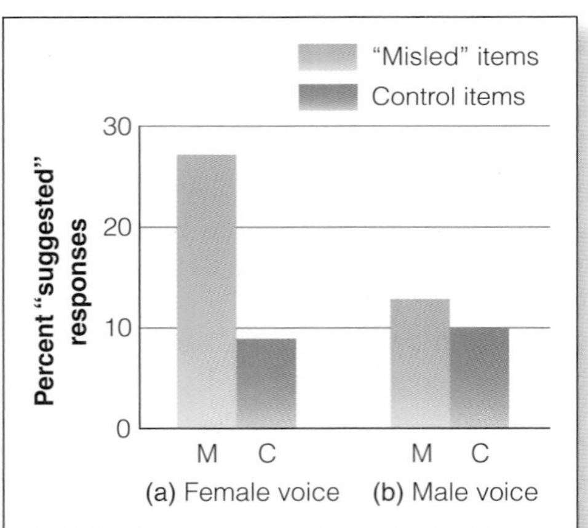

• **FIGURE 8.17** Results of Lindsay's (1990) source monitoring experiment. (a) Effect of misleading information provided by the female voice on responses to misled (M) and control (C) items. (b) There was no difference, compared to control, when the male voice presented misleading information.

The results for another group of participants, who heard a male voice tell the second story, are shown in Figure 8.17b. In this case, misled items received only 13 percent incorrect responses, which was not significantly different from the 10 percent incorrect responses for the control items. This lack of source monitoring errors occurred because the male voice was different from the female voice, so it was easier to distinguish which information came from which story. Thus, using the same female voice for both stories created source monitoring errors that led participants to believe they had seen something that they hadn't seen.

TABLE 8.2 Explanations for the Misinformation Effect

Explanation	Basic Principle
Memory trace replacement (Loftus)	MPI replaces original memory.
Retroactive interference	MPI interferes with (but does not eliminate) original memory.
Source monitoring error	MPI is mistakenly identified as what was originally experienced.

Although the mechanism that causes the misinformation effect is still being discussed by researchers, there is no doubt that the effect is real and that experimenters' suggestions can influence participants' reports in memory experiments (Table 8.2). Some of the most dramatic demonstrations of the effect of experimenter suggestion show that it can cause people to believe that events occurred early in their lives even though these events never happened.

CREATING FALSE MEMORIES FOR EARLY EVENTS IN PEOPLE'S LIVES

Ira Hyman, Jr., and coworkers (1995) created false memories for long ago events in an experiment in which they contacted the parents of their participants and asked them to provide descriptions of actual events that happened when the participants were children. The experimenters then also created descriptions of false events, ones that never happened, such as a birthday that included a clown and a pizza, and spilling a bowl of punch at a wedding reception.

Participants, who as college students were far removed from these childhood experiences, were given some of the information from the parents' descriptions and were told to elaborate on them. They were also given some of the information from the false events and were told to elaborate on them as well. The result was that 20 percent of the false events were "recalled" and described in some detail by the participants. For example, the following conversation occurred when an interviewer (I) asked a participant (P) what he remembered about a false event.

I: At age 6 you attended a wedding reception, and while you were running around with some other kids you bumped into a table and turned a punch bowl over on a parent of the bride.

P: I have no clue. I have never heard that one before. Age 6?

I: Uh-huh.

P: No clue.

I: Can you think of any details?

P: Six years old; we would have been in Spokane, um, not at all.

I: OK.

However, in a second interview that occurred 2 days later, the participant responded as follows:

I: The next one was when you were 6 years old and you were attending a wedding.

P: The wedding was my best friend in Spokane, T___. Her brother, older brother, was getting married, and it was over here in P___, Washington, 'cause that's where her family was from, and it was in the summer or the spring because it was really hot outside, and it was right on the water. It was an outdoor wedding, and I think we were running around and knocked something over like the punch bowl or something and um made a big mess and of course got yelled at for it.

I: Do you remember anything else?

P: No.

I: OK.

● **FIGURE 8.18** Photographs of a first- or second-grade class, similar to the one shown here (which shows slightly older children), were shown to participants in Lindsay et al.'s (2004) experiment.

What is most interesting about this participant's response is that he didn't remember the wedding the first time, but did remember it the second time. Apparently, hearing about the event and then waiting caused the event to emerge as a false memory. This can be explained by familiarity. When questioned about the wedding the second time, the participant's familiarity with the wedding from the first exposure caused him to accept the wedding as having actually happened. This is like Jacoby's "becoming famous overnight" experiment, in which familiarity led participants to erroneously label Sebastian Weissdorf and other nonfamous people as being famous. Both of these cases illustrate source monitoring errors because the participants attributed the source of their familiarity to something that never happened.

Recently, Stephen Lindsay and coworkers (2004) did an experiment that used the procedure described above, but with one additional twist. Participants were presented with descriptions of real childhood experiences supplied by their parents and another experience that never occurred (placing a toy called Slime, a brightly colored gelatinous compound, in their first-grade teacher's desk). Additionally, Lindsay had one group of participants look at a photograph of their first- or second-grade class, like the one in ● Figure 8.18, as they were being presented with the story about placing the slime toy in the teacher's desk. The result of this experiment was that the group of participants who saw the picture experienced more than twice as many false memories as the group who did not see the picture. There are a number of reasons this might have occurred, but the important point for our purposes is that adding the picture enhanced the false memory effect. We will return to this result in the Something to Consider section at the end of the chapter.

Why Do People Make Errors in Eyewitness Testimony?

We have seen, from the results of numerous laboratory studies, that memory is fallible. But nowhere is this fallibility more evident and significant than in the area of **eyewitness testimony**—testimony by an eyewitness to a crime about what he or she saw during commission of the crime. Eyewitness testimony is one of the most convincing types of evidence to a jury, but unfortunately many innocent people have been incarcerated based on mistaken identification by eyewitnesses. These mistaken identifications occur for a number of reasons. Some errors are caused by difficulties in perceiving a person's face and others by inaccurate memory for what was perceived. We will first look at the evidence for errors of eyewitness identification and then consider why these errors have occurred.

ERRORS OF EYEWITNESS IDENTIFICATION

In the United States, 200 people per day become criminal defendants based on eyewitness testimony (Goldstein et al., 1989). Unfortunately, there are many instances in which errors of eyewitness testimony have resulted in the conviction of innocent people. As of December 2009, the use of DNA evidence has exonerated 248 people in the United States who were wrongly convicted of crimes after serving an average of 12 years in prison (Innocence Project, 2009). Seventy-five percent of these convictions were based on eyewitness testimony (Quinlivan et al., 2009; Scheck et al., 2000).

To put a human face on the problem of wrongful convictions due to faulty eyewitness testimony, consider the case of David Webb, who was sentenced to up to 50 years in prison for rape, attempted rape, and attempted robbery based on eyewitness testimony. After serving 10 months, he was released after another man confessed to the crimes. Charles Clark went to prison for murder in 1938, based on eyewitness testimony that, 30 years later, was found to be inaccurate. He was released in 1968 (Loftus, 1979).

Ronald Cotton was convicted of raping Jennifer Thompson in 1984, based on her testimony that she was extremely positive that he was the man who raped her. Even after Cotton was exonerated by DNA evidence that implicated another man, Thompson still "remembered" Cotton as being her attacker. Cotton was released after serving 10 years (Wells & Quinlivan, 2009).

The disturbing thing about these examples is not only that they occurred, but that they suggest that many other innocent people are currently serving time for crimes they didn't commit. These miscarriages of justice and many others, some of which have undoubtedly never been discovered, are based on the assumption, made by judges and jurors, that people see and report things accurately. In essence, many people in the criminal justice system have subscribed to the erroneous idea that memory is like a camera.

We have seen from laboratory research that memory is definitely not like a camera, and research using crime scene scenarios supports this idea. A number of experiments have presented participants with films of actual crimes or staged crimes and then asked them to pick the perpetrator from a photospread (photographs of a number of faces, one of which could be the perpetrator). In one study, participants viewed a security videotape in which a gunman was in view for 8 seconds and then were asked to pick the gunman from photographs. Every participant picked someone they thought was the gunman, even though his picture was not included in the photospread (Wells & Bradfield, 1998). In another study, using a similar experimental design, 61 percent of the participants picked someone from a photospread, even though the perpetrator's picture wasn't included (Kneller et al., 2001).

These studies show how difficult it is to accurately identify someone after viewing a videotape of a crime. But things become even more complicated when we consider some of the things that happen during actual crimes.

THE CRIME SCENE AND AFTERWARD

Even under ideal conditions, identifying faces is a difficult task and errors occur (Henderson et al., 2001). But other factors can intervene to make the task even more difficult.

Errors Associated with Attention Emotions often run high during commission of a crime, and this can affect what a person pays attention to and what the person remembers later. One important example of how attention can affect a witness's access to relevant information is **weapons focus**. The tendency to focus attention on a weapon results in a narrowing of attention, so witnesses might miss seeing relevant information such as the perpetrator's face.

Claudia Stanny and Thomas Johnson (2000) studied weapons focus by measuring how well participants remembered details of a filmed simulated crime. They found that participants were more likely to recall details of the perpetrator, the victim, and the weapon in the "no-shoot" condition (a gun was present but not fired) than

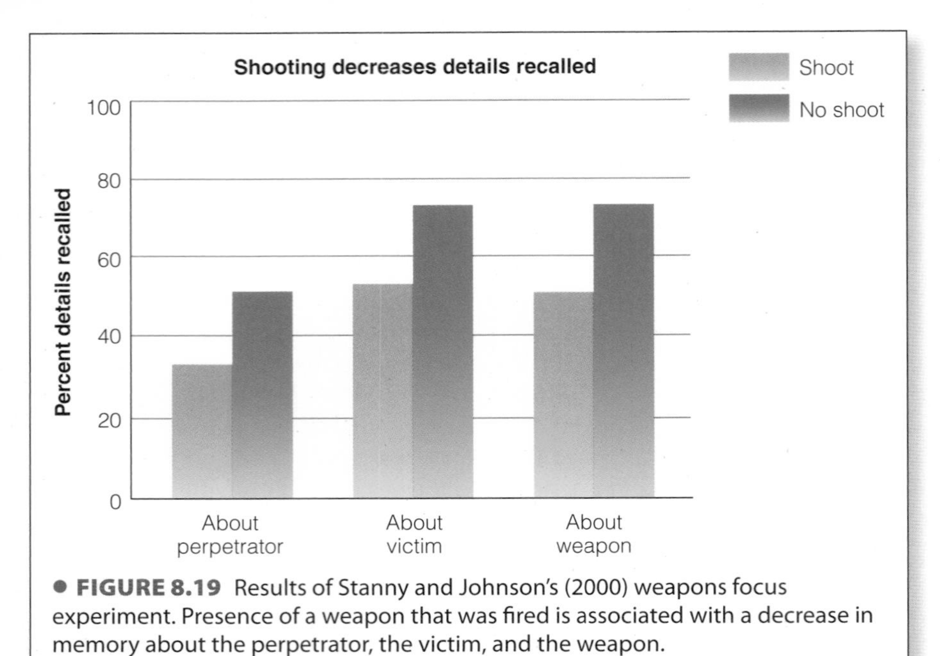

● **FIGURE 8.19** Results of Stanny and Johnson's (2000) weapons focus experiment. Presence of a weapon that was fired is associated with a decrease in memory about the perpetrator, the victim, and the weapon.

in the "shoot" condition (the gun was fired; ● Figure 8.19). Apparently, the presence of a weapon that was fired distracted attention from other things that were happening (also see Tooley et al., 1987).

Another explanation for the narrowing of attention caused by the weapons focus effect is that unusual objects attract attention. This idea is supported by an experiment by Kerri Pickel (2009), who found that people's ability to describe the perpetrator of a staged crime was affected more by the presence of a weapon if the perpetrator was female rather than male. Pickel relates this result to her participants' reporting it would be less likely for a woman to be carrying a gun than for a man to be carrying a gun. Whatever mechanism is responsible for the weapons focus effect (high arousal or unusualness, or both), the presence of weapons does attract attention and impair the ability to describe or identify perpetrators.

Errors Due to Familiarity Crimes not only involve a perpetrator and a victim, but often include innocent bystanders (some of whom, as we will see, may not even be near the scene of the crime). These bystanders add yet another dimension to the testimony of eyewitnesses because there is a chance that a bystander could be mistakenly identified as a perpetrator because of familiarity from some other context. A real-life example of misidentification based on familiarity is the case of Donald Thompson, a memory researcher who was talking about memory errors on a TV program at exactly the time that a woman was attacked in her home. The woman, who had been watching Thompson on the program, subsequently implicated Thompson as the person who had raped her, based on her memory for his face. Of course, Thompson had a perfect alibi because he was in the TV studio at the time of the crime (Schacter, 2001).

In another case, a ticket agent at a railway station was robbed and subsequently identified a sailor as being the robber. Luckily for the sailor, he was able to show that he was somewhere else at the time of the crime. When asked why he identified the sailor, the ticket agent said that he looked familiar. The sailor looked familiar not because he was the robber, but because he lived near the train station and had purchased tickets from the agent on a number of occasions. This was an example of a source monitoring error. The ticket agent thought the source of his familiarity with the sailor was seeing him during the holdup; in reality, the source of his familiarity was seeing him when he purchased tickets. The sailor had become transformed from a ticket buyer into a holdup man by the source monitoring error (Ross et al., 1994).

● Figure 8.20a shows the design for a laboratory experiment on familiarity and eyewitness testimony (Ross et al., 1994). Participants in the experimental group saw a film of a male teacher reading to students, and participants in the control group saw a film of a female teacher reading to students. Participants in both groups then saw a film of the female teacher getting robbed and were asked to pick the robber from a photospread. The photographs did not include the actual robber, but did include the male teacher, who resembled the robber. The results indicate that participants in the experimental group were three times more likely to pick the male teacher than were participants in the control group (Figure 8.20b). Even when the actual robber's face was included in the photospread, 18 percent of participants in the experimental group picked the teacher, compared to 10 percent in the control group (Figure 8.20c).

Errors Due to Suggestion From what we know about the misinformation effect, it is obvious that a police officer asking a witness "Did you see the white car?" could influence the witness's later testimony about what he or she saw. But suggestibility can also

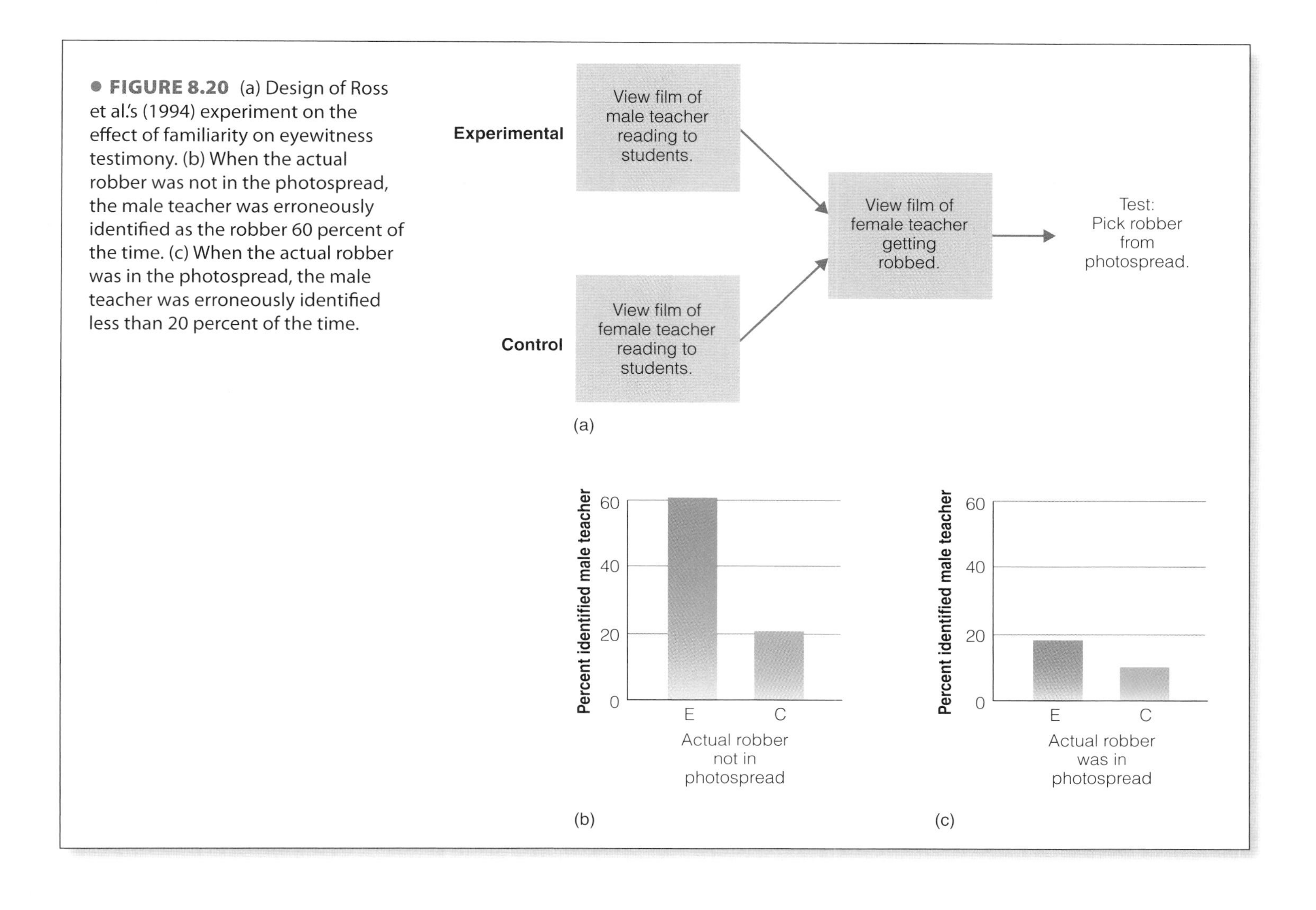

● **FIGURE 8.20** (a) Design of Ross et al.'s (1994) experiment on the effect of familiarity on eyewitness testimony. (b) When the actual robber was not in the photospread, the male teacher was erroneously identified as the robber 60 percent of the time. (c) When the actual robber was in the photospread, the male teacher was erroneously identified less than 20 percent of the time.

operate on a more subtle level. Consider the following situation. A witness to a crime is looking through a one-way window at a lineup of six men standing on a stage. The police officer says, "Which one of these men did it?" What is wrong with this question?

The problem with the police officer's question is that it carries the implication that the crime perpetrator is in the lineup. This suggestion increases the chances that the witness will pick someone, perhaps using the following type of reasoning: "Well, the guy with the beard looks more like the robber than any of the other men, so that's probably the one." Of course, looking *like* the robber and actually *being* the robber may be two different things, so the result may be identification of an innocent man. A better way of presenting the task is to let the witness know that the crime suspect may or may not be in the lineup.

Here is another situation, taken from a transcript of an actual criminal case, in which suggestion could have played a role.

> Eyewitness to a crime on viewing a lineup: "Oh, my God.... I don't know.... It's one of those two...but I don't know....Oh, man...the guy a little bit taller than number two.... It's one of those two, but I don't know."
>
> Eyewitness 30 minutes later, still viewing the lineup and having difficulty making a decision: "I don't know...number two?"
>
> Officer administering lineup: "Okay."
>
> Months later...at trial: "You were positive it was number two? It wasn't a maybe?"
>
> Answer from eyewitness: "There was no maybe about it.... I was absolutely positive." (Wells & Bradfield, 1998)

The problem with this scenario is that the police officer's response of "okay" may have influenced the witness to think that he or she had correctly identified the suspect. Thus, the

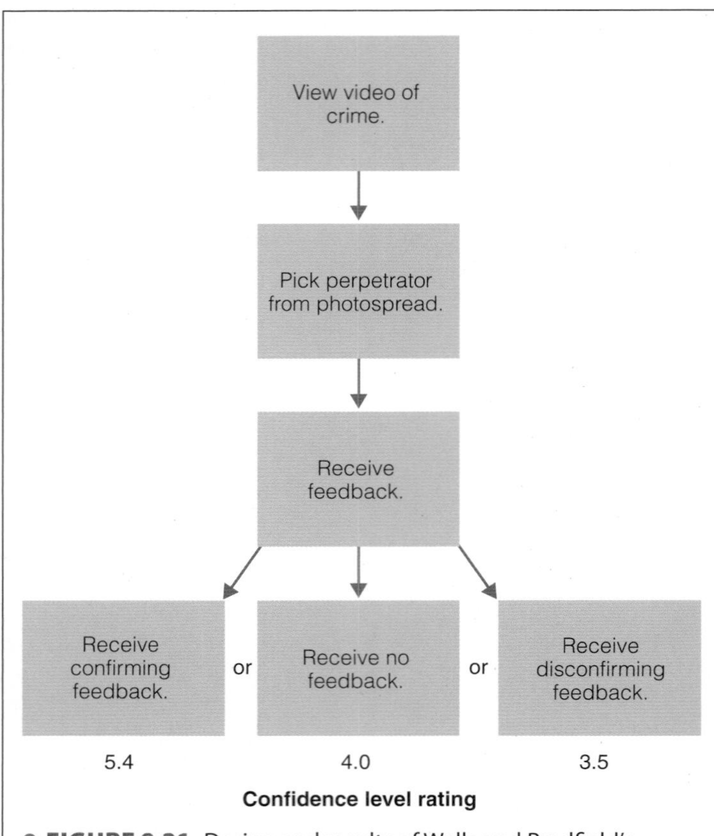

● **FIGURE 8.21** Design and results of Wells and Bradfield's (1998) "Good, You Identified the Suspect" experiment. The type of feedback from the experimenter influenced participants' confidence in their identification, with confirming feedback resulting in the highest confidence.

witness's initially uncertain response turns into an "absolutely positive" response. In a paper titled "Good, You Identified the Suspect," Gary Wells and Amy Bradfield (1998) had participants view a video of an actual crime and then asked them to identify the perpetrator from a photospread that did not actually contain a picture of the perpetrator (● Figure 8.21).

All of the participants picked one of the photographs, and following their choice, witnesses received either confirming feedback from the experimenter ("Good, you identified the suspect"), no feedback, or disconfirming feedback ("Actually, the suspect was number __"). A short time later, the participants were asked how confident they were about their identification. The results, shown at the bottom of the figure, indicate that participants who received the confirming feedback were more confident of their choice.

Wells and Bradfield call this increase in confidence due to confirming feedback after making an identification the **post-identification feedback effect**. This effect creates a serious problem in the criminal justice system, because jurors are strongly influenced by how confident eyewitnesses are about their judgments. Thus, faulty eyewitness judgments can result in picking the wrong person, and the post-identification feedback effect can increase witnesses' confidence that they made the right judgment (Douglass et al., 2009; Quinlivan et al., 2009; Wells & Quinlivan, 2009).

The Effect of Postevent Questioning Wells and Bradfield showed that postevent feedback can strengthen witnesses' confidence in their lineup identification. We will now describe an experiment by Jason Chan and coworkers (2009) that considers a related question: How does taking a recall test after witnessing an event and before being exposed to misleading postevent information influence memory for the event? The design of this experiment is shown in ● Figure 8.22. Participants first viewed a 40-minute episode of the television program *24*, in which Jack Bauer, played by Kiefer Sutherland, is trying to thwart a terrorist plot. The participants were then split into two groups. The *test group* took a cued recall test about the video, which contained questions like "What did the terrorist use to knock out the flight attendant?" (correct answers were not provided). The *no-test group* played a computer game. Both groups were then given distraction tasks, such as filling out a questionnaire and completing some tests unrelated to the TV program.

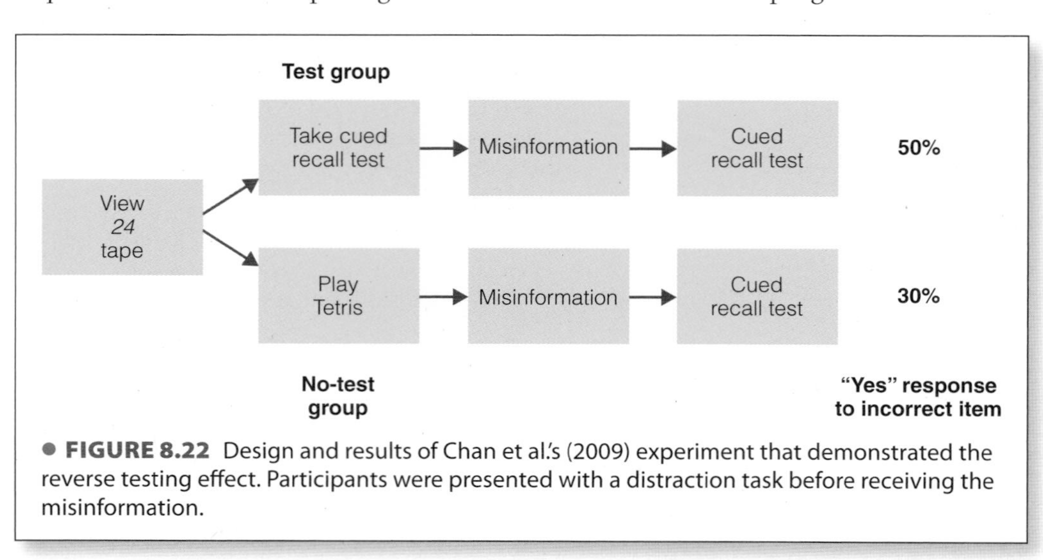

● **FIGURE 8.22** Design and results of Chan et al.'s (2009) experiment that demonstrated the reverse testing effect. Participants were presented with a distraction task before receiving the misinformation.

If the participants in both groups had been tested on their knowledge of the video at this point, which group do you think would remember more? Although this was not determined in the experiment, it is likely that the test group would have remembered more because of the practice provided by being tested. This is what we would predict based on the results of experiments on the *testing effect* described in Chapter 7 (page 180), which showed that taking tests after studying material increases memory for that material.

Instead of testing participants at this point, Chan presented an 8-minute audio that described some of the events in the TV program. Some events were described accurately, but some *misinformation items* differed from what happened in the video. For example, in the video the terrorist knocked out the flight attendant with a hypodermic syringe, but the misinformation item in the audio stated that the terrorist used a chloroform pad. The procedure in this part of the experiment is therefore similar to the procedure in the misinformation studies we described earlier. Finally, all participants took the cued recall test (the same one that the test group had taken earlier).

Imagine that you are one of the experimenters waiting for the results of the recall test. Which group would you predict would do better on the recall test—the test group or the no-test group? Stop for a moment and think about this before reading further.

Did you come up with an answer? Using common sense, and perhaps your knowledge of the testing effect, your answer might be that the test group, which took the recall test before being exposed to the misleading information, would perform better. However, the result, shown on the right, indicates that the opposite occurred. The number indicates the percentage of incorrectly described items (the misinformation items) from the video that participants indicated were in the original program. The test group said "yes" incorrectly to 50 percent of these items, compared to 30 percent for the no-test group.

This result, which Chan calls the **reverse testing effect**, shows that taking a recall test right after seeing the program increased participants' sensitivity to the misinformation. There are a number of possible reasons for this result. One reason is related to the reconsolidation effect we described in Chapter 7 (page 195). Remember that reactivating a memory can make it susceptible to being eliminated or modified. This can strengthen memories if the person is exposed to correct information (as might occur when reviewing information as you study for an exam), but it can distort memory if the person is exposed to different information (as occurs in the misinformation procedure).

According to this idea, testing that reactivates memory for an event makes the memory vulnerable to change. This mechanism would explain Chan's result, and may also help explain the experiment by Lindsay, in which participants who looked at a picture of their grade school class were more likely to be influenced by misinformation (see page 226). Perhaps when Lindsay's participants looked at the class picture, their memories were reactivated and so became more vulnerable to being affected by misinformation. (Review the description of Hupbach et al.'s experiment described on page 197 in Chapter 7. Can you see the parallel between the Hupbach experiment and this explanation of Lindsay's result?)

Chan also describes other possible mechanisms, but the main point for our purposes is that this effect occurs. The main reason this effect is important is that after witnessing a crime the witness is typically questioned about it, either at the scene or afterwards. This is, of course, necessary, but according to the results of Chan's experiment, thinking about this information makes it vulnerable to being changed by suggestion, misinformation, or other postevent experiences.

WHAT IS BEING DONE?

The first step toward correcting the problem of inaccurate eyewitness testimony is to recognize that the problem exists. This has been achieved, largely through the efforts of memory researchers and attorneys and investigators for unjustly convicted people. The next step is to propose specific solutions. Cognitive psychologists have made the following suggestions:

1. *When asking a witness to pick the perpetrator from a lineup, inform the witness that the perpetrator may not be in the particular lineup he or she is viewing.* As we have seen from the results of a number of studies, witnesses will usually pick

a person from a lineup even when the perpetrator is not present. When a witness assumes the perpetrator is in the lineup, this increases the chances that an innocent person who looks similar to the perpetrator will be selected. In one experiment, telling participants that the perpetrator may not be present in a lineup caused a 42 percent decrease in false identifications of innocent people (Malpass & Devine, 1981).

2. *When constructing a lineup, use "fillers" who are similar to the suspect.* Police investigators are reluctant to increase the similarity of people in lineups because they are afraid this will decrease the chances of identifying the suspect. However, when R. C. L. Lindsay and Gary Wells (1980) had participants view a tape of a crime scene and then tested them using high-similarity and low-similarity lineups, they obtained the results shown in ● Figure 8.23. Figure 8.23a shows that when the perpetrator was in the lineup, increasing similarity did decrease identification of the perpetrator, from 0.71 to 0.58. However, Figure 8.23b shows that when the perpetrator was not in the lineup, increasing similarity caused a large decrease in incorrect identification of an innocent person, from 0.70 to 0.31. Thus, increasing similarity does result in missed identification of some guilty suspects, but substantially reduces the erroneous identification of innocent people, when the perpetrator is not in the lineup.

3. *When presenting a lineup, use sequential rather than simultaneous presentation.* The usual depiction of lineups in movies—and the one most often used in police work—is 5 or 6 people standing in a line facing the witness, who is hidden behind a one-way window. The problem with this way of presenting a lineup is that it increases the chances that the witness will make a relative judgment—comparing people in the lineup to each other, so the question is "Who is most like the person I saw?" However, when each person in the lineup is presented sequentially—one at a time—then the witness compares each person not to the other people, but to the memory of what the witness saw. Lindsay and Wells (1985) found that for lineups in which the perpetrator was not present, an innocent person was falsely identified 43 percent of the time in the simultaneous lineup, but only 17 percent of the time in the sequential lineup. The beauty of the sequential lineup is that it does not decrease the chances of identifying the suspect when he or she is included in the lineup.

4. *Use a "blind" lineup administrator and get an immediate confidence rating.* When presenting a lineup, the person administering the lineup should not know who the suspect is. In addition, having witnesses immediately rate their confidence in their choice eliminates the possibility that the postevent feedback effect could increase their confidence.

5. *Improve interviewing techniques.* We have already seen that making suggestions to the witness ("Good, you identified the suspect") can cause errors. Cognitive psychologists have developed an interview procedure called the **cognitive interview**, which is based on what is known about memory retrieval. This interview procedure involves letting the witness talk with a minimum of interruption and also uses techniques that help witnesses recreate the situation present at the crime scene by having them place themselves back in the scene and recreate things like emotions they were feeling, where they were looking, and how the scene may have appeared when viewed from different perspectives. Comparisons of the results of cognitive interviews to routine police questioning have shown that the cognitive interview results in 25–60 percent more information than the usual police interview (Fisher et al., 1989; Geiselman et al., 1985, 1986).

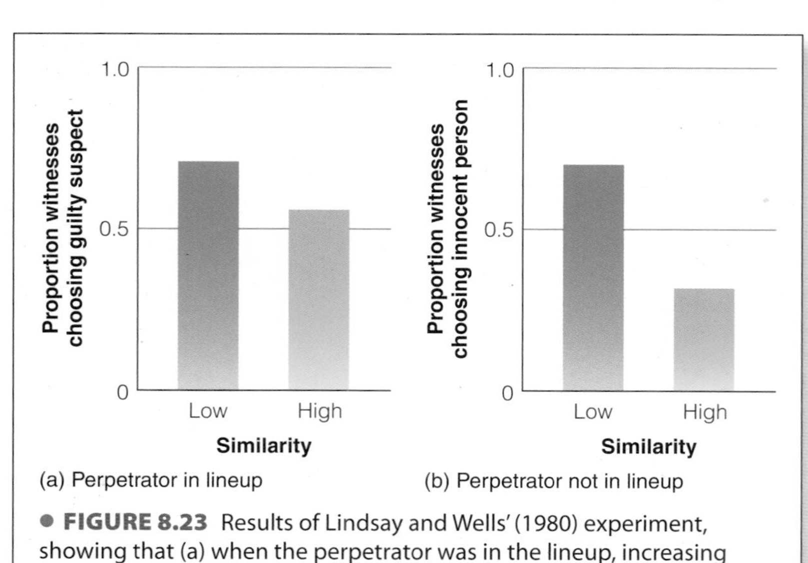

● **FIGURE 8.23** Results of Lindsay and Wells' (1980) experiment, showing that (a) when the perpetrator was in the lineup, increasing similarity decreased identification of the perpetrator, but (b) when the perpetrator was not in the lineup, increasing similarity caused an even greater decrease in incorrect identification of innocent people.

Recommendations like those described above led to the publication in 1999 of *Eyewitness Evidence: A Guide for Law Enforcement* by the U.S. Justice

Department (available at http://www.ojp.usdoj.gov/nij/pubs-sum/178240.htm), which includes many of these suggestions, plus others. One thing that is striking about these recommendations is that they are the direct outcome of psychological research. Thus, whereas one goal of cognitive psychology research is to determine basic mechanisms of memory, this research often has practical implications as well.

Something to Consider

CogLab
Forgot It All Along Effect

MEMORIES OF CHILDHOOD ABUSE

Eileen Lipsker was 28 years old in 1989 when, as she watched her young red-haired daughter draw pictures in their family room, she suddenly remembered a similar scene from 20 years earlier when, as an 8-year-old, she was playing with her red-haired friend Susan. This memory ended with the image of Eileen's father, George Franklin, raping and murdering her friend. Later, during therapy, memories surfaced of her father sexually abusing her (Terr, 1994). Based on these reports, George Franklin was convicted of first-degree murder in 1990 and was sentenced to life in prison.

This case is just one of many that began surfacing in the 1980s that shared a common theme: A memory of being abused or witnessing abuse appeared after many years of having no memory of these events, and a family member was accused and convicted based solely on the reported memory. Later, in some of the cases, it was determined that the abuse did not, in fact, happen. This was the outcome for George Franklin, whose conviction was later overturned on appeal.

How could this happen? One answer is suggested by the following scenario: Patient X enters therapy for an eating disorder and depression. The therapist believes that symptoms such as eating disorders and depression are caused by childhood sexual abuse that has been pushed out of memory (Blume, 1990; Fredrickson, 1992). This therapist, who belongs to a group of therapists that memory researchers have identified as "trauma-memory oriented therapists," tells the patient that memories of abuse can be buried—pushed out of consciousness because of their painful nature—and suggests trying some visualization exercises to help unlock this lost memory. In some cases, the therapist might ask the patient to obtain childhood family pictures because sometimes viewing them helps retrieve these memories.

From what you know about the possibility that memories can be created by suggestion, it is easy to see that the situation described above could provide powerful suggestions, which could lead the creation of a false memory for abuse. As we saw from the description of Lindsay et al.'s (2004) experiment on page 226, having the patient view pictures can further enhance the possibility of creating false memories.

Of course, it is also possible that the patient was abused, and that he or she is remembering something that actually happened. The incidence of childhood sexual abuse in the United States is shockingly high, with millions of people affected. Elizabeth Loftus (1993), a memory researcher who has extensively studied cases of memory of childhood sexual abuse, points out that the question is not whether childhood sexual abuse occurs, but how abuse is recalled by adults. She warns that uncritically accepting all allegations of abuse "no matter how dubious" could "lead to an increased likelihood that society in general will disbelieve the genuine cases of childhood sexual abuse that truly deserve our sustained attention" (p. 534).

Although research is being done toward being able to determine, by measuring brain activity, whether a memory is real or false (Schacter & Slotnick, 2004; Sederberg et al., 2007), at this point there is no test or procedure that can accurately differentiate between real memories and false memories. But given what we do know about memory, it is important to take into account the specific situation under which memories for long ago events are elicited. Thus, it is important to keep in mind the seriousness and high prevalence of abuse, but also not to lose sight of the possibility that memory can be created by suggestion.

TEST YOURSELF 8.3

1. Experiments showing that memory can be affected by suggestion have led to the proposal of the misinformation effect. How has the misinformation effect been demonstrated, and what mechanisms have been proposed to explain this effect?
2. How has it been shown that suggestion can influence people's memories for early events in their lives?
3. What is the evidence, both from "real life" and from laboratory experiments, that eyewitness testimony is not always accurate? Describe how the following factors have been shown to lead to errors in eyewitness testimony: weapons focus, familiarity, leading questions, feedback from a police officer, and postevent questioning.
4. What procedures have cognitive psychologists proposed to increase the accuracy of eyewitness testimony?
5. How does the suggestibility of memory pose problems for situations in which adults, during therapy, remember having been abused as children?

CHAPTER SUMMARY

1. A.J. is an example of someone with exceptional memory for personal events; normally, however, people remember some things about their lives and forget other things.
2. Autobiographical memory (AM) has been defined as recollected events that belong to a person's past. It consists of both episodic and semantic components, with episodic components more likely to be present for memories of more recent events.
3. The multidimensional nature of AM has been studied by showing that people who have lost their visual memory due to brain damage experience a loss of AM. Also supporting the multidimensional nature of AM is Cabeza's experiment, which showed that a person's brain is more extensively activated when viewing photographs taken by the person him- or herself than when viewing photographs taken by someone else.
4. When people are asked to remember events over their lifetime, transition points are particularly memorable. Also, people over 40 tend to have good memory for events they experienced from adolescence to early adulthood. This is called the reminiscence bump.
5. The following hypotheses have been proposed to explain the reminiscence bump: (a) self-image, (b) cognitive, and (c) cultural life script.
6. Emotions are often associated with events that are easily remembered. The link between emotions and memory has been demonstrated behaviorally and physiologically. The amygdala is a key structure for emotional memories.
7. Brown and Kulik proposed the term *flashbulb memory* to refer to a person's memory for the circumstances surrounding hearing about shocking, highly charged events. They proposed that these flashbulb memories are vivid and detailed, like photographs.
8. A number of experiments indicate that it is not accurate to equate flashbulb memories with photographs because, as time passes, people make many errors when reporting flashbulb memories. Studies of memories for hearing about the *Challenger* explosion showed that people's responses became more inaccurate with increasing time after the event.
9. Talarico and Rubin's study of people's memory for when they first heard about the 9/11 terrorist attack indicates that memory errors increased with time, just as for other memories, but that people remained more confident of the accuracy of their 9/11 memory. Another 9/11 study, by Davidson and coworkers, also showed that memory for 9/11 declined with time, but found that people had better memory for the events surrounding 9/11 than for another, more ordinary event that had occurred at the same time. The difference in these results might be explained by differences in the procedures used in these two experiments.
10. According to the constructive approach to memory, originally proposed by Bartlett based on his "War of the Ghosts" experiment, what people report as memories are constructed based on what actually happened plus additional factors such as the person's knowledge, experiences, and expectations.
11. Source monitoring is the process of determining the origins of our memories, knowledge, or beliefs. A source monitoring error occurs when the source of a memory is misidentified. Cryptomnesia (unconscious plagiarism) is an example of a source monitoring error.
12. Familiarity (Jacoby's "becoming famous overnight" experiment) and world knowledge (Marsh's gender stereotype experiment) can result in source monitoring errors.

13. General world knowledge can cause memory errors. Inference is one of the mechanisms of the constructive process of memory. The following show that inference based on world knowledge can cause memory errors: (a) pragmatic inference, (b) Bransford and Johnson's "pounding nail" experiment, and (c) the baseball story experiment.
14. Our knowledge about what is involved in a particular experience is a schema for that experience. The experiment in which participants were asked to remember what was in an office illustrates how schemas can cause errors in memory reports.
15. A script is our conception of the sequence of actions that usually occur during a particular experience. The "dentist experiment," in which a participant is asked to remember a paragraph about going to the dentist, illustrates how scripts can result in memory errors.
16. The experiment in which people were asked to recall a list of words related to sleep illustrates how our knowledge about things that belong together (for example, that *sleep* belongs with *bed*) can result in reporting words that were not on the original list.
17. Although people often think that it would be an advantage to have a photographic memory, the cases of S. and A.J. show that it may not be an advantage to be able to remember everything perfectly. The fact that our memory system does not store everything may even add to the survival value of the system.
18. Memory experiments in which misleading postevent information (MPI) is presented to participants indicate that memory can be influenced by suggestion. An example is Loftus's traffic accident experiment. The following explanations have been proposed to explain the errors caused by misleading postevent information: (a) memory trace replacement hypothesis, (b) effect of retroactive interference, and (c) effect of source monitoring errors. Lindsay's experiment provides support for the source monitoring explanation, but the reasons for the effect of MPI are still being debated by memory researchers.
19. An experiment by Hyman, in which he created false memories for a party, showed that it is possible to create false memories for early events in a person's life. A similar experiment by Lindsay showed that this false memory effect for early events can be made stronger by showing the participants a picture of their first- or second-grade class.
20. There is a great deal of evidence that eyewitness testimony about crimes can be prone to memory errors. Some of the reasons for errors in eyewitness testimony are (a) not paying attention to all relevant details, because of the emotional situation during a crime (weapons focus is one example of such an attentional effect); (b) errors due to familiarity, which can result in misidentification of an innocent person due to source monitoring error; (c) errors due to suggestion during questioning about a crime (the "Good, you identified the suspect" experiment illustrates how a police officer's responses can cause memory errors); (d) increased confidence due to postevent feedback (the post-identification feedback effect); and (e) postevent questioning (the reverse testing effect).
21. Cognitive psychologists have suggested a number of ways to decrease errors in eyewitness testimony.
22. The problem of childhood sexual abuse is serious and widespread. There is the potential, however, that false memories for abuse can be created by some of the techniques used by therapists to try to help patients remember events in their past. The problem of differentiating between accurate memories of abuse and false memories created in the therapy situation is a serious one because there is no test or procedure that can accurately differentiate between real memories and false memories.

Think ABOUT IT

1. What do you remember about how you heard about the terrorist attacks of September 11, 2001? How confident are you that your memory of these events is accurate? Given the results of experiments on flashbulb memories described in this chapter, what do you think the chances are that your memories might be in error? Are there any ways that you could check the accuracy of your memories?
2. What do you remember about what you did on the most recent major holiday (Thanksgiving, Christmas, New Year's, your birthday, etc.)? What do you remember about what you did on the same holiday 1 year earlier? How do these memories differ in terms of (a) how difficult they were to remember, (b) how much detail you can remember, and (c) the accuracy of your memory? (How would you know if your answer to part c is correct?)
3. There have been a large number of reports of people unjustly imprisoned because of errors in eyewitness testimony, with more cases being reported every day, based on DNA evidence. Given this situation, how would you react to the proposal that eyewitness testimony no longer be admitted as evidence in courts of law?
4. Interview people of different ages regarding what they remember about their lives. How do your results fit with the results of AM experiments, especially regarding the idea of a reminiscence bump in older people?
5. The process of reconsolidation was discussed at the end of Chapter 7. How might this idea provide a physiological explanation for the effects of suggestibility on memory that we discussed in this chapter?

If You WANT TO KNOW MORE

1. **True and false memories in the brain.** Can we distinguish between true and false memories by looking at activity in the brain? One idea, called the sensory reactivation hypothesis, is that true memories involve activation of sensory areas that were activated when the original memory was formed.

   Schacter, D. L., & Slotnick, S. D. (2004). The cognitive neuroscience of memory distortion. *Neuron, 44*, 149–160.

   Sederberg, P. B., et al. (2007). Gamma oscillations distinguish true from false memories. *Psychological Science, 18*, 927–932.

   Wheeler, M. E., & Buckner, R. L. (2004). Functional-anatomic correlates of remembering and knowing. *NeuroImage, 21*, 1337–1349.

   Wheeler, M. E., Petersen, S. E., & Buckner, R. L. (2000). Memory's echo: Vivid remembering reactivates sensory-specific cortex. *Proceedings of the National Academy of Sciences, 97*, 11125–11129.

2. **Social influence, source monitoring and the misinformation effect.** Source monitoring and the misinformation effect can be influenced by social factors.

   Assefi, S. L., & Garry, M. (2003). Absolut® memory distortions: Alcohol placebos influence the misinformation effect. *Psychological Science, 14*, 77–80.

   Hoffman, H. G., Granhag, P. A., See, S. T. K., & Loftus, E. F. (2001). Social influences on reality-monitoring decisions. *Memory and Cognition, 29*, 394–404.

3. **Memory distortions caused by personal bias.** In a very readable book, Daniel Schacter describes a number of ways that memory can be distorted. In one chapter he discusses how memory can be distorted by biases related to personal and social factors, such as how people perceive themselves and how they think about events in their lives.

   Schacter, D. L. (2001). *The seven sins of memory.* New York: Houghton Mifflin.

4. **Confabulation.** People with damage to their frontal lobes often engage in a process called confabulation, which involves making outlandish false statements. One characteristic of confabulation is that the person believes that even the most impossible-sounding statements are true. It has been suggested that this may tell us something about the role of the frontal lobes in normal memory.

   Moscovitch, M. (1995). Confabulation. In D. L. Schacter (Ed.), *Memory distortion* (pp. 226–251). Cambridge, MA: Harvard University Press.

5. **Mechanisms of the misinformation effect.** The chapter you just read reviews three ideas about the mechanisms responsible for the misinformation effect. This paper presents another idea, which argues against the memory trace replacement hypothesis.

   McCloskey, M., & Zaragoza, Z. (1985). Misleading postevent information and memory for events: Arguments and evidence against memory impairment hypothesis. *Journal of Experimental Psychology: General, 114*, 3–18.

6. **Suggestibility in children.** We have seen that adults can be influenced by suggestion. Young children pose additional problems, especially when they are called on to present testimony in court.

   Bruck, M., Ceci, S. J., & Hembrooke, H. (2002). The nature of children's true and false narratives. *Developmental Review, 22*, 520–554.

   Principe, G. F., Kanaya, T., Ceci, S. J., & Singh, M. (2006). Believing is seeing: How rumors can engender false memories in preschoolers. *Psychological Science, 17*, 243–248.

7. **The Moses illusion.** The Moses illusion occurs when people answer "two" to the question "How many animals of each kind did Moses take on the ark?" even though they know that Noah was the one with the ark. A number of different hypotheses have been proposed to explain this effect.

   Park, H., & Reder, L. M. (2004). Moses illusion: Implications for human cognition. In R. F. Pohl (Ed.), *Cognitive illusions* (pp. 275–291). Hove, UK: Psychology Press.

8. **Memory distortions in coerced false confessions.** Some people who confess to crimes they did not commit come to believe that they did commit the crime and can even create vivid memories of the crime. The following paper describes this striking phenomenon in terms of source monitoring.

   Henkel, L. A., & Coffman, K. J. (2004). Memory distortions in coerced false confessions: A source monitoring framework analysis. *Applied Cognitive Psychology, 10*, 567–588.

Key TERMS

Amygdala, 208
Autobiographical memory (AM), 205
Cognitive hypothesis, 207
Cognitive interview, 232
Constructive nature of memory, 213
Cryptomnesia, 215
Cultural life script, 207
Cultural life script hypothesis, 207
Eyewitness testimony, 226
Flashbulb memory, 209
Memory trace replacement hypothesis, 224
Misinformation effect, 222
Misleading postevent information (MPI), 222

Media RESOURCES

The *Cognitive Psychology* Book Companion Website

www.cengage.com/international

Prepare for quizzes and exams with online resources—including a glossary, flashcards, tutorial quizzes, crossword puzzles, and more.

CogLab

To experience these experiments for yourself, go to coglab.wadsworth.com. Be sure to read each experiment's setup instructions before you go to the experiment itself. Otherwise, you won't know which keys to press.

Primary Labs

Remember/know Distinguishing between remembered items in which there is memory for learning the item and items that just seem familiar (p. 214).

False memory How memory for words on a list sometimes occurs for words that were not presented (p. 220).

Forgot it all along effect How it is possible to remember something and also have the experience of having previously forgotten it (p. 233).

DEMONSTRATION Reading Sentences (continued from page 217)

The sentences below are the ones you read in the demonstration on page 217 but with one or two words missing. Without looking back at the original sentences, fill in the blanks with the words that were in the sentence you initially read.

The flimsy shelf _____ under the weight of the books.
The children's snowman _____ when the temperature reached 80.
The absent-minded professor _____ his car keys.
The new baby _____ all night.
The karate champion _____ the cinder block.

After doing this, turn to page 218 and read the text beginning at the top of the page.

9 Knowledge

Our ability to categorize some of these animals as "cats" and some as "dogs" helps us know which ones are more likely to fetch a thrown ball and which ones might rub up against a person's leg while purring. Research on how people place objects into categories such as "cat" or "dog"—and also more specifically, "Siamese" or "beagle"—is important for understanding how knowledge about the world is represented in the mind.

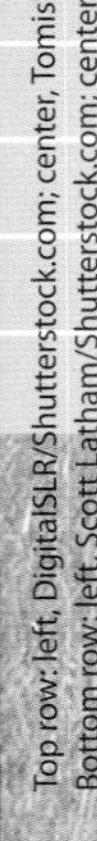
Top row: left, DigitalSLR/Shutterstock.com; center, Tomislav Stajduhar/Shutterstock.com; right, Gladkova Svetlana/Shutterstock.com. Center row: left, Patrick Lecarpentier/Shutterstock.com; center and right, Bruce Goldstein.
Bottom row: left, Scott Latham/Shutterstock.com; center, Bruce Goldstein; right, Tamara Bauer/iStockPhoto.com.

SOME QUESTIONS WE WILL CONSIDER

- Why is it difficult to decide if a particular object belongs to a particular category, such as "chair," by looking up its definition? (241)
- How are the properties of various objects "filed away" in the mind? (243, 256)
- How is information about different categories stored in the brain? (260)
- Can young infants respond to the categories "cat" and "dog"? (263)

IMAGINE THAT YOU FIND YOURSELF IN AN UNFAMILIAR TOWN, WHERE YOU HAVE NEVER been before. As you walk down the street, you notice that many things are not exactly the same as what you would encounter if you were in your own town. On the other hand, there are lots of things that seem familiar. Cars pass by, there are buildings on either side of the street and a gas station on the corner, and a cat dashes across the street and makes it safely to the other side. Luckily, you know a lot about cars, buildings, gas stations, and cats, so you have no trouble understanding what is going on.

You know about the various components of this street scene because your mind is full of concepts. A **concept** is a mental representation that is used for a variety of cognitive functions, including memory, reasoning, and using and understanding language (Solomon et al., 1999). Thus, when you think about cats, you are drawing on your concept, or mental representation, of cats, which includes information about what cats are, what they usually look like, how they behave, and so on.

By far the most commonly studied function of concepts is **categorization**, which is the process by which things are placed into groups called **categories**. For example, when you see vehicles in the street you can place them into categories such as cars, SUVs, Chevrolets, Fords, American cars, and foreign cars. Categories are not simply convenient ways of sorting objects. They are tools that are essential for our understanding of the world.

One of the most important functions of categories is to help us to understand individual cases we have never seen before. For example, being able to say that the furry animal across the street is a "cat" provides a great deal of information about it (● Figure 9.1). Categories have therefore been called "pointers to knowledge" (Yamauchi & Markman, 2000). Once you know that something is in a category, whether "cat," "gas station," or "impressionist painting," you know a lot of general things about it and can focus your energy on specifying what's special about this particular object (see Solomon et al., 1999; Spalding & Murphy, 1996).

Being able to place things in categories can also help us understand behaviors that we might otherwise find baffling. For example, if we see a man with the left side of his face painted black and the right side painted gold, we might wonder what is going on. However, once we note that the person is heading toward the football stadium and it is Sunday afternoon, we can categorize the person as a "Pittsburgh Steelers fan." Placing him in that category explains his painted face and perhaps other strange behaviors that happen to be normal on game day in Pittsburgh (Solomon et al., 1999).

These various uses of categories testify to their importance in everyday life. It is no exaggeration to say that if there were no such thing as categories, we would have a very difficult time dealing with the world. Consider what it would mean if every time you saw a different object, you knew nothing about it other than what you could find out by investigating it individually. Clearly, life would become extremely complicated if we weren't able to rely on the knowledge provided to us by categories. Given the importance of categories, cognitive psychologists have been interested in determining the process involved in categorizing objects.

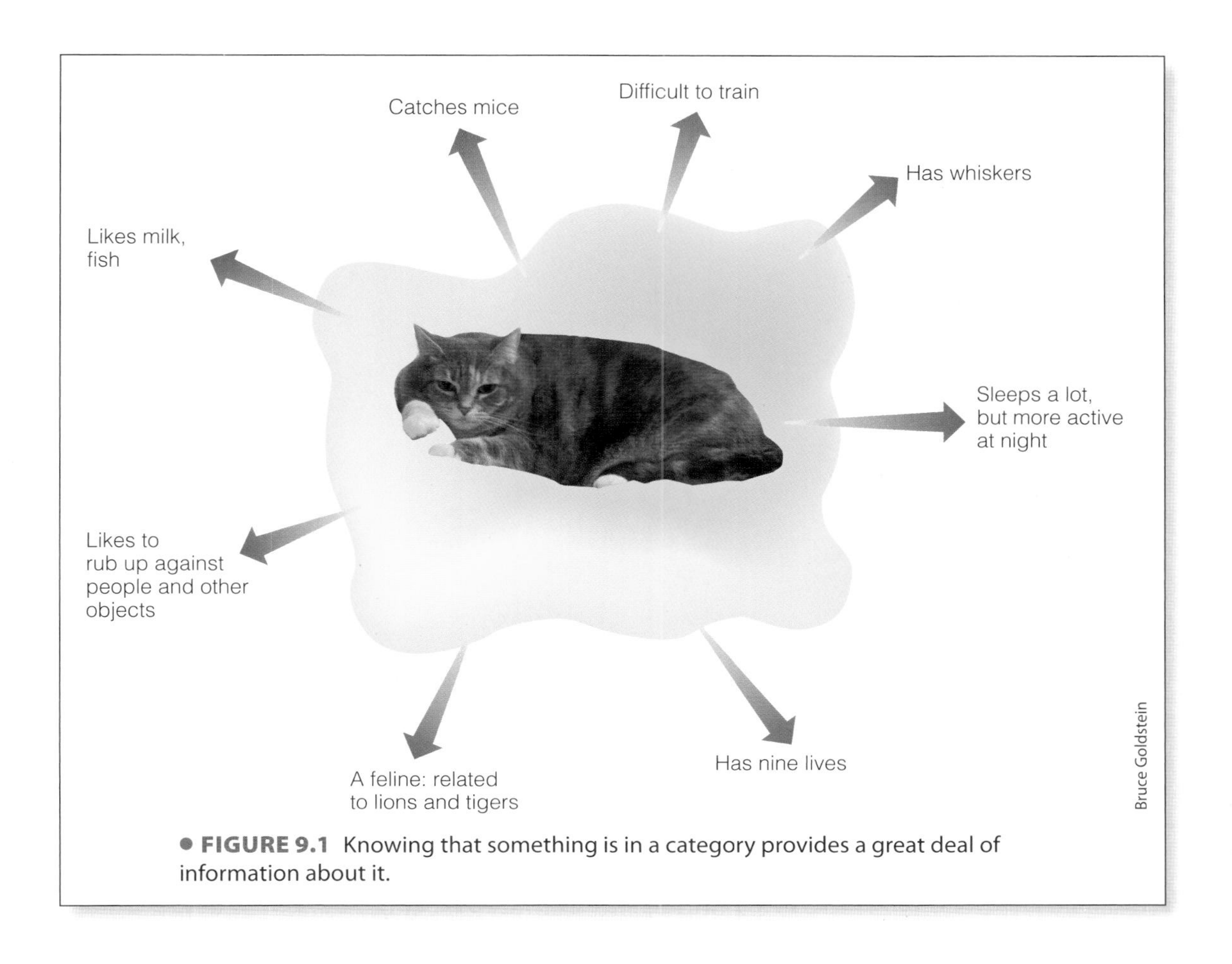

FIGURE 9.1 Knowing that something is in a category provides a great deal of information about it.

How Are Objects Placed Into Categories?

A time-honored approach to determining the characteristics of an object is to look up its definition. We begin by describing how cognitive psychologists have shown that this "definitional approach" to sorting objects into categories doesn't work. We then consider another approach, which is based on determining how similar an object is to other objects in a category.

WHY DEFINITIONS DON'T WORK FOR CATEGORIES

According to the **definitional approach to categorization**, we can decide whether something is a member of a category by determining whether a particular object meets the definition of the category. Definitions work well for some things, such as geometric objects. Thus, defining a square as "a plane figure having four equal sides" works. However, for most natural objects (such as birds, trees, and plants) and many human-made objects (like chairs), definitions do not work well at all.

The problem is that not all of the members of everyday categories have the same features. So, although the dictionary definition of a chair as "a piece of furniture consisting of a seat, legs, back, and often arms, designed to accommodate one person" may sound reasonable, there are objects we call "chairs" that don't meet that definition. For example, although the objects in • Figure 9.2a and b would be classified as chairs by this definition, the ones in Figures 9.2c and d would not. Most chairs may have legs and a back, as specified in the definition, but most people would still call the disc-shaped furniture in Figure 9.2c a chair, and might go so far as saying that the rock formation in Figure 9.2d is being used as a chair.

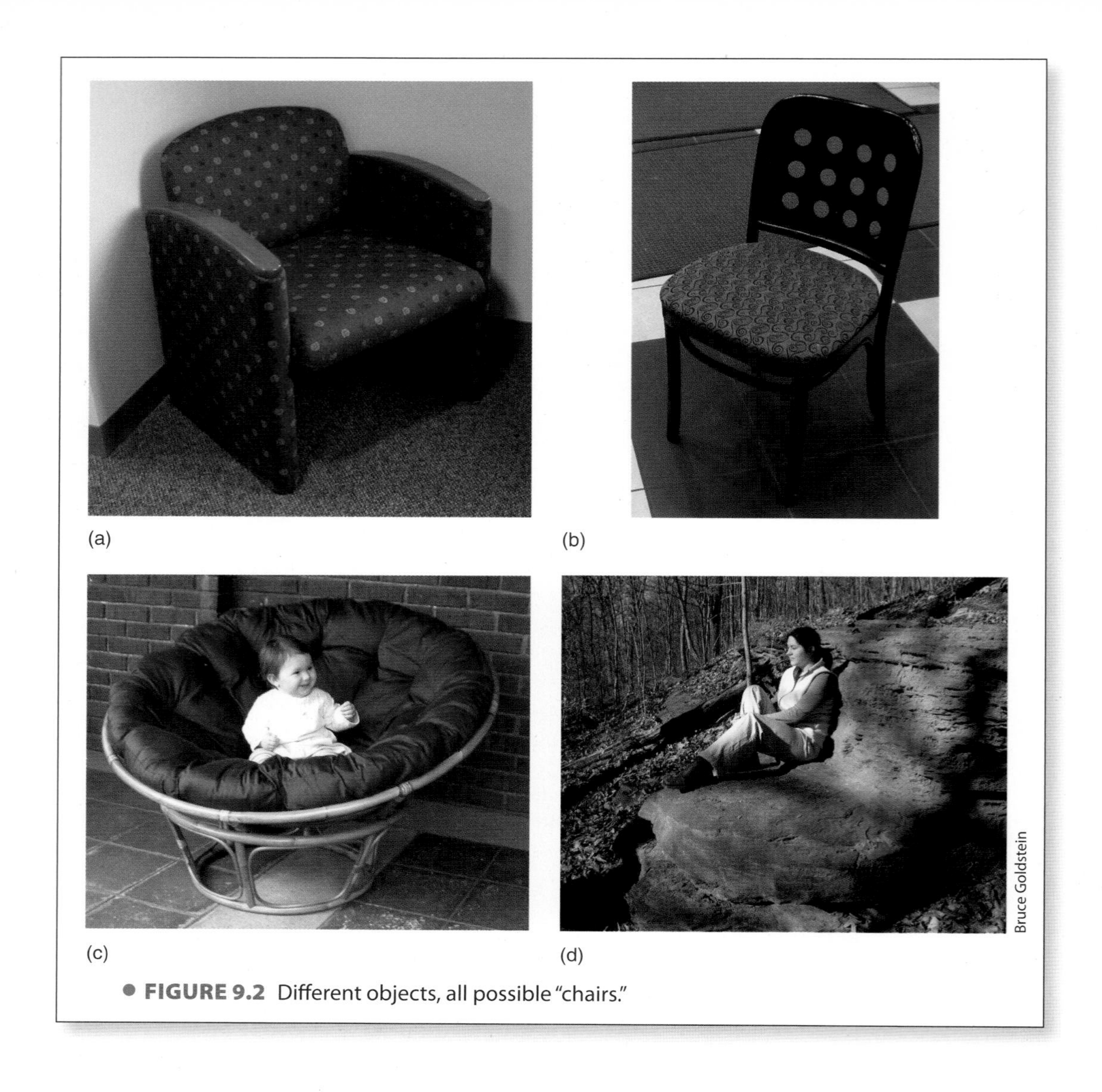

(a) (b) (c) (d)

● **FIGURE 9.2** Different objects, all possible "chairs."

The philosopher Ludwig Wittgenstein (1953) noted this problem with definitions and offered a solution:

> Consider for example the proceedings we call "games." I mean board-games, card-games, ball-games, Olympic games, and so on. For if you look at them you will not see something in common to *all,* but similarities, relationships, and a whole series of them at that. I can think of no better expression to characterize these similarities than "family resemblances."

Wittgenstein proposed the idea of **family resemblance** to deal with the problem that definitions often do not include all members of a category. Family resemblance refers to the idea that things in a particular category resemble one another in a number of ways. Thus, instead of setting definite criteria that every member of a category must meet, the family resemblance approach allows for some variation within a category. Chairs may come in many different sizes and shapes and be made of different materials, but every chair does resemble other chairs in some way. Looking at category membership in this way, we can see that the chair in Figure 9.2a and the beanbag chair in Figure 9.2c do have in common that they offer a place to sit, a way to support a person's back, and perhaps a place to rest the arms while sitting.

The idea of family resemblance has led psychologists to propose that categorization is based on determining how similar an object is to some standard representation of a category. We begin considering the idea of comparison to a standard by introducing the prototype approach to categorization.

● **FIGURE 9.3** Three real birds—a sparrow, a robin, and a blue jay—and a "prototype" bird that is the average representation of the category "birds."

THE PROTOTYPE APPROACH: FINDING THE AVERAGE CASE

CogLab
Prototypes

According to the **prototype approach to categorization**, membership in a category is determined by comparing the object to a prototype that represents the category. A **prototype** is a "typical" member of the category.

What is a typical member of a particular category? Elinor Rosch (1973) proposed that the "typical" prototype is based on an average of members of a category that are commonly experienced. For example, the prototype for the category "birds" might be based on some of the birds you usually see, such as sparrows, robins, and blue jays, but doesn't necessarily look exactly like a particular type of bird. Thus, the prototype is not an actual member of the category, but is an "average" representation of the category (● Figure 9.3).

Of course, not all birds are like robins, blue jays, or sparrows. Owls, buzzards, and penguins are also birds. Rosch describes these variations within categories as representing differences in **prototypicality. High prototypicality** means that a category member closely resembles the category prototype (it is like a "typical" member of the category). **Low prototypicality** means that the category member does not closely resemble a typical member of the category. Rosch (1975a) quantified this idea by presenting participants with a category title, such as "bird" or "furniture," and a list of about 50 members of the category. The participants' task was to rate the extent to which each member represented the category title on a 7-point scale, with a rating of 1 meaning that the member is a very good example of what the category is, and a rating of 7 meaning that the member fits poorly within the category or is not a member at all.

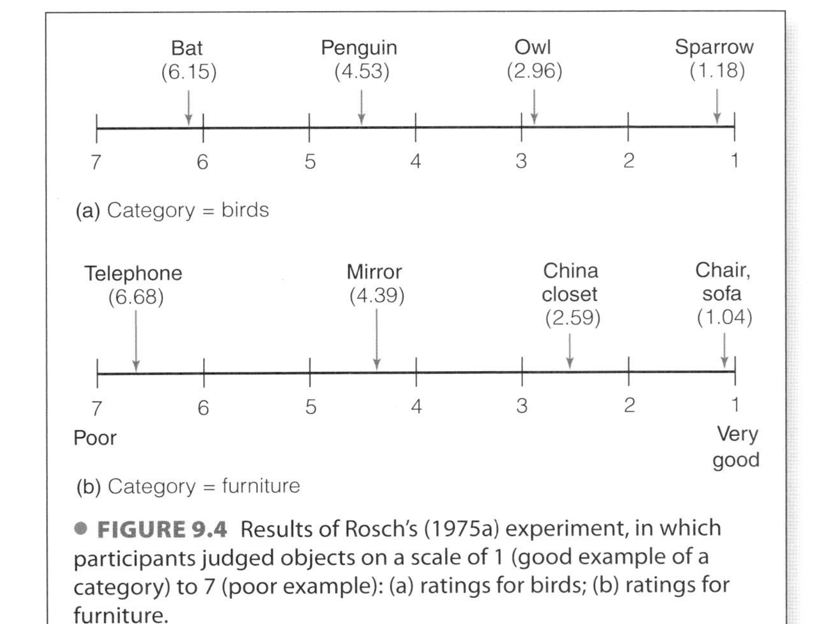

● **FIGURE 9.4** Results of Rosch's (1975a) experiment, in which participants judged objects on a scale of 1 (good example of a category) to 7 (poor example): (a) ratings for birds; (b) ratings for furniture.

Results for some of the objects in two different categories are shown in ● Figure 9.4. The 1.18 rating for *sparrow* reflects the fact that most people would agree that a sparrow is a good example of a bird (Figure 9.4a). The 4.53 rating for *penguin* and 6.15 for *bat* reflects the fact that penguins and bats are not considered good examples of birds. Similarly, *chair* and *sofa* (rating = 1.04) are considered very good examples of furniture, but *mirror* (4.39) and *telephone* (6.68) are poor examples (Figure 9.4b). The idea that sparrows are a better example of "bird" than penguins or bats is not very surprising. But Rosch went beyond this obvious result by doing a series of experiments that demonstrated differences between good and bad examples of a category.

Prototypical Objects Have High Family Resemblance

How well do good and poor examples of a category compare to other items within the category? The following demonstration is based on an experiment by Rosch and Carolyn Mervis (1975).

DEMONSTRATION Family Resemblance

Rosch and Mervis's (1975) instructions were as follows: For each of the following common objects, list as many characteristics and attributes that you feel are common to these objects. For example, for *bicycles* you might think of things they have in common like *two wheels, pedals, handlebars, you ride on them, they don't use fuel,* and so on. For *dogs* you might think of things they have in common like *having four legs, barking, having fur,* and so on. Give yourself about a minute to write down the characteristics for each of the following items: chair; sofa; mirror; telephone

If you responded like Rosch and Mervis's participants, you assigned many of the same characteristics to *chair* and *sofa*. For example, chairs and sofas share the characteristics of having legs, having backs, you sit on them, they can have cushions, and so on. It is likely, however, that your list contains far less overlap for *mirror* and *telephone*, which are also members of the category "furniture" (see Figure 9.4b). When an item's characteristics have a large amount of overlap with the characteristics of many other items in a category, this means that the family resemblance of these items is high; little overlap means the family resemblance is low.

Rosch and Mervis showed that there was a strong relationship between family resemblance and prototypicality, because items high on prototypicality had high family resemblance. Thus, good examples of the category "furniture," such as chair and sofa, share many attributes with other members of this category; poor examples, like mirror and telephone, do not. In addition to the connection between prototypicality and family resemblance, researchers have determined the following connections between prototypicality and behavior.

Statements About Prototypical Objects Are Verified Rapidly Edward Smith and coworkers (1974) used a procedure called the *sentence verification technique* to determine how rapidly people could answer questions about an object's category.

METHOD Sentence Verification Technique

The procedure for the **sentence verification technique** is simple. Participants are presented with statements and asked to answer "yes" if they think the statement is true and "no" if they think it isn't. Try this yourself, for the following two statements:

An apple is a fruit.

A pomegranate is a fruit.

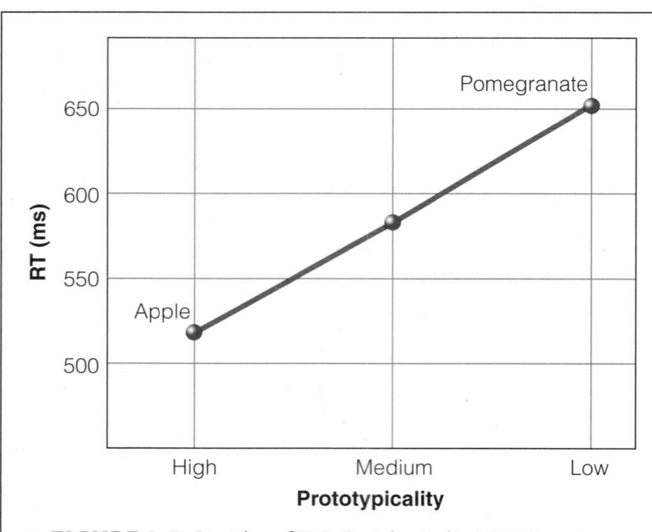

● **FIGURE 9.5** Results of E. E. Smith et al.'s (1974) sentence verification experiment. Reaction times were faster for objects rated higher in prototypicality.

When Smith and coworkers (1974) used this technique, they found that participants responded faster for objects that are high in prototypicality (like *apple* for the category "fruit") than they did for objects that are low in prototypicality (like *pomegranate;* ● Figure 9.5). This ability to judge highly prototypical objects more rapidly is called the **typicality effect.**

Prototypical Objects Are Named First When participants are asked to list as many objects in a category as possible, they tend to list the most prototypical members of the category first (Mervis et al., 1976). Thus, for "birds," sparrows would be named before penguins.

Prototypical Objects Are Affected More by Priming Priming occurs when presentation of one stimulus facilitates the response to another stimulus that usually follows closely in time (see Chapter 6, page 156). Rosch (1975b) demonstrated that prototypical members of a category are affected by a priming stimulus more than are

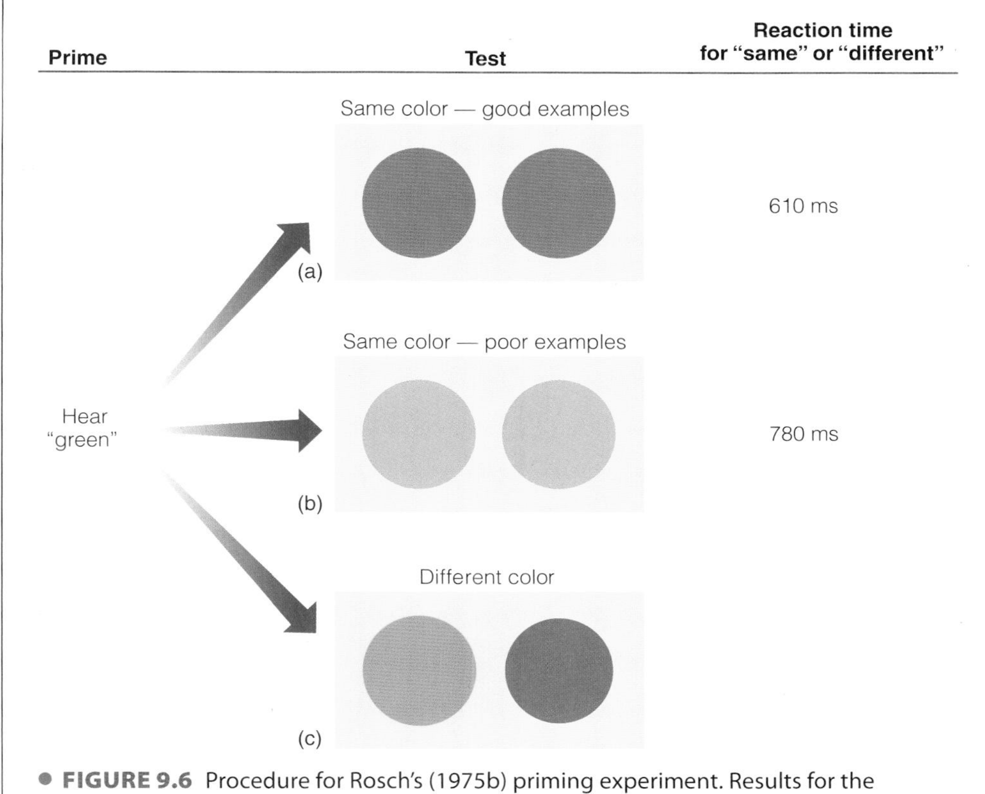

● **FIGURE 9.6** Procedure for Rosch's (1975b) priming experiment. Results for the conditions when the test colors were the same are shown on the right. (a) The person's "green" prototype matches the good green, but (b) is a poor match for the light green.

nonprototypical members. The procedure for Rosch's experiment is shown in ● Figure 9.6. Participants first heard the prime, which was the name of a color, such as "green." Two seconds later they saw a pair of colors side by side and indicated, by pressing a key as quickly as possible, whether the two colors were the same or different.

The side-by-side colors were paired in three different ways: (1) Colors were the same and were good examples of the category (primary reds, blues, greens, etc.; Figure 9.6a); (2) colors were the same, but were poor examples of the category (less rich versions of the good colors, such as light blue, light green, etc.; Figure 9.6b); (3) colors were different, with the two colors coming from different categories (for example, pairing orange with blue; Figure 9.6c).

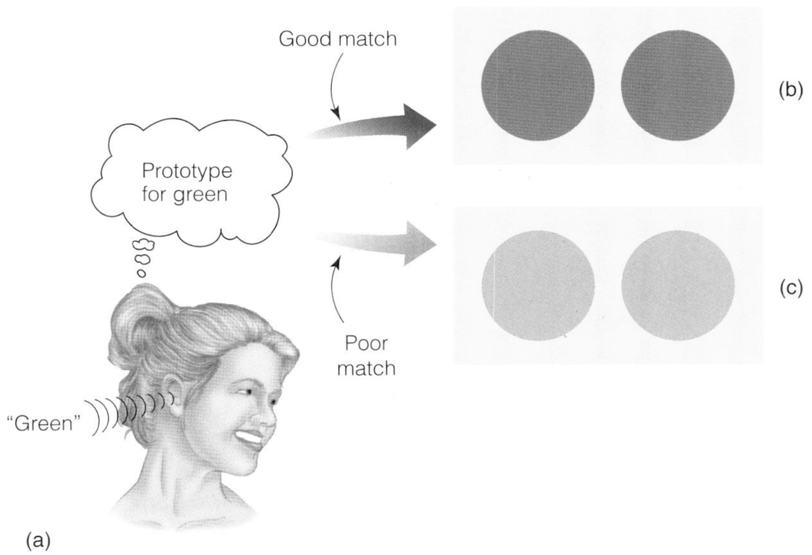

● **FIGURE 9.7** How Rosch explains the finding that priming resulted in faster "same" judgments for prototypical colors than for nonprototypical colors.

The most important result occurred for the two "same" groups, because in this condition, priming resulted in faster "same" judgments for the prototypical (good) colors (reaction time, RT = 610 ms) than to the nonprototypical (poor) colors (RT = 780 ms). Thus, when participants heard the word *green*, they judged two patches of primary green as being the same more rapidly than two patches of light green.

Rosch explains this result as follows: When participants hear the word *green*, they imagine a "good" (highly prototypical) green (● Figure 9.7a). The principle behind priming is that the prime will facilitate the participants'

TABLE 9.1 Some Effects of Prototypicality

Effect	Description	Experimental Result
Family resemblance	Things in a category resemble each other in a number of ways.	Higher ratings for high prototypical items when people rate how "good" a member of the category it is (Rosch, 1975).
Typicality	People react rapidly to members of a category that are "typical" of the category.	Faster reaction time to statements like "A _____ is a bird" for high-prototypical items (like robin) than for low-prototypical items (like ostrich) (Smith et al., 1974).
Naming	People are more likely to list some objects than others when asked to name objects in a category.	High-prototypical items are named first when people list examples of a category (Mervis et al., 1976).
Priming	Presentation of one stimulus affects responses to a stimulus that follows.	Faster same–different color judgments for high-prototypical items (Rosch, 1975b).

response to a stimulus if it contains some of the information needed to respond to the stimulus. This apparently occurs when the good greens are presented in the test (Figure 9.7b), but not when the poor greens are presented (Figure 9.7c). Thus, the results of the priming experiments support the idea that participants create images of good prototypes in response to color names. Table 9.1 summarizes the various ways, previously discussed, that prototypicality affects behavior.

The prototype approach to categorization, and in particular Rosch's pioneering research, represented a great advance over the definitional approach because it provided a wealth of experimental evidence that all items within a category are not the same. Another approach to categorization, called the *exemplar approach*, also takes into account the wide variation among items that belong to a particular category.

THE EXEMPLAR APPROACH: THINKING ABOUT EXAMPLES

The **exemplar approach to categorization**, like the prototype approach, involves determining whether an object is similar to a standard object. However, whereas the standard for the prototype approach is a single "average" member of the category, the standard for the exemplar approach involves many examples, each one called an exemplar. **Exemplars** are actual members of the category that a person has encountered in the past. Thus, if a person has encountered sparrows, robins, and blue jays in the past, each of these would be an exemplar for the category "birds."

The exemplar approach can explain many of Rosch's results, which were used to support the prototype approach. For example, the exemplar approach explains the typicality effect (in which reaction times on the sentence verification task are faster for better examples of a category than for poorer examples) by proposing that objects that are like more of the exemplars are classified faster. Thus, a sparrow is similar to many exemplars, so it is classified faster than a penguin, which is similar to few exemplars. This is basically the same as the idea of family resemblance, described for prototypes, that states that "better" objects will have higher family resemblance.

WHICH APPROACH WORKS BETTER: PROTOTYPES OR EXEMPLARS?

Which approach—prototypes or exemplars—provides a better description of how people use categories? One advantage of the exemplar approach is that by using real examples, it can more easily take into account atypical cases such as flightless birds. Rather than comparing a penguin to an "average" bird, we remember that there are some birds that don't fly. This ability to take into account individual cases means that the exemplar approach doesn't discard information that might be useful later. Thus, penguins, ostriches, and other birds that are not typical can be represented as exemplars, rather than becoming lost in the overall average that creates a prototype. The exemplar approach can also deal more easily with variable categories like games. Although it is difficult to imagine what the prototype might be for a category that contains football, computer games, solitaire, marbles, and golf, the exemplar approach requires only that we remember some of these varying examples.

Based on the results of a number of research studies, some researchers have concluded that people may use both approaches. It has been proposed that as we initially learn about a category, we may average exemplars into a prototype; then, later in learning, some of the exemplar information becomes stronger (Keri et al., 2002; Malt, 1989). Thus, early in learning we would be poor at taking into account "exceptions," such as ostriches or penguins, but later, exemplars for these cases would be added to the category (Minda & Smith, 2001; Smith & Minda, 2000).

Other research indicates that the exemplar approach may work best for small categories, such as "U.S. presidents" or "Mountains taller than 15,000 feet," and the prototype approach may work best for larger categories, such as "birds" or "automobiles." We can describe this blending of prototypes and exemplars in commonsense terms with the following example: We know generally what cats are (the prototype), but we know specifically our own cat the best (an exemplar; Minda & Smith, 2001).

Is There a Psychologically "Privileged" Level of Categories?

As we have considered the prototype and exemplar approaches, we have used examples of categories such as "furniture," which contains members such as beds, chairs, and tables. But, as you can see in • Figure 9.8, the category "chairs" can contain smaller categories such as kitchen chairs and dining room chairs. This kind of organization, in which larger, more general categories are divided into smaller, more specific categories, creating a number of levels of categories, is called a **hierarchical organization**.

One question cognitive psychologists have asked about this organization is whether there is a "basic" level that is more psychologically important or "privileged" than other levels. The research we will describe indicates that although it is possible to demonstrate that there is a basic level of categories with special psychological properties, the basic level may not be the same for everyone. We begin by describing Rosch's research, in which she introduced the idea of basic level categories.

ROSCH'S APPROACH: WHAT'S SPECIAL ABOUT BASIC LEVEL CATEGORIES?

Rosch's research starts with the observation that there are different levels of categories, ranging from general (like "furniture") to specific (like "kitchen table"), as shown in Figure 9.8, and that when people use categories they tend to focus on one of these

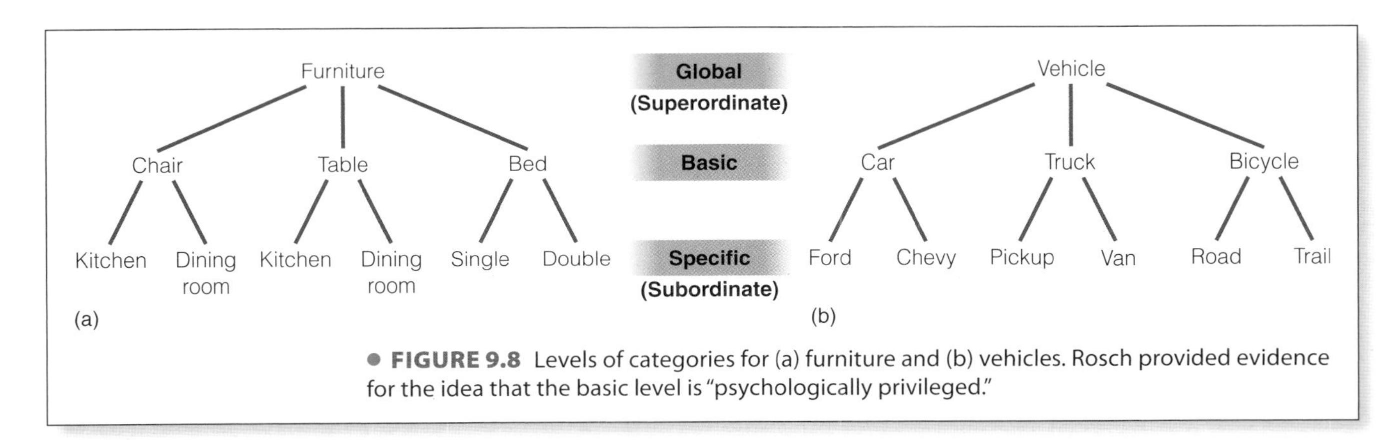

• **FIGURE 9.8** Levels of categories for (a) furniture and (b) vehicles. Rosch provided evidence for the idea that the basic level is "psychologically privileged."

levels. She distinguished three levels of categories: the **superordinate level**, which we will call the **global level** (for example, "furniture"), the **basic level** (for example, "table"), and the **subordinate level**, which we will call the **specific level** (for example, "kitchen table"). The following demonstration illustrates some characteristics of the different levels.

DEMONSTRATION Listing Common Features

This demonstration is a repeat of the task you did in the Family Resemblance demonstration on page 244, but with different categories. For the following categories, list as many features as you can that would be common to all or most of the objects in the category. For example, for "table" you might list "has legs."

1. furniture
2. table
3. kitchen table

If you responded like the participants in the Rosch, Mervis, and coworkers (1976) experiment, who were given the same task, you listed only a few features that were common to all furniture, but many features that were shared by all tables and by all kitchen tables. Rosch's participants listed an average of 3 common features for the global level category "furniture," 9 for basic level categories such as "table," and 10.3 for specific level categories such as "kitchen table" (● Figure 9.9).

LEVEL	EXAMPLE	NUMBER OF COMMON FEATURES
Global	Furniture	3
		↑ *Lose a lot of information.*
Basic	Table	9
		↓ *Gain just a little information.*
Specific	Kitchen table	10.3

● **FIGURE 9.9** Category levels, examples of each level, and average number of common features listed by participants in Rosch, Mervis, et al.'s (1976) experiment.

Rosch reasoned that because a greater number of features provides more information about a category, starting at the basic level and moving up to the global level causes the loss of a lot of information (9 features at the basic level versus 3 features at the global level). However, going from basic to specific provides a gain of only a little information (9 features versus 10.3 features).

Rosch proposed that the basic level is psychologically special because going above it (to global) results in a large loss of information and going below it (to specific) results in little gain of information. Here is another demonstration that is relevant to the idea of a basic level.

DEMONSTRATION Naming Things

Look at ● Figure 9.10 and, as quickly as possible, write down or say a word that identifies each picture.

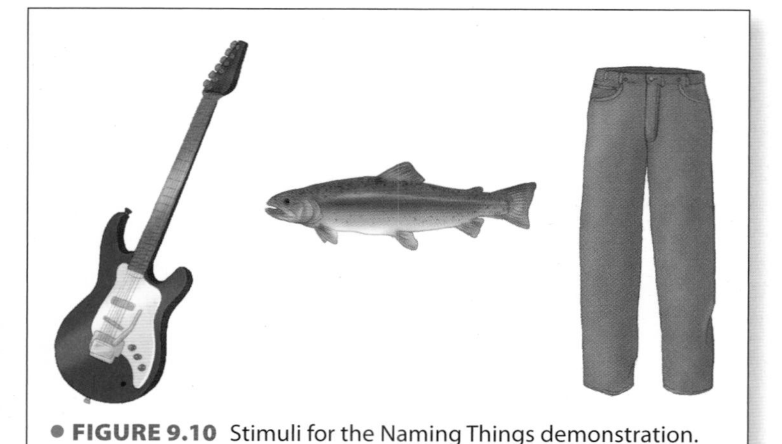

● **FIGURE 9.10** Stimuli for the Naming Things demonstration.

What names did you assign to each object? When Rosch, Mervis, and coworkers (1976) did a similar experiment, they found that people tended to pick a basic level name. They said "guitar" (basic level) rather than musical instrument (global) or rock guitar (specific), "fish" rather than animal or trout, and "pants" rather than clothing or jeans.

In another experiment, Rosch, Simpson, and Miller (1976) showed participants a category label, such as "car" or "vehicle," and then, after a brief delay, presented a picture. The participants' task was to indicate, as rapidly as possible, whether the picture was a member of the category. The results showed that they accomplished this task more rapidly for basic level categories (such as car) than for global level categories (such as vehicle). Thus, they would respond "yes" more rapidly when the picture of an automobile was preceded by the word *car* than when the picture was preceded by the word *vehicle*.

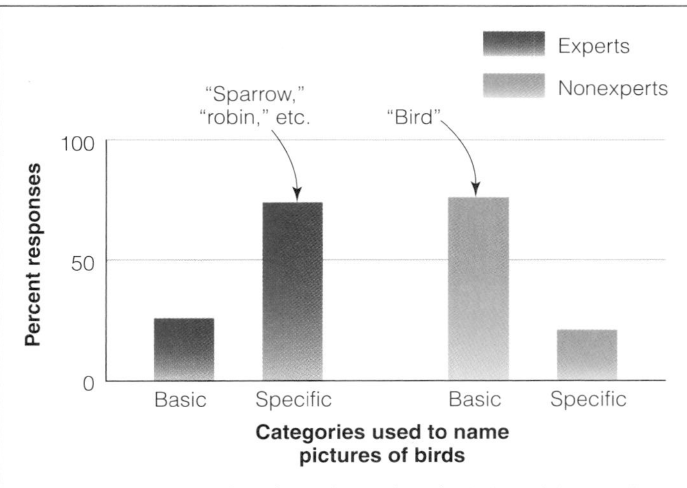

FIGURE 9.11 Results of Tanaka and Taylor's (1991) "expert" experiment. Experts (left pair of bars) used more specific categories to name birds, whereas nonexperts (right pair of bars) used more basic categories.

HOW KNOWLEDGE CAN AFFECT CATEGORIZATION

Rosch's experiments, which were carried out on college undergraduates, showed that there is a level of category, which she called "basic," that reflects college undergraduates' everyday experience. This has been demonstrated by many researchers in addition to Rosch. Thus, when J. D. Coley and coworkers (1997) asked Northwestern University undergraduates to name, as specifically as possible, 44 different plants on a walk around campus, 75 percent of the responses used labels like "tree," rather than more specific labels like "oak tree."

But instead of asking college undergraduate to name plants, what if Coley had taken a group of horticulturalists around campus? Do you think they would have said "tree" or "oak tree"? An experiment by James Tanaka and Marjorie Taylor (1991) asked a similar question for birds. They asked bird experts and nonexperts to name pictures of objects. There were objects from many different categories (tools, clothing, flowers, etc.), but Tanaka and Taylor were interested in how the participants responded to the four bird pictures.

The results (● Figure 9.11) show that the experts responded by specifying the birds' species (robin, sparrow, jay, or cardinal), but the nonexperts responded by saying "bird." Apparently the experts had learned to pay attention to features of birds that nonexperts were unaware of. Thus, in order to fully understand how people categorize objects, it is necessary to consider not only the properties of the objects, but the learning and experience of the people perceiving these objects (also see Johnson & Mervis, 1997).

From the result of Tanaka's bird experiment, we can guess that a horticulturist walking around campus would be likely to label plants more specifically than people who had little specific knowledge about plants. In fact, members of the Guatemalan Itza culture, who live in close contact with their natural environment, call an oak tree an "oak tree," not a "tree" (Coley et al., 1997).

Thus, the level that is "special"—meaning that people tend to focus on it—is not the same for everyone. Generally, people with more expertise and familiarity with a particular category tend to focus on more specific information that Rosch associated with the specific level. This result isn't that surprising, because our ability to categorize is learned from experience; it depends on which objects we typically encounter and what characteristics of objects we pay attention to. We will return to this idea of levels of categories in the Something to Consider section at the end of the chapter, when we consider how young infants categorize objects.

TEST YOURSELF 9.1

1. Why is the use of categories so important for our day-to-day functioning?
2. Describe the definitional approach to categories. Why does it initially seem like a good way of thinking about categories, but then become troublesome when we consider the kinds of objects that can make up a category?
3. What is the prototype approach? What experiments did Rosch do that demonstrated connections between prototypicality and behavior?
4. What is the exemplar approach to categorization? How does it differ from the prototype approach, and how might the two approaches work together?
5. What does it mean to say that there are different levels within a category? What arguments did Rosch present to support the idea that one of these levels is "privileged"? How has research on categorization by experts led to modifications of Rosch's ideas about which category is "basic" or "privileged"?

Representing Relationships Between Categories: Semantic Networks

We have seen that categories can be arranged in a hierarchy of levels, from global (at the top) to specific (at the bottom). In this section, our main concern is to explain how categories or concepts are organized in the mind. The approach we will be describing, called the **semantic network approach**, proposes that concepts are arranged in networks.

INTRODUCTION TO SEMANTIC NETWORKS: COLLINS AND QUILLIAN'S HIERARCHICAL MODEL

One of the first semantic network models was based on the pioneering work of Ross Quillian (1967, 1969), whose goal was to develop a computer model of human memory. We will describe Quillian's approach by looking at a simplified version of his model proposed by Allan Collins and Quillian (1969).

● Figure 9.12 shows Collins and Quillian's network. The network consists of nodes that are connected by links. Each node represents a category or concept, and concepts are placed in the network so that related concepts are connected. In addition, properties associated with each concept are indicated at the nodes.

The links connecting the nodes indicate that they are related to each other in the mind. Thus, the model shown in Figure 9.12 indicates that there is an association in the mind between "canary" and "bird," and between "bird" and "animal." It is a **hierarchical model**, because it consists of levels arranged so that more specific concepts, such as "canary" and "salmon," are at the bottom, and more general concepts are at higher levels.

We can illustrate how this network works, and how it proposes that knowledge about concepts is organized in the mind, by considering how we would retrieve the properties of canaries from the network. We start by entering the network at the concept node for "canary." At this node, we obtain the information that a canary can sing and is yellow. To access more information about "canary," we move up the link and learn that a canary is a bird and that a bird has wings, can fly, and has feathers. Moving up another level, we find that a canary is also an animal, which has skin and can move, and finally we reach the level of living things, which tells us it can grow and is living.

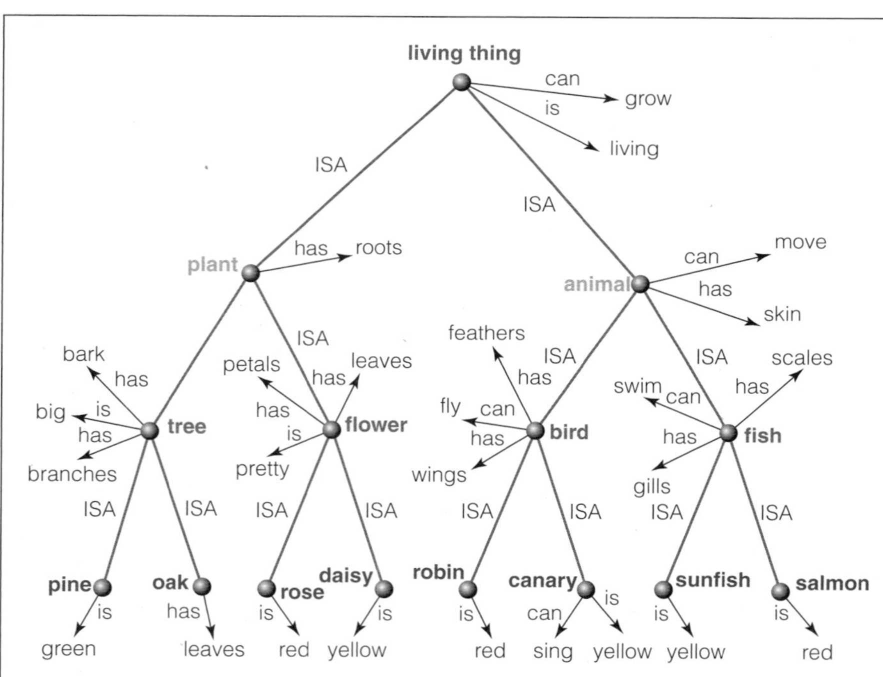

● **FIGURE 9.12** Collins and Quillian's (1969) semantic network. Concepts are indicated by colors. Properties of concepts are indicated at the nodes for each concept. Additional properties of a concept can be determined by moving up the network, along the lines connecting the concepts. For example, moving from "canary" up to "bird" indicates that canaries have feathers and wings and can fly. (Source: Adapted from T. T. Rogers & J. L. McClelland, *Semantic Cognition: A Parallel Distributed Processing Approach,* Cambridge, MA: MIT Press, 2004.)

You might wonder why we have to travel from "canary" to "bird" to find out that a canary can fly. That information could have been placed at the canary node, and then we would know it right away. But Collins and Quillian proposed that including "can fly" at the node for every bird (canary, robin, vulture, etc.) was inefficient and would use up too much storage space. Thus, instead of indicating the properties "can fly" and "has feathers" for every kind of bird, these properties are placed at the node for "bird" because this property holds for most birds. This way of storing shared properties just once at a higher level node is called **cognitive economy**.

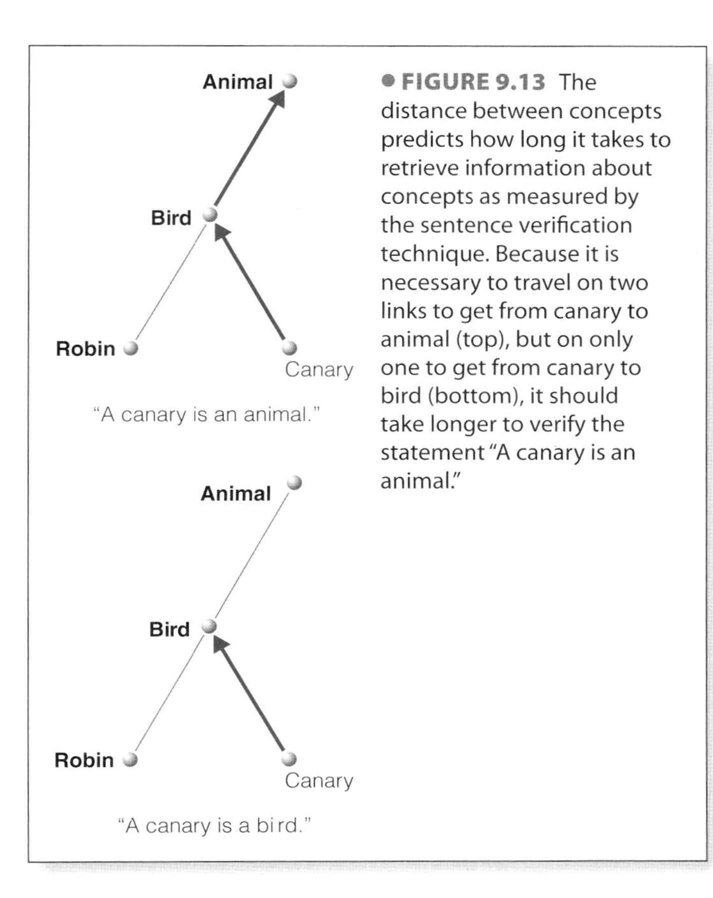

● **FIGURE 9.13** The distance between concepts predicts how long it takes to retrieve information about concepts as measured by the sentence verification technique. Because it is necessary to travel on two links to get from canary to animal (top), but on only one to get from canary to bird (bottom), it should take longer to verify the statement "A canary is an animal."

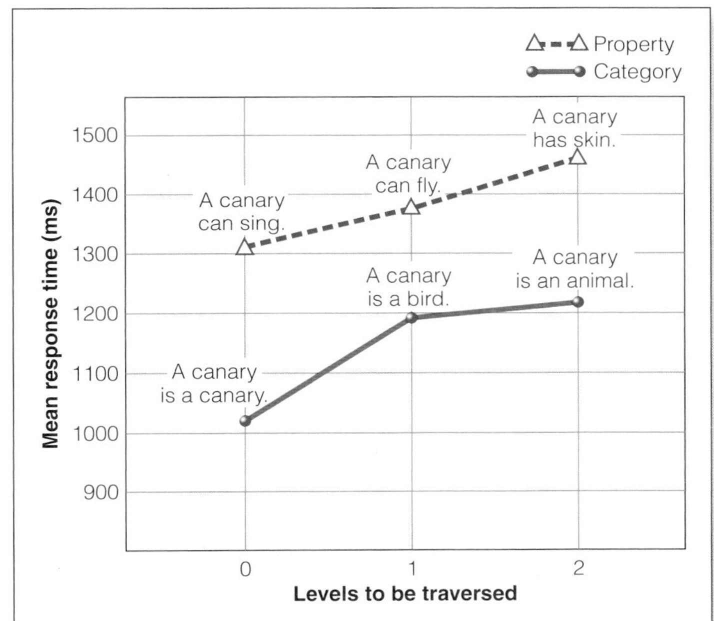

● **FIGURE 9.14** Results of Collins and Quillian's (1969) experiment that measured reaction times to statements that involved traversing different distances in the network. Greater distances are associated with longer reaction times, both when verifying statements about properties of canaries (top) and about categories of which the canary is a member (bottom). (Source: A. M. Collins et al., "Retrieval Time From Semantic Memory," *Journal of Verbal Learning and Verbal Behavior, 8,* 240–247, Fig. 2. Copyright © 1969, Elsevier Ltd. Reproduced by permission.

Although cognitive economy makes the network more efficient, it does create a problem because not all birds fly. To deal with this problem while still achieving the advantages of cognitive economy, Collins and Quillian added exceptions at lower nodes. For example, the node for "ostrich," which is not shown in this network, would indicate the property "can't fly."

How do the elements in this semantic network correspond to the actual operation of the brain? Remember from our discussion of models in cognitive psychology in Chapter 1 (page 17) that elements of models do not necessarily correspond to specific structures in the brain. Thus, the links and nodes we have been describing do not necessarily correspond to specific nerve fibers or locations in the brain. This model, and other network models we will be describing, are concerned with how concepts and their properties are *associated* in the mind. In fact, physiological findings relevant to these models, such as neurons that respond best to specific categories (see page 260), were not available until many years after these models were proposed.

Putting aside any possible connection between the network and actual physiology, we can ask how accurately Collins and Quillian's model represents how concepts are organized in the mind. The beauty of the network's hierarchical organization, in which general concepts are at the top and specific ones are at the bottom, is that it results in the testable prediction that the time it takes for a person to retrieve information about a concept should be determined by the distance that must be traveled through the network. Thus, the model predicts that when using the sentence verification technique, in which participants are asked to answer "yes" or "no" to statements about concepts (see Method: Sentence Verification Technique, page 244), it should take longer to answer "yes" to the statement "A canary is an animal" than to "A canary is a bird." This prediction follows from the idea that it is necessary to travel along two links to get from "canary" to "animal" but only one to get to "bird" (● Figure 9.13).

Collins and Quillian (1969) tested this prediction by measuring the reaction time to a number of different statements and obtained the results shown in ● Figure 9.14. As predicted, statements that required further travel from "canary" resulted in longer reaction times.

Another property of the theory, which leads to further predictions, is spreading activation. **Spreading activation** is activity that spreads out along any link that is connected to an activated node. For example, moving through the network from "robin" to "bird" activates the node at "bird" and the link we use to get from robin to bird, as indicated by the blue arrow in ● Figure 9.15. But according to the idea of spreading activation, this activation also spreads to other nodes in the network, as indicated by the dashed lines. Thus, activating the canary-to-bird pathway activates additional concepts that are connected to "bird," such as "animal" and other types of birds. The result of this spreading activation is that the additional concepts that receive this activation become "primed" and so can be retrieved more easily from memory.

The idea that spreading activation can influence priming was studied by David Meyer and Roger Schvaneveldt (1971) in a paper published shortly after Collins and Quillian's model was proposed. They used a method called the *lexical decision task*.

● **FIGURE 9.15** How activation can spread through a network as a person searches from "robin" to "bird" (blue arrow). The dashed lines indicate activation that is spreading from the activated bird node. Circled concepts, which have become primed, are easier to retrieve from memory because of the spreading activation.

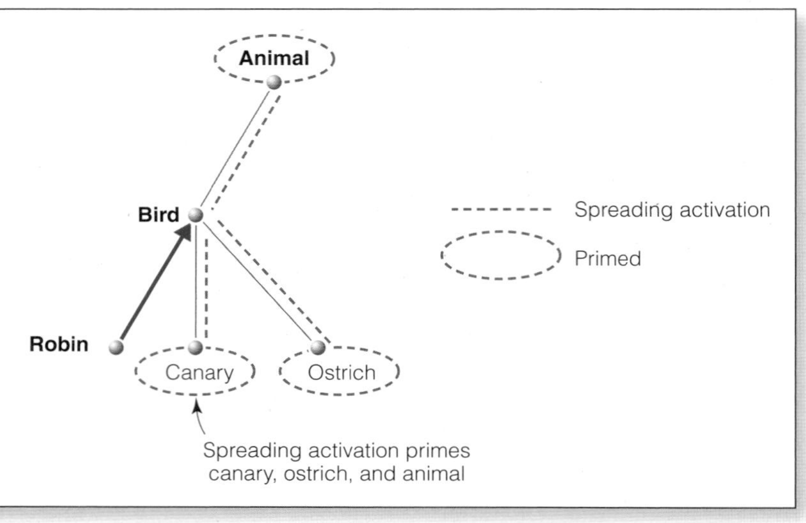

METHOD Lexical Decision Task

CogLab
Lexical Decision

In the **lexical decision task**, participants read stimuli, some of which are words and some of which are not words. Their task is to indicate as quickly as possible whether each entry is a word or a nonword. For example, the correct responses for bloog would be "no" and for bloat would be "yes."

Myer and Schvaneveldt used a variation of the lexical decision task by presenting participants with two strings of letters, one above the other, as in ● Figure 9.16. The participants' task was to press, as quickly as possible, the "yes" key when both strings were words or the "no" key when one or both were not words. Thus, the two nonwords shown in Figure 9.16a or the word and nonword in Figure 9.16b would require a "no" response, but the two stimuli in Figure 9.16c and d would require a "yes" response.

The key variable in this experiment was the association between the pairs of real words. In some trials the words were closely associated (like *bread* and *wheat*), and in some trials they were weakly associated (*chair* and *money*). The result, shown in ● Figure 9.17, was that reaction time was faster when the two words were associated. Meyer and Schvaneveldt proposed that this might have occurred because retrieving one word from memory triggered a spread of activation to other nearby locations in a network. Because more activation would spread to words that were related, the response to the related words was faster than the response to unrelated words.

	(a)	(b)	(c)	(d)
Stimuli	Fundt Glurb	Bleem Dress	Chair Money	Bread Wheat
Correct response	"No"	"No"	"Yes"	"Yes"

● **FIGURE 9.16** Stimuli and correct responses for Meyer and Schvaneveldt's (1971) priming experiment.

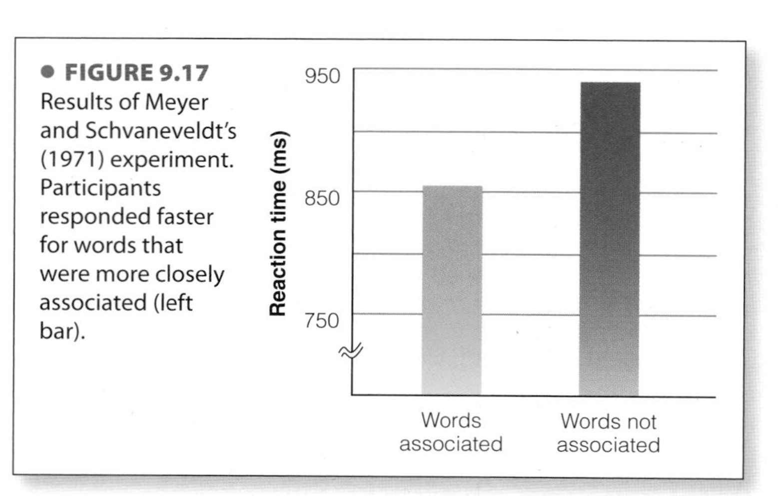

● **FIGURE 9.17** Results of Meyer and Schvaneveldt's (1971) experiment. Participants responded faster for words that were more closely associated (left bar).

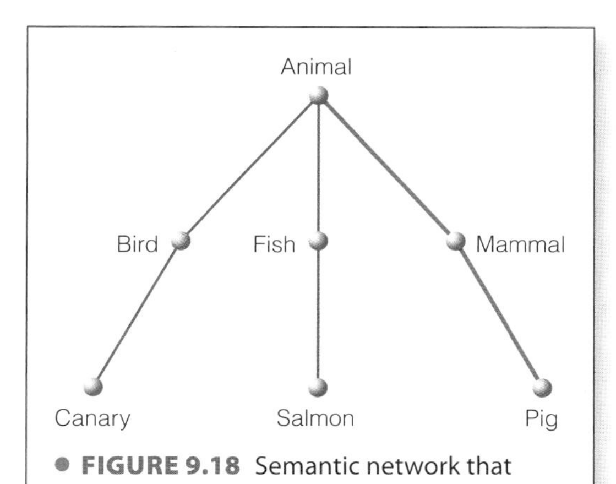

● **FIGURE 9.18** Semantic network that shows that "pig" is closer to "mammal" than to "animal."

CRITICISM OF THE COLLINS AND QUILLIAN MODEL

Although Collins and Quillian's model was supported by the results of a number of experiments, such as their reaction time experiment (Figure 9.14) and Meyer and Schvaneveldt's priming experiment, it didn't take long for other researchers to call the theory into question. They pointed out that the theory couldn't explain the typicality effect, in which reaction times for statements about an object are faster for more typical members of a category than for less typical members (see page 244; Rips et al., 1973). Thus, the statement "A canary is a bird" is verified more quickly than "An ostrich is a bird," but the model predicts equally fast reaction times because "canary" and "ostrich" are both one node away from "bird."

Researchers also questioned the concept of cognitive economy because of evidence that people may, in fact, store specific properties of concepts (like "has wings" for "canary") right at the node for that concept (Conrad, 1972). In addition, Lance Rips and coworkers (1973) obtained sentence verification results such as the following:

- A pig is a mammal. RT = 1,476 ms
- A pig is an animal. RT = 1,268 ms

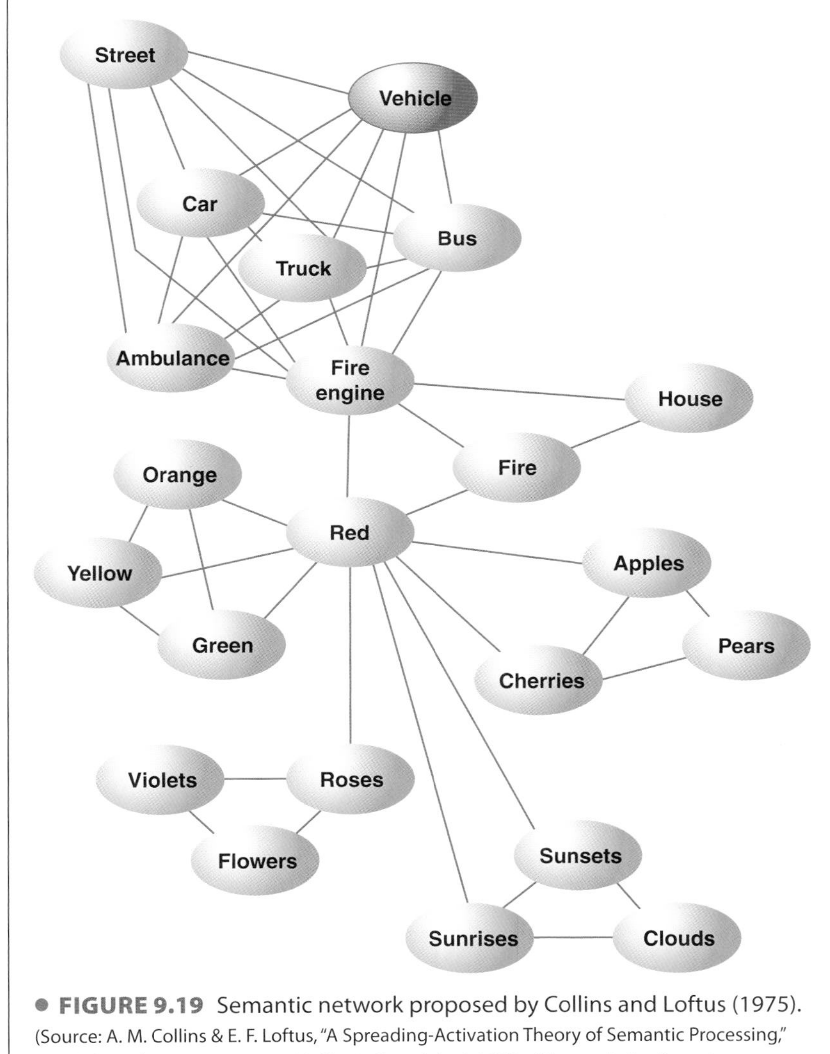

● **FIGURE 9.19** Semantic network proposed by Collins and Loftus (1975). (Source: A. M. Collins & E. F. Loftus, "A Spreading-Activation Theory of Semantic Processing," *Psychological Review, 82,* 407–428, Fig. 1. Copyright © 1975 with permission from the American Psychological Association.)

"A pig is an animal" is verified more quickly, but as we can see from the network in ● Figure 9.18, the Collins and Quillian model predicts that "A pig is a mammal" should be verified more quickly because a link leads directly from "pig" to "mammal," but we need to travel one link past the mammal node to get to "animal." Sentence verification results such as these, plus the other criticisms of the theory, led Collins and Elizabeth Loftus (1975) to propose a new semantic network model designed to handle the results that the Collins and Quillian model couldn't explain.

THE COLLINS AND LOFTUS MODEL: PERSONAL EXPERIENCE AFFECTS NETWORKS

Collins and Loftus (1975) proposed a model that resulted in networks like the one in ● Figure 9.19, in which concepts that are more closely related are connected by shorter lines. For example, the network in Figure 9.19 indicates that "vehicle" is connected to "car," "truck," and "bus" by short links (because these are closely related concepts), but is connected to "fire engine" and "ambulance" (which are less typical vehicles than car, truck, or bus) by longer links. These shorter links predict faster reaction times for the more typical vehicles.

The Collins and Loftus model abandons the hierarchical structure used by Collins and Quillian in favor of a structure based on a person's experience. This means that the spacing between various concepts can differ for various people depending on their experience and knowledge about specific concepts.

In addition to proposing experientially based links between concepts, Collins and Loftus also proposed a number of additional modifications to the Collins and Quillian model to deal with problems like cognitive economy and the pig-mammal problem. The details of their proposed modifications aren't that important. What is important is that these modifications made it possible to explain just about any result of categorization experiments. Collins and Loftus describe their theory as "a fairly complicated theory with enough generality to apply to results from many different experimental paradigms" (1975, p. 427). Although you might think that being able to explain just about any result would be an advantage, this property of the model led some researchers to criticize it, as we will see in the next section.

ASSESSMENT OF SEMANTIC NETWORK THEORIES

Why would a model be criticized if it can explain just about any result? We can answer this question by considering the following properties of good psychological theories:

1. *Explanatory power.* The theory can explain why a particular result occurred by making a statement like "Behavior A occurred because.... "
2. *Predictive power.* The theory can predict the results of a particular experiment by making a statement like "Under these circumstances, Behavior B will occur."
3. *Falsifiability.* The theory or part of the theory can potentially be shown to be wrong if a particular experimental result occurs. This means that it should be possible to design an experiment that can potentially yield results that would be predicted by the theory, and also that can potentially yield results that are *not* predicted by the theory.
4. *Generation of experiments.* Good theories usually stimulate a great deal of research to test the theory, to determine ways of improving the theory, to use new methods suggested by the theory, or study new questions raised by the theory.

When we evaluate the original Collins and Quillian theory against these criteria, we find that although it does explain and predict some results (see the data in Figure 9.16), there are many results it can't explain, such as the typicality effect and the longer reaction times for sentences like "A pig is a mammal." These failures to accurately explain and predict are what led Collins and Loftus to propose their theory.

But Collins and Loftus's theory has been criticized for being so flexible that it is difficult to falsify. We can understand why this is a problem by considering the networks in • Figure 9.20, which show the node for "fire engine" and some of its links for two different people. The "fire engine" node would be more easily activated by related

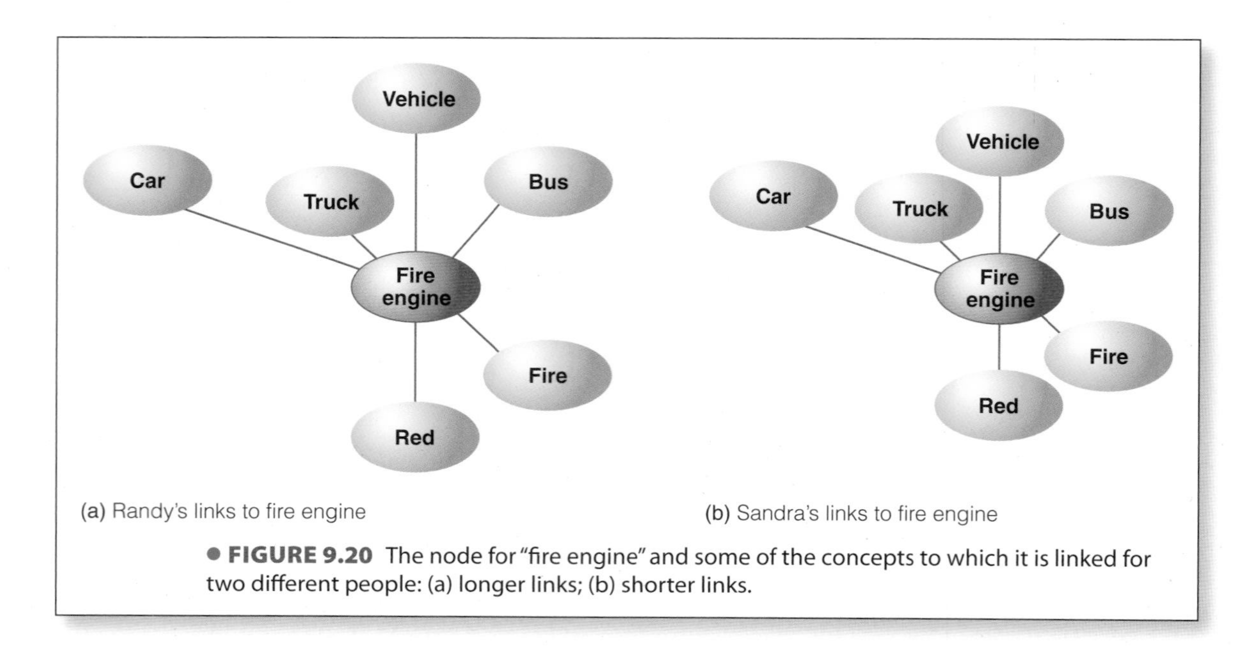

• FIGURE 9.20 The node for "fire engine" and some of the concepts to which it is linked for two different people: (a) longer links; (b) shorter links.

concepts for the network in (b) than in (a) because the links are shorter in (b). But the lengths of the links can be determined by a number of factors, including a person's past experience with fire engines or other types of vehicles. Unfortunately, there are no definite rules for determining these lengths—or, for that matter, for determining things like how long activation remains after it spreads, or how much total activation is needed to trigger a node. This means that by appropriately adjusting factors such as the length of the links and how long activation lasts, the model can "explain" many different results.

But if a theory can explain almost any result by adjusting various properties of the model, what has it really explained? This question is what led P. N. Johnson-Laird and coworkers (1984) to criticize semantic network theories and to conclude that these theories are "too powerful to be refuted by empirical evidence." This is a way of saying that it is difficult to falsify the theories. (See Anderson & Bower, 1973, and Glass & Holyoak, 1975, for additional semantic network theories.)

One of the characteristics of science is that models are constantly being revised to meet the challenges posed by new results or by criticisms such as Johnson-Laird's assessment of semantic network theory. But sometimes, instead of simply revising an existing theory, researchers propose a whole new approach. This is what happened in the 1980s, when a new approach called *connectionism* started moving to the forefront.

Representing Concepts in Networks: The Connectionist Approach

Criticism of semantic networks, combined with new advances in understanding how information is represented in the brain, led to the emergence of a new approach to explaining how knowledge is represented in the mind. In two volumes, both titled *Parallel Distributed Processing: Explorations in the Microstructure of Cognition* (McClelland & Rumelhart, 1986; Rumelhart & McClelland, 1986), James McClelland and David Rumelhart proposed a new approach called connectionism. This approach has gained favor among many researchers because (1) it is based on how information is represented in the brain; and (2) it can explain a number of findings, including how concepts are learned and how damage to the brain affects people's knowledge about concepts.

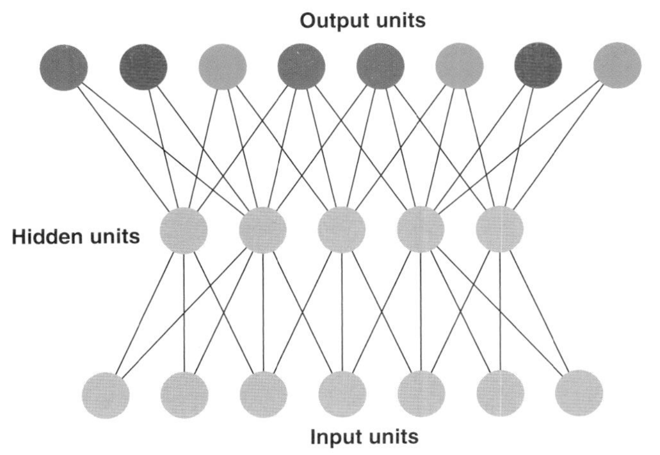

● **FIGURE 9.21** A parallel distributed processing (PDP) network showing input units, hidden units, and output units. Incoming stimuli activate the input units, and signals travel through the network, activating the hidden and output units. Activity of the output units is indicated by their colors, with blue and green representing low activity and red, higher activity. The patterns of activity that occur in the output units are determined both by the initial activity of the input units and by the connection weights that determine how strongly the hidden and output units will be activated by incoming activity. Connection weights are not shown in this figure.

WHAT IS A CONNECTIONIST MODEL?

Connectionism is an approach to creating computer models for representing concepts and their properties based on characteristics of the brain. These models are also called **parallel distributed processing (PDP)** models because, as we will see shortly, they propose that concepts are represented by activity that is distributed across a network.

An example of a simple **connectionist network** is shown in ● Figure 9.21. The circles are **units**. These units are inspired by the neurons found in the brain. The lines are connections that transfer information between units, and are roughly equivalent to axons in the brain. Like neurons, some units can be activated by stimuli from the environment, and some can be activated by signals received from other units. Units activated by stimuli from the environment (or stimuli presented by the experimenter) are **input units**. In the simple network illustrated here, input units send signals to **hidden units**, which send signals to **output units**.

An additional feature of a connectionist network is **connection weights**. A connection weight determines how signals sent from one unit either increase or decrease the activity of the next unit. These weights correspond to what happens at a synapse that transmits signals from one neuron to another (Figure 2.4, page 27). In Chapter 7 we saw that some synapses can transmit signals more strongly than others and therefore cause a high firing rate in the next neuron (Figure 7.16, page 190). Other synapses can cause a decrease in the firing rate of the next neuron. Connection weights in a connectionist network operate in the same way. High connection weights result in a strong tendency to excite the next unit, lower weights cause less excitation, and negative weights can decrease excitation or inhibit activation of the receiving unit. Activation of units in a network therefore depends on two things: (1) the signal that originates in the input units and (2) the connection weights throughout the network.

The effect of connection weights is illustrated by the differences in activation of the output units in the network in Figure 9.21, indicated by the colors, with highly activated units indicated by red, and less activated units by blue and green. Although the connection weights are not shown, differences between different connections are what is causing the differences in activity of the units. It is these differences, and the pattern of activity they create, that are responsible for a basic principle of connectionism: *A stimulus presented to the input units is represented by the pattern of activity that is distributed across the other units.* If this sounds familiar, it is because it is similar to the distributed representations in the brain we have described for neural coding (Chapter 2, page 36), attention (Chapter 4, page 107), and memory (Chapter 5, page 140; Chapter 7, page 191). Now that we have used the simple network in Figure 9.21 to introduce the basic principles of connectionist networks, we will consider how some specific concepts are represented in the more complex connectionist network shown in ● Figure 9.22.

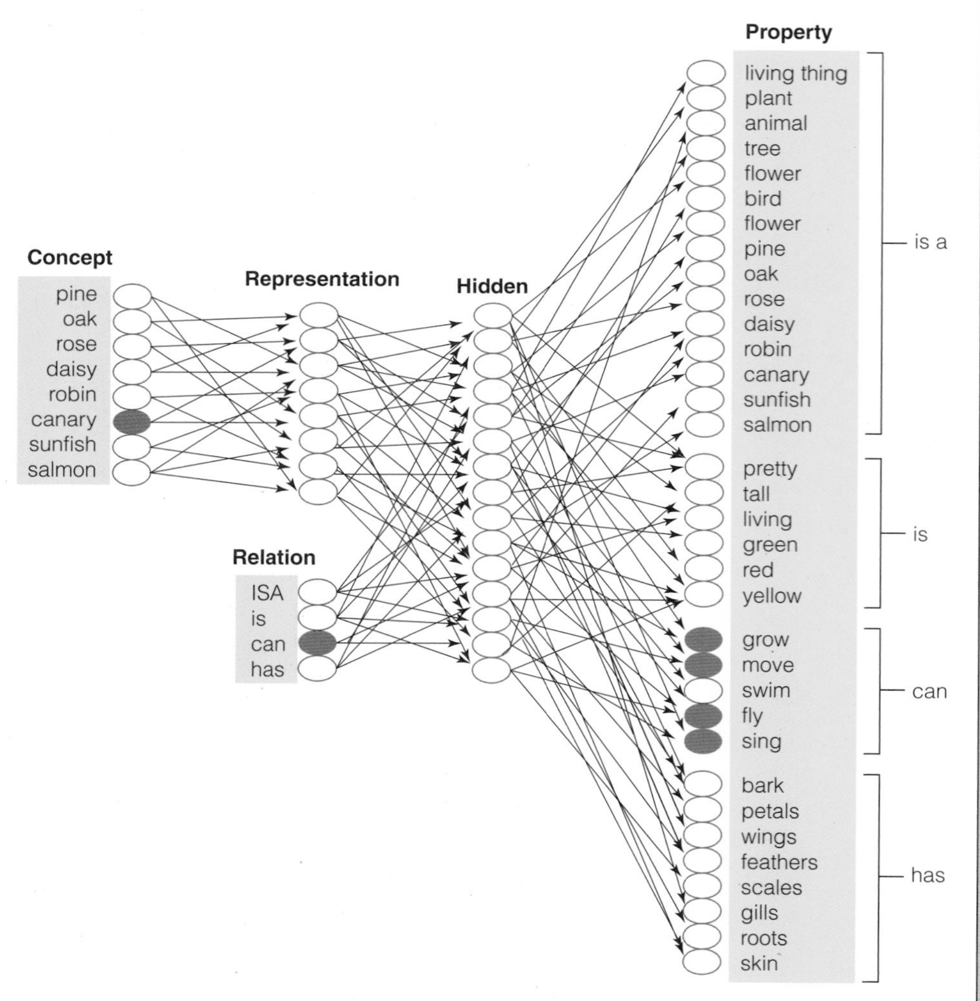

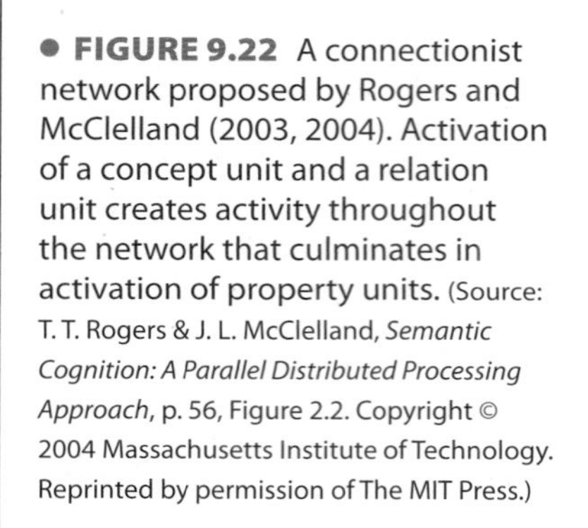

● **FIGURE 9.22** A connectionist network proposed by Rogers and McClelland (2003, 2004). Activation of a concept unit and a relation unit creates activity throughout the network that culminates in activation of property units. (Source: T. T. Rogers & J. L. McClelland, *Semantic Cognition: A Parallel Distributed Processing Approach*, p. 56, Figure 2.2. Copyright © 2004 Massachusetts Institute of Technology. Reprinted by permission of The MIT Press.)

HOW ARE CONCEPTS REPRESENTED IN A CONNECTIONIST NETWORK?

The model in Figure 9.22 was proposed by James McClelland and Timothy Rogers (2003) to show how different concepts and their properties can be represented in a connectionist network. Although this model is more complex than the one in Figure 9.21, it has similar components: units, links, and connection weights (although the connection weights are not shown).

First, let's compare this model to Quillian and Collins' hierarchical model in Figure 9.12. The first thing to notice is that both models are dealing with the same concepts. Specific concepts, such as "canary" and "salmon," shown in blue in Figure 9.12, are represented on the far left as concept units in Figure 9.22. Also, notice that the properties of the concepts are indicated in both networks by the following four relation statements: "is a" (A canary is a bird); "is" (A canary is yellow); "can" (A canary can fly); and "has" (A canary has wings). But whereas the hierarchical network indicates these properties at the network's nodes, the connectionist network indicates these properties by activity in the property units on the far right.

Let's now put our connectionist network to work by presenting a concept, "canary," and a relation statement, "can," indicated by the red units in Figure 9.22. The network's goal is to complete the following fill-in-the-blank statement: "A canary can _____." We can see that this has been achieved by noting that the units for "grow," "move," "fly," and "sing" have been activated. Try your hand at connecting the concepts and relation statements on the left with properties on the right by doing the following demonstration.

DEMONSTRATION Activation of Property Units in a Connectionist Network

Looking at the network in Figure 9.22, focus on the concept units, the relation units, and the property units. Ignore all of the other units in between. Your task is simply to ask the network questions by indicating a concept and a relation, and then to note which property units should be activated when the network answers the question. Determine which property units will be activated by the following:

Concept unit	Relation unit	Property units
• Salmon	is a	?
• Pine tree	has	?
• Daisy	is	?

The demonstration illustrates how a concept's properties can be represented by activation of property units in our connectionist network. The connectionist model proposes that a concept like "canary" is represented not only by activity of the property units, but also by the pattern of activation of other units within the network. How is this pattern determined? The answer to this question involves the connection weights, as we will see when we consider what happens inside the network when we activate a concept unit and a relation unit.

If we activate "canary" and "can," these units send activity to the representation and hidden units. The effect of this activation on the rest of the network depends on the connection weights between the various units in the network. If all of the connection weights were 1.0, then many of the units would be activated, including many incorrect property units. For example, if you start at *canary* and *can* and follow the links, signals would get through to incorrect property units like "tall," "daisy," and "green."

For this model to work, the connection weights have to be adjusted so that when concept unit "canary" and relation unit "can" are activated, only "grow," "move," "fly," and "sing" are activated. This adjustment of weights is achieved by a learning process. Before learning, the weights are incorrect, as in our example, so activating "canary" causes an erroneous response in the property units. According to connectionism, these erroneous responses are noted and sent back through the network, by a process called *back propagation*. **Back propagation** is the process by which **error signals** are sent back to the hidden and representation units to provide information about how the connection weights should be changed so that the correct property units will be activated.

We won't explain the specifics of how these back-propagated error signals provide information for changing the connection weights, because the answer is complex and is still a topic of investigation by researchers. Instead we will describe the process behaviorally. Consider a young child watching a robin on a branch. Just below the tree, a cat is approaching. The robin sees the cat and flies away. The young child may have thought the bird would not react to the cat but, in observing this situation, learned that robins avoid cats. Children also learn about properties of robins from their parents. If they see a canary and say "robin," the parent might correct them and say "That is a canary" and "Robins have red breasts." Thus, a child's learning about concepts begins with little information and some incorrect ideas, which are slowly modified in response both to observation of the environment and to feedback from others. Similarly, the connectionist network's learning about concepts begins with incorrect connection weights, which are slowly modified in response to error signals. In this way, the network slowly learns that things that look like birds can fly, things that look like fish can swim, and things that look like trees stay still while other things move around them.

The connectionist network's learning process therefore consists of initially weak and undifferentiated activation of property units, with many errors (for example, the input "canary" causing activation of the property unit "tall"). Error signals are then sent back through the network. These signals result in changes in connection weights, so the next activation of "canary" results in a new activation pattern. Changes to the connections are small after each learning experience. The new pattern is closer to the correct pattern but still isn't correct, so the process is repeated until the network assigns the correct properties to "canary." The pattern of activation distributed across the network that results in activation of the correct property units is the pattern that represents "canary."

Although this "educated" network might work well for canaries, what happens when a robin flies by and alights on the branch of a pine tree? To be useful, this network needs to be able to represent not just canaries, but also robins and pine trees. Thus, to create a network that can represent many different concepts, the network is not trained just on "canary." Instead, presentations of "canary" are interleaved with presentations of "robin," "pine tree," and so on, with small connection weights made after each presentation.

Because the network has to respond correctly to many different concepts, the network's learning process has to be designed in such a way that changing the connection weights to obtain a better response to "canary" doesn't result in a worse response to "pine tree." This is achieved by changing the weights very slowly on each trial, so that changing the weights in response to one concept causes little disruption of the weights for the other concepts that are being learned at the same time. Eventually, after thousands of trials, the weights in the network become adjusted so that the network generates the correct activation of property units for many different concepts.

We can appreciate how this learning process occurs over many trials by looking at the results of a computer simulation. The network in Figure 9.22 was presented with a number of different concepts and relation statements, one after another, and the activity of the units and connection weights between units were calculated by the computer. • Figure 9.23 indicates the activation of the eight representation units in response to different inputs. At the beginning of the process, the experimenter set the connection weights so that activity was about the same in each unit (Learning trials = 0). This corresponds to the initially weak and undifferentiated activation we discussed earlier.

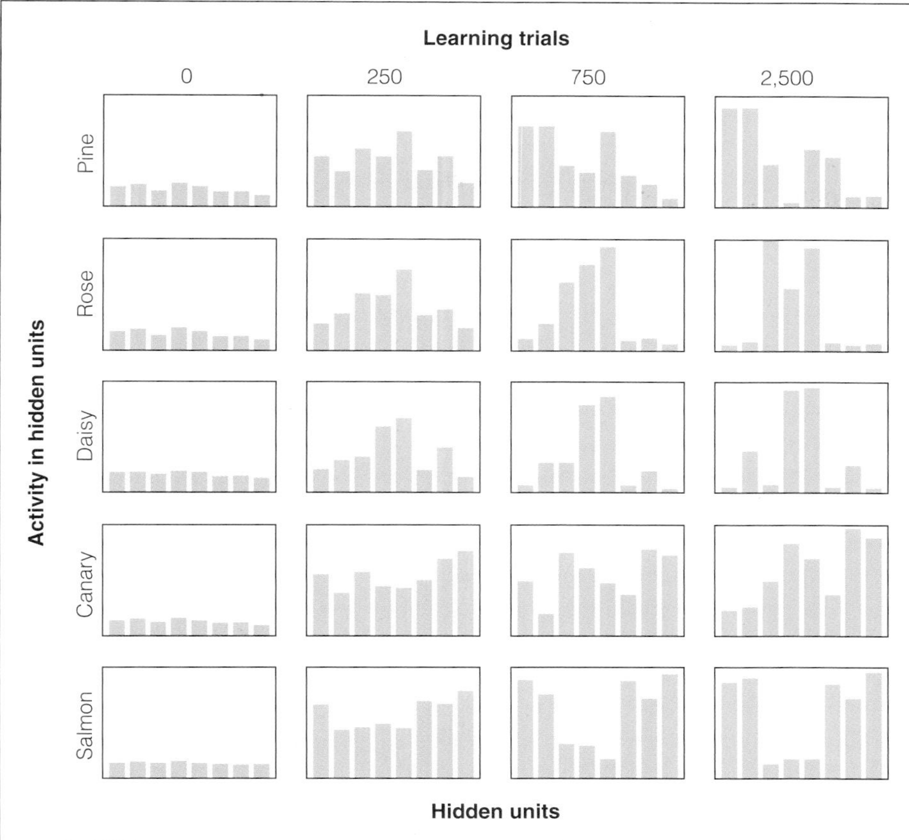

• **FIGURE 9.23** Learning in a connectionist network. Bars represent activity in the eight representation units. Notice how the pattern of activation changes as learning progresses. (Source: J. L. McClelland & T. T. Rogers, "The Parallel-Distributed Processing Approach to Semantic Cognition," *Nature Reviews Neuroscience, 4*, 310–320. Copyright © 2003. Reprinted by permission.)

As learning progressed, with each concept being presented one after another and the computer changing the weights just slightly after each trial in response to error signals, the patterns became adjusted, so by Trial 250 the patterns for "salmon" and "canary" begin to look different. By Trial 2,500 it is easy to tell the difference between the patterns for "salmon" and "canary" or between "canary" and "daisy." Note that the two flowers, "rose" and "daisy," have similar but slightly different patterns.

Although our description has been based on one particular connectionist network, most networks have similar properties. Connectionist networks are created by a learning process that shapes the networks so they are eventually capable of handling a wide range of inputs. Information about each concept in a connectionist network is contained in the *distributed* pattern of activity across a number of units.

Notice how different this operation of the connectionist network is from the operation of Collins and Quillian's hierarchical network, in which concepts and their properties are represented by activation of different nodes. Representation in a connectionist network is far more complex, involving many more units for each concept, but it is also much more like what happens in the brain.

Because of the resemblance between connectionist networks and the brain, and the fact that connectionist networks have been developed that can simulate normal cognitive functioning for processes such as language processing, memory, and cognitive development (Rogers & McClelland, 2004; Seidenberg & Zevin, 2006), many researchers believe that the idea that knowledge is represented by distributed activity holds great promise. The following results also support the idea of connectionism:

1. *The operation of connectionist networks is not totally disrupted by damage.* Because information in the network is distributed across many units, damage to the system does not completely disrupt its operation. This property, in which disruption of performance occurs only gradually as parts of the system are damaged, is called **graceful degradation**. It is similar to what often happens in actual cases of brain damage, in which damage to the brain causes only a partial loss of functioning. Some researchers have suggested that studying the way networks respond to damage may suggest strategies for rehabilitation of human patients (Farah et al., 1993; Hinton & Shallice, 1991; Olson & Humphreys, 1997; Plaut, 1996).
2. *Connectionist networks can explain generalization of learning.* Because similar concepts have similar patterns, training a system to recognize the properties of one concept (such as "canary") also provides information about other, related concepts (such as "robin" or "sparrow"). This is similar to the way we actually learn about concepts because learning about canaries enables us to predict properties of different types of birds we've never seen (see McClelland et al., 1995).

While active research on connectionism continues in many laboratories, some researchers point out that there are limits to what connectionist networks can explain. They are especially critical of the idea of the back propagation error-correcting mechanism, because it isn't clear exactly how it works, and it has been difficult to find a similar mechanism in the brain (see O'Reilly, 1996, who proposes a possible mechanism, and the commentary following Rogers & McClelland, 2008). Whatever the final verdict on connectionism, this approach has stimulated a great deal of research, some of which has added to our understanding of both normal cognition and how brain damage affects cognition.

Now that we have described how concepts are represented by a computer model based on the operation of the brain, we will describe some recent discoveries about how concepts are represented in the brain. This research involves recording from single neurons in the monkey, studying the effects of brain damage in humans, and measuring brain activity by brain scanning in humans.

Categories and the Brain

How are different categories (or concepts) represented in the brain? Research on this question has focused largely on visual objects like the ones we have been discussing in this chapter—things like plants, animals, vehicles, and trees.

SPECIFIC OR DISTRIBUTED ACTIVITY?

One possible answer to the question of how objects are represented is that different categories of objects are represented by activity in specific areas of the brain. Two examples of areas for specific categories are the fusiform face area (FFA) that responds strongly to faces and the parahippocampal place area (PPA) that responds to houses, rooms, and places (see page 32). Supporting the connection between the fusiform area and faces is the condition prospoagnosia, the inability to recognize faces, which occurs in people who have suffered damage to the temporal lobe.

But saying that one group of things, such as faces, is represented by activity in one area of the brain and another group, like houses or rooms, is represented in another area doesn't go far enough. For one thing, we know that brain representations are usually distributed, so that even if a particular stimulus causes a large amount of activity in one area, it also causes activity in many other areas as well.

One reason for this distributed representation is that objects consist of many different properties. Consider, for example, the cat in Figure 9.1. It has perceptual properties such as color, texture, and form. It has motor properties, which would include how cats move when they are walking, running, and catching mice. It has behavioral properties, which include catching mice, sleeping during the day, and other aspects of cat behavior. Cats also can evoke affective responses, such as a particular person's emotional response to cats. Thus, the representation of the cat consists of a distributed representation that would include activity in sensory areas (for what the cat looks like when stationary and moving), motor areas (for how it moves), higher level areas (that represent knowledge about the cat's behavior and other qualities), and emotional areas (for the emotional response elicited by the cat) (Barbey & Barsalou, 2009).

CATEGORY INFORMATION IN SINGLE NEURONS

The representation of categories in the brain has been studied by recording from single neurons. To illustrate this, we will describe an experiment by David Freedman and coworkers (2001, 2003, 2008). Freedman trained monkeys to classify stimuli like the ones in ● Figure 9.24, which consisted of mixtures of "cat" and "dog" stimuli. In this

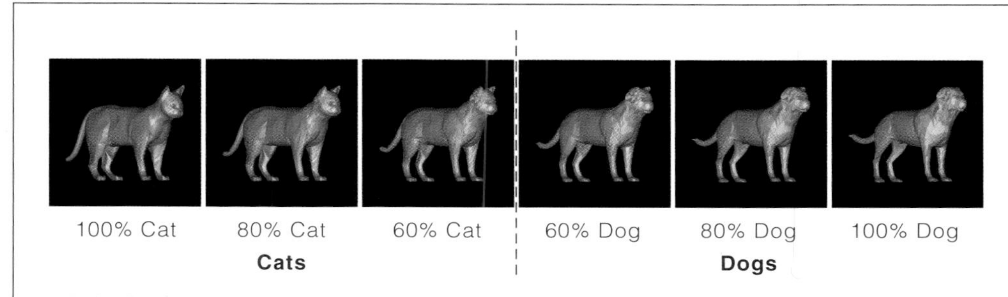

● **FIGURE 9.24** Some of the stimuli used in Freedman's experiment. The far left stimulus is 100 percent cat, the far right is 100 percent dog, and the others are mixtures of the two. The dashed line is the border between the category "cat" and the category "dog." (Source: Adapted from D. J. Freedman et al., "A Comparison of Primate Prefrontal and Inferior Temporal Cortices During Visual Categorization," *Journal of Neuroscience*, 23(12), 5235–5246, Figure 1b. Copyright 2003 Society for Neuroscience.)

example, the stimulus on the left is 100 percent cat, the one on the right is 100 percent dog, and the others are mixtures of the two. Using stimuli like these, plus many others that also mixed dog and cat properties, Freedman trained the monkeys to respond to stimuli that were more than 50 percent "cat" as being in the cat category, and to respond to the rest as dogs. After several months of training, the monkeys were able to categorize a 60 percent cat/40 percent dog stimulus as "cat" about 90 percent of the time. Likewise, monkeys correctly classified 60 percent dog stimuli as "dog" about 90 percent of the time.

Once the monkeys had learned to categorize the stimuli, they were tested using the procedure in ● Figure 9.25a. First a sample stimulus (either a cat or a dog) was presented; then, after a 1-second delay, a test stimulus was presented. The monkey's task was to release a lever if it judged the test stimulus to be in the same category as the sample stimulus. As the monkeys were doing this, Freedman recorded from neurons in an area of the temporal lobe called the inferotemporal (IT) cortex, which responds to forms, and from neurons in the prefrontal (PF) cortex, which is involved in memory and other cognitive processes (see Chapter 5, page 138).

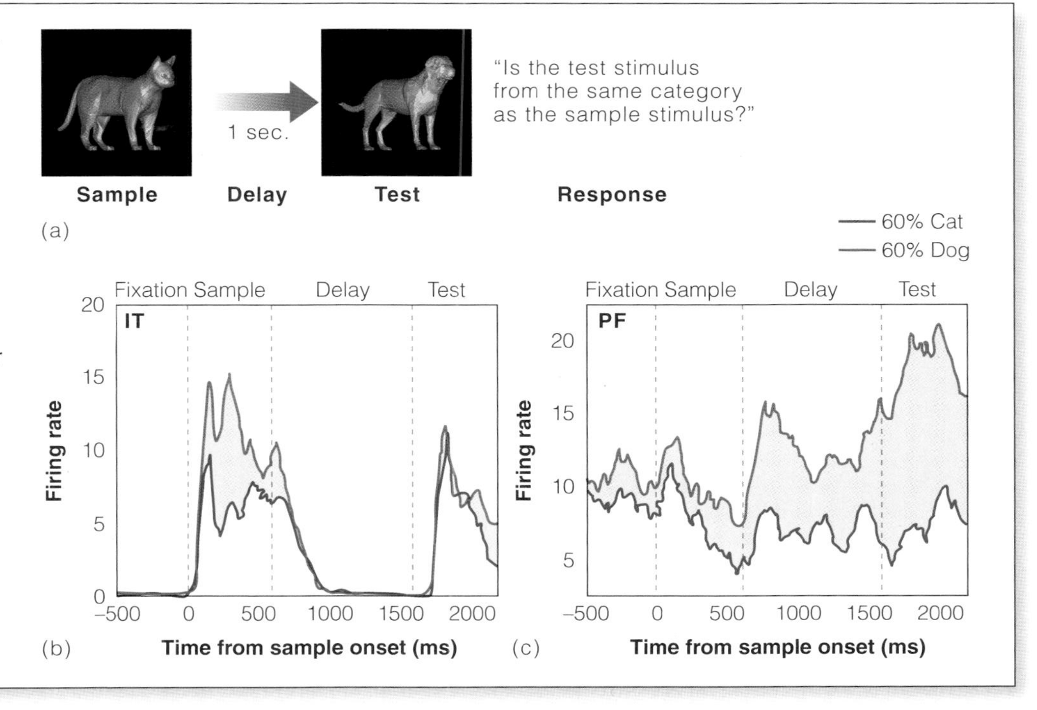

● **FIGURE 9.25** (a) Testing procedure for determining if monkeys can categorize cats and dogs. (b) Activity recorded from a neuron in the monkey's IT cortex during the testing sequence. This neuron responds more to a 60 percent dog stimulus than to a 60 percent cat stimulus during presentation of the sample. (c) Activity recorded from a neuron in the monkey's PF cortex during the testing sequence. This neuron responds better to the dog stimulus during the delay and test periods. (Source: D. J. Freedman et al., "A Comparison of Primate Prefrontal and Inferior Temporal Cortices During Visual Categorization," *Journal of Neuroscience, 23*, 5235–5246, Figure 4, 2003. Reprinted by permission.)

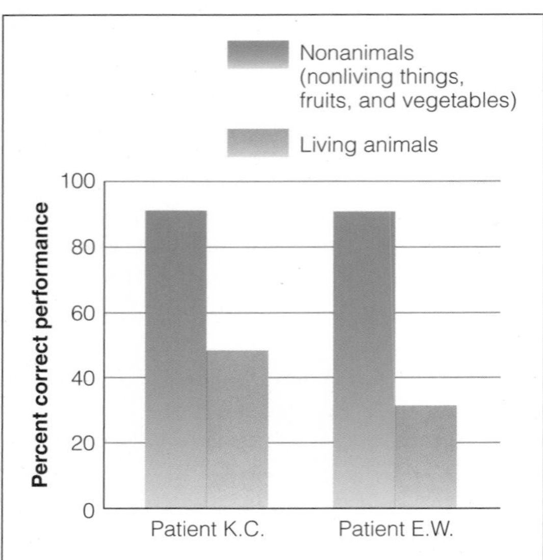

• **FIGURE 9.26** Performance on a naming task for patients K.C. and E.W., both of whom had category-specific knowledge impairment. They were able to correctly name pictures of nonliving things (like car and table) and fruits and vegetables (like tomato and pear), but performed poorly when asked to name pictures of animals. (Source: B. Z. Mahon & A. Caramazza, "Concepts and Categories: A Cognitive Neuropsychological Perspective," *Annual Review of Psychology, 60*, 27–51, Figure 1, 2009. Reprinted by permission.)

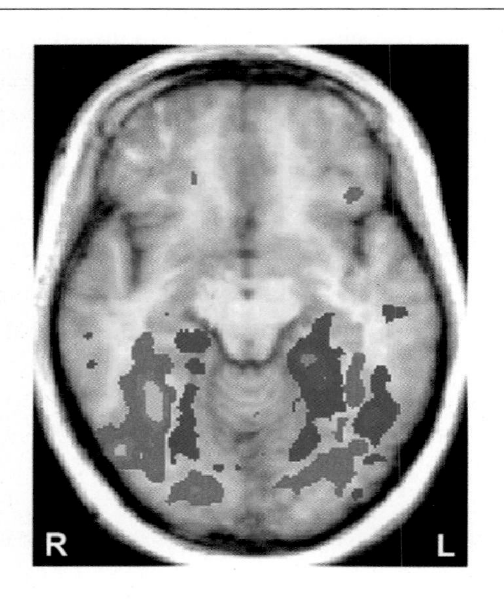

• **FIGURE 9.27** Cross section of the brain, looking up from the bottom, showing brain activation measured by fMRI. Yellow-red areas were activated by naming pictures of animals; blue-green areas were activated by naming pictures of tools. (Source: A. Martin, "The Representation of Object Concepts In The Brain, *Annual Review of Psychology, 58*, 25–45, 2007.)

The results of this experiment for an IT neuron are shown in Figure 9.25b. This figure shows the response of the neuron to 60 percent dog stimuli and 60 percent cat stimuli. During presentation of the sample, when the monkey is just looking at the stimuli, this neuron fires more to the dog stimuli. During the delay and test periods, when the monkey is holding the information about the stimuli in memory and then making a category judgment, this neuron responds in the same way to the dog and cat stimuli.

The results for the PF cortex neuron are shown in Figure 9.27c. During presentation of the sample, this neuron responds slightly better to the dog stimuli, although the difference is small and not significant. During the delay, however, the neuron fires much more rapidly to the dog (this would correspond to holding properties of the dog in working memory, see page 139). During the test, when the monkey is making a decision, the difference in response becomes even larger.

Freedman's results show that different areas of the cortex respond to different aspects of stimuli. The IT cortex, which distinguishes between dogs and cats during presentation of the stimuli, appears to be responding to the features and shapes of the dog and cat stimuli. The PF cortex, which distinguishes between dogs and cats during the delay and while the monkey is making a decision, appears to be responding to more abstract properties of the stimuli that are characteristic of dogs in general or of cats in general.

NEUROPSYCHOLOGY OF CATEGORIES

Another line of research on categorization has involved neuropsychology—studies of the behavior of people with brain damage. Neurosychological research on how categories are represented in the brain has focused on patients with **category-specific knowledge impairment**, in which the patient has trouble recognizing objects in one category. • Figure 9.26 shows the results for two patients, K.C. and E.W., who have difficulty naming animals, but can name nonliving things and fruits and vegetables (Blundo et al., 2006; Caramazza & Shelton, 1998; Mahon & Carmazza, 2009).

These patients appeared to have problems not only in telling the difference between different animals, but also in knowing the properties of animals. Thus, K.C. and E.W. not only had trouble naming different kinds of animals, but also had difficulty answering questions about animals, such as "Does a whale have legs?" or "Are dogs domestic animals?" However, they were able to answer similar questions about nonanimals (Mahon & Caramazza, 2009).

BRAIN SCANNING AND CATEGORIES

Differences between responses to living and nonliving things have also been demonstrated using brain scanning in humans. • Figure 9.27 shows areas that are activated by looking at pictures of animals (red-yellow areas) and by looking at pictures of tools (blue-green areas) (Chao et al., 2002; Martin, 2007; also see Chao et al., 1999). This difference in areas of the brain that are activated in response to animals and to tools has also been observed when words are presented instead of pictures. Thus, words such as *crow*, *pigeon*, and *horse*, which refer to living things, activate one area of the brain, and words such as *flute*, *fork*, and *crayon*, which refer to man-made objects that people use, activate another area (Wheatley et al., 2005).

When we consider the specific areas that are activated by animals and tools, an interesting result emerges. Areas activated by animals also respond well to the kinds of motion associated with animals, such as walking and running; areas activated by tools respond well to the kinds of motion associated with tools, such as banging with a hammer or sawing a piece of wood.

These findings confirm our description at the beginning of this section of the distributed nature of categories in the brain. Our knowledge about categories is distributed in many areas of the brain, including areas that respond to what an object looks like and also areas that respond to other properties associated with the object, such as what it is used for and how it moves. To emphasize this point, let's consider another class of objects—food. When Kyle Simmons and coworkers (2005) showed observers pictures of food, such as cookies and hamburgers, these pictures activated both areas in the visual cortex associated with the food's shape and also other areas associated with taste. Another study showed that pictures of food also activate the amygdala, an area associated with experiencing emotion (see Chapter 8, page 208), and the prefrontal cortex, which may be responding to how appealing a particular food it (Kilgore et al., 2003). Food, just like objects in other categories, is represented in the brain by responding in an array of neurons, distributed throughout the brain, which all together represent our knowledge about the object.

(a) **Familiarization**

(b) **Preference test**

● **FIGURE 9.28** Procedure for determining whether an infant has formed the category "cat." (a) The infant is shown pictures of 5 pairs of cats for 15 seconds per pair during familiarization. Two pairs are shown here. (b) The infant is then shown another cat paired with a dog during the preference test. Greater looking time for the dog provides evidence that the infant has placed the dog in a different category than "cat." (Source: Based on Quinn et al., 1993. Photos © Cathy Britcliffe/iStockphoto.com; Silberkorn/iStockphoto.com; GlobalP/iStockphoto.com; Olga Utlyakova, 2010/used under license from Shutterstock.com; A. Krotov, 2010/used under license from Shutterstock.com; Eric Isselée, 2010/used under license from Shutterstock.com.)

Something to Consider

Categorization in Infants

All of the research we have described in this chapter involves language. Questions such as "What do you call that?" "Is that a word or a nonword?" and "What are the characteristics of bicycles?" all involve understanding language and being able to use it. Does this mean that categorization is based on language and, therefore, that infants don't start placing things into categories until they can speak? The answer to this question is a resounding "no." Research has shown that even newborn infants are capable of primitive categorization (they have one category for "mother" and another for "other women") and that more sophisticated categorization begins appearing at about 2 months of age. The major method used to study categorization in very young infants is the *familiarization/novelty preference procedure*.

METHOD Familiarization/Novelty Preference Procedure

The **familiarization/novelty preference procedure** makes use of the fact that when given a choice between a familiar object and a novel one, infants generally will look longer at the novel object. The first step in a categorization experiment is *familiarization*, in which infants are exposed to a number of different examples within one category. For example, infants might see a number of different kinds of cats, as shown in ● Figure 9.28a, in which a number of pairs of cats are presented to the infant. (In another set of experiments it is determined that the infants can tell the difference between the cats, so during familiarization they are seeing stimuli that look different to them but share the characteristics that make them "cats.")

The second part of the experiment is the *preference test*, in which an example the infants have never seen before from the familiarized category (cats, in our example) is presented along with an example from another category, such as dogs (Figure 9.28b). If the infant looks longer at the dog, it is inferred that the infant has grouped the novel cat with all of the other cats (so it belongs to the category "cats"), but has not included the dog in that category (the dog is in another category).

Using this procedure, Paul Quinn and Mark Johnson (2000) have shown that infants as young as 2 months of age can mentally represent a category of mammals (such as cats, dogs, horses) that excludes furniture (such as chairs, couches, beds). This represents categorization at the broad, global level that we discussed earlier in the chapter (see page 247). However, infants this age don't yet form separate categories for cats, rabbits, and dogs, so they haven't yet formed intermediate, basic level categories.

By 3 to 4 months of age, infants begin forming basic level categories, as indicated by experiments like those described in the Methods section, which show that after being familiarized with cats, infants look more at a dog than at a novel cat (Furrer & Younger, 2005; Oakes & Ribar, 2005; Quinn et al., 1993; Younger & Fearing, 1999). This ability to categorize at the basic level is not completely developed by 3 to 4 months, however. After familiarization with cats, if infants this age are tested with a novel cat and a novel lion, the infants do not look more at the novel lion. Thus, while the infants can form a category "cat" that is separate from the category "dog," their "cat" category does not exclude lions, perhaps because lions have some catlike qualities. Slightly older infants (6 to 7 months) do respond differently to cats and lions (Eimas & Quinn, 1994).

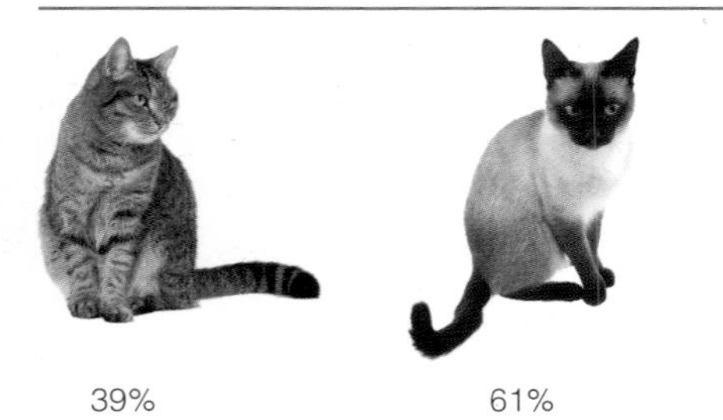

• **FIGURE 9.29** Procedure for determining whether an infant has formed specific categories for "tabby" and "Siamese." (a) A number of pairs of tabbies are shown during familiarization. One pair is shown here. (b) After the pairs of tabbies, a new tabby is paired with a Siamese during the preference test. Percentages indicate the amount of time spent looking at each picture during the preference test. (Source: Data from Quinn, 2004. Photos ZTS, 2010/used under license from Shutterstock.com; Paul Cotney, 2010/used under license from Shutterstock.com; AngiePhotos/iStockphoto.com; kovalvs/iStockphoto.com.)

At 6 to 7 months, infants can form even more specific categories. • Figure 9.29 shows the results of an experiment that used the same procedure as shown in Figure 9.28, except the cats in the familiarization part of the experiment were different examples of one kind of cat (all tabbies). In the preference test, when a new tabby cat was paired with a new Siamese, infants looked more at the new Siamese (Quinn, 2004). This result supports the idea that 6- to 7-month-old infants have formed categories for specific types of cats.

However, just as 3- to 4-month-old infants' capacity to categorize at the basic level is not fully developed (their cat category was separate from dogs, but not from lions), the 6- to 7-month-old infants' ability to categorize at the specific level is only partially developed. This is indicated by the finding that when the procedure is reversed, so the infants are familiarized with Siamese cats and then tested by presenting a Siamese and a tabby, they do not show a preference for the tabby. Thus, 6- to 7-month-old infants can form a category "tabby" that does not include "Siamese," but not a category "Siamese" that does not include "tabby." The reason why the tabby-Siamese experiment doesn't work in reverse isn't clear. The ability to distinguish between tabby and Siamese categories in both directions develops at a later age, although experiments determining the exact age at which this occurs have not yet been done.

These results for infants ranging from 2 months to 7 months of age demonstrate a progression from first being able to form global categories, then basic categories, and finally, specific categories (Quinn & Tanaka, 2007; Younger & Fearing, 2000). Thus, categories become more "fine-tuned" as infants get older.

The development of categorization does not, of course, end at 7 months. The early development we have described sets the stage for the development of more sophisticated concepts, a process that accelerates once language develops. This process enables young children to begin associating specific properties, such as the ones shown for the cat in Figure 9.1, with their categories. As children continue to acquire more knowledge (for example, that cats give birth to kittens, and that kittens are born with their eyes closed), this knowledge is incorporated into the mental representation of cats that was initially formed during infancy. This continuing "enrichment" of concepts is an important part of the cognitive developmental process that turns the perceptual categories of infants into the more knowledge-based ones of children and adults (Murphy, 2002; Quinn, 2008).

TEST YOURSELF 9.2

1. What is the basic idea behind the semantic network approach? What is the goal of this approach, and how did the network created by Collins and Quillian accomplish this goal?
2. What is the evidence for and against the Collins and Quillian model? How did Collins and Loftus modify the model to deal with criticisms of the Collins and Quillian model, and how were these modifications received by other researchers?
3. What are some of the properties of a good psychological theory? How have these properties been applied to semantic network theories?
4. What is a connectionist network? Describe how a connectionist network learns, considering specifically how connection weights are adjusted. Also consider how the way information is represented in a connectionist network differs from the way it is represented in a semantic network.
5. How are categories represented in the brain? Describe evidence from single neuron recording in monkeys, the effects of brain damage in humans, and human brain imaging.
6. How is the ability of young infants to form categories measured? Trace the development between 2 and 7 months of infants' ability to categorize. What abilities are added after 7 months?

CHAPTER SUMMARY

1. Categories are "pointers to knowledge." Once you know that something is in a category, you know a lot of general things about it and can focus your energy on specifying what is special about this particular object.
2. The definitional approach to categorization doesn't work because most categories contain members that do not conform to the definition. The philosopher Wittgenstein proposed the idea of family resemblances to deal with the fact that definitions do not include all members of a category.
3. The idea behind the prototypical approach to categorization is that we decide whether an object belongs to a category by deciding whether it is similar to a standard representative of the category, called a prototype. A prototype is formed by averaging category members a person has encountered in the past.
4. Prototypicality is a term used to describe how well an object resembles the prototype of a particular category.
5. The following is true of high-prototypical objects: (a) They have high family resemblance; (b) statements about them are verified rapidly; (c) they are named first; and (d) they are affected more by priming.
6. The exemplar approach to categorization involves determining whether an object is similar to an exemplar. An exemplar is an actual member of a category that a person has encountered in the past.
7. An advantage of the exemplar approach is that it doesn't discard information about atypical cases within a category, such as penguin in the bird category. The exemplar approach can also deal more easily with categories that contain widely varying members, like games.
8. Researchers have concluded that people use both approaches to categorization. Prototypes may be more important as people initially learn about categories; later, exemplar information may become more important. Exemplars may work better for small categories (U.S. presidents), and prototypes may work better for larger categories (birds).
9. The kind of organization in which larger, more general categories are divided into smaller, more specific categories is called hierarchical organization.
10. Experiments by Rosch indicate that a basic level of categories (such as guitar, as opposed to musical instrument or rock guitar) is a "privileged" level of categorization that reflects people's everyday experience.
11. Experiments in which experts were tested show that the basic level of categorization can depend on a person's degree of expertise.
12. The semantic network approach proposes that concepts are arranged in networks that represent the way concepts are organized in the mind. Collins and Quillian's model is a network that consists of nodes connected by links. Concepts and properties of concepts are located at the nodes. Properties that hold for most members of a concept are stored at higher level nodes. This is called cognitive economy.
13. Collins and Quillian's model is supported by the results of experiments using the sentence verification technique.

The spreading activation feature of the model is supported by priming experiments.

14. The Collins and Quillian model has been criticized for several reasons: It can't explain the typicality effect, the idea of cognitive economy doesn't always hold, and it can't explain all results of sentence verification experiments.
15. Collins and Loftus proposed another semantic network model, designed to deal with criticisms of the Collins and Quillian model. This model was, in turn, criticized because it was so flexible that it could explain any result.
16. The connectionist approach proposes that concepts are represented in networks that consist of input units, hidden units, and output units. Information about concepts is represented in these networks by a distributed activation of these units. This approach is therefore also called the parallel distributed processing (PDP) approach.
17. Connectionist networks learn the correct distributed pattern for a particular concept through a gradual learning process that involves adjusting the weights that determine how activation is transferred from one unit to another.
18. Connectionist networks have a number of features that enable them to reproduce many aspects of human concept formation.
19. The idea that concepts are represented by specialized brain areas has been supported by single neuron recording (Freedman's monkey experiments), neuropsychological evidence (category-specific knowledge impairments), and by the results of brain scanning experiments in humans (animals versus tools). The conclusion from this evidence is that knowledge about concepts is distributed over many areas of the brain.
20. Newborn infants are capable of crude categorization. The familiarity/novelty preference procedure has been used to determine the development of categorization from global to basic to specific between 2 and 7 months of age. Further learning during childhood adds more specific knowledge to categories.

Think ABOUT IT

1. In this chapter we have seen how networks can be constructed that link different levels of concepts. In Chapter 7 we saw how organizational trees can be constructed that organize knowledge about a particular topic (see Figures 7.5 and 7.6). Create a tree that represents the material in this chapter by linking together things that are related. How is this tree similar to or different from the semantic network in Figure 9.12? Is your tree hierarchical? What information does it contain about each concept?
2. Do a survey to determine people's conception of "typical" members of various categories. For example, ask several people to name, as quickly as possible, three typical "birds" or "vehicles" or "beverages." What do the results of this survey tell you about what level is "basic" for different people? What do the results tell you about the variability of different people's conception of categories?
3. Try asking a number of people to name the objects pictured in Figure 9.10. Rosch, who ran her experiment in the early 1970s, found that the most common responses were guitar, fish, and pants. Notice whether the responses you receive are the same as or different from the responses reported by Rosch. If they are different, explain why you think this might have occurred.

If You WANT TO KNOW MORE

1. **More on concepts.** If you want to read more about concepts, see *The Big Book of Concepts*, which starts by asserting that "concepts are the glue that holds our mental world together."

   Murphy, G. (2004). *The big book of concepts.* Cambridge, MA: MIT Press.

2. **Culture and categorization.** Cross-cultural research on members of the Itza culture indicates that culture can affect which level of categories is considered basic. Thus, a basic category for members of one culture may differ from what is basic for members of another culture.

   Medin, D. L., & Atran, S. (2004). The native mind: Biological categorization and reasoning in development and across cultures. *Psychological Review, 111*, 960–983.

3. **Personal and institutional categories.** People and major institutions create their own categories, some of which apply only to them individually. This type of categorization is related to the increased use of the Internet.

   Gleshko, R. J., Maglio, P. P., Matlock, T., & Barsalou, L. W. (2008). Categorization in the wild. *Trends in Cognitive Sciences, 12*, 129–135.

Key TERMS

Back propagation, 258
Basic level, 248
Categorization, 240
Category, 240
Category-specific knowledge impairment, 262
Cognitive economy, 250
Concept, 240
Connection weight, 255
Connectionism, 255
Connectionist network, 255
Definitional approach to categorization, 241
Error signal, 258
Exemplar, 246
Exemplar approach to categorization, 246
Familiarization/novelty preference procedure, 263
Family resemblance, 242
Global (superordinate) level, 248
Graceful degradation, 259
Hidden units, 255
Hierarchical model, 250
Hierarchical organization, 247
High prototypicality, 243
Input units, 255
Lexical decision task, 252
Low prototypicality, 243
Output units, 255
Parallel distributed processing (PDP), 255
Prototype, 243
Prototype approach to categorization, 243
Prototypicality, 243
Semantic network approach, 250
Sentence verification technique, 244
Specific (subordinate) level, 248
Spreading activation, 251
Typicality effect, 244
Units, 255

Media RESOURCES

The *Cognitive Psychology* Book Companion Website

www.cengage.com/international

Prepare for quizzes and exams with online resources—including a glossary, flashcards, tutorial quizzes, crossword puzzles, and more.

CogLab

CogLab

To experience these experiments for yourself, go to coglab.wadsworth.com. Be sure to read each experiment's setup instructions before you go to the experiment itself. Otherwise, you won't know which keys to press.

Primary Labs

Prototypes A method for studying the effect of concepts on responding (p. 243).

Lexical decision Demonstration of the lexical decision task, which has been used to provide evidence for the concept of spreading activation (p. 252).

Related Lab

Absolute identification Remembering levels that have been associated with a stimulus.

10 Imagery

“Visual imagery” occurs when a person visually imagines something that isn’t physically present. This picture represents the finding that although visual perception and visual imagery share many properties, experiences associated with visual imagery can be less detailed and more fragile than experiences associated with visual perception.

Bruce Goldstein

Some Questions We Will Consider

► How do "pictures in your head" that you create by imagining an object compare to the experience you have when you see the actual object? (272)

► What happens in your brain when you create visual images with your eyes closed? (279)

► How does damage to the brain affect the ability to form visual images? (282)

► How can we use visual imagery to improve memory? (286)

Let's return for a moment to Raphael, who, at the beginning of Chapter 1, was walking across campus talking to Susan on his cell phone (see Figure 1.1, page 4 for a retrieval cue!). One of Raphael's problems is that he has left Susan's book at home; as he realizes this, he thinks, "I can see it sitting there on my desk, where I left it." Raphael's ability to "see" Susan's book, even though it is not present, is an example of **visual imagery**—seeing in the absence of a visual stimulus.

Another example of visual imagery is my experience of being able to visually remember seeing the Pacific Ocean after cresting a mountain in California (page 158). This example was used to introduce the idea that mental time travel is a characteristic of episodic memory. Although mental time travel does not have to involve visual imagery, it often does, as it did for my "seeing what was on the other side of the mountain" experience. But imagery doesn't have to involve such drama! Consider, for example, the following demonstration.

DEMONSTRATION Experiencing Imagery

Answer the following questions:

- How many windows are there in front of the house or apartment where you live?
- How is the furniture arranged in your bedroom?
- Are an elephant's ears rounded or pointy?
- Is the green of grass darker or lighter than the green of a pine tree?

How did you go about answering these questions? Many people report that they experience visual images when answering questions such as these. On a more practical level, they might create images to help pack suitcases in the trunk of their car or rearrange furniture in the living room (Hegarty, 2010).

Mental imagery, or the ability to recreate the sensory world in the absence of physical stimuli, also occurs in senses other than vision. People have the ability to imagine tastes, smells, and tactile experiences. Most people can imagine melodies of familiar songs in their head, so it is not surprising that musicians often report strong auditory imagery and that the ability to imagine melodies has played an important role in musical composition. Paul McCartney says that the song "Yesterday" came to him as a mental image when he woke up with the tune in his head. Another example of auditory imagery is orchestra conductors' using a technique called the "inner audition" to practice without their orchestras by imagining a musical score in their minds. When they do this, they imagine not only the sounds of the various instruments but also their locations relative to the podium.

Just as auditory imagery has played an important role in the creative process of music, visual imagery has resulted in both scientific insights and practical applications. One of the most famous accounts of how visual imagery led to scientific discovery is the story related by the 19th-century German chemist Friedrich August Kekule. Kekule said that the structure of benzene came to him in a dream in which he saw a writhing chain that formed a circle that resembled a snake, with its head swallowing its tail. This visual image gave Kekule the insight that the carbon atoms that make up the benzene molecule are arranged in a ring.

A more recent example of visual imagery leading to scientific discovery is Albert Einstein's description of how he developed the theory of relativity by imagining himself traveling beside a beam of light (Intons-Peterson, 1993). On a less cosmic level, the golfer Jack Nicklaus has described how he discovered an error in the way he gripped his club as he was practicing golf swings in a dream (Intons-Peterson, 1993).

One message of these examples is that imagery provides a way of thinking that adds another dimension to the verbal techniques usually associated with thinking. But what is most important about imagery is that it is associated not just with discoveries by famous people, but also with most people's everyday experience. In this chapter we will focus on visual imagery, because most of the research on imagery has been on this type of imagery. We will describe the basic characteristics of visual imagery and how it relates to other cognitive processes such as thinking, memory, and perception. This connection between imagery and cognition in general is an important theme in the history of psychology, beginning in the early days of scientific psychology in the 19th century.

Imagery in the History of Psychology

We can trace the history of imagery back to the first laboratory of psychology, founded by Wilhelm Wundt (see Chapter 1, page 8).

EARLY IDEAS ABOUT IMAGERY

Wundt proposed that images were one of the three basic elements of consciousness, along with sensations and feelings. He also proposed that because images accompany thought, studying images was a way of studying thinking. This idea of a link between imagery and thinking gave rise to the **imageless thought debate**, with some psychologists taking up Aristotle's idea that "thought is impossible without an image," and others contending that thinking can occur without images.

Evidence supporting the idea that imagery was not required for thinking was Francis Galton's (1883) observation that people who had great difficulty forming visual images were still quite capable of thinking (also see Richardson, 1994, for more modern accounts of imagery differences between people). Other arguments both for and against the idea that images are necessary for thinking were proposed in the late 1800s and early 1900s, but these arguments and counterarguments ended when behaviorism toppled imagery from its central place in psychology (Watson, 1913; see Chapter 1, page 9). The behaviorists branded the study of imagery as unproductive because visual images are invisible to everyone except the person experiencing them. The founder of behaviorism, John Watson, described images as "unproven" and "mythological" (1928), and therefore not worthy of study. The dominance of behaviorism from the 1920s through the 1950s pushed the study of imagery out of mainstream psychology. However, this situation changed when the study of cognition was reborn in the 1950s.

IMAGERY AND THE COGNITIVE REVOLUTION

The history of cognitive psychology that we described in Chapter 1 recounts events in the 1950s and 1960s that came to be known as the cognitive revolution. One of the keys to the success of this "revolution" was that cognitive psychologists developed ways to measure behavior that could be used to infer cognitive processes. One example of a method that linked behavior and cognition is Alan Paivio's (1963) work on memory. Paivio showed that it was easier to remember concrete nouns, like *truck* or *tree*, that can be imaged, than it is to remember abstract nouns, like *truth* or *justice*, that are difficult to image. One technique Paivio used was *paired-associate learning*.

METHOD Paired-Associate Learning

In a **paired-associate learning** experiment, participants are presented with pairs of words, like *boat-hat* or *car-house*, during a study period. They are then presented, during the test period, with the first word from each pair. Their task is to recall the word that was paired with it during the study period. Thus, if they were presented with the word *boat*, the correct response would be *hat*.

Paivio (1963, 1965) found that memory for pairs of concrete nouns is much better than memory for pairs of abstract nouns. To explain this result, Paivio proposed the **conceptual peg hypothesis**. According to this hypothesis, concrete nouns create images that other words can "hang onto." For example, if presenting the pair *boat-hat* creates an image of a boat, then presenting the word *boat* later will bring back the boat image, which provides a number of places on which participants can place the hat in their mind (see Paivio, 2006, for an updating of his ideas about memory.)

CogLab Mental Rotation

Whereas Paivio inferred cognitive processes by measuring memory, Roger Shepard and J. Metzler (1971) inferred cognitive processes by using *mental chronometry*, determining the amount of time needed to carry out various cognitive tasks. In Shepard and Metzler's experiment, which we described in Chapter 5 (see page 134), participants saw pictures like the ones in ● Figure 10.1. Their task was to indicate, as rapidly as possible, whether the two pictures were of the same object or of different objects. This experiment showed that the time it took to decide that two views were of the same object was directly related to how different the angles were between the two views (see Figure 5.19). This result was interpreted as showing that participants were mentally rotating one of the views to see whether it matched the other one. What was important about this experiment was that it was one of the first to apply quantitative methods to the study of imagery and to suggest that imagery and perception may share the same mechanisms. (References to "mechanisms" include both mental mechanisms, such as ways of manipulating perceptual and mental images in the mind, and brain mechanisms, such as which structures are involved in creating perceptual and mental images.)

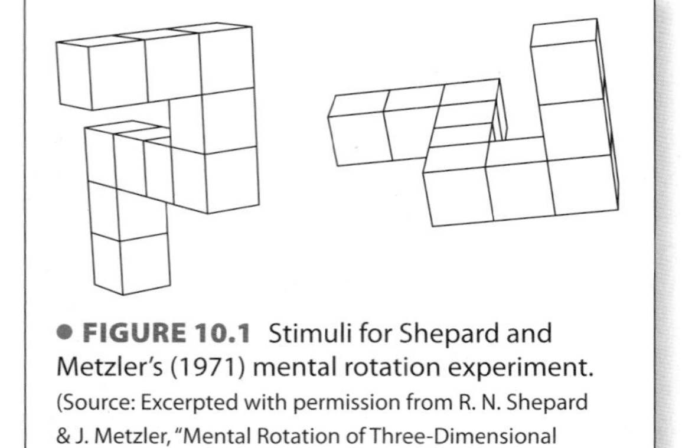

● **FIGURE 10.1** Stimuli for Shepard and Metzler's (1971) mental rotation experiment. (Source: Excerpted with permission from R. N. Shepard & J. Metzler, "Mental Rotation of Three-Dimensional Objects," *Science, 171,* 701–703, Fig. 1A & B. Copyright © 1971 AAAS.)

We will now describe research that illustrates similarities between imagery and perception, and also the possibility that there is a basic difference between how imagery and perception are represented in the mind. As we will see, these comparisons of imagery and perception have involved a large number of behavioral and physiological experiments, which demonstrate both similarities and differences between imagery and perception.

Imagery and Perception: Do They Share the Same Mechanisms?

The idea that imagery and perception may share the same mechanisms is based on the observation that although mental images differ from perception in that they are not as vivid or long lasting, imagery shares many properties with perception. Shepard and Metzler's results showed that mental and perceptual images both involve spatial representation of the stimulus. That is, the spatial experience for both imagery and

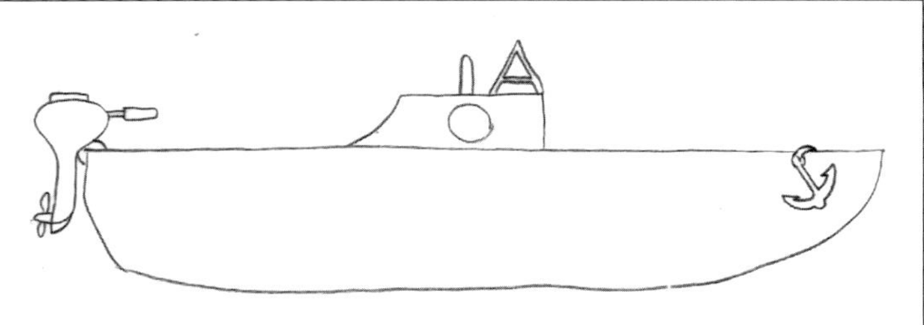

● **FIGURE 10.2** Stimulus for Kosslyn's (1973) image-scanning experiment. (Source: S. M. Kosslyn, "Scanning Visual Images: Some Structural Implications," *Perception & Psychophysics, 14,* 90–94, Fig. 1. Copyright © 1973 The Psychonomic Society Publications. Reproduced with permission.)

perception matches the layout of the actual stimulus. This idea, that there is a spatial correspondence between imagery and perception, is supported by a number of experiments by Stephen Kosslyn involving a task called **mental scanning**, in which participants create mental images and then scan them in their minds.

KOSSLYN'S MENTAL SCANNING EXPERIMENTS

Stephen Kosslyn has done enough research on imagery to fill three books (Kosslyn, 1980, 1994; Kosslyn et al., 2006), and he has proposed some influential theories of imagery based on parallels between imagery and perception. In one of his early experiments, Kosslyn (1973) asked participants to memorize a picture of an object, such as the boat in ● Figure 10.2, and then to create an image of that object in their mind and to focus on one part of the boat, such as the anchor. They were then asked to look for another part of the boat, such as the motor, and to press the "true" button when they found this part or the "false" button when they couldn't find it.

Kosslyn reasoned that if imagery, like perception, is spatial, then it should take longer for participants to find parts that are located farther from the initial point of focus because they would be scanning across the image of the object. This is actually what happened, and Kosslyn took this as evidence for the spatial nature of imagery. But, as often happens in science, another researcher proposed a different explanation. G. Lea (1975) proposed that as participants scanned, they may have encountered other interesting parts, such as the cabin, and this distraction may have increased their reaction time.

To answer this concern, Kosslyn and coworkers (1978) did another scanning experiment, this time asking participants to scan between two places on a map. Before reading about Kosslyn's experiment, try the following demonstration.

DEMONSTRATION Mental Scanning

Imagine a map of your state that includes three locations, the place where you live, a city that is far away, and another city that is closer but which does not fall on a straight line connecting your location and the far city. For example, for my state, I imagine Pittsburgh, the place where I am now; Philadelphia, all the way across the state (contrary to some people's idea, Pittsburgh is not a suburb of Philadelphia!); and Erie, which is closer than Philadelphia but not in the same direction (● Figure 10.3).

Your task is to create a mental image of your state and starting at your location, to form an image of a black speck moving along a straight line between your location and the closer city. Be aware of about how long it took to arrive at this city. Then repeat the same procedure for the far city, again noting about how long it took to arrive.

Erie
PENNSYLVANIA
Pittsburgh
Philadelphia

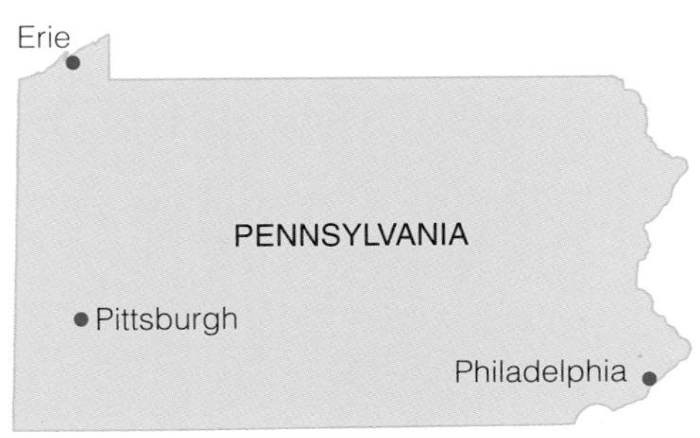

● **FIGURE 10.3** Example of a state map for "mental travel across a state" demonstration. Use your own state for this demonstration.

Kosslyn's participants used the same procedure as you did for the demonstration but were told to imagine an island, like the one in ● Figure 10.4a, that contained seven different locations. By having participants scan between every possible pair of locations (a total of 21 trips), Kosslyn determined the relationship between reaction time and distance shown in Figure 10.4b. Just as in the boat experiment, it took longer to scan between greater distances on the image, a result that supports the idea that visual imagery is spatial in nature. However, as convincing as Kosslyn's results were, Zenon Pylyshyn (1973) proposed another explanation, which started what has been called the **imagery debate**—a debate about whether imagery is based on spatial mechanisms,

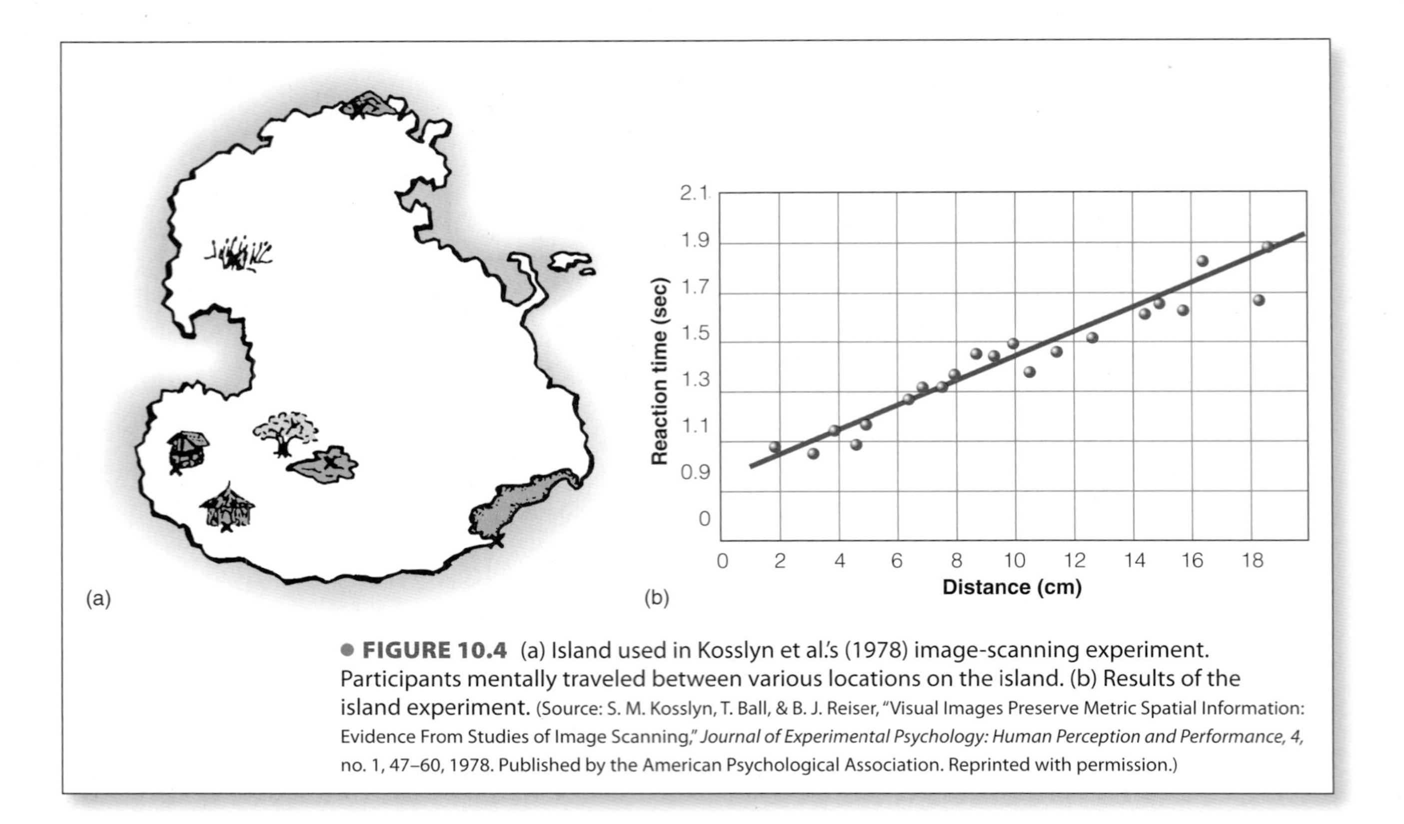

• **FIGURE 10.4** (a) Island used in Kosslyn et al.'s (1978) image-scanning experiment. Participants mentally traveled between various locations on the island. (b) Results of the island experiment. (Source: S. M. Kosslyn, T. Ball, & B. J. Reiser, "Visual Images Preserve Metric Spatial Information: Evidence From Studies of Image Scanning," *Journal of Experimental Psychology: Human Perception and Performance, 4,* no. 1, 47–60, 1978. Published by the American Psychological Association. Reprinted with permission.)

such as those involved in perception, or is based on mechanisms related to language, called *propositional mechanisms*.

THE IMAGERY DEBATE: IS IMAGERY SPATIAL OR PROPOSITIONAL?

Much of the research we have described so far in this book is about determining the nature of the mental representations that lie behind different cognitive experiences. For example, when we considered short-term memory in Chapter 5, we presented evidence that information in STM is often represented in auditory form, as when you rehearse a telephone number you have just looked up in the phone book or online.

Kosslyn interpreted the results of his research on imagery as supporting the idea that the mechanism responsible for imagery involves a **spatial representation**, a representation in which different parts of an image can be described as corresponding to specific locations in space. But Pylyshyn (1973) disagreed, saying that just because we *experience* imagery as spatial, that doesn't mean that the *underlying representation* is spatial. After all, one thing that is clear from research in cognitive psychology is that we often aren't aware of what is going on in our mind. The spatial experience of mental images, argues Pylyshyn, is an **epiphenomenon**—something that accompanies the real mechanism but is not actually part of the mechanism.

An example of an epiphenomenon is lights flashing as a mainframe computer carries out its calculations. The lights may indicate that *something* is going on inside the computer, but they don't necessarily tell us what is actually happening. In fact, if all of the light bulbs blew out, the computer would continue operating just as before. Mental images, according to Pylyshyn, are similar—they indicate that *something* is happening in the mind, but don't tell us *how* it is happening.

Pylyshyn proposed that the mechanism underlying imagery is not spatial but propositional. A **propositional representation** is one in which relationships can be represented by abstract symbols, such as an equation, or a statement such as "The cat is under the table." In contrast, a spatial representation would involve a spatial layout

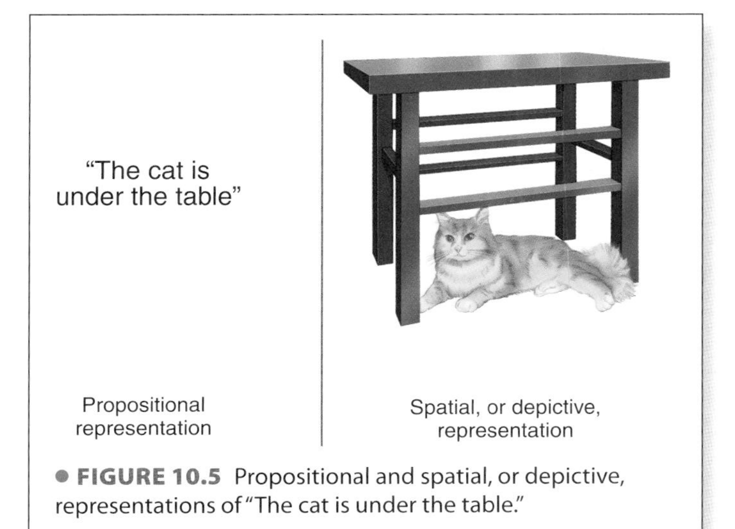

● **FIGURE 10.5** Propositional and spatial, or depictive, representations of "The cat is under the table."

showing the cat and the table that could be represented in a picture (● Figure 10.5). Representations that are like realistic pictures that resemble an object, so that part of the representation correspond to parts of the object, are called **depictive representations**.

We can understand the propositional approach better by returning to the depictive representation of Kosslyn's boat in Figure 10.2. ● Figure 10.6 shows how the visual appearance of this boat can be represented propositionally. The words indicate parts of the boat, the length of the lines indicate the distances between the parts, and the words in parentheses indicate the spatial relations between the parts. A representation such as this would predict that when starting at the motor, it should take longer to scan and find the anchor than to find the porthole because it is necessary to travel across three links to get to the porthole (dashed line) and four links to get to the anchor (dotted line). This kind of explanation proposes that imagery operates in a way similar to the semantic networks we described in Chapter 9 (see page 250).

In addition to suggesting that Kosslyn's results can be explained in terms of propositional representations, Pylyshyn also suggested that one reason that scanning time increases as the distance between two points on an image increases is that participants are responding to Kosslyn's tasks based on what they know about what usually happens when they are looking at a real scene. According to Pylyshyn (2003), "When asked to imagine something, people ask themselves what it would look like to see it, and they then simulate as many aspects of this staged event as they can" (p. 113). People know that in the real world it takes longer to travel longer distances, just as I know it takes longer to drive to Philadelphia than to Erie, so, Pylyshyn suggests, they simulate this result in Kosslyn's experiment. This is called the **tacit knowledge explanation** because it states that participants unconsciously use knowledge about the world in making their judgments.

Although Pylyshyn was in the minority (most researchers accept the spatial representation explanation of visual imagery), his criticisms couldn't be ignored, and researchers from the "spatial" camp proceeded to gather more evidence. For example,

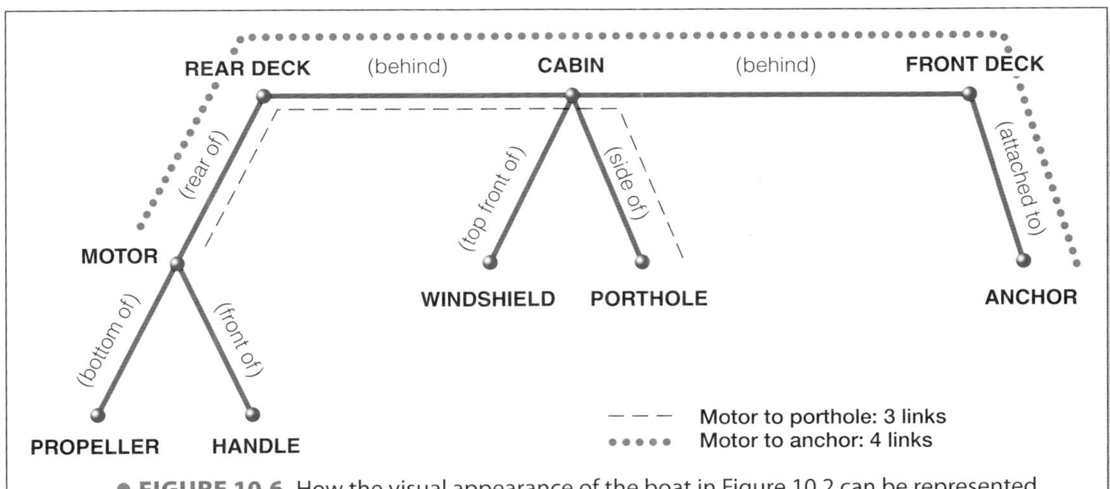

● **FIGURE 10.6** How the visual appearance of the boat in Figure 10.2 can be represented propositionally. Paths between motor and porthole (dashed line) and motor and anchor (dotted line) indicate the number of nodes that would be traversed between these parts of the boat. (Source: Reprinted from S. M. Kosslyn, "Mental Imagery," in S. M. Kosslyn & D. N. Osherson, *An Invitation to Cognitive Science,* 2nd edition, volume 2: *Visual Cognition,* pp. 267–296, Fig. 7.6. Copyright © 1995 with permission from MIT Press.)

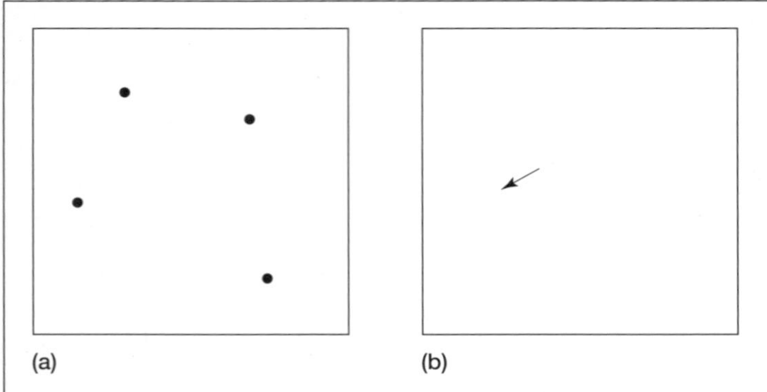

● **FIGURE 10.7** Stimuli for Finke and Pinker's (1982) experiment. The display in (a) was presented first, followed, after a 2-second delay, by the arrow in (b). The participants' task was to determine whether the arrow pointed to any of the dots that had been presented in the first display. (Source: Reprinted from R. A. Finke & S. Pinker, "Spontaneous Imagery Scanning in Mental Extrapolation," *Journal of Experimental Psychology: Learning, Memory and Cognition, 8,* 2, 142–147, Fig. 1, Copyright © 1982 with permission from the American Psychological Association.)

to counter the tacit knowledge explanation of Kosslyn's mental scanning results, Ronald Finke and Stephen Pinker (1982) briefly presented a four-dot display, like the one in ● Figure 10.7a, and then, after a 2-second delay (with the dots no longer present), presented an arrow, as in Figure 10.7b. The participants' task was to indicate whether the arrow was pointing to any of the dots they had previously seen.

Although the participants were not told to use imagery or to scan outward from the arrow, they took longer to respond for greater distances between the arrow and the dot. In fact, the results look very similar to the results of other scanning experiments. Finke and Pinker argue that because their participants wouldn't have had time to memorize the distances between the arrow and the dot before making their judgments, it is unlikely that they used tacit knowledge about how long it should take to get from one point to another.

We've discussed both the spatial and the propositional approaches to imagery because these two explanations provide an excellent example of how data can be interpreted in different ways. Pylyshyn's criticisms stimulated a large number of experiments that have taught us a great deal about the nature of visual imagery (also see Intons-Peterson, 1983). The weight of the evidence supports the idea that imagery is served by a spatial mechanism, and that it shares mechanisms with perception. We will now look at additional evidence that supports the idea of spatial representation.

COMPARING IMAGERY AND PERCEPTION

We begin by describing another experiment by Kosslyn. This one looks at how imagery is affected by the size of an object in a person's visual field.

Size in the Visual Field If you were to observe an automobile from far away, it would fill only a portion of your visual field, and it would be difficult to see small details such as the door handle. But as you move closer, it fills more of your visual field, and you can perceive details like the door handle more easily (● Figure 10.8). With these observations about perception in mind, Kosslyn wondered whether this relationship between viewing distance and the ability to perceive details also occurs for mental images.

To answer this question, Kosslyn (1978) asked participants to imagine animals next to each other, such as an elephant and a rabbit, and told them to imagine that they

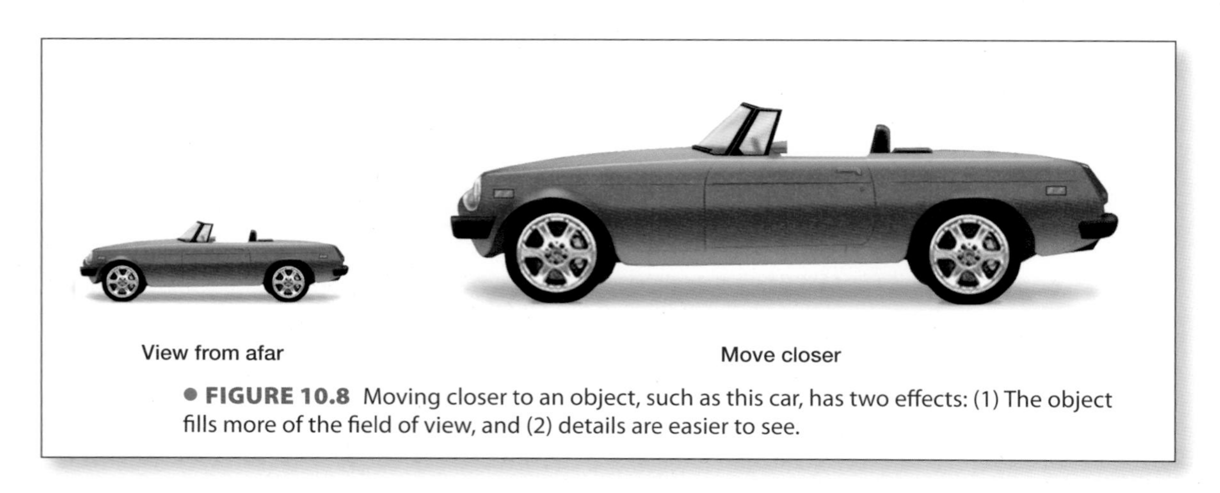

● **FIGURE 10.8** Moving closer to an object, such as this car, has two effects: (1) The object fills more of the field of view, and (2) details are easier to see.

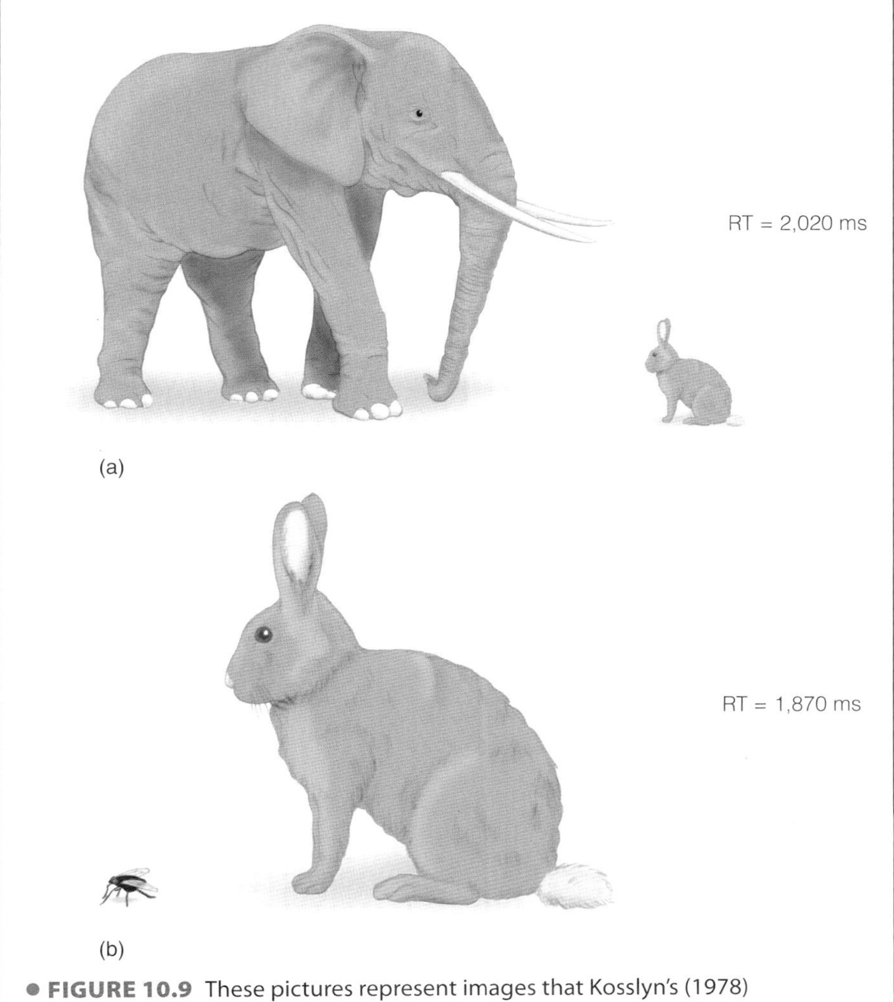

● **FIGURE 10.9** These pictures represent images that Kosslyn's (1978) participants created, which filled different portions of their visual field. (a) Imagine elephant and rabbit, so elephant fills the field. (b) Imagine rabbit and fly, so rabbit fills the field. Reaction times indicate how long it took participants to answer questions about the rabbit.

were standing close enough to the larger animal so that it filled most of their visual field (● Figure 10.9a). He then posed questions such as "Does a rabbit have whiskers?" and asked his participants to find that part of the animal in their mental image and to answer as quickly as possible. When he repeated this procedure but told participants to imagine a rabbit and a fly next to each other, participants created larger images of the rabbit, as shown in Figure 10.9b. The result of these experiments, shown alongside the pictures, was that participants answered questions about the rabbit more rapidly when it filled more of the visual field.

In addition to asking participants to respond to details in visual images, Kosslyn also asked them to do a **mental walk task**, in which they were to imagine that they were walking toward their mental image of an animal. Their task was to estimate how far away they were from the animal when they began to experience "overflow"—when the image filled the visual field or when its edges started becoming fuzzy. The result was that participants had to move closer for small animals (less than a foot for a mouse) than for larger animals (about 11 feet for an elephant), just as they would have to do if they were walking toward actual animals. This result provides further evidence for the idea that images are spatial, just like perception.

Interactions of Imagery and Perception

Another way to demonstrate connections between imagery and perception is to show that they interact with one another. The basic rationale behind this approach is that if imagery affects perception, or perception affects imagery, this means that imagery and perception both have access to the same mechanisms.

The classic demonstration of interaction between perception and imagery dates back to 1910, when Cheves Perky did the experiment pictured in ● Figure 10.10. Perky asked her participants to "project" visual images of common objects onto a screen, and then to describe these images. Unbeknownst to the participants, Perky was back-projecting a very dim image of this object onto the screen. Thus, when participants were asked to create an image of a banana, Perky projected a dim image of a banana onto the screen. Interestingly, the participants' descriptions of their images matched the images that Perky was projecting. For example, they described the banana as being oriented vertically, just as was the projected image. Even more interesting, not one of Perky's 24 participants noticed that there was an actual picture on the screen. They had apparently mistaken an actual picture for a mental image.

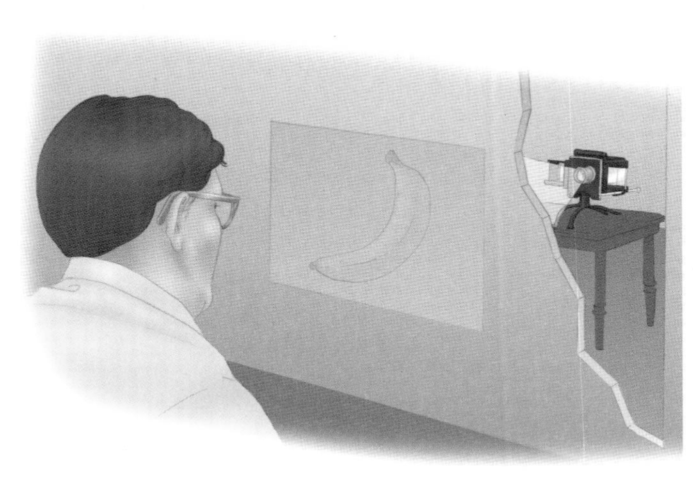

● **FIGURE 10.10** Participant in Perky's (1910) experiment. Unbeknownst to the participants, Perky was projecting dim images onto the screen.

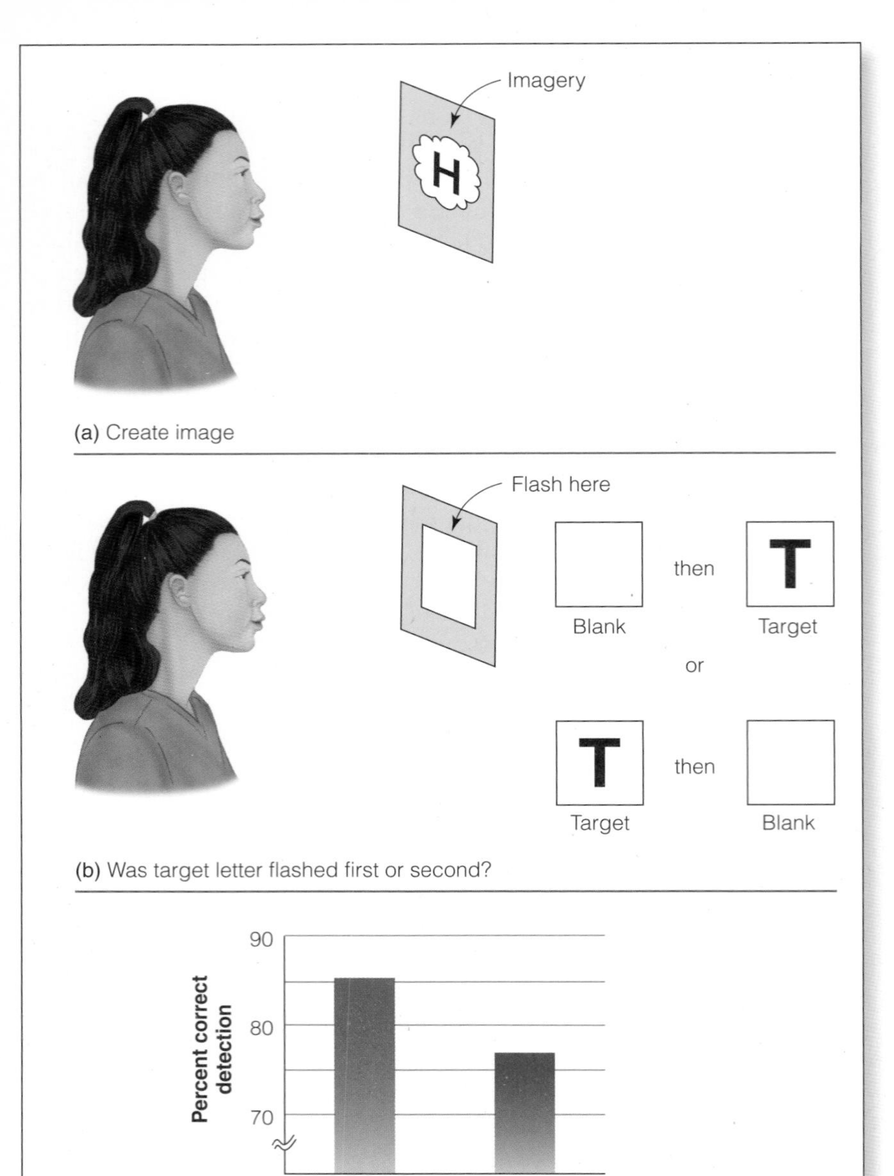

● **FIGURE 10.11** Procedure for Farah's (1985) letter visualization experiment. (a) Participant visualizes *H* or *T* on the screen. (b) Then two squares flash one after the other on the same screen. As shown on the right, the target letter can be in the first square or in the second one. The participants' task is to determine whether the test letter was flashed in the first or in the second square. (c) Results showing that accuracy was higher when the letter in (b) was the same as the one that had been imagined in (a). (Source: R. N. Shepard & J. Metzler, "Mental Rotation of Three-Dimensional Objects," *Science, 171*, 701–703, Fig. 1A & B. Copyright © 1971 American Association for the Advancement of Science. Reproduced with permission.)

Modern researchers have replicated Perky's result (see Craver-Lemley & Reeves, 1992; Segal & Fusella, 1970) and have demonstrated interactions between perception and imagery in a number of other ways. Martha Farah (1985) instructed her participants to imagine either the letter *H* or *T* on a screen (● Figure 10.11a). Once they had formed clear images on the screen, they pressed a button that caused two squares to flash, one after the other (Figure 10.11b). One of the squares contained a target letter, which was either an *H* or a *T*. The participants' task was to indicate whether the letter was in the first square or the second one. The results, shown in Figure 10.11c, indicate that the target letter was detected more accurately when the participant had been imagining the same letter rather than the different letter. Farah interpreted this result as showing that perception and imagery share mechanisms. Many other experiments have demonstrated similar interactions between perception and imagery (see Kosslyn & Thompson, 2000).

IS THERE A WAY TO RESOLVE THE IMAGERY DEBATE?

You might think, from the evidence of parallels between imagery and perception and of interactions between them, that the imagery debate would have been settled once and for all in favor of the spatial explanation. But John Anderson (1978) warned that despite this evidence, we still can't rule out the propositional explanation, and Martha Farah (1988) pointed out that it is difficult to rule out Pylyshyn's tacit knowledge explanation just on the basis of the results of behavioral experiments like the ones we have been describing. She argued that it is always possible that participants can be influenced by their past experiences with perception, so they could unknowingly be simulating perceptual responses in imagery experiments. For example, in the mental walk experiments, in which participants were supposed to be imagining that they were walking toward their mental image of an animal, participants could be using their knowledge from prior experience in perceiving animals to conclude that they would have to be closer to a mouse than to an elephant before these animals would fill up their field of view.

But Farah suggested a way out of this problem: Instead of relying solely on behavioral experiments, we should investigate how the brain responds to visual imagery. The reason Farah was able to make this proposal was that by the 1980s, evidence about the physiology of imagery was becoming available from neuropsychology—the study of patients with brain damage—and from electrophysiological measurements. In addition, beginning in the 1990s, brain imaging experiments provided additional data regarding the physiology of imagery. We will describe measurements of the brain's response to imagery in the next section.

TEST YOURSELF 10.1

1. Is imagery just a "laboratory phenomenon," or does it occur in real life?
2. Make a list of the important events in the history of the study of imagery in psychology, from the imageless thought debate of the 1800s to the studies of imagery that occurred early in the cognitive revolution in the 1960s.
3. How did Kosslyn use the technique of mental scanning (in the boat and island experiments) to demonstrate similarities between perception and imagery? Why were Kosslyn's experiments criticized, and how did Kosslyn answer Pylyshyn's criticism with additional experiments?
4. Describe the spatial (or depictive) and propositional explanations of the mechanism underlying imagery. How can the propositional explanation interpret the results of Kosslyn's boat and island image-scanning experiments?
5. What is the tacit knowledge explanation of imagery experiments? What experiment was done to counter this explanation?
6. How have experiments demonstrated interactions between imagery and perception? What additional evidence is needed to help settle the imagery debate, according to Farah?

Imagery and the Brain

As we look at a number of types of physiological experiments, we will see that a great deal of evidence points to a connection between imagery and perception, but the overlap is not perfect. We begin by looking at the results of research that has measured the brain's response to imagery and will then consider how brain damage affects the ability to form visual images.

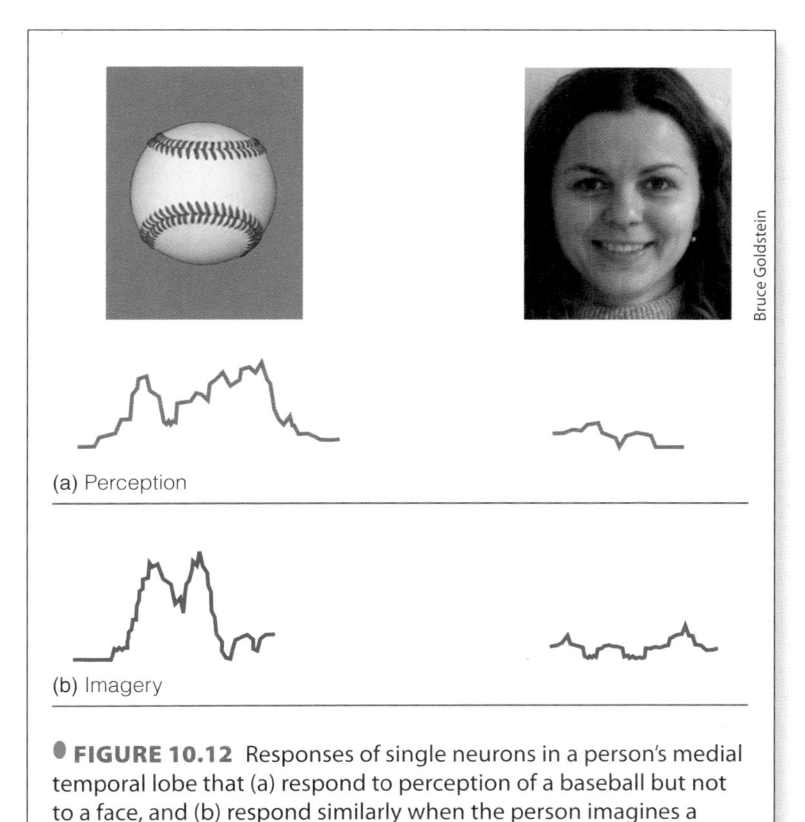

● **FIGURE 10.12** Responses of single neurons in a person's medial temporal lobe that (a) respond to perception of a baseball but not to a face, and (b) respond similarly when the person imagines a baseball or a face. (Source: Based on G. Kreiman, C. Koch, & I. Fried, "Imagery Neurons in the Human Brain," *Nature 408*, 357–361, November 16, 2000.)

IMAGERY NEURONS IN THE BRAIN

Studies in which activity is recorded from single neurons in humans are rare. But Gabriel Kreiman and coworkers (2000) were able to study patients who had electrodes implanted in various areas in their medial temporal lobe (see Figure 7.17) in order to determine the source of severe epileptic seizures that could not be controlled by medication.

They found neurons that responded to some objects but not to others. For example, the records in ● Figure 10.12a show a particular neuron that responds to a picture of a baseball, but does not respond to a picture of a face. Not only does this neuron respond to seeing baseballs but not faces, it also fires to baseballs and not faces when the person closes his eyes and *imagines* a baseball (good firing) or a face (no firing), as shown in Figure 10.12. Kreiman calls these neurons **imagery neurons**. What's especially significant about these imagery neurons is that they respond both to *perceiving* an object and to *imagining* it.

BRAIN IMAGING

Beginning in the early 1990s, a large number of brain imaging experiments were carried out in which brain activity was measured, using either PET or fMRI, as participants were creating visual images or during a baseline condition in which they were not creating images. Subtracting the baseline response from the imagery response indicated which areas of the brain were activated by imagery (see Method: Brain Imaging, Chapter 2, page 30).

One of the early brain imaging experiments to study imagery was carried out by LeBihan and coworkers (1993), who demonstrated that both perception and imagery activate the visual cortex. ● Figure 10.13 shows how activity in the striate cortex increased both when a person observed presentations of actual visual stimuli (marked "Perception") *and* when the person was imagining the stimulus ("Imagery"). In another brain imaging experiment, asking participants to think about questions that involve imagery, such as "Is the green of the trees darker than the green of the grass?" generated a greater response in the visual cortex than the response generated to nonimagery questions, such as "Is the intensity of electrical current measured in amperes?" (Goldenberg et al., 1989).

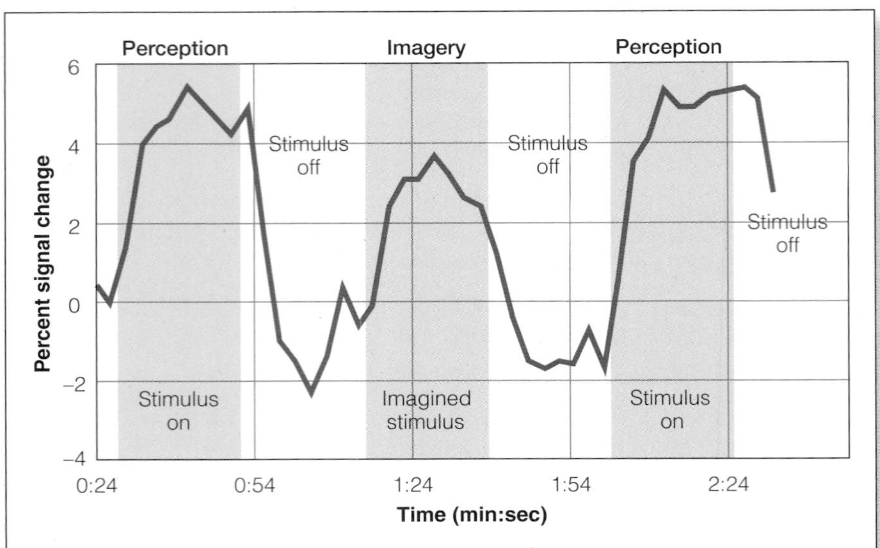

● **FIGURE 10.13** Brain activity measured using fMRI. Activity increases to presentation of a visual stimulus (shaded area marked "Stimulus on") and also increases when participants were imagining the stimulus (area marked "Imagined stimulus"). In contrast, activity is low when there is no stimulus (Source: D. LeBihan et al., "Activation of Human Primary Visual Cortex During Visual Recall: A Magnetic Resonance Imaging Study," *Proceedings of the National Academy of Sciences, USA, 90*, 11802–11805, 1993.)

● **FIGURE 10.14** Procedure for Ganis et al.'s (2004) experiment. A trial begins with the name of an object that was previously studied, in this case "tree." In the imagery condition, participants had their eyes closed and had to imagine the tree. In the perception condition, participants saw a faint picture of the object. Participants then heard instructions. The *W* in this example means they were to judge whether the object was "wider than tall." (Source: G. Ganis, W. L. Thompson, & S. M. Kosslyn, "Brain Areas Underlying Visual Mental Imagery and Visual Perception: An fMRI Study," *Cognitive Brain Research, 20*, 226–241. Copyright © 2004 Elsevier Ltd. Reproduced by permission.)

A number of recent brain imaging experiments have demonstrated overlap between brain areas activated by perceiving an object and those activated by creating a mental image of the object, but along with this overlap, differences have also been observed between the areas activated by perception and by imagery. For example, Giorgio Ganis and coworkers (2004) used fMRI to measure activation under two conditions, perception and imagery. For the perception condition, participants observed a drawing of an object, like the tree in ● Figure 10.14. For the imagery condition, participants were told to imagine a picture that they had studied before, when they heard a tone. For both the perception and imagery tasks, participants had to answer a question such as "Is the object wider than it is tall?"

Results of Ganis's experiment are shown in ● Figure 10.15, which shows activation at three different locations in the brain. Figure 10.15a shows activation in the frontal lobe for perception and imagery in the two center columns, and for the difference between perception and imagery in the right column. The absence of color in the right column indicates there is no difference between the activation caused by perception and by imagery. The same result also occurs for activation further back in the brain (Figure 10.15b). However, in Figure 10.15c, which shows activity nearer the back of the brain, the color in the far right column indicates that some areas respond more for perception than for imagery. This greater activity for perception isn't surprising because this is the location of the visual

● **FIGURE 10.15** Brain scan results from Ganis et al. (2004). The vertical lines through the brains in the far left column indicate where activity was being recorded. The columns labeled "Perception" and "Imagery" indicate responses in the perception and imagery conditions. "Perception-Imagery" indicates the difference between activation in these two conditions. (a) Responses of areas in the frontal lobe. The absence of color in this record indicates that activation was the same. (b) Responses further back in the brain. Activation was the same in this area as well. (c) Responses from the back of the brain, including the primary visual area. The color in the far right record indicates that there was a greater response in the perception condition. (Source: Reprinted from G. Ganis, W. L. Thompson, & S. M. Kosslyn, "Brain Areas Underlying Visual Mental Imagery and Visual Perception: An fMRI Study," *Cognitive Brain Research, 20,* 226–241, 2004.)

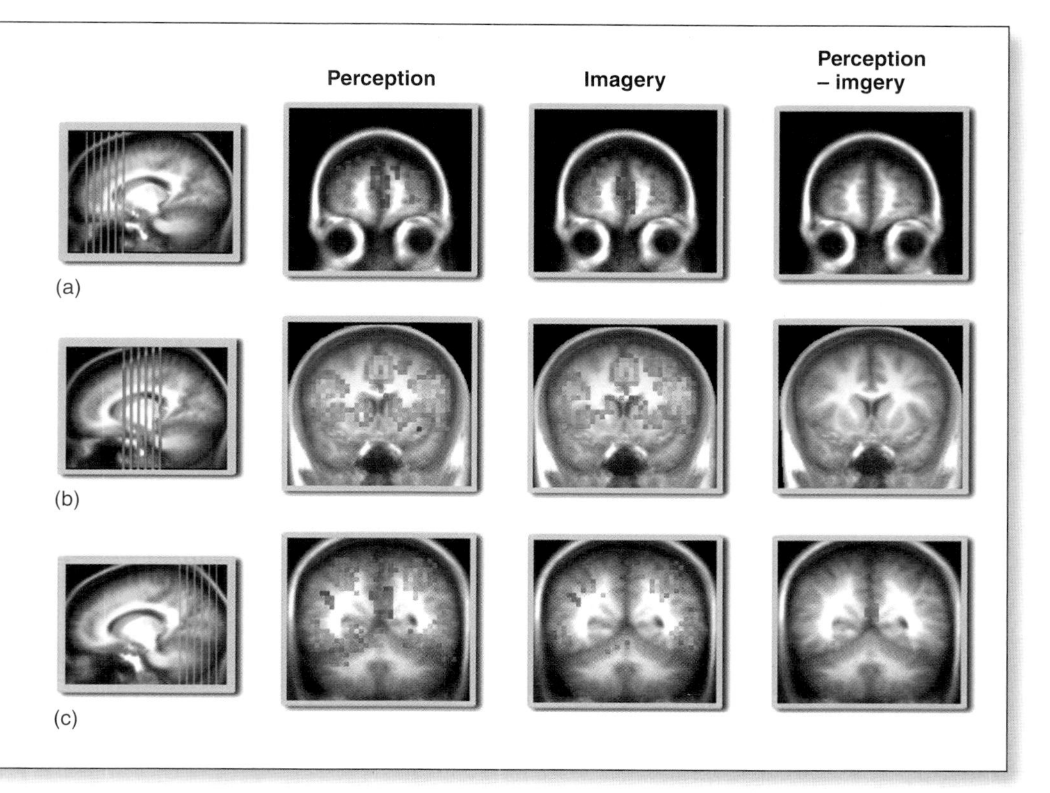

receiving area, where signals from the retina first reach the cortex. Thus, there is almost complete overlap of the activation caused by perception and imagery in the front of the brain, but some differences near the back of the brain.

Other experiments have also concluded that there are similarities but some differences between brain activation for perception and imagery. For example, an fMRI experiment by Amir Amedi and coworkers (2005) showed overlap, but also found that when participants were creating images using visual imagery, some areas associated with nonvisual areas such as hearing and touch were *deactivated*. That is, during imagery, their activation was decreased. Amedi suggests that the reason for this might be that visual mental images are more fragile than real perception, so this deactivation helps quiet down irrelevant activity that might interfere with the mental image.

The differences in activation that are observed when comparing perception and imagery are not that surprising. After all, seeing an object is different from imagining it. But what is most noteworthy in all of these experiments is the great degree of overlap between activation for perception and for imagery (also see Slotnick et al., 2005). This overlap supports the idea that imagery and perception share some mechanisms.

TRANSCRANIAL MAGNETIC STIMULATION

Although the brain imaging experiments we have just described are consistent with the idea that imagery and perception share the same mechanisms, showing that an area of the brain is activated by imagery does not *prove* that this activity *causes* imagery. Pylyshyn argues that just as the spatial experience of mental images is an epiphenomenon (see page 274), brain activity can also be an epiphenomenon. According to Pylyshyn, brain activity in response to imagery may indicate that *something* is happening, but may have nothing to do with *causing* imagery. To deal with this possibility, Stephen Kosslyn and coworkers (1999) did an experiment using a technique called **transcranial magnetic stimulation** (TMS).

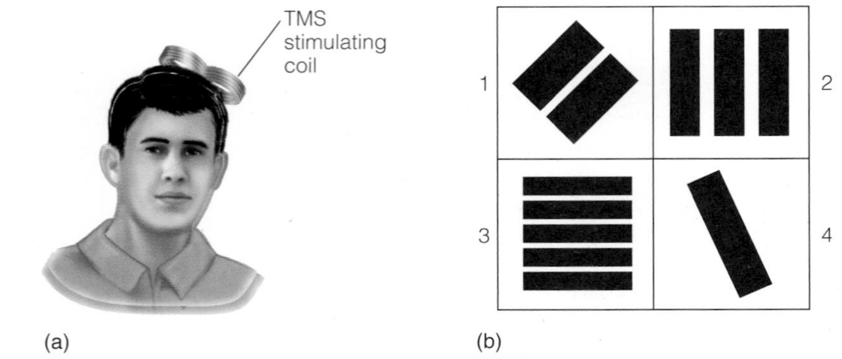

(a) (b)

FIGURE 10.16 (a) Transcranial magnetic stimulation apparatus; (b) stimuli.

METHOD Transcranial Magnetic Stimulation (TMS)

One way to investigate whether an area of the brain is involved in determining a particular function is to remove that part of the brain in animals or study cases of brain damage in humans (see pages 71, 73). Of course, we cannot purposely remove a portion of a person's brain, but it is possible to temporarily disrupt the functioning of a particular area by applying a pulsating magnetic field to the skull using a stimulating coil, as shown in Figure 10.16a. A series of pulses presented to a particular area of the brain for a few seconds decreases or eliminates brain functioning in that area for seconds or minutes. A participant's behavior is tested while the brain area is deactivated. If the behavior is disrupted, it is concluded that the deactivated area of the brain is causing that behavior.

Kossyln and coworkers (1999) presented transcranial magnetic stimulation to the visual area of the brain while participants were carrying out either a perception task or an imagery task. For the perception task, participants briefly viewed a display like the one in Figure 10.16b and were asked to make a judgment about the stripes in two of the quadrants. For example, they might be asked to indicate whether the stripes in quadrant 3 were longer than the stripes in quadrant 2. The imagery task was the same, but instead of actually looking at the stripes while answering the questions, the participants closed their eyes and based their judgments on their mental image of the display.

Kosslyn measured participants' reaction time to make the judgment, both when transcranial magnetic stimulation was being applied to the visual area of the brain and also during a control condition when the stimulation was directed to another part of the brain. The result indicated that stimulation caused participants to respond more slowly, and that this slowing effect occurred both for perception and for imagery. Based on this result, Kosslyn concluded that the brain activation that occurs in response to imagery is not an epiphenomenon and that brain activity in the visual cortex plays a causal role in both perception and imagery.

"I can get to within 15 feet of the horse in my imagination before it starts to overflow."

"The horse starts to overflow at an imagined distance of about 35 feet."

FIGURE 10.17 Results of mental walk task for patient M.G.S. *Left*: Before her operation, she could mentally "walk" to within 15 feet before the image of the horse overflowed her visual field. *Right*: After removal of the right occipital lobe, the size of the visual field was reduced, and she could mentally approach only to within 35 feet of the horse before it overflowed her visual field. (Source: Reprinted from M. J. Farah, "The Neural Basis of Mental Imagery," in M. Gazzaniga, ed., *The Cognitive Neurosciences,* 2nd ed., Cambridge, MA: MIT Press, pp. 965–974, Fig. 66.2. Copyright © 2000, with permission of The MIT Press.)

NEUROPSYCHOLOGICAL CASE STUDIES

How can we use studies of people with brain damage to help us understand imagery? One approach is to determine how brain damage affects imagery. Another approach is to determine how brain damage affects both imagery and perception, and to note whether both are affected in the same way.

Removing Part of the Visual Cortex Decreases Image Size

Patient M.G.S. was a young woman who was about to have part of her right occipital lobe removed as treatment for a severe case of epilepsy. Before the operation, Martha Farah and coworkers (1993) had M.G.S. perform the mental walk task that we described earlier, in which she imagined walking toward an animal and estimated how close she was when the image began to overflow her visual field. Figure 10.17 shows that before the

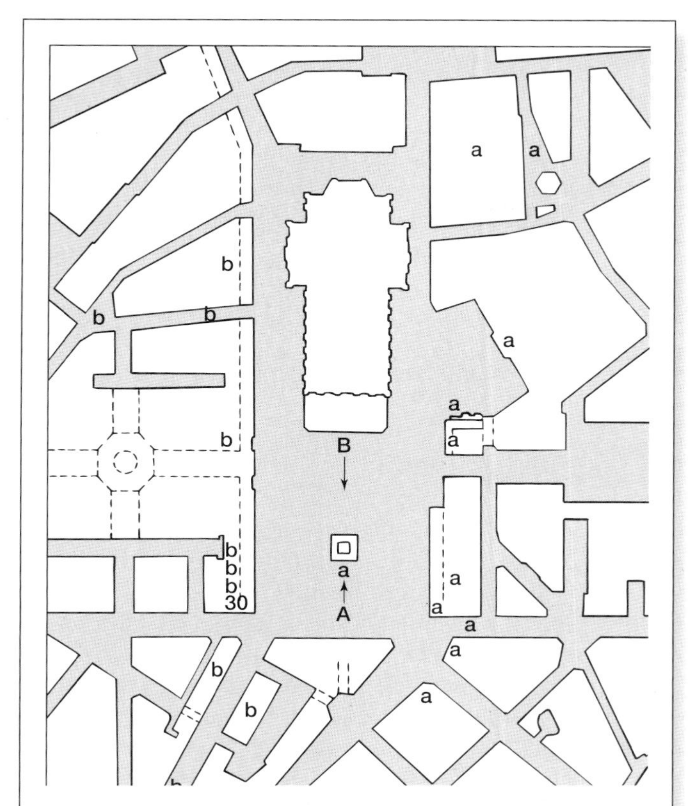

● **FIGURE 10.18** Piazza del Duomo in Milan. When Bisiach and Luzzatti's (1978) patient imagined himself standing at A, he could name objects indicated by *a*'s. When he imagined himself at B, he could name objects indicated by *b*'s. (Source: Reprinted from E. Bisiach & G. Luzzatti, "Unilateral Neglect of Representational Space," *Cortex, 14,* 129–133. Copyright © 1978 with permission from Cortex.)

operation, M.G.S. felt she was about 15 feet from an imaginary horse before its image overflowed. But when Farah had her repeat this task after her right occipital lobe had been removed, the distance increased to 35 feet. This occurred because removing part of the visual cortex reduced the size of her field of view, so the horse filled up the field when she was farther away. This result supports the idea that the visual cortex is important for imagery.

Perceptual Problems Are Accompanied by Problems With Imagery A large number of cases have been studied in which a patient with brain damage has a perceptual problem and also has a similar problem in creating images. For example, people who have lost the ability to see color due to brain damage are also unable to create colors through imagery (DeRenzi & Spinnler, 1967; DeVreese, 1991).

Damage to the parietal lobes can cause a condition called **unilateral neglect**, in which the patient ignores objects in one half of the visual field, even to the extent of shaving just one side of his face, or eating only the food on one side of her plate. E. Bisiach and G. Luzzatti (1978) tested the imagery of a patient with unilateral neglect by asking him to describe things he saw when imagining himself standing at one end of the Piazza del Duomo in Milan, a place with which he had been familiar before his brain was damaged (● Figure 10.18).

The patient's responses showed that he neglected the left side of his mental image, just as he neglected the left side of his perceptions. Thus, when he imagined himself standing at A, he neglected the left side and named only objects to his right (small *a*'s). When he imagined himself standing at B, he continued to neglect the left side, again naming only objects on his right (small *b*'s).

The correspondence between the physiology of mental imagery and the physiology of perception, as demonstrated by brain scans in normal participants and the effects of brain damage in participants with neglect, supports the idea that mental imagery and perception share physiological mechanisms. However, not all physiological results support a one-to-one correspondence between imagery and perception.

Dissociations Between Imagery and Perception When we discussed perception in Chapter 3, we described dissociations, in which people with brain damage had one function present and another function absent (see Method: Dissociations in Neuropsychology, Chapter 3, page 73). Cases have also been reported of dissociations between imagery and perception. For example, C. Guariglia and coworkers (1993) studied a patient whose brain damage had little effect on his ability to perceive but caused neglect in his mental images (his mental images were limited to just one side, as in the case just described).

Another case of normal perception but impaired imagery is the case of R.M., who had suffered damage to his occipital and parietal lobes (Farah et al., 1988). R.M. was able to recognize objects and to draw accurate pictures of objects that were placed before him. However, he was unable to draw objects from memory, a task that requires imagery. He also had trouble answering questions that depend on imagery, such as verifying whether the sentence "A grapefruit is larger than an orange" is correct.

Dissociations have also been reported with the opposite result, so that perception is impaired but imagery is relatively normal. For example, Marlene Behrmann and coworkers (1994) studied C.K., a 33-year-old graduate student who was struck by a car as he was jogging. C.K. suffered from visual agnosia, the inability to visually recognize objects. Thus, he labeled the pictures in ● Figure 10.19a as a "feather duster" (the dart),

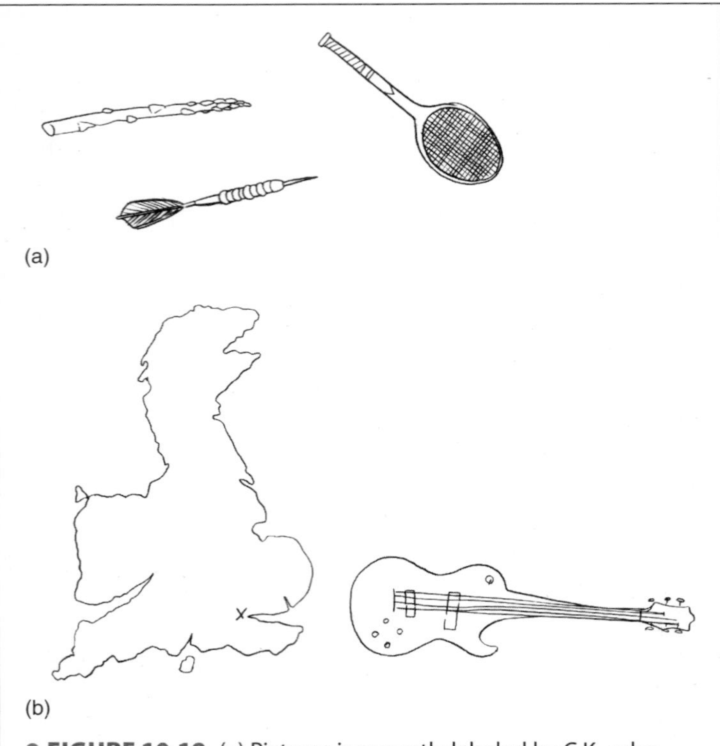

• **FIGURE 10.19** (a) Pictures incorrectly labeled by C.K., who had visual agnosia. (b) Drawings from memory by C.K.
(Source: Reprinted from M. Behrmann et al., "Intact Visual Imagery and Impaired Visual Perception in a Patient With Visual Agnosia," *Journal of Experimental Psychology: Human Perception and Performance, 30,* 1068–1087, Figs. 1 & 6. Copyright © 1994 with permission from the American Psychological Association.)

a "fencer's mask" (the tennis racquet), and a "rose twig with thorns" (the asparagus). These results show that C.K. could recognize parts of objects but couldn't integrate them into a meaningful whole. But despite his inability to name pictures of objects, C.K. was able to draw objects from memory in rich detail, a task that depends on imagery (Figure 10.19b). Interestingly, when he was shown his own drawings after enough time had passed so he had forgotten the actual drawing experience, he was unable to identify the objects he had drawn.

Making Sense of the Neuropsychological Results The neuropsychological cases present a paradox: On one hand, there are many cases that show close parallels between perceptual deficits and deficits in imagery. On the other hand, there are a number of cases in which dissociations occur, so that perception is normal but imagery is poor (Guariglia's patient and R.M.), or perception is poor but imagery is normal (C.K.). The cases in which imagery and perception are affected differently by brain damage provide evidence for a double dissociation between imagery and perception (Table 10.1). The presence of a double dissociation is usually interpreted to mean that the two functions (perception and imagery, in this case) are served by different mechanisms (see page 73). However, this conclusion contradicts the other evidence we have presented that shows that imagery and perception share mechanisms.

One way to explain this paradox, according to Behrmann and coworkers (1994), is that the mechanisms of perception and imagery overlap only partially, with the mechanism for perception being located at both lower and higher visual centers and the mechanism for imagery being located mainly in higher visual centers (• Figure 10.20). According to this idea, visual perception necessarily involves *bottom-up processing,* which starts when light enters the eye and an image is focused on the retina, and then continues as signals are sent along the visual pathways to the visual cortex and then to higher visual centers.

The visual cortex is crucial for perception because it is here that objects begin being analyzed into components like edges and orientations. This information is then sent to higher visual areas, where perception is "assembled" and some top-down processing, which involves a person's prior knowledge, may also be involved (see page 52). In contrast, imagery *originates* as a top-down process, in higher brain areas that are responsible for memory. Mental images are therefore "preassembled"; they do not depend on activation of cortical areas, such as the visual cortex, because there is no input that needs to be processed.

TABLE 10.1 Dissociations between perception and imagery

Case	Perception	Imagery
Guariglia (1993)	OK	Neglect (image limited to one side).
Farah et al. (1993) (R.M.)	OK. Recognizes objects and can draw pictures.	Poor. Can't draw from memory or answer questions based on imagery.
Behrmann et al. (1994) (C.K.)	Poor. Visual agnosia so can't recognize objects.	OK. Can draw object from memory.

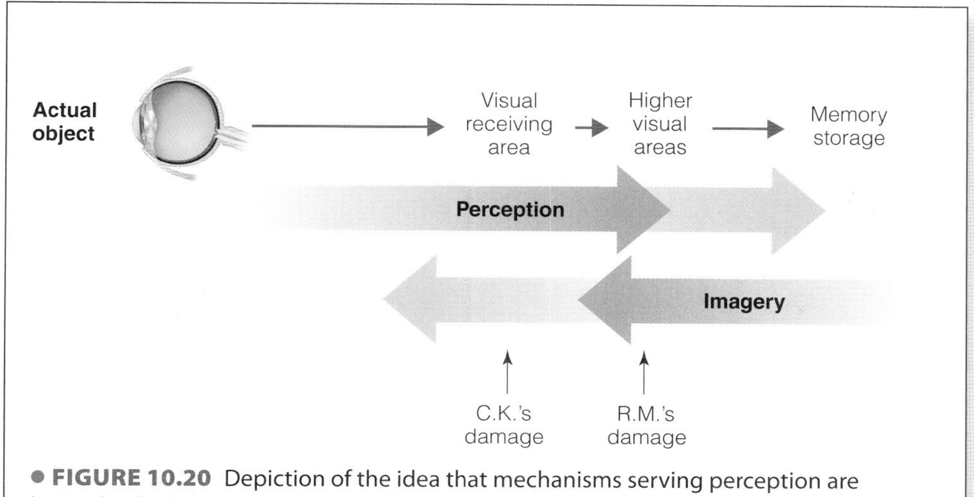

● **FIGURE 10.20** Depiction of the idea that mechanisms serving perception are located at both lower and higher visual centers and that mechanisms serving imagery are located mainly at higher levels (Behrmann et al., 1994). The general locations of damage for C.K. and R.M. are indicated by the vertical arrows. These locations can explain why C.K. has a perceptual problem but can still create images, and why R.M. has trouble creating images but can still perceive.

Based on this explanation, we can hypothesize that C.K.'s difficulty in perceiving is caused by damage early in the processing stream, but that he can still create images because higher-level areas of his brain are intact. Similarly, we can hypothesize that R.M.'s difficulty in creating mental images is caused by damage to higher-level areas, where mental images originate, but that he can perceive objects because areas earlier in the processing stream are still functioning.

Although this explanation works for C.K. and R.M., it can't explain the case of M.G.S., the woman who had part of her visual cortex removed (see Figure 10.17). Even though M.G.S.'s damage was earlier in the cortex, she experienced changes in both perception and imagery. Cases such as this emphasize the challenge of interpreting the results of neuropsychological research. It is likely that further research will lead to modifications in the explanation shown in Figure 10.20, or perhaps a new explanation altogether.

CONCLUSIONS FROM THE IMAGERY DEBATE

The imagery debate provides an outstanding example of a situation in which a controversy motivated a large amount of research. Most psychologists, looking at the behavioral and physiological evidence, have concluded that imagery and perception are closely related and share some (but not all) mechanisms (but see Pylyshyn, 2001, 2003, who doesn't agree).

The idea of shared mechanisms follows from all of the parallels and interactions between perception and imagery. The idea that not all mechanisms are shared follows from some of the fMRI results, which show that the overlap between brain activation is not complete; some of the neuropsychological results, which show dissociations between imagery and perception; and also from differences between the experience of imagery and perception. For example, perception occurs automatically when we look at something, but imagery needs to be generated with some effort. Also, perception is stable—it continues as long as you are observing a stimulus—but imagery is fragile—it can vanish without continued effort.

Another example of a difference between imagery and perception is that it is harder to manipulate mental images than images that are created perceptually. This was demonstrated by Deborah Chalmers and Daniel Reisberg (1985), who asked their participants to create mental images of ambiguous figures such as the one in ● Figure 10.21, which can be seen as a rabbit or a duck. Perceptually, it is fairly easy to "flip" between these two perceptions. However, Chalmers and Reisberg found that participants who were holding a mental image of this figure were unable to flip from one perception to another. Later research has shown that people can manipulate simpler mental images. For example, Ronald Finke and coworkers (1989) showed that when participants followed instructions to imagine a capital letter D, and then rotate it 90 degrees to the left and place a capital letter J at the bottom, they reported seeing an umbrella. Also, Fred Mast and Kosslyn (2002) showed that people who were good at imagery were able to rotate mental images of ambiguous figures if they were provided with extra information such as drawings of parts of the images that are partially rotated. So the experiments on manipulating images lead to the same conclusion as all of the other experiments we have described: Imagery and perception have many features in common, but there are also differences between them.

● **FIGURE 10.21** What is this, a rabbit (facing right) or a duck (facing left)?

Using Imagery to Improve Memory

It is clear that imagery can play an important role in memory. But how can you harness the power of imagery to help you remember things better? In Chapter 7 we saw that encoding is aided by forming connections with other information and described an experiment in which participants who created images based on two paired words (like *boat* and *tree*) remembered more than twice as many words as participants who just repeated the words (see Bower & Winzenz, Figure 7.3, page 177). Another principle of memory we described in Chapter 7 was that organization improves encoding. The mind tends to spontaneously organize information that is initially unorganized, and presenting information that is organized improves memory performance. We will now describe a method based on these principles, which involves placing images at locations.

PLACING IMAGES AT LOCATIONS

The power of imagery to improve memory is tied to its ability to create organized locations upon which memories for specific items can be placed. An example of the organizational function of imagery from ancient history is provided by a story about the Greek poet Simonides. According to legend, 2,500 years ago Simonides presented an address at a banquet, and just after he left the banquet, the roof of the hall collapsed, killing most of the people inside. To compound this tragedy, many of the bodies were so severely mutilated that they couldn't be identified. But Simonides realized that as he had looked out over the audience during his address, he had created a mental picture of where each person had been seated at the banquet table. Based on this image of people's locations around the table, he was able to determine who had been killed.

What is important about this rather gory example is that Simonides realized that the technique he had used to help him remember who was at the banquet could be used to remember other things as well. He found that he could remember things by imagining a physical space, like the banquet table, and placing, in his mind, items to be remembered in the seats surrounding the table. This feat of mental organization enabled him to later "read out" the items by mentally scanning the locations around the table, just as he had done to identify the people's bodies. Simonides had invented what is now called the **method of loci**—a method in which things to be remembered are placed at different locations in a mental image of a spatial layout. The following demonstration illustrates how to use the method of loci to remember something from your own experience.

DEMONSTRATION Method of Loci

Pick a place with a spatial layout that is very familiar to you, such as the rooms in your house or apartment, or the buildings on your college campus. Then pick five to seven things that you want to remember—either events from the past or things you need to do later today. Create an image representing each event, and place each image at a location in the house. If you need to remember the events in a particular order, decide on a path you would take while walking through the house or campus, and place the images representing each event along your walking path so they will be encountered in the correct order. After you have done this, retrace the path in your mind, and see if encountering the images helps you remember the events. To really test this method, try mentally "walking" this path a few hours from now.

Placing images at locations can help with retrieving memories later. For example, to help me remember a dentist appointment later in the day, I could visually place a huge pair of teeth in my living room. To remind myself to go to the gym and work out, I could imagine an elliptical trainer on the stairs that lead from the living room to the second floor, and to represent the *NCIS* TV show that I want to watch later tonight, I could imagine one of the characters in the show sitting on the landing at the top of the stairs.

CogLab
Link Word

ASSOCIATING IMAGES WITH WORDS

The pegword technique involves imagery, as in the method of loci, but instead of visualizing items in different locations, you associate them with concrete words. The first step is to create a list of nouns, like the following: one–bun; two–shoe; three–tree; four–door; five–hive; six–sticks; seven–heaven; eight–gate; nine–mine; ten–hen. It's easy to remember these words in order because they were created by rhyming them with the numbers. Also, the rhyming provides a retrieval cue (see page 178) that helps remember each word. The next step is to pair each of these things to be remembered with each pegword by creating a vivid image of your item-to-be-remembered with the object represented by the word.

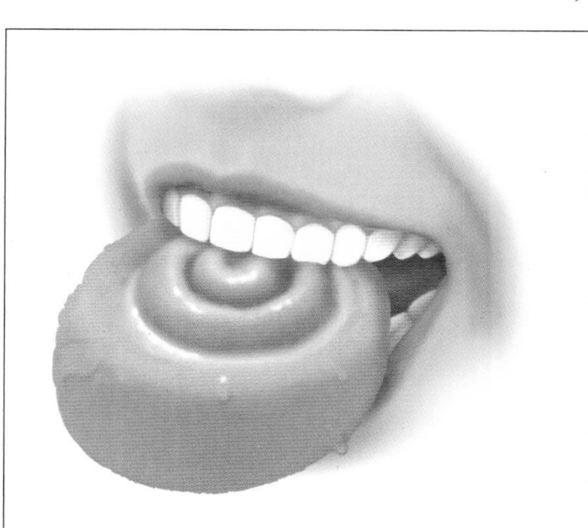

● **FIGURE 10.22** An image that pairs a bun and teeth, which could be used to remember a dentist appointment, using the pegword technique.

● Figure 10.22 shows an image that might help me remember the dentist appointment. For remembering other items, I might picture an elliptical trainer inside a shoe, and the letters *NCIS* in a tree. The beauty of this system is that it makes it possible to immediately identify an item based on its order on the list. So if I want to identify the third thing I need to do today, I go straight to *tree*, which translates into my image of the letters *N*, *C*, *I*, and *S* dangling in a tree, and this reminds me to watch the program *NCIS* on TV.

Imagery techniques like the ones just described are often the basis behind books that claim to provide the key to improving your memory (see Crook & Adderly, 1998; Lorayne & Lucas, 1996; Treadeau, 1997). Although these books do provide imagery-based techniques that work, people who purchase these books in the hope of discovering an easy way to develop "photographic memory" are often disappointed. Although imagery techniques do work, they do not provide easy, "magical" improvements in memory, but rather require a great deal of practice and perseverance (Schacter, 2001).

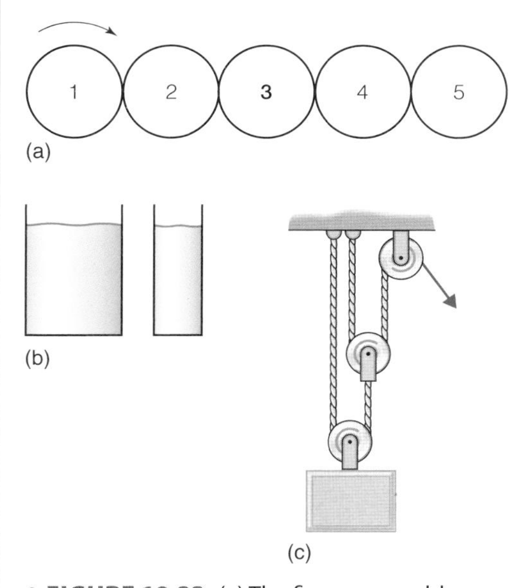

● **FIGURE 10.23** (a) The five-gear problem; (b) the water-pouring problem; (c) the pulley problem. See demonstration for details.
(Source: Adapted from M. Hegarty, "Mechanical Reasoning by Mental Simulation," *TRENDS in Cognitive Science, 8,* no. 6, June 2004, 280–281. Copyright © Elsevier Ltd. Reproduced by permission.)

➔ Something to Consider

Mental Representation of Mechanical Systems

Visual imagery, which has played an important role in scientific discoveries such as determining the structure of benzene and Einstein's theory of relativity (page 271), is also an important mechanism for solving mechanical problems (Hegarty, 2004). For example, consider the problems in the following demonstration.

DEMONSTRATION Mechanical Problems

Try solving the three problems in ● Figure 10.23. (a) The five-gear problem: If each of these gears meshes with the one next to it, and gear #1 is turning clockwise, in what direction is gear #5 turning? (b) The water-pouring problem: The two glasses are the same height and are filled to the same level. When these two glasses are tilted, will the water begin pouring out of the glasses at the same angle of tilt or at different angles? If the angles are different, which glass will pour first? (c) The pulley problem: If you pull on the free end of the rope (at the arrow), will the lower pulley turn clockwis

How did you solve these problems? One approach to solving mechanical problems is to use **mental simulation**, in which the operation of the mechanical system is mentally represented. If you used this procedure for the five-gear problem, you probably imagined gear #1 turning clockwise, gear #2 turning counterclockwise, gear #3 clockwise, and so on. Another way to solve the gear problem is by using a **rule-based approach**, which would involve applying a rule such as "When one gear turns, the one next to it rotates in the opposite direction" or "All odd-numbered gears rotate in the same direction."

These two ways of solving the gear problem are analogous to the two sides of the visual imagery debate we have been discussing in this chapter. The *mental simulation approach* is analogous to the idea that visual imagery involves a *spatial representation*. The *rule-based approach* is analogous to the idea that visual imagery involves a *propositional representation*. In our discussion of the imagery debate, we discussed a large amount of evidence favoring the spatial representation explanation of imagery. However, things are not as one-sided for solving mechanical problems. As we saw for the gear problem, both spatial representation and rule-based approaches can be used to solve the problem.

Let's now consider the water-pouring problem. The answer to this problem is that water will start pouring from the wide glass first. ● Figure 10.24a shows that this is the case, by superimposing the narrow and the wide glasses. From this diagram, you can see that whereas water is about to pour from the wide glass, it is still below the edge of the narrow glass. Thus, the narrow glass would need to be tilted farther before the water will begin to pour.

You may have found that this problem was harder to solve than the five-gear problem. In fact, Daniel Schwartz and Tamara Black (1999) found that when they asked participants for the answer to the water-pouring problem, without giving them time to either reason out the problem or use mental imagery, most of the participants answered incorrectly that both glasses would pour at the same angle (Figure 10.24b). However, when participants were told to close their eyes and imagine the glasses being tilted, almost all of them were able to "see" that the narrow glass would have to be tilted farther than the wide glass (Figure 10.24c).

This result is relevant to the tacit knowledge explanation that Pylyshyn used to explain people's performance in visual imagery tasks (see page 275). Because most people do not know the answer to the water-pouring problem beforehand, its solution by using imagery cannot depend on tacit knowledge.

The water-pouring problem, like the five-gear problem, can be solved without using imagery. One way to do this is to use a diagram like the one in Figure 10.24a. Imagery,

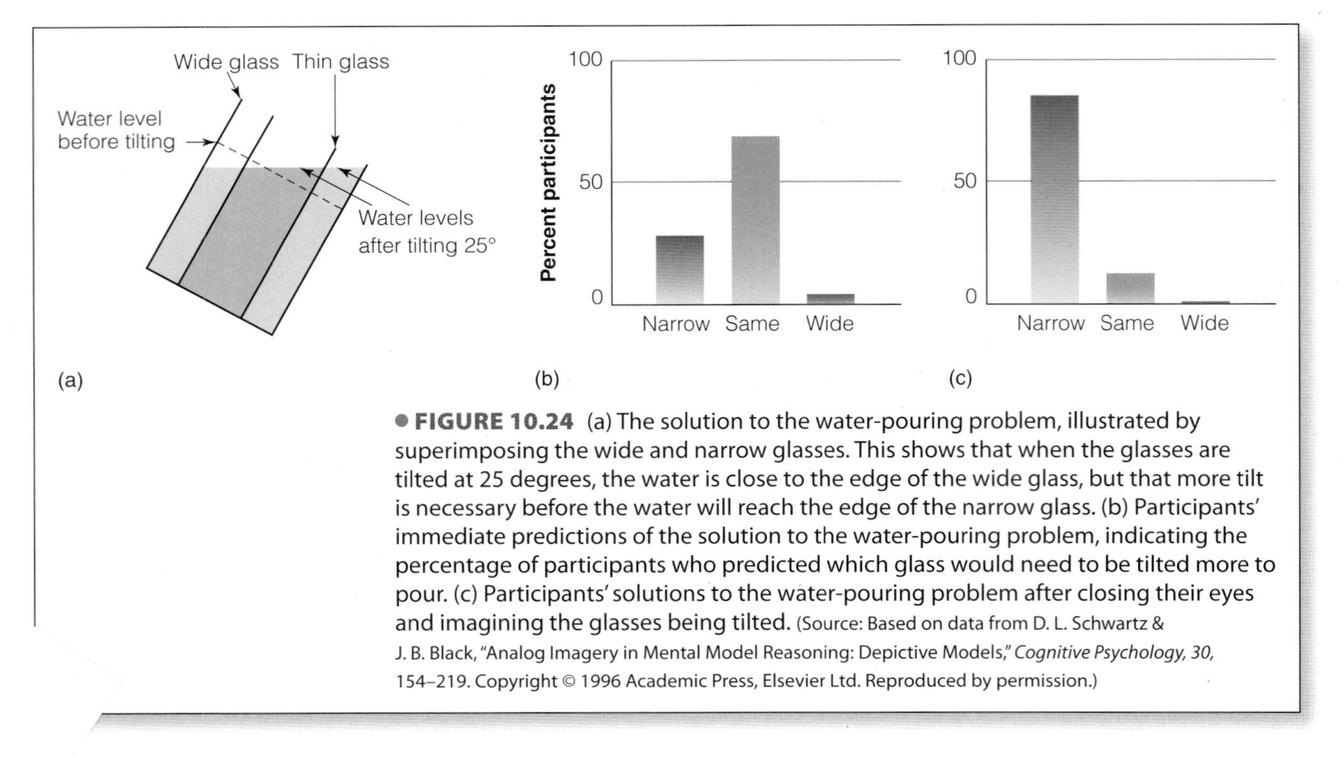

● **FIGURE 10.24** (a) The solution to the water-pouring problem, illustrated by superimposing the wide and narrow glasses. This shows that when the glasses are tilted at 25 degrees, the water is close to the edge of the wide glass, but that more tilt is necessary before the water will reach the edge of the narrow glass. (b) Participants' immediate predictions of the solution to the water-pouring problem, indicating the percentage of participants who predicted which glass would need to be tilted more to pour. (c) Participants' solutions to the water-pouring problem after closing their eyes and imagining the glasses being tilted. (Source: Based on data from D. L. Schwartz & J. B. Black, "Analog Imagery in Mental Model Reasoning: Depictive Models," *Cognitive Psychology, 30,* 154–219. Copyright © 1996 Academic Press, Elsevier Ltd. Reproduced by permission.)

therefore, is an effective way to solve mechanical problems, but is not the only way. In fact, there is evidence that people solve some mechanical problems by first using mental simulation and then later shift to using rules (Schwartz & Black, 1996).

Another question we can ask, in addition to *when* imagery is used to solve mechanical problems, is *how* is it used? The answer to this question may depend on the specific problem. For example, Mary Hegarty (1992) found that when asked to solve the pulley problem in Figure 10.23c, participants took longer to determine the motion of the lower pulley than the upper pulley. Based on this result, plus measurements of where the participants were looking as they solved the problem, she concluded that, rather than imagining the pulley system all at once, participants first determined the direction of the upper pulley, then how this movement affected the second pulley, and so on. In other words, participants considered each individual component of the system in sequence, to determine how later components, like the lower pulley, moved.

We have seen that imagery can be an effective way (and sometimes the most effective way) of solving mechanical problems, and also that there is often more than one way to solve a problem. When we discuss problem solving in Chapter 12, we will return to this idea that there is often more than one way to solve a particular problem, but that some ways are more effective than others.

TEST YOURSELF 10.2

1. Describe how experiments using the following physiological techniques have provided evidence of parallels between imagery and perception: (a) brain imaging; (b) deactivation of part of the brain; (c) neuropsychology; and (d) recording from single neurons.
2. Some of the neuropsychological results demonstrate parallels between imagery and perception, and some results do not. How has Behrmann explained these contradictory results?
3. What are some differences between imagery and perception? What have most psychologists concluded about the connection between imagery and perception?
4. Under what conditions does imagery improve memory? Describe techniques that use imagery as a tool to improve memory. What is the basic principle that underlies these techniques?
5. What is the evidence that solving mechanical problems can involve mental simulation? How is this evidence related to visual imagery?

CHAPTER SUMMARY

1. Mental imagery is experiencing a sensory impression in the absence of sensory input. Visual imagery is "seeing" in the absence of a visual stimulus. Imagery has played an important role in the creative process and as a way of thinking, in addition to purely verbal techniques.
2. Early ideas about imagery included the imageless thought debate and Galton's work with visual images, but imagery research stopped during the behaviorist era. Imagery research began again in the 1960s, with the advent of the cognitive revolution.
3. Kosslyn's mental scanning experiments suggested that imagery shares the same mechanisms as perception (that is, creates a depictive representation in the person's mind), but these results and others were challenged by Pylyshyn, who stated that imagery is based on a mechanism related to language (that is, it creates a propositional representation in a person's mind).
4. One of Pylyshyn's arguments against the idea of a depictive representation is the tacit knowledge explanation, which states that when asked to imagine something, people ask themselves what it would look like to see it and then simulate this staged event.
5. Finke and Pinker's "flashed dot" experiment argued against the tacit knowledge explanation. The following experiments also demonstrated parallels between imagery and perception: (a) size in the visual field (visual walk task); (b) interaction between perception and imagery (Perky's 1910 experiment; Farah's H/T experiment); and (c) physiological experiments.

6. Parallels between perception and imagery have been demonstrated physiologically by the following methods: (a) recording from single neurons (imagery neurons); (b) brain imaging (demonstrating overlapping activation in the brain); (c) transcranial magnetic stimulation experiments (comparing the effect of brain inactivation on perception and imagery); and (d) neuropsychological case studies (removal of visual cortex affects image size; unilateral neglect).
7. There is also physiological evidence for differences between imagery and perception. This evidence includes (a) differences in areas of the brain activated and (b) brain damage causing dissociations between perception and imagery.
8. Most psychologists, taking all of the above evidence into account, have concluded that imagery is closely related to perception and shares some (but not all) mechanisms.
9. The use of imagery can improve memory in a number of ways: (a) visualizing interacting images; (b) organization using the method of loci; and (c) associating items with nouns using the pegword technique.
10. Problems involving mechanical reasoning can be solved using either mental simulation or rule-based approaches. Experiments with the water-pouring problem show it is unlikely that tacit knowledge is involved in using imagery to solve this problem. Experiments with the pulley problem indicate that people may direct their attention to individual components of the problem, one after the other.

Think ABOUT IT

1. Look at an object for a minute; then look away, create a mental image of it, and draw a sketch of the object based on your mental image. Then draw a sketch of the same object while you are looking at it. How do the two sketches differ? What kinds of information about the object were you able to include in the sketch that was based on your mental image? What information was omitted, compared to the sketch you created by looking at the object?
2. Write a description of an object as you are looking at it. Then compare the written description with the information you can obtain by looking at the object or at a picture of the object. Is it true that "a picture is worth a thousand words"? How does your comparison of written and visual representations relate to the discussion of propositional versus depictive representations in this chapter?
3. Try using one of the techniques described at the end of this chapter to create images that represent things you have to do later today or during the coming week. Then, after some time passes (anywhere from an hour to a few days), check to see whether you can retrieve the memories for these images and if you can remember what they stand for.
4. Describe the connection between the description of the visual process in Figure 10.20 and the result of Ganis's fMRI experiment shown in Figure 10.15, in which brain activation caused by imagery and by perception was compared.

If You WANT TO KNOW MORE

1. **Auditory imagery.** Auditory imagery occurs when you mentally rehearse a telephone number or when a particular song keeps running through your mind. Recent research has demonstrated a connection between auditory imagery and brain activity.

Kraemer, D. J. M., Macrae, C. N., Green, A. E., & Kelly, W. M. (2005). Sound of silence activates auditory cortex. *Nature, 434*, 158.

Zatorre, R. J., Halpern, A. R., Perry, D. W., Meyer, E., & Evans, A. C. (1996). Hearing in the mind's ear: A PET investigation of musical imagery and perception. *Journal of Cognitive Neuroscience, 8*, 29–46.

2. **Visual imagery.** Although we have discussed visual imagery extensively in this chapter, it is worth looking at Stephen Kosslyn's books on the topic. His latest one is the following.

Kosslyn, S., Thompson, W. L., & Ganis, G. (2006). *The case for mental imagery*. New York: Oxford University Press.

3. **Mechanical reasoning and working memory.** The relationship between solving mechanical problems, imagery, and working memory has been studied by determining how placing a load on the visuospatial sketch pad component of working memory affects the ability to solve these problems. These experiments are analogous to the Demonstration on page 135 of Chapter 5.

Sims, V. K., & Hegarty, M. (1997). Mental animation in the visuospatial sketch pad: Evidence from dual task studies. *Memory & Cognition, 25*, 321–333.

Key TERMS

Conceptual peg hypothesis, 272
Depictive representation, 275
Epiphenomenon, 274
Imageless thought debate, 271
Imagery debate, 273
Imagery neuron, 279
Mental imagery, 270
Mental scanning, 273
Mental simulation, 288
Mental walk task, 277
Method of loci, 286
Paired-associate learning, 272
Pegword technique, 287
Propositional representation, 274
Rule-based approach (to mechanical reasoning), 288
Spatial representation, 274
Tacit knowledge explanation, 275
Transcranial magnetic stimulation (TMS), 281
Unilateral neglect, 283
Visual imagery, 270

Media RESOURCES

The *Cognitive Psychology* Book Companion Website

www.cengage.com/international

Prepare for quizzes and exams with online resources—including a glossary, flashcards, tutorial quizzes, crossword puzzles, and more.

CogLab

CogLab

To experience these experiments for yourself, go to coglab.wadsworth.com. Be sure to read each experiment's setup instructions before you go to the experiment itself. Otherwise, you won't know which keys to press.

Primary Labs

Mental rotation How a stimulus can be rotated in the mind to determine whether its shape matches another stimulus (p. 272).

Link word A demonstration of how imagery can be used to help learn foreign vocabulary (p. 287).

11 Language

Having a conversation involves perceiving and understanding words, following rules governing how words can be combined to form sentences, reacting to what the other person is saying, and inferring what they mean. All these things are occurring as the characters played by George Clooney and Vera Farmiga are talking in the film *Up in the Air.* It is, however, unlikely that they are paying attention to these cognitive processes. They are just having a conversation!

Some Questions We Will Consider

- ▶ How do we understand individual words, and how are words combined to create sentences? (297)
- ▶ How can we understand sentences that have more than one meaning? (304)
- ▶ How do we understand stories? (309)
- ▶ Does language affect the way a person perceives colors? (316)

Leaving the Chinese restaurant, I opened my fortune cookie and pulled out a thin slip of paper. On one side it said "Learn Chinese," followed by a phrase and its translation; on the other side it said:

> Everything you add to the truth
> Subtracts from the truth

As I pondered this statement, it occurred to me how amazing language is and how, like every cognitive capacity we have described so far, it involves knowledge that we bring to a situation. Understanding the saying I pulled out of my fortune cookie requires, for example, an understanding of the concept of "truth," but what makes it interesting is the question it poses: How can adding something to a true statement make it less true? One answer to this question is based on the classic "fish story." A fisherman boasts that he caught a big fish (which may be true) but then adds to the truth by exaggerating the fish's length (which makes his account less true). If we have the knowledge of the "fish story" idea that "adding to the truth" generally implies adding something *false* to the truth, then the initially puzzling statement from my fortune cookie makes perfect sense.

There is no question that knowledge is an integral part of language. For one thing, we come into the world without it, and have to learn it. Anyone who has observed infants for any length of time realizes that they understand language before they can produce it. Then when they begin talking, the process begins with single words, progresses to short phrases, and culminates in sentences that increase in complexity as the infant, then child, learns more on the path to adulthood.

What Is Language?

Long before individuals have acquired the knowledge needed to determine the meaning of my fortune cookie, they will have acquired the ability to create sentences and string them together into paragraphs that express their thoughts in either written or spoken form. This ability to understand words and then string them together to express thoughts makes possible the remarkable feat of transmitting thoughts from one person to another. This ability is captured in the following definition of **language**: *a system of communication using sounds or symbols that enables us to express our feelings, thoughts, ideas, and experiences.*

But this definition doesn't go far enough, because it conceivably could include some forms of animal communication. Cats "meow" when their food dish is empty; monkeys have a repertoire of "calls" that stand for things such as "danger" or "greeting"; bees perform a "waggle dance" at the hive to indicate the location of flowers. Although there is some evidence that monkeys may be able to use language in a way similar to humans (see "If You Want to Know More: Animal Language," page 321), most animal communication lacks the properties of human language. Let's expand on our definition by considering some of the properties that make human language unique.

THE CREATIVITY OF HUMAN LANGUAGE

Human language goes far beyond a series of fixed signals that transmit a single message such as "feed me," "danger," or "go that way for flowers." Language provides a way of arranging a sequence of signals—sounds for spoken language, letters and written words for written language, and physical signs for sign language—to transmit, from one person to another, things ranging from the simple and commonplace ("My car is over there") to messages that have perhaps never been previously written or uttered in the entire history of the world ("I'm thinking of getting my car repaired because I'm quitting my job in February and taking a trip across the country to celebrate Groundhog Day with my cousin Zelda").

Language makes it possible to create new and unique sentences because it has a structure that is (1) hierarchical and (2) governed by rules. The hierarchical nature of language means that it consists of a series of small components that can be combined to form larger units. For example, words can be combined to create phrases, which in turn can create sentences, which themselves can become components of a story. The rule-based nature of language means that these components can be arranged in certain ways ("What is my cat saying?" is permissible in English), but not in other ways ("Cat my saying is what?" is not). These two properties—a hierarchical structure and rules—endow humans with the ability to go far beyond the fixed calls and signs of animals, to communicate whatever they want to express.

THE UNIVERSALITY OF LANGUAGE

Although people do "talk" to themselves, as when Hamlet wondered "To be or not to be" or when you daydream in class, the predominant staging ground for language is one person conversing with another. Consider the following:

- People's need to communicate is so powerful that when deaf children find themselves in an environment where nobody speaks or uses sign language, they invent a sign language themselves (Goldin-Meadow, 1982).
- Everyone with normal capacities develops a language and learns to follow its complex rules, even though they are usually not aware of these rules. Although many people find the study of grammar to be very difficult, they have no trouble using language.
- Language is universal across cultures. There are more than 5,000 different languages, and there isn't a single culture that is without language. When European explorers first set foot in New Guinea in the 1500s, the people they discovered, who had been isolated from the rest of the world for eons, had developed more than 750 different languages, many of them quite different from one another.
- Language development is similar across cultures. No matter what the culture or particular language, children generally begin babbling at about 7 months, a few meaningful words appear by the first birthday, and the first multiword utterances occur at about age 2 (Levelt, 2001).
- Even though a large number of languages are very different from one another, we can describe them as being "unique but the same." They are unique in that they use different words and sounds, and they may use different rules for combining these words (although many languages use similar rules). They are the same in that all languages have words that serve the functions of nouns and verbs, and all languages include a system to make things negative, to ask questions, and to refer to the past and present.

STUDYING LANGUAGE

The scientific study of language traces its beginnings to the 1800s, when Paul Broca (1861) and Carl Wernicke (1874) identified areas in the frontal and temporal lobes that are involved in understanding and producing language. When we described this work in Chapter 2, we saw that this early research provided evidence that functions are localized in specific areas of the brain. We also saw that more recent physiological research, using new technologies such as brain scanning, has shown that language processing does not occur only in the areas originally identified by Broca and Wernicke, but is distributed over a large area of the brain (see page 35). Some research focusing on behavioral aspects of language was also being done during the first part of the 20th century, but large-scale research on cognitive aspects of language began only with the cognitive revolution of the 1950s.

This chapter focuses mainly on behavioral research, and it is in the 1950s that we take up the story. At that time behaviorism was still the dominant approach in psychology (see page 9), and in 1957 B. F. Skinner, the main proponent of behaviorism, published a book called *Verbal Behavior* in which he proposed that language is learned through reinforcement. According to this idea, just as children learn appropriate behavior by being rewarded for "good" behavior and punished for "bad" behavior, children learn language by being rewarded for using correct language and punished (or not rewarded) for using incorrect language.

In the same year, the linguist Noam Chomsky published a book titled *Syntactic Structures* in which he proposed that human language is coded in the genes. According to this idea, just as humans are genetically programmed to walk, they are programmed to acquire and use language. Chomsky concluded that despite the wide variations that exist across languages, the underlying basis of all language is similar. Most important for our purposes, Chomsky saw studying language as a way to study the properties of the mind and therefore disagreed with the behaviorist idea that the mind is not a valid topic of study for psychology.

Chomsky's disagreement with behaviorism led him to publish a scathing review of Skinner's *Verbal Behavior* in 1959. In his review, he presented arguments against the behaviorist idea that language can be explained in terms of reinforcements and without reference to the mind. One of Chomsky's most persuasive arguments was that as children learn language, they produce sentences that they have never heard and that have never been reinforced. (A classic example of a sentence that has been created by many children, and that is unlikely to have been taught or reinforced by parents, is "I hate you, Mommy.") Chomsky's criticism of behaviorism was an important event in the cognitive revolution and began changing the focus of the young discipline of psycholinguistics, the field concerned with the psychological study of language. (Also see "If You Want to Know More: The Beginnings of Psycholinguistics," page 321.)

The goal of psycholinguistics is to discover the psychological processes by which humans acquire and process language (Clark & Van der Wege, 2002; Gleason & Ratner, 1998; Miller, 1965). The four major concerns of psycholinguistics are as follows:

1. *Comprehension.* How do people understand spoken and written language? This includes how people process language sounds; how they understand words, sentences, and stories expressed in writing, speech, or sign language; and how people have conversations with one another.
2. *Speech production.* How do people produce language? This includes the physical processes of speech production and the mental processes that occur as a person creates speech.
3. *Representation.* How is language represented in the mind and in the brain? This includes how people group words together into phrases and make connections between different parts of a story, as well as how these processes are related to the activation of the brain.
4. *Acquisition.* How do people learn language? This includes not only how children learn language, but also how people learn additional languages, either as children or later in life.

Because of the vast scope of psycholinguistics, we are going to restrict our attention to the first three of these concerns, describing research on how we understand language and how we produce it. (See "If You Want to Know More: Language Acquisition," page 322, for suggested readings about language acquisition.) We begin by considering each of the components of language: small components such as *sounds* and *words*, then combinations of words that form *sentences*, and finally "texts"—*stories* that are created by combining a number of sentences. At the end of the chapter, we describe some of the factors involved in how people participate in and understand conversations. Finally, we look at cross-cultural research that considers how language affects thought, and how thought might affect language.

Perceiving Words, Phonemes, and Letters

One of the most amazing things about words is how many we know and how rapidly we acquire them. Infants produce their first words during their second year (sometimes a little earlier, sometimes later) and, after a slow start, begin adding words rapidly until, by the time they have become adults, they can understand more than 50,000 different words (Altmann, 2001; Dell, 1995). Our knowledge about words is stored in our **lexicon**, which is a person's knowledge of what words mean, how they sound, and how they are used in relation to other words.

COMPONENTS OF WORDS

The words on this page are made up of letters, but the units of language are defined not in terms of letters, but by sounds and meanings. The two smallest units of language are phonemes, which refer to sounds, and morphemes, which refer to meanings.

Phonemes When you say words, you produce sounds called phonemes. A **phoneme** is the shortest segment of speech that, if changed, changes the meaning of a word. Thus, the word *bit* contains the phonemes /b/, /i/, and /t/ (phonemes are indicated by phonetic symbols that are set off with slashes), because we can change *bit* into *pit* by replacing /b/ with /p/, to *bat* by replacing /i/ with /a/, or to *bid* by replacing /t/ with /d/.

Note that because phonemes refer to sounds, they are not the same as letters, which can have a number of different sounds (consider the "e" sound in "we" and "wet"), and which can be silent in certain situations (the "e" in "some"). Because different languages use different sounds, the number of phonemes varies in different languages. There are only 11 phonemes in Hawaiian, about 47 in English, and as many as 60 in some African dialects.

Morphemes **Morphemes** are the smallest units of language that have a definable meaning or a grammatical function. For example, "truck" consists of a number of phonemes, but only one morpheme, because none of the components that create the word truck mean anything. Similarly, even though "table" has two syllables, "tabe" and "ul," it also consists of only a single morpheme, because the syllables alone have no meaning. In contrast "bedroom" has two syllables and two morphemes, "bed" and "room." Endings such as "s" and "ed," which contribute to the meaning of a word, are morphemes. Thus even though "trucks" has just one syllable, it consists of two morphemes, "truck" (which indicates a type of vehicle) and "s" (which indicates more than one).

PERCEIVING SPOKEN PHONEMES AND WORDS, AND WRITTEN LETTERS

One of the central characteristics of language, which we will encounter throughout this chapter, is how its various components are affected by the context within which they are heard or seen. For example, a word's meaning can depend on the other words around it. Thus, the word *bug* means one thing in the sentence "The bug crawled up the blade of grass" and something else in the sentence "The computer program had a bug in it."

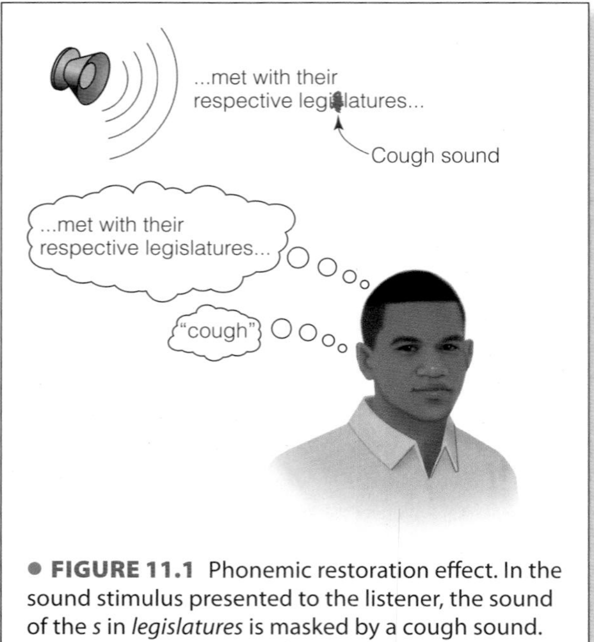

● **FIGURE 11.1** Phonemic restoration effect. In the sound stimulus presented to the listener, the sound of the *s* in *legislatures* is masked by a cough sound. What the person hears is indicated below. Although the person hears the cough, he also hears the *s*.

We will consider how context affects meaning in a moment, but first let's focus on *perception*—our ability to sense words and parts of words as individual units. For example, perceiving the spoken word *bug* in the two sentences above would involve hearing the sounds that make up that word as separate from the sounds of the other words in the sentence, and also sensing what the word sounds like. We don't have to know the meaning of the word *bug* to perceive it, although, as we will see, sometimes knowing the meaning can help us perceive it. We begin our discussion of perception by considering how we hear phonemes.

Speech: Perceiving Phonemes The powerful effect of context on perception is illustrated by the demonstration that a phoneme that is part of a sentence can be heard even if the sound of the phoneme is covered up by an extraneous noise. Richard Warren (1970) demonstrated this by having participants listen to a recording of the sentence "The state governors met with their respective legislatures convening in the capital city." Warren replaced the first /s/ in "legislatures" with the sound of a cough and asked his participants to indicate where in the sentence the cough occurred (● Figure 11.1). No participant identified the correct position of the cough, and, even more significantly, none of them noticed that the /s/ in "legislatures" was missing. This effect, which Warren called the **phonemic restoration effect**, was experienced even by students and staff in the psychology department who knew that the /s/ was missing. This "filling in" of the missing phoneme based on the context produced by the sentence and the portion of the word that was presented is an example of top-down processing.

Warren also showed that the phonemic restoration effect can be influenced by the meaning of the words that *follow* the missing phoneme. For example, the last word of the phrase "There was time to *ave ..." (where the * indicates the presence of a cough or some other sound) could be *shave*, *save*, *wave*, or *rave*, but participants heard the word *wave* when the remainder of the sentence had to do with saying good-bye to a departing friend. This example of how our knowledge of the meanings of words and the likely meanings of sentences affects speech perception is another example of top-down processing. The effect of knowledge on speech perception has also been demonstrated by finding that more restoration occurs for a real word like *prOgress* (where the capital letter indicates the masked phoneme) than for a similar "pseudoword" like *crOgress* (Samuel, 1990). We will now consider how our knowledge of the meanings of words helps us to perceive them.

Speech: Perceiving Words One of the challenges posed by the problem of perceiving words is that not everyone says words in the same way. People talk with different accents and at different speeds, and most important, people often take a relaxed approach to pronouncing words when they are speaking naturally. For example, if you were talking to a friend, how would you say "Did you go to class today?" Would you say "Did you" or "Dijoo"? You have your own ways of producing various words and phonemes, and other people have theirs. For example, analysis of how people actually speak has determined that there are 50 different ways to pronounce the word *the* (Waldrop, 1988).

The way people pronounce words in conversational speech makes about half of the words unintelligible when taken out of context and presented alone. Irwin Pollack and J. M. Pickett (1964) demonstrated this by recording the conversations of participants who sat in a room, waiting for the experiment to begin. When the participants were then presented with recordings of single words taken out of their own conversations, they could identify only half the words, even though they were listening to their own voices! The fact that the people in this experiment were able to identify words as they were talking to each other, but couldn't identify the same words when the words were isolated, illustrates that their ability to perceive words in conversations is aided by the context provided by the words and sentences that make up the conversation.

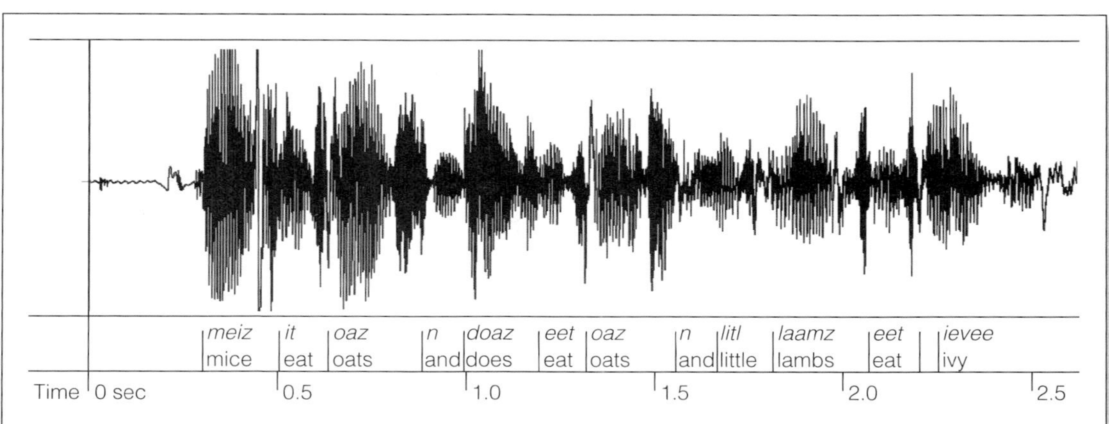

● **FIGURE 11.2** Sound energy for the phrase "Mice eat oats and does eat oats and little lambs eat ivy." The italicized words just below the sound record indicate how this phrase was pronounced by the speaker. The vertical lines next to the words indicate where each word begins. Note that it is difficult or impossible to tell from the sound record where one word ends and the next begins. (Speech signal courtesy of Peter Howell.)

One of the fascinating aspects of this effect is that if we were to analyze the sound energy that occurs when people are having conversations, we might come to the opposite conclusion—that it would be *more* difficult to perceive words when they are surrounded by other words in a sentence. The reason we might think this is that words in conversations are not separated from one another by spaces, or pauses, even though it may sound as though they are. We can see why this is so by remembering our discussion in Chapter 3, in which we saw that a record of the physical energy produced by conversational speech reveals either no physical breaks in the signal or breaks that don't correspond to the breaks we perceive between words (● Figure 11.2). The process of perceiving individual words in the continuous flow of the speech signal is called **speech segmentation**.

Our ability to perceive individual words, even though there are often no pauses between words in the sound signal, is aided by a number of factors. In Chapter 3 we pointed out that when we listen to an unfamiliar foreign language, it is often difficult to distinguish one word from the next, but if we know a language, individual words stand out (see page 57). This observation illustrates that knowing the meanings of words helps us perceive them. Perhaps you have had this experience, when words that you happen to know in a foreign language seem to "pop out" from what appears to be an otherwise continuous stream of speech.

Another example of how meaning is responsible for organizing sounds into words is provided by these two sentences.

Jamie's mother said, "Be a *big girl* and eat your vegetables."
The thing *Big Earl* loved most in the world was his car.

"Big girl" and "Big Earl" are both pronounced the same way, so hearing them differently depends on the overall meaning of the sentence in which these words appear. This example is similar to the familiar "I scream, you scream, we all scream for ice cream" that many people learn as children. The sound stimuli for "I scream" and "ice cream" are identical, so the different organizations must be achieved by the meaning of the sentence in which these words appear.

Although segmentation is aided by knowing the meanings of words and being aware of the context in which these words occur, listeners also use other information to achieve segmentation. As we learn a language, we learn that certain sounds are more likely to follow one another within a word, and other sounds are more likely to be separated by the space between two words. For example, consider the words *pretty baby*. In English it is more likely that *pre* and *ty* will follow each other in the same word (***pre-ty***) and that *ty* and *ba* will be separated by a space so will be in two different words (pret***ty*** ***ba***by). Thus, the space in the phrase *prettybaby* is most likely to be between *pretty* and

TABLE 11.1 Perceiving Phonemes, Words, and Letters

Effect	Description	Conclusion
Phonemic restoration	A phoneme in a spoken word in a sentence can be perceived even if it is obscured by noise.	Knowledge of meaning helps "fill in the blanks."
Words isolated from conversational speech	It is difficult to perceive isolated words.	The context provided by the rest of the conversation aids in the perception of words.
Speech segmentation	Individual words are perceived in spoken sentences even though the speech stimulus usually doesn't indicate breaks between words.	Knowledge of the meanings of words in a language and other characteristics of speech, such as sounds that usually go together in a word, help create speech segmentation.
Word superiority	Letters presented visually are easier to recognize when in a word.	Letters are affected by their surroundings.

baby. There is evidence that young children learn these rules about what sounds go together in words and what sounds are more likely to be separated into two different words (Gomez & Gerkin, 1999, 2000; Saffran et al., 1999).

CogLab
Word Superiority

Reading: Perceiving Letters Although most of the research we will be describing in this chapter involves spoken language, it is worth noting that the effect of context in perceiving phonemes and words has also been demonstrated to play a role in perceiving written letters. The **word superiority effect** refers to the finding that letters are easier to recognize when they are contained in a word than when they appear alone or are contained in a nonword. This effect was first demonstrated by G. M. Reicher in 1969 using the following procedure.

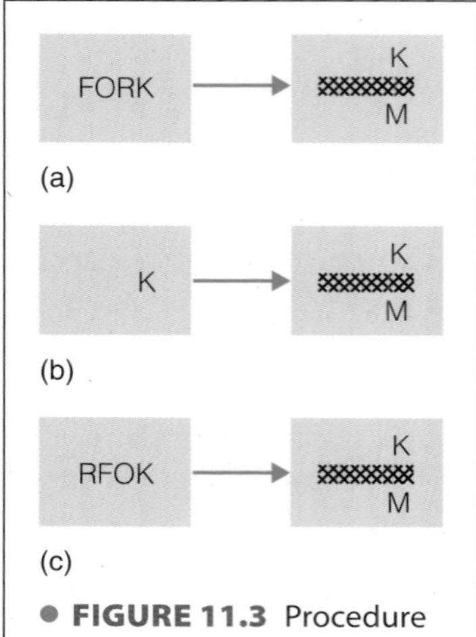

● **FIGURE 11.3** Procedure for an experiment that demonstrates the word superiority effect. First the stimulus is presented, then a random pattern and two letters. Three types of stimuli are shown: (a) word condition; (b) letter condition; and (c) nonword condition.

METHOD Word Superiority Effect

A stimulus that is either (a) a word (such as *FORK*), (b) a single letter (such as *K*), or (c) a nonword (such as *RFOK*) is flashed briefly. It is followed immediately by a random pattern where the stimulus was and two letters, one that appeared in the original stimulus (*K* in this example) and another that did not (*M* in this example). The pattern and letters are flashed rapidly, and the participants' task is to pick the letter that was presented in the original stimulus. In the example in ● Figure 11.3a, the word *FORK* was presented, so *K* would be the correct answer. *K* would also be the correct answer if the *K* were originally presented alone (Figure 11.3b) or if it were presented in a nonword such as *RFOK* (Figure 11.3c). Identifying the *K* more quickly and accurately when preceded by the word *FORK* is evidence for the word superiority effect.

When Reicher's participants were asked to choose which of the two letters they had seen in the original stimulus, they did so more quickly and accurately when the letter had been part of a word, as in Figure 11.3a, than when the letter had been presented alone, as in Figure 11.3b, or as part of a nonword, as in Figure 11.3c. This more rapid processing of letters within a word—the word superiority effect—means that letters in words are not processed one by one but that each letter is affected by its surroundings. Table 11.1 summarizes the effects of context on perceiving phonemes, words and letters.

Understanding Words

In the last section, we focused on how we *perceive* phonemes. We will now describe some of the factors that influence how we *understand* the meanings of words. We begin by considering the effect of **word frequency**—the relative usage of a word in a particular language—and follow with a discussion of how we understand words that have more than one meaning.

THE WORD FREQUENCY EFFECT

Some words occur more frequently in a particular language than others. For example, in English, *home* occurs 547 times per million words, and *hike* occurs only 4 times per million words. The word frequency effect refers to the fact that we respond more rapidly to high-frequency words like *home* than to low-frequency words like *hike*. One way this has been demonstrated is through the *lexical decision task*, introduced in Chapter 9 (see page 252). In this task, participants are asked to read stimuli and decide whether or not they are words, as illustrated in the following demonstration.

DEMONSTRATION Lexical Decision Task

CogLab Lexical Decision

The **lexical decision task** involves reading a list that consists of words and nonwords. Your task is to indicate as quickly as possible whether each entry in the two lists below is a word. Try this yourself by silently reading List 1 and saying "yes" each time you encounter a word. Either time yourself to determine how long it takes you to get through the list or just notice how difficult the task is.

List 1
Gambastya, revery, voitle, chard, wefe, cratily, decoy, puldow, faflot, oriole, voluble, boovle, chalt, awry, signet, trave, crock, cryptic, ewe, himpola

Now try the same thing for List 2.

List 2
Mulvow, governor, bless, tuglety, gare, relief, ruftily, history, pindle, develop, grdot, norve, busy, effort, garvola, match, sard, pleasant, coin, maisle

The task you have just completed (taken from D. W. Carroll, 2004; also see Hirsh-Pasek et al., 1993) is called a lexical decision task because you had to decide whether each group of letters was a word in your lexicon.

When researchers presented this task under controlled conditions, they found that people read high-frequency words faster than low-frequency words (Savin, 1963). Thus, it is likely that you were able to carry out the lexical decision task more rapidly for List 2, which contains high-frequency words such as *history* and *busy*, than for List 1, which contains low-frequency words such as *decoy* and *voluble*.

This slower response for less frequent words has also been demonstrated by measuring people's eye movements as they are reading. The eye movements that occur during reading consist of *fixations*, during which the eye stops on a word for about a quarter of a second (250 ms), and rapid movements of the eyes, called *saccades*, which propel the eye to the next fixation.

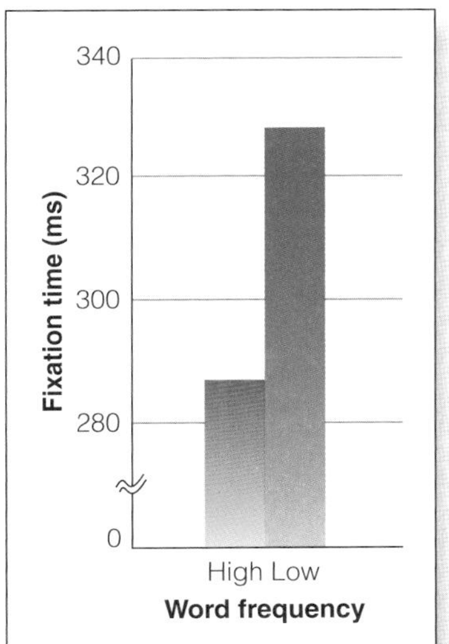

● **FIGURE 11.4** Results of Rayner et al.'s (2003) experiment. The bars indicate how long participants looked at target words such as *pretty* and *demure*. These results show that participants fixated low-frequency words longer than high-frequency words. (Source: Based on K. Rayner et al., "Reading Disappearing Text: Cognitive Control of Eye Movements," *Psychological Science, 14,* 385–388, 2003.)

In a recent eye movement study, Keith Rayner and coworkers (2003) had participants read sentences that contained either a high- or a low-frequency target word. For example, the sentence "Sam wore the horrid coat though his pretty girlfriend complained" contains the high-frequency target word *pretty*. The other version of the sentence was exactly the same, but with the high-frequency word *pretty* replaced by the low-frequency word *demure*. The results, shown in ● Figure 11.4, indicate that readers looked at the low-frequency words (such as *demure*) about 40 ms longer than the high-frequency words (such as *pretty*). One reason could be that the readers needed more time to access the meaning of the low-frequency words. The word frequency effect, therefore, demonstrates how our past experience with words influences our ability to access their meaning.

LEXICAL AMBIGUITY

Words can often have more than one meaning, a situation called lexical ambiguity. For example, the word *bug* can refer to insects, or hidden listening devices, or being annoyed, among other things. When ambiguous words appear in a sentence, we usually use the context of the sentence to determine which definition applies. For example, if Susan says "My mother is bugging me," we can be pretty sure that *bugging* refers to the fact that Susan's mother is annoying her, as opposed to sprinkling insects on her or installing a hidden listening device in her room (although we might need further context to totally rule out this last possibility).

Context often clears up ambiguity so rapidly that we are not aware of its existence. However, David Swinney (1979) showed that people briefly access multiple meanings of ambiguous words before the effect of context takes over (also see Tanenhaus et al., 1979). He did this by presenting participants with a tape recording of sentences such as the following:

> Rumor had it that, for years, the government building had been plagued with problems. The man was not surprised when he found several spiders, roaches, and other bugs in the corner of the room.

If you had to predict which meaning listeners would use for *bugs* in this sentence, *insect* would be the logical choice because the sentence mentions spiders and roaches. However, using a technique called *lexical priming*, Swinney found that right after the word *bug* was presented, his listeners had accessed two meanings.

METHOD Lexical Priming

Remember from Chapter 6 (page 161) that priming occurs when seeing a stimulus makes it easier to respond to that stimulus when it is presented again. The basic principle behind priming is that the first presentation of a stimulus activates a representation of the stimulus, and a person can respond more rapidly to the stimulus if this activation is still present when the stimulus is presented again.

Priming involving the naming of words is called **lexical priming**. Because lexical priming involves the *meaning* of words, priming effects can occur when a word is followed by another word with a similar meaning. For example, presenting the word *ant* before presenting the word *bug* can cause a person to respond faster to the word *bug* than if an unrelated word like *cloud* had preceded it. The presence of a lexical priming effect would, therefore, indicate whether two words, like *ant* and *bug*, have similar meanings in a person's mind.

Swinney used lexical priming by presenting the passage about the government building to participants and, as they were hearing the word *bug*, presenting a word or a nonword on a screen (● Figure 11.5a). The words he presented were either related to the "insect" meaning of *bug* (*ant*), related to the "hidden listening device" meaning (*spy*), or not related at all (*sky*). The participant was told to indicate as quickly as possible whether the item flashed on the screen was a word or a nonword. (This is the lexical decision task described on page 252.)

Swinney's result, shown in Figure 11.5b, was that participants responded with nearly the same speed to both *ant* and *spy* (the small difference between them is not significant), and the response to both of these words was significantly faster than the response to *sky*. This faster responding to words associated with two of the meanings of *bug* means that even though there is information in the sentence indicating that *bug* is an insect, listeners accessed both the "listening device" and "insect" meanings of *bug* as it was being presented. This effect was short-lived, however. The effect vanished when Swinney repeated the same test but, instead of presenting the word or nonword simultaneously with *bug*, waited about 200 ms before presenting the test words. Thus, within about 200 ms after hearing *bug*, the "insect" meaning had been selected from the ones initially activated. Context does, therefore, help determine the appropriate meaning of a word in a sentence, but it exerts its influence after a slight delay during which other meanings of a word are briefly accessed. (See Lucas, 1999, for more on how context affects the meaning of words.)

These effects, summarized in Table 11.2, combined with the effects in Table 11.1, illustrate one of the main messages of this chapter: Although the study of language

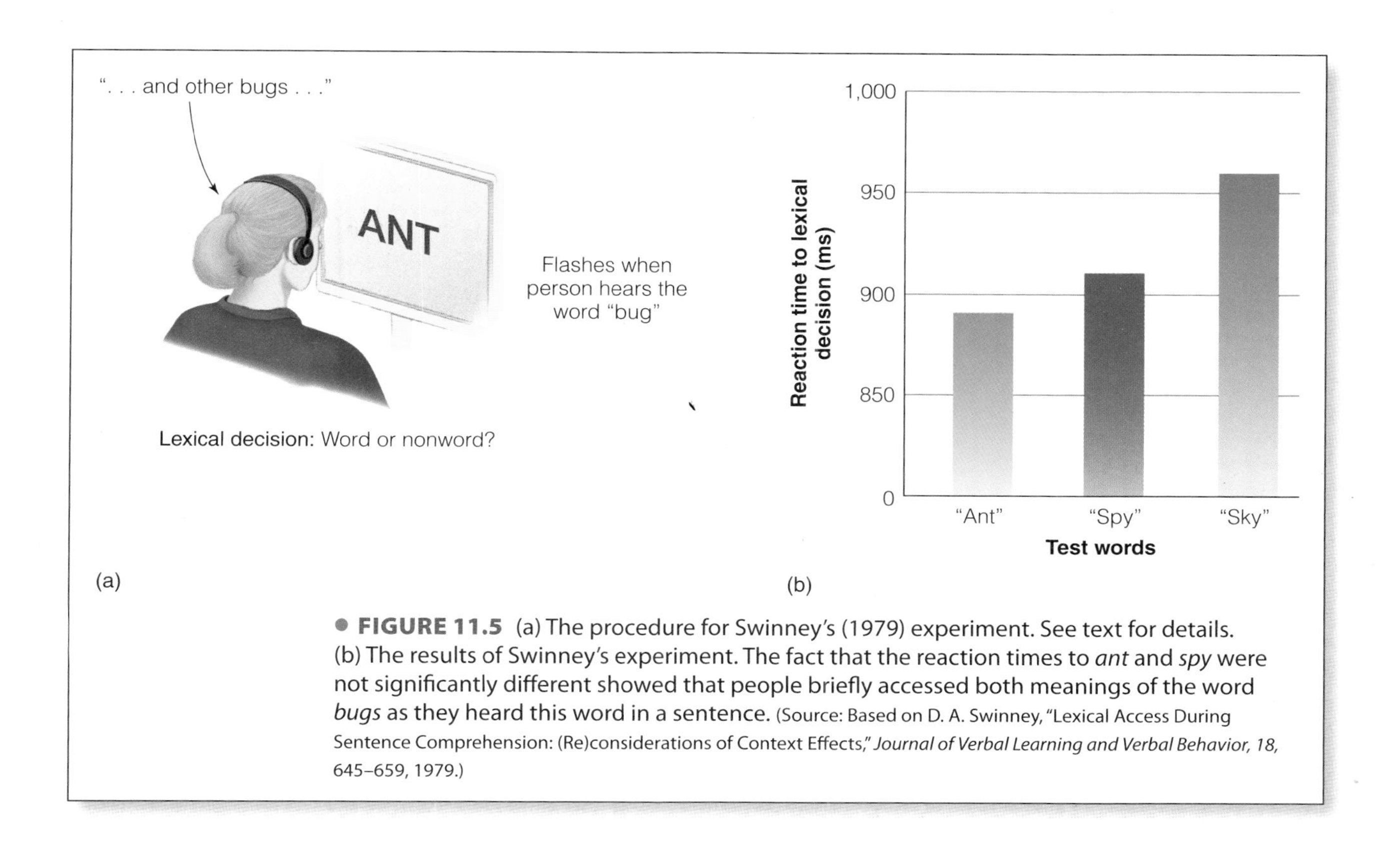

● **FIGURE 11.5** (a) The procedure for Swinney's (1979) experiment. See text for details. (b) The results of Swinney's experiment. The fact that the reaction times to *ant* and *spy* were not significantly different showed that people briefly accessed both meanings of the word *bugs* as they heard this word in a sentence. (Source: Based on D. A. Swinney, "Lexical Access During Sentence Comprehension: (Re)considerations of Context Effects," *Journal of Verbal Learning and Verbal Behavior, 18,* 645–659, 1979.)

is often described in terms of its individual components—such as letters, words, and sentences—these components are not processed in isolation. As we discuss how we understand sentences in the next section, we will see more examples of how each of these components interacts with and influences the others.

TEST YOURSELF 11.1

1. What is special about human language? Consider why human language is unique and what it is used for.
2. What events are associated with the beginning of the modern study of language in the 1950s?
3. What is psycholinguistics? What are its concerns, and what part of psycholinguistics does this chapter focus on?
4. What are the two components of words?
5. Describe the following demonstrations of how context helps with the perception of words and components of words: (1) phonemic restoration effect; (2) isolating words from conversations (Pollack and Pickett experiment); (3) speech segmentation.

TABLE 11.2 Understanding Words

Effect	Description	Conclusion
Word frequency	Words vary in the frequency with which they are used in a particular language (examples: *pretty, demure*).	High-frequency words are read faster than low-frequency words (lexical decision task; eye movements).
Lexical ambiguity	Many words have more than one meaning (example: *bug*).	When a word is used in a sentence, multiple meanings are accessed rapidly, but then the content of the sentence quickly determines the correct meaning.

6. What is the word superiority effect?
7. How does the frequency of words (word frequency effect) aid in accessing words? How does Swinney's experiment about "bugs" indicate that the meanings of ambiguous words can take precedence over context, at least for a short time? Be sure you understand lexical ambiguity and lexical priming.

Understanding Sentences

Although the last section was about words, we ended up discussing sentences as well. This isn't surprising because words rarely appear in isolation. They appear together in sentences in which all of the words combine to create meaning. To understand how words work together to create the meaning of a sentence, we first need to distinguish between two properties of sentences: semantics and syntax.

Semantics is the meanings of words and sentences; **syntax** specifies the rules for combining words into sentences. Changing the sentence "The cats won't eat" into "The cats won't bake" is an error of semantics because the meaning doesn't make sense; changing the sentence to "The cats won't eating" is an error of syntax because the grammar is not correct. Another example of the operation of syntax is word order: The sentence "The cat chased the bird" follows the rules of English syntax, but "Cat bird the chased" does not.

We saw in Chapter 2 that meaning (semantics) and form (syntax) are associated with different areas of the brain. Thus, damage to some brain areas makes it difficult for a person to understand what a sentence means, while damage to other areas makes it difficult for a person to produce grammatically correct sentences. As we describe the process of determining the meaning of a sentence, we will see that both semantics and syntax are involved.

PARSING AND A TRIP DOWN THE GARDEN PATH

As we read or listen to a sentence, we encounter a series of words, one following another. As this happens, the meaning of a sentence unfolds, derived from both the meanings of the words and how the words are grouped together in phrases. The grouping of words into phrases, called **parsing**, is a central process for determining the meaning of a sentence.

How does this process of grouping words into phrases occur? One way that psychologists study the process of understanding a sentence is by presenting sentences that can have more than one meaning. An example of this is **temporary ambiguity**, in which the initial words of a sentence can lead to more than one meaning. For exam0ple, consider the following phrase:

Amanda believed the senator ...

As the sentence continues, here are two ways it could unfold:

Choice 1: ... during his speech.

or

Choice 2: ... was lying to the committee.

The same initial phrase can lead to two very different meanings. Choice 1 indicates when Amanda thought the senator was telling the truth (during his speech); Choice 2 indicates what she thought the senator was doing (he was lying). By the time each of these sentences is completed, the meaning has become clear. However, one of the key principles of sentence comprehension is that people often don't wait until the end of a sentence to decide what it means. They typically decide on meanings as the sentence is unfolding. This means that a person may decide on one meaning and then have to revise it once the sentence is completed.

Here is another sentence that illustrates the way we assign meanings as we go along:

Cast iron sinks quickly rust.

How did you interpret this sentence as you read it? Initially, after *cast iron sinks*, the sentence appears to be about a cast iron sink that you might find in a kitchen or workroom; then at *quickly*, the sentence appears to be about a heavy piece of metal sinking in water; but after *rusts*, the sentence's meaning changes back to being about that kitchen or workroom sink.

This is an example of a **garden path sentence**, so called because it leads the reader "down the garden path" (down a path that seems right, but turns out to be wrong). A basic question about this "garden path" process is how readers decide which meanings to pick as the sentence unfolds. This process involves parsing, because the meaning of the sentence depends on how the words are grouped into phrases. Two approaches to understanding how the parsing mechanism works have been proposed. One assigns the central role to syntax, with semantics coming into play later; the other proposes that syntax and semantics work simultaneously to determine the meaning of a sentence.

THE SYNTAX-FIRST APPROACH TO PARSING

As its name implies, the **syntax-first approach to parsing** focuses on how parsing is determined by syntax—the grammatical structure of the sentence. The syntax-first approach states that the parsing mechanism groups phrases together based on structural principles. One of these principles is called *late closure*. The principle of **late closure** states that when a person encounters a new word, the person's parsing mechanism assumes that this word is part of the current phrase, so each new word is added to the current phrase for as long as possible (Frazier, 1987).

Consider, for example, our garden path sentence about cast iron. Let's look at how the grouping of words into phrases proceeds as we add words to the sentence. Words between two vertical lines are in the same phrase.

1. |Cast iron|

These words go together, indicating a type of iron.

2. |Cast iron sinks|

The added word *sinks*, when grouped as here, could be a noun meaning "kitchen sinks" or a verb meaning "sinks to the bottom." The fact that *sinks* can have two meanings is an example of lexical ambiguity.

3. |Cast iron sinks quickly|

Quickly is added to the phrase *cast iron sinks*. This, and the examples above, are examples of late closure, because each word in turn is added to the current phrase. Adding *quickly* to this phrase indicates that the meaning of *sinks* is "sinks to the bottom."

4. |Cast iron sinks| |quickly rust|

Adding *rust* changes the meaning, making it necessary to adjust the parsing so that *quickly* becomes part of a new phrase. Once the sentence is completed, we can see that in step 3 late closure led us astray ("down the garden path"). To be sure you understand late closure, try the following demonstration.

DEMONSTRATION Late Closure

For the following sentences, determine (1) where the first phrase ends (determine this by reading the whole sentence); and (2) the word or words that are erroneously added to the first phrase during the initial reading because of late closure (determine this by noticing how the sentence could be misinterpreted as it is being read). For answers, see page 325.

1. The shopper felt the fur coat was overpriced.

2. Because he always jogs a mile seems like a short distance to him.

3. The mechanic maintained the truck was working beautifully.

Notice what is happening in these sentences. The syntax-based principle of late closure leads the reader astray, but then a correction is made after the real meaning of the sentence becomes clear. In other words, syntax (structure) controls things and then, if necessary, semantics (meaning) jumps in to rearrange the parsing. We will now describe an approach to parsing that was proposed to account for evidence indicating that semantics doesn't just "jump in" to rearrange confusing parsing. This approach proposes that all information, both syntactic and semantic, is taken into account simultaneously as we read or listen to a sentence, so any corrections that need to occur take place as the sentence is unfolding (Altmann, 1998; Altmann & Steedman, 1988; MacDonald et al., 1994). This idea is called the **interactionist approach to parsing.**

THE INTERACTIONIST APPROACH TO PARSING

The crucial question in comparing the syntax-first approach and the interactionist approach is not *whether* semantics is involved, but *when* semantics comes into play. Is semantics activated only after syntax has determined the initial parsing (syntax-first approach), or does semantics come into play as a sentence is being read (interactionist approach)? One way to demonstrate an early role for semantics is to show how parsing can be influenced by the meaning of words in a sentence.

Sentence Understanding Influenced by the Meanings of Words We will look at some sentences that have the same structure but that, depending on the meanings of the words, can either be ambiguous or not ambiguous. Consider, for example, the following sentence:

The spy saw the man with the binoculars.

This sentence has two meanings, which represent different relationships between the words in the sentence. The relation between the phrases is indicated by the arrows.

Grouping 1: [The spy saw the man] [with the binoculars]

Meaning: The spy with the binoculars is looking at a man (● Figure 11.6a).

Grouping 2: [The spy saw] [the man with the binoculars]

Meaning: The spy is looking at a man who has a pair of binoculars (Figure 11.6b).

But if we change just one word, as in the following sentence, only one meaning becomes reasonable.

The bird saw the man with the binoculars.

Because organizing the sentence as in Grouping 1, above, would require birds to look through binoculars, this interpretation isn't even considered, and the grouping corresponds to Grouping 2, above. The important point here is that the structure of the bird sentence is the same as that of the spy sentence, but our knowledge of the properties of spies and of birds influences the way we interpret the relationships between the words in the sentence. This supports the interactionist approach because it demonstrates that semantics can be important in determining parsing right at the beginning of the sentence.

Sentence Understanding Influenced by the Environmental Setting Our interpretation of a sentence is influenced not only by the meaning of the words in the sentence, but also by the meaning of a scene we may be observing. To investigate how observing particular objects in a scene can influence how we interpret a sentence, Michael Tanenhaus and coworkers (1995) presented participants with objects on a table, as in ● Figure 11.7a. Participants looked at this display, which shows an apple on a towel, another towel, a pencil, and a box. This display, called the *one-apple condition*, is visible to the participant as he or she listens to the following instructions:

Put the apple on the towel in the box.

The beginning of this sentence (*Put the apple on the towel*) sounds as if it indicates that the apple should be moved to the other towel. But after hearing the last

● **FIGURE 11.6** Two possible interpretations of "The spy saw the man with the binoculars."

part of the sentence (*in the box*), the correct meaning emerges, which is that the apple should be placed in the box. To infer what was happening in the participants' mind, Tanenhaus measured their eye movements as they were listening to the instructions, using a portable eye tracker like the one in Figure 4.26 (page 101). Figure 11.7b shows the result. Upon hearing "Put the apple on the towel," the person looks at the apple (eye movement 1) and then at the other towel (eye movement 2), indicating that the person's initial interpretation is that the apple should be moved to the other towel. However,

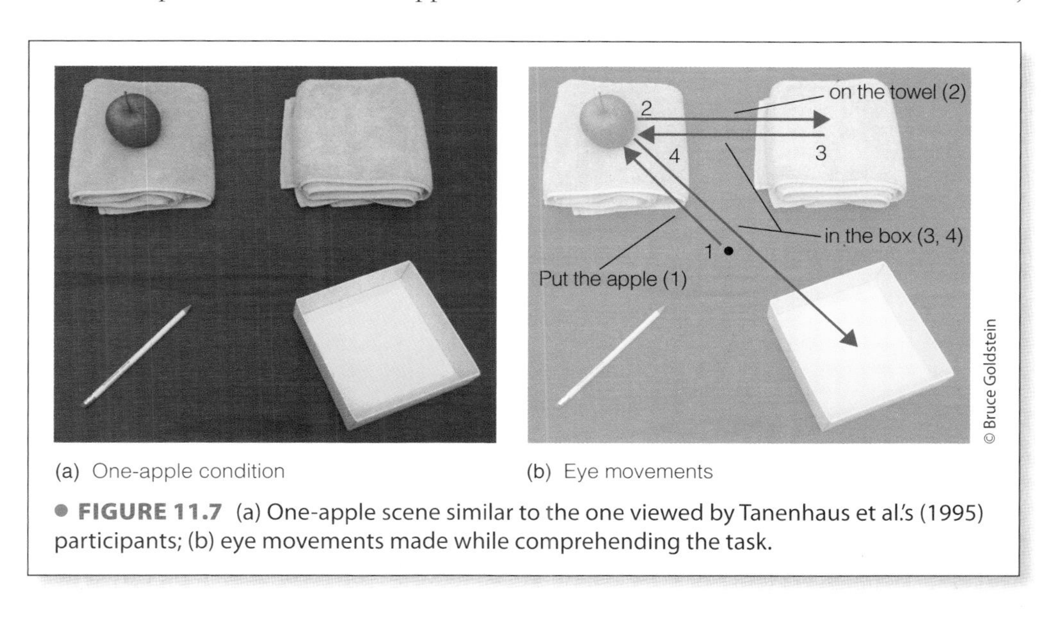

(a) One-apple condition (b) Eye movements

● **FIGURE 11.7** (a) One-apple scene similar to the one viewed by Tanenhaus et al.'s (1995) participants; (b) eye movements made while comprehending the task.

(a) Two-apple condition

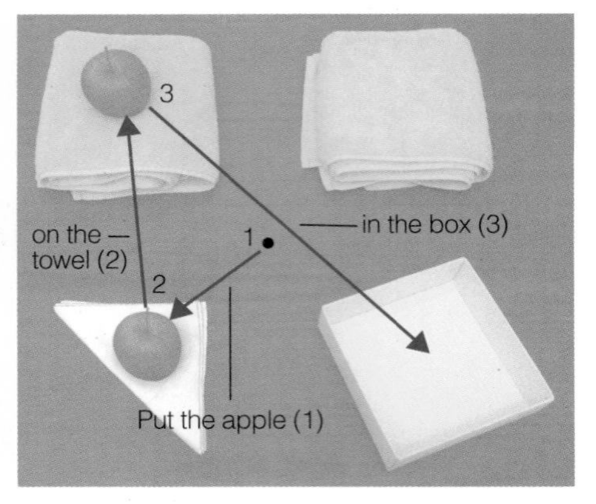

(b) Eye movements

● **FIGURE 11.8** (a) Two-apple scene similar to the one for the Tanenhaus et al. (1995) study; (b) eye movements while comprehending the task.

upon hearing "in the box," the person quickly makes a correction and looks back at the apple (eye movement 3) and then at the box (eye movement 4), indicating the new interpretation that the apple should be placed in the box.

Tanenhaus also measured participants' eye movements as they listened to these instructions while looking at the objects in ● Figure 11.8a, which is the same as the other scene, except the pencil has been replaced by an apple on a napkin. This is called the *two-apple condition.* When eye movements were measured while observing this scene (Figure 11.8b), many participants looked first at the apple on the napkin in response to "Put the apple" (eye movement 1), and then moved to the apple that is on the towel in response to "on the towel" (eye movement 2). Then, upon hearing "in the box," the eyes moved to the box (eye movement 3). Notice the difference in this situation, compared to when there was just one apple. In this case, *on the towel* is interpreted as indicating not that the apple should be placed on the other towel, but that the apple that is on the towel should be picked up and moved.

This result provides a contrast between the syntax-first approach and the interactionist approach. The syntax-first approach would predict that, based on the structure of the sentence, the initial interpretation should be that the apple is to be placed on the towel. This does occur in the one-apple condition, but the syntax-first approach also predicts that it should occur in the two-apple condition, because meaning is still determined by the structure of the sentence (which is the same in the two conditions). The fact that a different result occurs in the two-apple condition means that the listener is taking *both* the syntactic information in the sentence *and* information provided by the scene into account (also see Altmann & Kamide, 1999, and Chambers et al., 2004).

Although the controversy regarding whether the syntax-first approach or the interactionist approach is correct is still not resolved (Bever et al., 1998; Rayner & Clifton, 2002), evidence such as the results of the Tanenhaus experiment indicate that information in addition to the structure of the sentence helps determine what a sentence means. This is important, because in real life we rarely encounter sentences in isolation. Rather, we encounter sentences while we are in specific environments, or as we are listening to a conversation or reading a story.

That sentences occur within a context is particularly important for reading, because sentences are typically part of a larger text or story. Thus, when we read a particular sentence, we already know a great deal of information about what is happening from what we have read before. This brings us to the next level of the study of language—the study of how we understand text and stories (commonly called *discourse processing* or *text processing*). As we will see, most research in text processing is concerned with how readers' understanding of a story is determined by information provided by many sentences taken together.

Understanding Text and Stories

Just as sentences are more than the sum of the meanings of individual words, stories are more than the sum of the meanings of individual sentences. In a well-written story, sentences in one part of the story are related to sentences in other parts of the story. Thus, the reader's task is to use these relationships between sentences to create a coherent, understandable story.

An important part of the process of creating a coherent story is making inferences—determining what the text means by using our knowledge to go beyond the information provided by the text. We have seen that inference is an important part of many types of cognition. For example, in Chapter 3 we described how we take into account what we know about the environment to perceive what is in a scene. We also saw, in Chapter 8, how we use inference (often without realizing it) to retrieve memories of what has happened in the past. In fact, a number of the memory experiments we described involved remembering short passages, such as Bransford and Johnson's (1973) experiment in which one of the stories was about John trying to fix a birdhouse (see page 218).

• **FIGURE 11.9** *Goodbye, Sheep* by Greg Stones. Determining what is happening here depends on past knowledge about spaceships, sheep, and the relation between perceived size and distance, among other things.

MAKING INFERENCES

One of the passages Bransford and Johnson's participants read was

> John was trying to fix the birdhouse. He was pounding the nail when his father came out to watch him and help him do the work.

We saw that after reading that passage, participants were likely to indicate that they had previously seen the following passage: "John was using a hammer to fix the birdhouse when his father came out to watch him and help him do the work." They thought they had seen this passage, even though they had never read that John was using a hammer, because they *inferred* that John was using a hammer from the information that he was *pounding* the nail (Bransford & Johnson, 1973). People use a similar creative process to make a number of different types of inferences as they are reading a text. The following demonstration illustrates how inference operates not only when reading text but also when interpreting a story being told by a picture.

DEMONSTRATION Making Up a Story

Assume that the picture in • Figure 11.9 is an illustration in a book; your assignment is to describe what is happening, in story form. "Once upon a time" would be a good way to begin.

What knowledge did you use to create your story? Perhaps "flying saucers" and "attractor beams" were involved, and you might have surmised that before the sheep became airborne it was peacefully grazing with its friends on the ground. You might also have assumed, since the airborne sheep appears smaller than the ones on the ground, that it is farther away, which would mean that the flying saucer is moving toward the mountains. Because this information is not specifically indicated in the picture, a creative process involving prior knowledge and inference is needed to create meaning from this picture. We will now consider some of the specific ways inference is involved in creating meaning from written text.

One role of inference is to create connections between parts of a story. This process is typically illustrated with excerpts from narrative texts. *Narrative* refers to texts in which there is a story that progresses from one event to another, although stories can also include flashbacks of events that happened earlier. An important property of any narrative is **coherence**—the representation of the text in a person's mind so that information in one part of the text is related to information in another part of the text. Coherence can be created by a number of different types of inference.

Anaphoric Inference Inferences that connect an object or person in one sentence to an object or person in another sentence are called **anaphoric inferences**. For example, consider the following:

> Riffifi, the famous poodle, won the dog show. She has now won the last three shows she has entered.

Anaphoric inference occurs when we infer that *She* at the beginning of the second sentence and the other *she* near the end both refer to Riffifi. In the previous "John and the birdhouse" example, knowing that *He* in the second sentence refers to John is another example of anaphoric inference.

We usually have little trouble making anaphoric inferences because of the way information is presented in sentences and our ability to make use of knowledge we bring to the situation. But the following quote from a *New York Times* interview with former heavyweight champion George Foreman (also known for lending his name to a popular line of grills) puts our ability to create anaphoric inference to the test.

> What we really love to do on our vacation time is go down to our ranch in Marshall, Texas. We have close to 500 acres. There are lots of ponds and I take the kids out and we fish. And then, of course, we grill them. (Stevens, 2002)

Based just on the structure of the sentence, we might conclude that the kids were grilled, but we know the chances are pretty good that the fish were grilled, not George Foreman's children! Readers are capable of creating anaphoric inferences even under adverse conditions because they add information from their knowledge of the world to the information provided in the text.

Instrument Inference Inferences about tools or methods are **instrument inferences**. For example, when we read the sentence "William Shakespeare wrote *Hamlet* while he was sitting at his desk," we infer from what we know about the time Shakespeare lived that he was probably using a quill pen (not a laptop computer!) and that his desk was made of wood. Similarly, inferring from the passage about John and the birdhouse that he is using a hammer to pound the nails would be an instrument inference.

Causal Inference Inferences that the events described in one clause or sentence were caused by events that occurred in a previous sentence are **causal inferences** (Goldman et al., 1999; Graesser et al., 1994; van den Broek, 1994). For example, when we read the sentences

> Sharon took an aspirin. Her headache went away.

we infer that taking the aspirin caused the headache to go away (Singer et al., 1992). This is an example of a fairly obvious inference that most people in our culture would make based on their knowledge about headaches and aspirin.

Other causal inferences are not so obvious and may be more difficult to figure out. For example, what do you conclude from reading the following sentences?

> Sharon took a shower. Her headache went away.

You might conclude, from the fact that the headache sentence directly follows the shower sentence, that the shower had something to do with eliminating Sharon's headache. However, the causal connection between the shower and the headache is weaker than the connection between the aspirin and the headache in the first pair of sentences. Making the shower–headache connection requires more work from the reader. You might infer that the shower relaxed Sharon, or perhaps her habit of singing in the shower was therapeutic. Or you might decide there actually isn't much connection between the two sentences.

Inferences create connections that are essential for creating coherence in texts, and making these inferences can involve creativity by the reader. Thus, reading a text involves more than just understanding words or sentences. It is a dynamic process that involves transformation of the words, sentences, and sequences of sentences into a meaningful story. Sometimes this is easy, sometimes harder, depending on the skill and intention of both the reader and the writer (Goldman et al., 1999; Graesser et al., 1994; van den Broek, 1994).

We have been describing the process of text comprehension so far in terms of how people bring their knowledge to bear to infer connections between different parts of a story. Another approach to understanding how people understand stories is to consider the nature of the mental representation that people form as they read a story. This is called the *situation model* approach to text comprehension.

SITUATION MODELS

A situation model is a mental representation of what a text is about (Johnson-Laird, 1983). This approach proposes that the mental representation people form as they read a story does not consist of information about phrases, sentences, or paragraphs; instead, it is a representation of the situation in terms of the people, objects, locations, and events that are being described in the story (Barsalou, 2008, 2009; Graesser & Wiemer-Hastings, 1999; Zwaan, 1999).

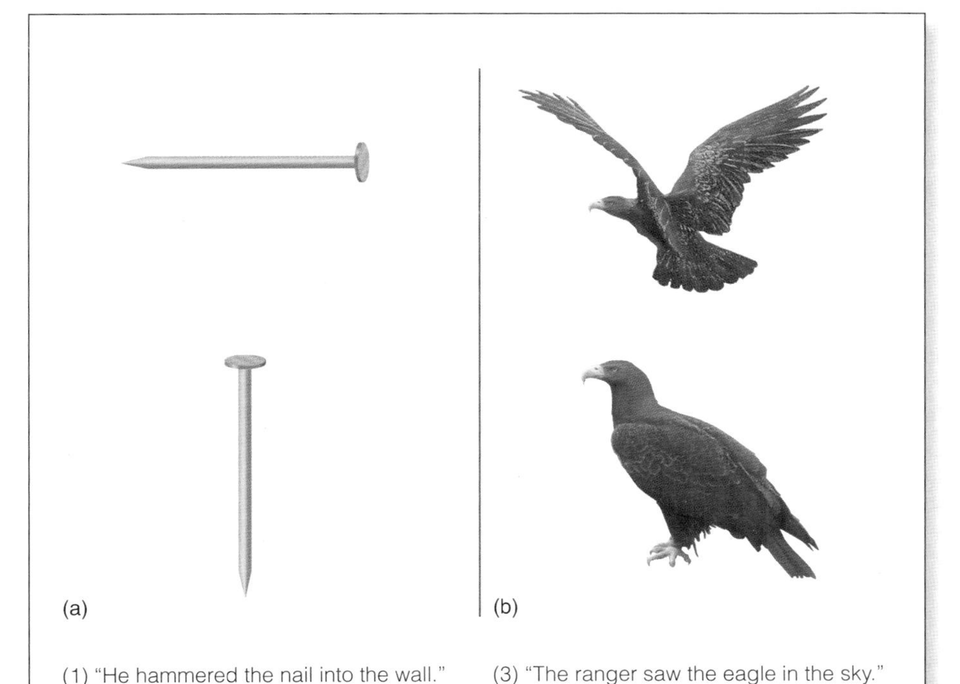

● **FIGURE 11.10** Stimuli similar to those used in (a) Stanfield and Zwaan's (2001) "orientation" experiment, and (b) Zwaan et al.'s (2002) "shape" experiment. Participants heard sentences and were then asked to indicate whether the picture was the object mentioned in the sentence.

Mental Representations as Simulations

What exactly is the "mental representation of what the text is about"? One way this question has been answered is to suggest that a person *simulates* the perceptual and motor (movement) characteristics of the objects and actions in a story. This idea has been tested by having participants read a sentence that describes a situation involving an object and then indicate as quickly as possible whether or not a picture shows the object mentioned in the sentence. For example, consider the following two sentences.

1. He hammered the nail into the wall.
2. He hammered the nail into the floor.

In ● Figure 11.10a, the horizontal nail matches the orientation that would be expected for sentence 1, and the vertical nail matches the orientation for sentence 2. Robert Stanfield and Rolf Zwaan (2001) presented these sentences, followed by either a matching picture or a nonmatching picture. Because the pictures both show nails and the task was to indicate whether

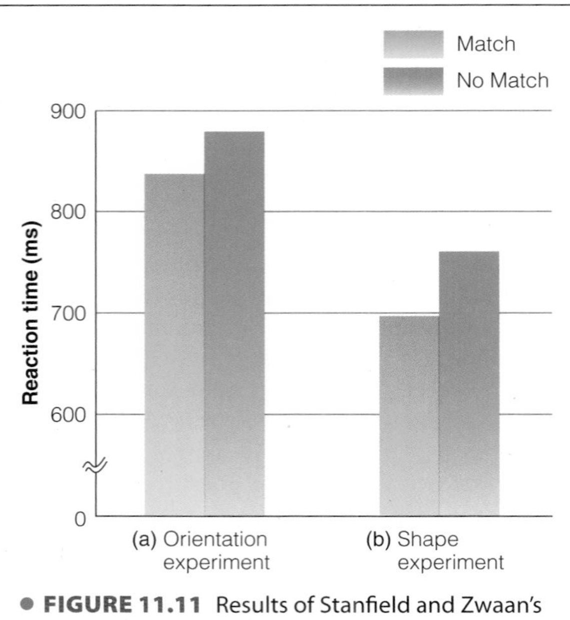

● **FIGURE 11.11** Results of Stanfield and Zwaan's (2001) and Zwaan et al.'s (2002) experiments. Participants responded "yes" more rapidly for the orientation (in a) and the shape (in b) that was more consistent with the sentence. (Source: Based on R. A. Stanfield & R. A. Zwaan, "The Effect of Implied Orientation Derived From Verbal Content on Picture Recognition," *Psychological Science, 12,* 153–156, 2001.)

the picture shows the object mentioned in the sentence, the correct answer was "yes" no matter which nail was presented. However, participants responded "yes" more rapidly when the picture's orientation matched the situation described in the picture (● Figure 11.11a).

The pictures for another experiment, involving object shape, are shown in Figure 11.10b. The sentences for these pictures are

1. The ranger saw the eagle in the sky.
2. The ranger saw the eagle in its nest.

In this experiment, by Zwaan and coworkers (2002), the picture of an eagle with wings outstretched elicited a faster response when it followed sentence 1 than when it followed sentence 2. Again, reaction times were faster when the picture matched the situation described in the sentence. This result, shown in Figure 11.11b, corresponds to the result for the orientation experiment, and both experiments support the idea that the participants created perceptions that matched the situation as they were reading the sentences.

The idea that readers create situation models has also been applied to stories. For example, William Horton and David Rapp (2003) tested this idea using short passages like the following:

1. Melanie ran downstairs and threw herself onto the couch.
2. An exciting horror movie was on television.
3. She opened a bag of chips and dug right in.
4. She watched a vampire stalk the helpless victim.
5. She had never seen this movie before.

Participants were then presented with one of the following endings.

Blocked story continuation (● Figure 11.12a):

6a. Melanie's mother appeared in front of the TV.
7a. She told Melanie not to forget about her homework.

or

Unblocked story continuation (Figure 11.12b):

6b. Melanie's mother appeared behind the TV.
7b. She told Melanie not to forget about her homework.

Participants read the story line by line from a computer screen. After sentence 7, a warning tone sounded, indicating that the target question was going to be presented. The target question for the story above was "Was the victim being stalked by a vampire?" The participant's task was to answer "yes" or "no" as quickly as possible by pressing the correct key on the computer keyboard.

The situation model prediction is that participants who read the blocked story continuation should react more slowly to the test question because the TV screen, which contained the answer, was blocked, so Melanie wouldn't be able to see the vampire stalking its victim. The result, shown in Figure 11.12c, confirms this prediction—responding was slower in the blocked condition. This supports the idea that readers represent story events in a manner similar to actual perception. That is, they experience a story as if they are experiencing the situation described in the text.

The experiments we have described so far have emphasized perception. But the situation model approach also includes the idea that a reader or listener simulates the motor characteristics of the objects in a story. According to this idea, a story that involves movement will result in simulation of this movement as the person is comprehending the story. For example, reading a story about a bicycle elicits not only the perception of what a bicycle looks like, but also properties associated with movement, such as how

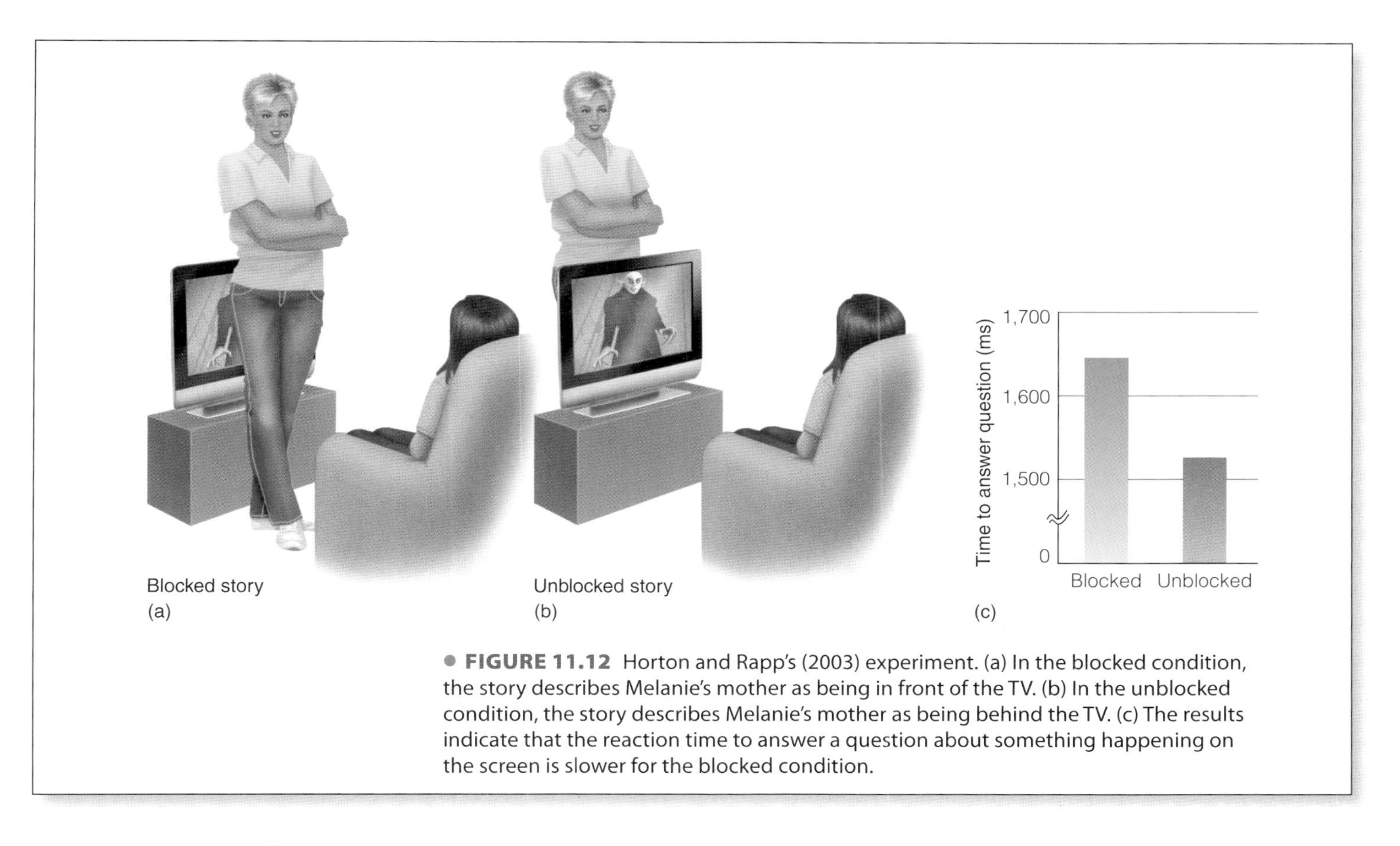

● **FIGURE 11.12** Horton and Rapp's (2003) experiment. (a) In the blocked condition, the story describes Melanie's mother as being in front of the TV. (b) In the unblocked condition, the story describes Melanie's mother as being behind the TV. (c) The results indicate that the reaction time to answer a question about something happening on the screen is slower for the blocked condition.

a bicycle is propelled (by peddling) and the physical exertion involved in riding the bicycle under different conditions (climbing hills, racing, coasting). This corresponds to the idea, introduced in Chapter 9, that knowledge about a category goes beyond simply identifying a typical object in that category; it also includes various properties of the object, such as how the object is used, what it does, and sometimes even emotional responses it elicits. This way of looking at the reader's response adds a richness to events in a story that extends beyond simply understanding what is going on (Barsalou, 2008; Fischer & Zwaan, 2008).

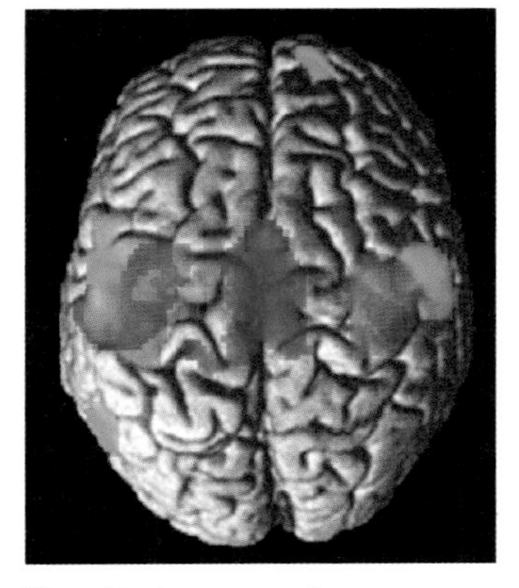

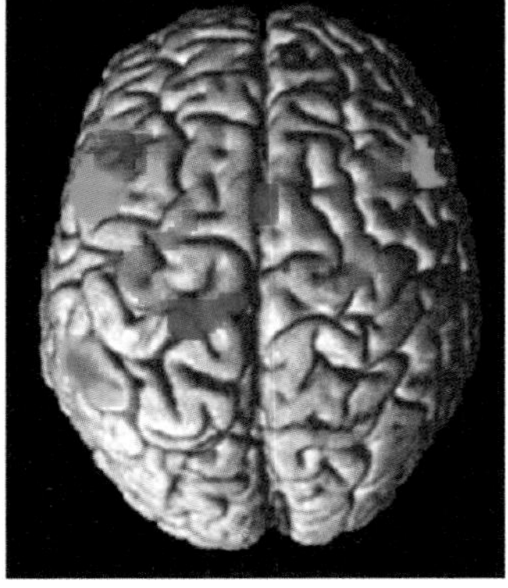

● **FIGURE 11.13** Hauk et al. (2004) results. Colored areas indicate the area of the brain activated by (a) foot, finger, and tongue movements; (b) leg, arm, and face words. (Source: O. Hauk, I. Johnsrude, & F. Pulvermuller, "Somatotopic Representation of Action Words in Human Motor and Premotor Cortex," *Neuron, 41,* 301–307, 2004. Reprinted with permission from Elsevier.)

The Physiology of Simulations How are these simulations reflected in activity in the brain? To answer this question, let's first consider an experiment by Olaf Hauk and coworkers (2004) in which participants' brain activity was measured using fMRI under two conditions: (1) as they moved their right or left foot, left or right index finger, or tongue; (2) as they read "action words" such as kick (foot action), pick (finger or hand action), or lick (tongue action).

The results show areas of the cortex activated by the actual movements (● Figure 11.13a) and by reading the action words (Figure 11.13b). The activation is more extensive for actual movements, but the activation caused by reading the words occurs in approximately the same areas of the brain. For example, leg words and leg movements elicit activity near the brain's center line, whereas arm words and finger movements elicit activity further from the center line. The conclusion from this study is that reading about an action causes activity in the brain that is similar to the activity that occurs when carrying out the action.

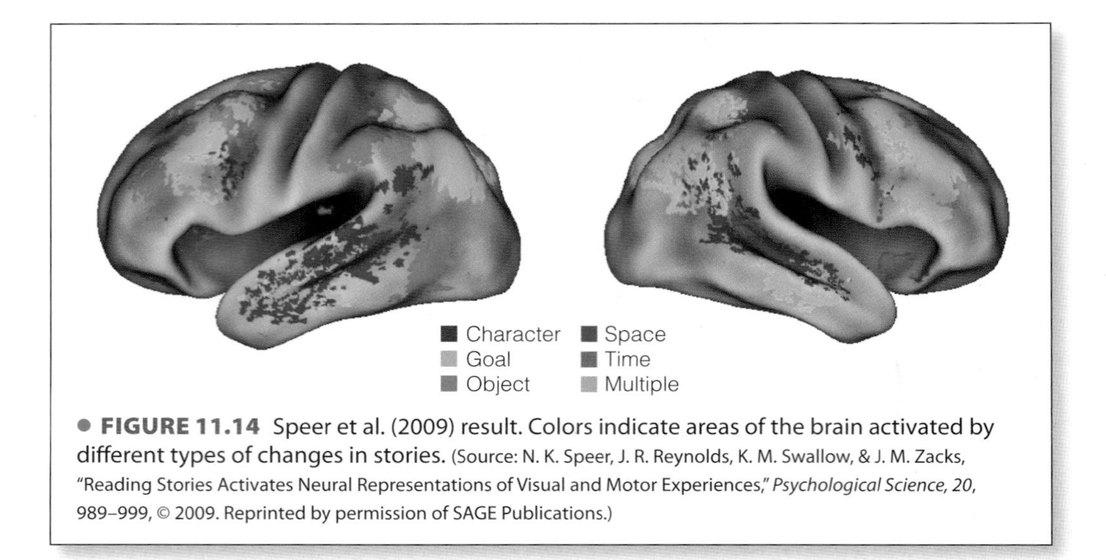

• **FIGURE 11.14** Speer et al. (2009) result. Colors indicate areas of the brain activated by different types of changes in stories. (Source: N. K. Speer, J. R. Reynolds, K. M. Swallow, & J. M. Zacks, "Reading Stories Activates Neural Representations of Visual and Motor Experiences," *Psychological Science, 20,* 989–999, © 2009. Reprinted by permission of SAGE Publications.)

This correspondence between brain activity caused by performing actions and by reading action words has also been studied for reading stories. Nicole Speer and coworkers (2009) had participants read a selection from the book *One Boy's Day* (Barker & Wright, 1951), which describes the everyday activities of Raymond, a 7-year-old boy. The participants' brain activity was measured as they read the story.

Speer analyzed the story to determine where changes in various aspects of the story occurred. For example, a *spatial change* occurred when Raymond moved from one location to another. An *object change* occurred when Raymond interacted with a new object. Thus, the sentence "He picked up his English workbook and returned to his desk" starts with an object change and ends with a spatial change. Speer also identified *character changes* (when a different character is mentioned), *goal changes* (when a character starts an action to achieve a new goal), and *time* (words like *immediately* or *slowly*).

• Figure 11.14 shows the results of this experiment. Colors indicate the area of the brain activated by each type of change. Two things are clear: (1) reading a story activates many areas in the cortex; and (2) specific actions cause activity in different areas, although there is also overlap. This correlation between events in the story and activity in the brain supports the central proposal of the situation model approach—that reading creates representations of the situations described in a story.

The overall conclusion from research on how people comprehend stories is that understanding a text or story is a creative and dynamic process. Understanding stories involves understanding sentences by determining how words are organized into phrases; then determining the relationships between sentences, often using inference to link sentences in one part of a story to sentences in another part; and finally, creating mental representations or simulations that involve both perceptual and motor properties of objects and events in the story. As we will now see, a creative and dynamic process also occurs when two or more people are having a conversation.

Producing Language: Conversations

Although language can be produced by a single person talking alone, as when a person recites a monologue or gives a speech, the most common form of language production is conversation—two or more people talking with one another. Conversation, or dialogue, provides another example of a cognitive skill that seems easy but contains underlying complexities.

In a conversation, other people are involved, so each person needs to take into account what other people are saying (Pickering & Garrod, 2004). This is an impressive accomplishment because we often don't know what other people are going to say.

Nonetheless, we are usually able to respond to their statements almost immediately. One way that people deal with this difficulty is by coordinating their conversations on both semantic and syntactic levels.

SEMANTIC COORDINATION

When people are talking about a topic, each person brings his or her own knowledge to the conversation. Such conversations go more smoothly when the participants bring *shared* knowledge. Thus, when people are talking about current events, it helps if everyone has been keeping up with the news; it is more difficult when one of the people has just returned from 6 months of meditation in an isolated monastery.

But even when everyone brings similar knowledge to a conversation, it helps when speakers take steps to guide their listeners through the conversation. One way of achieving this is by following the *given–new contract*. The given–new contract states that the speaker should construct sentences so that they include two kinds of information: (1) *given information*—information that the listener already knows; and (2) *new information*—information that the listener is hearing for the first time (Haviland & Clark, 1974). For example, consider the following two sentences.

> Sentence 1. Ed was given an alligator for his birthday.
> *Given information (from previous conversation)*: Ed had a birthday.
> *New information*: He got an alligator.
>
> Sentence 2. The alligator was his favorite present.
> *Given information (from sentence 1)*: Ed got an alligator.
> *New information*: It was his favorite present.

Notice how the new information in the first sentence becomes the given information in the second sentence.

Susan Haviland and Herbert Clark (1974) demonstrated the consequences of not following the given–new contract by presenting pairs of sentences and asking participants to press a button when they thought they understood the second sentence in each pair. They found that it took longer for participants to comprehend the second sentence in pairs like this one:

> We checked the picnic supplies.
> The beer was warm.

than it took to comprehend the second sentence in pairs like this one:

> We got some beer out of the trunk.
> The beer was warm.

The reason comprehending the second sentence in the first pair takes longer is that the given information (that there were picnic supplies) does not mention beer. Thus, the reader or listener needs to make an inference that beer was among the picnic supplies. This inference is not required in the second pair because the first sentence includes the information that there is beer in the trunk.

SYNTACTIC COORDINATION

When two people exchange statements in a conversation, it is common for them to use similar grammatical constructions. Kathryn Bock (1990) provides the following example, taken from a recorded conversation between a bank robber and his lookout, which was intercepted by a ham radio operator as the robber was removing the equivalent of $1 million from a bank vault in England.

> Robber: "... *you've got to hear* and witness it *to realize how bad it is.*"
> Lookout: "You *have got to experience exactly* the same position as me, mate, *to understand how I feel.*" (from Schenkein, 1980, p. 22)

Bock has added italics to the statements to illustrate how the lookout has copied the form of the robber's statement. This copying of form reflects a phenomenon called

syntactic priming—hearing a statement with a particular syntactic construction increases the chances that a sentence will be produced with the same construction. Syntactic priming is important because it can lead people to coordinate the grammatical form of their statements during a conversation. Holly Branigan and coworkers (2000) illustrated syntactic priming by using the following procedure to set up a give-and-take between two people.

METHOD Syntactic Priming

In a syntactic priming experiment, two people engage in a conversation, and the experimenter determines whether production of a specific grammatical construction by one person increases the chances that the same construction will be used by the other person.

Participants in Branigan's experiment were told that the experiment was about how people communicate when they can't see each other. They thought they were working with another participant who was on the other side of a screen (the person on the left in ● Figure 11.15a).

● **FIGURE 11.15** The Branigan et al. (2000) experiment. (a) The participant, on the right, picks, from the cards laid out on the table, a card with a picture that matches the statement read by the confederate. (b) The participant then picks a card from the pile of response cards on the left and describes the picture on the response card to the confederate. (Source: Based on H. P. Branigan, M. J. Pickering, & A. A. Cleland, "Syntactic Co-ordination in Dialogue," *Cognition, 75,* B13–B25, 2000.)

In reality, the person on the other side of the screen was a confederate who was working with the experimenter.

The confederate began the experiment by making a *priming statement*, as shown on the left of Figure 11.15a. This statement was in one of the following two forms:

The girl gave the book to the boy.
The girl gave the boy the book.

The participant had two tasks: (1) find the *matching card*, from the ones laid out on the table, that corresponded to the confederate's statement, as shown on the right in Figure 11.15a; and (2) pick a *response card* from the deck on the left and describe it to the confederate, as shown in Figure 11.15b. We can conclude that syntactic priming has occurred if the form of the participant's description of this new picture matches the form of the confederate's description of the previous picture.

Branigan found that on 78 percent of the trials, the form of the participant's description matched the form of the confederate's priming statement. Thus, if the participant heard the confederate say "The girl gave the boy the book," this increased the chances that the participant would describe a response card like the one shown in Figure 11.15b as "The father brought his daughter a present" (rather than "The father brought a present for his daughter" or some other construction). This supports the idea that speakers are sensitive to the linguistic behavior of other speakers and adjust their behaviors to match. This coordination of syntactic form between speakers reduces the computational load involved in creating a conversation because it is easier to copy the form of someone else's sentence than it is to create your own form from scratch.

Let's summarize what we have said about conversations: Conversations are dynamic and rapid, but a number of processes make them easier. On the semantic side, people take other people's knowledge into account (if they don't, confusion can result). On the syntactic side, people coordinate or align the syntactic form of their statements. This makes speaking easier and frees up resources to deal with the task of alternating between understanding and producing messages that is the hallmark of successful conversations.

Something to Consider

Culture, Language, and Cognition

How do you say *blue* in Russian? The answer to that question depends on the shade of blue. Light blues, like the ones on the left of ● Figure 11.16, are called *goloboy*, and darker blues, like the ones on the right, are called *siniy*. Thus, the Russian language defines *goloboy* and *siniy* as different colors, and Russian children learn these labels for the two blues as they are learning the names of the other colors. This contrasts with English, in which all of the colors in Figure 11.16 are called *blue*.

Do these differences in the way colors are labeled in Russian and English lead to differences in the way these colors are perceived? According to the Sapir-Whorf hypothesis, which was proposed by anthropologist Edward Sapir and linguist Benjamin Whorf, the nature of a culture's language can affect the way people think (Whorf, 1956). Although there was little evidence to support this when Whorf made his proposal, recent experiments have provided evidence that favors the idea that language can influence cognition (Davidoff, 2001; Gentner & Goldin-Meadow, 2003; Roberson et al., 2000).

One of these experiments, by Jonathan Winawer and coworkers (2007), compared the way Russian-speaking and English-speaking participants discriminated between different shades of blue. ● Figure 11.17 shows the stimuli. Participants saw three blue

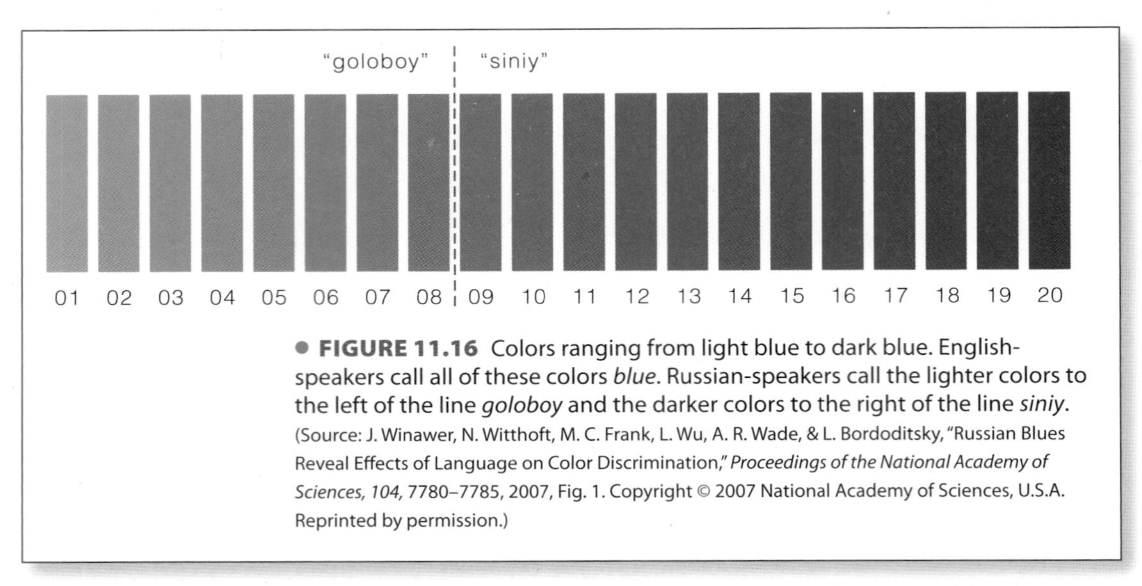

● **FIGURE 11.16** Colors ranging from light blue to dark blue. English-speakers call all of these colors *blue*. Russian-speakers call the lighter colors to the left of the line *goloboy* and the darker colors to the right of the line *siniy*. (Source: J. Winawer, N. Witthoft, M. C. Frank, L. Wu, A. R. Wade, & L. Bordoditsky, "Russian Blues Reveal Effects of Language on Color Discrimination," *Proceedings of the National Academy of Sciences, 104,* 7780–7785, 2007, Fig. 1. Copyright © 2007 National Academy of Sciences, U.S.A. Reprinted by permission.)

squares and were instructed to pick, as quickly and accurately as possible, the square on the bottom that matched the color of the square on the top. On some trials, the two squares on the bottom were from the same Russian category. This is shown in Figure 11.17a, in which both bottom squares would both be called *siniy*. On other trials, the two squares on the bottom were from different Russian categories. This is shown in Figure 11.17b, in which the left square is *siniy* and the right one is *goloboy.*

● Figure 11.18 shows that the Russian-speaking participants responded more quickly when the two bottom squares were from different categories (*goloboy/siniy*) than when the squares were from the same category. The English-speaking participants did not respond more quickly when the colors were in different Russian categories.

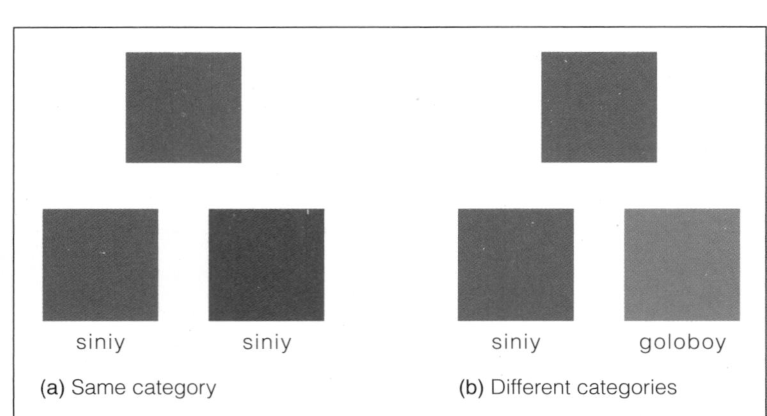

● **FIGURE 11.17** Sample stimuli from the Winawer et al. (2007) experiment. (a) The two bottom squares are from the same Russian category. (b) The two bottom squares are from different Russian categories. The color names shown here were not visible in the experiment. The participant's task was to indicate which of the two squares on the bottom matches the one on the top. Russian participants made this judgment more rapidly if the two bottom squares were in different categories, as in (b). (Source: J. Winawer, N. Witthoft, M. C. Frank, L. Wu, A. R. Wade, & L. Bordoditsky, "Russian Blues Reveal Effects of Language on Color Discrimination," *Proceedings of the National Academy of Sciences, 104,* 7780–7785, 2007, Fig. 1. Copyright © 2007 National Academy of Sciences, U.S.A. Reprinted by permission.)

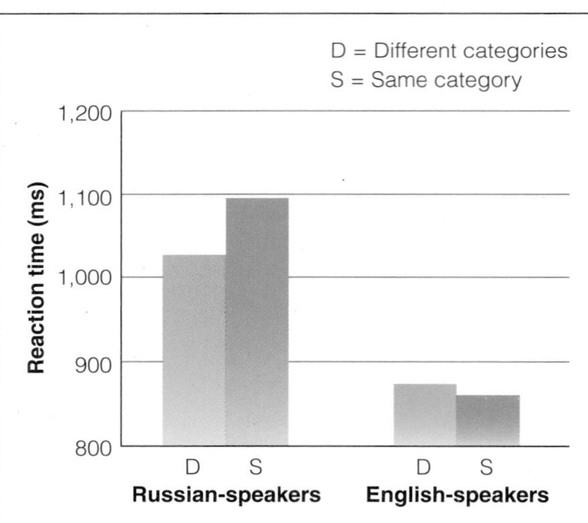

● **FIGURE 11.18** Results of the Winawer et al. (2007) experiment. The Russian-speaking participants responded faster when the bottom stimuli were from different categories than when they were from the same category (left pair of bars). This difference did not occur for English-speaking participants (right pair of bars). (Source: J. Winawer, N. Witthoft, M. C. Frank, L. Wu, A. R. Wade, & L. Bordoditsky, "Russian Blues Reveal Effects of Language on Color Discrimination," *Proceedings of the National Academy of Sciences, 104,* 7780–7785, 2007, Fig. 2. Copyright © 2007 National Academy of Sciences, U.S.A. Reprinted by permission)

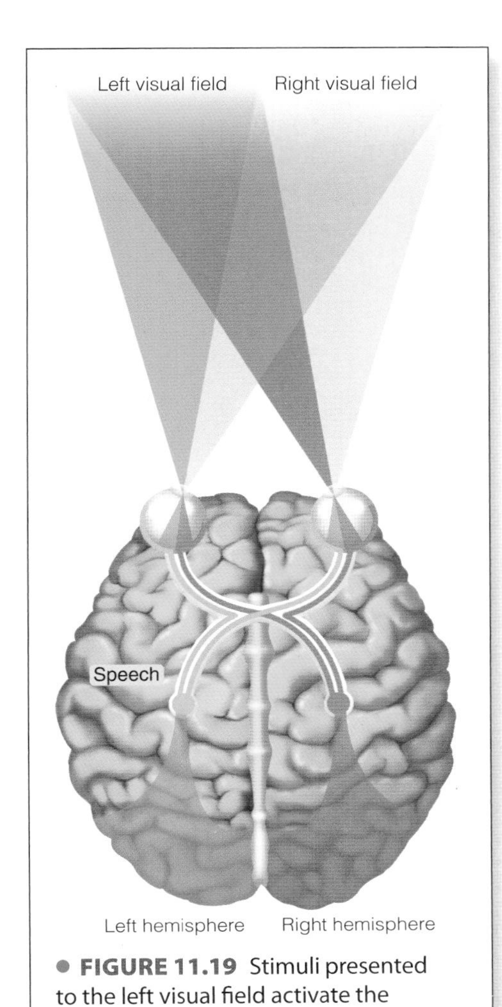

● **FIGURE 11.19** Stimuli presented to the left visual field activate the right hemisphere of the brain. Stimuli presented to the right visual field activate the left hemisphere.

According to Winawer, the Russians' faster response when stimuli were from different categories occurred because their language distinguishes between *goloby* and *siniy*. One way of looking at this is that learning the different labels makes it more likely that the colors will be perceived as different, and this makes it easier to quickly determine which square matches the one on the top. This effect does not occur for English-speakers because all of the colors are simply *blue*. These results, therefore, support the Sapir-Whorf idea that language can affect cognition.

Another approach to studying the relation between color perception and language was pursued by Aubrey Gilbert and coworkers (2006), who did an experiment to determine if there is a difference between how colors are processed in the left and right hemispheres of the brain. The basic idea behind this approach is that language is processed in the left hemisphere. Thus, if language does affect color perception, it would be more likely to do so when colors are viewed in the right visual field (which projects to the left hemisphere) than in the left visual field (● Figure 11.19).

To test this idea, Gilbert and coworkers presented participants with a display like the one in ● Figure 11.20a, in which all the squares in the wheel were the same (green in this example) except for a target square (blue). On some trials the target was from the same category as the other squares (for example, all squares were green, but the target was a slightly different green). On other trials, the target was from a different category, as in the example in Figure 11.20a. The participants' task was to push a button indicating whether the target was on the left or right side of the wheel.

The results, shown in Figure 11.20b, indicate that when the display was viewed in the left (nonlanguage) visual field (left pair of bars), the reaction time to identify the target was the same whether the target was from the same category or from a different category. Because objects in the left visual field activate the right hemisphere, language would not be involved. However, when the display was in the right visual field, reaction times were faster when the target was from a different category (right pair of bars). If the category labels *blue* and *green* are determined by language, this is what we would expect. Thus, when the nonlanguage (right) hemisphere is activated, no category effect occurs, but when the language (left) hemisphere is activated, a category effect does occur. So, does language affect perception? From the results of this experiment, the answer would seem to be that it depends on which part of the brain is involved (Reiger & Kay, 2009).

Other experiments have demonstrated differences in how Westerners and East Asians think about objects (Iwao & Gentner, 1997), numbers (Lucy & Gaskins, 1997), and space (Levinson, 1996) and how processing numbers when doing

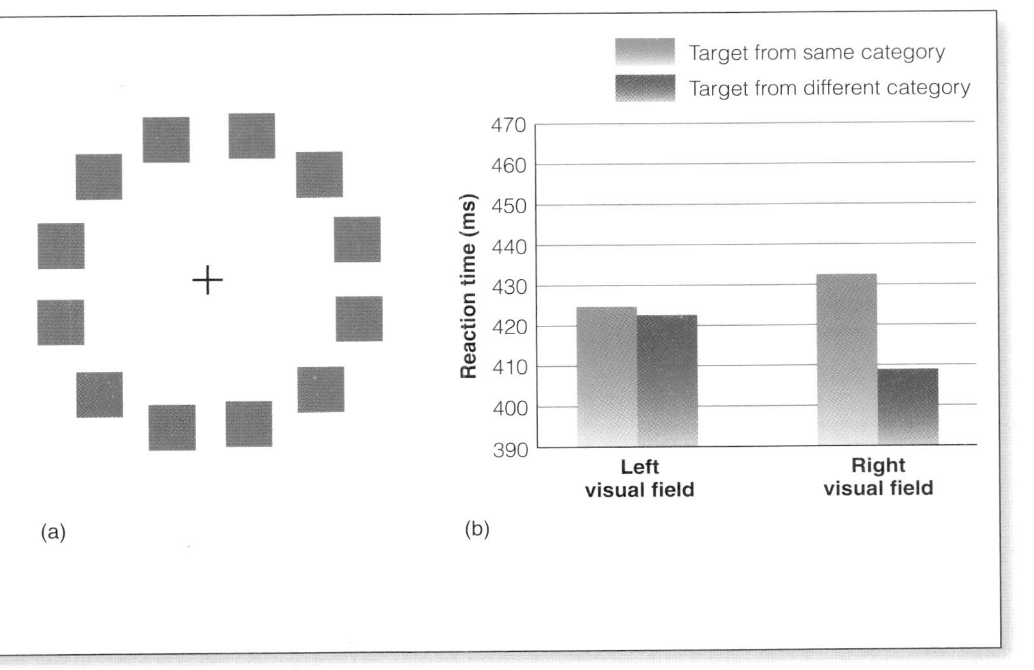

● **FIGURE 11.20** (a) Color wheel used in Gilbert et al.'s (2006) experiment. The participants' task was to indicate, as quickly as possible, which side contained the "odd" color. (b) Result of the experiment. The left pair of bars shows that when the color wheel was in the left visual field, reaction times were the same whether the odd color was in the same or different category as the other colors. The right pair of bars shows that when the wheel was presented in the right visual Field, reaction times were faster when the odd color was from a different category (for example, blue vs. green). (Source: A. L. Gilbert, T. Regier, P. Kay, & R. B. Ivry, "Whorf Hypothesis Is Supported in the Right Visual Field but Not the Left," *Proceedings of the National Academy of Sciences, 103,* 489–494, 2006, Fig. 1. Copyright © 2006 National Academy of Sciences, U.S.A. Reprinted by permission.)

arithmetic problems is related to language differences between Chinese-speaking and English-speaking participants (Tang et al., 2006). See "If You Want to Know More: Language, Culture, and the Representation of Space" and "Culture and Categories," page 322 for more references on the connection between language and thinking.

TEST YOURSELF 11.2

1. Why do we say that there is more to understanding a sentence than simply adding up the meanings of the words that make up the sentence?
2. Describe the syntax-first explanation and the interactionist explanation of parsing. What are the roles of syntax and semantics in each explanation? What evidence supports the interactionist approach?
3. Why do we say that understanding a story involves more than adding up the meanings of the sentences that make up the story?
4. What is coherence? Inference? What are the different types of inference, and what is their relation to coherence?
5. What are the assumptions behind the situation model? Describe what the following evidence tells us about this approach to understanding stories: (1) reaction times for pictures that match or don't match the orientations or shapes of objects in a story; (2) reaction times to answer questions about "blocked" and "unblocked" stories; (3) brain activation for action words compared to actual action; (4) brain activation for changes in different types of events in a story.
6. Describe how semantic coordination and syntactic coordination facilitate conversations. Be sure you understand syntactic priming and what it demonstrates about language production.
7. What is the Sapir-Whorf hypothesis? Describe the experiment on color perception that supports this hypothesis. Also describe the evidence that indicates that the hypothesis may hold for only one side of the visual field.

CHAPTER SUMMARY

1. Language is a system of communication that uses sounds or symbols to express feelings, thoughts, ideas, and experiences. Human language can be distinguished from animal communication by its creativity, hierarchical structure, governing rules, and universality.
2. Modern research in the psychology of language blossomed in the 1950s and 1960s, with the advent of the cognitive revolution. One of the central events in the cognitive revolution was Chomsky's critique of Skinner's behaviorist analysis of language.
3. All the words a person knows are his or her lexicon. Phonemes and morphemes are two basic units of words.
4. The effect of meaning on the perception of phonemes is illustrated by the phonemic restoration effect. Meaning, as well as a person's experience with other aspects of language, is important for achieving speech segmentation.
5. The ability to understand words is influenced by word frequency and the context provided by the sentence.
6. Lexical ambiguity refers to the fact that a word can have more than one meaning and that the word's meaning in a sentence may not be clear. Lexical priming experiments show that all meanings of a word are activated immediately after the word is presented but then context quickly determines the appropriate meaning.
7. The meaning of a sentence is determined by both semantics (the meanings of words) and syntax (the rules for using words in sentences).
8. Parsing is the process by which words in a sentence are grouped into phrases. Grouping into phrases is a major determinant of the meaning of a sentence. This process has been studied by using ambiguous sentences.
9. Two mechanisms proposed to explain parsing are (1) the syntax-first approach and (2) the interactionist approach. The syntax-first approach emphasizes the role of syntactic principles, such as late closure, in

determining how a sentence is parsed. The interactionist approach proposes that both semantics and syntax operate simultaneously to determine parsing. This approach is supported by the way words with different meanings affect the interpretation of a sentence and by eye movement studies.

10. Coherence enables us to understand stories. Coherence is largely determined by inference. Three major types of inference are anaphoric, instrument, and causal.
11. The situation model approach to text comprehension proposes that people represent the situation in a story in terms of the people, objects, locations, and events described in the story. There is both behavioral and physiological evidence that supports this idea.
12. Conversations, which involve give-and-take between two or more people, are made easier by two mechanisms of cooperation between participants in a conversation: semantic coordination and syntactic coordination. Syntactic priming experiments provide evidence for syntactic coordination.
13. There is evidence that a culture's language can influence the way people perceive and think. Experiments comparing color discrimination in Russian-speaking and English-speaking participants have revealed differences in color perception related to language. Other experiments show that these differences may occur mainly when colors are presented to the right hemisphere so that the left (language) hemisphere is activated.

Think ABOUT IT

1. How do the ideas of coherence and connection apply to some of the movies you have seen lately? Have you found that some movies are easy to understand whereas others are more difficult? In the movies that are easy to understand, does one thing appear to follow from another, whereas in the more difficult ones, some things seem to be left out? What is the difference in the "mental work" needed to determine what is going on in these two kinds of movies? (You can also apply this kind of analysis to books you have read.)
2. Next time you are able to eavesdrop on a conversation, notice how the give-and-take among participants follows (or does not follow) the given–new contract. Also, notice how people change topics and how that affects the flow of the conversation. Finally, see if you can find any evidence of syntactic priming. One way to "eavesdrop" is to be part of a conversation that includes at least two other people. But don't forget to say something every so often!
3. One of the interesting things about languages is the use of "figures of speech," which people who know the language understand but which nonnative speakers often find baffling. One example is the sentence "He brought everything but the kitchen sink." Can you think of other examples? If you speak a language other than English, can you identify figures of speech in that language that might be baffling to English-speakers?
4. Newspaper headlines are often good sources of ambiguous phrases. For example, consider the following, which were actual headlines: "Milk drinkers are turning to powder," "Iraqi head seeks arms," "Farm bill dies in house," and "Squad helps dog bite victim." See if you can find examples of ambiguous headlines in the newspaper, and try to figure out what it is that makes the headlines ambiguous.
5. People often say things in an indirect way, but listeners can often still understand what they mean. See if you can detect these indirect statements in normal conversation. (Examples: "Do you want to turn left here?" to mean "I think you should turn left here"; "Is it cold in here?" to mean "Please close the window.")

If You WANT TO KNOW MORE

1. **The beginnings of psycholinguistics.** An influential paper called "Some Preliminaries to Psycholinguistics" was published in 1965. This paper makes the case that language is far too complex to be explained by rewards and punishments. This paper is still well worth reading, both for the points it makes about language and for the effective way these points are made.

   Miller, G. A. (1965). Some preliminaries to psycholinguistics. *American Psychologist, 20*, 15–20.

2. **Animal language.** Can monkeys use language in a way similar to humans? This is a controversial question, with some psychologists answering "yes" and others "no."

   Savage-Rumbaugh, S., & Lewin, R. (1994). *Kanzi, the ape at the brink of the human mind.* New York: Wiley.

3. **Indirect statements.** People use indirect statements all the time (see the preceding Think About It). There is evidence that indirect statements are more prevalent in some cultures than in others.

   Holtgraves, T. (1998). Interpreting indirect replies. *Cognitive Psychology, 37*, 1–27.

4. **Bilingualism.** When people speak two or more languages, are these languages stored together or separately? This question, as well as other questions about the mechanisms

involved in bilingualism, has been studied both behaviorally and physiologically.

Kroll, J. F., & Tokowicz, N. (2005). Models of bilingual representation and processing: Looking back and to the future. In J. F. Kroll & A. M. B. De Groot (Eds.), *Handbook of bilingualism: Psycholinguistic approaches* (pp. 531–553). New York: Oxford University Press.

Perani, D., & Abutalebi, J. (2005). The neural basis of first and second language processing. *Current Opinion in Neurobiology, 15*, 202–206.

Petitto, L. A., Katerelos, M., Levy, B. G., Gauna, K., Tétreault, K., & Ferraro, V. (2001). Bilingual signed and spoken language acquisition from birth: Implications for the mechanisms underlying early bilingual language acquisition. *Journal of Child Language, 28*, 453–496.

Snow, C. E. (1998). Bilingualism and second language acquisition. In J. B. Gleason & N. B. Ratner (Eds.), *Psycholinguistics* (2nd ed., pp. 453–481). Ft. Worth, TX: Harcourt.

5. **Psychology of reading.** Much of our use of language involves reading. This involves vision or touch (in the case of Braille) and places demands on memory that are different than for spoken language.

Price, C. J., & Mechelli, A. (2005). Reading and reading disturbance. *Current Opinion in Neurobiology, 15*, 231–238.

Starr, M. S., & Rayner, K. (2001). Eye movements during reading: Some current controversies. *Trends in Cognitive Sciences, 5*, 156–163.

6. **Language, culture, and the representation of space.** ● Figure 11.21 indicates three ways of expressing spatial relationships. Different cultures favor different systems, and there is evidence that language plays an important role in this.

Majid, M., Bowerman, M., Kita, S., Haun, D. B. M., & Levinson, S. C. (2004). Can language restructure cognition? *Trends in Cognitive Sciences, 8*, 108–114.

7. **Culture and categories.** Which two objects in ● Figure 11.22 would you place together? Which two of the following words would you place together: *panda, monkey, banana*? Research has shown that Chinese and Americans sort these items differently and that these differences may be related to language.

Chiu, L.-H. (1972). A cross-cultural comparison of cognitive styles in Chinese and American children. *International Journal of Psychology, 7*, 235–242.

Ji, L., Peng, K., & Nisbett, R. E. (2000). Culture, control, and perception of relationships in the environment. *Journal of Personality and Social Psychology, 78*, 943–955.

8. **Speech errors.** The study of speech errors, or "slips of the tongue," has revealed that these errors are related to both the basic structure of language and a person's prior knowledge.

Bock, K. (1995). Sentence production: From mind to mouth. In J. C. Miller & P. D. Eimas (Eds.), *Speech, language, and communication* (pp. 181–216). San Diego: Academic Press.

Dell, G. S. (1995). Speaking and misspeaking. In L. Gleitman & M. Liberman (Eds.), *An invitation to cognitive science* (Vol. 1, pp. 183–208). Cambridge, MA: MIT Press.

9. **Language acquisition.** Children usually begin learning language before they can speak, produce their first words

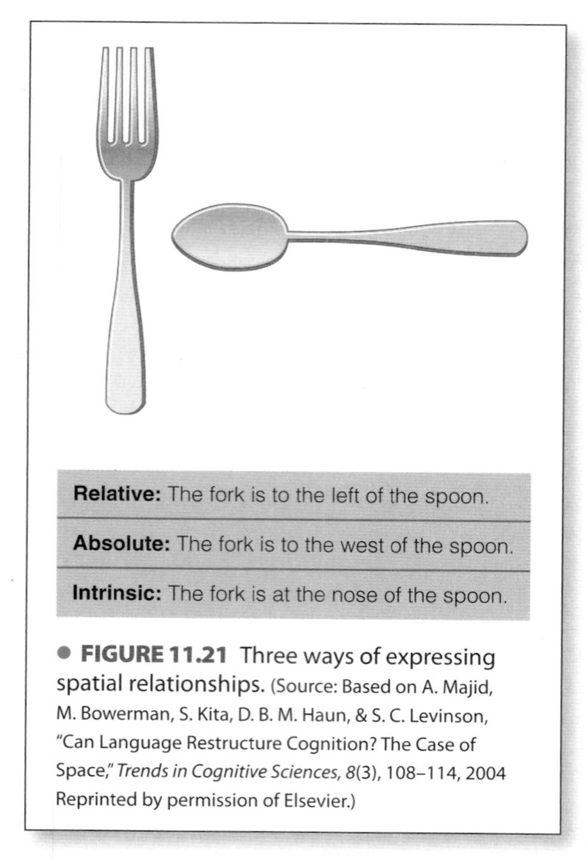

● **FIGURE 11.21** Three ways of expressing spatial relationships. (Source: Based on A. Majid, M. Bowerman, S. Kita, D. B. M. Haun, & S. C. Levinson, "Can Language Restructure Cognition? The Case of Space," *Trends in Cognitive Sciences, 8*(3), 108–114, 2004 Reprinted by permission of Elsevier.)

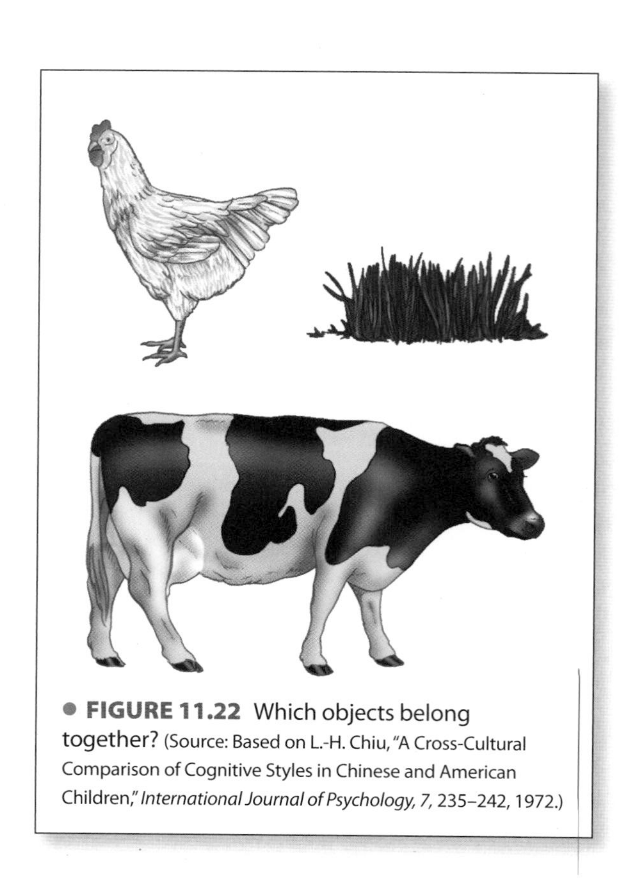

● **FIGURE 11.22** Which objects belong together? (Source: Based on L.-H. Chiu, "A Cross-Cultural Comparison of Cognitive Styles in Chinese and American Children," *International Journal of Psychology, 7*, 235–242, 1972.)

at about 1 year, and have mastered the basic structures of language by about 3 years of age.

Carroll, D. W. (2004). *Psychology of language* (4th ed.). Belmont, CA: Wadsworth.

Gleason, J. B., & Ratner, N. B. (1998). Language acquisition. In J. B. Gleason & N. B. Ratner (Eds.), *Psycholinguistics* (2nd ed., pp. 347–407). Fort Worth, TX: Harcourt.

Key TERMS

Anaphoric inference, 310
Causal inference, 310
Coherence, 310
Garden path sentence, 305
Given–new contract, 315
Inference, 309
Instrument inference, 310
Interactionist approach to parsing, 306
Language, 294
Late closure, 305
Lexical ambiguity, 301
Lexical decision task, 301
Lexical priming, 302
Lexicon, 297
Morpheme, 297
Parsing, 304
Phoneme, 297
Phonemic restoration effect, 298
Psycholinguistics, 296
Sapir-Whorf hypothesis, 317
Semantics, 304
Situation model, 311
Speech segmentation, 299
Syntactic priming, 316
Syntax, 304
Syntax-first approach to parsing, 305
Temporary ambiguity, 304
Word frequency, 300
Word frequency effect, 301
Word superiority effect, 300

Media RESOURCES

The Cognitive Psychology Book Companion Website

www.cengage.com/international

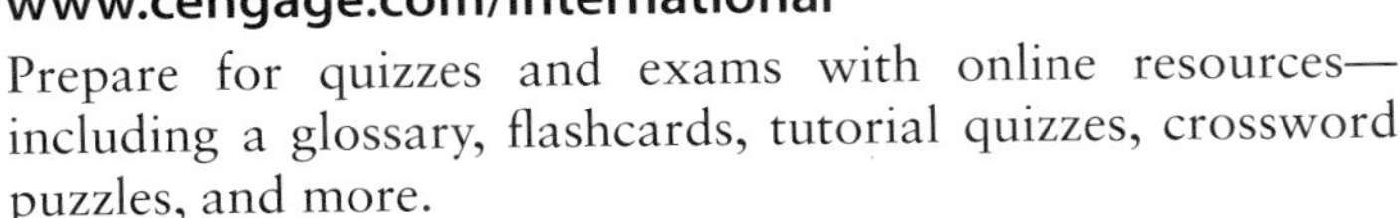

Prepare for quizzes and exams with online resources—including a glossary, flashcards, tutorial quizzes, crossword puzzles, and more.

CogLab

To experience these experiments for yourself, go to coglab.wadsworth.com. Be sure to read each experiment's setup instructions before you go to the experiment itself. Otherwise, you won't know which keys to press.

Primary Labs

Word superiority How speed of identifying a letter compares when the letter is isolated or in a word. (p. 300)

Lexical decision Demonstration of the lexical decision task. (p. 301)

Related Labs

Categorical perception—identification Demonstration of categorical perception based on the identification of different sound categories.

Categorical perception—discrimination Demonstration of categorical perception based on the ability to discriminate between sounds.

DEMONSTRATION Answers to Late Closure Demonstration on page 305

1. |The shoppers felt| |the fur coat was overpriced|
   Words added to first phrase: |the fur coat|
2. |Because he always jogs| |a mile seems like a short distance to him|
   Words added to first phrase: |a mile|
3. |The mechanic maintained| |the truck was working beautifully|
   Words added to first phrase: |the truck|

12 Thinking: Problem Solving

A problem occurs when there is an obstacle between a present state and a goal, and it is not immediately obvious how to get around the obstacle. The maze shown here is the obstacle to reaching the shelter in the middle. Research in problem solving has focused on determining the mental processes that occur as a person is solving a problem and on determining ways to make it easier to solve problems.

Bob Krist/Corbis

Some Questions We Will Consider

- What makes a problem hard? (326)
- Is there anything special about problems that seem to be solved in a flash of "insight"? (327)
- How can analogies be used to help solve problems? (340)
- How do experts in a field approach problems differently than nonexperts? (346)

The following is a story about physicist Richard Feynman, who received the Nobel Prize in Physics for his work in nuclear fission and quantum dynamics and who had a reputation as a scientific genius.

> A physicist working at the California Institute of Technology in the 1950s is having trouble deciphering some of Feynman's notes. He asks Murray Gell-Mann, a Nobel Laureate and occasional collaborator of Feynman, "What are Feynman's methods?" Gell-Mann leans coyly against the blackboard and says—"Dick's method is this. You write down the problem. You think very hard." [Gell-Mann shuts his eyes and presses his knuckles periodically to his forehead.] "Then you write down the answer." (adapted from Gleick, 1992, p. 315)

This is an amusing way of describing Feynman's genius, but leaves unanswered the question of what was really going on inside his head while he was thinking "very hard." Although we may not know the answer to this question for Feynman, research on problem solving has provided some answers for people in general. In this chapter we will describe some of the ways cognitive psychologists have described the mental processes that occur as people work toward determining the solution to a problem.

What Is a Problem?

What problems have you had to solve lately? When I ask students in my cognitive psychology class this question, I get answers such as the following: problems for math, chemistry, or physics courses; getting writing assignments in on time; dealing with roommates, friends, and relationships in general; deciding what courses to take, what career to go into; whether to go to graduate school or look for a job; how to pay for a new car. Many of these things fit the following definition: A **problem** occurs when there is an obstacle between a present state and a goal and it is not immediately obvious how to get around the obstacle (Lovett, 2002). Thus, a *problem*, as defined by psychologists, is difficult, and the solution is not immediately obvious.

You may notice, however, that my students' list includes two different types of problems. One type, such as solving a math or physics problem, is called a well-defined problem. **Well-defined problems** usually have a correct answer; certain procedures, when applied correctly, will lead to a solution. Another type of problem, such as dealing with relationships or picking a career, is called an ill-defined problem. **Ill-defined problems**, which occur frequently in everyday life, do not necessarily have one "correct" answer, and the path to their solution is often unclear (Pretz et al., 2003). We will consider ill-defined problems at the end of the chapter when we discuss creative problem solving. Our main concern will be well-defined problems, because psychological research has focused on this type of problem. We begin by considering the approach of the Gestalt psychologists, who introduced the study of problem solving to psychology in the 1920s.

The Gestalt Approach: Problem Solving as Representation and Restructuring

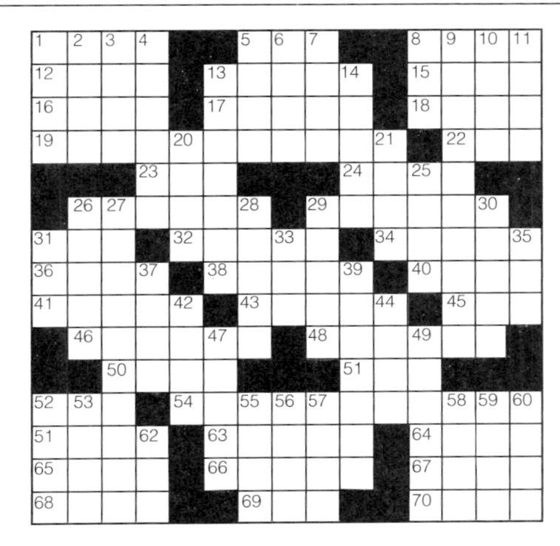

● **FIGURE 12.1** This is a picture of how a crossword puzzle is represented on the page. In addition, there are clues for filling in the horizontal and vertical words.

We introduced the Gestalt psychologists in Chapter 3 by describing their laws of perceptual organization. The Gestalt psychologists were interested not only in perception, but also in learning, problem solving, and even attitudes and beliefs (Koffka, 1935). But even as they considered other areas of psychology, they still took a perceptual approach. Problem solving, for the Gestalt psychologists, was about (1) how people represent a problem in their mind and (2) how solving a problem involves a *reorganization* or *restructuring* of this representation.

REPRESENTING A PROBLEM IN THE MIND

What does it mean to say that a problem is "represented" in the mind? One way to answer this question is to begin with how problems are presented. Consider, for example, a crossword puzzle (● Figure 12.1). This type of problem is represented on the page by a diagram and clues about how to fill in the open squares. How this problem is represented in the mind is probably different for different people, but it is likely to differ from how it is represented on the page. For example, as people try to solve this problem, they may choose to represent only a small part of the puzzle at a time. Some people might focus on filling in horizontal words and then use these words to help determine the vertical words. Others might pick one corner of the puzzle and search in their mind for both verticals and horizontals that fit together. Each of these ways of going about solving the problem involves a different way of representing it in the mind.

One of the central ideas of the Gestalt approach is that success in solving a problem is influenced by how it is represented in the person's mind. This idea—that the solution to a problem depends on how it is represented—is illustrated by the problem in ● Figure 12.2. This problem, which was posed by Gestalt psychologist Wolfgang Kohler (1929), asks us to determine the length of the segment marked x if the radius of the circle has a length r. (A number of problems will be posed in this chapter. The answers appear at the end of the chapter. See Figure ● 12.25, page 356, for the answer to the "circle" problem. For this problem, the answer is also stated in the next paragraph, so don't read any further if you want to try to solve it.)

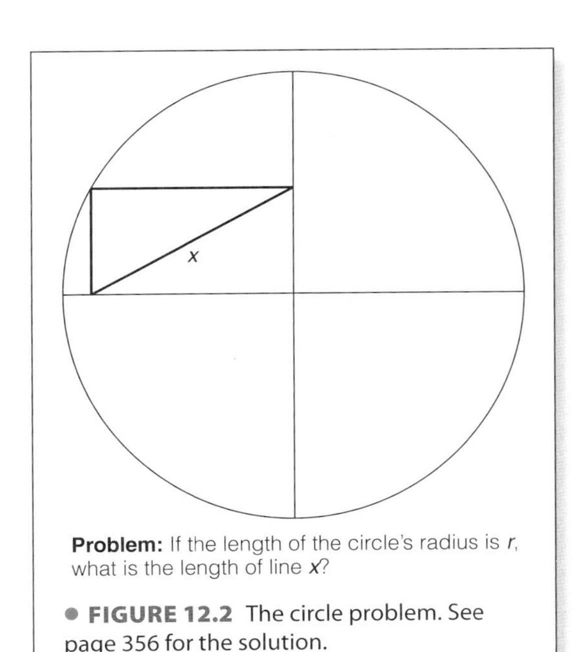

Problem: If the length of the circle's radius is r, what is the length of line x?

● **FIGURE 12.2** The circle problem. See page 356 for the solution.

One way to describe how this problem is represented on the page is "a circle with vertical and horizontal lines that divide the circle into quarters, with a small triangle in the upper left quadrant." The key to solving this problem is to change the last part of the representation to "a small rectangle in the upper left quadrant, with x being the diagonal between the corners." Once x is recognized as the diagonal of the rectangle, the representation can be reorganized by creating the rectangle's other diagonal (Figure 12.25). Once we realize that this diagonal is the radius of the circle, and that both diagonals of a rectangle are the same length, we can conclude that the length of x equals the length of the radius, r.

What is important about this solution is that it doesn't require mathematical equations. Instead, the solution is obtained by first *perceiving* the object and then *representing* it in a different way. The Gestalt psychologists called the process of changing the problem's representation **restructuring**.

RESTRUCTURING AND INSIGHT

The Gestalt psychologists also introduced the idea that restructuring is associated with **insight**—the sudden realization of a problem's solution. Reflecting this emphasis on insight, the solution to most of the problems posed by Gestalt psychologists involves suddenly discovering a crucial element that leads to the solution (Dunbar, 1998).

The Gestalt psychologists assumed that people solving their problems were experiencing insight because the solutions usually seemed to come to them all of a sudden. Modern researchers have debated whether insight actually exists. Some point out that people often experience problem solving as an "Aha!" experience—at one point they don't have the answer, and the next minute they have solved the problem—which is one of the characteristics associated with insight problems (Bowden et al., 2005; Kounios et al., 2008). Other researchers have emphasized the lack of evidence, other than anecdotal reports, to support the specialness of the insight experience (Weisberg, 1995; Weisberg & Alba, 1981, 1982).

Janet Metcalfe and David Wiebe (1987) did an experiment designed to distinguish between insight problems and noninsight problems. Their starting point was the idea that there should be a basic difference in how participants feel they are progressing toward a solution as they are working on an insight problem versus a noninsight problem. They predicted that participants working on an insight problem, in which the answer appears suddenly, should not be very good at predicting how near they are to a solution. Participants working on a noninsight problem, which involves a more methodical process, would be more likely to know when they are getting closer to the solution.

To test this hypothesis, Metcalfe and Wiebe gave participants insight problems, as in the demonstration below, and noninsight problems and asked them to make "warmth" judgments every 15 seconds as they were working on the problems. Ratings closer to "hot" (7 on a 7-point scale) indicated that they believed they were getting close to a solution; ratings closer to "cold" (1 on the scale) indicated that they felt that they were far from a solution. Here are some examples of insight problems.

DEMONSTRATION Two Insight Problems

TRIANGLE PROBLEM The triangle shown in ● Figure 12.3a points to the top of the page. Show how you can move three of the circles to get the triangle to point to the bottom of the page. (For the answer, see ● Figure 12.26 on page 356.)

As you work on this problem, see whether you can monitor your progress. Do you feel as though you are making steady progress toward a solution until eventually it all adds up to the answer, or as though you are not really making much progress but then suddenly experience the solution like an "Aha!" experience? Once you have tried the triangle problem, try the following problem and monitor your progress in the same way.

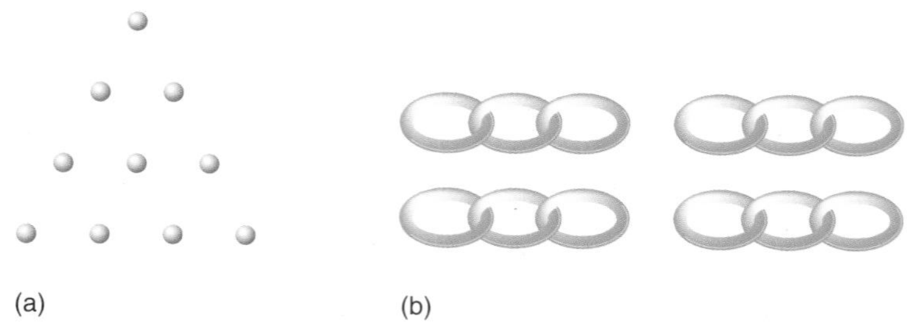

(a) (b)

● **FIGURE 12.3** (a) Triangle problem and (b) chain problem for "Two Insight Problems" demonstration.

CHAIN PROBLEM A woman has four pieces of chain. Each piece is made up of three links, as shown in Figure 12.3b. She wants to join the pieces into a single closed loop of chain. To open a link costs 2 cents and to close a link costs 3 cents. She has only 15 cents. How does she do it? (For the answer, see ● Figure 12.27 on page 356.)

For noninsight problems, Metcalfe and Wiebe used algebra problems like the following, which were taken from a high school mathematics text.

Solve for x: $(1/5)x + 10 = 25$
Factor $16y^2 - 40yz + 25z^2$

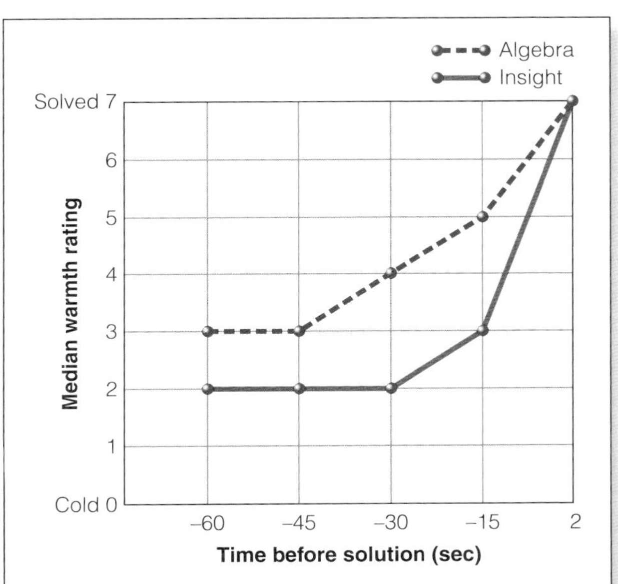

● **FIGURE 12.4** Results of Metcalfe and Wiebe's (1987) experiment showing participants' judgments of how close they were to solving insight problems and algebra problems during the minute just before solving the problem. (Source: Based on J. Metcalfe & D. Wiebe, "Intuition in Insight and Noninsight Problem Solving," *Memory and Cognition, 15,* 238–246, 1987.)

The results of their experiment are shown in ● Figure 12.4, which indicates the median warmth ratings for all of the participants during the minute just before they solved the two kinds of problems.

For the insight problems (solid line), warmth ratings remain low at 2 or 3 until just before the problem is solved. Notice that 15 seconds before the solution, the median rating is a relatively cold 3 for the insight problems. In contrast, for the algebra problems (dashed line), the ratings gradually increased until the problem was solved. Thus, Metcalfe and Wiebe demonstrated a difference between insight and noninsight problems. The solution for problems that have been called insight problems does, in fact, occur suddenly, as measured by people's reports of how close they feel they are to a solution.

The Gestalt psychologists believed that restructuring was usually involved in solving insight problems, so they focused on these types of problems. Their research strategy was to devise problems and situations that made it difficult for people to achieve the restructuring needed to solve the problem. They hoped to learn about processes involved in problem solving by studying *obstacles* to problem solving.

OBSTACLES TO PROBLEM SOLVING

One of the major obstacles to problem solving, according to the Gestalt psychologists, is **fixation**—people's tendency to focus on a specific characteristic of the problem that keeps them from arriving at a solution. One type of fixation that can work against solving a problem is focusing on familiar uses of an object.

Restricting the use of an object to its familiar functions is called **functional fixedness** (Jansson & Smith, 1991). The **candle problem**, first described by Karl Duncker (1945), illustrates how functional fixedness can hinder problem solving. In his experiment, he asked participants to use various objects to complete a task. The following demonstration asks you to try to solve Duncker's problem by imagining that you have the specified objects.

DEMONSTRATION The Candle Problem

You are in a room with a corkboard on the wall. You are given the materials in ● Figure 12.5—some candles, matches in a matchbox, and some tacks. Your task is to mount a candle on the corkboard so it will burn without dripping wax on the floor. Try to figure out how you would solve this problem before reading further, and then check your answer in ● Figure 12.28 (page 356).

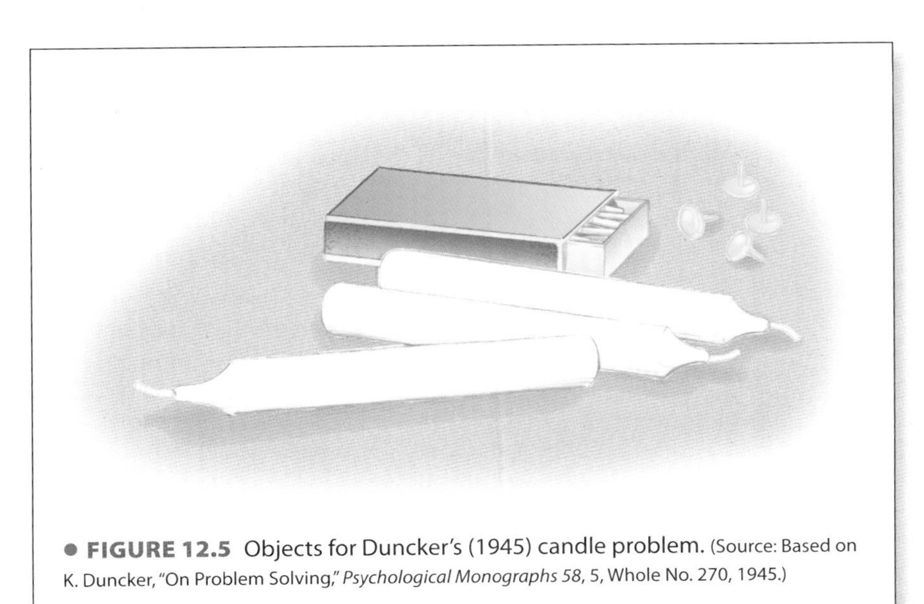

● **FIGURE 12.5** Objects for Duncker's (1945) candle problem. (Source: Based on K. Duncker, "On Problem Solving," *Psychological Monographs 58,* 5, Whole No. 270, 1945.)

The solution to the problem occurs when the person realizes that the matchbox can be used as a support rather than as a container. When Duncker did this experiment, he presented one group of participants with small cardboard boxes containing the materials (candles, tacks, and matches) and presented another group with the same materials, but outside the boxes, so the boxes were empty.

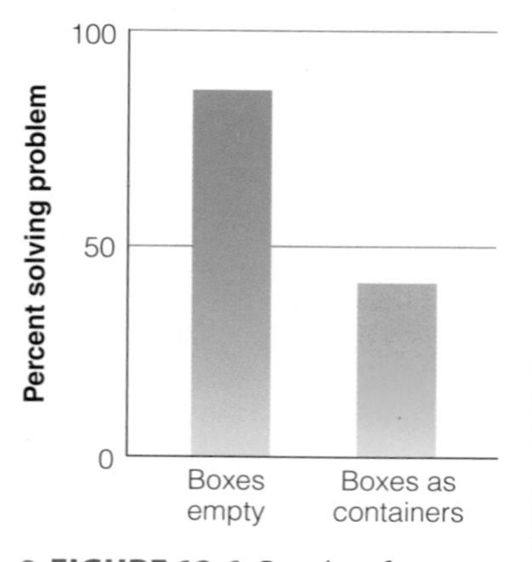

● **FIGURE 12.6** Results of Adamson's (1952) replication of Duncker's candle problem. (Source: Based on R. E. Adamson, "Functional Fixedness as Related to Problem Solving," *Journal of Experimental Psychology, 44,* 288–291, 1952.)

When he compared the performance of the two groups, he found that the group that had been presented with the boxes as containers found the problem more difficult than did the group that was presented with empty boxes. Robert Adamson (1952) repeated Duncker's experiment and obtained the same result: Participants who were presented with empty boxes were twice as likely to solve the problem as participants who were presented with boxes that were used as containers (● Figure 12.6).

The fact that seeing the boxes as containers inhibited using them as supports is an example of functional fixedness. Another demonstration of functional fixedness is provided by Maier's (1931) **two-string problem**, in which the participants' task was to tie together two strings that were hanging from the ceiling. This is difficult because the strings are separated, so it is impossible to reach one of them while holding the other (● Figure 12.7). Other objects available for solving this problem were a chair and a pair of pliers.

To solve this problem, participants needed to tie the pliers to one of the strings to create a pendulum, which could then be swung to within the person's reach. Two things are particularly significant about this problem. First, 60 percent of the participants did not solve the problem because they focused on the usual function of pliers and did not think of using them as a weight. Second, when Maier set the string into motion by "accidentally" brushing against it, 23 of 37 participants who hadn't solved the problem after 10 minutes proceeded to solve it within 60 seconds. Seeing the string swinging from side to side apparently triggered the insight that the pliers could be used as a weight to create a pendulum. In Gestalt terms, the solution to the problem occurred once the participants *restructured* their representation of how to achieve the solution (get the strings to swing from side to side) and their representation of the function of the pliers (they can be used as a weight to create a pendulum).

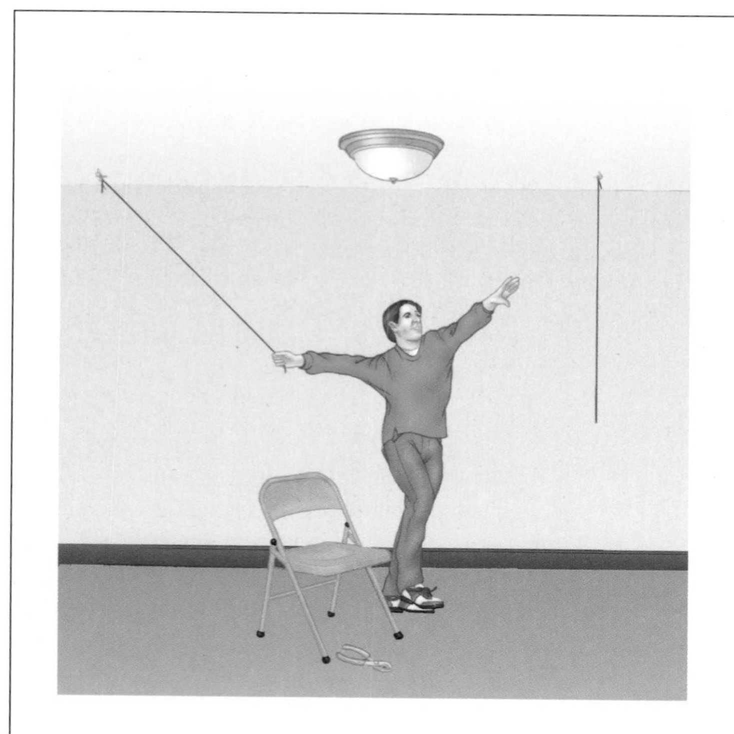

● **FIGURE 12.7** Maier's (1931) two-string problem. As hard as Sebastian tries, he can't grab the second string. How can he tie the two strings together? (Source: Based on N. R. F. Maier, "Reasoning in Humans: II. The Solution of a Problem and Its Appearance in Consciousness," *Journal of Comparative Psychology, 12,* 181–194, 1931.)

Both the candle problem and the two-string problem were difficult because of people's preconceptions about the uses of objects. These preconceptions are a type of **mental set**, a preconceived notion about how to approach a problem, which is determined by a person's experience or what has worked in the past. In these experiments mental set was created by people's knowledge about the usual use of objects.

The Gestalt psychologists also showed how mental set can arise out of the situation created as a person solves a problem. An example is provided by the Luchins **water-jug problem**, in which participants are given three jugs of different capacities and are required to use these jugs to measure out a specific quantity of water, as shown in ● Figure 12.8 (Luchins, 1942). Problem 1 is solved by first filling the 127-cup jug (B) and then pouring the water from B into A once and into C two times, thereby subtracting 27 cups and leaving 100 in jug B. This solution, which can be stated by the formula

$$\text{Desired quantity} = B - A - 2C$$

works for all of the problems in Figure 12.8. However, problems 7 and 8 can be solved more simply by using only jugs A and C. For problem 7: Pour A (15) and C (3) into a container to arrive at 18 (Desired quantity = A + C). For problem 8: Fill jug A (28) and then pour from A into C (3), to leave 25 in A (Desired quantity = A – C).

A. S. Luchins (1942) had some participants begin with problem 1 and do each problem in sequence through problem 8 (the mental set group), and had other participants solve only problems 7 and 8 (the no mental set group). ● Figure 12.9 compares the performance of the two groups. All of the participants in the *no mental set group* used the shorter solution for problems 7 and 8, whereas

	Capacities (cups)			
Problem	Jug A	Jug B	Jug C	Desired quantity
1	21	127	3	100
2	14	163	25	99
3	18	43	10	5
4	9	42	6	21
5	20	59	4	31
6	20	50	3	24
7	15	39	3	18
8	28	59	3	25

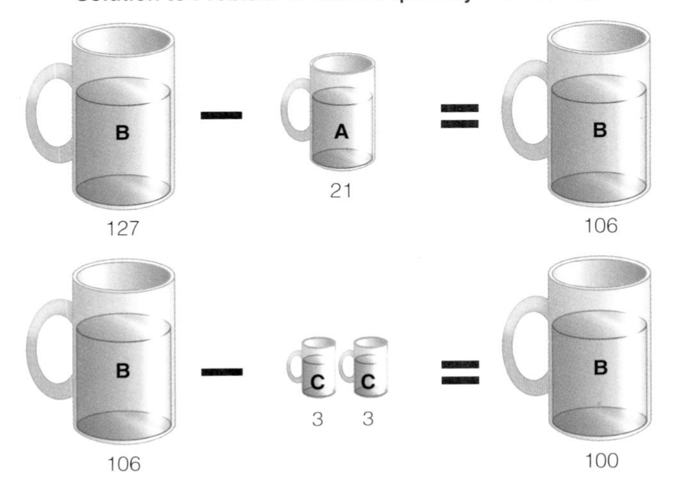

• **FIGURE 12.8** Luchins' (1942) water-jug problem. Each problem specifies the capacities of jugs A, B, and C, and a final desired quantity. The task is to use the jugs to measure out the final quantity. The solution to problem 1 is shown. All of the other problems can be solved using the same pattern of pourings, indicated by the equation, but there are more efficient ways to solve 7 and 8. (Source: Based on A. S. Luchins, "Mechanization in Problem Solving—the Effect of Einstellung," *Psychological Monographs, 54*, 6, 195, 1942.)

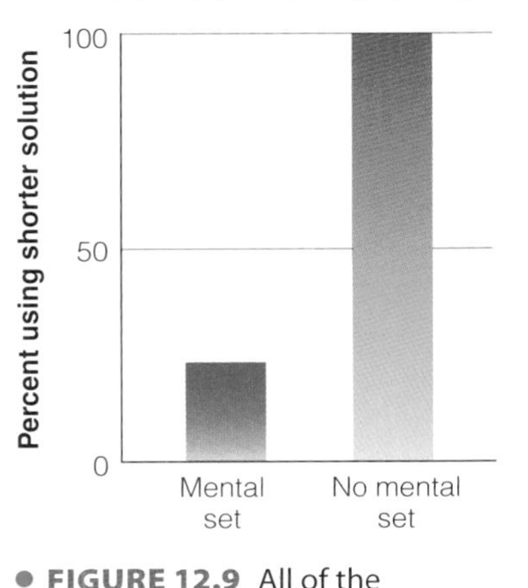

• **FIGURE 12.9** All of the participants who began the Luchins' water-jug problem with problem 7 used the shorter solution (right bar), but less than a quarter of those who had established a mental set by beginning with problem 1 used the shorter solution to solve problem 7 (left bar). (Source: Based on A. S. Luchins, "Mechanization in Problem Solving—the Effect of Einstellung," *Psychological Monographs, 54*, 6, 195, 1942.)

only 23 percent in the *mental set group* used this solution for these problems. Clearly, participants in the mental set group learned the procedure described by the formula B – A – 2C as they solved problems 1 to 6 and simply continued to apply that procedure to solve problems 7 and 8. The mental set created by solving problems 1 to 6 inhibited them from using the simpler solution for 7 and 8.

The Gestalt psychologists were the pioneers of problem-solving research. Between about 1920 and 1950, they described problems and solutions illustrating how mental set can influence problem solving and how solving a problem often involves creating a new representation. This idea that problem solving depends on how the problem is represented in the mind is one of the enduring contributions of Gestalt psychology. Modern research has taken this idea as a starting point for the information-processing approach to the study of problem solving.

Modern Research on Problem Solving: The Information-Processing Approach

In our description of the history of cognitive psychology in Chapter 1, we noted that in 1956 there were two important conferences, one at the Massachusetts Institute of Technology and one at Dartmouth University, that brought together researchers from many disciplines to discuss new ways to study the mind. At both of these conferences, Alan Newell and Herbert Simon described their "logic theorist" computer program that was designed to simulate human problem solving. This marked the beginning of a research program that described problem solving as a process that involves *search*. That is, instead of just considering the initial structure of a problem and then the new structure achieved when the problem is solved, Newell and Simon described problem solving as a search that occurs between the posing of the problem and its solution.

The idea of problem solving as a search is part of our language. People commonly talk about problems in terms of "searching for a way to reach a goal," "getting around roadblocks," "hitting a dead end," and "approaching a problem from a different angle" (Lakoff & Turner, 1989). We will introduce Newell and Simon's approach by describing the *Tower of Hanoi problem*.

NEWELL AND SIMON'S APPROACH

Newell and Simon (1972) saw problems in terms of an **initial state**—conditions at the beginning of the problem—and a **goal state**—the solution of the problem. ● Figure 12.10a shows the initial state of the **Tower of Hanoi problem** as three discs stacked on the left peg, and the goal state as these discs stacked on the right peg. Try solving this problem by following the instructions in the demonstration.

DEMONSTRATION Tower of Hanoi Problem

In addition to specifying initial and goal states of a problem, Newell and Simon also introduced the idea of **operators**—actions that take the problem from one state to another. For the Tower of Hanoi problem, the following rules specify which actions are allowed and which are not (see Figure 12.10b):

1. Discs are moved one at a time from one peg to another.
2. A disc can be moved only when there are no discs on top of it.
3. A larger disc can never be placed on top of a smaller disc.

As you try solving this problem, count the number of moves it takes to get from the initial to the goal state.

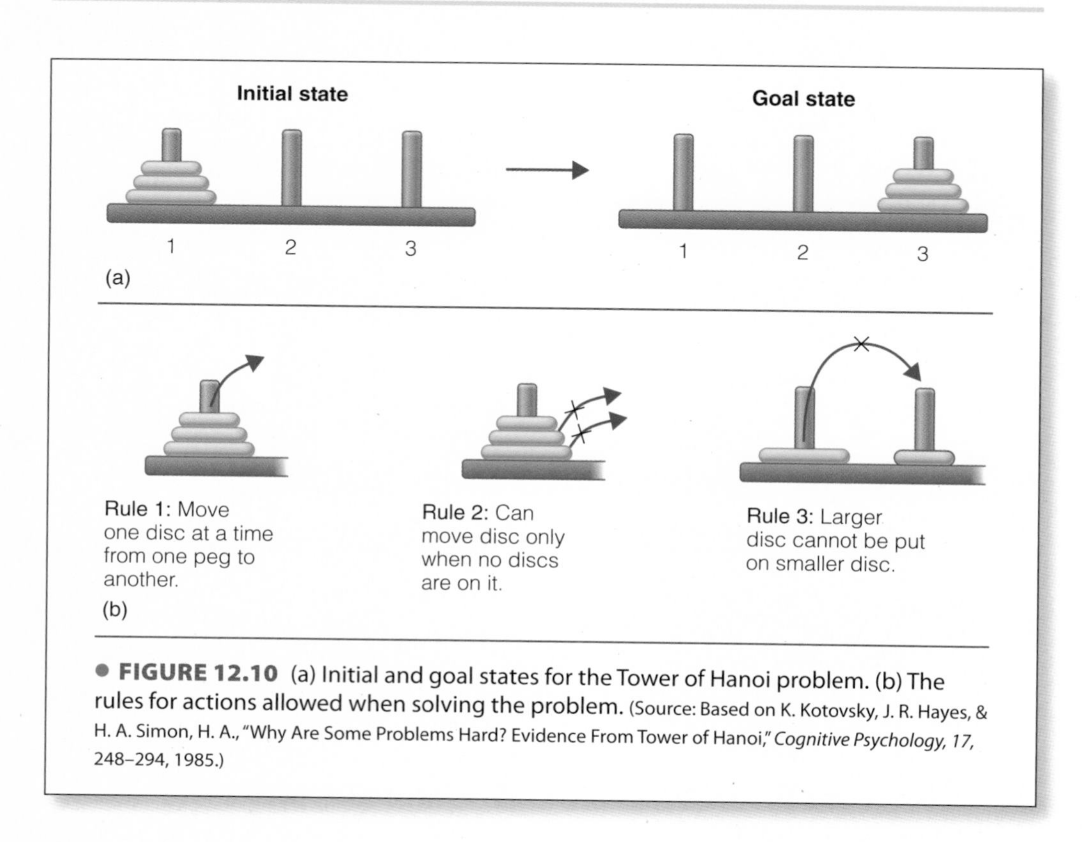

● **FIGURE 12.10** (a) Initial and goal states for the Tower of Hanoi problem. (b) The rules for actions allowed when solving the problem. (Source: Based on K. Kotovsky, J. R. Hayes, & H. A. Simon, H. A., "Why Are Some Problems Hard? Evidence From Tower of Hanoi," *Cognitive Psychology, 17*, 248–294, 1985.)

This problem is called the Tower of Hanoi problem because of a legend that there are monks in a monastery near Hanoi who are working on this problem. Their version of it, however, is vastly more complex than ours, with 64 discs on peg 1. According to the legend, the world will end when the problem is solved. Luckily, this will take close to a trillion years to accomplish even if the monks make one move every second and every move is correct (Raphael, 1976).

As you tried solving the problem, you may have realized that there were a number of possible ways to move the discs as you tried to reach the goal state. Newell and Simon conceived of problem solving as involving a sequence of choices of steps, with each step creating an **intermediate state**. Thus, a problem starts with an initial state, continues through a number of intermediate states, and finally reaches the goal state. The initial state, goal state, and all the *possible* intermediate states for a particular problem is called the **problem space**. (See Table 12.1 for a summary of the terms used by Newell and Simon.)

The problem space for the Tower of Hanoi problem is shown in ● Figure 12.11. The initial state is marked 1 and the goal state is marked 8. All of the other possible configurations of discs on pegs are intermediate states. From the diagram, you can see that there are a number of possible paths for getting from the initial state to the goal state, but that one of these paths is shorter than the others. By choosing the path along the right side of the problem space (states 2, 3, 4, 5, 6, and 7), as indicated by the arrow, it is possible to reach the goal state by making just seven moves.

Given all of the possible ways to reach the goal, how can we decide which moves to make, especially when starting out? It is important to realize that the problem-solver does not have a picture of the problem space, like the one in Figure 12.11, when trying to solve the problem. According to Newell and Simon, the person has to search the problem space to find a solution, and they proposed that one way to direct the search is to use a strategy called **means-end analysis**. The primary goal of means-end analysis is to reduce the difference between the initial and goal states. This is achieved by creating **subgoals**—intermediate states that are closer to the goal.

Our overall goal in applying means-end analysis to the Tower of Hanoi problem is to reduce the size of the difference between initial and goal states. An initial

TABLE 12.1 Key Terms for Newell-Simon Approach to Problem Solving

Term	Description	Example from Tower of Hanoi
Initial state	Conditions at the beginning of a problem.	All three discs on the left peg.
Goal state	Solution to the problem.	All three discs on the right peg.
Intermediate state	Conditions after each step is made toward solving a problem.	After moving the small disc to the right peg there are two other discus on left peg and the small one is on the right.
Operators	Actions that take the problem from one state to another. Operators are usually governed by rules.	Rule: A larger disc can't be placed on a smaller one.
Problem space	All possible states that could occur when solving a problem.	See Figure 12.11.
Means-end analysis	A way of solving a problem in which the goal is to reduce the difference between the initial and goal states.	Establishing subgoals, each of which moves the solution closer to the goal state.
Subgoals	Small goals that help create intermediate states that are closer to the goal. Occasionally, a subgoal may appear to increase the distance to the goal state but in the long run can result in the shortest path to the goal.	Subgoal 4: To free up the medium-sized disc, need to move the small disc from the middle peg back to the peg on the left.

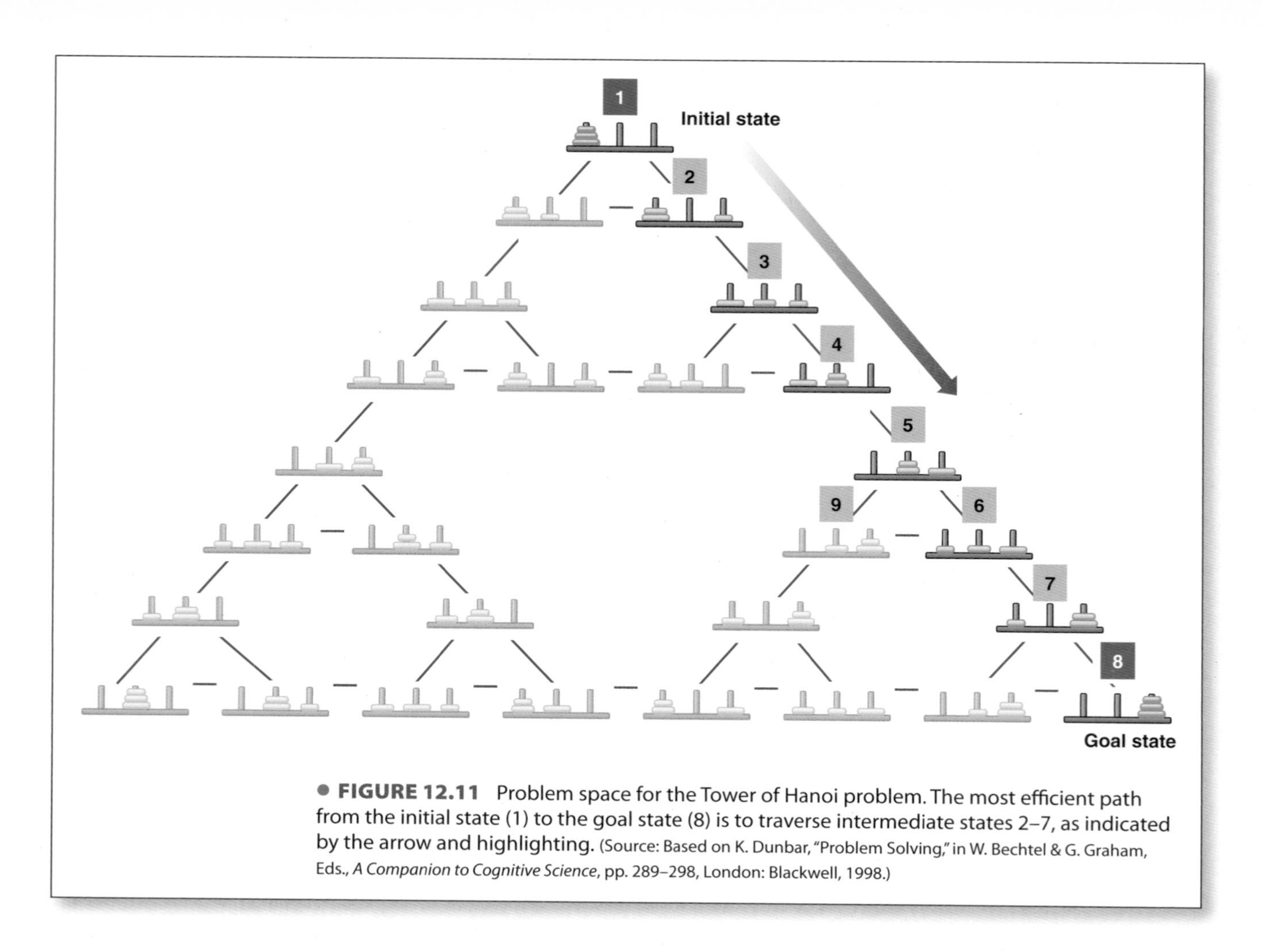

• **FIGURE 12.11** Problem space for the Tower of Hanoi problem. The most efficient path from the initial state (1) to the goal state (8) is to traverse intermediate states 2–7, as indicated by the arrow and highlighting. (Source: Based on K. Dunbar, "Problem Solving," in W. Bechtel & G. Graham, Eds., *A Companion to Cognitive Science*, pp. 289–298, London: Blackwell, 1998.)

goal would be to move the large disc that is on the left over to the peg on the right. However, if we are to obey the rules, we can't accomplish this in just one step, because we can move only one disc at a time and can't move a disc if another disc is on top of it. To solve the problem we therefore set a series of subgoals, some of which may involve a few moves.

Subgoal 1: Free up the large disc so we can move it onto peg 3. Do this by (1) removing the small disc and placing it on the third peg (• Figure 12.12a; this is state 2 in the problem space in Figure 12.11). (2) Remove the medium disc and place it on the second peg (Figure 12.12b; state 3 in the problem space). This completes the subgoal of freeing up the large disc.

Subgoal 2: Free up the third peg so we can move the large disc onto it. Do this by moving the small disc onto the medium one (Figure 12.12c; state 4 in the problem space).

Subgoal 3: Move the large disc onto peg 3 (Figure 12.12d; state 5 in the problem space).

Now that we have reached state 5 in the problem space, let's stop and decide how to achieve subgoal 4, freeing up the medium-sized disc. We can move the small disc either onto peg 3 (state 9) or onto peg 1 (state 6). These two possible choices illustrate that to find the shortest path to the goal, we need to look slightly ahead. When we do this, we can see that we should not move the small disc to peg 3, because that blocks moving the medium disc there, which would be our next subgoal. Thus, we move the disc back to peg 1, which makes it possible to move the medium disc to peg 3

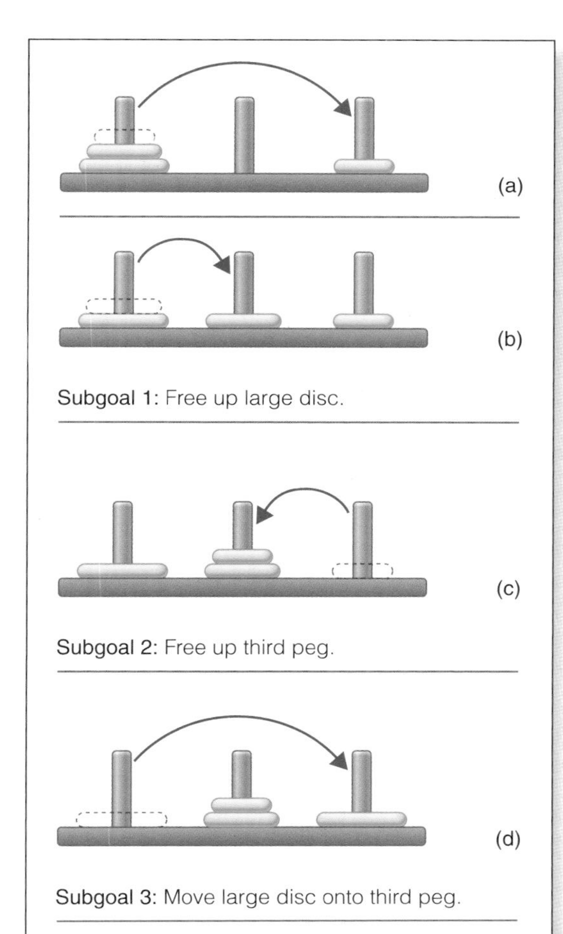

● **FIGURE 12.12** Initial steps in solving the Tower of Hanoi problem, showing how the problem can be broken down into subgoals. (Source: Based on K. Kotovsky, J. R. Hayes, & H. A. Simon, H. A., "Why Are Some Problems Hard? Evidence From Tower of Hanoi," *Cognitive Psychology, 17,* 248–294, 1985.)

● **FIGURE 12.13** Two possible routes from Pittsburgh to Copenhagen. The route through Paris (solid black line) immediately reduces the distance to Copenhagen, but doesn't satisfy the rules of the problem. The route through Atlanta (dashed red line) involves some backtracking but works because it satisfies the rules.

(state 7), and we have almost solved the problem! This procedure of setting subgoals and looking slightly ahead often results in an efficient solution to a problem.

Why is the Tower of Hanoi problem important? One reason is that it illustrates means-end analysis, with its setting of subgoals, and this approach can be applied to real-life situations. For example, I recently had to plan a trip from Pittsburgh to Copenhagen. Remember that in Newell and Simon's terminology, an operator is the action to get from one state to another. The operator for getting from Pittsburgh to Copenhagen is to take a plane, and one of the rules governing this operator is that if there isn't a direct flight (there isn't!), it is important to have enough time between flights to ensure that passengers and baggage can get from the first flight to the second one. Another rule is that the cost of the flights have to be within my budget.

My first step was to try to reduce the distance between myself and Copenhagen by taking the direct flight from Pittsburgh to Paris, and then transfer to a flight to Copenhagen. But there was only a gap of 90 minutes between flights, which violated the first rule, and waiting for a later flight increased the fare, which violated the second rule. The failure of the Pittsburgh-to-Paris idea led me to set a new subgoal: Find a city that has a direct flight to Copenhagen. The answer: Atlanta. So the new routing was Pittsburgh to Atlanta, then Atlanta to Copenhagen (● Figure 12.13). As it turned out, flights that met both of the rules were available, so the problem was solved. Notice that for this solution, the first subgoal involved traveling *away* from Copenhagen. Just as for subgoal 4 in the Tower of Hanoi example we had to move a disc away from the right peg to eventually get it there, I had to first fly away from Copenhagen to position myself to achieve my goal.

One of the main contributions of Newell and Simon's approach to problem solving is that it provided a way to specify the possible pathways from the initial to goal states. But research has shown that there is more to problem solving than specifying the problem space. As we will see in the next section, this research has shown that two problems with the same problem space can vary greatly in difficulty.

THE IMPORTANCE OF HOW A PROBLEM IS STATED

How a problem is stated can affect its difficulty. We can appreciate this by considering two similar problems: the acrobat problem and the reverse acrobat problem.

The Acrobat Problem

Three circus acrobats developed an amazing routine in which they jumped to and from each other's shoulders to form human towers (● Figure 12.14). The routine was quite spectacular because it was performed atop three very tall flagpoles. It was made even more impressive because the acrobats were very different in size: The large acrobat weighed 400 pounds; the medium acrobat, 200 pounds; and the small acrobat, a mere 40 pounds. These differences forced them to follow these safety rules:

1. Only one acrobat may jump at a time.
2. Whenever two acrobats are on the same flagpole, one must be standing on the shoulders of the other.
3. An acrobat may not jump when someone is standing on his or her shoulders.
4. A bigger acrobat may not stand on the shoulders of a smaller acrobat.

At the beginning of their act, the medium acrobat was on the left, the large acrobat in the middle, and the small acrobat on the right (initial state; Figure 12.14a). At the end of the act, they were arranged small, medium, and large from left to right (goal state; Figure 12.14b). How did they manage to do this while obeying the safety rules?

The acrobat problem can be solved by making just 5 moves, as indicated by the solution shown in ● Figure 12.29a (page 357). K. Kotovsky and coworkers (1985) found that it took their participants an average of 5.63 minutes to solve this problem. However, when they made one small change in the problem, it became much more difficult.

The Reverse Acrobat Problem

The reverse acrobat problem is the same as the acrobat problem, except that rule 4 above was changed to state that a smaller acrobat cannot stand on a larger one.

Although this version of the problem can be solved in the same number of steps as the original acrobat problem (see Figure 12.29b), Kotovsky's participants took an average of 9.51 minutes to solve the reverse acrobat problem. There are a number of possible reasons that the reverse acrobat problem is more difficult. One possibility is that the idea of a 400-pound acrobat standing on the shoulders of a 40-pound acrobat is not consistent with our knowledge of the real world, in which it would be highly unlikely that the small acrobat could support the large one. In addition, it may be harder to visualize larger acrobats on top of smaller ones, which would make the problem more difficult by increasing the load on the problem-solver's memory. Whatever the reason, these results show that to understand problem solving, we need to go beyond analyzing the structure of the problem space.

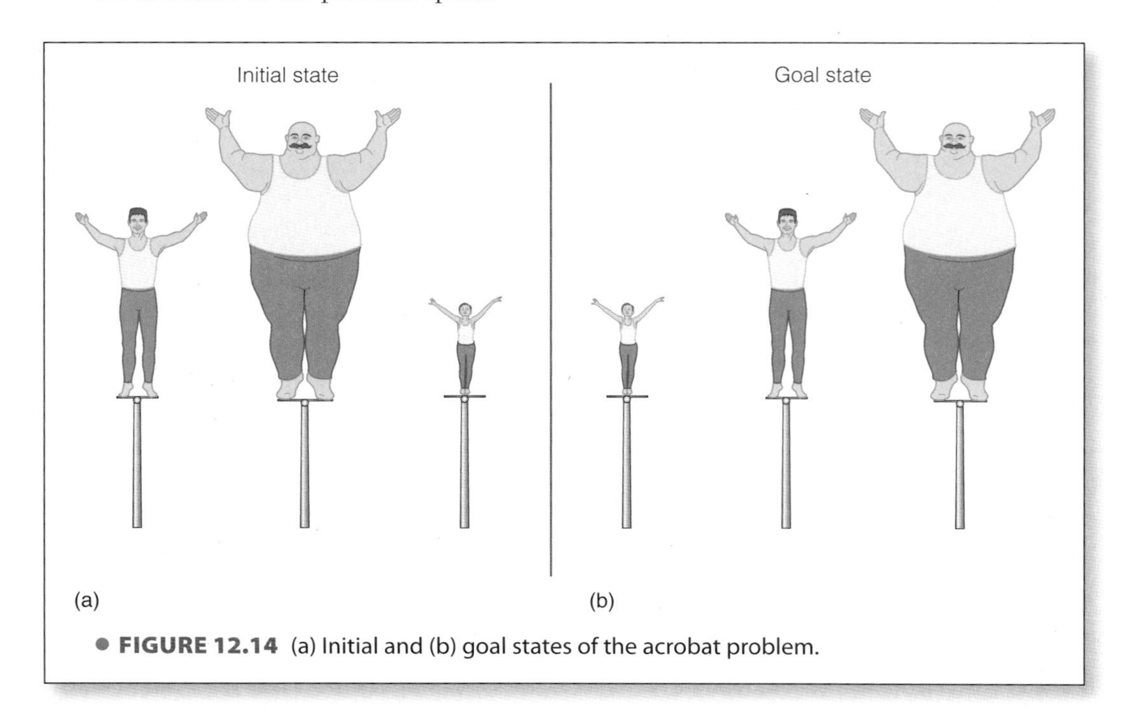

● **FIGURE 12.14** (a) Initial and (b) goal states of the acrobat problem.

We will now consider the **mutilated checkerboard problem**, which provides another example of how the way a problem is stated can influence its difficulty.

DEMONSTRATION The Mutilated Checkerboard Problem

A checkerboard consists of 64 squares. These 64 squares can be completely covered by placing 32 dominos on the board so that each domino covers two squares. If we eliminate two corners of the checkerboard, as shown in ● Figure 12.15, can we now cover the remaining squares with 31 dominos?

See whether you can solve this problem. A solution would be either a "yes" or "no" answer plus a statement of the rationale behind your answer.

Craig Kaplan and Herbert Simon (1990) used this problem and variations of it to study how the way a problem is stated affects its difficulty. There were four conditions in their experiment. Each group received a different version of the problem. The four conditions, shown in ● Figure 12.16, were (1) *blank*—a board with all blank squares; (2) *color*—alternating black and pink squares as might appear on a regular checkerboard; (3) *black and pink*—the words *black* and *pink* on the board; and (4) *bread and butter*—the words *bread* and *butter* on the board.

The key to solving the problem is to realize that when a domino is placed on the board so it covers just two squares, it is always covering two squares that are different (pink and black, for example). There is no way to place a domino so it covers two pink squares or two black squares. Therefore, for 31 dominos to cover the board there must be 31 pink squares and 31 black squares. However, this isn't the case, because two pink squares were removed. Thus, the board can't be covered by 31 dominos.

All four versions of the checkerboard problem have the same board layout and the same solution. What is different is the information on the squares (or lack of information on the blank board) that can be used to provide participants with the insight that a domino covers two squares and that these squares must be different colors. Not surprisingly, participants who were presented boards that emphasized the difference between

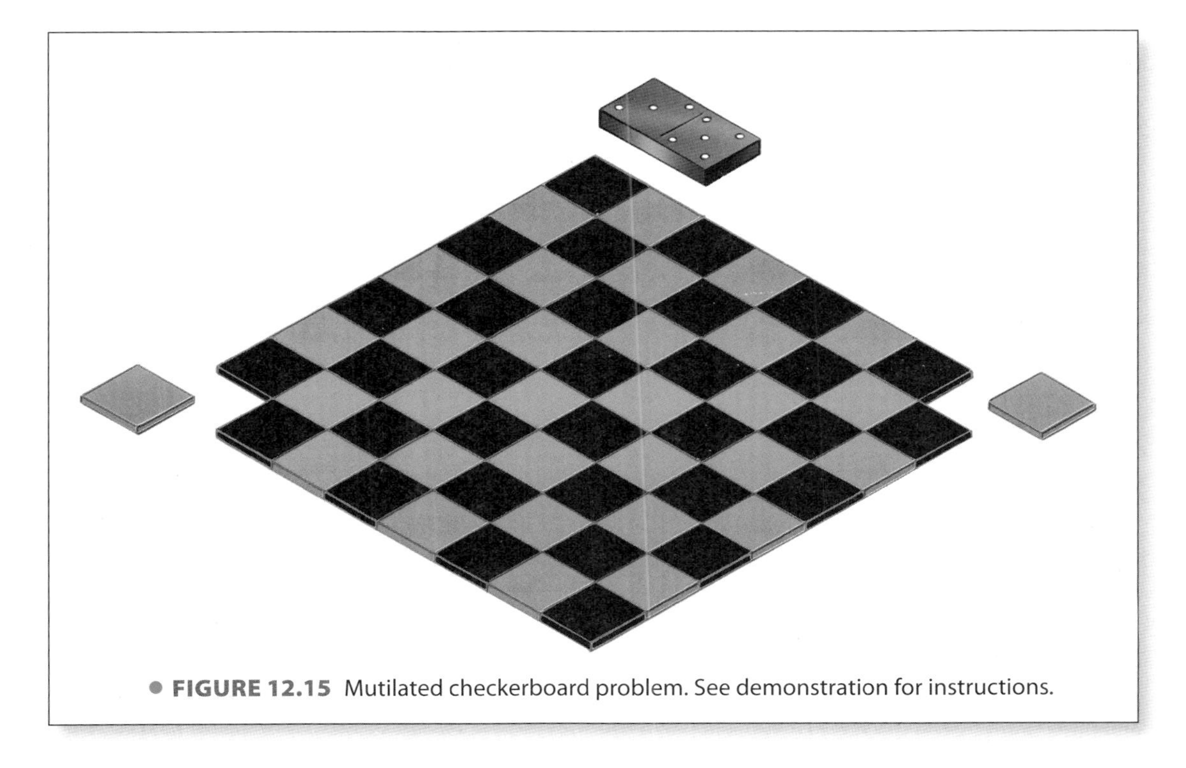

● **FIGURE 12.15** Mutilated checkerboard problem. See demonstration for instructions.

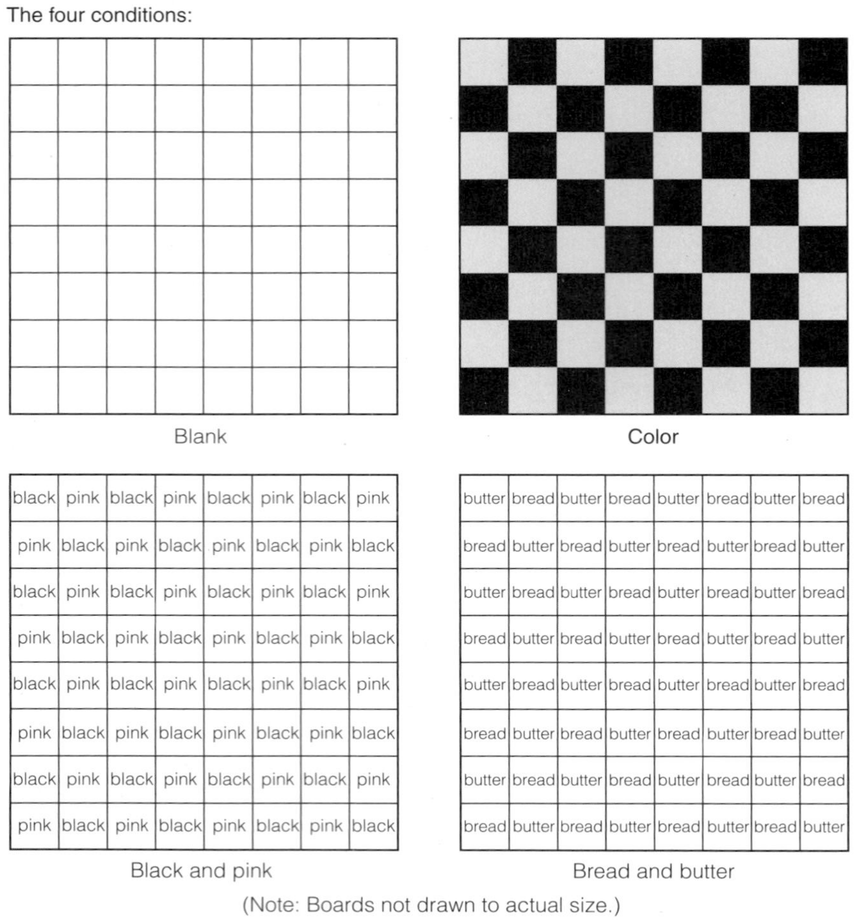

The four conditions:

Blank

Color

black	pink	black	pink	black	pink	black	pink
pink	black	pink	black	pink	black	pink	black
black	pink	black	pink	black	pink	black	pink
pink	black	pink	black	pink	black	pink	black
black	pink	black	pink	black	pink	black	pink
pink	black	pink	black	pink	black	pink	black
black	pink	black	pink	black	pink	black	pink
pink	black	pink	black	pink	black	pink	black

Black and pink

butter	bread	butter	bread	butter	bread	butter	bread
bread	butter	bread	butter	bread	butter	bread	butter
butter	bread	butter	bread	butter	bread	butter	bread
bread	butter	bread	butter	bread	butter	bread	butter
butter	bread	butter	bread	butter	bread	butter	bread
bread	butter	bread	butter	bread	butter	bread	butter
butter	bread	butter	bread	butter	bread	butter	bread
bread	butter	bread	butter	bread	butter	bread	butter

Bread and butter

(Note: Boards not drawn to actual size.)

● **FIGURE 12.16** Conditions in Kaplan and Simon's (1990) study of the mutilated checkerboard problem. (Source: C. A. Kaplan & H.A. Simon, "In Search of Insight," *Cognitive Psychology, 22,* 374–419, Figure 2. Copyright © 1990 Elsevier Ltd. Reproduced with permission.)

adjoining squares, found the problem to be easier to solve. The bread-and-butter condition emphasized the difference the most, because bread and butter are very different but are also associated with each other. The blank board had no information about the difference, because all squares were the same.

Participants in the bread-and-butter group solved the problem twice as fast as those in the blank group and required fewer hints, which the experimenter provided when participants appeared to be at a "dead end." The bread-and-butter group required an average of 1 hint, and the blank group required an average of 3.14 hints. The performance of the color and the black-and-pink groups fell between these two. This shows that solving a problem becomes easier when information is provided that helps point people toward the correct representation of the problem.

To achieve a better understanding of participants' thought processes as they were solving the problem, Kaplan and Simon used a technique introduced by Simon called the **think-aloud protocol.**

METHOD Think-Aloud Protocol

In the think-aloud protocol procedure, participants are asked to say out loud what they are thinking while doing a problem. They are instructed not to describe what they are doing, but to verbalize new thoughts as they occur. One goal of a think-aloud protocol is to determine what information the person is attending to while solving a problem. The following is an example of the instructions given to a participant:

> In this experiment we are interested in what you say to yourself as you perform some tasks that we give you. In order to do this we will ask you to talk aloud as you work on the problems. What I mean by talk aloud is that I want you to say out loud everything that you say to yourself silently. Just act as if you are alone in the room speaking to yourself. If you are silent for any length of time, I will remind you to keep talking aloud. . . . Any questions? Please talk aloud while you solve the following problem. (Ericsson & Simon, 1993)

Here is an example of the verbalizations from Kaplan and Simon's experiment. This participant was in the bread-and-butter condition.

Participant: Just by trial and error I can only find 31 places. . . . I dunno, maybe someone else would have counted the spaces and just said that you could fit 31, but if you try it out on the paper, you can only fit 30. (Pause)

Experimenter: Keep trying.

Participant: Maybe it has to do with the words on the page? I haven't tried anything with that. Maybe that's it. OK, dominos, umm, the dominos can only fit . . . alright, the dominos can fit over two squares, and no matter which way you put it because it cannot go diagonally, it has to fit over a butter and a bread. And because you crossed out two breads, it has to leave two butters left over so it doesn't . . . only 30, so it won't fit. Is that the answer?

Notice that the person was stuck at first, and then suddenly got the answer after realizing that the words *bread* and *butter* were important. By recording people's thought processes as they are solving the problem, the think-aloud protocol reveals a shift in how the person perceived elements of the problem. This is very similar to the Gestalt psychologists' idea of restructuring. For example, remember the circle problem in Figure 12.2. The key to solving that problem was realizing that the line x was the same length as the radius of the circle. Similarly, the key to solving the mutilated checkerboard problem is realizing that adjoining squares are paired, because a domino always covers two different-colored squares in a normal checkerboard. Thus, in Gestalt terms, we could say that the person creates a representation of the problem that makes it easier to solve.

Kaplan and Simon used two different colors to help their participants realize that pairing of adjacent squares is important. But this has also been achieved in another way—by telling the following story, which has parallels to the checkerboard problem.

The Russian Marriage Problem

In a small Russian village, there were 32 bachelors and 32 unmarried women. Through tireless efforts, the village matchmaker succeeded in arranging 32 highly satisfactory marriages. The village was proud and happy. Then one drunken night, two bachelors, in a test of strength, stuffed each other with pirogies and died. Can the matchmaker, through some quick arrangements, come up with 31 heterosexual marriages among the 62 survivors? (adapted from Hayes, 1978, p. 180)

The answer to this problem is obvious. Losing two males makes it impossible to arrange 31 heterosexual marriages. Of course, this is exactly the situation in the mutilated checkerboard problem, except instead of males and females being paired up, light and dark squares are. People who read this story are usually able to solve the mutilated checkerboard problem if they realize the connection between the couples in the story and the alternating squares on the checkerboard. This process of noticing connections between similar problems and applying the solution for one problem to other problems is called the method of analogy. In the next section we will look more closely at how analogy has been used in problem solving.

TEST YOURSELF 12.1

1. What is the psychological definition of a problem? Distinguish between well-defined and ill-defined problems.
2. What is the basic principle behind the Gestalt approach to problem solving? Describe how the following problems illustrate this principle, and also what else these problems demonstrate about problem solving: the circle (radius) problem; the candle problem; the two-string problem; the water-jug problem.
3. What is insight, and what is the evidence that insight does, in fact, occur as people are solving a problem?
4. Describe Newell and Simon's approach to problem solving, in which "search" plays a central role. How does means-end analysis as applied to the Tower of Hanoi problem illustrate this approach?
5. How do the acrobat problem and Kaplan and Simon's mutilated checkerboard experiment illustrate that the way a problem is stated can affect a person's ability to solve the problem? What are the implications of this research for Newell and Simon's "problem space" approach?

Using Analogies to Solve Problems

A person is faced with a problem and wonders how to proceed. Questions such as "What move should I make?" or "How should I begin thinking about this problem?" arise. One tactic that is sometimes helpful is to consider whether another problem that the person has solved before is similar to the new problem, and ask "Can I apply the same methods to solving this problem?" This technique of using the solution to a similar problem to guide solution of a new problem is called **analogical problem solving**.

Using the Russian marriage problem to help solve the mutilated checkerboard problem is an example of an effective use of analogy to solve a problem. Research on analogical problem solving has considered some of the conditions in which using analogies to solve problems is effective.

ANALOGICAL TRANSFER

The starting point for much of the research on analogical problem solving has been to first determine how well people can transfer their experience from solving one problem to solving another, similar problem. This transfer from one problem to another is called **analogical transfer**. To study analogical transfer, participants who are trying to solve a **target problem** are presented with a problem or a story, called the **source problem** or **source story**, that shares some similarities with the target problem and that illustrates a way to solve the target problem.

The mutilated checkerboard problem described in the last section provides an example of analogical transfer. The checkerboard problem is the target problem, and the Russian marriage problem is the source problem. In this example, evidence that analogical transfer occurs is provided when presentation of the Russian marriage problem enhances the ability to solve the mutilated checkerboard problem. In this example, analogical transfer is good, because participants readily see that the principle governing the solution of the Russian marriage problem is similar to the principle that needs to be applied to solve the checkerboard problem. However, as we will now see, good analogical transfer does not always occur.

ANALOGICAL PROBLEM SOLVING AND THE DUNCKER RADIATION PROBLEM

A problem that has been widely used in research on analogical problem solving is Karl Duncker's **radiation problem**.

DEMONSTRATION Duncker's Radiation Problem

Suppose you are a doctor faced with a patient who has a malignant tumor in his stomach. It is impossible to operate on the patient, but unless the tumor is destroyed the patient will die. There is a kind of ray that can be used to destroy the tumor. If the ray reaches the tumor at a sufficiently high intensity, the tumor will be destroyed. Unfortunately, at this intensity the healthy tissue that the ray passes through on the way to the tumor will also be destroyed. At lower intensities the ray is harmless to healthy tissue, but it will not affect the tumor either. What type of procedure might be used to destroy the tumor and at the same time avoid destroying the healthy tissue (Gick & Holyoak, 1980)?

If after thinking about this problem for a while, you haven't come up with a suitable answer, you are not alone. When Duncker (1945) originally posed this problem, most of his participants could not solve it, and Mary Gick and Keith Holyoak (1980,

1983) found that only 10 percent of their participants arrived at the correct solution, shown in ● Figure 12.17a (on page 342). The solution is to bombard the tumor with a number of low-intensity rays from different directions, which destroys the tumor without damaging the tissue the rays are passing through. The solution to this problem is actually the procedure used in modern radiosurgery, in which a tumor is bombarded with 201 gamma ray beams that intersect at the tumor (Tarkan, 2003; Figure 12.17b).

Notice how the radiation problem and its solution fit with the Gestalt idea of representation and restructuring. The initial representation of the problem is a single ray that destroys the tumor but also destroys healthy tissue. The restructured solution involves dividing the single ray into many smaller rays.

After confirming Duncker's finding that the radiation problem is extremely difficult, Gick and Holyoak (1980, 1983) had another group of participants read and memorize "The Fortress" story below, giving them the impression that the purpose was to test their memory for the story.

Fortress Story

A small country was ruled from a strong fortress by a dictator. The fortress was situated in the middle of the country, surrounded by farms and villages. Many roads led to the fortress through the countryside. A rebel general vowed to capture the fortress. The general knew that an attack by his entire army would capture the fortress. He gathered his army at the head of one of the roads, ready to launch a full-scale direct attack. However, the general then learned that the dictator had planted mines on each of the roads. The mines were set so that small bodies of men could pass over them safely, since the dictator needed to move his troops and workers to and from the fortress. However, any large force would detonate the mines. Not only would this blow up the road, but it would also destroy many neighboring villages. It therefore seemed impossible to capture the fortress.

However, the general devised a simple plan. He divided his army into small groups and dispatched each group to the head of a different road. When all was ready he gave the signal and each group marched down a different road. Each group continued down its road to the fortress so that the entire army arrived together at the fortress at the same time. In this way, the general captured the fortress and overthrew the dictator. (See Figure 12.17c.)

The fortress story is analogous to the radiation problem because the dictator's fortress corresponds to the tumor and the small groups of soldiers sent down different roads correspond to the low-intensity rays that can be directed at the tumor. After Gick and Holyoak's participants read the story, they were told to begin work on the radiation problem. Thirty percent of the people in this group were able to solve the radiation problem, an improvement over the 10 percent who solved the problem when it was presented alone. However, what is significant about this experiment is that 70 percent of the participants were still unable to solve the problem, even after reading an analogous source story. This result highlights one of the major findings of research on using analogies as an aid to problem solving: Even when exposed to analogous source problems, most people do not make the connection between the source problem and the target problem.

However, when Gick and Holyoak's participants were told to think about the story they had read, their success rate more than doubled, to 75 percent. Since no new information was given about the story, apparently the information needed to recognize the analogy was available in people's memories but had simply not been retrieved (Gentner & Colhoun, in press). These results led Gick and Holyoak to propose that the process of analogical problem solving involves the following three steps:

1. *Noticing* that there is an analogous relationship between the source story and the target problem. This step is obviously crucial in order for analogical problem solving to work. However, as we have seen, most participants need some prompting before they notice the connection between the source problem and the target problem. Gick and Holyoak consider this *noticing* step to be the most

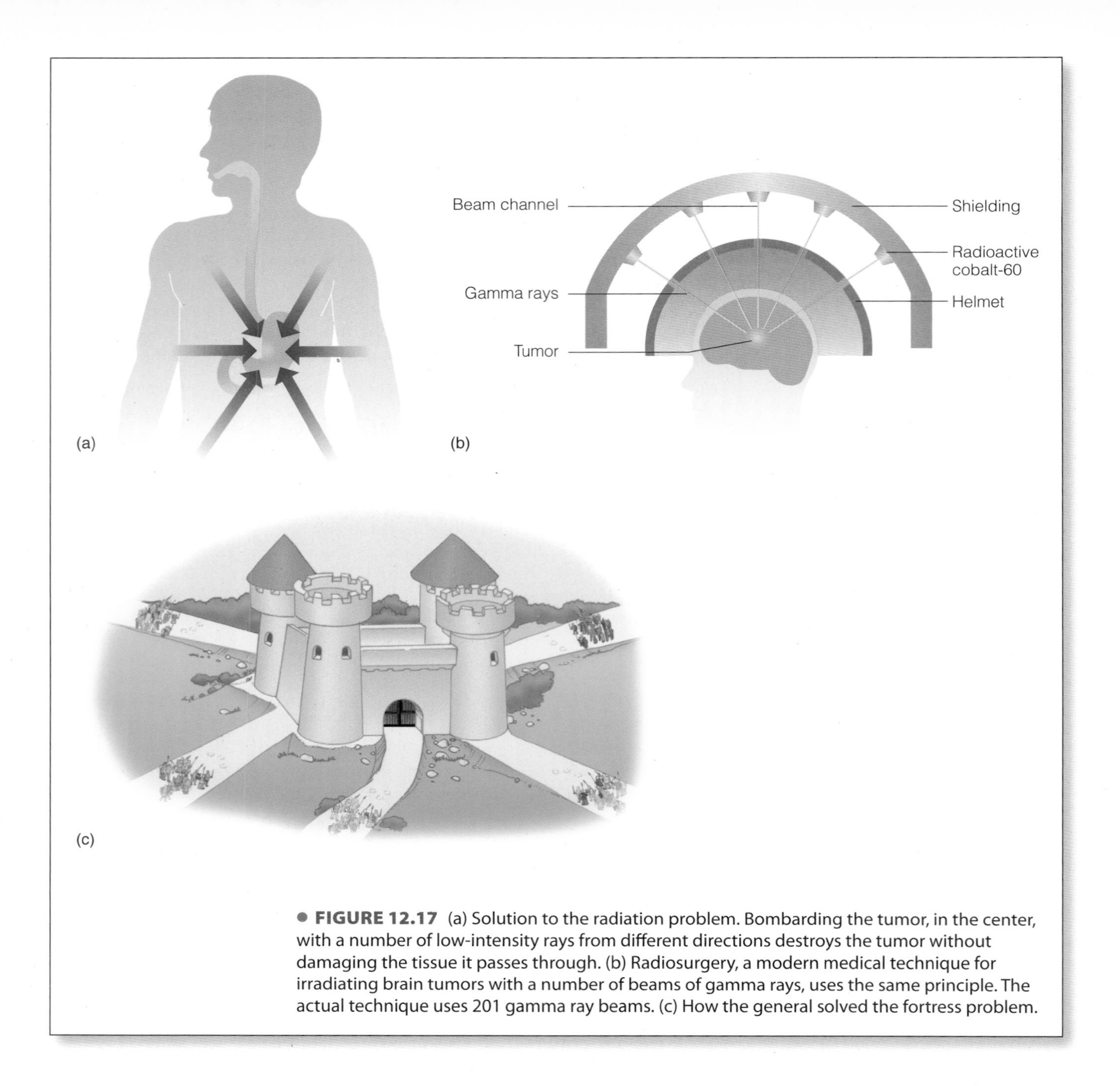

• **FIGURE 12.17** (a) Solution to the radiation problem. Bombarding the tumor, in the center, with a number of low-intensity rays from different directions destroys the tumor without damaging the tissue it passes through. (b) Radiosurgery, a modern medical technique for irradiating brain tumors with a number of beams of gamma rays, uses the same principle. The actual technique uses 201 gamma ray beams. (c) How the general solved the fortress problem.

difficult of the three steps to achieve. A number of experiments have shown that the most effective source stories are those that are most similar to the target problem (Catrambone & Holyoak, 1989; Holyoak & Thagard, 1995). This similarity could make it easier to notice the analogical relationship between the source story and the target problem, and could also help achieve the next step—mapping.

2. *Mapping* the correspondence between the source story and the target problem. To use the story to solve the problem, the participant has to map corresponding parts of the story onto the test problem by connecting elements in one story (for example, the dictator's fortress) to elements in the target problem (the tumor).
3. *Applying* the mapping to generate a parallel solution to the target problem. This would involve, for example, generalizing from the many small groups of soldiers approaching the fortress from different directions to the idea of using many weaker rays that would approach the tumor from different directions.

Once they determined that analogies can help with problem solving, but that hints are required to help participants notice the presence of the source problem, Gick and Holyoak (1983) proceeded to look for factors that help facilitate the *noticing* and *mapping* steps. One thing that makes noticing difficult is that people often focus on **surface features**, specific elements that make up the problem, such as the rays and the tumor. Surface features of the source problem and the target problem can be very different. For example, there is a big difference between a tumor and a fortress, and between rays and marching soldiers.

To test the idea that making the surface features more similar might help participants notice the relationship between the source story and the target story, Holyoak and Kyunghee Koh (1987) created a problem that had surface features similar to the radiation problem.

Effect of Making Surface Features More Similar The lightbulb problem is a problem with surface features similar to the radiation problem. The following is a shortened version of this problem.

Lightbulb Problem

In a physics lab at a major university, a very expensive lightbulb, which would emit precisely controlled quantities of light, was being used in some experiments. One morning Ruth, the research assistant, came into the lab and found that the lightbulb no longer worked. She noticed that the filament inside the bulb had broken into two parts. The surrounding glass bulb was completely sealed, so there was no way to open it. Ruth knew that the lightbulb could be repaired if a brief, high-intensity laser beam could be used to fuse the two parts of the filament into one.

However, a high-intensity laser beam would also break the fragile glass surrounding the filament. At lower intensities the laser would not break the glass, but neither would it fuse the filament. What type of procedure might be used to fuse the filament with the laser and at the same time avoid breaking the glass? (adapted from Holyoak & Koh, 1987)

Holyoak and Koh (1987) used the radiation problem as the source problem and the lightbulb problem as the target problem. Participants in one group were taught about the radiation problem and its solution in an introductory psychology class, just prior to being given the lightbulb problem. Participants in the control group did not know about the radiation problem. The result was that 81 percent of participants who knew about the radiation problem solved the lightbulb problem, but only 10 percent of the participants in the control group solved it. Holyoak and Koh hypothesized that this excellent analogical transfer from the radiation problem to the lightbulb problem occurred because of the high surface similarity between rays (radiation problem) and lasers (lightbulb problem).

Effect of Varying the Structural Features Having determined that similar surface features enhanced analogical transfer, Holyoak and Koh did another experiment in which they investigated the effect of varying the structural features of the problem. **Structural features** are the underlying principle that governs the solution. In the lightbulb and radiation problems the structural features are similar: (a) weak laser beams are used to avoid breaking the glass bulb (lightbulb problem); (b) weak rays are used to avoid damaging healthy tissue (radiation problem).

Holyoak and Koh kept surface features constant by using the lightbulb problem as the source problem and the radiation problem as the target problem, and varied structure by presenting two versions of the lightbulb problem. Both versions began with the story about the broken filament surrounded by glass, and the information that the filament could be repaired by fusing it with a high-intensity laser beam. But the problem that needed to be solved in order to fix the filament was different in the two versions. The first version, called the *fragile-glass version*, was essentially the same as the original lightbulb problem. In this version, the structural features of the lightbulb and radiation problems were similar.

TABLE 12.2 Fragile-Glass Condition: Structural Features Similar

Problems	Surface Features	Structural Features
Source problem: Fragile-glass version of lightbulb problem: Glass will break if laser is too strong.	Laser beam and filament	Need high-intensity radiation to fix filament without damaging surrounding glass with a high intensity beam.
Target problem: Radiation problem	Rays and tumor	Need high-intensity radiation to fix tumor without damaging surrounding body with a high-intensity beam.

FRAGILE-GLASS VERSION
(Source and target problems have similar structural features)

Problem: A high-intensity laser beam would break the fragile glass surrounding the filament. At lower intensities the laser would not break the glass, but neither would it fuse the filament.

Ruth's solution: Ruth placed several lasers in a circle around the lightbulb and administered low-intensity laser beams from several directions all at once. The beams all converged on the filament, where their combined effect was enough to fuse it. Because each spot on the surrounding glass received only a low-intensity beam from each laser, the glass was left intact.

The structural features of this problem are similar to the structural features of the radiation problem, as indicated in the far right column of Table 12.2. Sixty-nine percent of the participants who read this solution were able to solve the radiation problem.

In the second version of the problem, called the *insufficient-intensity version*, the structural features of the lightbulb and radiation problems are different.

INSUFFICIENT-INTENSITY VERSION
(Source and target problems have different structural features)

Problem: The laser generated only low-intensity beams that were not strong enough to fuse the filament. A much more intense laser beam was needed.

Ruth's solution: Ruth placed several lasers in a circle around the lightbulb and administered low-intensity laser beams from several directions all at once. The beams all converged on the filament, where their combined effect was enough to fuse it.

The structural features of this problem are different from the structural features of the radiation problem, as indicated in the far right column of Table 12.3. Only 33 percent of the participants who read this solution were able to solve the radiation problem. The conclusion from comparing the results from these two versions of the lightbulb problem is that analogical transfer is better when the structural features of the source and target problems are more similar.

All of these experiments taken together show that transfer is aided by making surface features more similar and by making structural features more similar. But the fact remains that it is often difficult for people to apply analogies to solving problems, especially in situations in which surface and structural similarities are not as obvious as in the lightbulb and radiation problems. One way to help people notice structural similarities is through a training procedure called *analogical encoding*.

ANALOGICAL ENCODING

Dedre Gentner and Susan Goldin-Meadow (2003) have shown that it is possible to get people to discover similar structural features by using a technique called **analogical encoding**, in which participants compare two cases that illustrate a principle. The idea behind analogical encoding is that when learners compare cases, they become more likely to see the underlying structure.

TABLE 12.3 Insufficient-Intensity Version: Structural Features Different

Problems	Surface Features	Structural Features
Source problem: Insufficient-intensity version of lightbulb problem: Laser beams are too weak to fuse filament.	Laser beam and filament	Need high-intensity radiation, but intensity of individual laser is too low.
Target problem: Radiation problem	Rays and tumor	Need high-intensity radiation to fix tumor without damaging surrounding body with a high-intensity beam.

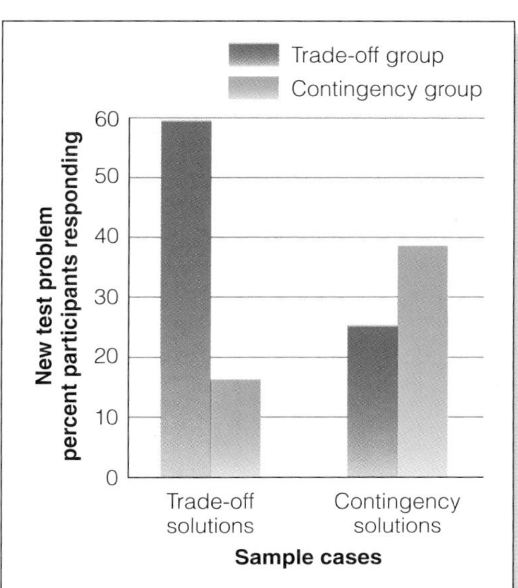

● **FIGURE 12.18** Results of Gentner and Goldin-Meadow's (2003) study of negotiating strategies. In the test case, participants who had compared trade-off examples were more apt to find trade-off solutions, whereas those who had compared contingency examples were more apt to find contingency solutions. (Source: Based on D. Gentner & S. Goldin-Meadow, Eds., *Language in Mind*, Cambridge, MA: MIT Press, 2003.)

Gentner and Goldin-Meadow's experiment involved a problem in negotiation. In the first part of the experiment, participants were taught about the negotiation strategies of *trade-off* and *contingency*. The strategy of trade-off is illustrated by a story about two sisters quarreling over an orange. Eventually they decide to compromise by cutting the orange in half. However, later they realize that one wanted just the juice and the other wanted just the peel, so another solution would be for one sister to receive the juice, and the other the peel. The trade-off between juice and peel is a better solution than the compromise solution because both sisters get what they want. (This story is attributed to management consultant Mary Parker Follet in Gentner & Goldin-Meadow, 2003.)

The strategy of *contingency* is illustrated by a situation in which an author wants 18 percent royalties, but the publisher wants to pay only 12 percent. The compromise solution would be halfway between, at 15 percent. The contingent solution would be to tie royalties to sales, so that the rate would be 12 percent if sales are low, but would increase if sales rise to higher levels.

After being familiarized with these negotiating strategies, one group of participants received two sample cases, both of which described trade-off solutions. The participants' task was to compare these two cases to arrive at a successful negotiation. Another group did the same thing, but their examples involved the contingency principle. Then both groups were given a new case, which potentially could be solved by either negotiating principle.

The results of this experiment are shown in ● Figure 12.18. When presented with the new test problem, participants tended to use the negotiating strategy that was emphasized in the sample cases they had read previously. Gentner concluded from these results that having people compare source stories is an effective way to get them to pay attention to structural features that enhance their ability to solve other problems.

ANALOGY IN THE REAL WORLD

So far, our examples of analogy problems have involved laboratory research. But what about the use of analogy in the real world? Many real-world examples of analogical problem solving illustrate what Kevin Dunbar (2001) has called the **analogical paradox**: Participants in psychological experiments tend to focus on surface features in analogy problems, whereas people in the real world frequently use deeper, more structural features. Dunbar reached this conclusion by using a technique called in vivo research.

METHOD In Vivo Problem-Solving Research

In vivo problem-solving research involves observing people to determine how they solve problems in real-world situations. This method has been used to study the use of analogy in a number of different settings, including laboratory meetings of a university research group and brainstorming sessions in which the goal was to develop a new product. Discussions recorded during these meetings have been analyzed for statements indicating that analogy is being used to help solve a problem. The advantage of the in vivo approach is that it captures thinking in naturalistic settings. A disadvantage is that it is time-consuming, and, as with most observational research, it is difficult to isolate and control specific variables.

When Dunbar and coworkers (Dunbar, 1999; Dunbar & Blanchette, 2001) videotaped molecular biologists and immunologists during their lab meetings, they found that researchers used analogies from 3 to 15 times in a 1-hour laboratory meeting. An example of an analogy from these laboratory meetings is the statement "If *E. coli* works like this, maybe your gene is doing the same thing." Similarly, when Bo Christensen and Christian Schunn (2007) recorded meetings of design engineers who were creating new plastic products for medical applications, they found that the engineers proposed an analogy about every 5 minutes. Thus, analogies play an important role both in solving scientific problems and in designing new products. When we discuss creativity later in this chapter, we will describe a famous example of how analogical thinking led to the development of a well-known product.

Although we understand some of the mental processes that occur as a person works toward the solution to a problem, what actually happens is still somewhat mysterious. We do know, however, that one factor that can sometimes make problem solving easier is practice or training. Some people can become very good at solving certain kinds of problems because they become experts in an area. We will now consider what it means to be an expert and how being an expert affects problem solving.

How Experts Solve Problems

Experts are people who, by devoting a large amount of time to learning about a field and practicing and applying that learning, have become acknowledged as being extremely knowledgeable or skilled in the particular field. For example, by spending 10,000–20,000 hours playing and studying chess, some chess players have reached the rank of grand master (Chase & Simon, 1973a, 1973b). Not surprisingly, experts tend to be better than nonexperts at solving problems in their field. Research on the nature of expertise has focused on determining differences between the way experts and nonexperts go about solving problems.

DIFFERENCES BETWEEN HOW EXPERTS AND NOVICES SOLVE PROBLEMS

Experts in a particular field usually solve problems faster with a higher success rate than do novices (people who are beginners or who have not had the extensive training of experts; Chi et al., 1982; Larkin et al., 1980). But what is behind this faster speed and greater success? Are experts smarter than novices? Are they better at reasoning in general? Do they approach problems in a different way? Cognitive psychologists have answered these questions by comparing the performance and methods of experts and novices, and have reached the following conclusions.

Experts Possess More Knowledge About Their Fields In Chapter 5 we discussed Chase and Simon's (1973a, 1973b) research on how well chess masters and novices can reproduce positions on a chessboard that they have seen briefly. The results showed that experts excelled at this task when the chess pieces were arranged in actual game positions, but were no better than novices when the pieces were arranged randomly (see Figure 5.9). The reason for the experts' superior performance for actual positions is that the chess masters were able to recognize these specific arrangements of pieces. A chess master has about 50,000 patterns in his or her memory, compared to 1,000 patterns for a good player and few or none for a poor or beginning player (Bedard & Chi, 1992). But what is important for the purposes of problem solving is not just that the expert's mind contains lots of knowledge, but that this knowledge is organized so it can be accessed when needed to work on a problem.

Experts' Knowledge Is Organized Differently From Novices' The difference in organization between experts and novices is illustrated by an experiment by Michelene Chi and coworkers (1982; also see Chi et al., 1981). They presented 24 physics problems to a group of experts (physics professors) and a group of novices (students with one semester of physics) and asked them to sort the problems into groups based on their similarities. • Figure 12.19 shows diagrams of problems that were grouped together by an expert and by a novice. We don't need a statement of the actual problems to see from the diagrams that the novice sorted the problems based on surface characteristics such as how similar the objects in the problem were. Thus, two problems that included inclined planes were grouped together, even though the physical principles involved in the problems were quite different.

The expert, in contrast, sorted problems based on structural features, such as general principles of physics. The expert perceived two problems as similar because they both involved the principle of conservation of energy, even though the diagrams indicate that one problem involved a spring and another an inclined plane. Thus, novices categorized problems based on their *surface features* (what the objects looked like) and the experts categorized them based on their *deep structure* (the underlying principles involved). Experts' ability to organize knowledge has been found to be important not only for chess masters and physics professors, but for experts in many other fields as well (Egan & Schwartz, 1979; Reitman, 1976).

Experts Spend More Time Analyzing Problems Experts often get off to what appears to be a slow start on a problem, because they spend time trying to understand the problem rather than immediately trying to solve it (Lesgold, 1988). Although this may slow them down at the beginning, this strategy usually pays off in a more effective approach to the problem.

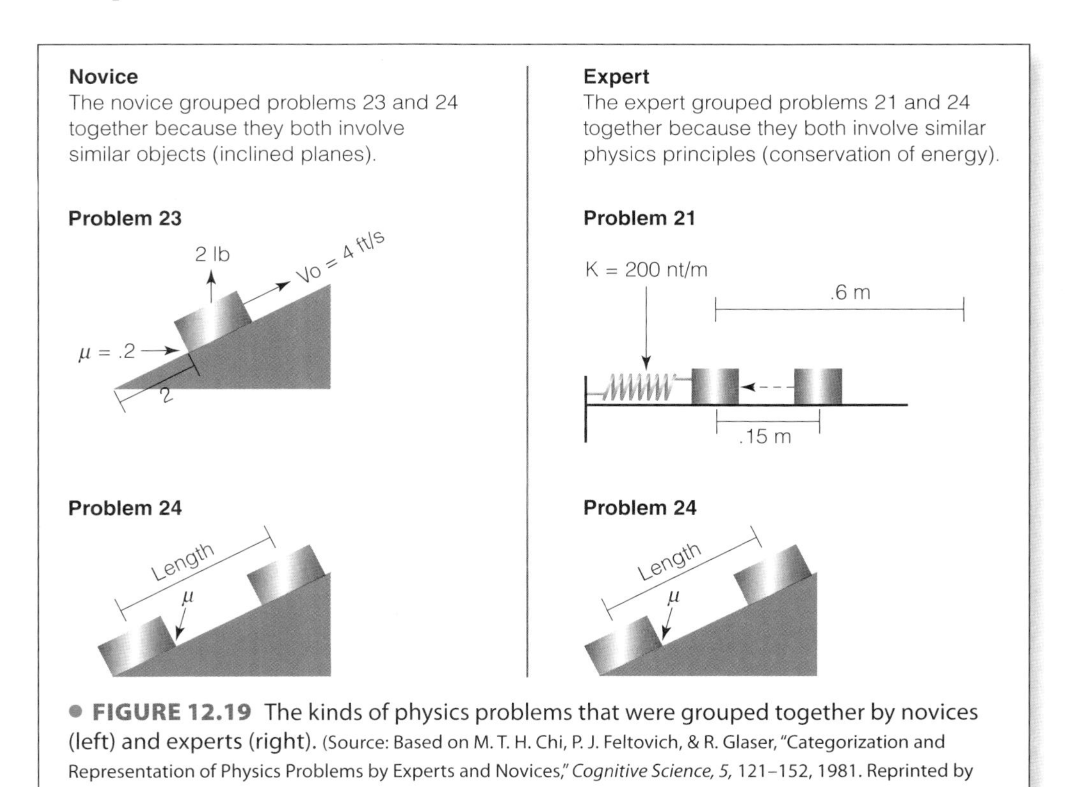

• **FIGURE 12.19** The kinds of physics problems that were grouped together by novices (left) and experts (right). (Source: Based on M. T. H. Chi, P. J. Feltovich, & R. Glaser, "Categorization and Representation of Physics Problems by Experts and Novices," *Cognitive Science, 5,* 121–152, 1981. Reprinted by permission of Taylor & Francis Group.)

EXPERTISE IS ONLY AN ADVANTAGE IN THE EXPERT'S SPECIALTY

Although there are many differences between experts and novices, it appears that these differences hold only when problems are within an expert's field. When James Voss and coworkers (1983) posed a real-world problem involving Russian agriculture to expert political scientists, expert chemists, and novice political scientists, they found that the expert political scientists performed best and that the expert chemists performed as poorly as the novice political scientists. In general, experts are experts only within their own field and perform like anyone else outside of their field (Bedard & Chi, 1992). This makes sense when we remember that the superior performance of experts occurs largely because they possess a larger and better organized store of knowledge about their specific field.

Before leaving our discussion of expertise, we should note that being an expert is not always an advantage. One disadvantage is that knowing about the established facts and theories in a field may make experts less open to new ways of looking at problems. This may be why younger and less experienced scientists in a field are often the ones responsible for revolutionary discoveries (Kuhn, 1970; Simonton, 1984). Thus, it has been suggested that being an expert may be a disadvantage when confronting a problem that requires flexible thinking—a problem whose solution may involve rejecting the usual procedures in favor of other procedures that might not normally be used (Frensch & Sternberg, 1989).

Creative Problem Solving

There's a story about a physics student who, in answer to the exam question "Describe how the height of a building can be measured using a barometer," wrote "Attach the barometer to a string and lower it from the top of the building. The length of string needed to lower the barometer to the ground indicates the height of the building." The professor was looking for an answer that involved measuring barometric pressure on the ground and on top of the building, using principles learned in class. He therefore gave the student a zero for his answer.

The student protested the grade, so the case was given to another professor, who asked the student to provide an answer that would demonstrate his knowledge of physics. The student's answer was that the barometer could be dropped from the roof measuring how long it took to hit the ground. Using a formula involving the gravitational constant it would be possible to determine how far the barometer fell. With further prodding from the appeals professor the student also suggested another solution: Put the barometer in the sun and measure the length of its shadow and the length of the building's shadow. The height of the building could be determined using proportions.

Upon hearing these answers, both of which could result in correct solutions, the appeals professor asked the student whether he knew the answer the professor was looking for, which involved the principle of barometric pressure. The student replied that he did, but was tired of just repeating back information to get a good grade (Lubart & Mouchiroud, 2003).

There are a number of points to this story, one of which is that sometimes being too creative can get you into trouble. But the main point is that this student's answers to the professor's question, although perhaps not what the professor was looking for, surely qualified as being creative. The definition of creativity is hard to pin down, but most people would agree that it involves innovative thinking, generating novel ideas, or making new connections between existing ideas to create something new (Csikszentmihalyi, 1996; Ward et al., 1995, 1997).

Creativity is often associated with **divergent thinking**—thinking that is open-ended, involving a large number of potential "solutions" and no "correct" answer (although some proposals might work better than others; see Guilford, 1956; Ward et al., 1997).

Divergent thinking can be contrasted with **convergent thinking**, which is thinking that works toward finding a solution to a specific problem that usually has a correct answer. In this case, thinking *converges* on the correct answer. Divergent thinking is most closely associated with ill-defined problems and convergent thinking with well-defined problems (see page 326).

Although creativity is highly valued in our society and has been responsible for many inventions and scientific discoveries, we have only a limited understanding of the processes involved in creativity. We do know, however, that some of the principles we have discussed with regard to problem solving in general also operate during the creative process.

In our earlier discussion of Gestalt psychologists' research on obstacles to problem solving, we discussed fixation. An example of how fixation almost derailed a promising project occurred when Sony temporarily abandoned work on music CDs in the mid-1970s because the 18 hours of music that could potentially fit on a CD the size of the 12-inch diameter long-playing records in use at the time was not considered commercially viable. Their problem was that they were fixated on the current medium of recorded music, taking as their starting point the LP record. Once they overcame that fixation and realized that CDs could be smaller, they returned to the project and revolutionized the music industry (Ward, 2004).

David Jansson and Steven Smith (1991) studied the effect of fixation on creative design by presenting engineering design students with design problems and telling them to generate as many designs as possible in 45 minutes. One of the problems was to design an inexpensive, spill-proof coffee cup. It was specified that the design could not include a straw or mouthpiece. Half the students were assigned to the "fixation group" and were presented with a sample design like the one in ● Figure 12.20a, which they were told illustrated what *not* to do. Notice that this sample design includes a mouthpiece and straw—two features specifically forbidden by the design specifications. Another group of students, the control group, was given the same task and specification, but did not see a sample design.

The average number of designs per person was approximately the same for the two groups, but the fixation group's designs included many more instances of cups with straws and mouthpieces (Figure 12.20b). Apparently, they were influenced by the sample design, even though they were told not to include straws or mouthpieces. This effect, which Jansson and Smith call **design fixation**, is analogous to the Gestalt psychologists' demonstrations of how fixation can inhibit problem solving (see page 329).

Another carryover from our discussion of problem solving to creativity is the process of analogical thinking. A famous example is the story of George de Mestral, who in 1948 went for a nature hike with his dog and returned home with burrs covering his pants and the dog's fur. To discover why the burrs were clinging so tenaciously, de Mestral inspected the burrs under a microscope. What he saw was many tiny hooklike structures, which led him to design a fabric fastener with many small hooks on one side and soft loops on the other side. In 1955 he patented his design and called it Velcro!

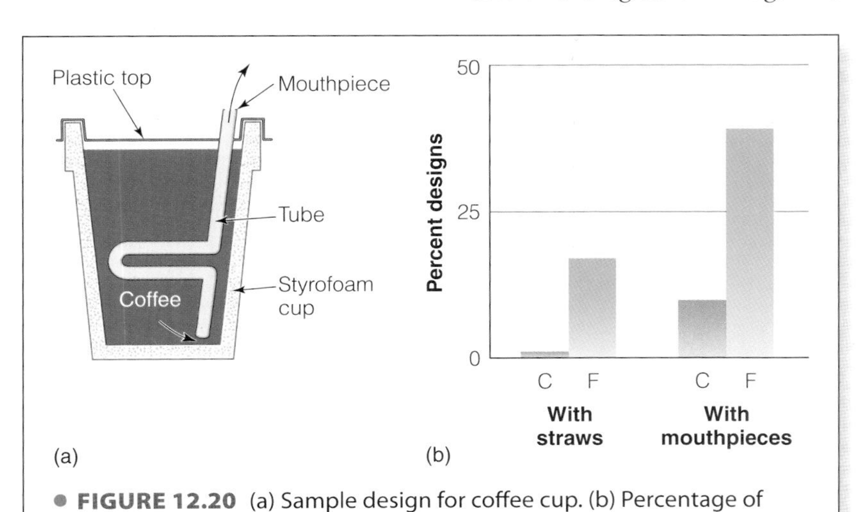

● **FIGURE 12.20** (a) Sample design for coffee cup. (b) Percentage of designs with straws and mouthpieces for the control group (C), which didn't see the sample design, and the fixation group (F), which did. (Source: Based on D. G. Jansson & S. M. Smith, "Design Fixation," *Design Studies, 12*, 3–11, 1991. Reprinted by permission of Elsevier.)

This story illustrates not only how analogy stimulated a new invention but that coming up with the initial idea is often just the beginning of the creative process. It took de Mestral 7 years of trial and error to transform his innovative insight into a marketable product. Creativity therefore involves having unique insights and also being able to follow through to transform that insight into a product—be it a work of art, an idea for a scientific experiment, or a commercially viable invention.

Although de Mestral was a particularly creative individual, you don't have to be a famous inventor

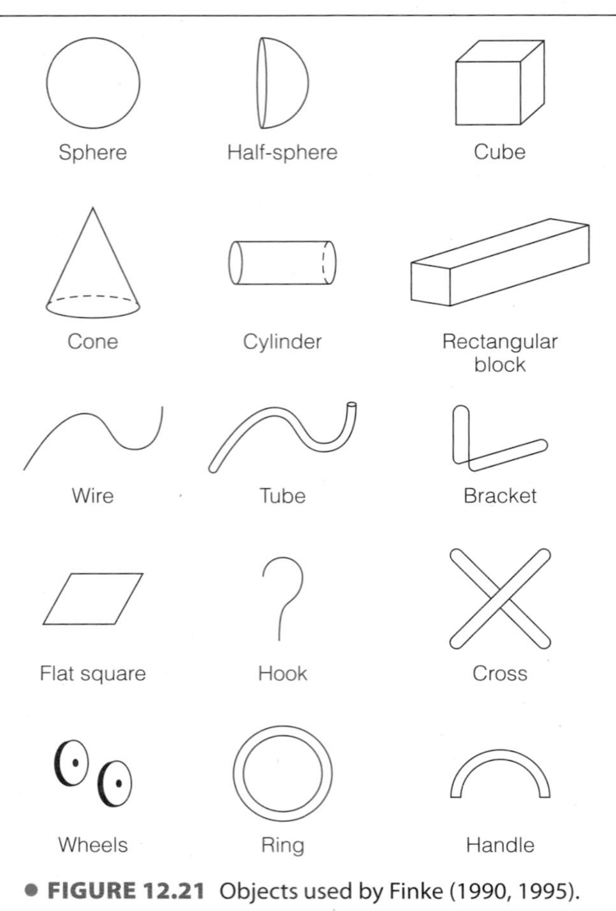

• **FIGURE 12.21** Objects used by Finke (1990, 1995). (Source: R. A. Finke, "Creative Insight and Preinventive Forms," Figure 8.1, in R. J. Sternberg & J. E. Davidson, Eds., *The Nature of Insight*, pp. 255–280, Cambridge, MA: MIT Press, 1995. Copyright © 1995 MIT Press. Reproduced with permission from the MIT Press.)

to be creative. Cognitive psychologist Ronald Finke developed a technique called **creative cognition** to train people to think creatively. The following demonstration illustrates Finke's technique.

DEMONSTRATION Creating an Object

• Figure 12.21 shows 15 object parts and their names. Close your eyes and touch the page three times, in order to randomly pick three of these object parts. After reading these instructions, take 1 minute to construct a new object using these three parts. The object should be interesting-looking and possibly useful, but try to avoid making your object correspond to a familiar object, and don't worry what it might be used for. You can vary the size, position, orientation, and material of the parts, as long as you don't alter the basic shape (except for the wire and the tube, which can be bent). Once you come up with something in your mind, draw a picture of it.

This exercise is patterned after one devised by Ronald Finke (1990, 1995), who randomly selected three of the object parts from Figure 12.21 for his participants. After the participants had created an object, they were provided with the name of one of the object categories from Table 12.4 and were given 1 minute to interpret their object. For example, if the category was tools and utensils, the person had to interpret their form as a screwdriver, a spoon, or some other tool or utensil. To do this for your form, pick a category, and then decide what your object could be used for and describe how it functions. • Figure 12.22 shows how a single form that was constructed from the half-sphere, wire, and handle could be interpreted in terms of each of the eight categories in Table 12.4.

Finke called these "inventions" *preinventive forms* because they are ideas that precede the creation of a finished creative product. Just as it took de Mestral years to develop Velcro after his initial insight, preinventive forms need to be developed further before becoming useful "inventions."

In an experiment in which participants created 360 objects, a panel of judges rated 120 of these objects as being "practical inventions" (the objects received high ratings for "practicality") and rated 65 as "creative inventions" (they received high ratings for both practicality and originality; Finke, 1990, 1995). Remarkably, Finke's participants had received no training or practice, were not preselected for "creativity," and were not even told they were expected to be creative.

TABLE 12.4 Object Categories in Preinventive Form Studies

Category	Examples
1. Furniture	Chairs, tables, lamps
2. Personal items	Jewelry, glasses
3. Scientific instruments	Measuring devices
4. Appliances	Washing machines, toasters
5. Transportation	Cars, boats
6. Tools and utensils	Screwdrivers, spoons
7. Toys and games	Baseball bats, dolls
8. Weapons	Guns, missiles

Adapted from Finke, 1995.

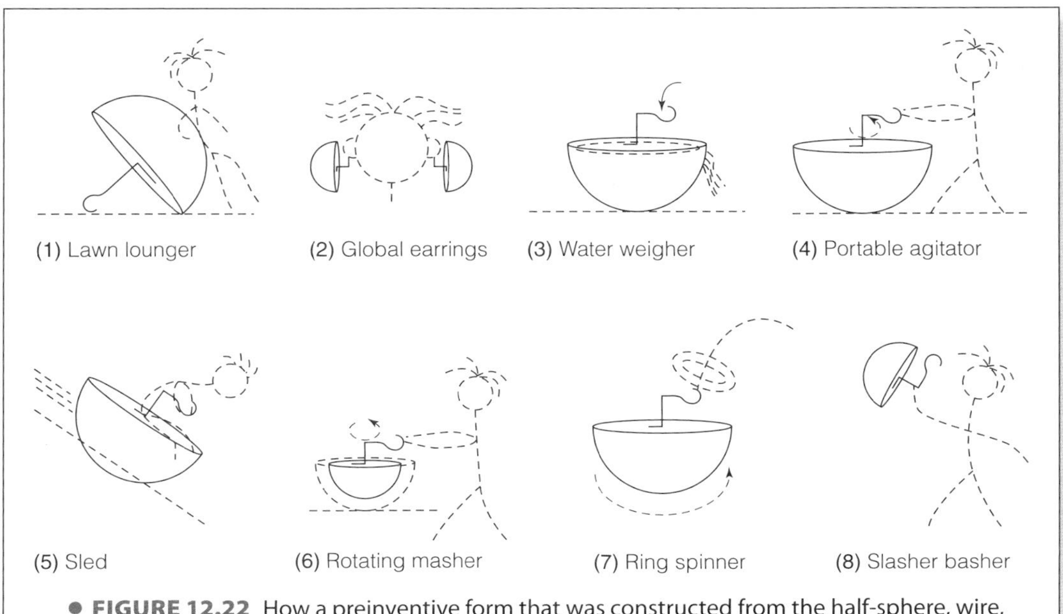

● **FIGURE 12.22** How a preinventive form that was constructed from the half-sphere, wire, and handle can be interpreted in terms of each of the eight categories in Table 12.4. (Source: R. A. Finke, "Creative Insight and Preinventive Forms," Figure 8.6, in R. J. Sternberg and J. E. Davidson, eds., *The Nature of Insight*, pp. 255-280. Copyright © 1995 MIT Press. Reproduced with permission from the MIT Press.)

Finke demonstrated not only that you don't have to be an "inventor" to be creative, but also that many of the processes that occur during creative cognition are similar to the cognitive process from other areas of cognitive psychology. For example, Finke found that people were more likely to come up with creative uses for preinventive objects that they had created themselves than for objects created by other people. This occurred even though participants were instructed not to consider uses for the forms as they were creating them. This result is similar to the generation effect we discussed in Chapter 7—people remember material better when they generate it themselves (page 178). This advantage for self-generated material also occurs for retrieval cues (page 183).

Another relevant cognitive principle is the idea that fixations can inhibit problem solving. Having participants combine objects rapidly and without reference to uses lessens the chance that fixations, caused by prior experience, will inhibit creativity. Although there is certainly something special about creativity, it appears we can understand some aspects of creativity in terms of general cognitive principles.

➔ Something to Consider

Does Large Working Memory Capacity Result in Better Problem Solving? It Depends!

Having high working memory capacity is generally considered to be a good thing. We saw in Chapter 5 that high working memory capacity is associated with higher intelligence and good performance on comprehension tests. (See Something to Consider: The Advantages of Having a More Efficient Working Memory, page 141.) It would therefore seem to follow that people with high working memory capacity should be better at solving problems. It turns out that this is true under some, but not all, conditions.

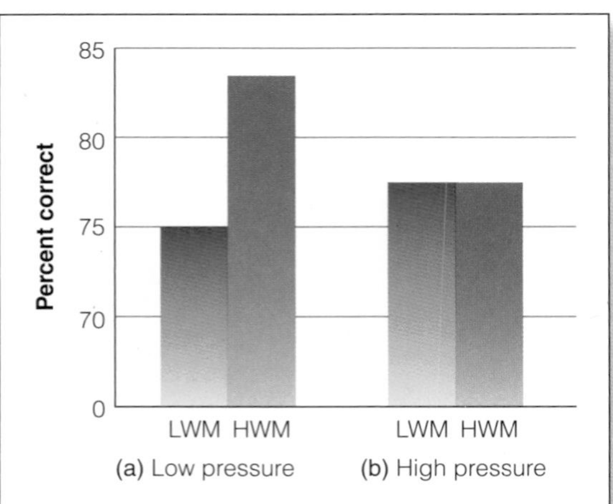

• **FIGURE 12.23** Mathematics problem-solving performance for high working memory and low working memory participants under (a) low pressure and (b) high pressure conditions. High working memory participants performed better under low pressure conditions but lost their advantage under high pressure. (Source: Based on S. L. Beilock & T. H. Carr, "When High-Powered People Fail," *Psychological Science, 16,* 101–105, 2005.)

First, let's consider when it is an advantage to have high working memory capacity. Sian Beilock and Thomas Carr (2005) investigated the relationship between working memory capacity and mathematical problem solving by first measuring participants' working memory capacity (see Method: Reading Span, page 142) to divide them into low working memory (LWM) and high working memory (HWM) groups. Then they presented participants with a modular arithmetic problem. Modular arithmetic problems are stated as follows: 51≡19 (mod 4). One way to solve the problem is by subtracting the second number from the first (51 – 19) and then dividing by the last number (32 divided by 4). The task is to respond "True" if the answer is a whole number (which would be the case in this example) or "False" if there is a remainder.

• Figure 12.23a shows the results for participants who were simply told to try their best on the task. These instructions were worded to create no pressure, so this was called the "low pressure condition." In this condition, HWM participants performed better than the LWM participants.

Figure 12.23b shows the results for participants who were given instructions calculated to create a great deal of pressure to perform well. These instructions indicated that they would receive money for increasing their score above a target level, that they had to perform well in order for another person "on their team" who had already done well to receive money, and that they were being videotaped so math teachers could examine their performance. The net result of these instructions, which created the "high pressure condition," was to increase feelings of pressure and anxiety. It is clear from the results for this condition that the increase in pressure had no effect on the performance of LWM participants but caused a decline in the performance of HWM participants, effectively eliminating the advantage they had in the low pressure condition.

Why would HWM participants "choke under pressure," while LWM participants didn't? The answer appears to be related to the fact that people with high working memory generally favor complex strategies for solving problems. When pressure is low, HWM participants are therefore more likely to work through each problem using the subtraction and division procedure described above. Beilock calls this the "algorithm" procedure because it is a step-by-step procedure that is guaranteed to result in the correct answer, if applied correctly (see page 62 for more on algorithms). In contrast, LWM participants are more likely to use a simpler "shortcut strategy" such as a rule like "Both numbers are even, so the result of subtraction would be even and probably divisible by the mod number."

Thus, under low pressure, the HWM participants have an advantage because they have enough working memory to do the more complex and more accurate calculation, but when under high pressure, these participants switch to faster but less accurate rules (Beilock & DeCaro, 2007). This switch to the less accurate procedure is why the HWM advantage vanishes under high pressure conditions.

Why should increasing the pressure cause HWM participants to switch strategies? One reason might be that the pressure and the anxiety it creates cause the HWM participants to use more of their WM to deal with their anxiety, and this effectively robs them of the working memory advantage that enabled them to use the more complex algorithm (DeCaro et al., 2010). Beilock (2008) describes this "choking under pressure" effect in terms of *distraction*, much like what occurs when a person is trying to pay attention to two things at once (see Divided Attention, page 91). According to this idea, anxiety caused by stress competes for WM capacity that under less stressful conditions could be focused solely on the math problem.

Given these negative effects of stress on HWM participants, it is important to ask whether there are ways to combat this problem. One possibility is to use strategies that direct attention away from the stress. Marci DeCaro and coworkers (2010) tested this idea by having participants verbalize the steps they were using to solve the problems, as

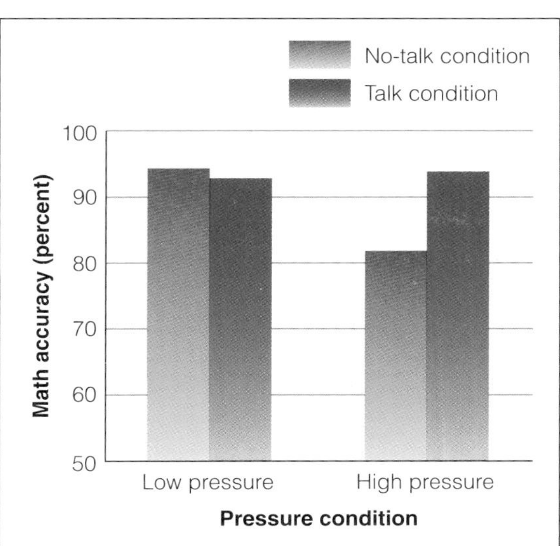

● **FIGURE 12.24** The effect of talking out loud during problem solving. *Left pair of bars*: No effect of talking under low pressure conditions. *Right pair of bars*: Pressure causes a decrease in performance for the no-talk condition, but not for the talk condition. (Source: M. S. DeCaro, K. E. Rotar, M. S. Kendra, & S. L. Beilock, "Diagnosing and Alleviating the Impact of Performance Pressure on Mathematical Problem Solving," *Quarterly Journal of Experimental Psychology, 16,* published online February 5, 2010.)

they were working on the problems (see Method: Think-Aloud Protocol, page 338). The idea is that talking should focus the person's attention on the problem and away from the stress. The results of this experiment are shown in ● Figure 12.24, which compares the performance of a group of participants who described what they were doing as they were solving the problem (the talk group) with that of a group that did not describe what they were doing (the no-talk group).

The left pair of bars shows that there was no difference in performance between the talk and no-talk groups under low pressure conditions. The right pair of bars shows that increasing the pressure caused a decrease in performance in the no-talk group, but didn't affect the performance of the talk group. Thus, carrying out a task that focuses attention on solving the problem and distracts attention away from the stress-producing situation is one way to combat the negative effects of stress. Although DeCaro did not separate her participants into HWM and LWM groups, she suggests that this procedure would probably be especially effective for people with high working memory.

Another technique that has been suggested for combating the effects of stress is *practice*. Beilock and Carr (2001) have shown that practicing a golf putting task while being videotaped eliminates choking when performing the task under pressure. In another experiment, participants who practiced math problems before taking a test were less affected by stress (Beilock et al., 2004). The idea that practice should reduce the effect of stress makes sense. After all, "studying" is a form of practice, and it seems likely that people who really know the material because they have studied will be less affected by stress. But more research is needed to determine under what conditions practice helps, what kinds of tasks are most helped by practice, and the kinds of practice that are most effective.

TEST YOURSELF 12.2

1. What is the basic idea behind analogical problem solving? How effective is it to present a source problem and then the target problem, without indicating that the source problem is related to the target problem?
2. What are the three steps in the process of analogical problem solving? Which of the steps appears to be the most difficult to achieve?
3. How do the surface features and structural features of problems influence a person's ability to make effective use of analogies in problem solving? Describe experiments relevant to this question, and also techniques that have been used to improve analogical problem solving.
4. What is the analogical paradox? How has analogical problem solving been studied in the real world?
5. What is an expert? What are some differences between the way experts and nonexperts go about solving problems? How good are experts at solving problems outside of their field?
6. What is convergent thinking? What is divergent thinking? How are these two types of thinking related to creativity? Describe experiments that have shown (a) how fixation can affect creativity; (b) de Mestral's use of analogy to invent Velcro; and (c) Finke's creative cognition procedure.
7. Under what conditions are people with high working memory capacity better at solving math problems than are people with low working memory capacity? Under what conditions do they lose this advantage? Why does this probably occur?

CHAPTER SUMMARY

1. A problem occurs when there is an obstacle between a present state and a goal and it is not immediately obvious how to get around the obstacle.
2. The Gestalt psychologists focused on how people represent a problem in their mind. They devised a number of problems to illustrate how solving a problem involves a restructuring of this representation and to demonstrate factors that pose obstacles to problem solving.
3. The Gestalt psychologists introduced the idea that reorganization is associated with insight—a sudden realization of a problem's solution. Insight has been demonstrated experimentally by tracking how close people feel they are to solving insight and noninsight problems.
4. Functional fixedness is an obstacle to problem solving that is illustrated by Duncker's candle problem and Maier's two-string problem. Luchins' water-jug problem illustrates the mental set created while solving a problem.
5. Alan Newell and Herbert Simon were early proponents of the information-processing approach to problem solving. They saw problem solving as the searching of a problem space to find the path between the statement of the problem (the initial state) and the solution to the problem (the goal state). This search is governed by operators and is usually accomplished by setting subgoals. The Tower of Hanoi problem has been used to illustrate this process.
6. The acrobat problem and the reverse acrobat problem illustrate that how the problem is presented can influence problem difficulty. Research on the mutilated checkerboard problem also illustrates the importance of how a problem is presented.
7. Newell and Simon developed the technique of think-aloud protocols to study participants' thought process as they are solving a problem.
8. Analogical problem solving occurs when experience with a previously solved source problem or a source story is used to help solve a new target problem. Research involving Duncker's radiation problem has shown that even when people are exposed to analogous source problems or stories, most people do not make the connection between the source problem or story and the target problem.
9. Analogical problem solving is facilitated when hints are given regarding the relevance of the source problem, when the source and target problems have similar surface features, and when structural features are made more obvious. Analogical encoding is a process that helps people discover similar structural features.
10. The analogical paradox is that participants in psychological experiments tend to focus on surface features in analogy problems, whereas people in the real world frequently focus on deeper, more structural features. In vivo problem-solving research has shown that analogical problem solving is often used in real-world settings.
11. Experts are better than novices at solving problems in their field of expertise. They have more knowledge of the field, organize this knowledge based more on deep structure than on surface features, and spend more time analyzing a problem when it is first presented.
12. Creative problem solving is associated with divergent thinking rather than with convergent thinking. We have only a limited understanding of the processes involved in creative problem solving and creativity in general. There is evidence that fixation can inhibit creative problem solving, and that using analogical thinking can enhance it. A technique called creative cognition has been used to train people to think creatively.
13. Mathematics problem-solving performance is affected by working memory capacity. High working memory capacity is associated with better performance than low working memory capacity under low-stress conditions, but this advantage disappears under high-stress conditions.

Think ABOUT IT

1. Pick a problem you have had to deal with, and analyze the process of solving it into subgoals, as is done in means-end analysis.
2. Have you ever experienced a situation in which you were trying to solve a problem, but stopped working on it because you couldn't come up with the answer? Then, after a while, when you returned to the problem, you got the answer right away? What do you think might be behind this process?
3. On August 14, 2003, a power failure caused millions of people in the northeastern and midwestern United States and in eastern Canada to lose their electricity. A few days later, after most people had their electricity restored, experts still did not know why the power failure had occurred and said it would take weeks to determine the cause. Imagine that you are a member of a special commission that has the task of solving this problem, or some other major problem. How could the processes described in this chapter be applied to finding a solution? What would the shortcomings of these processes be for solving this kind of problem?
4. Think of some examples of situations in which you overcame functional fixedness and found a new use for an object.

If You WANT TO KNOW MORE

1. **Incubation and creative problem solving.** People often report that they are able to solve a problem if they take a break from working on it and then come back to it later. This effect, called incubation, can play a role in creative problem solving.

Dodds, R. A., Smith, S. M., & Ward, T. B. (2002). The use of environmental cues during incubation. *Creativity Research Journal, 14*, 287–304.

2. **Cognition, creativity, and entrepreneurship.** How do entrepreneurs come up with novel and useful ideas for business ventures? Some answers to this question can be found in the results of cognitive research.

Baron, R. A., & Ward, T. B. (2004). Expanding entrepreneurial cognition's toolbox: Potential contributions from the field of cognitive science. *Entrepreneurship Theory and Practice, 28*, 553–573.

Ward, T. B. (2004). Cognition, creativity and entrepreneurship. *Journal of Business Venturing, 19*, 173–188.

3. **Sleep inspires insight.** It is a common observation that a person can be thinking about a problem during the day without solving it, then "sleep on it" and be able to solve it the next morning. Research supports the idea that sleep can increase the ability to solve a problem by insight.

Wagner, U., Gais, S., Haider, H., Verleger, R., & Born, J. (2004). Sleep inspires insight. *Nature, 427*, 352–355.

Key TERMS

Acrobat problem, 335
Analogical encoding, 344
Analogical paradox, 345
Analogical problem solving, 340
Analogical transfer, 340
Analogy, 339
Candle problem, 329
Convergent thinking, 349
Creative cognition, 350
Design fixation, 349
Divergent thinking, 348
Experts, 346
Fixation, 329
Functional fixedness, 329
Goal state, 332
Ill-defined problem, 326
Initial state, 332
Insight, 327
Intermediate state, 333
In vivo problem-solving research, 345
Means-end analysis, 333
Mental set, 330
Mutilated checkerboard problem, 337
Operators, 332
Problem, 326
Problem space, 333
Radiation problem, 340
Restructuring, 327
Reverse acrobat problem, 335
Source problem (or source story), 340
Structural features, 343
Subgoals, 333
Surface features, 343
Target problem, 340
Think-aloud protocol, 338
Tower of Hanoi problem, 332
Two-string problem, 330
Water-jug problem, 330
Well-defined problem, 326

Media RESOURCES

The *Cognitive Psychology* Book Companion Website

www.cengage.com/international

Prepare for quizzes and exams with online resources—including a glossary, flashcards, tutorial quizzes, crossword puzzles, and more.

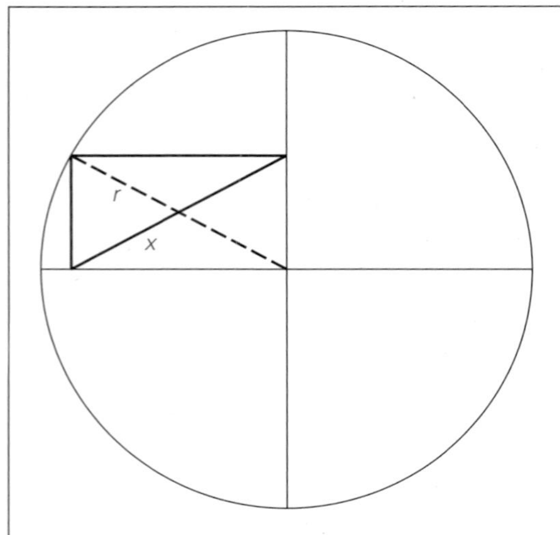

● **FIGURE 12.25** Solution to the circle problem. Note that the length of *x* is the same as the radius, *r,* because *x* and *r* are both diagonals of the rectangle.

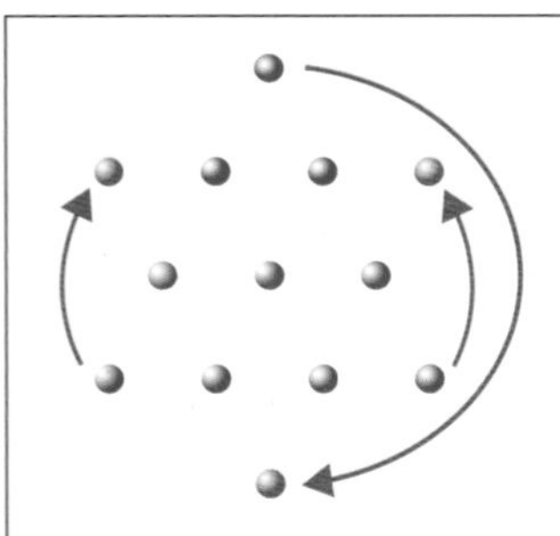

● **FIGURE 12.26** Solution to the triangle problem. Arrows indicate movement; colored circles indicate new positions.

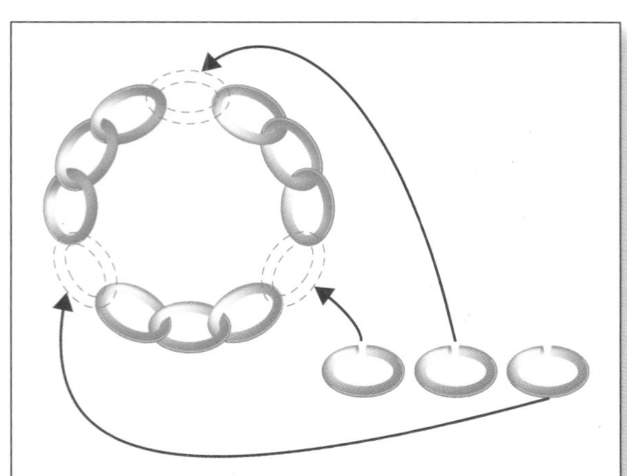

● **FIGURE 12.27** Solution to the chain problem. All the links in one chain are cut and separated (3 cuts @ 2 cents = 6 cents). The separated links are then used to connect the other three pieces and then closed (3 closings @ 3 cents = 9 cents). Total = 15 cents.

● **FIGURE 12.28** Solution to the candle problem.

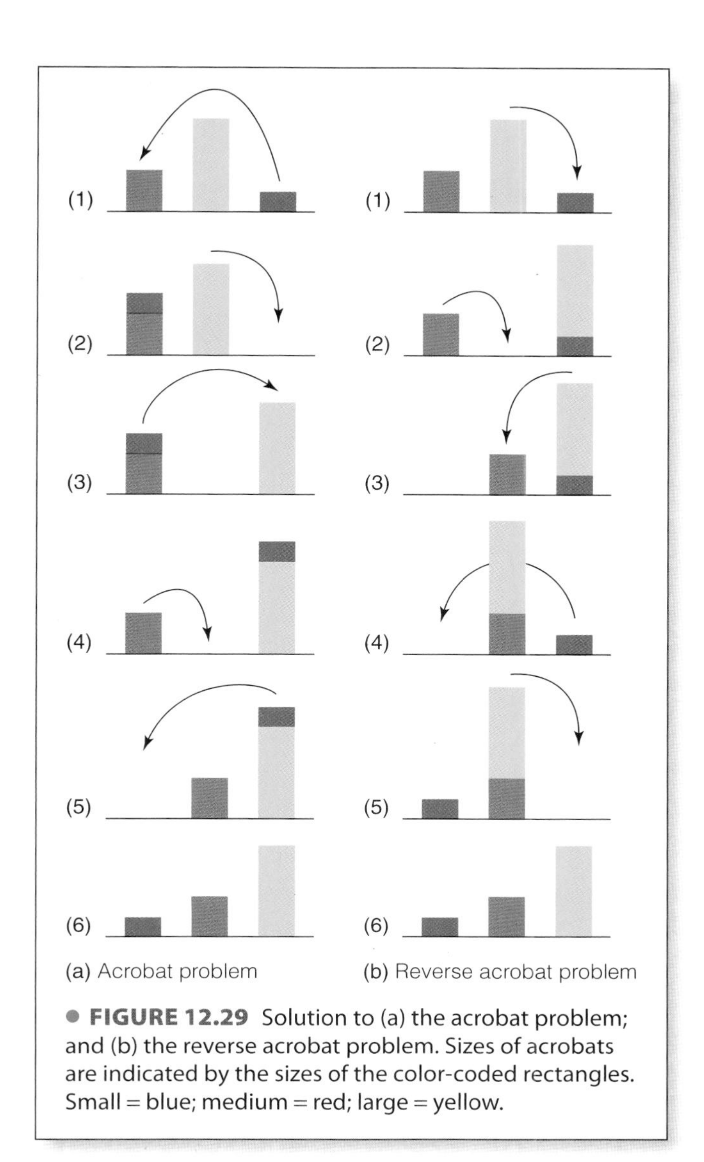

● **FIGURE 12.29** Solution to (a) the acrobat problem; and (b) the reverse acrobat problem. Sizes of acrobats are indicated by the sizes of the color-coded rectangles. Small = blue; medium = red; large = yellow.

13 Thinking: Reasoning and Decisions

These doctors are involved in reasoning, which is the process of drawing conclusions, and decision making, which is choosing between alternatives. Both of these processes come into play as the doctors decide on a diagnosis based on information in the X-ray and other information about the patient's history and symptoms.

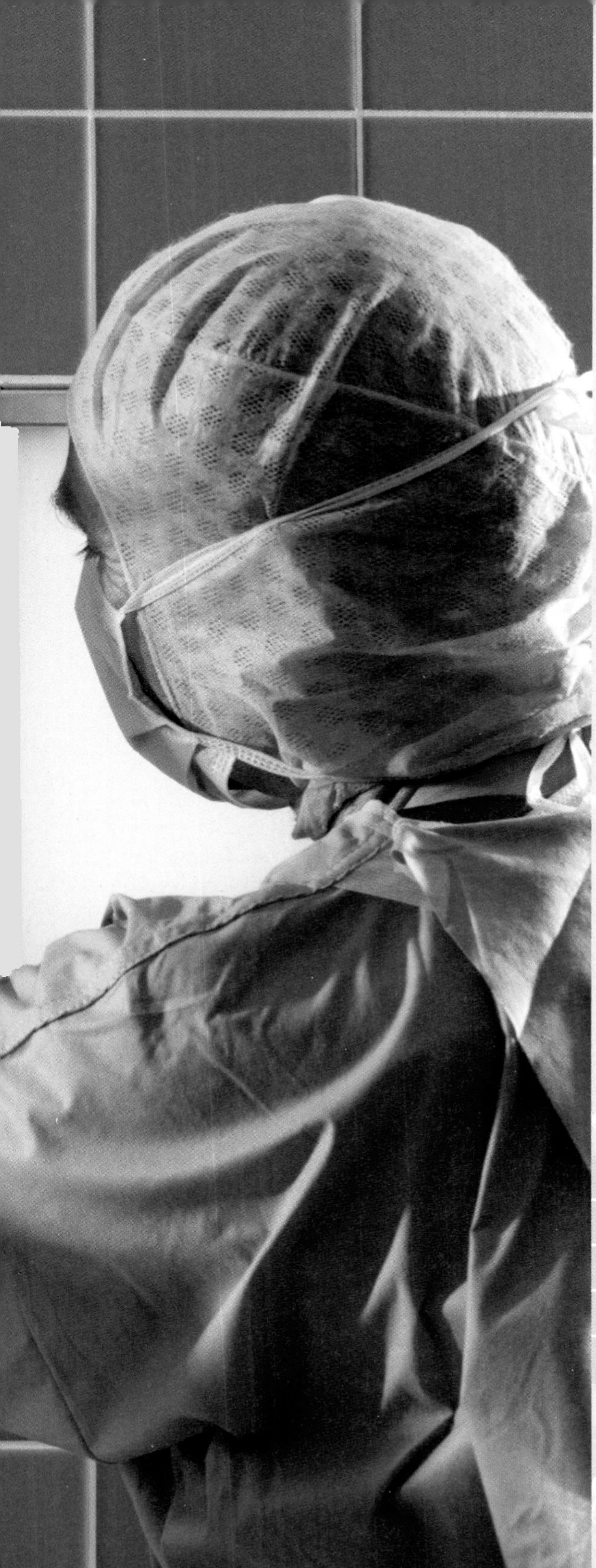

Heide Benser/Corbis

Some Questions We Will Consider

- What kinds of errors do people make in reasoning? (362)
- What kinds of reasoning "traps" do people get into when making decisions? (375)
- How do emotions influence decisions by contestants on shows like *Deal or No Deal*? (377)
- How does the fact that people sometimes feel a need to justify their decisions affect the process by which they make those decisions? (381)

Life is full of decisions—making choices between alternatives. What college to attend? Which movie to see? Which classes to take? Whether to sign on for more hours at the part-time job with finals coming up? Decisions such as these, both big and small, influence daily activities, and sometimes even the trajectory of a person's life.

But in addition to making decisions, we also engage in the closely related process of **reasoning**. Reasoning has been defined as the process of drawing conclusions (Leighton, 2004) and as the cognitive processes by which people start with information and come to conclusions that go beyond that information (Kurtz et al., 1999).

We can appreciate the process of reasoning by realizing that decisions are often the outcome of reasoning. Consider, for example, Raphael's problem that we described at the very beginning of the book (see page 4). He had to decide on an alternative form of transportation for when his car was in the shop. One way to decide between renting a car, bumming rides from his roommate, and taking the bus is to consider the pros and cons of each choice. Renting a car provides maximum flexibility but costs a lot. Whether or not this alternative makes sense depends on how much money is available and whether the added convenience is really worth the extra cost. Riding the bus is cheaper but involves a lot of waiting around outside. The third alternative, bumming rides from the roommate, seems like a bad choice because Raphael knows that he is unreliable. By taking these and other factors into account, Raphael reasons his way to a decision.

As we will see, reasoning is involved in many other situations besides making decisions. For example, we might use reasoning to help solve problems like the ones we described in Chapter 12. Reasoning is also involved in reading, as we make inferences about what is happening in a story based on what we know has happened earlier in the story.

We begin this chapter by focusing on how cognitive psychologists have studied two specific types of reasoning: deductive reasoning and inductive reasoning. We first consider **deductive reasoning**, which involves sequences of statements called **syllogisms**. For example, if we know that at least a C average is required to graduate from State U., and that Josie is graduating from State U., we can logically conclude that Josie has at least a C average.

We then consider **inductive reasoning**, in which we arrive at conclusions about what is *probably* true, based on evidence. Thus, if we know that Richard attended State U. for 4 years and that he is now the vice president of a bank, we might conclude it is likely that he graduated. Notice, however, that in this example, we cannot say that he *definitely* graduated (maybe he never completed all the requirements, and his mother, who is president of the bank, made him a vice president). Thus, we can make *definite* conclusions based on deductive reasoning and *probable* conclusions based on inductive reasoning. Studying both kinds of reasoning provides insights both about how the mind works and about everyday thinking.

Deductive Reasoning: Syllogisms and Logic

Aristotle is considered the father of deductive reasoning because he introduced the basic form of deductive reasoning called the *syllogism*. A syllogism includes two statements, called **premises**, followed by a third statement, called the **conclusion**. We will first consider **categorical syllogisms**, in which the premises and conclusion describe the relation between two categories by using statements that begin with *all*, *no*, or *some*. An example of a categorical syllogism is the following:

Syllogism 1

Premise 1: All birds are animals.
Premise 2: All animals eat food.
Conclusion: Therefore, all birds eat food.

If you were asked to evaluate this syllogism, would you decide it is an example of good reasoning? If you answered "yes," you would be correct. But what does it mean to say that "good reasoning" is involved here? The answer to this question involves considering the difference between *validity* and *truth* in syllogisms.

VALIDITY AND TRUTH IN SYLLOGISMS

The word *valid* is often used in everyday conversation to mean that something is true or might be true. For example, saying "Susan has a valid point" could mean that what Susan is saying is true, or possibly that it should be considered further. However, when used in conjunction with categorical syllogisms, the term **validity** has a very specific meaning: A syllogism is valid when its conclusion follows *logically* from its two premises.

Let's now consider another syllogism, that has exactly the same form as the first one:

Syllogism 2

All birds are animals. (All A are B)
All animals have four legs. (All B are C)
All birds have four legs. (All A are C)

In this example, the *form* of the premises and the conclusion is indicated in parentheses, using A, B, and C instead of birds, animals, and legs. From this, you can see that Syllogism 2 has the same form as Syllogism 1. Both syllogisms are therefore valid, because the conclusion follows from the two premises.

At this point you may feel that something is wrong. How can Syllogism 2 be valid when it is obvious that the conclusion is wrong, because birds don't have four legs? The answer is that validity and truth are two different things. Validity depends on the *form* of the syllogism, which determines whether the conclusion follows from the two premises. Truth, on the other hand, refers to the *content* of the premises, which have to be evaluated to determine whether they are consistent with the facts. The problem with Syllogism 2 is that the statement "All animals have four legs" is not true; that is, it is not consistent with what we know about the world. It is no coincidence, then, that the conclusion, "All birds have four legs," is not true either, even though the syllogism is valid.

The difference between validity and truth can make it difficult to judge whether reasoning is "logical" or not. Not only can valid syllogisms result in false conclusions, but syllogisms can be invalid even though each of the premises and the conclusion seem reasonable. For example, consider the following syllogism, in which each of the premises could be true and the conclusion could be true:

Syllogism 3

All of the students are tired.
Some tired people are irritable.
Some of the students are irritable.

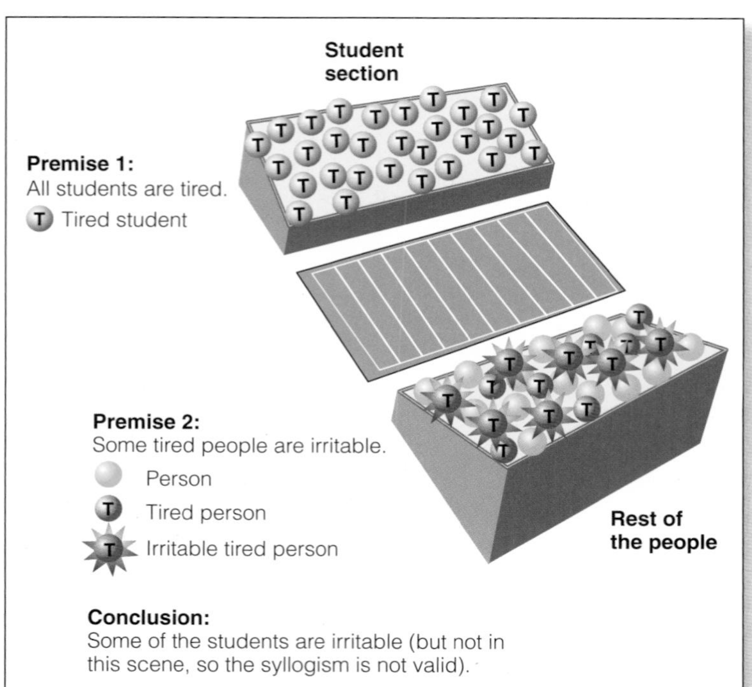

● **FIGURE 13.1** When we compare the places where people and students (who are also people!) are seated in the stadium, we can see that this seating arrangement is consistent with the first two premises of Syllogism 3. Note that in this example none of the students is irritable. Therefore the syllogism is not valid.

To understand why the conclusion does not logically follow from the two premises, consider ● Figure 13.1. All of the *students* are tired (Premise 1) and are sitting in the student section of the stadium. Some tired people, who are sitting across the field from the student section, are irritable (Premise 2). The fact that the tired and irritable people are sitting across the field from the students is consistent with the second premise because this premise just says some tired people are irritable, without mentioning students. Thus, just because the students are tired, and some tired people are irritable, the conclusion that some of the students are irritable does not follow. Because this conclusion does not logically follow from the premises, this syllogism is not valid.

The procedures for determining validity or lack of validity are complicated, and are more appropriately covered in a course in logic. The main message to take away from our discussion is that "good reasoning" and "truth" are not the same thing. This can have important implications for examples of reasoning that you might encounter. Consider, for example, the following statement:

> Listen to me. I know for a fact that all of the members of Congress from New York are against that new tax law. And I also know that some members of Congress who are against that tax law are taking money from special interest groups. What this means, as far as I can tell, is that some of the members of Congress from New York are taking money from special interest groups.

What is wrong with this argument? It happens to have exactly the same form as Syllogism 3, and as with Syllogism 3, it doesn't logically follow that just because all of the members of Congress from New York are against the new tax law (or all students are tired), and some members of Congress who are against the new tax law are taking money from special interest groups (or some people who are tired are irritable), that some members of Congress from New York are taking money from special interest groups (or some students are irritable). Thus, even though syllogisms may seem "academic," people often use syllogisms to "prove" their point, often without realizing that their reasoning might be invalid. It is therefore important to realize that even conclusions that might sound true are not necessarily the result of good reasoning.

We have been discussing categorical syllogisms, in which the statements begin with *all*, *no*, or *some*. Another type of syllogism, more commonly encountered in everyday experience, is the *conditional syllogism*.

CONDITIONAL SYLLOGISMS

Conditional syllogisms have two premises and a conclusion, like the ones we have been discussing, but the first premise has the form "If . . . then. . . ." This kind of deductive reasoning is common in everyday life. For example, let's say that you lent your friend Steve $20, but he has never paid you back. Knowing Steve, you might say to yourself that you knew this would happen. Stated in the form of a syllogism, your reasoning might look like this: If I lend Steve $20, then I won't get it back. I lent Steve $20. Therefore, I won't get my $20 back.

The four major types of conditional syllogisms are listed in Table 13.1. They are presented in abstract form (using p and q) and also in the form of a concrete "everyday" example. For conditional syllogisms, the notations p and q are typically used instead of the A and B used in categorical syllogisms. The symbol p, the first or "if" term, is called the **antecedent**, and q, the second or "then" term, is called the **consequent**.

TABLE 13.1 Four Syllogisms That Begin With the Same First Premise

First premise of all syllogisms:
If *p*, then *q*. (abstract version)
If I study, then I'll get a good grade. (concrete example)

Syllogism	Second Premise	Conclusion	Is It Valid?	Judged Correctly?
Syllogism 1: Affirming the antecedent	*p* (abstract) I studied. (concrete)	Therefore, *q* Therefore, I'll get a good grade.	Yes	97%
Syllogism 2: Denying the consequent	Not *q* I didn't get a good grade.	Therefore, not *p* Therefore, I didn't study.	Yes	60%
Syllogism 3: Affirming the consequent	*q* I got a good grade.	Therefore, *p* Therefore, I studied.	No	40%
Syllogism 4: Denying the antecedent	Not *p* I didn't study.	Therefore, not *q* Therefore, I didn't get a good grade.	No	40%

Syllogism 1 is called **affirming the antecedent** because the antecedent, *p* (If I study), is affirmed in the second premise (I studied). The conclusion of this syllogism (I got a good grade) is valid. Syllogism 2 is called **denying the consequent** because the consequent, *q* (I'll get a good grade) is negated in the second premise (I didn't get a good grade). The conclusion of this syllogism (I didn't study) is valid.

Syllogism 3 is called **affirming the consequent** because *q* is affirmed in the second premise (I got a good grade). The conclusion of this syllogism (I studied) is invalid, because even if you didn't study, it is still possible that you could have received a good grade. Perhaps the exam was easy, or maybe you knew the material because it was about your job experience. If that explanation is not convincing, consider the following syllogism, with "studying" and "good grade" in Syllogism 3, replaced by "robin" and "bird."

If it's a robin, then it's a bird.
It's a bird.
Therefore, it's a robin.

When stated in this way, it becomes more obvious that the affirming the consequent form of the syllogism is invalid.

Syllogism 4 is called **denying the antecedent** because *p* is negated in the second premise (I didn't study). The conclusion of this syllogism (I didn't get a good grade) is not valid. As in Syllogism 3, you can probably think of situations that would contradict the conclusion, in which a good grade was received even though the person didn't study. Again, the fact that this syllogism is invalid becomes more obvious when restated in terms of birds and robins:

If it's a robin, then it's a bird.
It's not a robin.
Therefore, it's not a bird.

How well can people judge the validity of these syllogisms? The results of many experiments, shown in the far right column of Table 13.1, indicate that most people (close to 100 percent in most experiments) correctly judge that Syllogism 1 is valid, but performance is lower on Syllogism 2, which is also valid, and 3 and 4, which are not valid. These percentages are the average results from many studies in which the syllogisms were stated abstractly, using the letters *p* and *q* for the antecedent and the consequent. In the next section we will describe a reasoning problem that has been studied both when stated in abstract form and also in terms of specific real-world examples.

CONDITIONAL REASONING: THE WASON FOUR-CARD PROBLEM

CogLab
Wason Selection Task

If reasoning from conditional syllogisms depended only on applying rules of formal logic, then it wouldn't matter whether the syllogism was stated in terms of abstract symbols, such as *p* and *q*, or in terms of real-world examples, such as studying or robins. However, research shows that people are often better at judging the validity of syllogisms when real-world examples are substituted for abstract symbols. As we look at this research, we will see that some real-world examples are better than others. Our main goal, however, is not simply to show that stating a problem in real-world terms makes it easier, but to consider how researchers have used various ways of stating a problem to propose mechanisms that explain *why* the real-world problems are easier. Many researchers have used a classic reasoning problem called the **Wason four-card problem.**

DEMONSTRATION Wason Four-Card Problem

Four cards are shown in ● Figure 13.2. Each card has a letter on one side and a number on the other side. Your task is to indicate which cards you would need to turn over to test the following rule: If there is a vowel on one side, then there is an even number on the other side.

If vowel, then even number.

● **FIGURE 13.2** The Wason four-card problem (Wason, 1966). Follow the directions in the demonstration and try this problem. (Source: Based on P. C. Wason, "Reasoning," in B. Foss, Ed., *New Horizons in Psychology*, pp. 135–151, Harmonsworth, UK: Penguin, 1966.)

When Wason (1966) posed this task (which we will call the abstract task), 53 percent of his participants indicated that the E must be turned over. This is correct because turning over the E directly tests the rule. (If there is an E, then there must be an even number, so if there is an odd number on the other side, this would prove the rule to be false.) However, another card needs to be turned over to fully test the rule. Forty-six percent of Wason's participants indicated that in addition to the E, the 4 would need to be turned over. The problem with this answer is that if a vowel is on the other side of the card, this is consistent with the rule, but if a consonant is on the other side, turning over the 4 tells us nothing about the rule, because having a consonant on one side and a vowel on the other does not violate the rule. As shown in ● Figure 13.3a, only 4 percent of Wason's participants came up with the correct answer—that the second card that needs to be turned over is the 7. Turning over the 7 is important because revealing a vowel would disconfirm the rule.

The key to solving the card problem is to be aware of the **falsification principle:** *To test a rule, it is necessary to look for situations that would falsify the rule.* As you can see from Table 13.2, the only two cards that have the potential to achieve this are the E and the 7. Thus, these are the only two cards that need to be turned over to test the rule.

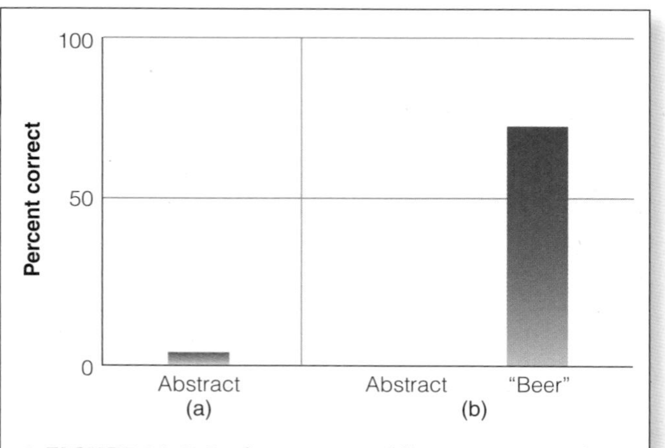

● **FIGURE 13.3** Performance on different versions of the four-card problem. (a) Abstract version (Wason, 1966) shown in Figure 13.2. (b) Abstract version and beer/drinking-age version (Griggs & Cox, 1982), shown in Figure 13.4. (Source: Based on P. C. Wason, "Reasoning," in B. Foss, Ed., *New Horizons in Psychology*, pp. 135–151, Harmondsworth, UK: Penguin, 1966; R. A. Griggs & J. R. Cox, "The Elusive Thematic-Materials Effect in Wason's Abstract Selection Task," *British Journal of Psychology, 73*, 407–420, 1982.)

The Role of "Regulations" in the Wason Task The Wason task has generated a great deal of research. One reason for the degree of interest in this problem is that it is a conditional reasoning task. (Note that the problem is stated as an "If ... then ..." statement.) But the main reason researchers are interested in this problem is that they want to determine if there are general reasoning mechanisms that are responsible for the improved performance when the task is stated in real-world terms. In one of these real-world experiments, Richard Griggs and James Cox (1982) stated the problem as follows:

TABLE 13.2 Outcomes of Turning Over Each Card in the Wason Task

The rule:
If there is a vowel on one side,
then there is an even number on the other side.

If turn over...	And the result is...	Then this ____ the rule
E	Even	confirms
E	Odd	**falsifies**
K	Even	is irrelevant to *
K	Odd	is irrelevant to
4	Vowel	confirms
4	Consonant	is irrelevant to
7	Vowel	**falsifies**
7	Consonant	is irrelevant to

* This outcome of turning over the card is irrelevant because the rule does not say anything about what should be on the card if a consonant is on one side. Similar reasoning holds for all of the other irrelevant cases.

Four cards are shown in ● Figure 13.4. Each card has an age on one side and the name of a beverage on the other side. Imagine you are a police officer who is applying the rule "If a person is drinking beer, then he or she must be over 19 years old." (The participants in this experiment were from Florida, where the drinking age was 19 at the time.) Which of the cards in Figure 13.4 must be turned over to determine whether the rule is being followed?

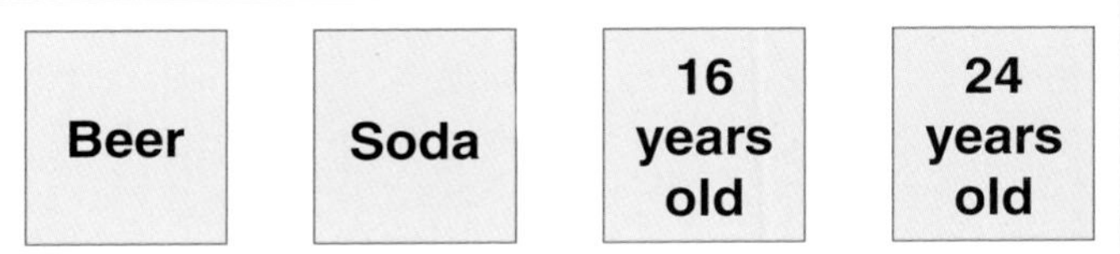

● **FIGURE 13.4** The beer/drinking-age version of the four-card problem. (Source: Based on R. A. Griggs & J. R. Cox, "The Elusive Thematic-Materials Effect in Wason's Abstract Selection Task," *British Journal of Psychology, 73*, 407–420, 1982.)

This beer/drinking-age version of Wason's problem is identical to the abstract version except that concrete everyday terms (beer, soda, and ages) are substituted for the letters and numbers. Griggs and Cox found that for this version of the problem, 73 percent of their participants provided the correct response: It is necessary to turn over the "beer" and the "16 years" cards. In contrast, none of their participants answered the abstract task correctly (Figure 13.3b). Why is the concrete task easier than the abstract task? Apparently, being able to relate the beer task to regulations about drinking makes it easier to realize that the "16 years" card must be turned over. (See Johnson-Laird et al., 1972, for another example of a "real world" version of the Wason problem.)

The Role of "Permissions" in the Wason Task Patricia Cheng and Keith Holyoak (1985) took the Wason task a step further by proposing the concept of *pragmatic reasoning schemas*. A pragmatic reasoning schema is a way of thinking about cause and effect in the world that is learned as part of experiencing everyday life. An example is the permission schema that states that if a person satisfies condition A (such as being the legal age for drinking), then he or she gets to carry out action B (being served alcohol). The permission schema "If you are 19, then you get to drink beer" is something that most of the participants in this experiment had learned, so they were able to apply that schema to the card task.

This idea that people apply a real-life schema like the permission schema to the card task makes it easier to understand the difference between the abstract version of the card task and the beer/drinking-age version. With the abstract task, the goal is to indicate whether an abstract statement about letters and numbers is true. But in the beer/drinking-age task, the goal is to be sure that a person has permission to drink alcohol. Apparently, activating the permission schema helps people focus attention on the card that would test that schema. Participants' attention is attracted to the "16 years old" card because they know that "beer" on the other side would be violating the rule that a person must be 19 years old to drink.

Entering	Transient	Cholera Typhoid Hepatitis	Typhoid Hepatitis

If entering, then cholera is listed.

● **FIGURE 13.5** Cholera version of the four-card problem. (Source: Based on P. W. Cheng & K. J. Holyoak, "Pragmatic Reasoning Schemas," *Cognitive Psychology, 17*, 391–416, 1985.)

To test the idea that a permission schema may be involved in reasoning about the card task, Cheng and Holyoak (1985) ran an experiment with two groups of participants who both saw the cards in ● Figure 13.5. One of the groups was read the following directions:

> You are an immigration officer at the International Airport in Manila, capital of the Philippines. Among the documents you have to check is a sheet called Form H. One side of this form indicates whether the passenger is entering the country or in transit, and the other side of the form lists names of tropical diseases. You have to make sure that if the form says "Entering" on one side, the other side includes cholera among the list of diseases.* Which of the following forms would you have to turn over to check? Indicate only those that you need to check to be sure. [*The asterisk is explained in the text that follows.]

Sixty-two percent of the participants in this group chose the correct cards, "Entering" and "Typhoid, Hepatitis." (If it isn't clear why "Typhoid, Hepatitis" is the second card, remember that "Entering" on the other side would disconfirm the rule.) Participants in the other group saw the same cards and heard the same instructions as the first group, but with the following changes: Instead of saying that the form listed tropical diseases, the instructions said that the form listed "inoculations the travelers had received in the past 6 months." In addition, the following sentence was added where indicated by the asterisk (*): "This is to ensure that entering passengers are protected against the disease."

The changes in the instructions were calculated to achieve a very important effect: Instead of checking just to see whether the correct diseases are listed on the form, the immigration officer is checking to see whether the travelers have the inoculations necessary to *give them permission* to enter the country. These instructions were intended to activate the participants' permission schema, and apparently this happened, because 91 percent of the participants in this condition picked the correct cards (● Figure 13.6).

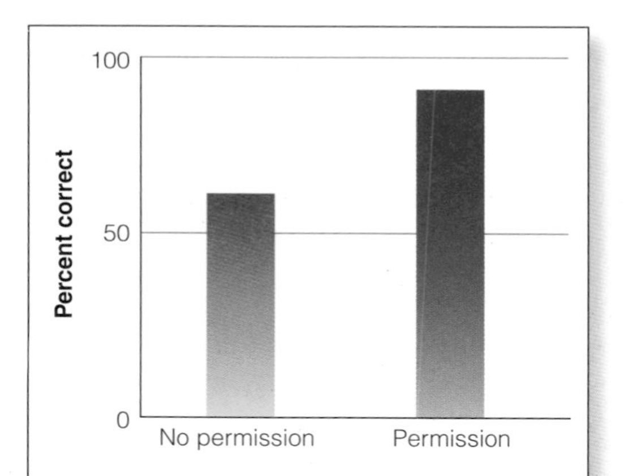

● **FIGURE 13.6** Results of Cheng and Holyoak's (1985) experiment that used two versions of the cholera problem. When "permissions" are implied by the instructions, performance is better. (Source: Based on P. W. Cheng & K. J. Holyoak, "Pragmatic Reasoning Schemas," *Cognitive Psychology, 17*, 391–416, 1985.)

An Evolutionary Approach to the Four-Card Problem One of the things we have learned from our descriptions of cognitive psychology research is that one set of data can be interpreted in different ways by different investigators. We saw this in the case of the misinformation effect in Chapter 8, in which memory errors were caused by presenting misleading postevent information (MPI) after a person witnessed an event (see page 222). We saw that one group of researchers explained these errors by stating that the MPI distorted existing memories (Loftus, 1993), but other researchers offered explanations based on the effect of retroactive interference and source monitoring errors (Lindsay, 1990).

Similarly, different explanations have been offered for the results of various experiments involving the Wason four-card problem. For example, one proposed alternative to a permission schema is that performance on the Wason task is governed by a built-in cognitive program for detecting cheating. Let's consider the rationale behind this idea.

Leda Cosmides and John Tooby (1992) are among psychologists who have an **evolutionary perspective on cognition**. They argue that we can trace many properties of our minds to the evolutionary principles of natural selection. According to natural selection, adaptive characteristics—characteristics that help people survive to pass their genes to the next generation—will, over time, become basic characteristics of humans. Charles Darwin originally proposed this theory based on observations of physical characteristics. For example, Darwin observed that birds in a specific area had beaks with shapes adapted to enable them to obtain the food that was available.

Applying this idea to cognition, it follows that a highly adaptive feature of the mind would, through a similar evolutionary process, become a basic characteristic of the mind. One such characteristic, according to the evolutionary approach, is related to **social exchange theory**, which states that an important aspect of human behavior is the ability for two people to cooperate in a way that is beneficial to both people. Thus, when caveman Morg lends caveman Eng his carving tool in exchange for some food that Eng has brought back from the hunt, both people benefit from the exchange.

Everything works well in social exchange as long as each person is receiving a benefit for whatever he or she is giving up. However, problems arise when someone cheats. Thus, if Morg gives up his carving tool, but Eng fails to give him the food, this does not bode well for Morg. It is essential, therefore, that people be able to detect cheating behavior so they can avoid it. According to the evolutionary approach, people who can do this will have a better chance of surviving, so "detecting cheating" has become a part of the brain's cognitive makeup.

The evolutionary approach proposes that the Wason problem can be understood in terms of cheating. Thus, people do well in the cholera task (Figure 13.5) because they can detect someone who cheats by entering the country without a cholera shot.

To test the idea that cheating (and not permission) is the important variable in the four-card problem, Cosmides and Tooby (1992) devised a number of four-card scenarios involving unfamiliar situations. Remember that one idea behind the permission schema is that people perform well because they are *familiar* with various rules.

To create unfamiliar situations, Cosmides and Tooby created a number of experiments that took place in a hypothetical culture called the Kulwane. Participants in these experiments read a story about this culture, which led to the conditional statement "If a man eats cassava root, then he must have a tattoo on his face." Participants saw the following four cards: (1) eats cassava roots; (2) eats molo nuts; (3) tattoo; and (4) no tattoo. Their task was to determine which cards they needed to turn over to determine whether the conditional statement above was being adhered to. This is a situation unfamiliar to the participants, and one in which cheating could occur, because a man who eats the cassava root without a tattoo would be cheating.

Cosmides and Tooby found that participants' performance was high on this task, even though the rule was unfamiliar. They also ran other experiments in which participants did better for statements that involved cheating than for other statements that could not be interpreted in this way (Cosmides, 1989; also see Gigerenzer & Hug, 1992).

However, in response to this proposal, other researchers have created scenarios that involve permission rules that are unfamiliar. For example, Ken Manktelow and David Over (1990) tested people using the rule "If you clean up spilt blood, you must wear gloves." Note that this is a "permission" statement that most people have not heard before. However, stating the problem in this way caused an increase in performance, just as in many of the other examples of the Wason task that we have described.

WHAT HAS THE WASON PROBLEM TAUGHT US?

The controversy continues among those who hold that permission is important, those who focus on cheating, and researchers who have proposed other explanations for the results of the Wason task. Evidence has been presented for and against each of these proposed mechanisms (Johnson-Laird, 1999; Manktelow, 1999).

We are left with the important finding that the context within which conditional reasoning occurs makes a big difference. Stating the four-card problem in terms of familiar situations can often generate better reasoning than abstract statements or statements that people cannot relate to. However, familiarity is not always necessary for conditional reasoning (as in the tattoo problem), and situations have also been devised in which people's performance is not improved, even in familiar situations (Evans & Feeney, 2004; Griggs, 1983; Manktelow & Evans, 1979).

Sometimes controversies such as this one are frustrating to read about because, after all, aren't we looking for "answers"? But another way to look at controversies is that they illustrate the complexity of the human mind and the challenge facing cognitive psychologists. Remember that at the beginning of this book we described an experiment by Donders that involved simply indicating when a light was presented or whether the light was presented on the right or on the left (see Chapter 1, page 6). We described Donders' experiment to illustrate the basic principle that cognitive psychologists must infer the workings of the mind from behavioral observations. It is fitting, therefore, that in this, the last chapter of the book, we are now describing a task that involves mental processes far more complex than judging whether a light has flashed, but that illustrates exactly the same principle: The workings of the mind must be inferred from behavioral observations.

We see, in this controversy over how people deal with the Wason task, how a number of different hypotheses about what is happening in the mind can be plausibly inferred from the same behavioral evidence. Perhaps, in the end, the actual mechanism will be something that has yet to be proposed, or perhaps the mind, in its complexity, has a number of different ways of approaching the Wason task, depending on the situation.

TEST YOURSELF 13.1

1. What is deductive reasoning? What does it mean to say that the conclusion to a syllogism is "valid"? How can a conclusion be valid but not true? True but not valid?
2. What is a categorical syllogism? What is the difference between validity and truth in categorical syllogisms?
3. What is a conditional syllogism? Which of the four types of syllogisms described in the chapter are valid, which are not valid, and how well can people judge the validity of each type?
4. What is the Wason four-card problem? Describe the falsification principle. What do the results of experiments that have used abstract and concrete versions of the problem indicate about the roles of (a) concreteness; (b) knowledge of regulations; and (c) permission schemas in solving this problem?
5. How has the evolutionary approach to cognition been applied to the Wason four-card problem? What can we conclude from all of the experiments on the Wason problem?

Inductive Reasoning: Reaching Conclusions From Evidence

In deductive reasoning, premises are stated as facts, such as "All robins are birds." However, in inductive reasoning, premises are based on observation of one or more specific cases, and we generalize from these cases to a more general conclusion.

THE NATURE OF INDUCTIVE REASONING

In inductive reasoning, conclusions are *suggested*, with varying degrees of certainty, but do not *definitely* follow from premises. This is illustrated by the following two inductive arguments:

> *Observation*: All the crows I've seen in Pittsburgh are black. When I visited my brother in Washington, DC, the crows I saw there were black too.
> *Conclusion*: I think it is a pretty good bet that all crows are black.
>
> *Observation*: Here in Tucson, the sun has risen every morning.
> *Conclusion*: The sun is going to rise in Tucson tomorrow.

Notice there is a certain logic to each argument, but the second argument is more convincing than the first. In evaluating inductive arguments, we do not consider validity, as we did for deductive arguments; instead, we decide how strong the argument is. Strong arguments result in conclusions that are more likely to be true, and weak arguments result in conclusions that are not as likely to be true. Remember that inductive arguments lead to what is *probably* true, not what is *definitely* true.

A number of factors can contribute to the strength of an inductive argument. Among them are the following:

- *Representativeness of observations:* How well do the observations about a particular category represent all of the members of that category? Clearly, the crows example suffers from a lack of representativeness because it does not consider crows from other parts of the country. If there are rare blue crows in California, then the conclusion is not true.

- *Number of observations:* The argument about the crows is made stronger by adding the Washington, DC, observations to the Pittsburgh observations. Adding more observations would strengthen it further. The conclusion about the sun rising in Tucson is extremely strong because it is supported by a very large number of observations.
- *Quality of the evidence:* Stronger evidence results in stronger conclusions. For example, although the conclusion "The sun will rise in Tucson" is extremely strong because of the number of observations, it becomes even stronger when we consider scientific descriptions of how the earth rotates on its axis and revolves around the sun. Thus, adding the observation "Scientific measurements of the rotation of the earth indicate that every time the earth rotates the sun will appear to rise" strengthens the conclusion even further.

Although our examples of inductive reasoning have been "academic" in nature, we often use inductive reasoning in everyday life, usually without even realizing it. For example, Sarah has observed, from a course she took with Professor X, that he asked a lot of questions about experimental procedures on his exams. Based on this observation, Sarah concludes that the exam she is about to take in another of Professor X's courses will probably be similar. In another example, Sam has bought merchandise from mail order company Y before and gotten good service, so he places another order based on the assumption that he will continue to get good service. Thus, anytime we make a prediction about *what will happen* based on our observations about *what has happened* in the past, we are using inductive reasoning.

It makes sense that we make predictions and choices based on past experience, especially when predictions are based on familiar situations such as studying for an exam or buying merchandise by mail. However, we make so many assumptions about the world, based on past experience, that we are using inductive reasoning constantly, often without even realizing it. For example, did you run a stress test on the chair you are sitting in to be sure it wouldn't collapse when you sat down? Probably not. You assumed, based on your past experience with chairs, that it would not collapse. This kind of inductive reasoning is so automatic that you are not aware that any kind of "reasoning" is happening at all. Think about how time-consuming it would be if you had to approach every experience as if you were having it for the first time. Inductive reasoning provides the mechanism for using past experience to guide present behavior.

When people use past experience to guide present behavior, they often use shortcuts to help them reach conclusions rapidly. After all, we don't have the time or energy to stop and gather every bit of information that we need to be 100 percent certain that every conclusion we reach is correct. These shortcuts take the form of *heuristics*—"rules of thumb" that are likely to provide the correct answer to a problem, but are not foolproof.

Using heuristics may sound familiar because we saw in Chapter 3 that people use heuristics to help them understand what they are seeing (see page 62). Similarly, people use a number of heuristics in reasoning that often lead to the correct conclusion, but sometimes do not. We will now describe two of these heuristics, the *availability heuristic* and the *representative heuristic*.

THE AVAILABILITY HEURISTIC

The following demonstration introduces the availability heuristic.

DEMONSTRATION Which Is More Prevalent?

Answer the following questions.

- Which are more prevalent in English, words that begin with the letter *r* or words in which *r* is the third letter?

- Some possible causes of death are listed below in pairs. Within each pair, which cause of death do you consider to be more likely for people in the United States? That is, if you randomly picked someone in the United States, would that person be more likely to die next year from cause A or cause B?

Cause A	Cause B
Homicide	Appendicitis
Auto-train collision	Drowning
Botulism	Asthma
Asthma	Tornado
Appendicitis	Pregnancy

When faced with a choice, we are often guided by what we remember from the past. The **availability heuristic** states that events that are more easily remembered are judged as being more probable than events that are less easily remembered (Tversky & Kahneman, 1973). Consider, for example, the problems we posed in the demonstration. When participants were asked to judge whether there are more words with *r* in the first position or the third, 70 percent responded that more words begin with *r*, even though in reality three times more words have *r* in the third position (Tversky & Kahneman, 1973; but see also Gigerenzer & Todd, 1999).

Table 13.3 shows the results of experiments in which participants were asked to judge the relative prevalence of various causes of death (Lichtenstein et al., 1978). For each pair, the more likely cause of death is listed in the left column (compare these to your answers in the demonstration above). The number in parentheses indicates the relative frequency of the more likely cause compared to the less likely cause. For example, 20 times more people die of homicide than die of appendicitis. The number on the right indicates the percentage of participants who picked the less likely alternative. For example, 9 percent of participants thought it was more likely that a person would die from appendicitis than as a result of homicide. In this case, therefore, a large majority of people, 91 percent, correctly picked homicide as causing more deaths. However, for the other causes of death, a substantial proportion of participants misjudged their relative likelihood. In these cases, large numbers of errors were associated with causes that had been publicized by the media. For example, 58 percent thought that more deaths were caused by tornados than by asthma, when in reality, 20 times more people die from asthma than from tornados. Particularly striking is that finding that 41 percent of participants thought botulism caused more deaths than asthma, even though 920 times more people die of asthma.

The explanation for these misjudgments appears linked to availability. When you try to think of words that begin with *r* or that have *r* in the third position, it is much easier to think of words that begin with *r* (*run*, *rain*, *real*) than words that have *r* in their third position (*word*, *car*, *arranged*). When people die of botulism or in a tornado, it is front-page news, whereas deaths from asthma go virtually unnoticed by the general public (Lichtenstein et al., 1978).

An experiment by Stuart McKelvie (1997) demonstrates the availability heuristic in another way. McKelvie presented lists of 26 names to participants. In the "famous men"

TABLE 13.3 Causes of Death

More Likely	Less Likely	Percent Picking Less Likely
Homicide (20)	Appendicitis	9
Drowning (5)	Auto-train collision	34
Asthma (920)	Botulism	41
Asthma (20)	Tornado	58
Appendicitis (2)	Pregnancy	83

Adapted from Lichtenstein et al., 1978.

condition, 12 of the names were famous men (Ronald Reagan, Mick Jagger) and 14 were nonfamous women. In the "famous women" condition, 12 of the names were famous women (Tina Turner, Beatrix Potter) and 14 were nonfamous men. When participants were asked to estimate whether there were more males or more females in the list they had heard, their answer was influenced by whether they had heard the famous male list or the famous female list. Seventy-seven percent of the participants who had heard the famous male list stated that there were more males in their list (notice that there were actually fewer), and 81 percent of the participants who had heard the famous female list stated that there were more females in their list. This result is consistent with the availability heuristic, because the famous names would be more easily remembered and would stand out when participants were asked to decide whether there had been more male or female names.

The previous examples illustrate how the availability heuristic can mislead us into reaching the wrong conclusion when less frequently occurring events stand out in our memory. There are many situations, however, in which we remember events that do occur frequently. For example, you might know from past observations that when it is cloudy and there is a certain smell in the air, it is likely to rain later in the day. Or you may have noticed that your boss is more likely to grant your requests when he or she is in a good mood.

Although observing correlations between events can be useful, sometimes people fall into the trap of creating illusory correlations. **Illusory correlations** occur when a correlation between two events appears to exist, but in reality there is no correlation or it is much weaker than it is assumed to be. Illusory correlations can occur when we expect two things to be related, so we fool ourselves into thinking they are related even when they are not. These expectations may take the form of a **stereotype**—an oversimplified generalization about a group or class of people that often focuses on the negative. A stereotype about the characteristics of a particular group may lead people to pay particular attention to behaviors associated with that stereotype, and this attention creates an illusory correlation that reinforces the stereotype. This phenomenon is related to the availability heuristic because selective attention to the stereotypical behaviors makes these behaviors more "available" (Chapman & Chapman, 1969; Hamilton, 1981).

We can appreciate how illusory correlations reinforce stereotypes by considering the stereotype that gay males are effeminate. A person who believes this stereotype might pay particular attention to effeminate gay characters on TV programs or in movies, and to situations in which they see a person who they know is gay acting effeminate. Although these observations support a correlation between being gay and being effeminate, the person has ignored the large number of cases in which gay males are not effeminate. This may be because these cases do not stand out or because the person chooses not to pay attention to them. Whatever the reason, selectively taking into account only the situations that support the person's preconceptions can create the illusion that a correlation exists, when there may be only a weak correlation or none at all.

THE REPRESENTATIVENESS HEURISTIC

CogLab
Typical Reasoning

While the availability heuristic is related to how *often* we expect events to occur, the representativeness heuristic is related to the idea that people often make judgments based on how much one event *resembles* another event.

Making Judgments Based on Resemblances The representativeness heuristic states that the probability that A is a member of class B can be determined by how well the properties of A resembles the properties we usually associate with class B. To put this in more concrete terms, consider the following demonstration.

DEMONSTRATION Judging Occupations

We randomly pick one male from the population of the United States. That male, Robert, wears glasses, speaks quietly, and reads a lot. Is it more likely that Robert is a librarian or a farmer?

When Amos Tversky and Daniel Kahneman (1974) presented this question in an experiment, more people guessed that Robert was a librarian. Apparently the description of Robert as wearing glasses, speaking quietly, and reading a lot matched these people's image of a typical librarian (see illusory correlations, above). Thus, they were influenced by the representativeness heuristic into basing their judgment on how closely they think the characteristics used to describe Robert (A in our definition of the representativeness heuristic) match those of a "typical" librarian (class B). However, they were ignoring another important source of information—the base rates of farmers and librarians in the population. The base rate is the relative proportion of different classes in the population. In 1972, when this experiment was carried out, there were many more male farmers than male librarians in the United States, so it is much more likely that Robert was a farmer (remember that he was randomly chosen from the population).

One reaction to the farmer–librarian problem might be that perhaps the participants were not aware of the base rates for farmers and librarians, so they didn't have the information they needed to make a correct judgment. The effect of knowing the base rate has been demonstrated by presenting participants with the following problem:

> In a group of 100 people, there are 70 lawyers and 30 engineers. What is the chance that if we pick one person from the group at random that the person will be an engineer?

Participants given this problem correctly guessed that there would be a 30 percent chance of picking an engineer. However, for some participants, the following description of the person who was picked was added:

> Jack is a 45-year-old man. He is married and has four children. He is generally conservative, careful, and ambitious. He shows no interest in political and social issues and spends most of his free time on his many hobbies, which include home carpentry, sailing, and mathematical puzzles.

Adding this description caused participants to greatly increase their estimate of the chances that the randomly picked person (Jack, in this case) was an engineer. Apparently, when only base rate information is available, people use that information to make their estimates. However, when any descriptive information is available, people disregard the base rate information, and this can potentially cause errors in reasoning. Note, however, that the right kind of descriptive information can increase the accuracy of a judgment. For example, if the description of Jack also noted that his last job involved determining the structural characteristics of a bridge that was being built, then this would greatly increase the chance that he was, in fact, an engineer. Thus, just as it is important to pay attention to base rate information, the information provided by descriptions can also be useful if it is relevant. When such information is available, then applying the representativeness heuristic can lead to correct judgments.

Making Judgments Without Considering the Conjunction Rule The following demonstration illustrates another characteristic of the representativeness heuristic.

DEMONSTRATION Description of a Person

Linda is 31 years old, single, outspoken, and very bright. She majored in philosophy. As a student, she was deeply concerned with issues of discrimination and social justice, and also participated in antinuclear demonstrations. Which of the following alternatives is more probable?

1. Linda is a bank teller.
2. Linda is a bank teller and is active in the feminist movement.

The correct answer to this problem is that Statement 1 has a greater probability of being true, but when Tversky and Kahneman (1983) posed this problem to their participants, 85 percent picked Statement 2. It is easy to see why they did this. They were influenced by the representativeness heuristic, because the description of Linda fits people's

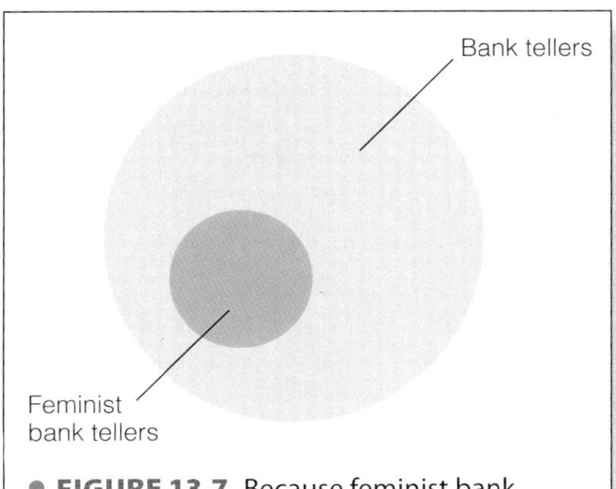

● **FIGURE 13.7** Because feminist bank tellers are a subset of bank tellers, it is always more likely that someone is a bank teller than a feminist bank teller.

idea of a typical feminist. However, in doing this they violated the **conjunction rule**, which states that the probability of a conjunction of two events (A and B) cannot be higher than the probability of the single constituents (A alone or B alone). For example, the probability that Anne has a red Corvette cannot be greater than the probability that she has a Corvette, because the two constituents together (Corvette *and* red) define a smaller number of cars than one constituent (Corvette) alone. Similarly, there are more bank tellers than feminist bank tellers; stating that Linda is a bank teller *includes* the possibility that she is a feminist bank teller (● Figure 13.7).

People tend to violate the conjunction rule even when it is clear that they understand it. The culprit is the representativeness heuristic. In the example just cited, the participants saw Linda's characteristics as more representative of "feminist bank teller" than "bank teller."

Incorrectly Assuming That Small Samples Are Representative People also make errors in reasoning by ignoring the importance of the size of the sample on which observations are based. The following demonstration illustrates the effect of sample size.

DEMONSTRATION Male and Female Births

A certain town is served by two hospitals. In the larger hospital about 45 babies are born each day, and in the smaller hospital about 15 babies are born each day. As you know, about 50 percent of all babies are boys. However, the exact percentage varies from day to day. Sometimes it may be higher than 50 percent, sometimes lower.

For a period of 1 year, each hospital recorded the days on which more than 60 percent of the babies born were boys. Which hospital do you think recorded more such days?

- The larger hospital?
- The smaller hospital?
- About the same

When participants were asked this question in an experiment (Tversky & Kahneman, 1974), 22 percent picked the larger hospital, 22 percent picked the smaller hospital, and 56 percent stated that there would be no difference. The group that thought there would be no difference was presumably assuming that the birthrate for males and females in both hospitals would be representative of the overall birthrate for males and females. However, the correct answer is that there would be more days with over 60 percent male births in the small hospital.

We can understand why this result would occur by considering a statistical rule called the **law of large numbers**, which states that the larger the number of individuals that are randomly drawn from a population, the more representative the resulting group will be of the entire population. Conversely, samples of small numbers of individuals will be less representative of the population. Thus, in the hospital problem it is more likely that the percentage of boys born on any given day will be near 50 percent in the large hospital and farther from 50 percent in the small hospital. To make this conclusion clear, imagine that there is a very small hospital that records only one birth each day. Over a period of a year there will be 365 births, with about 50 percent being boys and 50 percent being girls. However, on any given day, there will be either 100 percent boys or 100 percent girls—clearly percentages that are not representative of the overall population. People often assume that representativeness holds for small samples, and this results in errors in reasoning. (See Gigerenzer & Hoffrage, 1995; Gigerenzer & Todd, 1999, for additional perspectives on how statistical thinking and heuristics operate in reasoning.)

THE CONFIRMATION BIAS

One of the major roadblocks to accurate reasoning is the **confirmation bias**, our tendency to selectively look for information that conforms to our hypothesis and to overlook information that argues against it. This effect was demonstrated by Wason (1960), who presented participants with the following instructions:

> You will be given three numbers which conform to a simple rule that I have in mind.... Your aim is to discover this rule by writing down sets of three numbers together with your reasons for your choice of them. After you have written down each set, I shall tell you whether your numbers conform to the rule or not. When you feel highly confident that you have discovered the rule, you are to write it down and tell me what it is. (p. 131)

After Wason presented the first set of numbers, 2, 4, and 6, the participants began creating their own sets of three numbers and receiving feedback from Wason. Note that Wason told participants only whether the numbers they proposed fit *his* rule. The participants did not find out whether *their* rule was correct until they felt confident enough to actually announce their rule. The most common initial hypothesis was "increasing intervals of two." Because the actual rule was "three numbers in increasing order of magnitude," the rule "increasing intervals of two" is incorrect even though it creates sequences that satisfy Wason's rule.

The secret to determining the correct rule is to try to create sequences that *don't* satisfy the person's current hypothesis, but *do* satisfy Wason's rule. Thus, determining that the sequence 2, 4, 5 is correct, allows us to reject our "increasing intervals of two" hypothesis and formulate a new one. The few participants whose rule was correct on their first guess followed the strategy of testing a number of hypotheses themselves before announcing their rule, by creating sequences that were designed to *disconfirm* their current hypothesis. In contrast, participants who didn't guess the rule correctly on their first try tended to keep creating sequences that confirmed their current hypothesis.

The confirmation bias acts like a pair of blinders—we see the world according to rules we think are correct and are never dissuaded from this view because we seek out only evidence that confirms our rule. The confirmation bias is so strong that it can affect people's reasoning by causing them to ignore relevant information. Charles Lord and coworkers (1979) demonstrated this in an experiment that tested how people's attitudes are affected by exposure to evidence that contradicts those attitudes.

By means of a questionnaire, Lord identified one group of participants in favor of capital punishment and another group against it. Each participant was then presented with descriptions of research studies on capital punishment. Some of the studies provided evidence that capital punishment had a deterrent effect on murder; others provided evidence that capital punishment had no deterrent effect. When the participants reacted to the studies, their responses reflected the attitudes they had at the beginning of the experiment. For example, an article presenting evidence that supported the deterrence effect of capital punishment was rated as "convincing" by proponents of capital punishment and "unconvincing" by those against capital punishment. This is the confirmation bias at work—people's prior beliefs caused them to focus only on information that agreed with their beliefs and to disregard information that didn't.

TEST YOURSELF 13.2

1. What is inductive reasoning, and how is it different from deductive reasoning?
2. How is inductive reasoning involved in everyday experience?
3. How do the following cause errors in reasoning: availability heuristic; illusory correlations; representativeness heuristic; confirmation bias?
4. How can failure to take into account base rates and small sample sizes cause errors in reasoning?
5. What is the confirmation bias? Describe Wason's experiment on sequences of numbers and Lord's experiment on attitudes about capital punishment.

Decision Making: Choosing Among Alternatives

As we noted at the beginning of the chapter, we make decisions every day, from relatively unimportant ones (what clothes to wear, what movie to see) to those that can have great impact on our lives (what college to attend, whom to marry, what job to choose). The process of decision making can involve both inductive and deductive reasoning, so we have already considered some of the principles that apply to the study of how people make decisions.

When we discussed the availability and representativeness heuristics, we used examples in which people were asked to make judgments about things like causes of death or people's occupations. As we discuss decision making, our emphasis will be on how people make judgments that involve choices between different *courses of action*. These choices may involve personal decisions, such as deciding what school to attend or whether to fly or drive to a destination, or decisions made in conjunction with a profession, such as "Which advertising campaign should my company run?" or "Where should my law firm advertise to find another part-time student worker?" We begin by considering one of the basic properties of decision making: Decisions involve both benefits and costs.

THE UTILITY APPROACH TO DECISIONS

Much of the early theorizing on decision making was influenced by **expected utility theory.** This theory is based on the assumption that people are basically rational, so if they have all of the relevant information, they will make a decision that results in the maximum expected utility. **Utility** refers to outcomes that achieve a person's goals (Manktelow, 1999; Reber, 1995). The economists who studied decision making thought about utility in terms of monetary value; thus, the goal of good decision making was to make choices that resulted in the maximum monetary payoff.

One of the advantages of the utility approach is that it specifies procedures that make it possible to determine which choice would result in the highest monetary value. For example, if we know the odds of winning when playing a slot machine in a casino, and also know the cost of playing and the size of the payoff, it is possible to determine that, in the long run, playing slot machines is a losing proposition. But just because it is possible to predict the optimum strategy doesn't mean that people will follow that strategy. People regularly behave in ways that ignore the optimum way of responding based on probabilities. Even though most people realize that in the long run the casino wins, the huge popularity of gambling indicates that many people have decided to patronize casinos anyway. Observations such as this, as well as the results of many experiments, have led psychologists to conclude that people do not always make decisions that result in the desired outcome.

Here are some additional examples of situations in which people's decisions do not maximize the probability of a good outcome. Veronica Denes-Raj and Seymour Epstein (1994) offered participants the opportunity to earn up to $7 by receiving $1 every time they drew a red jelly bean from a bowl consisting of red and white jelly beans. When given a choice between drawing from a small bowl containing 1 red and 9 white beans (chances of drawing red = 10 percent; • Figure 13.8a) or from a

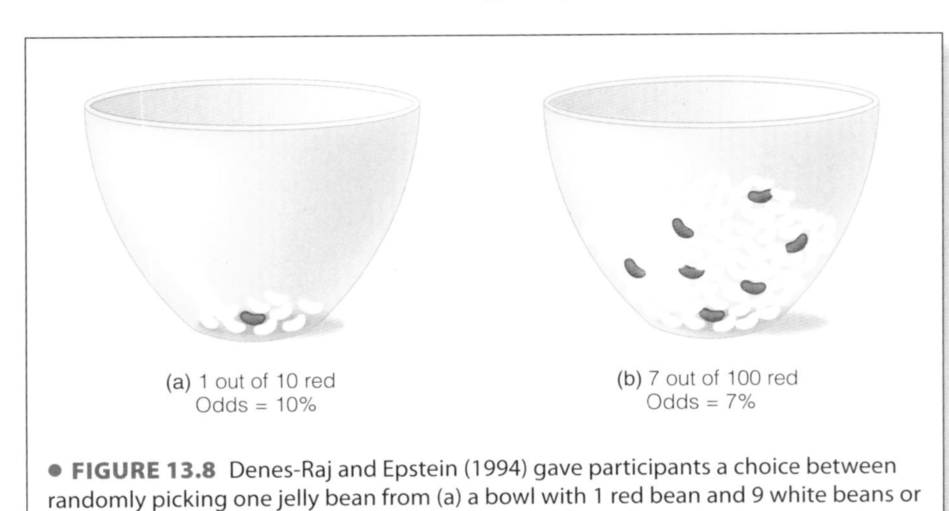

• **FIGURE 13.8** Denes-Raj and Epstein (1994) gave participants a choice between randomly picking one jelly bean from (a) a bowl with 1 red bean and 9 white beans or (b) a bowl with 7 red beans and 93 white beans (not all of the white beans are shown in this picture). Participants received money if they picked a red bean. (Source: Based on V. Denes-Raj & S. Epstein, "Conflict Between Intuitive and Rational Processing: When People Behave Against Their Better Judgment," *Journal of Personality and Social Psychology, 66*, 819–829, 1994.)

larger bowl containing a smaller proportion of red beans (for example, 7 red beans and 93 white beans, chances of drawing red = 7 percent; Figure 13.8b), many participants chose the larger bowl with the less favorable probability. When asked to explain, they reported that even though they knew the probabilities were against them, they somehow felt as if they had a better chance if there were more red beans. Apparently seeing more red beans overpowered their knowledge that the probability was lower (they were told how many red and white beans there were on each trial).

While deciding which bowl to pick jelly beans from is not a particularly important decision, participants' preference for the lower probability choice shows that they are influenced by considerations other than their knowledge of probabilities. A decision of greater consequence is the real-life decision of whether to travel by car or plane. Although it is well known that the odds are far greater of being killed in a car accident than in a plane crash, a decrease in air travel and an increase in driving occurred following the 9/11 terrorist attacks. According to one calculation, the number of Americans who lost their lives on the road by avoiding the risk of flying was higher than the total number of passengers killed on the four hijacked flights (Gigerenzer, 2004).

The idea that the utility approach does not describe how people make decisions is also supported by an analysis of how contestants respond in the TV game *Deal or No Deal*. In this game a contestant is shown a list of 26 amounts of money, ranging from one cent to a million dollars. Each of these amounts is contained in one of 26 briefcases, which are displayed on stage. The game begins when the contestant picks one of these briefcases to be his or her own. The contestant is entitled to whatever amount of money is contained in that briefcase. The problem, however, is that the contestant doesn't know how much is in the briefcase, and the only way to find out is to open the remaining 25 briefcases, one by one, until the contestant's briefcase is the only one left (• Figure 13.9).

The contestant indicates which of the remaining 25 briefcases to open, one by one. Each time the contestant decides on a briefcase number, the model next to that briefcase opens it and reveals how much money is inside. Each dollar amount that is revealed is taken off the list of 26 dollar amounts or values. Thus, by looking at the list of values, the contestant can tell which values are out of play (the values in briefcases that have been opened) and which values are still in play. One of the values still in play will be in the contestant's briefcase, but the contestant doesn't know which one.

After opening 6 briefcases, the contestant is offered a deal by the bank based on the 20 remaining prizes. At this point, the contestant must choose between taking the guaranteed amount offered by the bank (Deal) or continuing the game (No Deal). The only information that can help the contestant decide is the amount the bank is offering and the list of values that are still in play, one of which is in the contestant's briefcase. If the contestant rejects the bank's initial offer, then the contestant opens more briefcases, and the bank will make a new offer. Each time the bank makes an offer, the contestant considers the bank's offer and the values that are still in play, and decides whether to take the bank's deal or continue the game.

NBC-TV/THE KOBAL COLLECTION/PATTON, TRAE/The Picture Desk

• **FIGURE 13.9** A decision point early in a game on the television show *Deal or No Deal*. The host, Howie Mandel, on the right, has just asked the contestant, on the left, whether he wants to accept an offer made by the bank (Deal) or continue the game (No Deal). In the background, models stand next to numbered briefcases that have not yet been opened. Each of these briefcases contains an unknown amount of money. The contestant's briefcase, not shown here, also contains an unknown amount of money.

For example, consider the following situation, shown in Table 13.4, which occurred in an actual game for a contestant we will call contestant X. The amounts in the left column are the values that were inside the 21 briefcases that contestant X had opened. The amounts in the right column are the values inside the 5 briefcases that had not yet been opened. Four of these briefcases were on stage, and the remaining one belonged to contestant X. Based on these amounts, the bank made an offer of \$80,000. In other words, contestant X had a choice between definitely receiving \$80,000 or taking a chance at getting a higher amount listed in the right column. The rational choice would seem to be to take the \$80,000, because there was only a 1 in 5 chance of winning \$300,000 and all of the other amounts were less than \$80,000.

TABLE 13.4 Contestant X's Situation After Opening 21 Briefcases (the bank's offer at this point was $80,000)

Opened (No Longer in Play)		Remaining (Still in Play)
$0.01	$5,000	**$100**
$1	$10,000	
$5	$25,000	**$400**
$10	$75,000	
$25	$100,000	**$1,000**
$50	$200,000	
$75	$400,000	**$50,000**
$200	$500,000	
$300	$750,000	**$300,000**
$500	$1,000,000	
$750		

Unfortunately, contestant X didn't take the deal, and the next briefcase opened contained $300,000, taking it out of play. Contestant X then accepted the bank's new offer of $21,000, ending the game.

Thierry Post and coworkers (2008) analyzed contestants' responses in hundreds of games and concluded that the contestants' choices are determined not just by the amounts of money left in the briefcases, but by what has happened leading up to their decision. Post found that if things are going well for the contestant (they have opened a number of small money briefcases) and the bank begins offering more and more, the contestant is likely to be cautious and accept a deal early. In contrast, when contestants are doing poorly (having opened a number of large denomination briefcases) and the banks offers go down, they are likely to take more risks and keep playing. Post suggests that one reason for this behavior on the part of contestants who are doing poorly is that they want to avoid the negative feeling of being a loser. They therefore take more risks, in the hope of "beating the odds" and coming out ahead in the end. This is probably what happened to contestant X, with unfortunate results. What seems to be happening here is that contestants' decisions are swayed by their emotions. We will now describe a number of examples, many of which involve emotions and other factors that are not considered by utility theory.

HOW EMOTIONS AFFECT DECISIONS

Emotions can affect decisions in a number of different ways (Han & Lerner, 2009). Expected emotions are emotions that people *predict* they will feel for a particular outcome. For example, a *Deal or No Deal* contestant might think about a choice in terms of how good she will feel about accepting the bank's offer of $125,000 (even though she could potentially win $500,000), how great she will feel if she wins the $500,000, but also how bad she will feel if she doesn't accept the bank's offer and finds out there is only $10 in her briefcase.

Note that while expected emotion provides information about *probable* emotional outcomes of a decision, it doesn't involve actually *feeling* an emotion. Because emotion potentially provides information, this means that expected emotions can be part of a utility approach, because an outcome that results in a positive emotion will likely be a good outcome and one that results in a negative emotion will likely be a poor outcome (Lowenstein et al., 2003; Wilson & Gilbert, 2003).

Immediate emotions are emotions that are *experienced* at the time a decision is being made. There are two types of immediate emotions. Integral immediate emotions are emotions that are associated with the act of making a decision. For example, a *Deal or No Deal* contestant who is trying to decide whether to accept or turn down the bank's offer may feel extremely anxious. This anxiety is the integral emotion associated with making the decision, and it is probable that this emotion could affect the decision.

Incidental immediate emotions are emotions that are unrelated to the decision. Incidental emotions can be caused by a person's general disposition (the person is naturally happy, for example), or something that happened earlier in the day, or reacting to the general environment such as background music being played in a game show or the yells of the game show audience.

Each of these types of emotions can potentially have an effect on decisions, but only expected emotion, which involves some element of rational thought, can be handled within the expected utility framework. However, in the next section we will see that expected emotions may not accurately predict the actual emotion that would result from the outcome of a decision.

PEOPLE INACCURATELY PREDICT THEIR EMOTIONS

A basic characteristic of research on decisions is the phenomenon of risk aversion—the tendency to avoid taking risks. For example, a *Deal or No Deal* contestant who decides to accept the banker's offer rather than take a chance on winning big or losing it all may be motivated by risk aversion.

Expected emotions are one of the determinants of risk aversion, because one of the things that increase the chance of risk aversion is the tendency to believe that a particular loss will have a greater impact than a gain of the same size (Tversky & Kahneman, 1991). For example, if people believe it would be very disturbing to lose $100 but only slightly pleasant to win $100, then this would cause them to decline a bet for which the odds are 50-50, such as flipping a coin (win $100 for heads; lose $100 for tails). In fact, because of this effect, some people are reluctant to take a 50-50 bet in which winning pays $200 and losing pays $100, even though in accordance with utility theory, this would be a good bet (Kermer et al., 2006).

Deborah Kermer and coworkers (2006) studied this effect by doing an experiment that compared people's expected emotions with their actual emotions. They gave participants $5 and told them that based on a coin flip they would either win an additional $5 or lose $3. Participants rated their happiness before the experiment started and then predicted how their happiness would change if they won the coin toss (gain $5, so they have $10) or lost it (lose $3, so they have $2). The results of these ratings are indicated by the left pair of bars in • Figure 13.10. Notice that the participants predicted that the negative effect of losing $3 would be greater than the positive effect of winning $5.

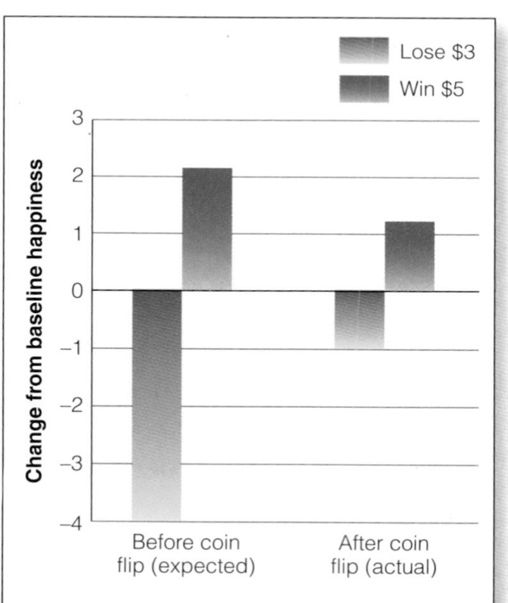

• **FIGURE 13.10** The results of Kermer et al.'s (2006) experiments showing that people overestimate the expected negative effect of losing (left red bar), compared to the actual effect of losing (right red bar). (Source: Based on D. A. Kermer, E. Driver-Linn, T. D. Wilson, & D. T. Gilbert, "Loss Aversion Is an Affective Forecasting Error," *Psychological Science, 17*, 649–653, 2006.)

After the coin toss, in which some participants won and some lost, they carried out a filler task for 10 minutes and then rated their happiness. The bars on the right show that the actual effect of losing was substantially less than predicted, but the positive effect of winning was only a little less than predicted. As a result, the positive effect of winning and negative effect of losing were about equal.

Why do people overestimate what their negative feelings will be? One reason is that when making their prediction they don't take into account the various coping mechanisms they may use to deal with adversity. For example, a person who doesn't get a job he wanted might rationalize the failure by saying "The salary wasn't what I really wanted" or "I'll find something better." In Kremer's experiment, participants predicting how they would feel if they lost focused on losing $5; after the outcome was determined, participants who actually lost focused on the fact that they still had $2 left.

The results of Kremer's experiment, plus others, show that the inability to correctly predict the emotional outcome of a decision can lead to inefficient decision making (Peters et al., 2006; Wilson & Gilbert, 2003). We will now see how emotions that aren't even related to making the decision can affect the decision.

INCIDENTAL EMOTIONS AFFECT DECISIONS

How might the fact that you feel happy or sad, or are in an environment that causes positive or negative feelings, affect your decisions? There is evidence that decision making is affected by these incidental emotions, even though they are not directly related to the decision. For example, in a paper titled "Clouds Make Nerds Look Good," Uri Simonsohn (2007) reports an analysis of university admissions decisions in which he found that applicants' academic attributes were more heavily weighted on cloudy days than on sunny days (nonacademic attributes won out on sunny days). In another study, he found that prospective students visiting an academically highly rated university were more likely to enroll if they had visited the campus on a cloudy day (Simonsohn, 2009).

An example of how emotions can affect the economic decisions of establishing selling and buying prices is provided in a study by Jennifer Lerner and coworkers (2004). Participants viewed one of three film clips, calculated to elicit emotions: (1) a person dying (sadness); (2) a person using a dirty toilet (disgust); and (3) fish at the Great Barrier Reef (neutral). Participants in the sadness and disgust groups were also asked to write about how they would feel if they were in the situation shown in the clip.

Lerner and coworkers then gave participants a highlighter set and determined (1) the price for which participants would be willing to sell the set (sell condition) and (2) the price at which they would be willing to choose the set instead of accepting the money (choice condition). The choice condition is roughly equivalent to setting the price they would pay for it.

The left bars in ● Figure 13.11 show that participants in the disgust and sadness group were willing to sell the set for less than the neutral group. Lerner suggests that this occurs because disgust is associated with a need to expel things and sad emotions are associated with a need for change. The right bars show that participants in the sad group were willing to pay more for the set. This also fits with the idea of sadness being associated with a need for change. The proposed reasons behind setting buying and selling prices are hypothetical at this point, but whatever the reasons, this study and others support the idea that a person's mood can influence economic decisions.

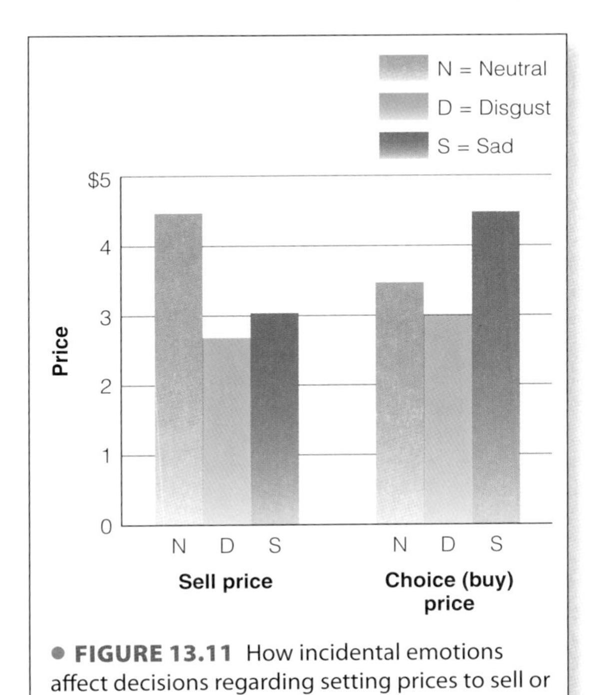

● **FIGURE 13.11** How incidental emotions affect decisions regarding setting prices to sell or buy an item. (Source: Based on data from J. S. Lerner, D. A. Small, & G. Lowenstein, "Heart Strings and Purse Strings: Effects of Emotions on Economic Transactions," *Psychological Science, 15*, 337–341, 2004).

DECISIONS CAN DEPEND ON HOW CHOICES ARE PRESENTED

Our discussion of deductive and inductive reasoning has shown that reasoning is affected by more than just the facts of the situation. This also happens in decision making when a person's judgments are affected by the way choices are stated. For example, take the decision about whether to become a potential organ donor. Although a poll has found that 85 percent of Americans approve of organ donation, only 28 percent have actually granted permission by signing a donor card. This signing of the card is called an **opt-in procedure**, because it requires the person to take an active step (Johnson & Goldstein, 2003).

The low American consent rate for organ donation also occurs in other countries, such as Denmark (4 percent), the United Kingdom (27 percent), and Germany (12 percent). One thing that these countries have in common is that they all use an opt-in procedure. However, in France and Belgium the consent rate is more than 99 percent. These countries use an opt-out procedure, in which everyone is a potential organ donor unless he or she requests not to be.

Besides having important ramifications for public health (in 1995 more than 45,000 people in the United States died waiting for a suitable donor organ), the difference between opt-in and opt-out procedures has important implications for the theory of decision making. According to the utility approach, people make decisions based on expected utility value; therefore, their decisions shouldn't depend on how the potential choices are stated.

However, the opt-in versus opt-out results indicate that the procedure used to identify people's willingness to be organ donors does have an effect.

An example of how the wording of a problem can influence a decision was demonstrated by Paul Slovic and coworkers (2000). They showed forensic psychologists and psychiatrists a case history of a mental patient, Mr. Jones, and asked them to judge the likelihood that the patient would commit an act of violence within 6 months of being discharged. The key variable in this experiment was the nature of a statement that presented information about previous cases. When they were told that "20 out of every 100 patients similar to Mr. Jones are estimated to commit an act of violence," 41 percent refused to discharge him. However, when told that "patients similar to Mr. Jones are estimated to have a 20 percent chance of committing an act of violence," only 21 percent refused to discharge him. Why did this difference occur? One possibility is that the first statement conjures up images of 20 people being beaten up, whereas the second is a more abstract probability statement that could be interpreted to mean that there is only a small chance that patients like Mr. Jones will be violent.

Here's another example of choosing between two alternatives, for you to try.

CogLab Risky Decisions

CogLab Decision Making

DEMONSTRATION What Would You Do?

Imagine that the United States is preparing for the outbreak of an unusual disease that is expected to kill 600 people. Two alternative programs to combat the disease have been proposed. Assume that the exact scientific estimates of the consequences of the programs are as follows:

- If Program A is adopted, 200 people will be saved.
- If Program B is adopted, there is a 1/3 probability that 600 people will be saved, and a 2/3 probability that no people will be saved.

Which of the two programs would you favor?

Now consider the following additional proposals for combating the same disease:

- If Program C is adopted, 400 people will die.
- If Program D is adopted, there is a 1/3 probability that nobody will die, and a 2/3 probability that 600 people will die.

Which of these two programs would you pick?

When offered the first pair of proposals, 72 percent of the students in an experiment by Tversky and Kahneman (1981) chose Program A and the rest picked Program B (● Figure 13.12). The choice of Program A represents a **risk aversion strategy**. The idea of saving 200 lives with certainty is more attractive than the risk that no one will be saved. However, when Tversky and Kahneman presented the descriptions of Programs C and D to another group of students, 22 percent picked Program C and 78 percent picked Program D. This represents a **risk-taking strategy**. The certain death of 400 people is less acceptable than a 2 in 3 chance that 600 people will die.

Tversky and Kahneman concluded that, in general, when a choice is framed in terms of gains (as in the first problem, which is stated in terms of saving lives), people use a risk aversion strategy, and when a choice is framed in terms of losses (as in the second problem, which is stated in terms of losing lives), people use a risk-taking strategy.

But if we look at the four programs closely, we can see that they are identical pairs (Figure 13.12). Programs A and C both result in 200 people living and 400 people dying. Yet 72 percent of the participants picked Program A and only 22 percent picked Program C. A similar situation occurs if we compare Programs B and D. Both lead to the same number of deaths, yet one was picked by 28 percent of the participants and the other by 78 percent. These results illustrate the **framing effect**—decisions are influenced by how the choices are stated, or *framed*.

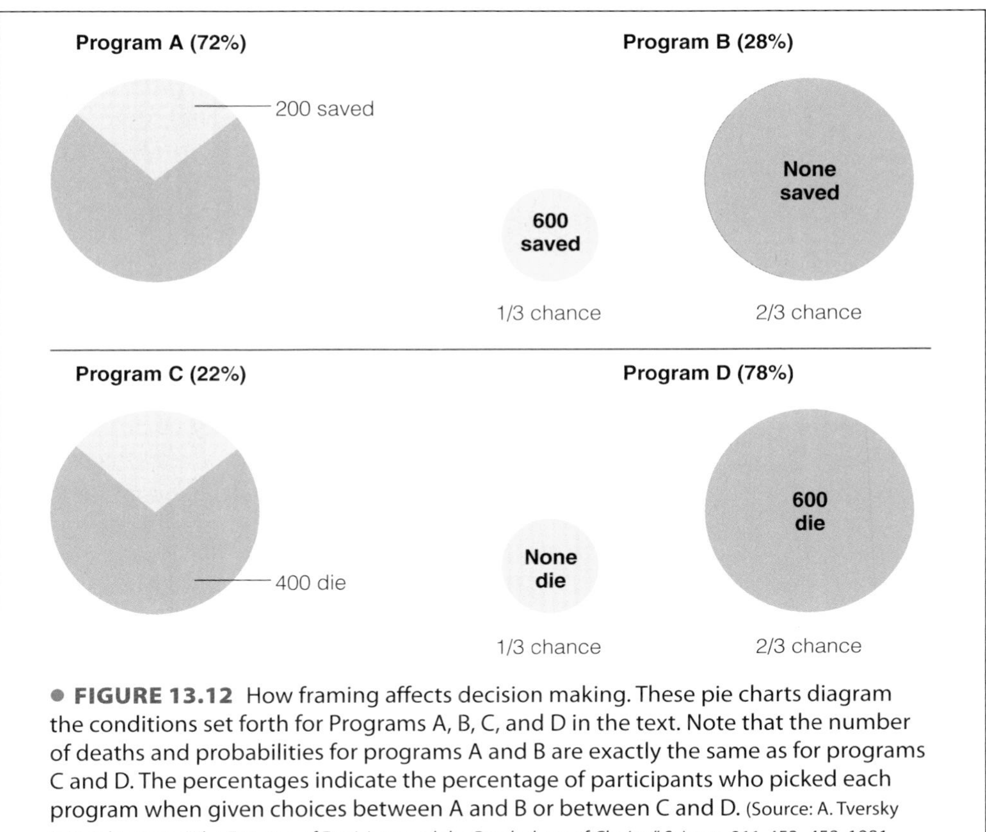

● **FIGURE 13.12** How framing affects decision making. These pie charts diagram the conditions set forth for Programs A, B, C, and D in the text. Note that the number of deaths and probabilities for programs A and B are exactly the same as for programs C and D. The percentages indicate the percentage of participants who picked each program when given choices between A and B or between C and D. (Source: A. Tversky & D. Kahneman, "The Framing of Decisions and the Psychology of Choice," *Science, 211*, 453–458, 1981. Reprinted by permission of AAAS.)

One reason people's decisions are affected by framing is that the way a problem is stated can highlight some features of the situation (for example, that people will die) and deemphasize others (Kahneman, 2003). It should not be a surprise that the way a choice is stated can influence cognitive processes, because this is similar to what happens when problems like the Wason task are stated in real-world terms. We also saw, in the chapter on problem solving, that the way a problem is stated can influence our ability to solve it (page 335). (Also see "If You Want to Know More: Physiology of Framing" on page 388.)

JUSTIFICATION IN DECISION MAKING

To end our consideration of decision making, we will consider yet another factor that influences how people make decisions. This factor is the need to justify the decision. We can illustrate this by considering an experiment by Tversky and Eldar Shafir (1992), in which they presented the following problem to two groups of students. The "pass" group saw the statement indicating that they passed; the "fail" group saw the statement indicating that they failed.

> Imagine that you have just taken a tough qualifying examination. It is the end of the semester, you feel tired and run-down, and you find out that [(*pass group*) you passed the exam; (*fail group*) you failed the exam and will have to take it again in a couple of months—after the Christmas holidays]. You now have the opportunity to buy a very attractive 5-day Christmas vacation package to Hawaii at an exceptionally low price. The special offer expires tomorrow. Would you
>
> - Buy the vacation package?
> - Not buy the vacation package?
> - Pay a $5 nonrefundable fee in order to retain the right to buy the vacation package at the same exceptional price the day after tomorrow?

TABLE 13.5 Choice Behavior and Knowledge of Exam Outcome

	Passed	Failed	Result in 2 Days
Buy vacation package	54 %	57 %	32 %
Don't buy	16	12	7
$5 to keep open option to buy later	30	31	61

The results for the two groups are shown in the columns headed "Passed" and "Failed" in Table 13.5. Notice that there is no difference between the two groups. Fifty-four percent of the participants in the "pass" group and 57 percent of those in the "fail" group opted to buy the vacation package.

The interesting result happened when a third group was given the same situation, except these participants were told that the outcome of the exam wouldn't be available for 2 more days. Only 32 percent of these participants opted for the package, and 61 percent decided they would pay the $5 so they could put off making the decision until they knew whether or not they had passed the exam. Thus, 61 percent of the participants in this group did not want to make a decision about the trip until they found out whether they had passed or failed, even though the results for the other two groups indicate that passing or failing made no difference in the actual decision about the vacation packages.

To explain this result, Tversky and Shafir suggest that once students know the outcome, they can then assign a reason for deciding to buy the vacation. Participants who passed could see the vacation as a reward; participants who failed could see the vacation as a consolation that would give them time to recuperate before taking the exam again.

Although there are other possible interpretations for these results, there is a great deal of other evidence that the decision-making process often includes looking for justification so the person can state a rationale for his or her decision. This is why doctors may carry out medical tests that might not lead to a different treatment but that provide additional evidence for the treatment they have recommended, thereby making it easier to justify the treatment to themselves, their patients, and, if necessary, to the courts (Tversky & Shafir, 1992).

The Physiology of Thinking

In this section we will consider the types of thinking we have discussed in this chapter and the previous one. We begin by asking the question, "How is the brain involved in problem solving, reasoning, and making decisions?" Because all of these forms of thinking involve a number of different cognitive capacities—including perception, memory, and the ability to focus and maintain attention—it isn't surprising that a number of different areas of the brain are involved. However, we will focus on one area in particular, the prefrontal cortex (PFC).

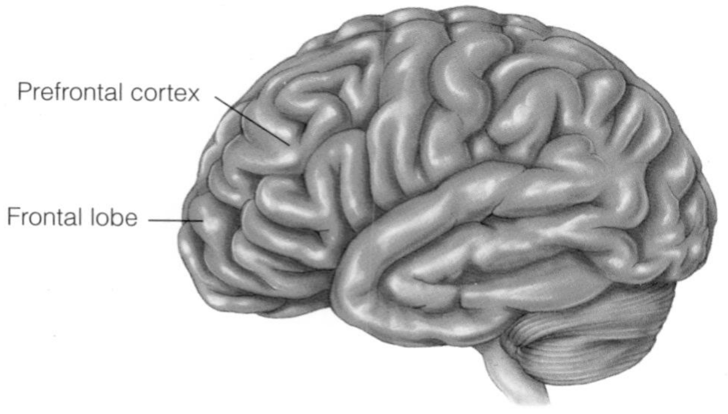

● **FIGURE 13.13** Brain showing location of the prefrontal cortex (PFC).

EFFECT OF DAMAGE TO THE PREFRONTAL CORTEX

The prefrontal cortex (● Figure 13.13) is activated by stimuli from all of the senses, by the retrieval of memories, and by the anticipation of future events, and can be affected by a person's emotional state (Wallis et al., 2001). It is not surprising, therefore, that the PFC plays a central role in determining complex behaviors that are involved in thinking. There is a great deal of neuropsychological evidence (recently supplemented by the results of brain scanning experiments) that shows that a wide range of cognitive functions related to thinking are affected by damage to the prefrontal cortex.

Planning and Perseveration One of the earliest reports of the effect of frontal lobe damage on functioning involved a young homemaker who had a tumor in her frontal lobe that made it impossible for her to plan a family meal, even though she was capable of cooking the individual dishes (Penfield & Evans, 1935). Results such as this led to the conclusion that the PFC plays an important role in planning future activities (Owen et al., 1990).

The prefrontal cortex has been linked to problem solving in a number of ways. Damage to the PFC interferes with people's ability to act with flexibility, a key requirement for solving problems. One symptom of PFC damage is a behavior called *perseveration* (see page 136), in which patients have difficulty switching from one pattern of behavior to another (Hauser, 1999; Munakata et al., 2003). For example, patients with damage to the PFC have difficulty when the rules change in a card-sorting task. Thus, if they begin by successfully separating out the blue cards from a pack, they continue picking the blue cards even after the experimenter tells them to shift to separating out the brown cards. Clearly, perseveration would play havoc with attempts to solve complex problems for which it is necessary to consider one possible solution and then shift to another possibility if the first one doesn't work.

Problem Solving Because damage to the PFC results in perseveration and poor planning ability, it is not surprising that PFC damage decreases performance on tasks such as the Tower of Hanoi problem (Morris et al., 1997), the Tower of London problem (a similar task that involves moving colored beads between two vertical rods; Carlin et al., 2000; Owen et al., 1990), and the Luchins water-jug problem (Colvin et al., 2001). Brain imaging has also shown that problem solving activates the PFC in normal participants (Rowe et al., 2001).

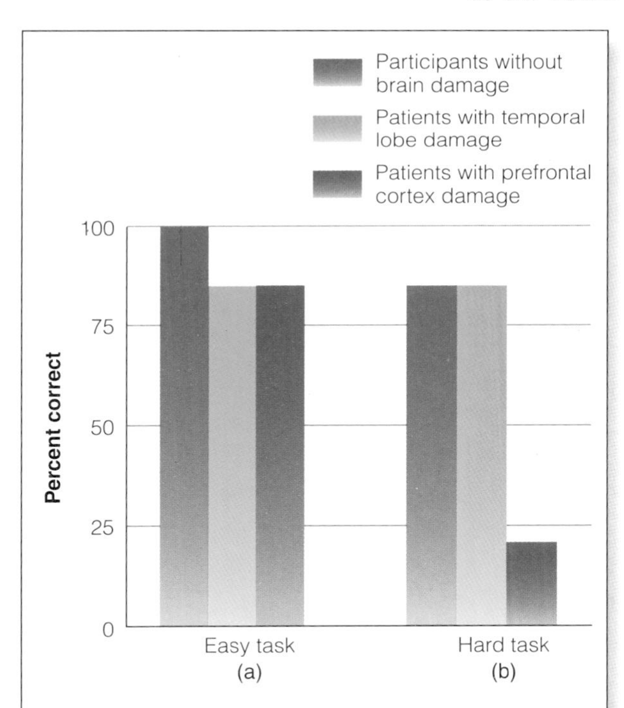

● **FIGURE 13.14** Effect of damage to the PFC on performance on a reasoning task. Participants without brain damage, participants with temporal lobe damage, and participants with PFC damage can all solve the easy task (left bars), but the PFC group's performance drops to a low level when the task is made more difficult (Source: Based on J. A. Waltz et al., "A System for Relational Reasoning in Human Prefrontal Cortex," *Psychological Science, 10*, 119–124, 1999. Reprinted by permission of John Wiley & Sons, Inc.)

Understanding Stories Other research has shown that the PFC is important for a number of cognitive tasks involving planning, reasoning, and making connections among different parts of a problem or a story. For example, when Tiziana Zalla and coworkers (2002) tested patients with PFC damage, they found that these patients were able to understand individual words and could identify events described in stories. However, they were unable to follow the order of events in the story or to make inferences that connected different parts of the story.

Reasoning There is also a large amount of evidence that the PFC is important for reasoning. This has been demonstrated by presenting a deductive reasoning task to people with PFC damage. Participants were presented with relationships such as "Sam is taller than Nate; Nate is taller than Roger" and asked to arrange the names in order of the people's heights. When James Waltz and coworkers (1999) presented these tasks to patients with PFC damage, patients with temporal lobe damage, and participants without brain damage, they found that all of these groups did well when the task was easy, like the previous one about Sam, Nate, and Roger (● Figure 13.14a). However, when the task was made more difficult by scrambling the order of presentation ("Beth is taller than Tina; Amy is taller than Beth"), the people without brain damage and the patients with temporal lobe damage still did well, but the PFC patients performed poorly (Figure 13.14b). This result confirms the conclusion of brain imaging studies, which show that as reasoning problems become more complex, reasoning activates larger areas of the PFC (Kroger et al., 2002). (Also see "If You Want to Know More: Neurons That Respond to Abstract Rules" on page 389.)

NEUROECONOMICS: THE NEURAL BASIS OF DECISION MAKING

A new approach to studying decision making, called **neuroeconomics**, combines research from the fields of psychology, neuroscience, and economics (Lee, 2006; Lowenstein et al., 2008; Sanfey et al., 2006). One outcome of this approach has been research that has identified areas of the brain that are activated as people make decisions while playing economic games. This research shows that decisions are often influenced by emotions, and that these emotions are associated with activity in specific areas of the brain.

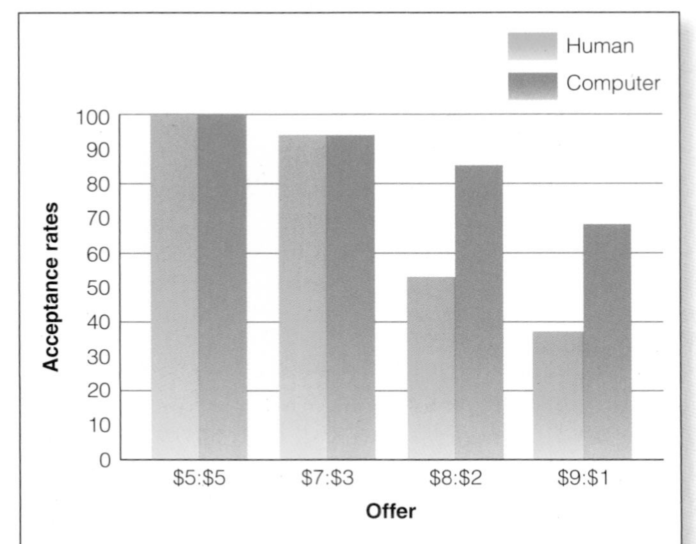

• **FIGURE 13.15** Behavioral results of Sanfey and coworkers' (2003) experiment, showing responders' acceptance rates in response to different offers made by human partners and computer partners. (Source: Based on A. G. Sanfey et al., "The Neural Basis of Economic Decision Making in the Ultimatum Game," *Science, 300*, 1755–1758, 2003.)

To illustrate the neuroeconomic approach, we will describe an experiment by Alan Sanfey and coworkers (2003) in which people's brain activity was measured as they played the ultimatum game. The **ultimatum game** is very simple. Two people play. One is designated as the *proposer* and the other as the *responder.* The proposer is given a sum of money, say $10, and makes an offer to the responder as to how this money should be split between them. If the responder accepts the offer, then the money is split according to the proposal. If the responder rejects the offer, neither player receives anything. Either way, the game is over after the responder makes his or her decision.

According to utility theory, the responder should accept the proposer's offer, no matter what it is. This is the rational response, because if you accept the offer you get something, but if you refuse, you get nothing (remember that the game is only one trial long, so there is no second chance).

In Sanfey's experiment, participants played 20 separate games as responder: 10 with 10 different human partners and 10 with a computer partner. The offers made by both the human and computer partners were determined by the experimenters, with some being "fair" (evenly split, so the responder received $5) and some "unfair" (the responder received $1, $2, or $3). The results of responders' interactions with their human partners (orange bars in • Figure 13.15) match the results of other research on the ultimatum game—all responders accept an offer of $5, most accept the $3 offer, and half or more reject the $1 or $2 offers.

Why do people reject low offers? When Sanfey and coworkers asked participants, many explained that they were angry because they felt the offers were unfair. Consistent with this explanation, when participants received exactly the same offers from their computer partner, more accepted "unfair" proposals (turquoise bars in Figure 13.15). Apparently, people are less likely to get angry with an unfair computer than with an unfair person.

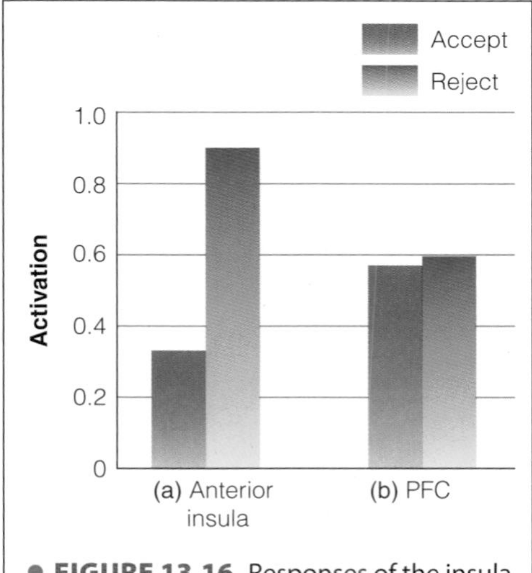

• **FIGURE 13.16** Responses of the insula and PFC to "fair" and "unfair" offers. (Source: Based on A. G. Sanfey et al., "Neuroeconomics: Cross-Currents in Research on Decision-Making," *Trends in Cognitive Sciences, 10*, 106–116, 2006. Reprinted by permission of Elsevier.)

In addition to testing people's behavior, Sanfey and coworkers measured brain activity in the responders as they were making their decisions. The results showed that the right anterior insula, an area located deep within the brain between the parietal and temporal lobes, was activated about three times more strongly when responders rejected an offer than when they accepted it (• Figure 13.16a). Also, participants with higher activation to unfair offers rejected a higher proportion of the offers. The fact that the insula responded during rejection is not surprising when we consider that this area of the brain is connected with negative emotional states, including pain, distress, hunger, anger, and disgust.

What about the prefrontal cortex, which plays such a large role in complex cognitive behaviors? The PFC is also activated by the decision task, but this activation is the same for offers that are rejected and offers that are accepted (Figure 13.16b). Sanfey hypothesizes that the function of the PFC may be to deal with the cognitive demands of the task, which involves the goal of accumulating as much money as possible. Looked at in this way, each of these brain areas represents a different goal of the ultimatum game—the emotional goal of resenting unfairness is handled by the anterior insula, and the cognitive goal of accumulating money is handled by the PFC.

The results of this experiment support the idea that it is important to take emotional factors into account when considering decision making. It also illustrates the value of combining both physiological and behavioral approaches to the study of decision making.

Something to Consider

Is What Is Good for You Also Good for Me?

When we discussed how framing affects decision making, we saw that people's decisions regarding programs to deal with the outbreak of a hypothetical disease depended on how the problem was stated (page 380). We now pose a similar type of medical problem, but in a more personal way, because the hypothetical decision you are asked to make could affect you personally (adapted from Zikmund-Fisher et al., 2006).

DEMONSTRATION A Personal Health Decision

Imagine that there will be a deadly flu going around your area next winter. Your doctor says that you have a 10 percent chance (10 out of 100) of dying from this flu. A new flu vaccine has been developed and tested. If administered, the vaccine will prevent you from catching the deadly flu. However, there is one serious risk involved: The vaccine is made from a somewhat weaker type of flu virus, so there is a 5 percent risk (5 out of 100) that the vaccine could kill you. Considering this information, decide between the following two alternatives:

- I will not take the vaccine, and I accept the 10 percent chance of dying from this flu.
- I will take the vaccine, and I accept the 5 percent chance of dying from the weaker flu in the vaccine.

When Brian Zikmund-Fisher and coworkers (2006) gave this choice to their participants, 48 percent said they would take the vaccine. This is an interesting result, because it means that 52 percent of the participants decided to do nothing, even though statistically this doubled their chances of dying.

This result is an example of the **omission bias**—the tendency to do nothing to avoid having to make a decision that could be interpreted as causing harm. However, Zikmund-Fisher's experiment asked participants not only to imagine that they were making a decision for themselves, as in the demonstration, but to make the decision while imagining themselves in the following three roles: (1) as a physician recommending a treatment for a patient; (2) as a hospital medical director setting treatment guidelines for all patients in the hospital; and (3) as a parent of a child who might receive the treatment. The results of this experiment, shown in • Figure 13.17, indicate that people are more likely to recommend that others receive the shot than they are to choose the shot for themselves.

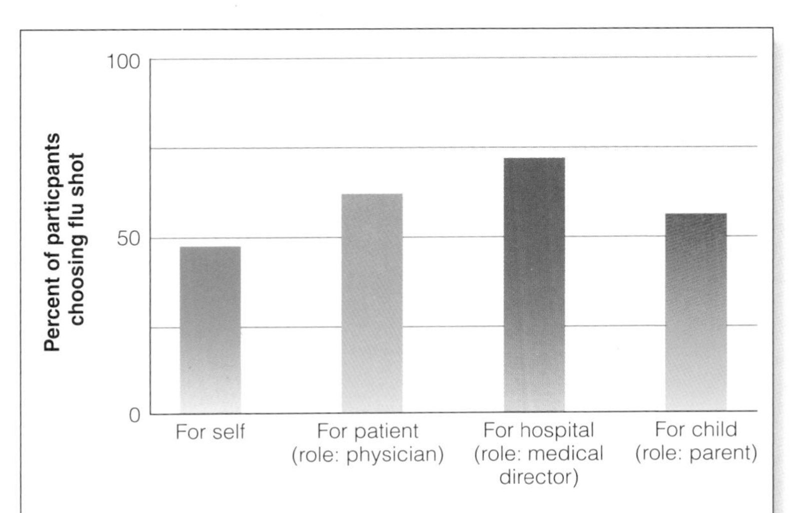

• **FIGURE 13.17** Effect of imagined decision-making role on willingness to choose the flu vaccine. (Source: Data from B. J. Zikmund-Fisher et al., "A Matter of Perspective: Choosing for Others Differs From Choosing for Yourself When Making Treatment Decisions," *Journal of General Internal Medicine, 21*, 618–622, 2006.)

Apparently, the decisions people make can be influenced by the person or group for whom they are making the decision. But why does this occur? Zikmund-Fisher and coworkers propose that when making decisions for others, people take into account the possibility that they will be held responsible if something bad happens. Looked at from this point of view, it is easy to understand why a medical director would be prone to recommend that hospital patients receive the vaccine, because it is easy to justify a decision that maximizes survival chances for a group of people.

The most important implication of these results may be what it suggests about how physicians should present choices to their patients. Physicians often feel that they should simply present the information and let their patients deal with making the decision. But perhaps physicians should be sensitive to some of the emotional factors facing patients who are being asked to make decisions about their own treatment. Zikmund-Fisher and coworkers suggest that physicians should consider asking patients to "reframe" their decision by thinking about it as if it were a decision they were making for someone else. The idea behind doing this would be to help the patient gain a better understanding of the trade-offs they face.

TEST YOURSELF 13.3

1. What is the utility approach to decisions? What are some examples of situations in which people do not behave to maximize the outcome, as the utility approach proposes?
2. Distinguish between expected emotions, integral immediate emotions, and incidental immediate emotions.
3. What is the connection between risk aversion and people's ability to predict their emotions? Describe the Kermer experiment in which participants rated their expected happiness before gambling and their actual happiness after the results were known.
4. What is some evidence that incidental emotions affect decisions? Consider the relationship between the weather and university admissions, and Lerner's experiment on the relationship between mood and setting buying and selling prices.
5. How do the way choices are presented and the need to justify decisions affect the decisions people make?
6. How is the prefrontal cortex involved in problem solving and reasoning?
7. What is neuroeconomics? Describe Sanfey and coworkers' (2003) experiment, and indicate what it adds to our understanding of decision making.
8. How are people's decisions about treatment options influenced by the person or group for whom they are making the decision?

CHAPTER SUMMARY

1. Reasoning is a cognitive process in which people start with information and come to conclusions that go beyond that information. Deductive reasoning involves syllogisms and can result in definite conclusions. Inductive reasoning is based on evidence and results in conclusions that are *probably* true.
2. Categorical syllogisms have two premises and a conclusion that describe the relation between two categories by using statements that begin with *all*, *no*, or *some*.
3. A syllogism is valid if its conclusion follows logically from its premises. The validity of a syllogism is determined by its form. This is different from *truth*, which is determined by the content of the statements in the syllogism and has to do with how statements correspond to known facts.
4. Conditional syllogisms have two premises and a conclusion, like categorical syllogisms, but the first premise has the form "If ... then...." The four basic types of conditional syllogism are (a) affirming the antecedent and (b) denying the consequent (both valid); (c) affirming the consequent and (d) denying the antecedent (both invalid).
5. The Wason four-card problem has been used to study how people think when evaluating conditional syllogisms. People make errors in the abstract version, but perform better when the problem is stated in real-world terms, as in the "drinking age" version. The key to solving the problem is to apply the falsification principle.
6. Based on experiments using different versions of the Wason problem, a number of mechanisms have been proposed to explain people's performance. These mechanisms include using permission schemas, and the evolutionary approach, which explains performance in terms of social exchange theory. Many experiments have provided evidence for and

against these explanations, leaving the controversy about how to explain the Wason problem still unresolved.

7. In inductive reasoning, conclusions follow not from logically constructed syllogisms, but from evidence. Conclusions are *suggested* with varying degrees of certainty. The strength of an inductive argument depends on the representativeness, number, and quality of observations on which the argument is based.
8. Inductive reasoning plays a major role in everyday life because we often make predictions about what we think will happen based on our observations about what has happened in the past.
9. The availability heuristic states that events that are more easily remembered are judged as being more probable than events that are less easily remembered. This heuristic can sometimes lead to correct judgments, and sometimes not. Errors due to the availability heuristic have been demonstrated by having people estimate the relative prevalence of various causes of death.
10. Illusory correlations and stereotypes, which can lead to incorrect conclusions about relationships between things, are related to the availability heuristic, because they draw attention to specific relationships and therefore make them more "available."
11. The representativeness heuristic is based on the idea that people often make judgments based on how much one event resembles another event. Errors due to this heuristic have been demonstrated by asking participants to judge a person's occupation based on descriptive information. Errors occur when the representativeness heuristic leads people to ignore base rate information. In other situations, judgment errors occur when people ignore the conjunction rule and the law of large numbers.
12. The confirmation bias is the tendency to selectively look for information that conforms to a hypothesis and to overlook information that argues against it. Operation of this bias was demonstrated by Wason's number sequence task. This bias also operates in real life when people's attitudes influence the way they evaluate evidence.
13. The utility approach to decision making is based on the idea that people are basically rational, so when they have all of the relevant information, they will make a decision that results in outcomes that are in their best interest. Evidence that people do not always act in accordance with this approach includes gambling behavior, choosing to drive in the face of evidence that it is more dangerous than flying, and the behavior of contestants on quiz shows like *Deal or No Deal*.
14. Emotions can affect decisions. Expected emotions are emotions a person predicts will happen in response to the outcome of a decision. Integral emotions are associated with the act of making a decision. Incidental emotions are unrelated to the decision, but may affect the decision nonetheless.
15. There is evidence that people are not always accurate in predicting their emotions. This can lead to risk aversion. An experiment by Kermer demonstrates the difference between predicted emotions and the actual emotions experienced after making a decision.
16. There is a large amount of evidence that incidental emotions can affect decisions. Examples include the relationship between the weather and college admissions, and Lerner's experiment showing a relationship between emotions like sadness and anger and decisions regarding how to set buying and selling prices.
17. Decisions can depend on how choices are presented, or *framed*. Evidence includes the differences in behavior for opt-in vs. opt-out procedures, the results of Slovic's experiment involving decisions about a mental patient, and people's response to the Tversky and Kahneman lethal disease problem. When a choice is framed in terms of gains, people use a risk aversion strategy, but when the choice is framed in terms of losses, people use a risk-taking strategy. Decision making is also influenced by people's tendency to want to justify their decision and state a rationale for the decision.
18. The prefrontal cortex (PFC) is one of the major areas of the brain involved in thinking. Damage to the PFC can cause perseveration and poor planning ability, resulting in poor performance on everyday tasks, problems such as the Tower of Hanoi and water-jug problems, and other problems that involve reasoning.
19. Neuroeconomics studies decision making by combining approaches from psychology, neuroscience, and economics. The results of a neuroeconomics experiment using the ultimatum game have shown that people's emotions can interfere with their ability to make rational decisions. Brain imaging indicates that the anterior insula is associated with the emotions that occur during the ultimatum game while the PFC may be involved in the cognitive demands of the task.
20. An experiment that involved asking people to make a risky decision about being vaccinated against a deadly disease has shown that people are more likely to recommend that others receive the vaccination than they are to choose to receive the vaccination themselves. This result has implications for how physicians talk about treatment options with their patients.

Think ABOUT IT

1. Astrology is popular with many people because they perceive a close connection between astrological predictions and events in their lives. Explain factors that might lead to this perception, even if a close connection does not, in fact, exist.

2. Think about a decision you have made recently. It can be a minor one, such as deciding which restaurant to go to on Saturday evening, or a more important one, such as picking an apartment or deciding which college to attend. Analyze this decision, taking into account the processes you went through to arrive at it and how you justified it in your mind as being a good decision.
3. Create deductive syllogisms and inductive arguments that apply to the decision you analyzed in the previous question.
4. Johanna has a reputation for being extremely good at justifying her behavior by a process that is often called "rationalization." For example, she justifies the fact that she eats anything she wants by saying "Ten years ago this food was supposed to be bad for you, and now they are saying it may even have some beneficial effects, so what's the point of listening to the so-called health experts?" or "That movie actor who was really into red meat lived to be 95." Analyze Johanna's arguments by stating them as inductive or deductive arguments; better yet, do the same for one of your own rationalizations.
5. From watching the news or reading the paper, what can you conclude about how the availability heuristic can influence our conceptions of the nature of the lives of different groups of people (for example, movie stars, rich people, various racial, ethnic, or cultural groups) and how accurate these conceptions might actually be?
6. Describe a situation in which you made a poor decision because your judgment was clouded by emotion or some other factor.

If You WANT TO KNOW MORE

1. **Using diagrams to determine the validity of syllogisms.** There are a number of ways to use diagrams to determine whether syllogisms are valid. One method uses Venn diagrams; another uses Euler circles.

Edwards, A. W. F. (2004). *Cogwheels of the mind: The story of Venn diagrams.* Baltimore: Johns Hopkins University Press.

Shin, S.-J. (1994). *The logical status of diagrams.* Cambridge, UK: Cambridge University Press.

2. **Culture and cognition.** Culture can affect inductive reasoning and how people solve syllogisms, reason inductively, and solve math problems.

Dehaene, S., Izard, V., Pica, P., & Spelke, E. (2006). Core knowledge of geometry in an Amazonian indigene group. *Science, 311*, 381–384.

Nisbett, R. E. (2003). *The geography of thought.* New York: Free Press.

Scribner, S. (1977). Modes of thinking and ways of speaking: Culture and logic reconsidered. In P. N. Johnson-Laird & P. C. Wason (Eds.), *Thinking: Readings in cognitive science* (pp. 483–500). Cambridge: Cambridge University Press.

Tang, Y., Zhang, W., Chen, K., Feng, S., Ji, Y., Shen, J., Reiman, E. M., & Liu, Y. (2006). Arithmetic processing in the brain shaped by cultures. *Proceedings of the National Academy of Sciences, 103*, 10775–10780.

3. **Reasoning and the law.** Juries are asked to come to a conclusion by evaluating evidence. New research indicates that a person's beliefs can affect his or her decision making. Also, the brain's response depends on whether the evidence is consistent or inconsistent with the person's beliefs.

Fugelsang, J. A., & Dunbar, K. N. (2004). A cognitive neuroscience framework for understanding causal reasoning and the law. *Philosophical Transactions of the Royal Society of London, B: Biological Sciences, 359*, 1749–1754.

4. **Regret and decision making.** The results of the ultimatum game experiments show that human decision making can be influenced by emotions. Other experiments have shown that people's decision making is influenced by a desire to avoid the regret they would experience if they made the wrong decision.

Coricelli, G., Critchley, H. D., Joffily, M., O'Doherty, J. P., Sirigu, A., & Dolan, R. J. (2005). Regret and its avoidance: A neuroimaging study of choice behavior. *Nature Neuroscience, 8*, 1255–1262.

5. **Another view of rationality.** We described the idea that people's reasoning and decision making can be negatively affected by bias and the use of heuristics. Some researchers have proposed another approach that sees people as behaving more rationally than this view gives them credit for.

Chase, V. M., Hertwig, R., & Gigerenzer, G. (1998). Views of rationality. *Trends in Cognitive Sciences, 2*, 206–214.

6. **Physiology of framing.** The framing effect is associated with activity in the amygdala, an area associated with emotions.

De Martino, B., Kumaran, D., Seymour, B., & Dolan, R. J. (2006). Frames, biases, and rational decision-making in the human brain. *Science, 313*, 684–687.

7. **Neural responses to purchases and preferences.** Choosing between Coke and Pepsi, or taking price into account when deciding whether or not to purchase something, can be related to activity in the brain.

Knutson, B., Rick, S., Wimmer, G. E., Prelec, D., & Lowenstein, G. (2007). Neural predictors of purchases. *Neuron, 53*, 247–156.

McClure, S. M., Li, J., Tomlin, D., Cypert, K. S., Montague, L. M., & Montague, P. R. (2004). Neural correlates of behavioral preference for culturally familiar drinks. *Neuron, 44*, 379–387.

8. **Unconscious determinants of attention in the brain.** The outcome of a decision can be encoded in activity in the prefrontal and parietal cortex for as long as 10 seconds before a person is aware of the decision.

Soon, C. S., Brass, M., Heinze, H.-J., & Haynes, J.-D. (2008). Unconscious determinants of free decisions in the human brain. *Nature Neuroscience, 11*, 543–545.

9. **Neurons that respond to abstract rules.** There are neurons in the monkey PFC that respond to abstract rules. This adds to the evidence that the PFC is important for problem solving.

Wallis, J. D., Anderson, K. C., & Miller, E. K. (2001). Single neurons in prefrontal cortex encode abstract rules. *Nature, 411*, 953–956.

Key TERMS

Affirming the antecedent, 363
Affirming the consequent, 363
Antecedent, 362
Availability heuristic, 370
Base rate, 372
Categorical syllogism, 361
Conclusion (of syllogism), 361
Conditional syllogism, 362
Confirmation bias, 374
Conjunction rule, 373
Consequent, 362
Decisions, 360
Deductive reasoning, 360
Denying the antecedent, 363
Denying the consequent, 363
Expected emotion, 377
Expected utility theory, 375
Evolutionary perspective on cognition, 366
Falsification principle, 364
Framing effect, 380
Illusory correlation, 371
Immediate emotion, 377
Incidental immediate emotion, 378
Inductive reasoning, 360
Integral immediate emotion, 377
Law of large numbers, 373
Neuroeconomics, 384
Omission bias, 385
Opt-in procedure, 379
Opt-out procedure, 379
Permission schema, 365
Pragmatic reasoning schema, 365
Premise, 361
Reasoning, 360
Representativeness heuristic, 371
Risk aversion, 378
Risk aversion strategy, 380
Risk-taking strategy, 380
Social exchange theory, 366
Stereotype, 371
Syllogism, 360
Ultimatum game, 384
Utility, 375
Validity, 361
Wason four-card problem, 364

Media RESOURCES

The *Cognitive Psychology* Book Companion Website

www.cengage.com/international

Prepare for quizzes and exams with online resources—including a glossary, flashcards, tutorial quizzes, crossword puzzles, and more.

CogLab

To experience these experiments for yourself, go to coglab.wadsworth.com. Be sure to read each experiment's setup instructions before you go to the experiment itself. Otherwise, you won't know which keys to press.

Primary Labs

Wason selection task Two versions of the Wason four-card problem. (p. 364)

Typical reasoning How the representativeness heuristic can lead to errors of judgment. (p. 371)

Risky decisions How decision making is influenced by framing effects. (p. 380)

Decision making An experiment that demonstrates how decisions can be affected by the context within which the decision is made. (p. 380)

Related Lab

Monty Hall A simulation of the Monty Hall three-door problem, which involves an understanding of probability.

Glossary

(Number in parentheses is the chapter in which the term first appears.)

Acrobat problem A problem involving acrobats that is similar to the Tower of Hanoi problem. Used to illustrate how the way a problem is stated can influence its difficulty. See also **Reverse acrobat problem.** (12)

Action pathway Neural pathway, extending from the occipital lobe to the parietal lobe, that is associated with neural processing that occurs when people take action. Corresponds to the *where* pathway. (3)

Action potential Electrical potential that travels down a neuron's axon. (2)

Affirming the antecedent A conditional syllogism of the following form: If *p*, then *q*; *p*; therefore, *q*. The antecedent, *p*, is affirmed in the second premise. This is a valid form of conditional syllogism. See Table 13.1. See also **Denying the consequent.** (13)

Affirming the consequent A conditional syllogism of the following form: If *p*, then *q*; *q*; therefore, *p*. This is an invalid form of conditional syllogism. See Table 13.1. See also **Denying the antecedent.** (13)

Algorithm A procedure that is guaranteed to solve a problem. (3)

Amygdala A subcortical structure that is involved in processing emotional aspects of experience, including memory for emotional events. (8)

Analogical encoding A technique in which people compare two problems that illustrate a principle. This technique is designed to help people discover similar structural features of cases or problems. (12)

Analogical paradox Participants in psychological experiments tend to focus on surface features in analogy problems, whereas people in the real world frequently use deeper, more structural features. (12)

Analogical problem solving The use of analogies as an aid to solving problems. Typically, a solution to one problem, the source problem, is presented that is analogous to the solution to another problem, the target problem. (12)

Analogical transfer The application of problem-solving strategies experienced in solving one problem to the solution of another, similar problem. (12)

Analogy Making a comparison in order to show a similarity between two different things. (12)

Analytic introspection A procedure used by early psychologists in which trained participants described their experiences and thought processes elicited by stimuli presented under controlled conditions. (1)

Anaphoric inference An inference that connects an object or person in one sentence to an object or person in another sentence. See also **Causal inference; Instrument inference.** (11)

Antecedent In a conditional syllogism, the term *p* in the conditional premise "If *p*, then *q*." See also **Consequent.** (13)

Anterograde amnesia Amnesia for events that occur after an injury—that is, the inability to form new memories. Compare to **retrograde amnesia**—the inability to remember information from the past. (6)

Articulatory rehearsal process Rehearsal process involved in working memory that keeps items in the phonological store from decaying. (5)

Articulatory suppression Interference with operation of the phonological loop that occurs when a person repeats an irrelevant word such as "the" while carrying out a task that requires the phonological loop. (5)

Artificial intelligence The ability of a computer to perform tasks usually associated with human intelligence. (1)

Attention Focusing on specific features, objects, or locations or on certain thoughts or activities. (4)

Attenuation theory of attention Anne Treisman's model of selective attention that proposes that selection occurs in two stages. In the first stage, an attenuator analyzes the incoming message and lets through the attended message—and also the unattended message, but at a lower (attenuated) strength. (4)

Attenuator In Treisman's model of selective attention, the attenuator analyzes the incoming message in terms of physical characteristics, language, and meaning. Attended messages pass through the attenuator at full strength, and unattended messages pass though with reduced strength. (4)

Audiovisual mirror neuron Neuron in the monkey premotor cortex that responds when a monkey performs an action and also when it hears the sound associated with this action (for example, the action associated with breaking a peanut, and the associated sound). Also see **Mirror neuron**. (3)

Auditory coding Representation of the sound of a stimulus in the mind. (5)

Autism A developmental disorder in which one of the major symptoms is withdrawal of contact from other people. People with autism often direct their attention differently from people without autism. (4)

Autobiographical memory (AM) Memory for dated events in a person's life. Autobiographical memory is usually considered to be a type of episodic memory, but has also been defined as including personal semantic memories. (8)

Automatic processing Processing that occurs automatically, without the person intending to do it, and that also uses few cognitive resources. Automatic processing is associated with easy or well-practiced tasks. (4)

Availability heuristic Basing judgments of the frequency of events on what events come to mind. (13)

Axon Part of the neuron that transmits signals from the cell body to the synapse at the end of the axon. (2)

Back propagation A process by which learning can occur in a connectionist network, in which an error signal is transmitted backward through the network. This backward-transmitted error signal provides the information needed to adjust the weights in the network to achieve the correct output signal for a stimulus. (9)

Balint's syndrome A condition caused by brain damage in which a person has difficulty focusing attention on individual objects. (4)

Base rate The relative proportions of different classes in a population. Failure to consider base rates can often lead to errors of reasoning. (13)

Basic level In Rosch's categorization scheme, the level below the global (superordinate) level (e.g., "table" or "chair" for the superordinate category "furniture"). According to Rosch, the basic level is psychologically special because it is the level above which much information is lost and below which little is gained. See also **Global (superordinate) level; Specific (subordinate) level**. (9)

Behavioral approach Studying the mind by measuring a person's behavior and explaining this behavior in behavioral terms. (1)

Behaviorism The approach to psychology, founded by John B. Watson, which states that observable behavior provides the only valid data for psychology. A consequence of this idea is that consciousness and unobservable mental processes are not considered worthy of study by psychologists. (1)

Bottleneck model Model of attention that proposes that incoming information is restricted at some point in processing, so only a portion of the information gets through to consciousness. Broadbent's model of attention is an example of a bottleneck model. (4)

Bottom-up processing Processing that starts with information received by the receptors. This type of processing can also be called data-based processing. (3)

Brain ablation A procedure in which a specific area is removed from an animal's brain. It is usually done to determine the function of this area by assessing the effect on the animal's behavior. (3)

Brain imaging Techniques such as functional magnetic resonance imaging (fMRI) and positron emission tomography (PET) that result in images of the brain that represent brain activity. In cognitive psychology, activity is measured in response to specific cognitive tasks. (2)

Broca's aphasia A condition associated with damage to Broca's area, in the frontal lobe, characterized by difficulty in using speech to express thoughts, but with a remaining facility for understanding speech. (2)

Broca's area An area in the frontal lobe associated with the production of language. Damage to this area causes Broca's aphasia. (2)

Candle problem A problem, first described by Duncker, in which a person is given a number of objects and is given the task of mounting a candle on a wall so it can burn without dripping wax on the floor. This problem was used to study functional fixedness. (12)

Categorical syllogism A syllogism in which the premises and conclusion describe the relationship between two categories by using statements that begin with *all*, *no*, or *some*. (13)

Categorization The process by which objects are placed in categories. (9)

Category Groups of objects that belong together because they belong to the same class of objects, such as "houses," "furniture," or "schools." (9)

Category-specific knowledge impairment A result of brain damage in which the patient has trouble recognizing objects in a specific category. (9)

Causal inference An inference that results in the conclusion that the events described in one clause or sentence were caused by events that occurred in a previous clause or sentence. See also **Anaphoric inference; Instrument inference.** (11)

Cell body Part of a cell that contains mechanisms that keep the cell alive. In some neurons, the cell body and the dendrites associated with it receive information from other neurons. (2)

Central executive The part of working memory that coordinates the activity of the phonological loop and the visuospatial sketch pad. (5)

Cerebral cortex The 3-mm-thick outer layer of the brain that contains the mechanisms responsible for higher mental functions such as perception, language, thinking, and problem solving. (2)

Change blindness Difficulty in detecting changes in similar, but slightly different, scenes that are presented one after another. The changes are often easy to see once attention is directed to them, but are usually undetected in the absence of appropriate attention. (4)

Choice reaction time Reacting to one of two or more stimuli. For example, in Donders' experiment (see Chapter 1), participants had to make one response to one stimulus and a different response to another stimulus. (1)

Chunk Used in connection with the idea of chunking in memory. A chunk is a collection of elements that are strongly associated with each other, but are weakly associated with elements in other chunks. (5)

Chunking Combining small units into larger ones, such as when individual words are combined into a meaningful sentence. Chunking can be used to increase the capacity of memory. (5)

Classical conditioning A procedure in which pairing a neutral stimulus with a stimulus that elicits a response causes the neutral stimulus to elicit that response. (1, 6)

Cocktail party effect The phenomenon that occurs when, in the process of focusing attention on one message or conversation, a message from another source enters consciousness. This can occur when a person is focusing attention on a conversation at a party and suddenly hears his or her name from across the room. (4)

Coding The form in which stimuli are represented in the mind. For example, information can be represented in visual, semantic, and phonological forms. See also **Neural code,** which refers to how stimuli are represented in the firing of neurons. (5)

Cognition The mental processes involved in perception, attention, memory, language, problem solving, reasoning, and making decisions. (1)

Cognitive economy A feature of some semantic network models in which properties of a category that are shared by many members of a category are stored at a higher level node in the network. For example, the property "can fly" would be stored at the node for "bird" rather than at the node for "canary." (9)

Cognitive hypothesis An explanation for the reminiscence bump, which states that memories are better for adolescence and early adulthood because encoding is better during periods of rapid change that are followed by stability. (8)

Cognitive interview A procedure used for interviewing crime scene witnesses that involves letting witnesses talk with a minimum of interruption, and also uses techniques that help witnesses recreate the situation present at the crime scene by having them place themselves back in the scene and recreate things like emotions they were feeling, where they were looking, and how the scene may have appeared when viewed from different perspectives. (8)

Cognitive load The amount of a person's cognitive resources needed to carry out a particular cognitive task. (4)

Cognitive map Mental conception of a spatial layout. (1)

Cognitive neuroscience Field involved in studying the neural basis of cognition. (2)

Cognitive psychology The branch of psychology concerned with the scientific study of the mental processes involved in perception, attention, memory, language, problem solving, reasoning, and decision making. In short, cognitive psychology is concerned with the scientific study of the mind and mental processes. (1)

Cognitive resources The idea that a person has a certain cognitive capacity, or resources, that can be used for carrying out various tasks. (4)

Cognitive revolution A shift in psychology, beginning in the 1950s, from the behaviorist approach to an approach in which the main thrust was to explain behavior in terms of the mind. One of the outcomes of the cognitive revolution was the introduction of the information-processing approach to studying the mind. (1)

Coherence The representation of a text or story in a reader's mind so that information in one part of the text or story is related to information in another part. (11)

Compatible flanker A stimulus in the display for a flanker compatibility task that is associated with a response that is the same as or compatible with the response that the participant is supposed to make to a target stimulus. See **Incompatible flanker**. (4)

Componential recovery, principle of The principle associated with recognition-by-components theory that states that if we can recover (see) an object's geons, we can identify the object. (3)

Concept A mental representation used for a variety of cognitive functions, including memory, reasoning, and using and understanding language. An example of a concept would be the way a person mentally represents "cat" or "house." (9)

Conceptual peg hypothesis A hypothesis, associated with Paivio's dual coding theory, that states that concrete nouns create images that other words can hang onto, which enhances memory for these words. (10)

Conceptual priming Priming that occurs when the enhancement caused by a priming stimulus is based on the meaning of the stimulus. For example, presentation of the word *furniture* causing a faster response to later presentation of the word *chair*. (6)

Conclusion The final statement in a syllogism, which follows from the two premises. (13)

Conditional syllogism Syllogism with two premises and a conclusion, like a categorical syllogism, but whose first premise is an "If...then..." statement. (13)

Confirmation bias The tendency to selectively look for information that conforms to our hypothesis and to overlook information that argues against it. (13)

Conjunction rule The probability of the conjunction of two events (such as feminist and bank teller) cannot be higher than the probability of the single constituents (feminist alone or bank teller alone). (13)

Connection weight In connectionist models, a connection weight determines the degree to which signals sent from one unit either increase or decrease the activity of the next unit. (9)

Connectionism A network model of mental operation that proposes that concepts are represented in networks that are modeled after neural networks. This approach to describing the mental representation of concepts is also called the parallel distributed processing (PDP) approach. See also **Connectionist network**. (9)

Connectionist network The type of network proposed by the connectionist approach to the representation of concepts. Connectionist networks are based on neural networks, but are not necessarily identical to them. One of the key properties of a connectionist network is that a specific category is represented by activity that is distributed over many units in the network. This contrasts with semantic networks, in which specific categories are represented at individual nodes. (9)

Consequent In a conditional syllogism, the term q in the conditional premise "If p, then q." See also **Antecedent**. (13)

Consolidation The process that transforms new memories into a state in which they are more resistant to disruption. See also **Standard model of consolidation**. (7)

Constructive nature of memory The idea that what people report as memories are constructed based on what actually happened plus additional factors, such as expectations, other knowledge, and other life experiences. (8)

Control processes In Atkinson and Shiffrin's modal model of memory, active processes that can be controlled by the person and may differ from one task to another. Rehearsal is an example of a control process. (5)

Controlled processing Processing that involves close attention. This term is especially associated with Schneider and Shiffrin's (1977) experiment, which showed that controlled processing was needed in the difficult, varied mapping condition of their experiment, even after extensive practice. (4)

Convergent thinking Thinking that works toward finding a solution to a specific problem that usually has a correct answer. Can be contrasted with **Divergent thinking.** (12)

Covert attention Occurs when attention is shifted without moving the eyes, commonly referred to as seeing something "out of the corner of one's eye." Contrasts with **Overt attention.** (4)

Creative cognition A technique developed by Finke to train people to think creatively. (12)

Cryptomnesia Unconscious plagiarism of the work of others. This has been associated with errors in source monitoring. (8)

Cued recall A procedure for testing memory in which a participant is presented with cues, such as words or phrases, to aid recall of previously experienced stimuli. See also **Free recall.** (7)

Cultural life script Life events that commonly occur in a particular culture. (8)

Cultural life script hypothesis The idea that events in a person's life story become easier to recall when they fit the cultural life script for that person's culture. (8)

Decay Process by which information is lost from memory due to the passage of time. (5)

Decisions Making choices between alternatives. (13)

Declarative memory Memory that involves conscious recollections of previously experienced events (episodic memory) or facts (semantic memory). (6)

Deductive reasoning Reasoning that involves syllogisms in which a conclusion logically follows from premises. See also **Inductive reasoning.** (13)

Deep processing Processing that involves attention to meaning and relating an item to something else. Deep processing is usually associated with elaborative rehearsal. See also **Depth of processing; Shallow processing.** (7)

Definitional approach to categorization The idea that we can decide whether something is a member of a category by determining whether the object meets the definition of the category. See also **Family resemblance.** (9)

Delayed partial report method Procedure used in Sperling's experiment on the properties of the visual icon, in which participants were instructed to report only some of the stimuli in a briefly presented display. A cue tone that was delayed for a fraction of a second after the display was extinguished indicated which part of the display to report. See also **Partial report method; Whole report method.** (5)

Delayed-response task A task in which information is provided, a delay is imposed, and then memory is tested. This task has been used to study short-term memory by testing monkeys' ability to hold information about the location of a food reward during a delay. (5)

Dendrites Structures that branch out from the cell body to receive electrical signals from other neurons. (2)

Denying the antecedent A conditional syllogism of the following form: If p, then q; not p; therefore, not q. This is an invalid form of conditional syllogism. See Table 13.1. See also **Affirming the consequent.** (13)

Denying the consequent A conditional syllogism of the following form: If p, then q; not q; therefore, not p. The consequent, q, is denied in the second premise. This is a valid form of conditional syllogism. See Table 13.1. See also **Affirming the antecedent.** (13)

Depictive representation Corresponds to spatial representation. So called because a spatial representation can be depicted by a picture. (10)

Depth of processing The idea that the processing that occurs as an item is being encoded into memory can be deep or shallow. Deep processing involves attention to meaning and is associated with elaborative rehearsal. Shallow processing involves repetition with little attention to meaning and is associated with maintenance rehearsal. See also **Levels of processing.** (7)

Design fixation Presenting a sample design influences the creation of new designs. (12)

Dichotic listening The procedure of presenting one message to the left ear and a different message to the right ear. (4)

Dictionary unit A component of Treisman's attenuation theory of attention. This processing unit contains stored words and thresholds for activating the words. The dictionary unit helps explain why we can sometimes hear a familiar word, such as our name, in an unattended message. See also **Attenuation theory of attention.** (4)

Digit span The number of digits a person can remember. Digit span is used as a measure of the capacity of short-term memory. (5)

Dissociation A situation in cases of brain damage, in which the damage causes a problem in one function while not affecting other functions. See also **Double dissociation; Single dissociation.** (3)

Distributed coding Representation of an object or experience by the pattern of firing of a number of neurons. (2)

Distributed processing Processing that involves a number of different areas of the brain. (2)

Divergent thinking Thinking that is open-ended, involving a large number of potential solutions. Can be contrasted with **Convergent thinking.** (12)

Divided attention The ability to pay attention to, or carry out, two or more different tasks simultaneously. (4)

Double dissociation A situation in which a single dissociation can be demonstrated in one person, and the opposite type of single dissociation can be demonstrated in another person (i.e., Person 1: function A is present; function B is damaged; Person 2: function A is damaged; function B is present). (3)

Early selection model Model of attention that explains selective attention by early filtering out of the unattended message. In Broadbent's early selection model, the filtering step occurs before the message is analyzed to determine its meaning. (4)

Echoic memory Brief sensory memory for auditory stimuli that lasts for a few seconds after a stimulus is extinguished. (5)

Elaborative rehearsal Rehearsal that involves thinking about the meaning of an item to be remembered or making connections between that item and prior knowledge. Compare to **Maintenance rehearsal.** (7)

Encoding The process of acquiring information and transferring it into memory. (5, 7)

Encoding specificity The principle that we learn information together with its context. This means that presence of the context can lead to enhanced memory for the information. (7)

Endogenous attention Occurs when a person consciously decides to scan the environment to find a specific stimulus or monitor what is happening. Can also occur for auditory stimuli. (4)

Epiphenomenon A phenomenon that accompanies a mechanism but is not actually part of the mechanism. An example of an epiphenomenon is lights that flash on a mainframe computer as it operates. (10)

Episodic buffer A component added to Baddeley's original working memory model that serves as a "backup" store that communicates with both LTM and the components of working memory. It holds information longer and has greater capacity than the phonological loop or visuospatial sketch pad. (5)

Episodic memory Memory for specific events that have happened to the person having the memory. These events are usually remembered as a personal experience that occurred at a particular time and place. Episodic and semantic memory together make up declarative memory. (6)

Error signal During learning in a connectionist network, the difference between the output signal generated by a particular stimulus and the output that actually represents that stimulus. (9)

Event-related potential (ERP) An electrical potential, recorded with disc electrodes on a person's scalp, that reflects the response of many thousands of neurons near the electrode that fire together. The ERP consists of a number of waves that occur at different delays after a stimulus is presented and that can be linked to different functions. For example, the N400 wave occurs in response to a sentence that contains a word that doesn't fit the meaning of the sentence. (2)

Evolutionary perspective on cognition The idea that many properties of our minds can be traced to the evolutionary principles of natural selection. See also **Social exchange theory.** (13)

Exemplar In categorization, members of a category that a person has experienced in the past. (9)

Exemplar approach to categorization The approach to categorization in which members of a category are judged against exemplars, examples of members of the category that the person has encountered in the past. (9)

Exogenous attention Attention that is automatically attracted by a sudden visual or auditory stimulus. (4)

Expected emotion Emotion that a person predicts he or she will feel for a particular outcome of a decision. (13)

Expected utility theory The idea that people are basically rational, so if they have all of the relevant information, they will make a decision that results in the maximum expected utility. (13)

Experience-dependent plasticity A mechanism that causes an organism's neurons to develop so they respond best to the type of stimulation to which the organism has been exposed. (3)

Expert Person who, by devoting a large amount of time to learning about a field and practicing and applying that learning, has become acknowledged as being extremely skilled or knowledgeable in that field. (12)

Explicit memory Memory that involves conscious recollections of events or facts that we have learned in the past. Also called *declarative memory* or *conscious memory*. (6)

Extrastriate body area (EBA) An area in the temporal cortex that is activated by pictures of bodies and parts of bodies, but not by faces or other objects. (2)

Eye tracker A device for measuring where people look (fixate) in a scene and how they move their eyes from one fixation point to another. (4)

Eyewitness testimony Testimony by eyewitnesses to a crime about what they saw during commission of the crime. (8)

Falsification principle The reasoning principle that to test a rule, it is necessary to look for situations that would falsify the rule. (13)

Familiarity, law of Law of perceptual organization that states that things are more likely to form groups if the groups appear familiar or meaningful. (3)

Family resemblance In considering the process of categorization, the idea that things in a particular category resemble each other in a number of ways. This approach can be contrasted with the definitional approach, which states that an object belongs to a category only when it meets a definite set of criteria. (9)

Feature detectors Neurons that respond to specific visual features, such as orientation, size, or the more complex features that make up environmental stimuli. (2)

Feature integration theory An approach to object perception developed by Anne Treisman that proposes that object perception occurs in a sequence of stages in which features are first analyzed and then combined to result in perception of an object. (4)

Feedback signal Neural signal that travels back from higher centers to influence incoming signals. (3)

Fixation In perception and attention, a pausing of the eyes on places of interest while observing a scene. (4)

Fixation In problem solving, people's tendency to focus on a specific characteristic of the problem that keeps them from arriving at a solution. See also **Design fixation; Functional fixedness.** (12)

Flanker compatibility task A procedure in which participants are instructed to respond to a target stimulus that is flanked, or surrounded, by distractor stimuli that they are supposed to ignore. The degree to which the distractor interferes with responding to the target is taken as an indication of whether the distractor stimuli are being processed. (4)

Flashbulb memory Memory for the circumstances surrounding hearing about shocking, highly charged events. It has been claimed that such memories are particularly vivid and accurate. See **Narrative rehearsal hypothesis** for another viewpoint. (8)

Focused attention stage The second stage of Treisman's feature integration theory. According to the theory, attention causes the combination of features into perception of an object. (4)

Framing effect Decisions are influenced by how the choices are stated. (13)

Free recall A procedure for testing memory in which the participant is asked to remember stimuli that were previously presented. See also **Cued recall.** (7)

Frontal lobe The lobe in the front of the brain that serves higher functions such as language, thought, memory, and motor functioning. (2)

Functional fixedness An effect that occurs when the ideas a person has about an object's function inhibit the person's ability to use the object for a different function. See also **Fixation** (in problem solving). (12)

Functional magnetic resonance imaging (fMRI) A brain imaging technique that measures how blood flow changes in response to cognitive activity. Unlike positron emission tomography, this technique does not involve the injection of a radioactive tracer. (2)

Fusiform face area (FFA) An area in the temporal lobe that contains many neurons that respond selectively to faces. (2)

Garden path sentence A sentence in which the meaning that seems to be implied at the beginning of the sentence turns out to be incorrect, based on information that is presented later in the sentence. (11)

Generation effect Memory for material is better when a person generates the material him- or herself, rather than passively receiving it. (7)

Geon The basic feature unit of the recognition-by-components approach to object perception. Geons are basic three-dimensional volumes. (3)

Gestalt psychologists A group of psychologists who proposed principles governing perception, such as laws of organization, and a perceptual approach to problem solving involving restructuring. (3, 12)

Given–new contract In a conversation, a speaker should construct sentences so that they contain both given information (information that the listener already knows) and new information (information that the listener is hearing for the first time). (11)

Global (superordinate) level The highest level in Rosch's categorization scheme (e.g., "furniture" or "vehicles"). See also **Basic level; Specific (subordinate) level.** (9)

Goal state In problem solving, the condition that occurs when a problem has been solved. (12)

Good continuation, law of Law of perceptual organization stating that points that, when connected, result in straight or smoothly curving lines are seen as belonging together. In addition, lines tend to be seen as following the smoothest path. (3)

Good figure, law of See **Pragnanz, law of.** (3)

Graceful degradation Disruption of performance due to damage to a system that occurs only gradually as parts of the system are damaged. This occurs in some cases of brain damage and also when parts of a connectionist network are damaged. (9)

Graded amnesia When amnesia is most severe for events that occurred just prior to an injury and becomes less severe for earlier, more remote events. (7)

Grandmother cell A neuron that responds only to a highly specific stimulus. This stimulus could be a specific image, such as a picture of a person's grandmother; a concept, such as the idea of grandmothers in general; or a person's real-life grandmother. See also **Specificity coding.** (2)

Heuristic A "rule of thumb" that provides a best-guess solution to a problem. (3)

Hidden units Units in a connectionist network that are located between input units and output units. See also **Connectionist network; Input units; Output units.** (9)

Hierarchical model As applied to network models of knowledge representation, a model that consists of levels arranged so that more specific concepts, like canary or salmon, are at the bottom and more general concepts, such as bird, fish, or animal, are at higher levels. (9)

Hierarchical organization Organization of categories in which larger, more general categories are divided into smaller, more specific categories. These smaller categories can, in turn, be divided into even more specific categories to create a number of levels. (9)

High prototypicality A category member that closely resembles the category prototype. See also **Prototypicality.** (9)

High-load task A task that uses most or all of a person's resources and so leaves little capacity to handle other tasks. (4)

Iconic memory Brief sensory memory for visual stimuli that lasts for a fraction of a second after a stimulus is extinguished. This corresponds to the sensory memory stage of the modal model of memory. (5)

Ill-defined problem A problem in which it is difficult to specify a clear goal state or specific operators. Many real-life problems are ill-defined problems. (12)

Illusory conjunctions A situation, demonstrated in experiments by Anne Treisman, in which features from different objects are inappropriately combined. (4)

Illusory correlation A correlation that appears to exist between two events, when in reality there is no correlation or it is weaker than it is assumed to be. (13)

Imageless thought debate The debate about whether thought is possible in the absence of images. (10)

Imagery debate The debate about whether imagery is based on spatial mechanisms, such as those involved in perception, or on propositional mechanisms that are related to language. (10)

Imagery neuron A type of category-specific neuron that is activated by imagery. (10)

Immediate emotion Emotion that is experienced at the time a decision is being made. (13)

Implicit memory Memory that occurs when an experience affects a person's behavior, even though the person is not aware that he or she has had the experience. Also called *nondeclarative memory.* (6)

Inattentional blindness Not noticing something even though it is in clear view, usually caused by failure to pay attention to the object or the place where the object is located. Also see **Change blindness.** (4)

Incidental immediate emotion Immediate emotion unrelated to the decision. An example is an emotion associated with a person's general disposition. Contrast with **Integral immediate emotion.** (13)

Incompatible flanker A stimulus in the display for a flanker compatibility task that is associated with a response that is different from the response that the participant is supposed to make to a target stimulus. See **Compatible flanker.** (4)

Inductive reasoning Reasoning in which a conclusion follows from a consideration of evidence. This conclusion is stated as being probably true, rather than definitely true, as can be the case for the conclusions from deductive reasoning. (13)

Inference The process by which readers create information that is not explicitly stated in the text. (11)

Information-processing approach The approach to psychology, developed beginning in the 1950s, in which the mind is described as processing information through a sequence of stages. (1)

Initial state In problem solving, the conditions at the beginning of a problem. (12)

Input units Units in a connectionist network that are activated by stimulation from the environment. See also **Connectionist network; Hidden units; Output units.** (9)

Insight Sudden realization of a problem's solution. (12)

Instrument inference An inference about tools or methods that occurs while reading text or listening to speech. See also **Anaphoric inference; Causal inference.** (11)

Integral immediate emotion Immediate emotion that is associated with the act of making a decision. Contrast with **Incidental immediate emotion.** (13)

Interactionist approach to parsing The approach to parsing that takes into account all information—both semantic and syntactic—to determine parsing as a person reads a sentence. This approach assigns more weight to semantics than does the syntax-first approach to parsing. (11)

Intermediate states In problem solving, the various conditions that exist along the pathways between the initial and goal states. (12)

In vivo problem-solving research Observing people to determine how they solve problems in real-world situations. This technique has been used to study the use of analogy in a number of different settings, including laboratory meetings of a university research group and design brainstorming sessions in an industrial research and development department. (12)

Korsakoff's syndrome A condition caused by prolonged vitamin B1 deficiency that leads to destruction of areas on the frontal and temporal lobes and causes severe impairments in memory. (6)

Landmark discrimination problem Problem in which the task is to remember an object's location and to choose that location after a delay. Associated with research on the *where* processing stream. (3)

Language A system of communication through which we code and express our feelings, thoughts, ideas, and experiences. (11)

Late closure In parsing, when a person encounters a new word, the parser assumes that this word is part of the current phrase. (11)

Late selection model A model of selective attention that proposes that selection of stimuli for final processing does not occur until after the information in the message has been analyzed for meaning. (4)

Law of large numbers The larger the number of individuals that are randomly drawn from a population, the more representative the resulting group will be of the entire population. (13)

Law(s) of familiarity, good continuation, good figure, perceptual organization, pragnanz, similarity, simplicity See inverted entries (e.g., **Familiarity, law of**).

Levels of processing (LOP) Part of levels-of-processing theory that states that there are different depths of processing that can be achieved as information is being encoded. See also **Depth of processing; Levels-of-processing theory.** (7)

Levels-of-processing theory The idea that memory depends on how information is encoded, with better memory being achieved when processing is deep than when processing is shallow. Deep processing involves attention to meaning and is associated with elaborative rehearsal. Shallow processing involves repetition with little attention to meaning and is associated with maintenance rehearsal. (7)

Lexical ambiguity When a word can have more than one meaning. For example, *bug* can mean an insect, a listening device, or to annoy. (11)

Lexical decision task A procedure in which a person is asked to decide as quickly as possible whether a particular stimulus is a word or a nonword. (9, 11)

Lexical priming Priming that involves the meaning of words. Typically occurs when a word is followed by another word with a similar meaning—for example, when presenting the word *ant* before the word *bug* causes a person to respond faster to the word *bug* than if *ant* had not preceded it. (11)

Lexicon A person's knowledge of what words mean, how they sound, and how they are used in relation to other words. (11)

Light-from-above heuristic The assumption that light is coming from above. This heuristic can influence how we perceive three-dimensional objects that are illuminated. (3)

Likelihood principle Part of Helmholtz's theory of unconscious inference that states that we perceive the object that is *most likely* to have caused the pattern of stimuli we have received. (3)

Localization of function Location of specific functions in specific areas of the brain. For example, areas have been identified that are specialized to process information involved in the perception of movement, form, speech, and different aspects of memory. (2)

Location-based attention Models of attention that propose that attention operates on whatever stimuli are at a particular location. This contrasts with *object-based attention*, in which attention is focused on a particular object. (4)

Logic theorist Computer program devised by Alan Newell and Herbert Simon that was able to solve logic problems. (1)

Long-term memory (LTM) A memory mechanism that can hold large amounts of information for long periods of time. Long-term memory is one of the stages in the modal model of memory. (6)

Long-term potentiation (LTP) The increased firing that occurs in a neuron due to prior activity at the synapse. (7)

Low-load task A task that uses few resources, leaving some capacity to handle other tasks. (4)

Low prototypicality A category member that does not closely resemble the category prototype. See also **Prototypicality**. (9)

Maintenance rehearsal Rehearsal that involves repetition without any consideration of meaning or making connections to other information. Compare to **Elaborative rehearsal.** (7)

Means-end analysis A problem-solving strategy that seeks to reduce the difference between the initial and goal states. This is achieved by creating subgoals, intermediate states that are closer to the goal. (12)

Medial temporal lobe (MTL) An area in the temporal lobe that consists of the hippocampus and a number of surrounding structures. Damage to the MTL causes problems in forming new long-term memories. (7)

Memory The processes involved in retaining, retrieving, and using information about stimuli, images, events, ideas, and skills, after the original information is no longer present. (5)

Memory consolidation Process by which experiences or information that has entered the memory system becomes strengthened so it is resistant to interference caused by trauma or other events. (1)

Memory trace replacement hypothesis The idea that misleading postevent information impairs or replaces memories that were formed during the original experiencing of an event. (8)

Mental approach to coding Determining how a stimulus or experience is represented in the mind. (5)

Mental imagery Experiencing a sensory impression in the absence of sensory input. (10)

Mental scanning A process of mental imagery in which a person scans a mental image in his or her mind. (10)

Mental set A preconceived notion about how to approach a problem, which is determined by a person's experience or what has worked in the past. (12)

Mental simulation Models that people create about what will happen following different decisions. (10, 12)

Mental time travel According to Tulving, the defining property of the *experience* of episodic memory, in which a person travels back in time in his or her mind to reexperience events that happened in the past. See also **Self-knowing.** (6)

Mental walk task A task used in imagery experiments in which participants are asked to form a mental image of an object and to imagine that they are walking toward this mental image. (10)

Method of loci A method for remembering things in which the things to be remembered are placed at different locations in a mental image of a spatial layout. See also **Pegword technique**. (10)

Microelectrodes Small wires that are used to record electrical signals from single neurons. (2)

Mind System that creates and controls mental functions such as perception, attention, memory, emotions, language, deciding, thinking, and reasoning, and that creates mental representations of the world. (1)

Mirror neuron Neuron in the premotor cortex, originally discovered in the monkey, that responds both when a monkey observes someone else (usually the experimenter) carrying out an action and when the monkey itself carries out the action. There is also evidence for mirror neurons in humans. (3)

Misinformation effect Misleading information presented after a person witnesses an event can change how the person describes that event later. (8)

Misleading postevent information (MPI) The misleading information that causes the misinformation effect. (8)

Modal model of memory The model proposed by Atkinson and Shiffrin that describes memory as a mechanism that involves processing information through a series of stages, including short-term memory and long-term memory. It is called the *modal model* because it contained features of many models that were being proposed in the 1960s. (5)

Model In cognitive psychology, a representation of the workings of the mind; often presented as interconnected boxes that each represent the operation of specific mental functions. (1)

Module An area of the brain that is specialized for a specific function. For example, the fusiform face area, extrastriate body area, and parahippocampal place area are modules for perceiving faces, bodies, and places, respectively. (2)

Morpheme The smallest unit of language that has a definable meaning or a grammatical function. For example, *truck* consists of a number of phonemes but only one morpheme, because none of the components that create the word *truck* means anything. (11)

Multiple trace hypothesis The idea, associated with memory consolidation, that the hippocampus is involved in retrieval of remote memories, especially episodic memories. This contrasts with the standard model of memory, which proposes that the hippocampus is involved only in the retrieval of recent memories. (7)

Mutilated checkerboard problem A problem that has been used to study how the statement of a problem influences a person's ability to reach a solution. (12)

Narrative rehearsal hypothesis The idea that we remember some life events better because we rehearse them. This idea was proposed by Neisser as an explanation for "flashbulb" memories. (8)

Natural selection, theory of The idea, originating with Darwin, that genetically based characteristics that enhance an animal's ability to survive, and therefore reproduce, will be passed on to future generations (3)

Nerve fiber See **Axon.** (2)

Nerve impulse An electrical response that is propagated down the length of an axon (nerve fiber). Also called an **Action potential.** (2)

Nerve net A network of continuously interconnected nerve fibers (as contrasted with neural networks, in which fibers are connected by synapses). (2)

Neural circuit Group of interconnected neurons that are responsible for neural processing. (2)

Neural code The representation of specific stimuli or experiences by the firing of neurons. (2)

Neuroeconomics An approach to studying decision making that combines research from the fields of psychology, neuroscience, and economics. (13)

Neuron Cell that is specialized to receive and transmit information in the nervous system. (2)

Neuron doctrine The idea that individual cells called neurons transmit signals in the nervous system, and that these cells are not continuous with other cells as proposed by nerve net theory. (2)

Neuropsychology The study of the behavioral effects of brain damage in humans. (3)

Neurotransmitter Chemical that is released at the synapse in response to incoming action potentials. (2)

Nondeclarative memory Memory that occurs when an experience affects a person's behavior, even though the person is not aware that he or she has had the experience. (6)

Object discrimination problem A problem in which the task is to remember an object based on its shape and choose it when presented with another object after a delay. Associated with research on the *what* processing stream. (3)

Object-based attention Model of attention proposing that the enhancing effects of attention can be located on a particular object. This contrasts with *location-based attention,* in which attention is focused on a location. (4)

Oblique effect The finding that vertical and horizontal orientations can be perceived more easily than other (slanted) orientations. (3)

Occipital lobe The lobe at the back of the brain that is devoted primarily to analyzing incoming visual information. (2)

Omission bias The tendency to do nothing to avoid having to make a decision that could be interpreted as causing harm. (13)

Operant conditioning Type of conditioning championed by B. F. Skinner, which focuses on how behavior is strengthened by presentation of positive reinforcers, such as food or social approval, or withdrawal of negative reinforcers, such as a shock or social rejection. (1)

Operators In problem solving, permissible moves that can be made toward a problem's solution. (12)

Opt-in procedure Procedure in which a person must take an active step to *choose* a course of action—for example, choosing to be an organ donor. (13)

Opt-out procedure Procedure in which a person must take an active step to *avoid* a course of action—for example, choosing not to be an organ donor. (13)

Output units Units in a connectionist network that contain the final output of the network. See also **Connectionist network; Hidden units; Input units.** (9)

Overt attention Shifting of attention by moving the eyes. Contrasts with **Covert attention.** (4)

Paired-associate learning A learning task in which participants are first presented with pairs of words, then one word of each pair is presented and the task is to recall the other word. (7, 10)

Parahippocampal place area (PPA) An area in the temporal lobe that contains neurons that are selectively activated by pictures of indoor and outdoor scenes. (2)

Parallel distributed processing (PDP) See **Connectionism;** see also **Connectionist network.** (9)

Parietal lobe The lobe at the top of the brain that contains mechanisms responsible for sensations caused by stimulation of the skin, and also some aspects of visual information. (2)

Parsing The mental grouping of words in a sentence into phrases. The way a sentence is parsed determines its meaning. (11)

Partial report method Procedure used in Sperling's experiment on the properties of the visual icon, in which participants were instructed to report only some of the stimuli in a briefly presented display. A cue tone immediately after the display was extinguished indicated which part of the display to report. See also **Delayed partial report method; Sensory memory; Whole report method.** (5)

Pegword technique A method for remembering things in which the things to be remembered are associated with concrete words. See also **Method of loci.** (10)

Perception Conscious experience that results from stimulation of the senses. (3)

Perception pathway Neural pathway, extending from the occipital lobe to the temporal lobe, that is associated with perceiving or recognizing objects. Corresponds to the *what* pathway. (3)

Perceptual organization The process of organizing elements of the environment into separate objects. (3)

Perceptual organization, laws of Rules proposed by the Gestalt psychologists to explain how small elements of a scene or a display become perceptually grouped to form larger units. These "laws" are described as "heuristics" in this book. (3)

Permission schema A pragmatic reasoning schema that states that if a person satisfies condition A, then they get to carry out action B. The permission schema has been used to explain the results of the Wason four-card problem. (13)

Perseveration Difficulty in switching from one behavior to another, which can hinder a person's ability to solve problems that require flexible thinking. Perseveration is observed in cases in which the prefrontal cortex has been damaged. (5)

Persistence of vision The continued perception of light for a fraction of a second after the original light stimulus has been extinguished. Perceiving a trail of light from a moving sparkler is caused by the persistence of vision. See also **Iconic memory.** (5)

Phoneme The shortest segment of speech that, if changed, changes the meaning of a word. (11)

Phonemic restoration effect When a phoneme in a word is heard even though it is obscured by a noise, such as a cough. This typically occurs when the word is part of a sentence. (11)

Phonological loop The part of working memory that holds and processes verbal and auditory information. See also **Central executive; Visuospatial sketch pad; Working memory.** (5)

Phonological similarity effect An effect that occurs when letters or words that sound similar are confused. For example, T and P are two similar-sounding letters that could be confused. (5)

Phonological store Component of the phonological loop of working memory that holds a limited amount of verbal and auditory information for a few seconds. (5)

Physical regularities Regularly occurring physical properties of the environment. For example, there are more vertical and horizontal orientations in the environment than oblique (angled) orientations. (3)

Physiological approach Studying the mind by measuring physiological and behavioral responses, and explaining behavior in physiological terms. (1)

Physiological approach to coding Determining how a stimulus or experience is represented by the firing of neurons. (5)

Positron emission tomography (PET) A brain imaging technique involving the injection of a radioactive tracer. (2)

Post-identification feedback effect An increase in confidence of memory recall due to confirming feedback after making an identification. This effect can occur after a person identifies someone in a lineup. (8)

Pragmatic inference Inference that occurs when reading or hearing a statement leads a person to expect something that is not explicitly stated or necessarily implied by the statement. (8)

Pragmatic reasoning schema A way of thinking about cause and effect in the world that is learned as part of experiencing everyday life. See also **Permission schema.** (13)

Pragnanz, law of Law of perceptual organization that states that every stimulus pattern is seen in such a way that the resulting structure is as simple as possible. Also called the *law of good figure* and the *law of simplicity.* (3)

Preattentive stage The first stage of Treisman's feature integration theory, in which an object is analyzed into its features. (4)

Precueing A procedure in which participants are given a cue that will usually help them carry out a subsequent task. This procedure has been used in visual attention experiments in which participants are presented with a cue that tells them where to direct their attention. (4)

Premise The first two statements in a syllogism. The third statement is the conclusion. (13)

Primacy effect In a memory experiment in which a list of words is presented, enhanced memory for words presented at the beginning of the list. See also **Recency effect.** (6)

Primary receiving area Area in the cortex that is the first to receive inputs from one of the senses. For example, the occipital cortex is the primary receiving area for vision. (2)

Priming A change in response to a stimulus caused by the previous presentation of the same or a similar stimulus. See also **Conceptual priming; Repetition priming.** (6)

Proactive interference (PI) When information learned previously interferes with learning new information. See also **Retroactive interference.** (5)

Problem A situation in which there is an obstacle between a present state and a goal state and it is not immediately obvious how to get around the obstacle. (12)

Problem space The initial state, goal state, and all the possible intermediate states for a particular problem. (12)

Procedural memory Memory for how to carry out highly practiced skills. Procedural memory is a type of implicit memory because although people can carry out a skilled behavior, they often cannot explain exactly how they are able to do so. (6)

Propaganda effect People are more likely to rate statements they have read or heard before as being true, just because of prior exposure to the statements. (6)

Propositional representation A representation in which relationships are represented by symbols, as when the words of language represent objects and the relationships between objects. (10)

Prosopagnosia Condition caused by damage to the temporal lobe that is characterized by an inability to recognize faces. (2)

Prototype A standard used in categorization that is formed by averaging the category members a person has encountered in the past. (9)

Prototype approach to categorization The idea that we decide whether something is a member of a category by determining whether it is similar to a standard representation of the category, called a prototype. (9)

Prototypicality The degree to which a particular member of a category matches the prototype for that category. See also **High prototypicality; Low prototypicality.** (9)

Psycholinguistics The field concerned with the psychological study of language. (11)

Radiation problem A problem posed by Duncker that involves finding a way to destroy a tumor by radiation without damaging other organs in the body. This problem has been widely used to study the role of analogy in problem solving. (12)

Reaction time The time it takes to react to a stimulus. This is usually determined by measuring the time between presentation of a stimulus and the response to the stimulus. Examples of responses are pushing a button, saying a word, moving the eyes, and the appearance of a particular brain wave. (1)

Reactivation A process that occurs during memory consolidation, in which the hippocampus replays the neural activity associated with a memory. During reactivation, activity occurs in the network connecting the hippocampus and the cortex. This activity results in the formation of connections between the cortical areas. (7)

Reading span The maximum number of sentences that a person can read while simultaneously holding the last word of each sentence in memory. Reading span has been used to measure both the storage and processing functions of working memory. (5)

Reasoning Cognitive processes by which people start with information and come to conclusions that go beyond that information. See also **Deductive reasoning; Inductive reasoning.** (13)

Recall test A test in which participants are presented with stimuli and then, after a delay, are asked to remember as many of the stimuli as possible. See also **Cued recall; Free recall.** (5)

Recency effect In a memory experiment in which a list of words is presented, enhanced memory for words presented at the end of the list. See also **Primacy effect.** (6)

Receptors Specialized neural structures that respond to environmental stimuli such as light, mechanical stimulation, or chemical stimuli. (2)

Recognition memory Identifying a stimulus that was encountered earlier. Stimuli are presented during a study period and then, later, the same stimuli plus other, new stimuli are presented. The participants' task is to pick the stimuli that were originally presented. (6)

Recognition-by-components (RBC) theory A feature-based approach to object perception that proposes that the recognition of objects is based on three-dimensional features called geons. See also **Geon.** (3)

Reconsolidation A process proposed by Nader and others that occurs when a memory is reactivated. This process is similar to the consolidation that occurs after initial learning, although it apparently occurs more rapidly. (7)

Recording electrode When used to study neural functioning, a very thin glass or metal probe that can pick up electrical signals from single neurons. Also see **Event-related potential (ERP).** (2)

Reference electrode Used in conjunction with a recording electrode to measure the difference in charge between the two. Reference electrodes are generally placed where the electrical signal remains constant, so any change in charge between the recording and reference electrodes reflects events happening near the tip of the recording electrode. (2)

Regularities in the environment Characteristics of the environment that occur frequently. For example, blue is associated with open sky, landscapes are often green and smooth, and verticals and horizontals are often associated with buildings. (3)

Rehearsal The process of repeating a stimulus over and over, usually for the purpose of remembering it, that keeps the stimulus active in short-term memory. (5, 7)

Release from proactive interference A situation in which conditions occur that eliminate or reduce the decrease in performance caused by proactive interference. See Wickens' experiment described in Chapter 5. (5)

Reminiscence bump The empirical finding that people over 40 years old have enhanced memory for events from adolescence and early adulthood, compared to other periods of their lives. (8)

Remote memory Memory for events that occurred long ago. (7)

Repeated recall Recall that is tested immediately after an event and then retested at various times after the event. (8)

Repeated reproduction A method of measuring memory in which a person reproduces a stimulus on repeated occasions so his or her memory is tested at longer and longer intervals after the original presentation of the material to be remembered. (8)

Repetition priming When an initial presentation of a stimulus affects the person's response to the same stimulus when it is presented later. (6)

Representativeness heuristic The probability that an event A comes from class B can be determined by how well A resembles the properties of class B. (13)

Restructuring The process of changing a problem's representation. According to the Gestalt psychologists, restructuring is the key mechanism of problem solving. (12)

Retina A network of neurons that lines the back of the eye. The transformation of light into electrical signals and the initial processing of visual information occur in the retina. (2)

Retrieval The process of remembering information that has been stored in long-term memory. (5, 7)

Retrieval cues Cues that help a person remember information that is stored in memory. (7)

Retroactive interference When more recent learning interferes with memory for something that happened in the past. See also **Proactive interference.** (8)

Retrograde amnesia Loss of memory for something that happened prior to an injury or traumatic event such as a concussion. See also **Anterograde amnesia.** (6)

Reverse acrobat problem A modification of the acrobat problem that is used to show how the way a problem is stated can influence its difficulty. (12)

Reverse testing effect Taking a recall test right after witnessing an event increases a participant's sensitivity to subsequently presented misinformation. (8)

Risk aversion The tendency to make decisions that avoid risk. (13)

Risk aversion strategy A decision-making strategy that is governed by the idea of avoiding risk. Often used when a problem is stated in terms of gains. See also **Risk-taking strategy.** (13)

Risk-taking strategy A decision-making strategy that is governed by the idea of taking risks. Often used when a problem is stated in terms of losses. See also **Risk aversion strategy.** (13)

Rule-based approach (to mechanical reasoning) Applying a rule to solve a mechanical reasoning problem. Contrasts with approaches that involve mental imagery. (10)

Saccadic eye movements Eye movements from one fixation point to another. See also **Fixation** (in perception and attention). (4)

Same-object advantage Occurs when the enhancing effect of attention spreads throughout an object, so that attention to one place on an object results in a facilitation of processing at other places on the object. (4)

Sapir-Whorf hypothesis The idea that the nature of language in a particular culture can affect the way people in that culture think. (11)

Savings method Method used to measure retention in Ebbinghaus's memory experiments. He read lists of nonsense syllables and determined how many repetitions it took to repeat the lists with no errors. He then repeated this procedure after various intervals following initial learning and compared the number of repetitions needed to achieve no errors. (1)

Scene schema A person's knowledge about what is likely to be contained in a particular scene. This knowledge can help guide attention to different areas of the scene. For example, knowledge of what is usually in an office may cause a person to look toward the desk to see the computer. (4)

Schema A person's knowledge about what is involved in a particular experience. See also **Script.** (8)

Script A type of schema. The conception of the sequence of actions that describe a particular activity. For example, the sequence of events that are associated with going to class would be a "going to class" script. See also **Schema.** (8)

Selective attention The ability to focus on one message and ignore all others. (4)

Self-image hypothesis The idea that memory is enhanced for events that occur as a person's self-image or life identity is being formed. This is one of the explanations for the reminiscence bump. (8)

Self-reference effect Memory for a word is improved by relating the word to the self. (7)

Semantic coding Coding in the mind in the form of meaning. An example of semantic coding would be remembering the meaning of something you have read, as opposed to what the letters or words looked like (visual coding) or sounded like (auditory coding). (5)

Semantic memory Memory for knowledge about the world that is not tied to any specific personal experience. Semantic and episodic memory together make up declarative memory. (6)

Semantic network approach The approach to understanding how concepts are organized in the mind that proposes that concepts are arranged in networks. (9)

Semantic regularities Characteristics associated with the functions carried out in different types of scenes. For example, food preparation, cooking, and perhaps eating occur in a kitchen. (3)

Semantics The meanings of words and sentences. Distinguished from **Syntax.** (11)

Sensory memory A brief stage of memory that holds information for seconds or fractions of a second. It is the first stage in the modal model of memory. See also **Iconic memory; Persistence of vision.** (5)

Sentence verification technique A technique in which the participant is asked to indicate whether a particular sentence is true or false. For example, sentences like "An apple is a fruit" have been used in studies on categorization. (9)

Serial position curve In a memory experiment in which participants are asked to recall a list of words, a plot of the percentage of participants remembering each word against the position of that word in the list. See also **Primacy effect; Recency effect.** (6)

Shadowing The procedure of repeating a message out loud as it is heard. Shadowing is commonly used in conjunction with studies of selective attention that use the dichotic listening procedure. (4)

Shallow processing Processing that involves repetition with little attention to meaning. Shallow processing is usually associated with maintenance rehearsal. See also **Deep processing; Depth of processing.** (7)

Short-term memory (STM) A memory mechanism that can hold a limited amount of information for a brief period of time, usually around 30 seconds, unless there is rehearsal (such as repeating a telephone number) that can maintain information in short-term memory. Short-term memory is one of the stages in the modal model of memory. (5)

Similarity, law of Law of perceptual organization that states that similar things appear to be grouped together. (3)

Simple reaction time Reacting to the presence or absence of a single stimulus (as opposed to having to choose between a number of stimuli before making a response). See also **Choice reaction time.** (1)

Simplicity, law of See **Pragnanz, law of.** (3)

Single dissociation A situation that occurs in cases of brain damage, in which the damage causes a problem in one function while not affecting other functions. A single dissociation occurs when one function is present and another is absent. See also **Double dissociation.** (3)

Situation model A mental representation of what a text is about. (11)

Size constancy The tendency to perceive an object as remaining the same size even if it is viewed from different distances. This leads to the conclusion that perception of an object's size does not depend solely on the size of its image on the receptors. (3)

Social exchange theory An important aspect of human behavior is the ability for two people to cooperate in a way that is beneficial to both people. According to the evolutionary perspective on cognition, application of this theory can lead to the conclusion that detecting cheating is an important part of the brain's cognitive makeup. This idea has been used to explain the results of the Wason four-card problem. (13)

Source misattribution Occurs when the source of a memory is misidentified. Equivalent to source monitoring error. (8)

Source monitoring The process by which people determine the origins of memories, knowledge, or beliefs. Remembering that you heard about something from a particular person would be an example of source monitoring. (8)

Source monitoring error Misidentifying the source of a memory. Equivalent to source misattribution. (8)

Source problem (or story) A problem or story that is analogous to the target problem and which therefore provides information that can lead to a solution to the target problem. See also **Analogical problem solving; Target problem.** (12)

Spacing effect The advantage in performance caused by short study sessions separated by breaks from studying. (7)

Spatial representation A representation in which different parts of an image can be described as corresponding to specific locations in space. See also **Depictive representation.** (10)

Specific (subordinate) level The level in Rosch's categorization scheme that is a level below the basic level (e.g., "kitchen table" for the basic category "table"). See also **Basic level; Global (superordinate) level.** (9)

Specificity coding The representation of a specific stimulus by the firing of neurons that respond only to that stimulus. An example would be the signaling of a person's face by the firing of a neuron that responds only to that person's face. See also **Grandmother cell.** (2)

Speech segmentation The process of perceiving individual words within the continuous flow of the speech signal. (3, 11)

Spreading activation Activity that spreads out along any link in a semantic network that is connected to an activated node. (9)

Standard model of consolidation Proposes that memory retrieval depends on the hippocampus during consolidation, but that once consolidation is complete, retrieval no longer depends on the hippocampus. (7)

State-dependent learning The principle that memory is best when a person is in the same state for encoding and retrieval. This principle is related to encoding specificity. (7)

Stereotype An oversimplified generalization about a group or class of people that often focuses on negative characteristics. See also **Illusory correlation.** (13)

Stimulus salience Bottom-up factors that determine attention to elements of a scene. Examples are color, contrast, and orientation. The meaningfulness of the images, which is a top-down factor, does not contribute to stimulus salience. See also **Salience map.** (4)

Stroop effect An effect originally studied by J. R. Stroop, using a task in which a person is instructed to respond to one aspect of a stimulus, such as the color of ink that a word is printed in, and ignore another aspect, such as what the word spells. The Stroop effect refers to the fact that people find this task difficult when the ink color differs from what the word spells. (4)

Structural features (modal model) Stages in the modal model of memory. These stages are sensory memory, short-term memory, and long-term memory. (5)

Structural features (problems) The underlying principle of a problem. For example, in the radiation problem, needing high intensity to fix something surrounded by material that could be damaged by high intensity. Contrast with **Surface features.** (12)

Structuralism An approach to psychology that explained perception as the adding up of small elementary units called sensations. (1, 3)

Subgoals In the means-end analysis approach to problem solving, intermediate states that move the process of solution closer to the goal. (12)

Subtraction technique The technique used in brain imaging in which baseline activity is subtracted from the activity generated by a specific task. The result is the activity due only to the task that is being studied. (2)

Surface features Specific elements that make up a problem. For example, in the radiation problem, the rays and the tumor are surface features. Contrast with **Structural features.** (12)

Syllogism A series of three statements: two premises followed by a conclusion. The conclusion can follow from the premises based on the rules of logic. See also **Categorical syllogism; Conditional syllogism.** (13)

Synapse Space between the end of an axon and the cell body or dendrite of the next axon. (2)

Synaptic consolidation A process of consolidation that involves structural changes at synapses that happen rapidly, over a period of minutes. See also **Consolidation; Systems consolidation.** (7)

Syntactic priming Hearing a statement with a particular syntactic construction increases the chances that a statement that follows will be produced with the same construction. (11)

Syntax The rules for combining words into sentences. Distinguished from **Semantics.** (11)

Syntax-first approach to parsing The approach to parsing that emphasizes the role of syntax. See also **Interactionist approach to parsing.** (11)

Systems consolidation A consolidation process that involves the gradual reorganization of circuits within brain regions and takes place on a long time scale, lasting weeks, months, or even years. See also **Consolidation; Synaptic consolidation.** (7)

Tacit knowledge explanation An explanation proposed to account for the results of some imagery experiments that states that participants unconsciously use knowledge about the world in making their judgments. This explanation has been used as one of the arguments against describing imagery as a depictive or spatial representation. (10)

Target problem A problem to be solved. In analogical problem solving, solution of this problem can become easier when the problem-solver is exposed to an analogous source problem or story. See also **Source problem.** (12)

Temporal lobe The lobe on the side of the brain that contains mechanisms responsible for language, memory, hearing, and vision. (2)

Temporary ambiguity A situation in which the meaning of a sentence, based on its initial words, is ambiguous because a number of meanings are possible, depending on how the sentence unfolds. "Cast iron sinks quickly rust" is an example of a sentence that creates temporary ambiguity. (11)

Testing effect Enhanced performance on a memory test caused by being tested on the material to be remembered. (7)

Think-aloud protocol A procedure in which participants are asked to say out loud what they are thinking while doing a problem. This procedure is used to help determine people's thought processes as they are solving a problem. (12)

Top-down processing Processing that involves a person's knowledge or expectations. This type of processing has also been called knowledge-based processing. (3)

Tower of Hanoi problem A problem involving moving discs from one set of pegs to another. It has been used to illustrate the process involved in means-end analysis. (12)

Transcranial magnetic stimulation (TMS) A procedure in which magnetic pulses are applied to the skull in order to temporarily disrupt the functioning of part of the brain. (10)

Transfer-appropriate processing When the type of task that occurs during encoding matches the type of task that occurs during retrieval. This type of processing can result in enhanced memory. (7)

Two-string problem A problem first described by Maier in which a person is given the task of attaching two strings together that are too far apart to be reached at the same time. This task was devised to illustrate the operation of functional fixedness. (12)

Typicality effect The ability to judge the truth or falsity of sentences involving high-prototypical members of a category more rapidly than sentences involving low-prototypical members of a category. See also **Sentence verification technique**. (9)

Ultimatum game A game in which a *proposer* is given a sum of money and makes an offer to a *responder* as to how this money should be split between them. The responder must choose to accept the offer or reject it. This game has been used to study people's decision-making strategies. (13)

Unconscious inference, theory of Helmholtz's idea that some of our perceptions are the result of unconscious assumptions that we make about the environment. (3)

Unilateral neglect A problem caused by brain damage, usually to the right parietal lobes, in which the patient ignores objects in the left half of his or her visual field. (10)

Units "Neuronlike processing units" in a connectionist network. See also **Hidden units; Input units; Output units.** (9)

Utility Outcomes that achieve a person's goals; in economic terms, the maximum monetary payoff. (13)

Validity Quality of a syllogism whose conclusion follows logically from its premises. (13)

Visual coding Coding in the mind in the form of a visual image. An example of visual coding would be remembering something by conjuring up an image of it in your mind. Also see **Semantic coding.** (5)

Visual icon See **Iconic memory**. (5)

Visual imagery A type of mental imagery involving vision, in which an image is experienced in the absence of a visual stimulus. (5, 10)

Visuospatial sketch pad The part of working memory that holds and processes visual and spatial information. See also **Central executive; Phonological loop; Working memory.** (5)

Wason four-card problem A conditional reasoning task developed by Wason that involves four cards. Various versions of this problem have been used to study the mechanisms that determine the outcomes of conditional reasoning tasks. (13)

Water-jug problem A problem, first described by Luchins, that illustrates how mental set can influence the strategies that people use to solve a problem. (12)

Weapons focus The tendency for eyewitnesses to a crime to focus attention on a weapon, which causes poorer memory for other things that are happening. (8)

Well-defined problem A problem that has a correct answer. There are usually procedures that, when applied correctly, will lead to a solution. See also **Ill-defined problem.** (12)

Wernicke's aphasia A condition, caused by damage to Wernicke's area, that is characterized by difficulty in understanding language, and fluent, grammatically correct, but incoherent speech. (2)

Wernicke's area Area in the temporal lobe associated with understanding language. Damage to this area causes Wernicke's aphasia. (2)

***What* pathway** Neural pathway, extending from the occipital lobe to the temporal lobe, that is associated with perceiving or recognizing objects. Corresponds to the perception pathway. (3)

***Where* pathway** Neural pathway, extending from the occipital lobe to the parietal lobe, that is associated with neural processing that occurs when people locate objects in space. Roughly corresponds to the action pathway. (3)

Whole report method Procedure used in Sperling's experiment on the properties of the visual icon, in which participants were instructed to report all of the stimuli they saw in a brief presentation. See also **Partial report method; Sensory memory.** (5)

Word frequency The relative usage of words in a particular language. For example, in English, *home* has higher word frequency than *hike*. (11)

Word frequency effect The phenomenon of faster reading time for high-frequency words than for low-frequency words. (11)

Word length effect The notion that it is more difficult to remember a list of long words than a list of short words. (5)

Word superiority effect The idea that letters are easier to identify when they are part of a word than when they are seen in isolation or in a string of letters that do not form a word. (11)

Working memory A limited-capacity system for temporary storage and manipulation of information for complex tasks such as comprehension, learning, and reasoning. (5)

References

Adamson, R. E. (1952). Functional fixedness as related to problem solving. *Journal of Experimental Psychology, 44*, 288–291.

Adrian, E. D. (1928). *The basis of sensation*. New York: Norton.

Adrian, E. D. (1932). *The mechanism of nervous action*. Philadelphia: University of Pennsylvania Press.

Aguirre, G. K., Zarahn, E., & D'Esposito, M. (1998). An area within human ventral cortex sensitive to "building" stimuli: Evidence and implications. *Neuron, 21*, 373–383.

Altmann, G. T. M. (1998). Ambiguity in sentence processing. *Trends in Cognitive Sciences, 2*, 146–152.

Altmann, G. T. M. (2001). The language machine: Psycholinguistics in review. *British Journal of Psychology, 92*, 129–170.

Altmann, G. T. M., & Kamide, Y. (1999). Incremental interpretation at verbs: Restricting the domain of subsequent reference. *Cognition, 73*, 247–264.

Altmann, G. T. M., & Steedman, M. J. (1988). Interaction with context during human sentence parsing. *Cognition, 30*, 191–238.

Amedi, A., Malach, R., & Pascual-Leone, A. (2005). Negative BOLD differentiates visual imagery and perception. *Neuron, 48*, 859–872.

Anderson, J. R. (1978). Arguments concerning representation for mental imagery. *Psychological Review, 85*, 249–277.

Anderson, J. R., & Bower, G. H. (1973). *Human associative memory*. Washington, DC: V. H. Winston.

Anderson, J. R., & Schooler, L. J. (1991). Reflections of the environment in memory. *Psychological Science, 2*, 396–408.

Annenberg/CPB Project/WNET-TV. (2000). *The mind* (2nd ed.) [Video]. F. J. Vattano, T. L. Bennett, & M. Butler (Eds.), Module 11: Clive Wearing, part 2: Living without memory.

Appelle, S. (1972). Perception and discrimination as a function of stimulus orientation: The "oblique effect" in man and animals. *Psychological Bulletin, 78*, 266–278.

Arkes, H. R., & Freedman, M. R. (1984). A demonstration of the costs and benefits of expertise in recognition memory. *Memory & Cognition, 12*, 84–89.

Atkinson, R. C., & Shiffrin, R. M. (1968). Human memory: A proposed system and its control processes. In K. W. Spence & J. T. Spence (Eds.), *The psychology of learning and motivation*. New York: Academic Press.

Awh, E., & Vogel, E. K. (2008). The bouncer in the brain. *Nature Neuroscience, 11*, 5–6.

Baddeley, A. D. (1996). Exploring the central executive. *Quarterly Journal of Experimental Psychology, 49A*, 5–28.

Baddeley, A. D. (2000a). The episodic buffer: A new component of working memory? *Trends in Cognitive Sciences, 4*, 417–423.

Baddeley, A. D. (2000b). Short-term and working memory. In E. Tulving & F. I. M. Craik (Eds.), *The Oxford handbook of memory* (pp. 77–92). New York: Oxford University Press.

Baddeley, A. D., Eysenck, M., & Anderson, M. C. (2009). *Memory*. New York: Psychology Press.

Baddeley, A. D., & Hitch, G. J. (1974). Working memory. In G. A. Bower (Ed.), *The psychology of learning and motivation* (pp. 47–89). New York: Academic Press.

Baddeley, A. D., Lewis, V. F. J., & Vallar, G. (1984). Exploring the articulatory loop. *Quarterly Journal of Experimental Psychology, 36*, 233–252.

Baddeley, A. D., Thomson, N., & Buchanan, M. (1975). Word length and the structure of short-term memory. *Journal of Verbal Learning and Verbal Behavior, 14*, 575–589.

Barbey, A. K., & Barsalou, L. W. (2009). Reasoning and problem solving: Models. *Encyclopedia of neuroscience* (pp. 35–43). Oxford: Academic Press.

Barker, R. G., & Wright, H. F. (1951). *One boy's day: A specimen record of behavior*. New York: Harper & Brothers.

Barlow, H. B. (1995). The neuron in perception. In M. S. Gazzaniga (Ed.), *The cognitive neurosciences* (pp. 415–434). Cambridge, MA: MIT Press.

Barsalou, L. W. (2008). Grounded cognition. *Annual Review of Psychology, 59*, 617–645.

Barsalou, L. W. (2009). Simulation, situated conceptualization and prediction. *Philosophical Transactions of the Royal Society B, 364*, 1281–1289.

Bartlett, F. C. (1932). *Remembering: A study in experimental and social psychology*. Cambridge, UK: Cambridge University Press.

Bechtel, W., Abrahamsen, A., & Graham, G. (1998). The life of cognitive science. In W. Bechtel & G. Graham (Eds.), *A companion to cognitive science* (pp. 2–104). Oxford, UK: Blackwell.

Bedard, J., & Chi, M. T. H. (1992). Expertise. *Current Directions in Psychological Science, 1*, 135–139.

Begg, I. M., Anas, A., & Farinacci, S. (1992). Dissociation of processes in belief: Source recollection, statement familiarity, and the illusion of truth. *Journal of Experimental Psychology: General, 121*, 446–458.

Behrmann, M., Moscovitch, M., & Winocur, G. (1994). Intact visual imagery and impaired visual perception in a patient with visual agnosia. *Journal of Experimental Psychology: Human Perception and Performance, 30*, 1068–1087.

Behrmann, M., & Shomstein, S. (2010). Attention: Object-based. In E. B. Goldstein (Ed.), *Sage encyclopedia of perception*. Thousand Oaks, CA: Sage.

Behrmann, M., & Tipper, S. P. (1999). Attention accesses multiple reference frames: Evidence from visual neglect. *Journal of Experimental Psychology: Human Perception and Performance, 25*, 83–101.

Beilock, S. L. (2008). Math performance in stressful situations. *Current Directions in Psychological Science, 17*, 339–343.

Beilock, S. L., & Carr, T. H. (2001). On the fragility of skilled performance: What

governs choking under pressure? *Journal of Experimental Psychology: General, 130*, 701–725.
Beilock, S. L., & Carr, T. H. (2005). When high-powered people fail. *Psychological Science, 16*, 101–105.
Beilock, S. L., & DeCaro, M. S. (2007). From poor performance to success under stress: Working memory, strategy selection, and mathematical problem solving under pressure. *Journal of Experimental Psychology: Learning, Memory and Cognition, 33*, 983–998.
Beilock, S. L., Kulp, C. A., Holt, L. E., & Carry, T. H. (2004). More on the fragility of performance: Choking under pressure in mathematical problem solving. *Journal of Experimental Psychology: General, 133*, 584–600.
Berntsen, D. (2009). Flashbulb memory and social identity. In O. Luminet & A. Curci (Eds.), *Flashbulb memories: New issues and new perspectives* (pp. 187–205). Philadelphia: Psychology Press.
Berntsen, D., & Rubin, C. (2004). Cultural life scripts structure recall from autobiographical memory. *Memory & Cognition, 32*, 427–442.
Bever, T. G., Sanz, M., & Townsend, D. J. (1998). The emperor's psycholinguistics. *Journal of Psycholinguistic Research, 27*, 261–284.
Biederman, I. (1987). Recognition by components: A theory of human image understanding. *Psychological Review, 94*, 115–147.
Binder, J. R., Frost, J. A., Hammeke, T. A., Cox, R. W., Rao, S. M., & Prieto, T. (1997). Human brain language areas identified by functional magnetic resonance imaging. *Journal of Neuroscience, 17*, 353–362.
Bisiach, E., & Luzzatti, G. (1978). Unilateral neglect of representational space. *Cortex, 14*, 129–133.
Blakemore, C., & Cooper, G. G. (1970). Development of the brain depends on the visual environment. *Nature, 228*, 477–478.
Bliss, T. V. P., Collingridge, G. L., & Morris, R. G. M. (2003). Introduction. *Philosophical Transactions of the Royal Society, Series B: Biological Sciences, 358*, 607–611.
Bliss, T. V. P., & Lomo, T. (1973). Long-lasting potentiation of synaptic transmission in the dentate area of the anaesthetized rabbit following stimulation of the perforant path. *Journal of Physiology (London), 232*, 331–336.
Blume, E. S. (1990). *Secret survivors: Uncovering incest and its aftereffects in women*. New York: Ballantine.
Blundo, C., Ricci, M., & Miller, L. (2006). Category-specific knowledge deficit for animals in a patient with herpes simplex encephalitis. *Cognitive Neuropsychology, 23*, 1248–1268.
Bock, K. (1990). Structure in language. *American Psychologist, 45*, 1221–1236.
Boden, M. A. (2006). *Mind as machine: A history of cognitive science*. New York: Oxford University Press.
Bolognani, S. A., Gouvia, P. A., Brucki, S. M., & Bueno, O. F. (2000). Implicit memory and its contribution to the rehabilitation of an amnesic patient: Case study. *Arquiuos de neuro-psiqustria, 58*, 924–930.
Boring, E. G. (1942). *Sensation and perception in the history of experimental psychology.* New York: Appleton-Century-Crofts.
Bowden, E. M., Jung-Beeman, M., Fleck, J., & Kounios, J. (2005). New approaches to demystifying insight. *Trends in Cognitive Sciences, 9*, 322–328.
Bower, G. H., Black, J. B., & Turner, T. J. (1979). Scripts in memory for text. *Cognitive Psychology, 11*, 177–220.
Bower, G. H., Clark, M. C., Lesgold, A. M., & Winzenz, D. (1969). Hierarchical retrieval schemes in recall of categorized word lists. *Journal of Verbal Learning and Verbal Behavior, 8*, 323–343.
Bower, G. H., & Winzenz, D. (1970). Comparison of associative learning strategies. *Psychonomic Science, 20*, 119–120.
Branigan, H. P., Pickering, M. J., & Cleland, A. A. (2000). Syntactic co-ordination in dialogue. *Cognition, 75*, B13–B25.
Bransford, J. D., & Johnson, M. K. (1972). Contextual prerequisites for understanding: Some investigations of comprehension and recall. *Journal of Verbal Learning and Verbal Behavior, 11*, 717–726.
Bransford, J. D., & Johnson, M. K. (1973). Consideration of some problems of comprehension. In W. C. Chase (Ed.), *Visual information processing* (pp. 383–438). New York: Academic Press.
Brewer, W. F. (1977). Memory for the pragmatic implication of sentences. *Memory & Cognition, 5*, 673–678.
Brewer, W. F., & Treyens, J. C. (1981). Role of schemata in memory for places. *Cognitive Psychology, 13*, 207–230.
Broadbent, D. E. (1958). *Perception and communication.* London: Pergamon Press.
Broca, P. (1861). Sur le volume et la forme du cerveau suivant les individus et suivant les races. *Bulletin Societé d'Anthropologie Paris, 2*, 139–207, 301–321, 441–446.
Brooks, L. (1968). Spatial and verbal components of the act of recall. *Canadian Journal of Psychology, 22*, 349–368.
Brown, J. (1958). Some tests of the decay theory of immediate memory. *Quarterly Journal of Experimental Psychology, 10*, 12–21.
Brown, R., & Kulik, J. (1977). Flashbulb memories. *Cognition, 5*, 73–99.
Brunet, A., Orr, S. P., Tremblay, J., Robertson, K., Nader, K., & Pitman, R. K. (2008). Effect of post-retrieval propranolol on psychophysiologic responding during subsequent script-driven traumatic imagery in post-traumatic stress disorder. *Journal of Psychiatric Research, 42*, 503–506.
Burton, A. M., Young, A. W., Bruce, V., Johnston, R. A., & Ellis, A. W. (1991). Understanding covert recognition. *Cognition, 39*, 129–166.
Butterworth, B., Shallice, T., & Watson, F. L. (1990). Short-term retention without short-term memory. In G. Vallar & T. Shalline (Eds.), *Neuropsychological impairments of short-term memory* (pp. 187–213). Cambridge, UK: Cambridge University Press.

Cabeza, R., & Nyberg, L. (2000). Imaging cognition II: An empirical review of 275 PET and fMRI studies. *Journal of Cognitive Neuroscience, 12*, 1–47.
Cabeza, R., Prince, S. E., Daselaar, S. M., Greenberg, D. L., Budde, M., Dolcos, F., et al. (2004). Brain activity during episodic retrieval of autobiographical and laboratory events: An fMRI study using novel photo paradigm. *Journal of Cognitive Neuroscience, 16*, 1583–1594.
Cabeza, R., & St. Jacques, P. (2007). Functional neuroimaging of autobiographical memory. *Trends in Cognitive Sciences, 11*, 219–227.
Cahill, L., Babinsky, R., Markowitsch, H. J., & McGaugh, J. L. (1995). The amygdala and emotional memory. *Nature, 377*, 295–296.
Cahill, L., Haier, R. J., Fallon, J., Alkire, M. T., Tang, C., Keator, D., et al. (1996). Amygdala activity at encoding correlated with long-term free recall of emotional information. *Proceedings of the National Academy of Sciences, USA, 93*, 8016–8021.
Calder, A. J., Beaver, J. D., Winston, J. S., Dolan, R. J., Jenkins, R., Eger, E., et al.

(2007). Separate coding of different gaze directions in the superior temporal sulcus and inferior parietal lobule. *Current Biology, 17*, 20–25.

Campbell, F. W., Kulikowski, J. J., & Levinson, J. (1966). The effect of orientation on the visual resolution of gratings. *Journal of Physiology (London), 187*, 427–436.

Caramazza, A., & Shelton, J. R. (1998). Domain-specific knowledge systems in the brain: The animate-inanimate distinction. *Journal of Cognitive Neuroscience, 10*, 1–34.

Carlin, D., Bonerba, J., Phipps, M., Alexander, G., Shapiro, M., & Grafman, J. (2000). Planning impairments in frontal lobe dementia and frontal lobe lesion patients. *Neuropsychologia, 38*, 655–665.

Carpenter, S. K., Pashler, H., & Cepeda, N. J. (2009). Using tests to enhance 8th grade students' retention of U.S. history facts. *Applied Cognitive Psychology, 23*, 760–771.

Carrasco, M. (2010). Attention: Covert. In E. B. Goldstein (Ed.), *Sage encyclopedia of perception*. Thousand Oaks, CA: Sage.

Carroll, D. W. (2004). *Psychology of language* (4th ed.). Belmont, CA: Wadsworth.

Catrambone, R., & Holyoak, K. J. (1989). Overcoming contextual limitations on problem-solving transfer. *Journal of Experimental Psychology: Learning, Memory, and Cognition, 15*, 1147–1156.

Chalmers, D., & Reisberg, D. (1985). Can mental images be ambiguous? *Journal of Experimental Psychology: Human Perception and Performance, 11*, 317–328.

Chambers, C. G., Tanenhaus, M. K., & Magnuson, J. S. (2004). Actions and affordances in syntactic ambiguity resolution. *Journal of Experimental Psychology: Learning Memory, and Cognition, 30*, 687–696.

Chan, J. C. K., & McDermott, K. B. (2006). Remembering pragmatic inferences. *Applied Cognitive Psychology, 20*, 633–639.

Chan, J. C. K., Thomas, A. K., & Bulevich, J. B. (2009). Recalling a witnessed event increases eyewitness suggestibility. *Psychological Science, 20*, 66–73.

Chao, L. L., Haxby, J. V., & Martin, A. (1999). Attribute-based neural substrates in temporal cortex for perceiving and knowing about objects. *Nature Neuroscience, 2*, 913–919.

Chao, L. L., Weisberg, J., & Martin, A. (2002). Experience-dependent modulation of category-related cortical activity. *Cerebral Cortex, 12*, 478–484.

Chapman, L. J., & Chapman, J. P. (1969). Genesis of popular but erroneous psychodiagnostic observations. *Journal of Abnormal Psychology, 74*, 272–280.

Chase, W. G., & Simon, H. A. (1973a). The mind's eye in chess. In W. G. Chase (Ed.), *Visual information processing*. New York: Academic Press.

Chase, W. G., & Simon, H. A. (1973b). Perception in chess. *Cognitive Psychology, 4*, 55–81.

Cheng, P. W., & Holyoak, K. J. (1985). Pragmatic reasoning schemas. *Cognitive Psychology, 17*, 391–416.

Cherry, E. C. (1953). Some experiments on the recognition of speech, with one and with two ears. *Journal of the Acoustical Society of America, 25*, 975–979.

Chi, M. T. H., Feltovich, P. J., & Glaser, R. (1981). Categorization and representation of physics problems by experts and novices. *Cognitive Science, 5*, 121–152.

Chi, M. T. H., Glaser, R., & Rees, E. (1982). Expertise in problem solving. In R. J. Sternberg (Ed.), *Advances in the psychology of human intelligence*. Hillsdale, NJ: Erlbaum.

Chiu, L.-H. (1972). A cross-cultural comparison of cognitive styles in Chinese and American children. *International Journal of Psychology, 7*, 235–242.

Chklovskii, D. B., Mel, B. W., & Svoboda, K. (2004). Cortical rewiring and information storage. *Nature, 431*, 782–788.

Chomsky, N. (1957). *Syntactic structures*. The Hague: Mouton.

Chomsky, N. (1959). A review of Skinner's *Verbal Behavior. Language, 35*, 26–58.

Christensen, B. T., & Schunn, C. D. (2007). The relationship of analogical distance to analogical function and pre-inventive structure: The case of engineering design. *Memory and Cognition, 35*, 29–38.

Clare, L., & Jones, R. S. P. (2008). Errorless learning in the rehabilitation of memory impairment: A critical review. *Neuropsychology Review, 18*, 1–23.

Clark, H. H., & Van der Wege, M. M. (2002). Psycholinguistics. In H. Pashler & S. Yantis (Eds.), *Stevens' handbook of experimental psychology* (3rd ed., pp. 209–259). New York: Wiley.

Colby, C. L., Duhamel, J.-R., & Goldberg, M. E. (1995). Oculocentric spatial representation in parietal cortex. *Cerebral Cortex, 5*, 470–481.

Coley, J. D., Medin, D. L., & Atran, S. (1997). Does rank have its privilege? Inductive inferences within folkbiological taxonomies. *Cognition, 64*, 73–112.

Collins, A. M., & Loftus, E. F. (1975). A spreading-activation theory of semantic processing. *Psychological Review, 82*, 407–428.

Collins, A. M., & Quillian, M. R. (1969). Retrieval time from semantic memory. *Journal of Verbal Learning and Verbal Behavior, 8*, 240–247.

Colvin, M. K., Dunbar, K., & Grafman, J. (2001). The effects of frontal lobe lesions on goal achievement in the water jug task. *Journal of Cognitive Neuroscience, 13*, 1129–1147.

Conrad, C. (1972). Cognitive economy in semantic memory. *Journal of Experimental Psychology, 92*, 149–154.

Conrad, R. (1964). Acoustic confusion in immediate memory. *British Journal of Psychology, 55*, 75–84.

Conway, A. R. A., Jarrold, C., Kane, M. J., Miyake, A., & Towse, J. N. (2007). *Variation in working memory: An introduction*. In A. R. A. Conway, C. Jarrold, M. J. Kane, A. Miyake, & J. N. Towse (Eds.), *Variation in working memory* (pp. 3–17). New York: Oxford University Press.

Conway, A. R. A., Kane, M. J., & Engle, R. W. (2003). Working memory capacity and its relation to general intelligence. *Trends in Cognitive Sciences, 7*, 547–552.

Conway, M. A. (1996). Autobiographical memory. In E. L. Bjork & R. A. Bjork (Eds.), *Handbook of perception and cognition: Vol. 10. Memory* (2nd ed., pp. 165–194). New York: Academic Press.

Coons, P. M., & Milstein, V. (1992). Psychogenic amnesia: A clinical investigation of 25 cases. *Dissociation, 5*, 73–79.

Coppola, D. M., White, L. E., Fitzpatrick, D., & Purves, D. (1998). Unequal distribution of cardinal and oblique contours in ferret visual cortex. *Proceedings of the National Academy of Sciences, 95*, 2621–2623.

Corbetta, M., & Shulman, G. L. (2002). Control of goal-directed and stimulus driven attention in the brain. *Nature Reviews Neuroscience, 3*, 201–215.

Cosmides, L. (1989). The logic of social exchange: Has natural selection shaped how humans reason? Studies with the Wason selection task. *Cognition, 31*, 187–226.

Cosmides, L., & Tooby, J. (1992). Cognitive adaptations for social exchange. In J. H. Barkow, L. Cosmides, & J. Tooby (Eds.), *The adapted mind* (pp. 179–228). Oxford, UK: Oxford University Press.

Courtney, S. M., Petit, L., Maisog, J. M., Ungerleider, L. G., & Haxby, J. V. (1998). An area specialized for spatial working memory in human frontal cortex. *Science, 279*, 1347–1351.

Cowan, N. (1988). Evolving conceptions of memory storage, selective attention, and their mutual constraints within the human information-processing system. *Psychological Bulletin, 104*, 163–191.

Cowan, N. (1999). An embedded-processes model of working memory. In A. M. P. Shah (Ed.), *Models of working memory* (pp. 62–101). Cambridge, UK: Cambridge University Press.

Cowan, N. (2001). The magical number 4 in short-term memory: A reconsideration of mental storage capacity. *Behavioral Brain Sciences, 24*, 87–185.

Cowan, N. (2005). *Working memory capacity.* New York: Psychology Press.

Craik, F. I. M., & Lockhart, R. S. (1972). Levels of processing: A framework for memory research. *Journal of Verbal Learning and Verbal Behavior, 11*, 671–684.

Craik, F. I. M., & Tulving, E. (1975). Depth of processing and retention of words in episodic memory. *Journal of Experimental Psychology: General, 104*, 268–294.

Craver-Lemley, C., & Reeves, A. (1992). How visual imagery interferes with vision. *Psychological Review, 99*, 633–649.

Crook, T. H., & Adderly, B. (1998). *The memory cure.* New York: Simon & Schuster.

Csikszentmihalyi, M. (1996). *Creativity: Flow and the psychology of discovery and invention.* New York: HarperCollins.

Daneman, M., & Carpenter, P. A. (1980). Individual differences in working memory and reading. *Journal of Verbal Learning and Verbal Behavior, 19*, 450–466.

Dapretto, M., Davies, M. S., Pfeifer, J. H., Scott, A. A., Sigman, M., et al. (2006). Understanding emotions in others: Mirror neuron dysfunction in children with autism spectrum disorders. *Nature Neuroscience, 9*, 28–30.

Darwin, C. J., Turvey, M. T., & Crowder, R. G. (1972). An auditory analogue of the Sperling partial report procedure: Evidence for brief auditory storage. *Cognitive Psychology, 3*, 255–267.

Davachi, L., Mitchell, J. P., & Wagner, A. C. (2003). Multiple routes to memory: Distinct medial temporal lobe processes build item and source memories. *Proceedings of the National Academy of Sciences, 100*, 2157–2162.

Davidoff, J. (2001). Language and perceptual categorization. *Trends in Cognitive Sciences, 5*, 382–387.

Davidson, P. S. R., Cook, S. P., & Glisky, E. L. (2006). Flashbulb memories for September 11th can be preserved in older adults. *Aging, Neuropsychology, and Cognition, 13*, 196–206.

Davidson, P. S. R., & Glisky, E. L. (2002). Is flashbulb memory a special instance of source memory? Evidence from older adults. *Memory, 10*, 99–111.

DeCaro, M. S., Rotar, K. E., Kendra, M. S., & Beilock, S. L. (2010). Diagnosing and alleviating the impact of performance pressure on mathematical problem solving. *Quarterly Journal of Experimental Psychology, 16* [published online February 5, 2010].

Deese, J. (1959). On the prediction of occurrence of particular verbal intrusions in immediate recall. *Journal of Experimental Psychology, 58*, 17–22.

DeGroot, A. (1965). *Thought and choice in chess.* The Hague, Netherlands: Mouton.

Dell, G. S. (1995). Speaking and misspeaking. In L. R. Gleitman & M. Liberman (Eds.), *An invitation to cognitive science* (Vol. 1, pp. 183–208). Cambridge, MA: MIT Press.

Della Sala, S., Gray, C., Baddeley, A., Allamano, N., & Wilson, L. (1999). Attention span: A tool for unwelding visuo-spatial memory. *Neuropsychologia, 37*, 1189–1199.

Denes-Raj, V., & Epstein, S. (1994). Conflict between intuitive and rational processing: When people behave against their better judgment. *Journal of Personality and Social Psychology, 66*, 819–829.

DeRenzi, E., Liotti, M., & Nichelli, P. (1987). Semantic amnesia with preservation of autobiographic memory: A case report. *Cortex, 23*, 575–597.

DeRenzi, E., & Spinnler, H. (1967). Impaired performance on color tasks inpatients with hemispheric lesions. *Cortex, 3*, 194–217.

Desimone, R., & Duncan, J. (1995). Neural mechanisms of selective visual attention. *Annual Review of Neuroscience, 18*, 193–222.

Deutsch, J. A., & Deutsch, D. (1963). Attention: Some theoretical considerations. *Psychological Review, 70*, 80–90.

DeValois, R. L., Yund, E. W., & Hepler, N. (1982). The orientation and direction selectivity of cells in macaque visual cortex. *Vision Research, 22*, 531–544.

DeVreese, L. P. (1991). Two systems for colour-naming defects: Verbal disconnection vs. colour imagery disorder. *Neuropsychologia, 29*, 1–18.

Deware, M. T., Cowan, N., & Sala, S. D. (2007). Forgetting due to retroactive interference: A fusion of Muller and Pilzecker's (1900) early insights into everyday forgetting and recent research on anterograde amnesia. *Cortex, 43*, 616–634.

Di Lollo, V. (2010). Feedback pathways. In E. B. Goldstein, *Sage encyclopedia of perception.* Thousand Oaks, CA: Sage.

di Pellegrino, G., Fadiga, L., Fogassi, L., Gallese, V., & Rizzolatti, G. (1992). Understanding motor events: A neurophysiological study. *Experimental Brain Research, 91*, 176–180.

Dick, F., Bates, E., Wulfeck, B., Utman, J. A., Dronkers, N., & Gernsbacher, M. A. (2001). Language deficits, localization, and grammar: Evidence for a distributive model of language breakdown in aphasic patients and neurologically intact individuals. *Psychological Review, 108*, 759–788.

Dingus, T. A., Klauer, S. G., Neale, V. L., Petersen, A., Lee, S. E., Sudweeks, J., et al. (2006). *The 100-Car Naturalistic Driving Study: Phase II. Results of the 100-Car Field Experiment* (Interim Project Report for DTNH22-00-C-07007, Task Order 6; Report No. DOT HS 810 593). Washington, DC: National Highway Traffic Safety Administration.

Dolcos, F., LaBar, K. S., & Cabeza, R. (2005). Remembering one year later: Role of the amygdala and the medial temporal lobe memory system in retrieving emotional memories. *Proceedings of the National Academy of Sciences, 102*, 2626–2631.

Douglass, A. B., Neuschatz, J. S., Imrich, J., & Wilkinson, M. (2009). Does post-identification feedback affect evaluations of eyewitness testimony and identification procedures? *Law and Human Behavior* [Published online July 8, 2009].

Downing, P. E., Jiang, Y., Shuman, M., & Kanwisher, N. (2001). Cortical area selective for visual processing of the human body. *Science, 293*, 2470–2473.

Dronkers, N. F., Wilkins, D. P., Van Valin, R. D. Jr., Redfern, B. B., & Jaeger, J. J. (2004). Lesion analysis of the brain

areas involved in language comprehension. *Cognition, 92*, 145–177.
Dudai, Y. (2006). Reconsolidation: The advantage of being refocused. *Current Opinion in Neurobiology, 16*, 174–178.
Dudai, Y., & Eisenberg, M. (2004). Rites of passage of the engram: Reconsolidation and the lingering consolidation hypothesis. *Neuron, 44*, 93–100.
Dunbar, K. (1998). Problem solving. In W. Bechtel & G. Graham (Eds.), *A companion to cognitive science* (pp. 289–298). London: Blackwell.
Dunbar, K. (1999). How scientists build models: In vivo science as a window on the scientific mind. In L. Magnani, N. Nersessian, & P. Thagard (Eds.), *Model-based reasoning in scientific discovery* (pp. 89–98). New York: Plenum.
Dunbar, K. (2001). The analogical paradox: Why analogy is so easy in naturalistic settings yet so difficult in the psychological laboratory. In D. Gentner, K. J. Holyoak, & B. Kokinov (Eds.), *Analogy: Perspectives form cognitive science*. Cambridge, MA: MIT Press.
Dunbar, K., & Blanchette, I. (2001). The *in vivo/in vitro* approach to cognition: The case of analogy. *Trends in Cognitive Sciences, 5*, 334–339.
Duncker, K. (1945). On problem solving. *Psychological Monographs, 58*(5, Whole No. 270).
Duzel, E., Cabeza, R., Picton, T. W., Yonelinas, A. P., Scheich, H., Heinze, H.-J., & Tulving, E. (1999). Task-related and item-related brain processes of memory retrieval. *Proceedings of the National Academy of Sciences, USA, 96*, 1794–1799.

Ebbinghaus, H. (1913). *Memory: A contribution to experimental psychology* (H. A. Ruger & C. E. Bussenius, Trans.). New York: Teachers College, Columbia University. (Original work, *Über das Gedächtnis*, published 1885)
Egan, D. E., & Schwartz, B. J. (1979). Chunking in recall of symbolic drawings. *Memory and Cognition, 7*, 149–158.
Egly, R., Driver, J., & Rafal, R. D. (1994). Shifting visual attention between objects and locations: Evidence from normal and parietal lesion subjects. *Journal of Experimental Psychology: General, 123*, 161–177.
Eich, E. (1995). Searching for mood dependent memory. *Psychological Science, 6*, 67–75.
Eich, E., & Metcalfe, J. (1989). Mood dependent memory for internal vs. external events. *Journal of Experimental Psychology: Learning, Memory and Cognition, 15*, 443–455.
Eimas, P. D., & Quinn, P. C. (1994). Studies on the formation of perceptually based basic-level categories in young infants. *Child Development, 65*, 111–126.
Epstein, R., Harris, A., Stanley, D., & Kanwisher, N. (1999). The parahippocampal place area: Recognition, navigation, or encoding? *Neuron, 23*, 115–125.
Ericsson, K. A., Chase, W. G., & Falloon, F. (1980). Acquisition of a memory skill. *Science, 208*, 1181–1182.
Ericsson, K. A., & Simon, H. A. (1993). *Protocol analysis*. Cambridge, MA: MIT Press.
Eriksen, B. A., & Eriksen, C. W. (1974). Effects of noise letters upon the identification of a target letter in a nonsearch task. *Perception and Psychohysics, 16*, 143–149.
Evans, J. St. B. T., & Feeney, A. (2004). In J. P. Leighton & R. J. Steinberg (Eds.), *The nature of reasoning* (pp. 78–102). Cambridge, UK: Cambridge University Press.

Farah, M. J. (1985). Psychophysical evidence for a shared representational medium for mental images and percepts. *Journal of Experimental Psychology: General, 114*, 91–103.
Farah, M. J. (1988). Is visual imagery really visual? Overlooked evidence from neuropsychology. *Psychological Review, 95*, 307–317.
Farah, M. J. (2000). The neural basis of mental imagery. In M. Gazzaniga (Ed.), *The cognitive neurosciences* (2nd ed., pp. 965–974). Cambridge, MA: MIT Press.
Farah, M. J., Levine, D. N., & Calvanio, R. (1988). A case study of mental imagery deficit. *Brain and Cognition, 8*, 147–164.
Farah, M. J., O'Reilly, R. C., & Vecera, S. P. (1993). Dissociated overt and covert recognition as an emergent property of a lesioned neural network. *Psychological Review, 100*, 571–588.
Fiez, J. A. (2001). Bridging the gap between neuroimaging and neuropsychology: Using working memory as a case study. *Journal of Clinical and Experimental Neuropsychology, 23*, 19–31.
Finke, R. A. (1990). *Creative imagery: Discoveries and inventions in visualization*. Hillsdale, NJ: Erlbaum.
Finke, R. A. (1995). Creative insight and preinventive forms. In R. J. Sternberg & J. E. Davidson (Eds.), *The nature of insight* (pp. 255–280). Cambridge, MA: MIT Press.
Finke, R. A., & Pinker, S. (1982). Spontaneous imagery scanning in mental exploration. *Journal of Experimental Psychology: Learning, Memory and Cognition, 8*, 142–147.
Finke, R. A., Pinker, S., & Farah, M. J. (1989). Reinterpreting visual patterns in visual imagery. *Cognitive Science, 13*, 51–78.
Fischer, M. H., & Zwaan, R. A. (2008). Embodied language: A review of the role of the motor system in language comprehension. *Quarterly Journal of Experimental Psychology, 61*, 825–850.
Fischl, B., & Dale, A. M. (2000). Measuring the thickness of the human cerebral cortex from magnetic resonance images. *Proceedings of the National Academy of Sciences, 97*, 11050–11055.
Fisher, R. P., Geiselman, R. E., Amador, M. (1989). Field test of the cognitive interview: Enhancing the recollection of actual victims and witnesses of crime. *Journal of Applied Psychology, 74*, 722–727.
Flexner, J. B., Flexner, L. B., & Stellar, E. (1963). Memory in mice as affected by intracerebral puromycin. *Science, 141*, 57–59.
Frankland, P. W., & Bontempi, B. (2005). The organization of recent and remote memories. *Neuroscience, 6*, 119–130.
Frase, L. T. (1975). Prose processing. In G. H. Bower (Ed.), *The psychology of learning and motivation* (Vol. 9). New York: Academic Press.
Frazier, L. (1987). Sentence processing: A tutorial review. In M. Coltheart (Ed.), *Attention and performance: Vol. 12. The psychology of reading* (pp. 559–586). Hove: Erlbaum.
Fredrickson, R. (1992). *Repressed memories: A journey to recovery from sexual abuse*. New York: Simon & Schuster.
Freedman, D. J., & Miller, E. K. (2008). Neural mechanisms of visual categorization: Insights from neurophysiology. *Neuroscience and Biobehavioral Reviews, 32*, 311–329.
Freedman, D. J., Riesenhuber, M., Poggio, T., & Miller, E. K. (2001). Categorical representation of visual stimuli in the primate prefrontal cortex. *Science, 291*, 312–316.
Freedman, D. J., Riesenhuber, M., Poggio, T., & Miller, E. K. (2003). A comparison of primate prefrontal and inferior

temporal cortices during visual categorization. *Journal of Neuroscience, 23*, 5235–5246.

Frensch, P. A., & Sternberg, R. J. (1989). Expertise and intelligent thinking: When is it worse to know better? In R. J. Sternberg (Ed.), *Advances in the psychology of human intelligence* (Vol. 5). Hillsdale, NJ: Erlbaum.

Friederici, A. D. (2002). Towards a neural basis of auditory sentence processing. *Trends in Cognitive Sciences, 6*, 78–84.

Friederici, A. D. (2009). Pathways to language: Fiber tracts in the human brain. *Trends in Cognitive Sciences, 13*, 175–181.

Friederici, A. D., Fiebach, C. J., Schlesewsky, M., Bornkessel, I. D., & von Cramon, D. Y. (2006). Processing linguistic complexity and grammaticality in the left frontal cortex. *Cerebral Cortex, 16*, 1709–1717.

Friedman-Hill, S. R., Robertson, L. C., & Treisman, A. (1995). Parietal contributions to visual feature binding: Evidence from a patient with bilateral lesions. *Science, 269*, 853–855.

Funahashi, S. (2006). Prefrontal cortex and working memory processes. *Neuroscience, 139*, 251–261.

Funahashi, S., Bruce, C. J., & Goldman-Rakic, P. S. (1989). Mnemonic coding of visual space in the primate dorsolateral prefrontal cortex. *Journal of Neurophysiology, 61*, 331–349.

Furmanski, C. S., & Engel, S. A. (2000). An oblique effect in human primary visual cortex. *Nature Neuroscience, 3*, 535–536.

Furrer, S. D., & Younger, B. A. (2005). Beyond the distributional input? A developmental investigation of asymmetry in infants' categorization of cats and dogs. *Developmental Science, 8*, 544–560.

Gais, S., Albouy, G., Boly, M., Dang-Vu, T. T., Darsaud, A., Desseilles, M., et al. (2007). Sleep transforms the cerebral trace of declarative memories. *Proceedings of the National Academy of Sciences, 104*, 18778–18783.

Gais, S., Lucas, B., & Born, J. (2006). Sleep after learning aids memory recall. *Learning and Memory, 13*, 259–262.

Gallese, V., Fadiga, L., Fogassi, L., & Rizzolatti, G. (1996). Action recognition in the premotor cortex. *Brain, 119*, 593–609.

Galton, F. (1883). *Inquiries into human faculty and its development.* London: Macmillan.

Ganis, G., Thompson, W. L., & Kosslyn, S. M. (2004). Brain areas underlying visual mental imagery and visual perception: An fMRI study. *Cognitive Brain Research, 20*, 226–241.

Gardiner, J. M. (2001). Episodic memory and autonoetic consciousness: A first-person approach. *Philosophical Transactions of the Royal Society of London B., 356*, 1351–1361.

Gauthier, I., Skudlarski, P., Gore, J. C., & Anderson, A. W. (2000). Expertise for cars and birds recruits brain areas involved in face recognition. *Nature Neuroscience, 3*, 191–197.

Gauthier, I., Tarr, M. J., Anderson, A. W., Skudlarski, P., & Gore, J. C. (1999). Activation of the middle fusiform "face area" increases with expertise in recognizing novel objects. *Nature Neuroscience, 2*, 568–573.

Geiselman, R. E., Fisher, R. P., MacKinnon, D. P., & Holland, H. L. (1985). Eyewitness memory enhancement in the police interview: Cognitive retrieval mnemonics versus hypnosis. *Journal of Applied Psychology, 70*, 401–412.

Geiselman, R. E., Fisher, R. P., MacKinnon, D. P., & Holland, H. L. (1986). Enhancement of eyewitness memory with the cognitive interview. *American Journal of Psychology, 99*, 385–401.

Gentner, D., & Colhoun, J. (in press). Analogical processes in human thinking and learning. In A. von Müller & E. Pöppel (Series Eds.) & B. Glatzeder, V. Goel, & A. von Müller (Vol. Eds.), *On thinking: Vol. 2. Towards a theory of thinking*. Berlin: Springer-Verlag.

Gentner, D., & Goldin-Meadow, S. (Eds.). (2003). *Language in mind.* Cambridge, MA: MIT Press.

Gibson, J. J. (1979). *The ecological approach to visual perception.* Boston: Houghton Mifflin.

Gick, M. L., & Holyoak, K. J. (1980). Analogical problem solving. *Cognitive Psychology, 12*, 306–355.

Gick, M. L., & Holyoak, K. J. (1983). Schema induction and analogical transfer. *Cognitive Psychology, 15*, 1–38.

Gigerenzer, G. (2004). Dread risk, September 11, and fatal traffic accidents. *Psychological Science, 15*, 286–287.

Gigerenzer, G., & Hoffrage, U. (1995). How to improve Bayesian reasoning without instruction: Frequency formats. *Psychological Review, 102*, 684–704.

Gigerenzer, G., & Hug, K. (1992). Domain-specific reasoning: Social contracts, cheating, and perspective change. *Cognition, 43*, 127–171.

Gigerenzer, G., & Todd, P. M. (1999). *Simple heuristics that make us smart.* Oxford, UK: Oxford University Press.

Gilbert, A. L., Regier, T., Kay, P., & Ivry, R. B. (2006). Whorf hypothesis is supported in the right visual field but not the left. *Proceedings of the National Academy of Sciences, 103*, 489–494.

Gilboa, A., Winocur, G., Grady, C. L., Hevenor, S. J., & Moscovitch, M. (2004). Remembering our past: Functional neuroanatomy of recollection of recent and very remote personal events. *Cerebral Cortex, 14*, 1214–1225.

Glanzer, M., & Cunitz, A. R. (1966). Two storage mechanisms in free recall. *Journal of Verbal Learning and Verbal Behavior, 5*, 351–360.

Glass, A. L., & Holyoak, K. J. (1975). Alternative conceptions of semantic memory. *Cognition, 3*, 313–339.

Gleason, J. B., & Ratner, N. B. (1998). Language acquisition. In J. B. Gleason & N. B. Ratner (Eds.), *Psycholinguistics* (2nd ed., pp. 347–407). Fort Worth, TX: Harcourt.

Gleick, J. (1992). *Genius: The life and science of Richard Feynman.* New York: Pantheon.

Gobbini, M. I., & Haxby, J. V. (2007). Neural systems for recognition of familiar faces. *Neuropsychologia, 45*, 32–41.

Gobet, F., Land, P. C. R., Croker, S., Cheng, P. C.-H., Jones, G., Oliver, I., & Pine, J. M. (2001). Chunking mechanisms in human learning. *Trends in Cognitive Science, 5*, 236–243.

Godden, D. R., & Baddeley, A. D. (1975). Context-dependent memory in two natural environments: On land and underwater. *British Journal of Psychology, 66*, 325–331.

Goldenberg, G., Podreka, I., Steiner, M., Willmes, K., Suess, E., & Deecke, L. (1989). Regional cerebral blood flow patterns in visual imagery. *Neuropsychologia, 27*, 641–664.

Goldin-Meadow, S. (1982). The resilience of recursion: A study of a communication system developed without a conventional language model. In E. Wanner & L. R. Gleitman (Eds.), *Language acquisition: The state of the art* (pp. 51–77). Cambridge, UK: Cambridge University Press.

Goldman, S. R., Graesser, A. C., & Van den Broek, P. (Eds.). (1999). *Narrative comprehension, causality, and coherence.* Mahwah, NJ: Erlbaum.

Goldman-Rakic, P. S. (1992, September). Working memory and the mind. *Scientific American*, p. 111–117.

Goldstein, A. G., Chance, J. E., & Schneller, G. R. (1989). Frequency of eyewitness identification in criminal cases: A survey of prosecutors. *Bulletin of the Psychonomic Society, 27*, 71–74.

Goldstein, E. B. (2010). *Sensation and perception* (8th ed.). Belmont, CA: Wadsworth/Cengage.

Goldstein, E. B., & Fink, S. I. (1981). Selective attention in vision: Recognition memory for superimposed line drawings. *Journal of Experimental Psychology: Human Perception and Performance, 7*, 954–967.

Gollin, E. S. (1960). Developmental studies of visual recognition of incomplete objects. *Perceptual and Motor Skills, 11*, 289–298.

Gomez, R. L., & Gerken, L. A. (1999). Artificial grammar learning by one-year-olds leads to specific and abstract knowledge. *Cognition, 70*, 109–135.

Gomez, R. L., & Gerken, L. A. (2000). Infant artificial language learning and language acquisition. *Trends in Cognitive Sciences, 4*, 178–186.

Goodale, M. (2010). Action and vision. In E. B. Goldstein, *Sage encyclopedia of perception*. Thousand Oaks, CA: Sage.

Graesser, A. C., Singer, M., & Trabasso, T. (1994). Constructing inferences during narrative text comprehension. *Psychological Review, 101*, 371–395.

Graesser, A. C., & Wiemer-Hastings, K. (1999). Situation models and concepts in story comprehension. In S. R. Goldman, A. C. Graesser, & P. Van den Broek (Eds.), *Narrative comprehension, causality, and coherence* (pp. 77–92). Mahwah, NJ: Erlbaum.

Graf, P., Shimamura, A. P., & Squire, L. R. (1985). Priming across modalities and priming across category levels: Extending the domain of preserved function in amnesia. *Journal of Experimental Psychology: Learning, Memory, and Cognition, 11*, 386–396.

Grant, H., Bredahl, L. S., Clay, J., Ferrie, J., Goves, J. E., Mcdorman, T. A., & Dark, V. J. (1998). Context-dependent memory for meaningful material: Information for students. *Applied Cognitive Psychology, 12*, 617–623.

Gray, J. A., & Wedderburn, A. I. (1960). Grouping strategies with simultaneous stimuli. *Quarterly Journal of Experimental Psychology, 12*, 180–184.

Greenberg, D. L., & Rubin, D. C. (2003). The neuropsychology of autobiographical memory. *Cortex, 39*, 687–728.

Grelotti, D. J., Gauthier, I., & Schultz, R. T. (2002). Social interest and the development of cortical face specialization: What autism teaches us about face processing. *Developmental Psychobiology, 40*, 213–225.

Griggs, R. A. (1983). The role of problem content in the selection task and in the THOG problem. In J. St. B. T. Evans (Ed.), *Thinking and reasoning: Psychological approaches*. London: Routledge & Kegan Paul.

Griggs, R. A., & Cox, J. R. (1982). The elusive thematic-materials effect in Wason's abstract selection task. *British Journal of Psychology, 73*, 407–420.

Grill-Spector, K., Knouf, N., & Kanwisher, N. (2004). The fusiform face area subserves face perception, not generic within-category identification. *Nature Neuroscience, 7*, 555–562.

Gross, C. G. (2002). The genealogy of the "grandmother cell." *Neuroscientist, 8*, 512–518.

Guariglia, C., Padovani, A., Pantano, P., & Pizzamiglio, L. (1993). Unilateral neglect restricted to visual imagery. *Nature, 364*, 235–237.

Guilford, J. (1956). The structure of intellect. *Psychological Bulletin, 53*, 267–293.

Haber, R. N. (1983). The impending demise of the icon: A critique of the concept of iconic storage in visual information processing. *The Behavioral and Brain Sciences, 6*, 1–11.

Haigney, D., & Westerman, S. J. (2001). Mobile (cellular) phone use and driving: A critical review of research methodology. *Ergonomics, 44*, 132–143.

Hamann, S. B., Ely, T. D., Grafton, S. T., & Kilts, C. D. (1999). Amygdala activity related to enhanced memory for pleasant and aversive stimuli. *Nature Neuroscience, 2*, 289–293.

Hamilton, D. L. (1981). Illusory correlation as a basis for stereotyping. In D. L. Hamilton (Ed.), *Cognitive processes in stereotyping and intergroup behavior*. Hillsdale, NJ: Erlbaum.

Han, S., & Lerner, J. S. (2009). Decision making. *Oxford Companion to the Affective Sciences*. New York: Oxford University Press.

Hanowski, R. J., Olson, R. L., Hickman, J. S., & Bocanegra, J. (2009, September). *Driver distraction in commercial vehicle operations*. Paper presented at the First International Conference on Driver Distraction and Inattention, Gothenburg, Sweden.

Hauk, O., Johnsrude, I., & Pulvermuller, F. (2004). Somatotopic representation of action words in human motor and premotor cortex. *Neuron, 41*, 301–307.

Hauser, M. D. (1999). Perseveration, inhibition and the prefrontal cortex: A new look. *Current Opinion in Neurobiology, 9*, 214–222.

Haviland, S. E., & Clark, H. H. (1974). What's new? Acquiring new information as a process in comprehension. *Journal of Verbal Learning and Verbal Behavior, 13*, 512–521.

Haxby, J. V., Hoffman, E. A., & Gobbini, M. I. (2000). The distributed human neural system for face perception. *Trends in Cognitive Science, 46*, 223–233.

Hayes, J. R. (1978). *Cognitive psychology.* Homewood, IL: Dorsey Press.

Hayhoe, M., & Ballard, D. (2005). Eye movements in natural behavior. *Trends in Cognitive Sciences, 9*, 188–194.

Hebb, D. O. (1948). *Organization of behavior.* New York: Wiley.

Hecaen, H., & Angelergues, R. (1962). Agnosia for faces (prosopagnosia). *Archives of Neurology, 7*, 92–100.

Hegarty, M. (1992). Mental animation: Inferring motion from static displays of mechanical systems. *Journal of Experimental Psychology: Learning, Memory, and Cognition, 18*, 1084–1102.

Hegarty, M. (2004). Mechanical reasoning by mental simulation. *Trends in Cognitive Sciences, 8*, 280–285.

Hegarty, M. (2010). Visual imagery. In E. B. Goldstein (Ed.), *Sage encyclopedia of perception* (pp. 1081–1085). Thousand Oaks, CA: Sage.

Helmholtz, H. von. (1911). *Treatise on physiological optics*. Leipzig: Voss. (Original work published 1866)

Helson, H. (1933). The fundamental propositions of Gestalt psychology. *Psychological Review, 40*, 13–32.

Henderson, A., Bruce, V., & Burton, A. M. (2001). Matching the faces of robbers captured on video. *Applied Cognitive Psychology, 15*, 445–464.

Henderson, J. M. (2003). Human gaze control during real-world scene perception. *Trends in Cognitive Sciences, 7*, 498–503.

Henderson, J. M., & Hollingworth, A. (2003). Global transsaccadic change blindness during scene perception. *Psychological Science, 14*, 493–497.

Henkel, L. A. (2004). Erroneous memories arising from repeated attempts to remember. *Journal of Memory and Language, 50*, 26–46.

Hinton, G. E., & Shallice, T. (1991). Lesioning an attractor network: Investigations of acquired dyslexia. *Psychological Review, 98*, 74–95.

Hirsh-Pasek, K., Reeves, L. M., & Golinkoff, R. (1993). Words and meaning: From primitives to complex organization. In J. B. Gleason & N. B. Ratner (Eds.), *Psycholinguistics* (p. 138). Fort Worth, TX: Harcourt Brace Jovanovich.

Hochberg, J. E. (1971). Perception. In J. W. Kling & L. A. Riggs (Eds.), *Experimental psychology* (3rd ed., pp. 396–450). New York: Holt, Rinehart and Winston.

Hoffman, E. J., Phelps, M. E., Mullani, N. A., Higgins, C. S., & Ter-Pogossian, M. M. (1976). Design and performance characteristics of a whole-body positron transaxial tomography. *Journal of Nuclear Medicine, 17*, 493–502.

Hollingworth, A. (2005). Memory for object position in natural scenes. *Visual Cognition, 12*, 1003–1016.

Holyoak, K. J., & Koh, K. (1987). Surface and structural similarity in analogical transfer. *Memory and Cognition, 15*, 332–340.

Holyoak, K. J., & Thagard, P. (1995). Analogical mapping by constraint satisfaction. *Cognitive Science, 13*, 295–355.

Horton, W. S., & Rapp, D. N. (2003). Out of sight, out of mind: Occlusion and the accessibility of information in narrative comprehension. *Psychonomic Bulletin & Review, 10*, 104–110.

Hubel, D. H. (1982). Exploration of the primary visual cortex, 1955–1978. *Nature, 299*, 515–524.

Hubel, D. H., & Wiesel, T. N. (1959). Receptive fields of single neurons in the cat's striate cortex. *Journal of Physiology, 148*, 574–591.

Hubel, D. H., & Wiesel, T. N. (1961). Integrative action in the cat's lateral geniculate body. *Journal of Physiology, 155*, 385–398.

Hubel, D. H., & Wiesel, T. N. (1965). Receptive fields and functional architecture in two non-striate visual areas (18 and 19) of the cat. *Journal of Neurophysiology, 28*, 229–289.

Huber, R., Ghilardi, M. F., Massimini, M., & Tononi, G. (2004). Local sleep and learning. *Nature, 430*, 78–81.

Hupbach, A., Gomez, R., Hardt, O., & Nadel, L. (2007). Reconsolidation of episodic memories: A subtle reminder triggers integration of new information. *Learning & Memory, 14*, 47–53.

Hyman, I. E., Jr., Husband, T. H., & Billings, J. F. (1995). False memories of childhood experiences. *Applied Cognitive Psychology, 9*, 181–197.

Iacoboni, M. (2009). Imitation, empathy, and mirror neurons. *Annual Review of Psychology, 60*, 653–670.

Iacoboni, M., Molnar-Szakacs, I., Gallese, V., Buccino, G., Mazziotta, J. C., & Rizzolatti, G. (2005). Grasping the intentions of others with one's own mirror neuron system. *PLoS Biology, 3*, e79.

Innocence Project. (2009). 248 exonerated. Retrieved December 18, 2009, from http://www.innocenceproject.org

Intons-Peterson, M. J. (1983). Imagery paradigms: How vulnerable are they to experimenters' expectations? *Journal of Experimental Psychology: Human Perception and Performance, 9*, 394–412.

Intons-Peterson, M. J. (1993). Imagery's role in creativity and discovery. In B. Roskos-Ewoldson, M. J. Intons-Peterson & R. E. Anderson (Eds.), *Imagery, creativity, and discovery: A cognitive perspective* (pp. 1–37). New York: Elsevier.

Ishai, A. (2008). Let's face it: It's a cortical network. *Neuroimage, 40*, 415–419.

Ishai, A., Pessoa, L., Bikle, P. C., & Ungerleider, L. G. (2004). Repetition suppression of faces is modulated by emotion. *Proceedings of the National Academy of Sciences, 101*, 9827–9832.

Iwao, M., & Gentner, D. (1997). A cross-linguistic study of early word meaning: Universal ontology and linguistic influence. *Cognition, 62*, 169–200.

Jacoby, L. L., Kelley, C. M., Brown, J., & Jaseckko, J. (1989). Becoming famous overnight: Limits on the ability to avoid unconscious inferences of the past. *Journal of Personality and Social Psychology, 56*, 326–338.

Jadhav, S. P., & Frank, L. M. (2009). Reactivating memories for reconsolidation. *Neuron, 62*, 745–746.

James, W. (1890). *The principles of psychology* (Vol. 1). New York: Henry Holt & Co. (Reprinted, 1981, Harvard University Press).

Jansson, D. G., & Smith, S. M. (1991). Design fixation. *Design Studies, 12*, 3–11.

Jenkins, J. J., & Russell, W. A. (1952). Associative clustering during recall. *Journal of Abnormal and Social Psychology, 47*, 818–821.

Johnson, E. J., & Goldstein, D. (2003). Do defaults save lives? *Science, 302*, 1338–1339.

Johnson, K. E., & Mervis, C. B. (1997). Effects of varying levels of expertise on the basic level of categorization. *Journal of Experimental Psychology: General, 126*, 248–277.

Johnson, M. K. (2006). Memory and reality. *American Psychologist, 61*, 760–771.

Johnson, M. K., Hashtroudi, S., & Lindsay, D. S. (1993). Source monitoring. *Psychological Bulletin, 114*, 3–28.

Johnson-Laird, P. N. (1983). *Mental models*. Cambridge, MA: Harvard University Press.

Johnson-Laird, P. N. (1999). Deductive reasoning. *Annual Review of Psychology, 50*, 109–135.

Johnson-Laird, P. N., Herrmann, D. J., & Chaffin, R. (1984). Only connections: A critique of semantic networks. *Psychological Bulletin, 96*, 292–315.

Johnson-Laird, P. N., Legrenzi, P., & Legrenzi, M. S. (1972). Reasoning and a sense of reality. *British Journal of Psychology, 63*, 395–400.

Jonides, J., Lacey, S. C., & Nee, D. E. (2005). Process of working memory in mind and brain. *Current Directions in Psychological Science, 14*, 2–5.

Jonides, J., Lewis, R. L., Nee, D. E., Lustig, C. A., Berman, M. G., & Moore, K. S. (2008). The mind and brain of short-term memory. *Annual Review of Psychology, 59*, 193–224.

Kahneman, D. (2003). A perspective on judgment and choice. *American Psychologist, 58*, 697–720.

Kandel, E. R. (2001). A molecular biology of memory storage: A dialogue between genes and synapses. *Science, 294*, 1030–1038.

Kandel, E. R. (2006). *In search of memory*. New York: Norton.

Kanwisher, N. (2003). The ventral visual object pathway in humans: Evidence from fMRI. In L. M. Chalupa & J. S. Werner (Eds.), *The visual neurosciences* (pp. 1179–1190). Cambridge, MA: MIT Press.

Kanwisher, N., McDermott, J., & Chun, M. M. (1997). The fusiform face area: A module in human extrastriate cortex specialized for face perception. *Journal of Neuroscience, 17*, 4302–4311.

Kaplan, C. A., & Simon, H. A. (1990). In search of insight. *Cognitive Psychology, 22*, 374–419.

Karpicke, J. D., Butler, A. C., & Roediger, H. L. (2009). Metacognitive strategies in student learning: Do students practise retrieval when they study on their own? *Memory, 17*, 471–479.

Keppel, G., & Underwood, B. J. (1962). Proactive inhibition in short-term retention of single items. *Journal of Verbal Learning and Verbal Behavior, 1*, 153–161.

Keri, S., Janka, Z., Benedek, G., Aszalos, P., Szatmary, B., Szirtes, G., & Lorincz, A. (2002). Categories, prototypes and memory systems in Alzheimer's disease. *Trends in Cognitive Sciences, 6*, 132–136.

Kermer, D. A., Driver-Linn, E., Wilson, T. D., & Gilbert, D. T. (2006). Loss aversion is an affective forecasting error. *Psychological Science, 17*, 649–653.

Kida, S., Josselyn, S. A., Peña de Oritz, S., Kogan, J. H., Chevere, I., Masushige, S., & Silva, A. J. (2002). CREB required for the stability of new and reactivated fear memories. *Nature Neuroscience, 5*, 348–355.

Kilgore, W. D. S., Young, A. D., Femia, L. A., Bogorodzki, P., Rogowska, J., & Yurgelun-Tod, D. A. (2003). Cortical and limbic activation during viewing of high- versus low-calorie foods. *NeuroImage, 19*, 1381–1394.

Kim, A., & Osterhout, L. (2005). The independence of combinatory semantic processing: Evidence from event-related potentials. *Journal of Memory and Language, 52*, 205–255.

Kingstone, A., Smilek, D., Ristic, J., Friesen, C. K., & Eastwood, J. D. (2003). Attention, researchers! It is time to take a look at the real world. *Current Directions in Psychological Sciences, 12*, 176–184.

Kleffner, D. A., & Ramachandran, V. S. (1992). On the perception of shape from shading. *Perception and Psychophysics, 52*, 18–36.

Klin, A., Jones, W., Schultz, R., & Volkmar, F. (2003). The enactive mind, or from actions to cognition: Lessons from autism. *Philosophical Transactions of the Royal Society of London B*, 345–360.

Kneller, W., Memon, A., & Stevenage, S. (2001). Simultaneous and sequential lineups: Decision processes of accurate and inaccurate eye witnesses. *Applied Cognitive Psychology, 15*, 659–671.

Koffka, K. (1935). *Principles of Gestalt psychology.* New York: Harcourt Brace & World.

Kohler, E., Keysers, C., Umilta, M. A., Fogassi, L., Gallese, V., & Rizzolatti, G. (2002). Hearing sounds, understanding actions: Action representation in mirror neurons. *Science, 297*, 846–848.

Kohler, W. (1929). *Gestalt psychology.* New York: Liveright.

Konorski, J. (1967). *Integrative activity of the brain: An interdisciplinary approach.* Chicago: University of Chicago Press.

Kornell, N., & Son, L . K. (2009). Learners' choices and beliefs about self-testing. *Memory, 17*, 493–501.

Kosslyn, S. M. (1973). Scanning visual images: Some structural implications. *Perception & Psychophysics, 14*, 90–94.

Kosslyn, S. M. (1978). Measuring the visual angle of the mind's eye. *Cognitive Psychology, 10*, 356–389.

Kosslyn, S. M. (1980). *Image and mind.* Cambridge, MA: Harvard University Press.

Kosslyn, S. M. (1994). *Image and brain: The resolution of the imagery debate.* Cambridge, MA: MIT Press.

Kosslyn, S. M. (1995). Mental imagery. In S. M. Kosslyn & D. N. Osherson (Eds.), *An invitation to cognitive science* (2nd ed., Vol. 2, pp. 267–296). Cambridge, MA: MIT Press.

Kosslyn, S. M., Ball, T., & Reiser, B. J. (1978). Visual images preserve metric spatial information: Evidence from studies of image scanning. *Journal of Experimental Psychology: Human Perception and Performance, 4*, 47–60.

Kosslyn, S. M., Pascual-Leone, A., Felician, O., Camposano, S., Keenan, J. P., Thompson, W. L., et al. (1999). The role of area 17 in visual imagery: Convergent evidence form PET and rTMS. *Science, 284*, 167–170.

Kosslyn, S. M., & Thompson, W. L. (2000). Shared mechanisms in visual imagery and visual perception: Insights from cognitive neuroscience. In M. Gazzanaga (Ed.), *The cognitive neurosciences* (2nd ed., pp. 975–985). Cambridge, MA: MIT Press.

Kosslyn, S. M., Thompson, W., L., & Ganis, G. (2006). *The case for mental imagery*. New York: Oxford University Press.

Kotovsky, K., Hayes, J. R., & Simon, H. A. (1985). Why are some problems hard? Evidence from Tower of Hanoi. *Cognitive Psychology, 17*, 248–294.

Kounios, J., Fleck, J. I., Green, D. L., Payne, L., Stevenson, J. L., Bowden, E. M., & Jong-Beeman, M. (2008). The origins of insight in resting-state brain activity. *Neuropsychologia, 46*, 281–291.

Kreiman, G., Koch, C., & Fried, I. (2000). Imagery neurons in the human brain. *Nature, 408*, 357–361.

Kroger, J. K., Sabb, F. W., Fales, C. L., Bookheimer, S. Y., Cohen, M. S., & Holyoak, K. J. (2002). Recruitment of anterior dorsolateral prefrontal cortex in human reasoning: A parametric study of relational complexity. *Cerebral Cortex, 12*, 477–485.

Kroll, N. (1970). Short-term memory while shadowing: Recall of visually and aurally presented letters. *Journal of Experimental Psychology, 85*, 220–224.

Kuhn, T. (1970). *The structure of scientific revolution* (2nd ed.). Chicago: University of Chicago Press.

Kurtz, K. J., Gentner, D., & Gunn, V. (1999). Reasoning. In B. M. Bly & D. E. Rumelhart (Eds.), *Cognitive science: Handbook of perception and cognition* (2nd ed., pp. 145– 200). San Diego, CA: Academic Press.

LaBar, K. S., & Phelps, E. A. (1998). Arousal-mediated memory consolidation: Role of the medial temporal lobe in humans. *Psychological Science, 9*, 490–493.

Lakoff, G., & Turner, M. (1989). *More than cool reason: The power of poetic metaphor.* Chicago: Chicago University Press.

Lamble, D., Kauranen, T., Laakso, M., & Summala, H. (1999). Cognitive load and detection thresholds in car following situations: Safety implications for using mobile (cellular) telephones while driving. *Accident Analysis and Prevention, 31*, 617–623.

Land, M. F., & Hayhoe, M. (2001). In what ways do eye movements contribute to everyday activities? *Vision Research, 41*, 3559–3565.

Land, M. F., Mennie, N., & Rusted, J. (1999). The roles of vision and eye movements in the control of activities of daily living. *Perception, 28*, 1311–1328.

Larkin, J. H., McDermott, J., Simon, D. P., & Simon, H. A. (1980). Expert and novice performance in solving physics problems. *Science, 208*, 1335–1342.

Lavie, N. (1995.) Perceptual load as a necessary condition for selective attention. *Journal of Experimental Psychology: Human Perception and Performance, 21*, 451–468.

Lavie, N. (2005). Distracted and confused? Selective attention under load. *Trends in Cognitive Sciences, 5*, 75–82.

Lavie, N., & Cox, S. (1997). On the efficiency of visual selective attention:

Efficient visual search leads to inefficient distractor rejection. *Psychological Science, 8*, 395–398.

Lea, G. (1975). Chronometric analysis of the method of loci. *Journal of Experimental Psychology: Human Perception and Performance, 2*, 95–104.

LeBihan, D., Turner, R., Zeffiro, T. A., Cuenod, A., Jezzard, P., & Bonnerdot, V. (1993). Activation of human primary visual cortex during visual recall: A magnetic resonance imaging study. *Proceedings of the National Academy of Sciences, USA, 90*, 11802–11805.

Lee, D. (2006). Neural basis of quasi-rational decision making. *Current Opinion in Neurobiology, 16*, 191–198.

Leighton, J. P. (2004). Defining and describing reasoning. In J. P. Leighton & R. J. Steinberg (Eds.), *The nature of reasoning* (pp. 3–11). Cambridge, UK: Cambridge University Press.

Lerner, J. S., Small, D. A., & Lowenstein, G. (2004). Heart strings and purse strings: Effects of emotions on economic transactions. *Psychological Science, 15*, 337–341.

Lesgold, A. M. (1988). Problem solving. In R. J. Sternberg & E. E. Smith (Eds.), *The psychology of human thoughts.* New York: Cambridge University Press.

Levelt, W. J. M. (1999). *Producing spoken language: A blueprint of the speaker.* Oxford, UK: Oxford University Press.

Levelt, W. J. M. (2001). Spoken word production: A theory of lexical access. *Proceedings of the National Academy of Sciences, 98*, 13464–13471.

Levin, D., & Simons, D. (1997). Failure to detect changes in attended objects in motion pictures. *Psychonomic Bulletin and Review, 4*, 501–506.

Levine, B., Turner, G. R., Tisserand, D., Hevenor, S. J., Graham, S. J., & McIntosh, A. R. (2004). The functional neuroanatomy of episodic and semantic autobiographical remembering: A prospective functional MRI study. *Journal of Cognitive Neuroscience, 16*, 1633–1646.

Levinson, S. C. (1996). Language and space. *Annual Review of Anthropology, 25*, 353–382.

Lewis, D. J., & Maher, B. A. (1965). Neural consolidation and electroconvulsive shock. *Psychological Review, 72*, 225–239.

Lichtenstein, S., Slovic, P., Fischoff, B., Layman, M., & Combs, B. (1978). Judged frequency of lethal events. *Journal of Experimental Psychology: Human Learning and Memory, 4*, 551–578.

Lindsay, D. S. (1990). Misleading suggestions can impair eyewitnesses' ability to remember event details. *Journal of Experimental Psychology: Learning, Memory, and Cognition, 16*, 1077–1083.

Lindsay, D. S., Hagen, L., Read, J. D., Wade, K. A., & Garry, M. (2004). True photographs and false memories. *Psychological Science, 15*, 149–154.

Lindsay, R. C. L., & Wells, G. L. (1980). What price justice? Exploring the relationship of lineup fairness to identification accuracy. *Law and Human Behavior, 4*, 303–313.

Lindsay, R. C. L., & Wells, G. L. (1985). Improving eyewitness identifications from lineups: Simultaneous versus sequential lineup presentation. *Journal of Applied Psychology, 70, 556–564.*

Loewenstein, R. J. (1991). Psychogenic amnesia and psychogenic fugue: A comprehensive review. In A. Tasman & S. M. Goldfinger (Eds.), *American Psychiatric Press Review of Psychiatry* (Vol. 10, pp. 189–221). Washington, DC: American Psychiatric Press.

Loftus, E. F. (1979). *Eyewitness testimony.* Cambridge, MA: Harvard University Press.

Loftus, E. F. (1993). Made in memory: Distortions in recollection after misleading information. In D. L. Medin (Ed.), *The psychology of learning and motivation: Advances in theory and research* (pp. 187–215). New York: Academic Press.

Loftus, E. F. (1998). Imaginary memories. In M. A. Conway, S. E. Gathercole, & C. Cornoldi (Eds.), *Theories of memory II* (pp. 135–145). Hove, UK: Psychology Press.

Loftus, E. F., Miller, D. G., & Burns, H. J. (1978). Semantic integration of verbal information into visual memory. *Journal of Experimental Psychology: Human Learning and Memory, 4*, 19–31.

Loftus, E. F., & Palmer, J. C. (1974). Reconstruction of an automobile destruction: An example of the interaction between language and memory. *Journal of Verbal Learning and Verbal Behavior, 13*, 585–589.

Lomber, S. G., & Malhotra, S. (2008). Double dissociation of "what" and "where" processing in auditory cortex. *Nature Neuroscience, 11*, 609–616.

Lorayne, H., & Lucas, J. (1996). *The memory book.* New York: Ballantine Books.

Lord, C. G., Ross, L., & Lepper, M. (1979). Biased assimilation and attitude polarization: The effects of prior theories on subsequently considered evidence. *Journal of Personality and Social Psychology, 46*, 1254–1266.

Lovatt, P., Avons, S. E., & Masterson, J. (2000). The word-length effect and disyllabic words. *Quarterly Journal of Experimental Psychology, 53A*, 1–22.

Lovatt, P., Avons, S. E., & Masterson, J. (2002). Output decay in immediate serial recall: Speech time revisited. *Journal of Memory and Language, 46*, 227–243.

Lovett, M. C. (2002). Problem solving. In D. L. Medin (Ed.), *Stevens' Handbook of Experimental Psychology* (3rd ed., pp. 317–362). New York: Wiley.

Lowenstein, G., O'Donoghue, T., & Rabin, M. (2003). Projection bias in predicting future utility. *Quarterly Journal of Economics, 118*, 1209–1248.

Lowenstein, G., Rick, S., & Cohen D. (2008). Neuroeconomics. *Annual Review of Psychology, 59*, 647–672.

Lubart, T. I., & Mouchiroud, C. (2003). Creativity: A source of difficulty in problem solving. In J. E. Davidson & R. J. Sternberg (Eds.), *The psychology of problem solving* (pp. 127–148). New York: Cambridge University Press.

Lucas, M. (1999). Context effects in lexical access: A meta-analysis. *Memory & Cognition, 27*, 385–398.

Luchins, A. S. (1942). Mechanization in problem solving—the effect of Einstellung. *Psychological Monographs, 54*(6), 195.

Luck, S. J., & Vecera, S. P. (2002). Attention. In H. Pashler & S. Yantis (Eds.), *Stevens' handbook of experimental psychology* (3rd ed., pp. 235–286). New York: Wiley.

Luck, S. J., & Vogel, E. K. (1997). The capacity of visual working memory for features and conjunctions. *Nature, 390*, 279–281.

Lucy, J. A., & Gaskins, S. (1997). Grammatical categories and the development of classification preferences: A comparative approach. In S. C. Levinson & M. Bowerman (Eds.), *Language acquisition and conceptual development.* Cambridge, UK: Cambridge University Press.

Luminet, O., & Curci, A. (Eds.). (2009). *Flashbulb memories: New issues and new perspectives.* Philadelphia: Psychology Press.

Luria, A. R. (1968). *The mind of a mnemonist* (L. Solotaroff, Trans.). New York: Basic Books.

MacDonald, M. C., Pearlmutter, N. J., & Seidenberg, M. S. (1994). Lexical nature of syntactic ambiguity resolution. *Psychological Review, 101*, 676–703.

Mack, A., & Rock, I. (1998). *Inattentional blindness*. Cambridge, MA: MIT Press.

MacKay, D. G. (1973). Aspects of the theory of comprehension, memory and attention. *Quarterly Journal of Experimental Psychology, 25*, 22–40.

Mahon, B. Z., & Caramazza, A. (2009). Concepts and categories: A cognitive neuropsychological perspective. *Annual Review of Psychology, 60*, 27–51.

Maier, N. R. F. (1931). Reasoning in humans: II. The solution of a problem and its appearance in consciousness. *Journal of Comparative Psychology, 12*, 181–194.

Majid, A., Bowerman, M., Kita, S., Haun, D. B. M., & Levinson, S. C. (2004). Can language restructure cognition? The case of space. *Trends in Cognitive Sciences, 8*(3), 108–114.

Malpass, R. S., & Devine, P. G. (1981). Eyewitness identification: Lineup instructions and absence of the offender. *Journal of Applied Psychology, 66*, 482–489.

Malt, B. C. (1989). An on-line investigation of prototype and exemplar strategies in classification. *Journal of Experimental Psychology: Learning, Memory and Cognition, 4*, 539–555.

Manktelow, K. I. (1999). *Reasoning and thinking*. Hove, UK: Psychology Press.

Manktelow, K. I., & Evans, J. St. B. T. (1979). Facilitation of reasoning by realism: Effect or non-effect? *British Journal of Psychology, 70*, 477–488.

Manktelow, K. I., & Over, D. E. (1990). Deontic thought and the selection task. In K. J. Gilhooly, M. T. G. Keane, R. H. Logie, & G. Erdos (Eds.), *Lines of thinking: Reflections on the psychology of thought* (Vol. 1). Chichester, UK: Wiley.

Mantyla, T. (1986). Optimizing cue effectiveness: Recall of 500 and 600 incidentally learned words. *Journal of Experimental Psychology: Learning Memory, and Cognition, 12*, 66–71.

Marino, A. C., & Scholl, B. (2005). The role of closure in defining the "objects" of object-based attention. *Perception & Psychophysics, 67*, 1140–1149.

Marsh, R., Cook, G., & Hicks, J. (2006). Gender and orientation stereotypes bias source-monitoring attributions. *Memory, 14*, 148–160.

Martin, A. (2007). The representation of object concepts in the brain. *Annual Review of Psychology, 58*, 25–45.

Mast, F. W., & Kosslyn, S. (2002). Visual mental images can be ambiguous: Insights from individual differences in spatial transformation abilities. *Cognition, 86*, 57–70.

McAdams, C. J., & Reid, R. C. (2005). Attention modulates the responses of simple cells in monkey primary visual cortex. *Journal of Neuroscience, 25*, 11023–11033.

McCarthy, J., Minsky, M. L., & Shannon, C. E. (1955). A proposal for the Dartmouth summer research project on artificial intelligence. Downloaded from http://www-formal.stanford.edu/jmc/history/dartmouth/dartmouth.html

McClelland, J. L., McNaughton, B. L., & O'Reilly, R.C. (1995). Why there are complementary learning systems in the hippocampus and neocortex: Insights from the successes and failures of connectionist models of learning and memory. *Psychological Review, 102*, 419–457.

McClelland, J. L., & Rogers, T. T. (2003). The parallel-distributed processing approach to semantic cognition. *Nature Reviews Neuroscience, 4*, 310–322.

McClelland, J. L., & Rumelhart, D. E. (1986). *Parallel distributed processing: Explorations in the microstructure of cognition*. Cambridge, MA: MIT Press.

McDaniel, M. A., Anderson, J. L., Derbish, M. H., & Morrisette, N. (2007). Testing the testing effect in the classroom. *European Journal of Cognitive Psychology, 19*, 494–513.

McDermott, K. B., & Chan, J. C. K. (2006). Effects of repetition on memory for pragmatic inferences. *Memory & Cognition, 34*, 1273–1284.

McKelvie, S. L. (1997). The availability heuristic: Effects of fame and gender on the estimated frequency of male and female names. *Journal of Social Psychology, 137*, 63–78.

McNab, F., & Klingberg, T. (2008). Prefrontal cortex and basal ganglia control access to working memory. *Nature Neuroscience, 11*, 103–107.

Mervis, C. B., Catlin, J., & Rosch, E. (1976). Relationships among goodness-of-example, category norms and word frequency. *Bulletin of the Psychonomic Society, 7*, 268–284.

Metcalfe, J., & Wiebe, D. (1987). Intuition in insight and noninsight problem solving. *Memory and Cognition, 15*, 238–246.

Meyer, D. E., & Schvaneveldt, R. W. (1971). Facilitation in recognizing pairs of words: Evidence of a dependence between retrieval operations. *Journal of Experimental Psychology, 90*, 227–234.

Miller, G. A. (1956). The magical number seven, plus or minus two: Some limits on our capacity for processing information. *Psychological Review, 63*, 81–97.

Miller, G. A. (1965). Some preliminaries to psycholinguistics. *American Psychologist, 20*, 15–20.

Miller, G. A. (2003). The cognitive revolution: A historical perspective. *Trends in Cognitive Sciences, 7*, 141–144.

Milner, A. D., & Goodale, M. A. (1995). *The visual brain in action*. New York: Oxford University Press.

Minda, J. P., & Smith, J. D. (2001). Prototypes in category learning: The effect of category size, category structure, and stimulus complexity. *Journal of Experimental Psychology: Learning, Memory, and Cognition, 27*, 775–799.

Mishkin, M., Ungerleider, L. G., & Macko, K. A. (1983). Object vision and spatial vision: Two central pathways. *Trends in Neuroscience, 6*, 414–417.

Misiak, H., & Sexton, V. (1966). *History of psychology: An overview*. New York: Grune & Stratton.

Mitchell, K. J., & Johnson, M. K. (2000). Source monitoring. In E. Tulving & F. I. M. Craik (Eds.), *The Oxford handbook of memory* (pp. 179–195). New York: Oxford University Press.

Moran, J., & Desimone, R. (1985). Selective attention gates visual processing in the extrastriate cortex. *Science, 229*, 782–784.

Moray, N. (1959). Attention in dichotic listening: Affective cues and the influence of instructions. *Quarterly Journal of Experimental Psychology, 11*, 56–60.

Morris, C. D., Bransford, J. D., & Franks, J. J. (1977). Levels of processing versus transfer appropriate processing. *Journal of Verbal Learning and Verbal Behavior, 16*, 519–533.

Morris, R. G., Miotto, E. C., Feigenbaum, J. D., Bullock, P., & Polkey, C. E. (1997). Planning ability after frontal and temporal lobe lesions in humans: The effects of selection equivocation and working memory load. *Cognitive Neuropsychology, 14*, 1007–1027.

Moscovitch, M., Rosenbaum, R. S., Gilboa, A., Addis, D. R., Westmacott, R., Grady, C., et al. (2005). Functional neuroanatomy of remote episodic, semantic and spatial memory: A unified account based on multiple trace theory. *Journal of Anatomy, 207*, 35–66.

Muller, G. E., & Pilzecker, A. (1900). Experimentelle Beitrage zur Lehr vom Gedachtniss *Zeitschrift für Psychologie, 1*, 1–300.

Munakata, Y., Morton, J. B., & Stedron, J. M. (2003). The role of prefrontal cortex in perseveration: Developmental and computational explorations. In P. Quinlan (Ed.), *Connectionist models of development*. East Sussex, UK: Psychology Press.

Murdoch, B. B., Jr. (1962). The serial position effect in free recall. *Journal of Experimental Psychology, 64*, 482–488.

Murphy, G. L. (2002). *The big book of concepts*. Cambridge, MA: MIT Press.

Murphy, K. J., Racicot, C. I., & Goodale, M. A. (1996). The use of visuomotor cues as a strategy for making perceptual judgements in a patient with visual form agnosia. *Neuropsychology, 10*, 396–401.

Murray, D. J. (1968). Articulating and acoustic confusability in short-term memory. *Journal of Experimental Psychology, 78*, 679–684.

Nadel, L., & Land, C. (2000). Memory traces revisited. *Neuroscience, 1*, 209–212.

Nadel, L., & Moscovitch, M. (1997). Memory consolidation, retrograde amnesia and the hippocampal complex. *Current Opinion in Neurobiology, 7*, 217–227.

Nader, K. (2003). Memory traces unbound. *Trends in Neurosciences, 26*, 65–72.

Nader, K., Schafe, G. E., & Le Doux, J. E. (2000a). Fear memories require protein synthesis in the amygdala for reconsolidation after retrieval. *Nature, 406*, 722–726.

Nader, K., Schafe, G. E., & Le Doux, J. E. (2000b). The labile nature of consolidation theory. *Nature, 1*, 216–219.

Nationwide Insurance. (2008, May). Driving while distracted public relations research. http://www.nationwide.com/pdf/dwd-2008-survey-results.pdf

Neisser, U. (1967). *Cognitive psychology*. New York: Appleton-Century-Crofts.

Neisser, U. (1988). New vistas in the study of memory. In U. Neisser & E. Winograd (Eds.), *Remembering reconsidered: Ecological and traditional approaches to the study of memory* (pp. 1–10). Cambridge, UK: Cambridge University Press.

Neisser, U., & Becklen, R. (1975). Selective looking: Attending to visually-specified events. *Cognitive Psychology, 7*, 480–494.

Neisser, U., & Harsch, N. (1992). Phantom flashbulbs: False recollections of hearing the news about *Challenger*. In E. Winograd & U. Neisser (Eds.), *Affect and accuracy in recall: Studies of "flashbulb" memories* (pp. 9–31). New York: Cambridge University Press.

Neisser, U., Winograd, E., Bergman, E. T., Schreiber, C. A., Palmer, S. E., & Weldon, M. S. (1996). Remembering the earthquake: Direct experience vs. hearing the news. *Memory, 4*, 337–357.

Newell, A., & Simon, H. A. (1956). The logic theory machine: A complex information processing system. *Transactions on information theory* (Institute of Radio Engineers), *IT-2*, No. 3, 61–79.

Newell, A., & Simon, H. A. (1972). *Human problem solving*. Englewood Cliffs, NJ: Prentice-Hall.

Norman, D. (1968). Toward a theory of memory and attention. *Psychological Review, 75*, 522–536.

Novick, J. M., Trueswell, J. C., & Thompson-Schill, S. L. (2005). Cognitive control and parsing: Reexamining the role of Broca's area in sentence comprehension. *Cognitive, Affective, and Behavioral Neuroscience, 5*, 263–281.

Nyberg, L., McIntosh, A. R., Cabeaa, R., Habib, R., Houle, S., & Tulving, E. (1996). General and specific brain regions involved in encoding and retrieval of events: What, where and when. *Proceedings of the National Academy of Sciences, USA, 93*, 11280–11285.

O'Reilly, R. C. (1996). Biologically plausible error-driven learning using local activation differences: The generalized recirculation algorithm. *Neural Computation, 8*, 895–938.

Oakes, L. M., & Ribar, R. J. (2005). A comparison of infants' categorization in paired and successive familiarization tasks. *Infancy, 7*, 85–98.

Olesen, P. J., Westerberg, H., & Klingberg, T. (2004). Increased prefrontal and parietal activity after training of working memory. *Nature Neuroscience, 7*, 75–79.

Oliva, A., & Torralba, A. (2007). The role of context in object recognition. *Trends in Cognitive Sciences, 11*, 521–527.

Olson, A. C., & Humphreys, G. W. (1997). Connectionist models of neuropsychological disorders. *Trends in Cognitive Sciences, 1*, 222–228.

Orban, G. A., Vandenbussche, E., & Vogels, R. (1984). Human orientation discrimination tested with long stimuli. *Vision Research, 24*, 121–128.

Osterhout, L., Kim, A., & Kuperberg, G. (in press). The neurobiology of sentence comprehension. In M. Spivey, M. Jonnisse, & K. McRae (Eds.), *The Cambridge handbook of the language sciences*. Cambridge, UK: Cambridge University Press.

Osterhout, L., McLaughlin, J., & Bersick, M. (1997). Event-related brain potentials and human language. *Trends in Cognitive Sciences, 1*, 203–209.

Owen, A. M., Downes, J. J., Sahakian, B. J., Polkey, C. E., & Robbins, T. W. (1990). Planning and spatial working memory following frontal lobe lesions in man. *Neuropsychologica, 28*, 1021–1034.

Paivio, A. (1963). Learning of adjective-noun paired associates as a function of adjective-noun word order and noun abstractness. *Canadian Journal of Psychology, 17*, 370–379.

Paivio, A. (1965). Abstractness, imagery, and meaningfulness in paired-associate learning. *Journal of Verbal Learning and Verbal Behavior, 4*, 32–38.

Paivio, A. (2006). *Mind and its evolution: A dual coding theoretical approach*. Hillsdale, NJ: Erlbaum.

Palmer, S. E. (1975). The effects of contextual scenes on the identification of objects. *Memory and Cognition, 3*, 519–526.

Parker, E. S., Cahill, L., & McGaugh, J. L. (2006). A case of unusual autobiographical remembering. *Neurocase, 12*, 35–49.

Parkhurst, D., Law, K., & Niebur, E. (2002). Modeling the role of salience in the allocation of overt visual attention. *Vision Research, 42*, 107–123.

Parkin, A. J. (1996). *Explorations in cognitive neuropsychology*. Oxford, UK: Blackwell.

Pavlov, I. (1927). *Conditioned reflexes*. New York: Oxford University Press.

Peigneux, P., Laureys, S., Fuchs, S., Gollette, F., Perrin, F., Reggers, J., et al. (2004). Are spatial memories strengthened in the human hippocampus during slow wave sleep? *Neuron, 44*, 535–545.

Penfield, W., & Evans, J. (1935). The frontal lobe in man: A clinical study of maximum removals. *Brain, 58*, 115–133.

Perfect, T. J., & Askew, C. (1994). Print adverts: Not remembered but memorable. *Applied Cognitive Psychology, 8*, 693–703.

Perky, C. W. (1910). An experimental study of imagination. *American Journal of Psychology, 21*, 422–254.

Peters, E., Vastfjall, D., Garling, T., & Slovic, P. (2006). Affect and decision making: A "hot" topic. *Journal of Behavioral Decision Making, 19*, 79–85.

Peters, J. (2004, November 26). "Hi, I'm your car. Don't let me distract you." *New York Times*.

Peterson, L. R., & Peterson, M. J. (1959). Short-term retention of individual verbal items. *Journal of Experimental Psychology, 58*, 193–198.

Peterson, S. W. (1992). The cognitive functions of underlining as a study technique. *Reading Research and Instrumentation, 31*, 49–56.

Pickel, K. L. (2009). The weapon focus effect on memory for female versus male perpetrators. *Memory, 17*, 664–678.

Pickering, M. J., & Garrod, S. (2004). Toward a mechanistic psychology of dialogue. *Behavioral and Brain Sciences, 27*, 169–226.

Pillemer, D. B. (1998). *Momentous events, vivid memories*. Cambridge, MA: Harvard University Press.

Pillemer, D. B., Picariello, M. L., Law, A. B., & Reichman, J. S. (1996). Memories of college: The importance of specific educational episodes. In D. C. Rubin (Ed.), *Remembering our past: Studies in autobiographical memory* (pp. 318–337). Cambridge, UK: Cambridge University Press.

Plaut, D. C. (1996). Relearning after damage in connectionist networks: Toward a theory of rehabilitation. *Brain and Language, 52*, 25–82.

Pollack, I., & Pickett, J. M. (1964). Intelligibility of excerpts from fluent speech: Auditory vs. structural context. *Journal of Verbal Learning and Verbal Behavior, 3*, 79–84.

Porter, S., & Birt, A. R. (2001). Is traumatic memory *special*? A comparison of traumatic memory characteristics with memory for other emotional life experiences. *Applied Cognitive Psychology, 15*, S101–S117.

Posner, M. I., & Keele, S. W. (1967). Decay of visual information from a single letter. *Science, 158*, 137–139.

Posner, M. I., Nissen, M. J., & Ogden, W. C. (1978). Attended and unattended processing modes: The role of set for spatial location. In H. L. Pick & I. J. Saltzman (Eds.), *Modes of perceiving and processing information*. Hillsdale, NJ: Erlbaum.

Posner, M. I., & Rothbart, M. K. (2007). Research on attention networks as a model for the integration of psychological science. *Annual Review of Psychology, 58*, 1–23.

Post, T., van den Assem, M. J., Baltussen, G., & Thaler, R. H. (2008). Deal or no deal? Decision making under risk in a large-payoff game show. *American Economic Review, 98*, 38–71.

Pretz, J. E., Naples, A. J., & Sternberg, R. J. (2003). Recognizing, defining, and representing problems. In J. E. Davidson & R. J. Sternberg (Eds.), *The psychology of problem solving* (pp. 3–30). Cambridge, UK: Cambridge University Press.

Pylyshyn, Z. W. (1973). What the mind's eye tells the mind's brain: A critique of mental imagery. *Psychological Bulletin, 80*, 1–24.

Pylyshyn, Z. W. (2001). Is the imagery debate over? If so, what was it about? In E. Dupoux (Ed.), *Language, brain, and cognitive development* (pp. 59–83). Cambridge, MA: MIT Press.

Pylyshyn, Z. W. (2003). Return of the mental image: Are there really pictures in the brain? *Trends in Cognitive Sciences, 7*, 113–118.

Quillian, M. R. (1967). Word concepts: A theory and simulation of some basic semantic capabilities. *Behavioral Science, 12*, 410–430.

Quillian, M. R. (1969). The Teachable Language Comprehender: A simulation program and theory of language. *Communications of the ACM, 12*, 459–476.

Quinlivan, D. S., Wells, G. L., & Neuschatz, J. S. (2009). Is manipulative intentnecessary to mitigate the eyewitness post-identification feedback effect? *Law and Human Behavior* [Published online April 24, 2009].

Quinn, P. C. (2004). Development of subordinate-level categorization in 3- to 7-month-old infants. *Child Development, 75*, 886–899.

Quinn, P. C. (2008). In defense of core competencies, quantitative change, and continuity. *Child Development, 79*, 1633–1638.

Quinn, P. C., Eimas, P. D., & Rosenkrantz, S. L. (1993). Evidence for representations of perceptually similar natural categories by 3-month-old and 4-month-old infants. *Perception, 22*, 463–475.

Quinn, P. C., & Johnson, M. H. (2000). Global-before-basic object categorization in connectionist networks and 2-month-old infants. *Infancy, 1*, 31–46.

Quinn, P. C., & Tanaka, J. W. (2007). Early development of perceptual expertise: Within-basic-level categorization experience facilitates the formation of subordinate-level category representations in 6- to 7-month-old infants. *Memory & Cognition, 35*, 1422–1431.

Raphael, B. (1976). *The thinking computer.* New York: Freeman.

Rathbone, C. J., Moulin, C. J. A., & Conway, M. A. (2008). Self-centered memories: The reminiscence bump and the self. *Memory & Cognition, 36*, 1403–1414.

Rayner, K., & Clifton, C. (2002). Language processing. In H. Pashler & S. Yantis (Eds.), *Stevens' handbook of experimental psychology* (3rd ed., pp. 261–316). New York: Wiley.

Rayner, K., Liersedge, S. P., White, S. J., & Vergilino-Perez, D. (2003). Reading disappearing text: Cognitive control of eye movements. *Psychological Science, 14*, 385–388.

Reber, A. S. (1995). *Penguin dictionary of psychology* (2nd ed.). New York: Penguin.

Redelmeier, D. A., & Tibshirani, R. J. (1997). Association between cellular-telephone calls and motor vehicle collisions. *New England Journal of Medicine, 336*, 453–458.

Reder, L. M., & Anderson, J. R. (1982). Effects of spacing and embellishment for the main points of a text. *Memory & Cognition, 10*, 97–102.

Reicher, G. M. (1969). Perceptual recognition as a function of meaningfulness of stimulus material. *Journal of Experimental Psychology, 81*, 275–280.

Reiger, T., & Kay, P. (2009). Language, thought, and color: Whorf was half right. *Trends in Cognitive Sciences, 13*, 439–446.

Reitman, J. (1976). Skilled perception in Go: Deducing memory structures from inter-response times. *Cognitive Psychology, 8*, 336–356.

Rensink, R. A. (2002). Change detection. *Annual Review of Psychology, 53*, 245–277.

Rensink, R. A., O'Regan, J. K., & Clark, J. J. (1997). To see or not to see: The need for attention to perceive changes in scenes. *Psychological Science, 8*, 368–373.

Richardson, A. (1994). *Individual differences in imaging: Their measurement, origins, and consequences*. Amityville, NY: Baywood.

Rips, L. J., Shoben, E. J., & Smith, E. E. (1973). Semantic distance and the verification of semantic relations. *Journal of Verbal Learning and Verbal Behavior, 12*, 1–20.

Rizzolatti, G., & Arbib, M. A. (1998). *Trends in Neurosciences, 21*, 188–194.
Rizzolatti, G., Fadiga, L., Gallese, V., & Fogassi, L. (1996). Premotor cortex and the recognition of motor actions. *Cognitive Brain Research, 3*, 131–141.
Rizzolatti, G., Forgassi, L., & Gallese, V. (2000). Cortical mechanisms subserving object grasping and action recognition: A new view on the cortical motor functions. In M. Gazzaniga (Ed.), *The new cognitive neurosciences* (pp. 539–552). Cambridge, MA: MIT Press.
Rizzolatti, G., Forgassi, L., & Gallese, V. (2006, November). Mirrors in the mind. *Scientific American*, pp. 54–63.
Roberson, D., Davies, I., & Davidoff, J. (2000). Color categories are not universal: Replications and new evidence from a stone-age culture. *Journal of Experimental Psychology: General, 129*, 369–398.
Robertson, L., Treisman, A., Freidman-Hill, S., & Grabowecky, M. (1997). The interaction of spatial and object pathways: Evidence from Balint's syndrome. *Journal of Cognitive Neuroscience, 9*, 295–317.
Rock, I. (1983). *The logic of perception.* Cambridge, MA: MIT Press.
Roediger, H. L. (1990). Implicit memory: Retention without remembering. *American Psychologist, 45*, 1043–1056.
Roediger, H. L., & Karpicke, J. D. (2006). Test-enhanced learning: Taking memory tests improves long-term retention. *Psychological Science, 17*, 249–255.
Roediger, H. L., & McDermott, K. B. (1995). Creating false memories: Remembering words not presented in lists. *Journal of Experimental Psychology: Learning, Memory, and Cognition, 21*, 803–814.
Rogers, T. B., Kuiper, N. A., & Kirker, W. S. (1977). Self-reference and the encoding of personal information. *Journal of Personality and Social Psychology, 35*, 677–688.
Rogers, T. T., & McClelland, J. L. (2004). *Semantic cognition: A parallel distributed processing approach.* Cambridge, MA: MIT Press.
Rogers, T. T., & McClelland, J. L. (2008). Precis of *Semantic Cognition, a Parallel Distributed Processing Approach* (including open peer commentary and response to commentaries). *Behavioral and Brain Sciences, 31*, 689–749.
Rogin, M. P. (1987). *Ronald Reagan, the movie and other episodes in political demonology.* Berkeley: University of California Press.
Rolls, E. T., & Tovee, M. J. (1995). Sparseness of the neuronal representation of stimuli in the primate temporal visual cortex. *Journal of Neurophysiology, 73*, 713–726.
Rosch, E. H. (1973). On the internal structure of perceptual and semantic categories. In T. E. Moore (Ed.), *Cognitive development and the acquisition of language* (pp. 111–144). New York: Academic Press.
Rosch, E. H. (1975a). Cognitive representations of semantic categories. *Journal of Experimental Psychology: General, 104*, 192–233.
Rosch, E. H. (1975b). The nature of mental codes for color categories. *Journal of Experimental Psychology: Human Perception and Performance, 1*, 303–322.
Rosch, E. H., & Mervis, C. B. (1975). Family resemblances: Studies in the internal structures of categories. *Cognitive Psychology, 7*, 573–605.
Rosch, E. H., Mervis, C. B., Gray, W. D., Johnson, D. M., & Boyes-Braem, P. (1976). Basic objects in natural categories. *Cognitive Psychology, 8*, 382–439.
Rosch, E. H., Simpson, C., & Miller, R. S. (1976). Structural bases of typicality effects. *Journal of Experimental Psychology: Human Perception and Performance, 2*, 491–502.
Rose, D. (1996). Reflections on (or by?) grandmother cells. *Perception, 25*, 881.
Rosenbaum, R. S., Köhler, S., Schacter, D. L., Moscovitch, M., Westmacott, R., Black, S. E., et al. (2005). The case of K.C.: Contributions of a memory-impaired person to memory theory. *Neuropsychologia, 43*, 989–1021.
Ross, D. F., Ceci, S. J., Dunning, D., & Toglia, M. P. (1994). Unconscious transference and mistaken identity: When a witness misidentifies a familiar but innocent person. *Journal of Applied Psychology, 79*, 918–930.
Rowe, J. B., Owen, A. M., Johnsrude, I. S., & Passingham, R. E. (2001). Imaging the mental components of a planning task. *Neuropsychologia, 39*, 315–327.
Rubin, D. C. (2005). A basic-systems approach to autobiographical memory. *Current Directions in Psychological Science, 14*, 79–83.
Rubin, D. C., Rahhal, T. A., & Poon, L. W. (1998). Things learned in early adulthood are remembered best. *Memory & Cognition, 26*, 3–19.
Rumelhart, D. E., & McClelland, J. L. (1986). *Parallel distributed processing: Explorations in the microstructure of cognition.* Cambridge, MA: MIT Press.
Rundus, D. (1971). Analysis of rehearsal processes in free recall. *Journal of Experimental Psychology, 89*, 63–77.

Sachs, J. (1967). Recognition memory for syntactic and semantic aspects of a connected discourse. *Perception and Psychophysics, 2*, 437–442.
Sacks, O. W. (1985). *The man who mistook his wife for a hat and other clinical tales.* New York: Summit Books.
Saffran, J. R., Aslin, R. N., & Newport, E. L. (1999). Statistical learning of tone sequences by human infants and adults. *Cognition, 70*, 27–52.
Samuel, A. G. (1990). Using perceptual-restoration effects to explore the architecture of perception. In G. T. M. Altmann (Ed.), *Cognitive models of speech processing* (pp. 295–314). Cambridge, MA: MIT Press.
Sanfey, A. G., Lowenstein, G., McClure, S. M., & Cohen, J. D. (2006). Neuroeconomics: Cross-currents in research on decision-making. *Trends in Cognitive Sciences, 10*, 106–116.
Sanfey, A. G., Rilling, J. K., Aronson, J. A., Nystrom, L. E., & Cohen, J. D. (2003). The neural basis of economic decision making in the Ultimatum Game. *Science, 300*, 1755–1758.
Sara, S. J. (2000). Strengthening the shaky trace through retrieval. *Neuroscience, 1*, 212–213.
Sara, S. J., & Hars, B. (2006). In memory of consolidation. *Learning & Memory, 13*, 515–521.
Savin, H. B. (1963). Word-frequency effects and errors in the perception of speech. *Journal of the Acoustical Society of America, 35*, 200–206.
Schacter, D. L. (1987). Implicit memory: History and current status. *Journal of Experimental Psychology: Learning, Memory and Cognition, 13*, 501–518.
Schacter, D. L. (2001). *The seven sins of memory.* New York: Houghton Mifflin.
Schacter, D. L., Norman, K. A., & Koutstaal, W. (1998). The cognitive neuroscience of constructive memory. *Annual Review of Psychology, 49*, 289–318.
Schacter, D. L., & Slotnick, S. D. (2004). The cognitive neuroscience of memory distortion. *Neuron, 44*, 149–160.
Scheck, B., Neufeld, P., & Dwyer, J. (2000). *Actual innocence.* New York: Doubleday.
Schenkein, J. (1980). A taxonomy for repeating action sequences in natural conversation. In B. Butterworth (Ed.), *Language production* (Vol. 1, pp. 21–47). San Diego, CA: Academic Press.

Schmolck, H., Buffalo, E. A., & Squire, L. R. (2000). Memory distortions develop over time: Recollections of the O. J. Simpson trial verdict after 15 and 32 months. *Psychological Science, 11*, 39–45.

Schneider, W., & Chein, J. (2003). Controlled and automatic processing: Behavioral and biological mechanisms. *Cognitive Science, 27*, 525–559.

Schneider, W., & Shiffrin, R. M. (1977). Controlled and automatic human information processing: I. Detection, search, and attention. *Psychological Review, 84*, 1–66.

Schrauf, R. W., & Rubin, D. C. (1998). Bilingual autobiographical memory in older adult immigrants: A test of cognitive explanations of the reminiscence bump and the linguistic encoding of memories. *Journal of Memory and Language, 39*, 437–457.

Schwartz, D. L., & Black, J. B. (1996). Analog imagery in mental model reasoning: Depictive models. *Cognitive Psychology, 30*, 154–219.

Schwartz, D. L., & Black, T. (1999). Inferences through imagined actions: Knowing by simulated doing. *Journal of Experimental Psychology: Learning, Memory, and Cognition, 25*, 116–136.

Schweickert, R., & Boruff, B. (1986). Short-term memory capacity: Magic number or magic spell? *Journal of Experimental Psychology: Learning, Memory and Cognition, 12*, 419–425.

Scoville, W. B., & Milner, B. (1957). Loss of recent memory after bilateral hippocampal lesions. *Journal of Neurology, Neurosurgery, and Psychiatry, 20*, 11–21.

Sederberg, P. B., Schulze-Bonhage, A., Madsen, J. R., Bromfield, E. B., Litt, B., Brandt, A., & Kahana, M. J. (2007). Gamma oscillations distinguish true from false memories. *Psychological Science, 18*, 927–932.

Segal, S. J., & Fusella, V. (1970). Influence of imaged pictures and sounds on detection of visual and auditory signals. *Journal of Experimental Psychology, 83*, 458–464.

Seidenberg, M. S., & Zevin, J. D. (2006). Connectionist models in developmental cognitive neuroscience: Critical periods and the paradox of success. In Y. Munakata & M. Johnson (Eds.), *Processes of change in brain and cognitive development: Attention and performance XXI*. Oxford, UK: Oxford University Press.

Shallice, T., & Warrington, E. K. (1970). Independent functioning of verbal memory stores: A neuropsychological study. *Quarterly Journal of Experimental Psychology, 22*, 261–273.

Shepard, R. N., & Metzler, J. (1971). Mental rotation of three-dimensional objects. *Science, 171*, 701–703.

Sheth, B., R., Nguyen, N., & Janvelyan, D. (2009). Does sleep *really* influence face recognition memory? *PLoS ONE, 4*(5): e5496. doi:10.1371/journal.pone.0005496

Shinkareva, S. V., Mason, R. A., Malave, V. L., Wang, W., Mitchel, T. M., & Just, M. A. (2008). Using fMRI brain activation to identify cognitive states associated with perception of tools and dwellings. *PLoS One, 3*(1), e1394.

Shomstein, S. (2010). Attention: Spatial. In E. B. Goldstein (Ed.), *Sage encyclopedia of perception*. Thousand Oaks, CA: Sage.

Shomstein, S., & Behrmann, M. (2006). Cortical systems mediating visual attention to both objects and spatial locations. *Proceedings of the National Academy of Sciences, 103*, 11387–11392.

Shulman, G. L., Ollinger, J. M., Akbudak, E., Conturo, T. E., Snyder, A. Z., Petersen, S. E., & Corbetta, M. (1999). Areas involved in encoding and applying directional expectations to moving objects. *Journal of Neuroscience, 19*, 9480–9496.

Simmons, W., K., Martin, A., & Barsalou, L. W. (2005). Pictures of appetizing foods activate gustatory cortices for taste and reward. *Cerebral Cortex, 15*, 1602–1608.

Simons, D. J., & Chabris, C. F. (1999). Gorillas in our midst: Sustained inattentional blindness for dynamic events. *Perception, 28*, 1059–1074.

Simonsohn, U. (2007). Clouds make nerds look good. *Journal of Behavioral Decision Making, 20*, 143–152.

Simonsohn, U. (2009). Weather to go to college. *Economic Journal, 20*, 1–11.

Simonton, D. K. (1984). Creative productivity and age: A mathematical model based on a two-step cognitive process. *Developmental Review, 4*, 77–111.

Singer, E. (2009). Manipulating memory. *Technology Review, 112*(May/June), 54–59.

Singer, M., Andrusiak, P., Reisdorf, P., & Black, N. L. (1992). Individual differences in bridging inference processes. *Memory & Cognition, 20*, 539–548.

Skinner, B. F. (1938). *The behavior of organisms*. New York: Appleton Century.

Skinner, B. F. (1957). *Verbal behavior*. New York: Appleton-Century Crofts.

Slameka, N. J., & Graf, P. (1978). The generation effect: Delineation of a phenomenon. *Journal of Experimental Psychology: Human Learning and Memory, 4*, 592–604.

Slotnick, S. D., Thompson, W. L., & Kosslyn, S. M. (2005). Visual mental imagery induces retinotopically organized activation of early visual areas. *Cerebral Cortex, 15*, 1570–1583.

Slovic, P., Monahan, J., & MacGregor, D. G. (2000). Violence risk assessment and risk communication: The effects of using actual cases, providing instructions, and employing probability versus frequency formats. *Law and Human Behavior, 24*, 271–296.

Smith, E. E., & Grossman, M. (2008). Multiple systems of category learning. *Neuroscience and Biobehavioral Reviews, 32*, 249–264.

Smith, E. E., Schoben, E. J., & Rips, L. J. (1974). Structure and process in semantic memory. *Psychological Review, 81*, 214–241.

Smith, J. D., & Minda, J. P. (2000). Thirty categorization results in search of a model. *Journal of Experimental Psychology: Learning, Memory, and Cognition, 26*, 3–27.

Smith, S. M., Glenberg, A. M., & Bjork, R. A. (1978). Environmental context and human memory. *Memory & Cognition, 6*, 342–353.

Smith, S. M., & Rothkopf, E. Z. (1984). Contextual enhancement and distribution of practice in the classroom. *Cognition and Instruction, 1*, 341–358.

Solomon, K. O., Medin, D. L., & Lynch, E. (1999). Concepts do more than categorize. *Trends in Cognitive Science, 3*, 99–105.

Spalding, T. L., & Murphy, G. L. (1996). Effects of background knowledge on category construction. *Journal of Experimental Psychology: Learning, Memory and Cognition, 22*, 525–538.

Speer, N. K., Reynolds, J. R., Swallow, K. M., & Zacks, J. M. (2009). Reading stories activates neural representations of visual and motor experiences. *Psychological Science, 20*, 989–999.

Spence, C., & Read, L. (2003). Speech shadowing while driving: On the difficulty of splitting attention between eye and ear. *Psychological Science, 14*, 251–256.

Sperling, G. (1960). The information available in brief visual presentations. *Psychological Monographs, 74*(11, Whole No. 498), 1–29.

Squire, L. R., & Zola-Morgan, S. (1998). Episodic memory, semantic memory, and amnesia. *Hippocampus, 8*, 205–211.

Stanfield, R. A., & Zwaan, R. A. (2001). The effect of implied orientation derived from verbal content on picture recognition. *Psychological Science, 12*, 153–156.

Stanny, C. J., & Johnson, T. C. (2000). Effects of stress induced by a simulated shooting on recall by police and citizen witnesses. *American Journal of Psychology, 113*, 359–386.

Stevens, K. (2002, May 7). Out of the kitchen, and other getaways. *New York Times*.

Strayer, D. L., & Johnston, W. A. (2001). Driven to distraction: Dual-task studies of simulated driving and conversing on a cellular telephone. *Psychological Science, 12*, 462–466.

Stroop, J. R. (1935). Studies of interference in serial verbal reactions. *Journal of Experimental Psychology, 18*, 643–662.

Super, H., Spekreijse, H., & Lamme, V. A. F. (2001). A neural correlate of working memory in the monkey primary visual cortex. *Science, 293*, 120–124.

Swinney, D. A. (1979). Lexical access during sentence comprehension: (Re) considerations of context effects. *Journal of Verbal Learning and Verbal Behavior, 18*, 645–659.

Talarico, J. M. (2009). Freshman flashbulbs: Memories of unique and first-time events in starting college. *Memory, 17*, 256–265.

Talarico, J. M., & Rubin, D. C. (2003). Confidence, not consistency, characterizes flashbulb memories. *Psychological Science, 14*, 455–461.

Talarico, J. M., & Rubin, D. C. (2009). Flashbulb memories result from ordinary memory processes and extraordinary event characteristics. In O. Luminet & A. Curci (Eds.), *Flashbulb memories: New issues and new perspectives*. Philadelphia: Psychology Press.

Talmi, D., Grady, C. L., Goshen-Gottstein, Y., & Moscovitch, M. (2005). Neuroimaging the serial position curve. *Psychological Science, 16*, 716–723.

Tanaka, J. W., & Taylor, M. (1991). Object categories and expertise: Is the basic level in the eye of the beholder? *Cognitive Psychology, 23*, 457–482.

Tanenhaus, M. K., Leiman, J. M., & Seidenberg, M. S. (1979). Evidence for multiple stages in the processing of ambiguous words in syntactic contexts. *Journal of Verbal Learning & Verbal Behavior, 18*, 427–440.

Tanenhaus, M. K., Spivey-Knowlton, M. J., Beerhard, K. M., & Sedivy, J. C. (1995). Integration of visual and linguistic information in spoken language comprehension. *Science, 268*, 1632–1634.

Tang, Y., Zhang, W., Chen, K., Feng, S., Ji, Y., Shen, J., et al. (2006). Arithmetic processing in the brain shaped by cultures. *Proceedings of the National Academy of Sciences, 103*(28), 10775–10780.

Tarkan, L. (2003, April 29). Brain surgery, without knife or blood, gains favor. *New York Times*, p. F5.

Teghtsoonian, R., Teghtsoonian, M., Berglund, B., & Berglund, U. (1978). Invariance of odor strength with sniff vigor: An olfactory analogue to size constancy. *Journal of Experimental Psychology: Human Perception and Performance, 4*, 144–152.

Ter-Pogossian, M. M., Phelps, M. E., Hoffman, E. J., & Mullani, N. A. (1975). A positron-emission tomograph for nuclear imaging (PET). *Radiology, 114*, 89–98.

Terr, L. C. (1994). *Unchained memories: The stories of traumatic memories lost and found*. New York: Basic Books.

Tolman, E. C. (1938). The determinants of behavior at a choice point. *Psychological Review, 45*, 1–41.

Tolman, E. C. (1948). Cognitive maps in rats and men. *Psychological Review, 55*, 189–208.

Tooley, V., Bringham, J. C., Maass, A., & Bothwell, R. K. (1987). Facial recognition: Weapon effect and attentional focus. *Journal of Applied Social Psychology, 17*, 845–859.

Treadeau, K. (1997). *Mega memory*. New York: William Morrow.

Treisman, A. M. (1964). Selective attention in man. *British Medical Bulletin, 20*, 12–16.

Treisman, A. M. (1986). Features and objects in visual processing. *Scientific American, 225*, 114–125.

Treisman, A. M. (1998). The perception of features and objects. In R. D. Wright (Ed.), *Visual attention* (pp. 26–54). New York: Oxford University Press.

Treisman, A. M. (2005, February 4). *Attention and binding*. Presentation to the Cognitive Science Group, University of Arizona.

Treisman, A. M., & Schmidt, H. (1982). Illusory conjunctions in the perception of objects. *Cognitive Psychology, 14*, 107–141.

Tulving, E. (1985). How many memory systems are there? *American Psychologist, 40*, 385–398.

Tulving, E., & Markowitsch, H. J. (1998). Episodic and declarative memory: Role of the hippocampus. *Hippocampus, 8*, 198–204.

Tulving, E., & Pearlstone, Z. (1966). Availability versus accessibility of information in memory for words. *Journal of Verbal Learning and Verbal Behavior, 5*, 381–391.

Tversky, A., & Kahneman, D. (1973). Availability: A heuristic for judging frequency and probability. *Cognitive Psychology, 5*, 207–232.

Tversky, A., & Kahneman, D. (1974). Judgment under uncertainty: Heuristics and biases. *Science, 185*, 1124–1131.

Tversky, A., & Kahneman, D. (1981). The framing of decisions and the psychology of choice. *Science, 211*, 453–458.

Tversky, A., & Kahneman, D. (1983). Extensional versus intuitive reasoning: The conjunction fallacy in probability judgment. *Psychological Review, 90*, 293–315.

Tversky, A., & Kahneman, D. (1991). Loss aversion in riskless choice. *Quarterly Journal of Economics, 106*, 1039–1061.

Tversky, A., & Shafir, E. (1992). Choice under conflict: The dynamics of deferred decision. *Psychological Science, 3*, 358–361.

Ungerleider, L. G., & Mishkin, M. (1982). Two cortical visual systems. In D. J. Ingle, M. A. Goodale, & R. J. Mansfield (Eds.), *Analysis of visual behavior* (pp. 549–580). Cambridge, MA: MIT Press.

Van den Broek, P. (1994). Comprehension and memory of narrative texts. In M. A. Gernsbacher (Ed.), *Handbook of psycholinguistics* (pp. 539–588). San Diego, CA: Academic Press.

Van Petten, C., & Luka, B. J. (2006). Neural localization of semantic context effects in electromagnetic and hemodynamic studies. *Brain and Language, 97*, 279–293.

Violanti, J. M. (1998). Cellular phones and fatal traffic collisions. *Accident Analysis and Prevention, 28*, 265–270.

Vo, M. L. H., & Henderson, J. M. (2009). Does gravity matter? Effects of semantic and syntactic inconsistencies on the allocation of attention during scene perception. *Journal of Vision, 9*(3), 1–15.

Vogel, E. K., McCollough, A. W., & Machizawa, M. G. (2005). Neural measures reveal individual differences in controlling access to working memory. *Nature, 438*, 500–503.

Voss, J. F., Greene, T. R., Post, T., & Penner, B. C. (1983). Problem-solving skill in the social sciences. In G. Bower (Ed.), *The psychology of learning and motivation.* New York: Academic Press.

Wagenaar, W. A. (1986). My memory: A study of autobiographical memory over six years. *Cognitive Psychology, 18,* 225–252.
Waldrop, M. M. (1988). A landmark in speech recognition. *Science, 240,* 1615.
Wallis, J. D., Anderson, K. C., & Miller, E. K. (2001). Single neurons in prefrontal cortex encode abstract rules. *Nature, 411,* 953–956.
Waltz, J. A., Knowlton, B. J., Holyoak, K. J., Boone, K. B., Mishkin, F. S., de Menezes Santos, M., et al. (1999). A system for relational reasoning in human prefrontal cortex. *Psychological Science, 10,* 119–124.
Ward, T. B. (2004). Cognition, creativity and entrepreneurship. *Journal of Business Venturing, 19,* 173–188.
Ward, T. B., Finke, R. A., & Smith, S. M. (1995). *Creativity and the mind: Discovering the genius within.* New York: Plenum.
Ward, T. B., Smith, S. M., & Vaid, J. (Eds.). (1997). *Creative thought: An investigation of conceptual structures and processes.* Washington, DC: American Psychological Association.
Warren, R. M. (1970). Perceptual restoration of missing speech sounds. *Science, 167,* 392–393.
Warrington, E. K., & Weiskrantz, L. (1968). New method of testing long-term retention with special reference to amnesic patients. *Nature, 217,* 972–974.
Wason, P. C. (1960). On the failure to eliminate hypotheses in a conceptual task. *Quarterly Journal of Experimental Psychology, 12,* 129–140.
Wason, P. C. (1966). Reasoning. In B. Foss (Ed.), *New horizons in psychology* (pp. 135–151). Harmondsworth, UK: Penguin.
Watson, J. B. (1913). Psychology as the behaviorist views it. *Psychological Review, 20,* 158–177.
Watson, J. B. (1928). *The ways of behaviorism.* New York: Harper and Brothers.
Watson, J. B., & Rayner, R. (1920). Conditioned emotional reactions. *Journal of Experimental Psychology, 3,* 1–14.
Wearing, D. (2005). *Forever today.* London: Doubleday.
Weisberg, R. W. (1995). Prolegomena to theories of insight in problem solving: A taxonomy of problems. In R. J. Sternberg & J. E. Davidson (Eds.), *The nature of insight* (pp. 157–196). Cambridge, MA: MIT Press.
Weisberg, R. W., & Alba, J. W. (1981). An examination of the alleged role of "fixation" in the solution of several "insight" problems. *Journal of Experimental Psychology: General, 110,* 169–192.
Weisberg, R. W., & Alba, J. W. (1982). Problem solving is not like perception: More on Gestalt theory. *Journal of Experimental Psychology: General, 111,* 326–330.
Wells, G. L., & Bradfield, A. L. (1998). "Good, you identified the suspect": Feedback to eyewitnesses distorts their reports of the witnessing experience. *Journal of Applied Psychology, 83,* 360–376.
Wells, G. L., & Quinlivan, D. S. (2009). Suggestive eyewitness identification procedures and the Supreme Court's reliability test in light of eyewitness science: 30 years later. *Law and Human Behavior, 33,* 1–24.
Wernicke, C. (1874) Der aphasische Symptomenkomplex. Breslau: Cohn.
Westmacott, R., & Moscovitch, M. (2003). The contribution of autobiographical significance to semantic memory. *Memory & Cognition, 31,* 761–774.
Wheatley, T., Weisberg, J., Beauchamp, M. S., & Martin, A. (2005). Automatic priming of semantically related words reduces activity in the fusiform gyrus. *Journal of Cognitive Neuroscience, 17,* 1871–1885.
Wheeler, M. E., Stuss, D. T., & Tulving, E. (1997). Toward a theory of episodic memory: The frontal lobes and autonoetic consciousness. *Psychological Bulletin, 121,* 331–354.
Whorf, B. J. (1956). The relation of habitual thought and behavior to language. In J. B. Carroll (Ed.), *Language, thought and reality: Essays by B. L. Whorf* (pp. 35–270). Cambridge, MA: MIT Press.
Wickelgren, W. A. (1965). Acoustic similarity and retroactive interference in short-term memory. *Journal of Verbal Learning and Verbal Behavior, 4,* 53–61.
Wickens, D. D., Dalezman, R. E., & Eggemeier, F. T. (1976). Multiple encoding of word attributes in memory. *Memory & Cognition, 4,* 307–310.
Wilding, J., & Valentine, E. R. (1997). *Superior memory.* Hove, UK: Psychology Press.
Williams, T. (1964). *The milk train doesn't stop here anymore.* Norwalk, CT: New Directions.
Wilson, T. D., & Gilbert, D. T. (2003). Affective forecasting. In L. Berkowitz (Ed.), *Advances in experimental social psychology* (Vol. 35, pp. 345–411). San Diego, CA: Academic Press.
Winawer, J., Witthoft, N., Frank, M. C., Wu, L., Wade, A. R., & Bordoditsky, L. (2007). Russian blues reveal effects of language on color discrimination. *Proceedings of the National Academy of Sciences, 104,* 7780–7785.
Wiseman, S., & Neisser, U. (1974). Perceptual organization as a determinant of visual recognition memory. *American Journal of Psychology, 87,* 675–681.
Wittgenstein, L. (1953). *Philosophical investigations* (G. E. M. Amnscombe, Trans.). Oxford, UK: Blackwell.
Wood, N., & Cowan, N. (1995). The cocktail party phenomenon revisited: How frequent are attention shifts to one's name in an irrelevant auditory channel? *Journal of Experimental Psychology: Human Perception and Performance, 21,* 255–260.

Yamauchi, T., & Markman, A. B. (2000). Inference using categories. *Journal of Experimental Psychology: Learning, Memory and Cognition, 26,* 776–795.
Younger, B. A., & Fearing, D. D. (1999). Parsing items into separate categories: Developmental change in infant categorization. *Child Development, 70,* 291–303.
Younger, B. A., & Fearing, D. D. (2000). A global-to-basic trend in early categorization: Evidence from a dual-category habituation task. *Infancy, 1,* 47–58.

Zalla, T., Phipps, M., & Grafman, J. (2002). Story processing in patients with damage to the prefrontal cortex. *Cortex, 38,* 215–231.
Zikmund-Fisher, B. J., Sarr, B., Fagerlin, A., & Ubel, P. A. (2006). A matter of perspective: Choosing for others differs from choosing for yourself when making treatment decisions. *Journal of General Internal Medicine, 21,* 618–622.
Zwaan, R. A. (1999). Situation models: The mental leap into imagined worlds. *Current Directions in Psychological Science, 8,* 15–18.
Zwaan, R. A., Stanfield, R. A., & Yaxley, R. H. (2002). Language comprehenders mentally represent the shapes of objects. *Psychological Science, 13,* 168–171.

Name Index

D

E

F

G

H

I

J

K

L

M

N

O

P

Q

R

S

T

U

V

W

Y

Z

Subject Index

A

B

C

D

E

F

G

H

I

J

K

L

P

R

S

T

U

V

W